W9-CNV-957

Critical Concepts

An Introduction to Politics

Second Edition

Edited by Janine Brodie

University of Alberta

Prentice
Hall

Toronto

To our Students

National Library of Canada Cataloguing in Publication Data

Main entry under title:
Critical concepts: an introduction to politics

2nd ed.

Includes index.
ISBN 0-13-040928-6

1. Political Science. I. Brodie, M. Janine, 1952– .

JA66.C75 2001   320   C2001-900473-7

Copyright © 2002 Pearson Education Canada Inc., Toronto, Ontario
All Rights Reserved. This publication is protected by copyright, and permission should be obtained from the publisher prior to any prohibited reproduction, storage in a retrieval system, or transmission in any form or by any means, electronic, mechanical, photocopying, recording, or likewise. For information regarding permission, write to the Permissions Department.

Original edition © 1999 Prentice-Hall Canada., Scarborough, Ontario

ISBN 0-13-040928-6

Vice President, Editorial Director: Michael Young
Editor-in-Chief: David Stover
Acquisitions Editor: Andrew Wellner
Developmental Editor: Martina van de Velde
Marketing Manager: Christine Cozens
Production Editor: Susan Adlam
Copy Editor: Imogen Brian
Production Coordinator: Wendy Moran
Art Direction: Mary Opper
Cover Design: Sarah Battersby
Cover Illustration: Martin O'Neill
Interior Design: Lisa LaPointe
Page Layout: Susan Thomas

Cartoons used with permission of Malcolm Mayes, *The Edmonton Journal*

3 4 5   06 05 04 03 02

Printed and bound in Canada.

Brief Table of Contents

Detailed Table of Contents

Preface

Two years have passed since the first edition of this introductory text was published. This second edition benefits from the feedback we have received both from instructors of introductory political science across Canada and from our students at the University of Alberta. This text was initially conceived as a primer on the key concepts that we believe students should master in their first course in political science. The text explores the key concepts evolving out of political thought, political institutions, organized political behaviour and civil society, and, finally, the rapidly changing international environment. In this second edition, we have expanded both the introductory section on political thought and the final section on global perspectives. In addition to including new chapters, all the previous chapters, debate boxes, and websites have been updated and the glossary of key political terms has been expanded. Our objective in this second edition, however, remains the same as in the first: to introduce students to the fundamentals of political science, to engage them with key and enduring debates, and to explore the conceptual shifts and uncertainties emerging in the current era of ever-intensifying globalization. Most importantly, the chapters in this text are designed to challenge students with the political issues they confront daily. Each chapter attempts to frame these issues as part of the disciplinary heritage of political science and to make them accessible to first-year students.

Introductory courses are often a challenge for political science instructors because of differing philosophies about how best to acquaint students with the complex world of politics. Some are convinced that an introductory course should concentrate on the foundations of political analysis, most notably the canons of Western political thought. These instructors emphasize the study of great thinkers. Others prefer a course that serves as an intensive institutional primer, reasoning that students require a working knowledge of the mechanics of political life before they can explore more advanced subject matter. These instructors focus on key political institutions such as constitutions, executives, and elected assemblies. Still others suggest that foundations and mechanics will come with time and that the primary goal of an introductory course should be to offer students a sampling of the many intriguing perspectives on the political world that political science offers. Each of these perspectives has merit considering the many dimensions of political life.

There is no equivalent in political science to the laws of supply and demand in economics or the laws of motion in physics. Neither is there a neutral doorway into the political world. Any entry to the study of politics is already saturated by, among other things, history, political ideas, institutional constraints, and power inequalities among political actors. Moreover, students come to their first course in political science already influenced by and engaged in the political world around them. Political science offers few road maps to move from the simple to the complex, in part because politics is always complex, especially for students who study politics at the dawn of the third millennium.

A Chinese proverb goes something like this: "May you live in interesting times." Students of politics have always lived in interesting times. The most enduring work in political science has taken up the challenges of "its time," both in order to make sense of political life and to change and improve it. Political scientists have studied the ravages of war, of industrialization, of colonialism, and of genocide. They have also advanced the causes of human rights, good governance, individual well-being, and peaceful co-existence within and between states. Today's students of politics will go on to face many similar challenges but they will also confront new ones in this emerging era of globalization.

Globalization consists of complex and multiple processes that reach from the transnational to the daily lives of the average citizen. While we may quibble about exact definitions, there is no doubt that we now find ourselves immersed in a process of complex social change. In fact, some argue that today's social changes are similar in magnitude and scope to those of the Industrial Revolution. Today, a space station prepares to explore the vastness of the universe, geneticists create new forms of life, and new technologies allow information and digital cash to travel around the globe at the speed of light. The world, it seems, is getting smaller. But, it also seems more fragmented and difficult to comprehend. Globalization, as this text emphasizes, is a contested concept in political science; it has many subtle and contradictory influences on political life. Some celebrate the globalization of national economies and cultures because it promises to transcend barriers to finding global political solutions to serious political problems such as famine, mass migration, global warming, and the HIV/AIDS epidemic.

At the same time, citizens and students of politics are becoming increasingly aware that globalization is challenging the continuing viability of sovereign and national democratic governance as we have come to understand these terms. These challenges are particularly unsettling for the discipline of political science. Modern political institutions, political processes, and theories of politics have been built up around the assumption of state sovereignty. Globalization, in other words, complicates the question of where to begin the study of politics as well as politics itself.

This introductory text is designed to address both the fundamentals of political science and many of the current challenges to governance in the twenty-first century. It examines the critical concepts that we believe students should master during their first encounter with political science. Each chapter introduces a critical political concept, describes its importance in the study of politics, and outlines the debates that the concept has engendered in political life and for the discipline of political science. Each chapter also explores how the contemporary political environment challenges the meaning and relevance of these concepts. The text acquaints students with traditional debates in political science as well as those recently introduced to the discipline by, for example, feminists, ecologists, and postmodernists.

The text is divided into four sections examining: 1) different ways of thinking about politics; 2) institutional structures, actors and issues; 3) civil society, political participation and social cleavages; and, 4) traditional and new ways of studying the international and the global. The contents of each section are as follows:

Part I, *Introductory Themes: The Politics of Ideas,* explores the broad contexts within which contemporary politics occurs. Chapter 1, Power, Politics, and Political Science, introduces many of the critical concepts, such as power, authority, and sovereignty, which will be developed in later chapters. Chapters 2 to 4, Democratic Theory, Modern Political Ideologies, and Radical Ideologies explore the foundations and critiques of liberal democratic governance and also describe how political ideas and ideologies influence both politics and the study of politics. The last chapter in this section, Ethics and Politics, reminds students that politics is always about choice and discusses how these choices are framed as ethical and moral.

Part II, *Institutions*, begins with Political Regimes, a chapter that outlines the elementary relationships among the historical development of the state, the market, regime types, and international political economy. The next chapter provides a detailed account of the evolution of the liberal democratic state and describes its three principal forms—the laissez-faire, welfare, and neoliberal state. The remaining chapters provide detailed accounts of the development of and challenges facing the central institutions of modern governance, especially in liberal democracies such as Canada. These include constitutions (Chapter 8), legislatures and executives (Chapter 9), the judiciary (Chapter 10), elections and electoral systems (Chapter 11), political parties and party systems (Chapter 12), the civil service (Chapter 13) and local government (Chapter 14). Each of the contributions to Part II describes the evolution and importance of these institutions as well as contemporary factors that have enhanced or eroded their influence and function.

Part III, *Political Influence*, explores less formal influences on political outcomes, including the most basic units of liberal democratic politics at the level of nation, community, group, and individual. The section begins with a look at the important contemporary issues of diversity, culture, and globalization (Chapter 15). Next examined are the issues of community, citizenship, and gender (Chapters 16, 17, and 18). The last two chapters discuss the topics of organizing political influence (Chapter 19), and new social movements (Chapter 20).

Part IV, *Global Perspectives*, shifts our focus to the international and transnational domains. This section includes more familiar foci and debates in the study of the international arena including foreign policy (Chapter 22), international organizations (Chapter 25), and multilateralism (Chapter 27). This section, however, also concentrates on new perspectives and actors in an increasingly global rather than international environment. The first chapter of the section, Chapter 21, reviews four popular theses about the future of post-Cold War politics. Chapter 23 explains the historical construction of inequalities between the North and the South. Chapter 24 explains what we mean by the controversial term *globalization* and outlines the key debates and changes associated it. Critical new players in the global arena—international financial institutions—are described in Chapter 26.

This text has been designed for a first-year political science course. It has a number of innovations that we believe will contribute to a successful first encounter with political science. Each chapter provides study questions, suggested further readings, and websites for further research on the topic. In addition, most of the chapters include debate or information boxes. Key terms are identified within the text, and defined in a glossary at the end of the book. **An instructor's guide and a test bank also accompany this text.**

Acknowledgments

Many people deserve our thanks and appreciation for their contributions to this project. First, the authors wish to thank Andy Wellner, Lisa Phillips, Laura Forbes, Martina van de Velde, Susan Adlam, and Imogen Brian. Undoubtedly, this second edition could not have been completed without the very capable support of the staff of the Department of Political Science at the University of Alberta—Cindy Anderson, Marilyn Calvert, Sharon Moroschan, and Tara Mish.

Two people deserve special recognition and a heartfelt thanks from all the contributors to this text. First, Malcolm Mayes, editorial cartoonist at the Edmonton Journal, has once again generously volunteered to lend his obvious talents, political insights, and, above all, his sense of humour to this project. Second, all of the authors and, especially the editor, owe deep gratitude to Sandra Rein, who both contributed a chapter to this edition and provided the lion's share of organizational energy to this project. We are all indebted to Sandra for keeping this project intact and on time with her characteristic persistence, abundant good humour, and professionalism.

Janine Brodie
Edmonton

Introductory Themes: The Politics of Ideas

There is rarely a simple answer for why political events unfold as they do. Political outcomes are the combined product of many forces that vary in strength and often clash and pull in opposite directions. Some of these factors are immediate and observable while others are more distant and concealed, lodged in historical legacies and political traditions. There is, however, one inescapable constant in political analyses. Everything political is embedded in ideas, in the way we understand the political world around us. All political and social interactions, both harmonious and conflict-ridden, are informed and directed by ideas. The five chapters in this introductory section of the text provide an introduction to the key concepts and different streams of political thinking that have structured politics in the West for millennia. First, a number of critical concepts that are fundamental to the study and practice of politics, such as power, sovereignty, and authority, are explained. We discuss their ongoing centrality in political life as well as how they are challenged by the political terrain of the early twenty-first century. Next, the similarities and differences among the most important streams of Western political thought are outlined and explained within their historical contexts. We explore why different political ideas arose when they did and how they have influenced political choices, patterns of conflict, and the creation of the core political institutions through which we have organized our common affairs for centuries. We will discover that the history of modern political thought is very much the history of democracy, the ongoing struggle of people to realize equality and freedom as they have understood these key concepts. We will also discover that, even today, the debate about how best to govern ourselves is linked to how we understand and place value on the individual, the community, and the division between the public and the private. Finally, we will visit the ageless challenge of ethics—questions of fairness and justice that are always at the centre of political choice and action. Politics, however constrained, is always about choice and the consequences of our choices.

DON'T PUSH IT,
PIERRE.

CHAPTER 1

POLITICS, POWER, AND POLITICAL SCIENCE

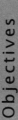

We often encounter the flat assertion that "power and politics are everywhere." And so they are, but this truism does not give us any guideposts indicating where or how to begin to study political power. The world of politics is complex, fascinating, and multi-dimensional. The study of politics can lead us to the most diverse of places, among them, the home, the workplace, political party organizations, and the bureaucracy. Political science is increasingly inclusive about what constitutes the appropriate terrain of politics and political study. But, in order to enter the complex world of politics, we have to carry with us some basic conceptual tools, not the least of which is an understanding of the concepts of power and politics.

JANINE
BRODIE

This chapter introduces many of the critical political concepts that will be revisited and explained in greater detail throughout this text. In particular, we discuss the relationship between politics and power. We then explore a few of the many faces of political power, among them, *power to, power over*, knowledge and power, sovereignty, and authority, especially Weber's distinctions among traditional, charismatic, and legal-rational authority. The chapter next introduces some of the dominant approaches to the study of politics—legal-institutional, pluralist, elitist, and class approaches. We begin our discussion of approaches by outlining the dominant assumptions of liberalism because each approach, either directly or indirectly, represents a conversation with liberalism's claims about the nature and organization of political life. Finally, we touch on some of the ways that the current era of globalization is challenging the meaning and continuing relevance of key components of modern governance.

Introduction

Aristotle, contemplating political life over two thousand years ago, made an enduring observation about the human condition. "Man," he said, "is by nature a political animal." Aristotle quite literally meant *man*, indeed only the men of Ancient Greece's ruling class. Contemporary political theorists now understand Aristotle's man as a representation of all people and politics as an ever-present force in all societies. Whenever two or more people come together, there is politics. Politics, whether we recognize it or not, flows through all social relationships. It is the glue that holds these relationships together. It also is the friction that erupts in disagreement and conflict, sometimes tearing communities and nations apart. Politics is all around us, not unlike the air we breathe. And, like air, it is often difficult to see, to capture, and to study. Politics, whether experienced at the level of the individual, the community, the country, or the globe, is constantly shifting. The push and pull of conflict and consensus means that political life is always moving in directions that we can never fully predict.

Uncertainty and unpredictability were for Karl Mannheim, writing over half a century ago, at the very heart of the definition of politics. He drew a fundamental distinction between administration and politics. The administration of our daily lives was routinized, ruled-based, and predictable—what he called the "routine affairs of the state." Politics, in contrast, was the play of irrational forces, social competition, and struggle. "The two main sources of irrationalism (uncontrolled competition and domination by force)," he argued, "constitute the realm of social life which is still unorganized and where politics becomes necessary" (1936, 115–116).

How then are we to understand, let alone study, something that is so fundamental to our daily lives and yet so fluid and so unpredictable? Some argue that an all-embracing approach to the study of politics, one that sees its operations and consequences everywhere, is not very useful. How are we to distinguish a political relationship from other kinds of relationships? If politics is everywhere, they point out, then it is nowhere.

The discipline of political science, however, rests on the basic premise that politics does have a number of defining characteristics that make it more tangible. While there is considerable debate about what these characteristics are, political scientists agree on at least one point of departure. Politics is about power, and political science is devoted to the study of its various uses, organization, and outcomes. Who has political power and why? How does it flow through institutions and societies and to what end? Where does political power come from? Can it be used to build a better society?

Politics and Power

THE PRIMARY LINK BETWEEN POLITICS AND POWER HAS BEEN A PERENNIAL ISSUE for students of politics. Niccolo Machiavelli (1469–1527) is sometimes called the first political scientist because he distinguished between the "is" and the "ought" of politics. While religious and moral codes tell us what action we ought to take, the grim realities of politics are more often concerned with what is. Almost five hundred years ago, Machiavelli, in his famous book, *The Prince*, advised the ruling elite of Italy to give up any notion of governing according to moral ideals and, instead, to use the power of both force and persuasion to disarm opponents. He believed that political survival and moral codes were often incompatible and that princes sometimes had to violate moral norms to hold onto political office. The end—staying in power—could justify amoral and brutal means. For Machiavelli, politics was mostly about the effective exercise and consolidation of political power and position. Early in the twentieth century, the great Soviet revolutionary, Vladimir Lenin, defined politics in a similar way as "who does what to whom" (quoted in Guy, 1995, 5). Perhaps the most often quoted definition of politics comes from Harold Lasswell, a distinguished American political scientist writing in the 1930s. For him, the study of politics was about "who gets what, when, and how" (1936).

Yet, to say that politics is about the exercise of power only begs the obvious question— what is power? Most political scientists agree about the ubiquity of power. As Amos Hawley explains, "every act is an exercise of power, every social relationship is a power equation, and every social group or system is an organization of power" (1963, 433). Think about how often in our everyday conversations or in the media we hear the word *power*. This person has power, that person is seduced by power, another person is on a power-trip, while Ford trucks have more power, and Mario Lemieux executed a perfect power play. Do these various usages convey the same or different meanings? In fact, we find little consensus in political science about the meaning of power. Like politics, it has many faces. There are literally dozens of definitions of power. At the most basic level, **power** is understood as "bringing about consequences." Power, in other words, makes something happen that probably would not happen in its absence. But, beyond that, there is widespread disagreement about the fundamentals of power. For example, how is power acquired? Is it through wealth, knowledge, cunning, good looks, force, race, or something else? How do we experience power? Is it through influence, coercion, control, or some other mechanism? Are we even aware when power is weighing down on us? How is power used? Who benefits—individuals, select groups, or the community? Who decides how power will be used? (Philp, 1985, 635).

Power To and Power Over

Political scientists have generally treated power in one of two ways, either as power to do something or as power over something. **Power to** connotes the realization of personal or collective goals or, in today's parlance, "being empowered." (Kourvetaris, 1997, 41). The popular notion that, in democratic systems, power ultimately rests in the hands of citizens conveys the idea of "power to" realize social consensus and collective goals through democratic institutions, such as elected legislative assemblies. Through democratic practices, in particular, voting, citizens are supposed to be able to hold their political leaders accountable for their actions and, if need be, throw them out of office.

For political cynics, this idea of "power to" is, at best, naive and, at worst, an outright sham. They argue that people are encouraged to believe that they can change political outcomes or govern themselves democratically when, in fact, the present and the future are already determined by the laws of the market, the capitalist class, political elites, faceless bureaucrats … the list is endless. Such fatalism, however, does not square with history. One need only think of the lone student staring down a tank in Tiananmen Square, the droves of Yugoslavians who stayed away from work and packed the streets until Milosevic left office, or Rosa Parks who refused to go to the back of the bus in a racist American south, to realize that people, individually and collectively, have the power to bring about political change. But, the fight for political change always exacts costs, whether it is the small investment of time to attend a political rally or write a letter to a public official or the ultimate cost of one's life. If the graveyard of history is filled with political elites, even larger graveyards are filled with those who opposed them. To paraphrase Marx, people engage with a political world marked by profound imbalances in political resources—in other words, under conditions not of their own choosing.

The notion of **power over**, in contrast, conveys the idea of disempowerment. It tells us that there are forces outside us that constrain and direct our actions, making us do things that we would not otherwise do and that might be contrary to our interests and well-being. Robert Dahl's definition of power is a good example of the idea of "power over." For Dahl, "A has power to the extent that A makes B do something that B would not otherwise do" (1961, 203). Dahl's thinking about power was very much influenced by the behavioural approach to politics that dominated Canadian and American political science thinking in the 1960s and 1970s. **Behaviouralism** highlighted individual political actors and their interactions rather than political institutions or systems of inequality embedded in society. Behaviouralists made great use of public opinion polling—large surveys of the attitudes and actions of both ordinary people and political leaders. Behaviouralism was informed by two fundamental assumptions which subsequently were strongly criticized as being inappropriate to the study of politics. First, behaviouralists believed that individuals, both citizens and leaders, were the basic units for the study of politics rather than systems and institutions. Second, behaviouralists assumed that, by studying individuals scientifically, that is with surveys and statistical calculations, they could discover fundamental laws about political behaviour. In much the same way that natural scientists were able to discover the laws or building blocks of nature, behaviouralists aspired to discover the laws of politics— laws that operated everywhere and at all times that could explain such things as, for example, how revolutions occur.

Political scientists, unfortunately, have proved time and again that politics defies regularity and prediction. We were not able to predict the collapse of Soviet-style communism, although this was arguably the greatest political event of the past fifty years. To be fair, economists wedded to the science of the market have not done much better, being unable to predict with precision the onset of the nine deep recessions that have hit capitalist economies since the Great Depression of the 1930s. The problem, it would seem, is not the discipline of study but, instead, the questionable assumption that the complexity of human relations can be reduced to timeless scientific generalities.

Ahistorical and individualized approaches to power contrast greatly with societal approaches, such as class analysis, that locate power and political conflict in the economy and the historical organization of societies. Consider, for example, the depiction of "power over" provided by Karl Marx and Friedrich Engels in the *Communist Manifesto*. "The history of all hitherto existing society," they write, "is the history of class struggles. Freeman and slave, patrician and plebeian, lord and serf, guildmaster and journeyman, in a word, oppressor and oppressed, stood in opposition to one another." Marx and Engels, and many after them, were trying to convey an important point: people are political animals; they are also born into specific historical contexts and patterns of politics before they take their first breath of air. At different times and in different places, to be born black, Aboriginal, female, or working-class was already to be in a position of being subjected to "power over" within the broader historical contexts of racism, colonialism, sexism, and capitalism. Political conflict based on these systemic patterns of domination was, and is, an inevitable result.

Power and Knowledge

More recently, some political theorists, particularly those associated with postmodern analyses, such as Michel Foucault, have rejected the idea that power is simply a thing to possess or to hold over other people. Foucault argued that thinking about power as something outside us, to be gained, lost, or used to empower or to disempower is not the only or perhaps the most appropriate way to think about power. Instead, he suggested that the "real power" of power is productive. For Foucault, we never stand outside power, but, instead, are created by it. Power runs through all social relations, indeed, through our bodies like capillaries. These capillaries of power can be so innocuous, even commonsensical, as to be undetectable.

Foucault's argument is that, for example, unequal gender relations are not created or maintained solely or primarily through force, although brute force always lies somewhere deep behind systems of exploitation. Instead, Foucault argues that, from birth, we are shaped by a particular historical image of what being male or female should look like. These images have shifted dramatically over time. For example, if a proper Victorian lady walked into your class today, she would have a hard time sorting out male and female and would probably deem the whole class sexual deviants and deserving of the full weight of productive power—social exclusion and legal penalty.

Foucault advanced the idea that power is embedded in the way we think about things, in knowledge systems that tell us what exists, who we are, what is true. He used the term *discourse* to convey the idea of the inseparability of power and knowledge. Foucault expanded modern thinking about power to include the ideas of disciplinary power and dividing practices. **Disciplinary power** exacts appropriate behaviours, not through force, but by defining what is normal. **Dividing practices** stigmatize those who do not fit the mould by naming them scientifically as being different or abnormal. Foucault was particularly interested in scientific discourse about human sexuality, mental illness, and criminal deviance. His research tried to show that particular ways of thinking about things, of common understandings of what is true, change over time and change our behaviour.

People exercise productive power over themselves and others quite unconsciously. For example, when a scientific discourse defines what is normal, we both discipline ourselves to fit this definition in order to avoid social rejection and, in turn, reject those who, through dividing practices, do not conform. Long before we act, we have power inscribed on us through these disciplinary and dividing practices. As Foucault explains, power and knowledge directly imply one another. This means that there can be no knowledge "out there" that is free of power relations to be used for good or evil. Claims to knowledge are also claims to power. Fields of knowledge categorize, discipline, and divide people for the purposes of social control. Modern governments, Foucault argued, use these various categories to manage populations.

Foucault's work focused on the dividing and disciplinary practices that came out of the scientific naming of homosexuals, the mentally ill, and criminals. More generally, Foucault argued that the accepted truths of knowledge and their resulting disciplinary practices are like a panopticon. The *panopticon* was a model prison designed so that the prisoners could always be watched but could never see the guard. The beauty of the design was that prisoners would eventually come to behave as if they were being watched even if they were not (Fink-Eitel 1992, 50). Foucault used the analogy of the panopticon to convey the idea that knowledge systems work in the same way, producing appropriate behaviours without coercing them.

Foucault's approach to power has been criticized for being too all-encompassing and for effectively foreclosing the possibility of individual action, political contestation, and political change. Foucault, however, resisted this interpretation of his work. He recognized that there were situations where opportunities for political opposition were limited but he called these examples of domination, rather than power. States of domination can be so complete, argued Foucault, that "the way one determines the behaviour of others is so well determined in advance, that there is nothing left to do." "Slavery," for example, "is not a power relationship when man is in chains" (quoted in Simons 1995, 82). Foucault's point, in other words, was that the exercise of power always presupposes resistance.

Foucault never had the opportunity to fully respond to his critics. He died of AIDS in the mid-1980s. His work remains important because it underlines the critical notion that knowledge contains power and the reverse. His conception of power challenges us to take responsibility for the power relations embedded in the way we think about ourselves and the world. Consider, for example, the power relations embedded in recent changes in thinking about social welfare recipients. For most of the postwar period, those receiving assistance did so as a right of citizenship which could be claimed by those in need. These citizens were seen to need state support because of a broad range of factors, many of them beyond the control of the individual. Disability, unemployment, injury, and illness are a few examples. Moreover, it was assumed that any one of us could fall victim to these unhappy fates.

Now, it is common to refer to these same citizens as welfare dependents. The term *dependence* conveys the idea that welfare recipients, like drug addicts, are lesser individuals and somehow responsible for their own plight. The dependency metaphor also invites certain kinds of policy responses and not others. It involves isolating the "dependents" and subjecting them to some kind of treatment such as retraining or workfare or creating disincentives to break their habit by reducing eligibility or benefits. Nowhere in this discourse are we invited to entertain the idea that most of those who do not depend on social assistance are "dependent" on the job market to save them from a similar fate (Brodie 1995; Fraser and Gordon, 1994). We are all dependent in one way or another but the discourse on welfare dependency stigmatizes those who depend on the state, however temporarily, to meet their basic needs for survival.

Authority

Other writers have located power in institutions and value systems. This approach also tends to emphasize the idea of power as authority rather than as force, although the two are usually mutually reinforcing. In cases of **authority**, individuals adjust their behaviour because they concede to the authority associated with an institution. Consider the following two scenarios. In the first scenario, you are driving down the street and a police officer demands that you stop your car. You are likely to comply. In the second scenario, an ordinary person demands that you stop your car. In this case, you may stop or, instead, lock your doors and speed down the street. What is the difference? The authority vested in a policeman's uniform. Authority is "socially approved power" that entails both legitimacy and impartiality (Kourvetaris, 1997, 51). Someone is accorded power and legitimacy, less for who they are personally, than for the institution that they represent, whether that be the police, the judiciary, or elected office. This legitimacy is often backed up by the threat of sanction or punishment. Most us of obey the law both because we believe in the rule of law and because we realize that failure to comply with the law might very well result in a fine or jail sentence.

Max Weber (1864–1920), one of the fathers of modern social science, argued that societies have been governed by three different kinds of authority: traditional, charismatic, and legal-rational. **Traditional authority** was the social glue that held together pre-industrial societies. Power was vested in certain individuals because of custom or heredity. The chief or the king was obeyed because that was how it was intended or how it had always been. While traditional authorities might take advice from others, including a god, their authority was individual and incontestable.

Charismatic authority was similarly vested in individuals. It, however, was grounded in the personal qualities of the charismatic leader rather than in tradition or in birth. Weber argued that charismatic leaders tend to gain authority during periods of profound crisis and social upheaval. Their authority, he argued, grows out of "a certain quality of an individual personality by virtue of which he is set apart from ordinary men and treated as endowed with supernatural, superhuman, or at least specifically exceptional powers and qualities" (quoted in Bendix, 1960, 88). The social upheaval of the Great Depression in the 1930s, which saw the rise of fascist dictators such as Hitler in Germany and Mussolini in Italy, provides obvious examples of what Weber meant by charismatic authority.

Weber saw both traditional and charismatic authority as fleeting in modern societies, which were increasingly governed by **legal-rationalism**. This kind of authority is based in the rule of law and in the bureaucratic and impersonal procedures of modern institutions such as the courts, constitutions, bureaucracy, and legislatures. Legal-rational authority is accorded to leaders who hold positions in and abide by the rules of these institutions. They, in turn, are considered legitimate by the public. In a legal-rational system, claims to authority, even by charismatic leaders, are unlikely to be considered legitimate unless they are framed within a system of legal-rationality. To put the point more clearly, no matter how charismatic an individual or how royal a blood-line, a person could not make claims to political leadership and authority in a legal-rational culture unless accorded legitimacy by, for example, a democratic election. For example, the fact that George W. Bush gained the American presidency in 2000 without winning the popular vote has led many to question his legitimacy and authority to rule.

Although these different kinds of authority tend to characterize different kinds of society, from the simple to the complex, all can be found in contemporary culture. A religious leader or one's parents or teachers make claims to traditional authority, although many traditionalists lament that these claims do not hold the force that they once did. Any day of the week you can find someone on television linking the problems of the world to the decline of religious deference or the authority of the family.

Charisma also remains a formidable force in political life. The international political stage still affords a role to charismatic leaders such as Saddam Hussein, who grounds his political power both in force and in the force of personality. Yet, in a world dominated by legal-rational authority, these leaders are condemned as illegitimate. Charisma, nonetheless, is an extremely valuable asset for political leaders. It is widely conceded that Al Gore could have walked away with the American presidential election if he had a larger measure of charisma. Closer to home, the reaction to the death of former Prime Minister Pierre Trudeau, in the fall of 2000 demonstrated that charisma often lives on in the hearts of citizens long after a politician leaves office. In the late 1960s, the enthusiasm generated by Trudeau's charisma, what was called "Trudeaumania," drew baby-boomers into Canadian political life. His appearance of youthfulness, dedication to a new pan-Canadianism, and his apparent disregard for traditional forms of authority, demonstrated when he made an irreverent pirouette behind Queen Elizabeth II, were part and parcel of his charismatic appeal to an entire generation.

State and Sovereignty

The rise of legal-rationalism is intimately tied to the ideas of sovereignty and the birth of the modern state. Traditional leaders, especially the rulers of feudal Europe, claimed sovereignty in their person. **Sovereignty** means supreme power. There is no question or debate about the right to exercise power where sovereignty has been established. In feudal societies, power and authority were dispersed and divisible, often shared and struggled for among the nobility, the monarch, and the Church. Gradually from the fifteenth to the seventeenth centuries, coinciding with the demise of feudalism and the ascendancy of capitalism, political power began to consolidate both territorially and practically within the early predecessors of the modern state. These predecessors took on two dominant personalities—the "absolute" monarchies of France, Prussia, Austria, Spain, and Russia and the "constitutional" monarchies and republics, based on representative government, which were beginning to take form in England and Holland (Held, 1996, 66). In absolute monarchies, the sovereignty of traditional hereditary monarchs such as King Louis XV of France, who ruled from 1715 to 1774, was effectively imposed on the state through the person of the King. Louis XV pronounced that "in my person alone resides the sovereign power, and it is from me alone that the courts hold their existence and their authority. That … authority can only be exercised in my name …. The rights and interests of the nation … are necessarily united with my own and can only rest in my hands" (quoted in Held, 1996, 67). Absolute monarchs maintained that their power was God-given and, thus, to disobey the monarch was to disobey God which was the greatest offence in pre-modern times.

Absolute monarchies eventually crumbled in the face of democratization, class conflict, and the idea of popular sovereignty, that is, the idea that political power ultimately rested in the hands of all citizens instead of leaders alone. Yet, even after the first tentative steps to democratization, echoes of absolutism could still be heard. Queen Victoria, for example, who ruled the British empire from 1837 to 1901, pronounced in 1848, the very year that the Canadian colonies saw open rebellion calling for responsible government, that "obedience to the laws and to the sovereign is obedience to a higher Power" (Kellogg, 2001, E3).

Absolute monarchies provided the institutional underpinnings of the modern state out of the remnants of feudal society. Primary among these were

- the territorial boundaries of the nation state and a uniform system of political rule;
- new means of law-making and enforcement;
- the centralization of political and administrative power;
- the creation of standing armies; and
- the formalization of international relations (Held, 1996, 68).

During the past four centuries, the modern state has taken on a number of different forms ranging from representative democracies to fascist dictatorships to communist regimes. Regardless of form, states share one defining characteristic—the non-negotiable claim to sovereignty. All modern states claim the supreme and indivisible power to rule over a national territory. This non-negotiable monopoly of state sovereignty was recognized formally in the Peace of Westphalia in 1648, which cast the world community as consisting of "sovereign states." These states controlled their own territories and could legitimately use force to repel threats to national security and sovereignty arising either from domestic politics or external threats (Held, 1996, 69). This idea of the fusion of power, sovereignty, authority, and legitimacy, which structures current thinking about politics, is clearly conveyed by Weber's often cited definition of the **state**. He called it "a human community that successfully claims monopoly of the legitimate use of physical force within a given territory" (quoted in Gerth and Mills, 1958, 78).

The consequences of ever-intensifying globalization, however, have led some to argue that the world is fast entering into a **post-sovereign** age, that is, a period when states are no longer sovereign over national territories. For example, the World Trade Organization (WTO) now has the binding legal capacity to overrule national laws which are deemed to interfere with the free flow of global trade. Similarly, environmental and migration issues are now beyond the capacity of any single state to resolve. And, as the Kosovo crisis demonstrated, the world community now takes the position that state sovereignty can be bypassed when there is evidence of gross human rights violations within a country. All of these and other factors point to the diminishing capacity of sovereign states to determine what happens inside their territorial boundaries.

To sum up, the study of politics revolves around a number of critical concepts, among them, power, authority, legitimacy, sovereignty, and the state. But political scientists have adopted quite distinct perspectives on how politics works within and among national territories. Next we will briefly review four broad approaches, each of which serves as a guidepost to explore the complex world of politics. Legal-institutionalism, pluralism, elite analysis, and class analysis are only four, among the many perspectives, that political scientists have adopted in order to compare and explain the political world around us. Approaches are simply perspectives. They highlight one part of the complex matrix of political life, often to the exclusion of others. Approaches to politics are neither true nor false, only more or less useful in helping us to understand political events. But, as we will see, using one approach rather than another forces us to accept a number of other assumptions about the nature of political actors, the basic structures of social organization, and the appropriate ways to achieve political change. Theories of politics are also theories of society, providing answers to questions such as what the basic units of political society are and how power is distributed. Almost all approaches, including the four detailed in this chapter, assume a liberal configuration of social and political life, as the next few paragraphs explain.

Liberalism

Liberalism, in its various manifestations, finds its logic in what Walzer appropriately terms, "the art of separation." Early liberal theorists sought to reconfigure feudal society, which was structured around ideas of hierarchy and interdependence, by recasting it as a "world of walls." Emerging alongside capitalism, liberalism recast the old feudal society as a segmented society— "they drew lines, marked off different realms and created the social/political map" with which we still live (Walzer, 1984, 315). The Church was separated from the state so that the latter could be governed by the principles of responsible government and, later, of liberal democracy. In turn, the state was mapped out as a separate sphere from the market, which operated under the capitalist rules of supply and demand. Finally, a line was drawn between the state and economy and the sphere of the private or social. This sphere included the grab bag of those things that were not explicitly in the public sphere or in the market— things such as the family, cultural activities, and voluntary groups.

Following from Marx's criticism of capitalism, Marxists fundamentally disagree that liberalism's separation of the market and of politics is an accurate reflection of how the political world actually works. Feminists also disagree that the private sphere of the family is devoid of politics and unconnected to the economy. Nonetheless, liberalism was ascendant, especially in the United States, when the social sciences became professional academic disciplines. These disciplines would carve out social life with unquestioning devotion to the liberal's world of walls. Economics would become the science of the market; political science the science of the public and the political, and sociology the science of the private and the social. Liberalism, it must be emphasized, was a political idea, a discourse if you like, about the appropriate organization of economic, social, and political life in the dying days of feudalism. Advanced and hotly debated by Western political theorists in the seventeenth century, liberalism eventually became embodied in the key institutions of liberal democracy,

FIGURE 1.1   *Liberalism: The Art of Separation in Public Policy*

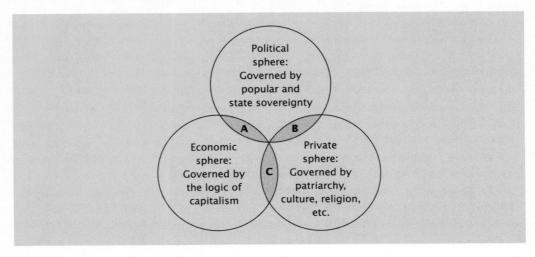

liberal democracy, among them, the judiciary, the constitution, representative government, citizenship, and democratic elections.

Liberalism's world of walls, as Figure 1.1 shows, severely constrained the social terrain afforded to the new science of politics. The political sphere was the public sphere, the world of public institutions and formal processes. The intersection of the three spheres of liberalism was limited. The liberal state intersected with the market (see A in figure) to the extent that it enforced such things as contracts and property law, controlled currency, set standards for measurement, and protected private property. Similarly, the state intervened in the private (see B) to the extent that it set conditions for legal marriage and custody of children, and intervened in the home in cases of extreme poverty or family violence. The state also mediated between the market and the private sphere (see C) through such things as the protection of collective bargaining for workers, consumer protection, and environmental controls.

Approaches to the Study of Politics

Legal-Institutionalism

It is not surprising, then, that early political scientists defined their task as explaining those things obviously contained within the political sphere, especially laws and institutions and formal political processes. Legal-institutionalism provided a descriptive and comparative analysis of the institutional infrastructure of the liberal state. Texts focused on questions such as the differences between parliamentary and congressional systems, federal and unitary systems, a separation of power versus a fusion of power, and written versus unwritten constitutions. A.V. Dicey's book, *An Introduction to the Study of the Law of the Constitution*, first published in 1908 and reprinted many times and in many languages since then, is a classic example of the legal-institutional approach.

Canada's early political scientists also emphasized the centrality of institutions in explaining the complex contours of Canadian politics. Professor Alexander Brady's text, *Canada,* published in 1932, provides a good example. In it, Brady explains that Canadians have maintained their political identity, although living in the shadow of the United States, largely because of their political institutions. Canadians' "rich inheritance of common law and constitutional custom," writes Brady, "combined with the rigid character of the British North America Act, have helped preserve them from an over-ready surrender to the methods and thought dominant in the continent. In political life [Canadians] have retained their identity" (1932, 82).

The questions posed by legal-institutionalism remain important to political scientists today. In fact, introductory textbooks such as this one devote a great deal of effort to clarifying the distinctions between different kinds of legal and political institutions. Nevertheless, events leading up to the Second World War created doubts that legal institutionalism could explain how politics worked. For example, the horrors of Nazi Germany could not be predicted or explained by studying its constitution. How could the politics of a country with a history of constitutionalism take such a turn? Could something similar be prevented in the future? The legal-institutional approach could not provide answers to these questions.

Advances in scientific polling, after World War II, also created doubts about whether liberal democracies actually worked in the way that legal-institutionalists assumed. In particular, this approach assumed that citizens behaved in the way that democratic theory prescribed. In theory, at least, citizens were active and informed, could identify and prioritize the political choices offered to them at election time, and voted accordingly. Early public opinion polls, however, showed that most citizens did not pay attention to politics, even fewer were active in political parties and other political organizations, most had trouble distinguishing between the political right and the political left and most did not understand the implications of particular policy choices. This mismatch between political theory and political behaviour encouraged political scientists, overwhelmingly located in the United States, to rethink the relationship between society and the state.

Pluralism

Postwar political science took on the task of developing an approach to politics that would explain the realities of modern politics and, at the same time, preserve the idea of the superiority of a democratic system. Strongly influenced by liberal political thinking, the **pluralist** school argued that, although the individual remained the basic unit of democratic politics, the sheer size and complexity of modern society had long ago ruled out a democratic politics revolving around the informed and active democratic citizen. The notion of a town hall democracy was no longer sustainable but this did not mean that democracy itself was dead. Instead, pluralists saw politics as the play for preferred policy outcomes among an endless variety of competing groups.

The pluralist's emphasis on groups reflected the relatively high rates of voluntary group membership in postwar United States as well as a strong tradition of group theory in American social thought. In the early 1900s, for example, Arthur Bentley tried to explain the political process through an analysis of group membership and competition. For Bentley groups represented interests, many of them overtly political. He argued that political society was best studied as a series of group interests arrayed against other group interests. The political world was composed of groups and little else. As Bentley explains, in the study of politics, "We shall always find the political interests and activities of any given group... . The society itself is nothing other than the complex of groups that compose it" (Bentley 1908, 222).

Postwar pluralist thinkers were less single-minded about the primacy of groups. Pluralists identified groups as the primary, instead of only, vehicle for exchanges between citizens and the state as well as the locus for democracy. Pluralist theory sees politics as operating from the bottom up, that is to say, politics is initiated by the citizens of a democratic polity. The governance of modern society, however, is far too complex and society too large to nurture the direct political participation of everyone in the political process. Instead, individuals join groups that promote their interests. Since modern citizens have many interests, they may hold membership in many different kinds of groups, ranging from a parent-teacher organization to an association to abolish capital punishment, a gun collectors club, or a lesbian and gay choir.

Many of the groups to which citizens belong have a direct interface with the public sphere but most do not. According to the pluralists, groups become politically active around political issues that concern or affect their members. They make coalitions and compete with other groups for preferred policy outcomes. No one group is a permanent player in pluralist politics. Neither does one group always win. Different groups with different resources move in and out of the political sphere when their interests are affected. Politics is a constant play of groups that both advance the interests of their respective memberships and check the power of other groups. Everyone gets to play and there are no winners assumed at the onset of a political debate. As prominent pluralist theorist Robert Dahl contended "all active and legitimate groups in the population can make themselves heard at some critical stage in the process of decision making" (1956, 137).

The pluralist approach was very much committed to promoting the idea that both the democratic citizen and the democratic system, although somewhat modified, were alive and well in postwar America. Their message was that democratic pluralism was a system of governance that could and should be emulated in countries emerging from the rubble of fascism and the Second World War as well as in new countries recently released from the bonds of European colonialism. Citizens were free to join groups, to advance their interests, and to choose group leaders, indeed to become leaders themselves to represent their interests in the policy process. As important, the state was not predisposed to favour one group over another. The game of politics, in other words, was not stacked for or against anyone. Pluralists viewed the state as neutral, serving to mediate among competing groups and to strike compromise and consensus in public policy. From a pluralist perspective the state processed group demands or inputs and converted them to public policies or outputs. Officials inside the state did not adopt policies which were self-serving and the institutions of government did not manipulate democratic processes to favour some groups over others. The strength of democracy on the ground, as it were, in clubs, groups, and communities, in turn, was a powerful preventive to the rise of authoritarian or corrupt regimes.

Elitism

At the same time that the pluralist school was advancing its celebration of democratic pluralism, the approach found powerful critics both inside and outside the United States. E.E. Schattschneider, an American political scientist and liberal thinker, criticized the pluralist school for misrepresenting the extent and nature of group membership in the United States. Most group members were decidedly middle class and most groups rarely engaged directly with politics. Schattschneider mused that if there were a pluralist heaven then "the heavenly chorus sings with a strong upper-class accent." Schattschneider also argued that political institutions were not neutral but, instead, set in motion what he termed a "mobilization of bias" (1960, 29). Others argued that the singular focus of the pluralist approach on the decision-making process obscured the fact that power is also exercised, perhaps even more strongly, when issues never make it to the public agenda and when no decision is made. In these cases inaction would obscure and preserve an unequal and power-saturated status quo (Bachrach and Baratz, 1970).

The most sustained criticism of the pluralist approach in the United States, however, came from the new elite theorists. They revived a long tradition of elite theorizing about the possibility of sustaining a meaningful democracy in modern societies. Elite theorists, for different reasons, argued that a select few, in all societies, manipulate the levers of government for their own advantage. President Dwight Eisenhower, just before departing office in 1960, warned the American public of the growing power of what he termed the "military-industrial complex." Himself a former general and war hero, Eisenhower argued that a triad of military leaders, arms manufacturers, and sympathetic public officials posed a threat to American democracy. Elite theorist C. Wright Mills fleshed out the "military-industrial complex" in his famous book *The Power Elite*, which appeared on bookshelves beside Robert Dahl's pluralist primer, *Preface to Democracy*, in 1956.

Elite theory has a long tradition in political theory and in the evolution of political science. It is based on a very different view of society than the one advanced in the pluralist model. While pluralism focused on individuals in groups, elitism proposed a stark divide between the few and the many. The few, the elite, occupy the most powerful positions in the central institutions of society—the military, religion, the economy, politics, and culture. The few hold the power while the many do not. There is little debate about the fact that there are leaders and followers in all societies—the questions posed by elite theory are, first, is this a good or bad thing, and second, do elites threaten democracy?

Plato advanced the idea that good governance was best achieved when an elite of "philosopher kings," endowed with wisdom, virtue, and prudence were given the exclusive power to rule. At the turn of this century, Italian sociologists Vilfredo Pareto (1848–1923) and Gaetano Mosca (1858–1941) claimed that elite rule was an inevitable fact of human existence. For these elite theorists, all societies were characterized by a fundamental truth— the few (elites) rule the many (masses). Pareto advanced this dichotomous model of society quite starkly. "Whatever certain theorists may like to think," he wrote, "human society in fact is not a homogeneous thing, and different individuals are physically, morally, and intellectually different" (1978, 247). A few excel and the great majority are average.

Mosca presents a similar depiction of social organization. "In all societies," he contends, "two classes of people appear—a class that rules and a class that is ruled." The first class performs "all political functions, monopolizes power and enjoys the advantages that power brings" and controls the second class (quoted in Knuttila, 1987, 50). Pareto and Mosca advanced the case that elite rule is a basic fact of human existence and inevitable. A meaningful democratic politics, therefore, was neither possible nor desirable. It is perhaps for this reason that the Italian fascists of the 1930s embraced these theorists, especially Mosca, and their anti-democratic thought.

Perhaps the most often cited elite theorist, Roberto Michels (1876–1936), also argued that elite rule was inevitable, although not necessarily desirable. Michels was active in social democratic politics and observed how elites captured the party organization, even though party ideology was committed to democracy. According to Michels, modern society was governed by what he called "the iron law of the oligarchy" (rule by a few). Modern societies require large and complex organizations which are characterized by specialization and a division of labour. The latter creates a hierarchy in which a few, because of their organizational position and skills, gain experience, expertise, power, and control. As the elite's skill set grows, it becomes increasingly distant from the rank-and-file of the organization who, in turn, grow apathetic and disempowered. It is through this process, according to Michels, that democracy inevitably leads to oligarchy, or elite rule (Knuttila, 1987, 52–3).

Michels' point was that elites gain their power because of their strategic position within modern organizations and not because of human nature. Most elite studies now identify powerful institutions and key figures within them as the starting point of their analyses. These studies often find that the elite of a variety of sectors, including politics, the military, the media, and business, are overwhelmingly white, wealthy, and male. They share similar backgrounds, attend the same elite schools, frequently interact socially and through marriage, and share similar values and opinions. But, these similarities do not necessarily demonstrate that we are governed by oligarchy or that the study of elites tells us all that we need to know about power and politics.

Pareto once mused that "history is the graveyard of elites" (1976, 249), and in some ways it is. There are few examples in politics where there are no leaders and followers. The starting point of elite theory, that society is composed of two groups—the elite and the masses—seems obvious and, thus, for many, is an appealing approach to the study of politics. Few would argue that the study of political and other institutional leadership is not important, but this does not mean we can explain politics through the narrow lens of elite analysis. Critics of elite theory argue that it over-emphasizes the cohesion of elites. As we know, there is considerable conflict and competition among the powerful. What factors determine the winners and losers in struggles among the elite? Others suggest that elite theory ignores the institutional constraints that make it impossible for elites to ignore the masses. Elected officials, for example, still have to get elected by the people. Finally, others, especially Marxist critics, suggest that elite analysis is simply a poorly theorized class analysis, which fails to locate elites in the broader historical and economic context and ignores the ever-present tensions arising from class conflict.

Class Analysis

There are many variations of class analysis but each envisions society as being divided into hierarchical strata or ranks which have unequal access to power, authority, and influence. Sociologists call this the study of social stratification. Political scientists, following from the work of Karl Marx see, in these social divisions, social classes, antagonistically grounded in the organization of the economy while followers of Max Weber see status groups that can be ranked on the basis of wealth and prestige. Karl Marx's theory of the capitalist organization of politics and society is explained in more detail later in this volume. Here we will concentrate on the concept of social class and its implications for the study of politics.

Although social stratification has always been recognized in political theory, Marx was the first to develop a comprehensive theory of social class. Marx, as we saw earlier in this chapter, believed that all societies were divided along class lines and that, moreover, classes were necessarily and always in conflict over the distribution of material resources in society. Marx provided an overarching explanation of history grounded in the historical organization of the economy. He argued that the "economic structure of society" was "the real foundation" from which arises a society's legal structure and politics (1970, 21).

Although Marx argued that a focus on the way economies are organized and the class divisions that result explained the politics of all societies, the bulk of his writings on social class pertain to the emergence of capitalism and industrialization in Europe. He contended that democratic government was the result of a political revolution of a new class— commercial and industrial capitalists or, as Marx called them, the bourgeoisie. At the same time, the emergence of capitalism created another new class—the working class or the proletariat—who sold their labour to capitalists and were exploited by them. Marx's careful analysis of the logic of capitalism led him to conclude that, in time, the middle class would be absorbed into the working class and the living conditions of the working class would become more and more desperate. The politics of capitalist societies would then revolve around a struggle between capitalists and workers. The working class of the world, through revolution, would ultimately win and establish a communist society. Capitalism, unlike previous systems, Marx concluded, had a distinctive identifying feature. As he and Engels put it in the *Communist Manifesto*, capitalism "has simplified the class antagonisms. Society as a whole is more and more splitting up into two great hostile camps, into two great classes directly facing each other, bourgeoisie and proletariat" (1952, 8).

Marx's work on social class and the inevitability of class conflict significantly influenced political science as well as the politics of the twentieth century. Nonetheless, many of the political developments of the twentieth century also suggested to many that Marx's analysis was too extreme and failed to account for many of the subsequent changes in the stratification of society. His work has been criticized for its *economic determinism*, that is, for reducing the explanation of all social phenomena to a single factor, the organization of the economy. Others argue that, contrary to Marx's prediction, the middle class did not disappear as capitalism matured, but instead, grew to be an important political force. White-collar workers and professionals do not fit easily into Marx's scheme of class conflict because they are neither capitalists nor working class in a traditional Marxist definition of these terms. Finally, others, following from the work of Max Weber, argue that social stratification occurs along many dimensions due to a variety of factors, not solely one's position in the organization of economic relations.

When Weber contemplated the ways that societies were stratified, he saw quite a different world than did Marx. The starkly oppressive conditions of emerging industrialization had been somewhat improved, the working class had organized into unions and socialist political parties, democracy had expanded, and, as Weber saw it, society was increasingly governed by legal-rational authority and large bureaucracies. He argued that social stratification could no longer be studied as a product of social class alone. For Weber, social class remained an important determinant of power but it was not the only factor. Modern society was divided into many status groups whose position on the social hierarchy was also determined by prestige and by political power. Prestige could involve things as intangible as tastes and patterns of consumption that are socially valued such as driving a Mercedes or being a celebrated author. This kind of social power, while not entirely unrelated to social class, is not reducible to economic relations alone.

Weber's work on status groups encouraged political scientists and sociologists to explain social divisions in influence and power on the basis of a variety of factors, including patterns of consumption, the social prestige assigned to some professions such as medicine or law, and factors such as ethnicity, gender, race, and religion. Weber's work also encouraged political scientists in the United States, where the Marxist tradition was not strong, to talk about class divisions in non-antagonistic ways. Social class was analyzed along a continuum—upper class, middle class, and lower class—without any notion of exploitation or conflict among these groups. Weber's work, nonetheless, underlined the many ways that power and influence are unequally distributed in society, quite often on the basis of characteristics we are assigned at birth, such as gender and race.

To sum up, the legal-institutional, pluralist, elite, and class approaches to the study of politics are only four among many ways to view the political world. They do, nonetheless, highlight many of the critical concepts in political science. Legal-institutionalism emphasizes the importance of formal political institutions and how constitutions structure the rules of the political game and thus, often, the outcome. Pluralists, in contrast, emphasize the informal ingredients of power, individual political actors and the competition among groups for their preferred policy outcomes. They emphasize the play of politics from the bottom up, from the citizen to the state, while elitism focuses on the opposite flow, from leadership down. Although the elite approach probably exaggerates the isolation and independence of elites from the vast majority, it does point to the ways that ordinary citizens are often distanced from the political world and lack the expertise and information to engage in effective political participation. Finally, the class approach points to the ways in which power and influence are unevenly distributed in societies on the basis of social structure, position, and identity. Whether we agree with Marx or with Weber about the singular or multiple causes of social stratification, the class/status approach tells us that we can never study the individual political actor outside the context of history or the broader social divisions of power and influence. Having traced many of the key perspectives of the political world, this chapter concludes with a discussion of some of the new challenges facing political science in the twenty-first century.

Politics in the Twenty-First Century

EACH OF THE CHAPTERS IN THIS VOLUME ADDRESSES THE CONTINUING usefulness of the above approaches to political science as well as new perspectives introduced into political analysis by, among other factors, globalization, postmodernism, feminism, and new social movements. The text is still very much focused on the traditional concerns of political science—the nation-state, primarily liberal democratic states such as Canada; national political institutions; national patterns of politics; and relationships between states. These themes have been the bread and butter of political science since its conception. Familiarity with these themes and the debates that they continue to generate are a necessary beginning point for any student of politics.

The chapters in this book also introduce the conceptual and practical problems that globalization and rapid technological change are now posing for political science and for contemporary politics generally. Currently political scientists, political activists, and citizens alike find themselves deeply involved in a prolonged process of fundamental change. Many of the critical concepts of political science are losing their initial intent and meaning— among them, state sovereignty, citizenship rights, social welfare, development, community, democracy, and political identity. All of these are said to have been "decentred, dislocated, and fragmented" by globalization (Hall, 1996, 596).

Mouffe goes so far as to suggest that "what is at stake for citizens of the late twentieth century is politics itself and the distinct possibility of its elimination" (1993, 1). But, if we are to believe Aristotle, we are still political animals. Politics will always be an integral part of our collective existence and of our daily lives. Indeed, as the fates of the many peoples of the world become ever increasingly interwoven, politics is perhaps more important and necessary than ever before. Globalization has, however, eroded familiar political institutions and patterns of politics without clearly signalling what will take their place.

Globalization is fast becoming one of the most overused and least understood words in contemporary speech. There are many definitions of globalization and, like definitions of power, each structures political relationships in different ways. Liberal economists and other supporters of global capitalism, for example, tend to define it in narrow liberal and market terms. From this liberal perspective, globalization represents progress, the opening of new markets, the end of political interference in the economy, new technologies, travel, more and cheaper goods, and so on. All of these advances, moreover, are accomplished through rapid technological advances which deem territorial borders increasingly irrelevant. This discourse obviously discounts the social and political consequences of globalization which are described in various chapters that follow.

Others depict globalization as a still-unfolding process that involves critical shifts in power and influence among institutions, countries, and people. In particular, social, economic, and political processes are increasingly flowing either over or through nation-states and national territories. These processes, in turn, challenge the continuing viability of state sovereignty and national democratic governance. The erosion of state sovereignty is particularly critical in the current era because much of our modern thinking about the political is tied to it. Democratic theory, approaches to power and politics, political institutions, and citizenship all have been built up around the assumption of state sovereignty which has held sway for the past four hundred years. The politics of the twenty-first century, however, makes it apparent that national electorates are increasingly at a loss to hold their governments accountable. As one analyst puts it, all the big decisions "are made outside of all national boundaries, even as they shape life within all such entities. It is as if global capitalism was headquartered somewhere off the globe" (Persky, 1992, 187).

Summary

This textbook provides an introduction to the critical concepts of political science, their origin, their ongoing importance in political life, and the challenges to their viability in the future. There is an old cliché that says "we can't understand where we are going, unless we understand where we have been." This cliché resonates in today's world. As we debate today's political issues, it is important to realize that similar questions vexed other societies and that, through politics, they arrived at either reasonable or horrible solutions. The kind of politics we will have in an era of globalization, as well as the solutions we find to global coexistence are still ours to create, although as Marx would remind us, not necessarily under conditions of our own choosing. Globalization challenges old assumptions and creates new political problems. It does not, however, release us from the responsibility of constantly revisiting the fundamental political questions of what is and, more important, what ought to be.

Discussion Questions

1. Think about your day. How often did you encounter politics? What kind of politics did you encounter? Were there some encounters that entailed more power than others? Why? In what ways could you have resisted that power?
2. Compare and contrast the approaches to politics discussed in this chapter.
3. As we enter a new millennium, describe the basic elements of what politics means to you. What will politics look like in the twenty-first century? Why?

References

Bachrach, Peter and Morton Baratz. 1970. *Power and Poverty: Theory and Practice.* New York: Oxford University Press.

Bauman, Zygmunt. 1985. "Social Class." in Adam Kuper and Jessica Kuper, eds. *The Social Science Encyclopedia.* London: Routledge.

Bendix, Reinhard. 1960. Max Weber: *An Intellectual Portrait.* Garden City, N.Y.: Doubleday.

Bentley, Arthur. 1935. *The Process of Government. Evanstown,* Illinois: Principia Press.

Bottomore, Tom. 1979. *Political Sociology.* London: Harper and Row Publishers.

Brady, Alexander. 1932. *Canada.* London: Ernest Benn Limited.

Brodie, Janine. 1995. *Politics on the Margins: Restructuring and the Canadian Women's Movement.* Halifax: Fernwood Publishing.

Dahl, Robert. 1956. *Preface to Democratic Theory.* Chicago: University of Chicago Press.

_____. 1961. *Who Governs.* New Haven, Conn.: Yale University Press.

Dicey, A.V. 1908. *An Introduction to the Study of the Law of the Constitution.* 7th edition. London: Macmillan.

Fink-Eitel, Hinrich. 1992. *Foucault: An Introduction.* Philadelphia: Pennbridge Books.

Foucault, Michel. 1977. *Power/Knowledge.* New York: Pantheon.

Fraser, Nancy, and Linda Gordon. 1994. "A Geneology of Dependency: Tracing a Keyword of the US Welfare State." *Signs,* 19, 2 (Winter).

Gerth, H.H. and C.W. Mills, eds. 1958. *From Max Weber: Essays in Sociology.* New York: Oxford University Press.

Guy, James John. 1995. *People, Politics, Government: Political Science: A Canadian Perspective.* Scarborough, ON: Prentice Hall.

Hall, Stuart. 1996. "The Question of Cultural Identity." in Stuart Hall, David Held, Don Hubert and Kenneth Thompson, eds. *Modernity: An Introduction to the Modern Social Sciences.* London: Blackwell.

Hawley, Amos. 1963. "Community Power and Urban Renewal Success." *American Journal of Sociology.* Vol. 68 (January).

Held, David. 1996. "The Development of the Modern State." in Stuart Hall, David Held, Don Hubert and Kenneth Thompson, eds. *Modernity: An Introduction to the Modern Social Sciences.* London: Blackwell.

Knuttila, Murray. 1987. *State Theories.* Toronto: Garamond.

Kourvetaris, George. 1997. *Political Sociology: Structure and Process.* Boston: Allyn and Bacon.

Lasswell, Harold. 1936. *Politics: Who Gets, What, When and How.* New York: McGraw-Hill.

Mannheim, Karl. 1936. *Ideology and Utopia.* New York: Harvest Books.

Michels, Roberto. 1962. *Political Parties.* New York: The Free Press.

Mouffe, Chantal. 1992. *Dimensions of Radical Democracy: Pluralism, Citizenship, Community.* London: Verso.

Pareto, Vilfredo. 1978. *Sociological Writings.* Oxford: Basil Blackwell.

Persky. Stan. 1992. "City Without Citizens." in Max Wyman, ed. *Vancouver Forum: Old Powers, New Forces.* Vancouver: Douglas McIntyre.

Philp, Mark. 1985. "Power." in Adam Kuper and Jessica Kuper, eds. *The Social Science Encyclopedia.* New York: Routledge.

Schattschneider, E.E. 1960. *The Semi-Sovereign People: A Realist's View of Democracy.* New York: Holt, Reinhart and Winston.

Simons, Jon. 1995. *Foucault and the Political.* New York: Routledge.

Walzer, Michael. 1984. "Liberalism and the Art of Separation." *Political Theory.* 12 (August).

Further Readings

Bottomore, Tom. 1979. *Political Sociology.* London: Harper and Row Publishers.

Hall, Stuart, David Held, Don Hubert and Kenneth Thompson, eds. 1996. *Modernity: An Introduction to the Social Sciences.* London: Blackwell.

Knuttila, Murray. 1987. *State Theories.* Toronto: Garamond.

Weblinks

American Political Science Association
www.apsanet.org

Canadian Political Science Association
www.sfu.ca/igs/CPSA.html

Department of Political Science, University of Alberta
www.ualbertaa.ca/~polisci/index.html

International Studies Association
www.isanet.org

CHAPTER 2

DEMOCRATIC THEORY

CATHERINE
KELLOGG

Objectives

This chapter examines one of the most "critical" concepts of the current era—democracy. **Democracy** is a critical concept because it highlights the question of the "public." The distinction between what is public and what is private has been extremely important to the study of politics. This chapter begins by showing how the concept of democracy involves the question of the public. The chapter then provides a brief history of democratic thought, from the philosophers of the *polis* of Ancient Greece to today's theorists of radical democracy. We find that dramatic shifts in thinking about democracy often occur in periods of social change, when societies are forced to reflect on themselves and on their assumptions about the fundamentals of social organization and governance. The current era of globalization is just such a period of reflection. Key assumptions about governing such as the nature of the capitalist market and its relationship with the state are now being revisited and reformulated. More specifically, contemporary thinkers are suggesting that many dimensions of human experience such as sexuality, the family, and "private" property are in fact political in nature, and are therefore public concerns. Some contemporary theorists of democracy question the distinction between public and private set down by the tradition of liberal democratic theory. In this sense, contemporary democracy is said to be "in crisis." As a way of trying to understand this current crisis, the chapter concludes by introducing ongoing debates in contemporary democratic thought.

Introduction

The word *democracy* comes from the Greek *demos* (people) and *kratos* (rule). In the classical literature we refer to, democracy means the "rule of the many." It is generally contrasted with the "rule of the few" (aristocracy) or the "rule of one" (monarchy). More recently, however, *democracy* is used to refer to its literal translation as "the rule of the people." Simply put, democracy is any form of government in which the rules of society are decided by the people who will be bound by them. This is how the concept of democracy implicates the public: it suggests that public affairs—the rules of society—should be decided by the public itself.

What is distinctive about theories of democracy is their common insistence that the authority of the state begins and ends with the public. At the root of the practice of democracy lies a faith in the capacity of people to decide key issues of governance for themselves. While this belief is the central tenet of democratic theory, it is not limited to classical democratic theorists such as Jean Jacques Rousseau or John Stuart Mill. It is also found in the editorial pages of our newspapers. Indeed, the view that governments should operate only through the "will" of the people is so widespread that the only regimes in the modern world considered legitimate are those based on popular consent.

Despite the widespread appeal of democracy, anyone who looks closely at this concept is bound to notice that it means many different things to different people. Indeed, Robert Dahl explains that a "term that means anything means nothing. And so it has become with 'democracy' which nowadays is not so much a term of restricted and specific meaning, as a vague endorsement of a popular idea" (Dahl, 1989, 2). Not only does the word itself imply the "populus" or the public, but democracy as an ideal receives seemingly unanimous support the world over. For instance, the vast majority of national constitutions in the world today claim to be democratic. It is precisely the popularity of this concept that leads our political leaders to use the word *democracy* when they are stuck for something to say. Like the British politician of the late nineteenth century who, when asked a difficult question, always mentioned the name of the popular Liberal party leader Gladstone because the five minutes of cheering that ensued gave him time to formulate an answer, the word *democracy* has been used to navigate politicians out of many tight spots. The word is often used simply as a synonym of "good." In short, democracy is hailed as the master principle of our age.

Theory and Crisis

DEMOCRATIC THEORY IS THE DOMINANT FRAME OR THEORY THROUGH WHICH WE organize and make meaningful the world of politics. In fact, constructing theories is nothing more than the process through which we organize and make our lives meaningful. Even when we are performing a mundane task, we are doing so within a set of assumptions that have rendered that activity meaningful in some way. In this sense, all social life is founded on theory; a compilation of ideas that tell a coherent story about a given human practice. Theory is an activity that goes on all the time, even when we are unaware of it. But at certain moments the theories making our lives meaningful no longer seem to fit our experience or make sense of the world. These are times of *crisis*.

For instance, if this morning you looked out the window at the sky and it was green, this usually uneventful experience would no longer be so. You would likely come up with a set of possible theories for why the sky was not blue this morning. Perhaps it was that the beer you drank last night was laced with hallucinogenic drugs, or that you are losing your grip on reality. Theory becomes visible when we are forced to become aware of a human practice that has in the past seemed most ordinary and most un-theoretical. Theory becomes visible when the ideas ordering ordinary human practices stop making sense.

Like every other kind of human activity, politics has its own set of theories. Political theories are interpretations—coherent stories that order and make sense of the world—about politics. In fact, the history of Western political thought can be understood as the history of the practice of theories of democracy. More precisely, the history of political thought can be understood as the history of waves of *crisis* that have forced human beings to reflect upon practices of human governance; democratic and otherwise.

One of the most interesting things about the current state of democratic theory is that it is now at a point of crisis. This crisis in democratic theory stems from a variety of factors including a crisis in contemporary practices of democracy. Many issues that until now were not understood to belong to the tradition of democratic thought have come into view. For instance, democracy has generally been taken to mean something as simple as the representation of citizens in legislatures where we are recognized as "formally" equal. But certain thinkers have begun to question whether formal equality can mean anything very profound when we are so demonstrably unequal to each other with respect to our access to other kinds of power. The power at work in the areas of our lives previously considered "private," for instance, our workplaces, our families, or the "private sector"—the capitalist market—is perhaps as important politically as are the formal processes of political decision making. Can we consider truly democratic a set of political and social arrangements that render us formally equal to each other when the way that we actually live our lives is increasingly unequal? What are the real requirements of democratic citizenship? In order to begin making sense of these questions, we will look at three historical "models" of democratic thought.

A History of Democratic Theory

DEMOCRACY MEANS, AND HAS MEANT, A GREAT NUMBER OF DIFFERENT THINGS TO different people. However, Canadian political theorist C.B. MacPherson tells us that "in looking at models of democracy . . . we should keep a sharp lookout for two things: [the theory's] assumptions about the whole society in which the democratic political system is to operate, and its assumptions about the essential nature of the people who are to make the system work (which for a democratic system means the people in general, not just a ruling or leading class)" (MacPherson, 1977, 5). The following section offers a brief history of democratic theories. It pays particular attention to the assumptions those theories make about the essential nature of both society and the people who inhabit it.

Ancient Greek Democracy

The development of democracy in Athens during its "golden age"—which lasted for about fifty years in the fifth century B.C.E.—has been the source of inspiration for much modern democratic political thought. For instance, the modern ideals of equality before the law, liberty, and respect are often traced to the ancient Greek *polis*. This small, self-contained institutional form nurtured intense communal life. The *polis* formed the ethical model for subsequent thinkers as diverse as Thomas Hobbes, John Locke, Alexis de Tocqueville, Jean-Jacques Rousseau, and G.W.F. Hegel.

The Greek word *polis* is the root for a range of English words, including *politics, politician, political,* and *police.* While there is no exact English equivalent, *polis* is commonly translated as both *state* and *city,* because it possesses attributes of both. Central to the life of the Athenian *polis* was smallness of scale. Although scholars do not agree on precise figures, it is estimated that some 300 000 people lived in Athens at its height. Only 40 000 however, were citizens. The rest of the population—women, children, foreign residents, and slaves—were excluded from the ranks of the citizen and from formal participation in political life. The "public" realm, then, was actually made up of a very small percentage of the inhabitants of the Greek city-state.

The small size of the *polis* allowed citizens to partake of a distinctive communal way of life. Spheres of life we now consider non-political—religion, art, sport, and commerce—were all considered within the purview of politics. They were therefore subject to democratic deliberation. The small size of the *polis* also provided its citizens with a sense of active involvement in public affairs that has not been widely duplicated at any other time. Greek direct democracy was probably the most *participatory* form of politics that Western civilization has ever seen.

Following approximately fifty years of flourishing, ancient Athens and its allies entered into a conflict with oligarchies that sided with Sparta. This conflict—known as the Peloponnesian Wars—ended with the complete defeat and occupation of democratic Athens. Precisely because the Greek city state or *polis* was in crisis, Plato and Aristotle were impelled to think about politics in a new way, and to write their important works. For instance, the trial and execution of Socrates—the political philosopher so admired by Plato—inspired Plato to question the validity of rule by those who were ignorant of the most pressing questions of the purpose of life. Perhaps, he suggested, Greek citizens were not truly able to rule themselves but required the leadership of those specifically trained in the art of state and soul-craft. Despite the democratic nature of the ancient Greek state, then, the political thinkers we most associate with ancient Greece—Plato, Aristotle, and Thucydides—were uniformly hostile to the direct democracy represented by the Greek *polis.*

Notwithstanding this hostility to democracy, both Plato and Aristotle were profoundly influenced by the participatory nature of the Greek city-state. Significantly, Aristotle argued that "man is a political animal." By this he meant that human beings can attain their full potential only by living in political association with each other. It is only through active involvement in the life of one's political community that citizens can know what is truly important. Thus we can see that, for the ancient Greeks, a good citizen was someone actively involved in the day-to-day running of their government.

The Middle Ages and Italian Republicanism

There is a strange silence in the history of democratic thought that begins shortly after the demise of Athenian democracy and ends with the early Renaissance. This period overlaps significantly with what we call the Medieval period, or the "Middle Ages," which are meant to mark the "middle" period between the collapse of the Roman Empire in the fifth century and the beginning of the Renaissance in the fourteenth. This silence in the history of political thought is a complex matter to explain, but in its simplest terms, the ascendency in the Western world of the Christian faith, as well as the rise of feudal forms of social organization, meant that the "good" citizen of the Ancient Greek *polis*, was replaced by the "true believer." The Greek world view—which suggested that political good could be found in active participation in public affairs—was replaced by one which insisted that the "highest good" was to be found only in the next world. The idea that humans could organize their common futures democratically was replaced by the idea that everyone's fate was predetermined by God.

By the middle part of the Medieval period, Europe was also dominated by **feudalism**. This form of social and economic organization was characterized by a strict hierarchy between the property-owning aristocracy and the landless peasants. This way of life emphasized the deeply held belief that people were fundamentally unequal; those who held power did so because they were essentially "better" than those that they ruled. Feudalism was set against the backdrop of the Holy Roman Empire; a complex web of kings and rulers who were understood to rule by "divine right." The authority of these rulers was said to come directly from God. In short, throughout the Middle Ages, European politics was heavily influenced by three great supra-national institutions: the Church, the Holy Roman Empire, and feudalism.

By the beginning of the sixteenth century, a number of political communities had established some form of popular control, especially in northern Italy. What eventually became the new "city-states" or city republics were run by elected councillors. Councillors were ultimately accountable to male householders with taxable property. This notion of accountability represented an important challenge to the prevailing understanding that rule was God-given. An outcome of this new social order was a return to the ideas of **civic republicanism** first articulated by Aristotle: the idea of active involvement in the state as a "good." For we recall that for Aristotle, human beings are essentially political, and they only flourish when they are involved in making the important decisions of public life. Central to this idea is the notion of a political community with a shared history and a shared destiny. Thus, the Renaissance (literally, *rebirth*) was so named because it recalled many of the ideas of ancient Greek democracy.

Capitalism and the Liberal Revolution

The slow movement out of the Middle Ages typified by these revived ideas led from the Renaissance to the Enlightenment. If the Reformation was a revolution against the traditional church, and the Renaissance was the revalorization of some of the ideas from Greek democracy, the Enlightenment was a revolution against traditional philosophy and science. It was a "movement" that sought to understand the world and humanity on a new basis. This period was accompanied by the growing belief that all people were equal because no matter what their social position, each possessed the enobling capacity for reason. The presumption of equality was revolutionary because it led people to challenge the validity of political institutions that distributed power and wealth unequally among citizens. Legitimate political power was seen to emanate from the people themselves; the people were seen to be the source of ultimate political and legal authority.

The Reformation and the Enlightenment were accompanied (and in some senses precipitated) by the end of feudal forms of life, and by the rise of *capitalism* and market economies. While feudal society did have market activity—there were individual transactions of labour goods and services—it was not a market economy. In feudalism, most economic activity was for the purposes of immediate consumption rather than for exchange. What was distinctive about capitalism was the newly emerging notion of "private property" and the accompanying right of an individual (or corporate entity) to exclude others from the use or benefit of it. Significantly, human labour itself also became a commodity which could be bought and traded on the market. The transformation from feudal forms of life (characterized by the predominance of the Church, absolutist sovereigns, and a landless peasantry) to a market of "free" producers and buyers was a complex one which had profound social, political, and cultural consequences. In short, the Reformation, the Enlightenment, and the emergence of capitalism were not separate events, but rather events that mutually reinforced each other.

These mutually reinforcing events are known together as the *liberal revolution*, a crisis in governing which marks the passing from feudal society to what we now recognize as capitalist modernity. An organic, hierarchical, traditional society was rapidly being replaced by an individualistic, fluid, and pluralist society in which reason replaced custom as a standard by which to judge policy and institutions. Perhaps the most graphic representations of this liberal revolution were the American Revolution of 1776 and the French Revolution of 1789. Both revolutions were dramatic uprisings against traditional, hierarchical forms of rule, and both were infused with the energy and enthusiasm of the liberal slogan: *liberty, equality, and solidarity.*

Early Liberal Democratic Theory

The dramatic changes in political rule in Europe and North America brought with them the most important variant of democratic thought: *liberal democratic theory*. This view was first articulated by theorists such as Thomas Hobbes, John Locke, and John Stuart Mill. The most important aspect of liberal democratic theory, and what distinguishes it from the models of democratic thought reviewed so far, was the belief in the importance of political, moral, and economic *liberty*. This variant of democratic theory clearly distinguished the public—understood as the institutions of the state—from the private. This was significantly different from the civic republicanism and the Greek *ethos* of the *polis* which preceded it. For both of the previous models, the *public* included some dimensions of human life which were consigned to the private sphere in the modern model.

The notion of freedom was very important to these liberal thinkers, but it was a very specific kind of freedom. As C.B. Macpherson explains, liberal democrats believed passionately in the freedom to pursue private property. Moreover, liberal democrats, no less than the democratic theorists who preceded them, had a distinct view of what constitutes human nature and a distinct view of the whole society in which the democratic political system operates.

According to liberal democrats, individuals are rational maximizers of self-interest. That is to say, for most liberal democrats, individuals will rationally choose what is in their own best interests, even when those interests are not necessarily those that grant them the most immediate satisfaction. For example, individuals will choose to live under a government that restricts some of their destructive activities, because it will also restrict the destructive activities of others. Thus, they will rationally choose to outlaw theft and to be policed, because they will weigh their own desires to rob against the possibility of being robbed by others.

One of the most passionate defenders of this perspective was Thomas Hobbes. While he was no advocate of democracy in principle, his justification of government was that state authority, rather than monarchs or God, was created by individuals acting out of self-interest. People created the authority of the state to protect them from each other. Hobbes believed that individuals ought willingly to surrender their rights of self-government to a powerful single authority. Democracy, in this view, was the mechanism by which citizens could check the powers of the state against arbitrarily punishing its citizens.

John Locke revised Hobbes' argument with the view that "government" should be conceived as an instrument for the defence of "life, liberty and estate" (Locke, 1965). One important difference between Hobbes and Locke is that whereas Hobbes emphasized democracy as a mechanism for protecting *individuals* from the state, Locke understood democracy as a mechanism for protecting the *market* from the state. And here is the second important assumption shared by classical liberal democrats: the society in which the democratic political system operates is understood to be a capitalist one. This is why, in Locke's view, the state should leave the "private" economic transactions of individuals entirely unregulated.

In the nineteenth century, John Stuart Mill developed his important objection to the purely formal dimensions of the position laid down by earlier liberal democrats. Mill went far beyond previous liberal democrats with respect to *moral* freedom. Mill formulated his theory with a view to protecting iconoclasts or "free thinkers" from the imposition of conventional or traditional morality. In this sense, Mill was passionately dedicated to the protection of minorities within a majoritarian system.

Classical liberal democrats, then, constructed a relatively coherent theory of democracy. In it, the major institutions of modern governance—in particular the various institutions of the state—were understood to be public, and therefore subject to collective control. The modern distinction between the public realm of the state, and the private, unregulated and apolitical realms of the family and the economy was vital to this theoretical framework.

Common Liberal Democratic Claims

Despite the important differences among the classical thinkers of liberal democracy, it is possible to outline seven main principles that they share:

1. *Individualism.* This view takes individuals, independent of groups or societies, as the basic building blocks of social life. Liberals reject the idea that the institutions that we encounter in our lives mould and create us in various ways, including as individuals.

2. *Equality.* Individuals are inherently equal. This contrasts with the premodern world view, in which people were understood to be demonstrably not equal—

DEBATE BOX

An Imaginary Election

1: Imagine that we read of an election occurring somewhere in the Third World in which the self-declared winner was the son of the former prime minister and that former prime minister was himself the former head of that nation's secret police.

2: Imagine that the self-declared winner lost the popular vote but won based on some old colonial holdover (electoral college) from the nation's predemocracy past.

3: Imagine that the self-declared winner's 'victory' turned on disputed votes cast in a province governed by his brother.

4: Imagine that the poorly drafted ballots of one district, a district heavily favouring the self-declared winner's opponent, led thousands of voters to vote for the wrong candidate.

5: Imagine that members of that nation's most despised caste, fearing for their lives/livelihoods, turned out in record numbers to vote in near universal opposition to the self-declared winner's candidacy.

6: Imagine that hundreds of members of that most despised caste were intercepted on their way to the polls by state police operating under the authority of the self-declared winner's brother.

7: Imagine that six million people voted in the disputed province and that the self-declared winner's "lead" was only 327 votes: Fewer, certainly, than the vote-counting machines' margin of error.

8: Imagine that the self-declared winner and his political party opposed a more careful by-hand inspection and re-counting of the ballots in the disputed province or in its most hotly disputed district.

9: Imagine that the self-declared winner, himself a governor of a major province, had the worst human rights record of any province in his nation and actually led the nation in executions.

10: Imagine that a major campaign promise of the self-declared winner was to appoint like-minded human rights violators to lifetime positions on the high court of that nation.

This description of the recent American presidential election appeared anonymously on the Internet after the U.S. presidential elections. It is clearly organized in such a way as to spoof North American descriptions of elections in the so-called "Third World." Does this description do a disservice to the importance of democratic processes?

some human beings were inherently vested with the right to rule, and others with the obligation to be ruled.

3. *Reason.* Individual equality derives from the unique human capacity for reason; the ability to deduce, the ability to ask for reasons. Reason is possessed by all humans.

4. *Rights.* Individuals have rights apart from their involvement in or existence in society. The state should only exist to promote those values and uphold these rights.

5. *Society.* Society is nothing but the individuals who compose it. In other words, the interests of the community are reducible to the interests of the people.

6. *Protection of property and rights.* Political institutions exist for the protection of individual rights and for the protection of private property.

7. *Freedom.* Freedom is conceived of as "negative"—individuals and markets should be free of coercive interference from the state, and from other people.

Contemporary Challenges

THE CONTEMPORARY PERIOD IS DOMINATED BY THE SO-CALLED "TRIUMPH" OF democracy worldwide. One does not have to look very far to discover, however, that we are not living in the best of all possible worlds. As Amnesty International points out, grotesque violations of human rights, such as torture, are used on citizens in almost half the countries in the world, many of which describe themselves as democratic.

The conversation about what constitutes "democracy" is thus far from over. While the majority of contemporary democratic theorists continue to be preoccupied with the major questions of liberalism, they have shifted their focus from freedom to equality. As well, there are some radical democratic critiques of the public/private distinction laid down by liberalism which bear important scrutiny. In the current era of globalization (and the subsequent waves of democratic protest against globalization), the fundamentals of democratic thought are being challenged. In the following section, we look at the debates among contemporary liberal democrats, who are divided over the question of what vision of "the good" should drive contemporary liberal democracies. One variant of contemporary liberal democracy suggests that democracy is a "good" because it provides a mechanism by which each individual is equally represented in processes of governing. These thinkers are opposed by those who suggest that this purely formal mechanism is inadequate because it covers over and in fact entrenches important *differences* between people. Finally, Marxist and radical democratic critiques of liberal democracy propose that without economic and social equality, political equality is next to meaningless.

Contemporary Liberal Democratic Theory

The transition from premodern absolutist states and traditional societies to modern liberal democratic representative democracies has been largely achieved in the Western world. Not surprisingly, therefore, liberal democrats are currently less concerned with the freedom of individuals from the arbitrary powers of the state than they are with the nature of the equality that democracies can deliver to their citizens. The most important debate among contemporary liberal democrats— known as the *liberal-communitarian debate* takes the liberal notion of equality as its central focus.

John Rawls, for example, suggests that the only "good" of democracies lies in their ability to formally recognize the equality of each citizen. More precisely, Rawls argues that the only idea of "the good" that we can agree upon, is a thinly conceived notion of political *tolerance.* Any other concept would be in some way threatening to the multicultural, diverse political culture in which we live. In other words, we can never agree that we *should* worship one particular kind of God, or even that we should worship at all; that we *should* hold certain kinds of values when raising our children, or that we *should* mate in these and not other ways. The only *should* we can agree upon is to be tolerant of a variety of ways in which to worship, instill values, make families and structures of kinship, and so on.

Noted communitarians such as Charles Taylor and Alisdair MacIntyre take issue with Rawls' vision of the "good." They say that this conception of democracy has no "end." It is not directed towards making us better patriots or even better people. The idea of tolerance, they argue, is nothing more than a *procedure* that suggests that we deal fairly and equally with each other. Recalling the civic republicanism first articulated by Aristotle, Taylor and MacIntyre maintain that political life involves much more than representation in democratic institutions; liberal democracies are forms of civic association in which we discover who we really are. In fact, they say that we don't discover our "identities" (as Canadians, as Muslims, or as lesbians) in isolation. We discover them in dialogue with each other; in the give and take of a "public" conversation. Communitarians take their point of departure from people's real sense of alienation from the formal public institutions that represent them. For example, Quebec nationalism, or Western Canadian alienation suggest that not everyone feels recognized by Canadian democratic institutions.

Rawls and other liberals respond that this is precisely the price that citizens must pay for living in a society that treats us all as equals regardless of our particular ethnic, racial, religious, sexual, or other identities. It is the very neutrality of the public sphere that protects our freedom as citizens. In this "liberal" view, our "freedom" and "equality" refer only to our common characteristics. These include our universal needs for such things as income, health care, education, religious freedom, and freedom of speech. Therefore our public institutions need not strive to recognize our particular cultural identities in treating us as free and equal citizens.

Rawls proposes that the principle of equality is complete in itself and that the differences between us are, in the final analysis, politically irrelevant. In contrast, Charles Taylor understands, in his unique situation as an Anglophone living in Quebec, that the demand for public recognition (by institutions such as the state or schools) by a people is more than simply a psychological quirk. It is a constitutive feature of liberal democracies. Taylor and other communitarians recall the civic republican tradition first articulated by Aristotle when they suggest that something more than empty "equality" ought to govern the public sphere, and that we might be better served to return to traditional religious or cultural values

However, both of these contemporary liberal democratic positions share the division between public and private laid down by the earlier liberal democrats. While communitarians

like Taylor want to infuse public institutions such as the judiciary or parliament with a
sensitivity to cultural differences between us, the question of the market, the family, or the
very real political and economic differences between people are conceived only as "cultural."
The question of economic equality—rather than political equality—does not appear as a
variable in this dispute.

Marxist and Radical Democratic Critiques

The focus on economic equality is another way of talking about the compatibility of
liberal democracy with capitalism. This compatibility has been questioned with most
insistence by Marxist and radical democratic critics. Marx argued that historically and
logically, capitalism is tied to the private ownership of the means of production—the right
of individuals or corporate entities to the exclusive use of land, money, and labour power.
This private ownership encourages wealth to accumulate predominantly in one class. It is
thus surely not accidental, Marx argued, that the "rights of private property" are at the
foundation of the whole constitutional and juridical superstructure we have come to know
as *liberal democracy*. Marx felt that capitalism can tolerate "democracy" because in the final
analysis, real power is not to be found in democratic institutions, but instead rests with
those who control the means of production.

Specifically, capitalists control the working class, not by means of exclusive political rights
but by means of exclusive property. This means that even in its best and most democratic
forms, capitalism can, and must, confine equality to a separate "political" sphere that does
not, and must not, intrude into the economic sphere or subvert economic *in*equality. People
in capitalist societies spend most of their waking lives in activities and relationships where
there is no democratic accountability at all. This is true not only in the workplace, where they
are likely to be under the direct control of others, but in all spheres of life that are subject
to "market" imperatives. Liberal democracies like Canada may indeed have a political
sphere governed by "democracy," but at the same time, large areas of human life lie entirely
outside the reach of democratic processes.

This critique of classical and modern liberal democratic theory has been most recently re-
elaborated by a new form of democratic theory known as *radical democracy*. Like Marxists, radical
democrats argue that traditional democracy has failed to deliver on its promise of real equality
and civic participation. And like Marxists, radical democrats claim that a thorough-going
understanding of democracy will entail extending the principles of democracy—freedom,
equality, and solidarity—into every area of daily life: work, education, leisure, the home.

But radical democrats differ from traditional Marxists by insisting that class is not the
only source of inequality in contemporary society. They argue that we are unequal in ways
that go beyond the economic. For instance, the great disparity in real economic and political
power between men and women, between white and non-white people, and between those
who live in the "North" and those who live in the "South" reflects the inability of our
"democratic" institutions to deliver any kind of substantive equality. Understanding
democracy as nothing more than free-market capitalism accompanied by multi-party elections
does a real disservice to the radical vision of emancipation offered by early liberal democratic

theory. Radical democrats insist that if the principles of liberal democracy are to be taken seriously, the limited scope of freedom and equality offered by contemporary liberal democracies must be challenged.

This new strain of political critique also responds to the challenge of *globalization*. For while the nation-state is still a key unit in the political order of the twenty-first century, in many important respects, it is under attack. This attack comes both from within, by those who look to subnational forms of authority as the focus of their activity, and from without by supranational forces such as transnational corporations, continental or hemispheric trade agreements and so on.

In the present era the nation state is less and less endowed with the power to curb the stark inequalities in social, political, and economic power both nationally and internationally. In this sense, the current era is witnessing a "contraction" in the realm of what we can meaningfully talk about as "public." Increasingly, the values of the private sphere—the capitalist market on the one hand, and the family on the other—dominate questions of public policy. Nations are required to be increasingly efficient and competitive (the dominant values of the market) and public discourses of morality (family values) dominate the public realm, at the same time as the accountability of the state to its citizens is increasingly restricted. This new era of so-called "global competitiveness" or globalization represents the crisis forcing democratic theorists to rethink the distinction between public and private at the heart of liberal conceptions of democracy. If the nation state becomes less and less able to act as an arbiter of social life, this rethinking may involve the creation of a global democracy beyond the level of the nation state.

Summary

This chapter has surveyed the way that democratic practices and theories have consistently raised the question of the relationship between what is "public" and what is "private." Beginning with a brief history of democratic thought, we found that dramatic shifts in thinking about democracy often occurred during periods of fundamental social change. We then investigated the direct and participatory nature of Greek democracy, the revitalization of that tradition in civic republicanism, and the re-articulation of democratic ideals of freedom and equality in early and contemporary liberal democratic thought. The fundamental premise of liberal democratic theory is the importance of individual, political, moral, and economic *freedom*. This democratic theory draws lines between the public and the private in terms we might currently recognize. Specifically, the family and the market are carved off from what was understood as "public" and placed in the category "private." They are thus outside the purview of those issues that traditionally concerned democratic politics.

More recently, liberal, Marxist, and radical democratic theorists, especially in Western democracies, have shifted the emphasis from freedom to equality in questioning how all citizens of a democratic society can participate equally. They have asked whether the formal political equality of the contemporary liberal democratic state is truly adequate to satisfy the important differences between us. Does democracy require *economic* or simply *political* equality? Does democracy imply the end of social discrimination? In the shift in emphasis from freedom to equality, many contemporary democratic theorists are challenging the validity of the claim that the market or the family are private and therefore outside the bounds of democratic deliberation. Despite the apparent success of democracy as the dominant ideal and practice of governing worldwide, then, some thinkers in liberal democracies have grown increasingly critical of the equality democratic states are able to deliver to their citizens.

Discussion Questions

1. Do you agree with the modern liberal perspective that it is only the neutrality of the public sphere that protects our freedom as citizens?

2. Do you think that democracy should imply economic as well as political equality in the way that Marxist and radical democrats suggest?

3. According to this chapter, theory is something that becomes evident when the human practices it orders and makes meaningful come into crisis. Can you think of a set of human practices less complex than democratic processes of governing to which this idea might apply?

4. According to this chapter, democracy is the dominant value of our age. What values are embedded within this term?

References

Aristotle.1948. *Politics* translated by Ernest Barker. Oxford: Oxford University Press.

Bernal, Martin. 1987. *Black Athena: The Afroasiatic Roots of Classical Civilization.* New Brunswick: Rutgers University Press.

Connolly, William. 1991. *Identity/Difference: Democratic Negotiation of Political Paradox.* Ithaca: Cornell University Press.

Dahl, Robert. 1989. *Democracy and Its Critic.* New Haven: Yale University Press.

Dworkin, Ronald. 1977. *Taking Rights Seriously.* Cambridge, Mass: Harvard University Press.

Held, David. 1987. *Models of Democracy.* Cambridge: Polity Press.

Hobbes, Thomas. 1977. *Leviathan.* Hammondsworth: Penguin.

Kymlicha, Will. 1995. *Multicultural Citizenship.* Oxford: Oxford University Press.

Locke, John. 1965. *Second Treatise on Government.* New York: Mentor Press.

MacPherson, C.B. 1965. *The Real World of Democracy.* Toronto: CBC Publications,.

———. 1977. *The Life and Times of Liberal Democracy.* Oxford: Oxford University Press.

Marx, Karl and Friedrich Engels. 1968. "The Communist Manifesto" in *Selected Works.* London: Lawrence and Wishart.

McIntryre, Alisdaire. 1981. *After Virtue.* Notre Dame: University of Notre Dame Press.

Mouffe, Chantal. 1994. *The Return to the Political.* London: Verso.

Philips, Anne. 1991. *Engendering Democracy*. Cambridge: Polity Press.

Rawls, John. 1971. *A Theory of Justice*. Cambridge: Harvard University Press.

Rousseau, Jean-Jacques. 1964. *A Discourse on the Origins of Inequality* New York: St. Martin's Press.

Sandel, Michael. 1984. *Liberalism and Its Critics*. Oxford: Clarendon Press.

Taylor, Charles. 1992. *Multiculturalism and the Politics of Recognition*. Princeton: Princeton University Press.

Trend, David ed. 1996. *Radical Democracy: Identity, Citizenship and the State*. London: Routledge.

Further Readings

Aristotle. 1948. *Politics* translated by Ernest Barker. Oxford: Oxford University Press.

Held, David. 1987. *Models of Democracy* Cambridge: Polity Press.

—————————. 1995. *Democracy and the Global Order*. Oxford: Polity Press.

MacPherson, C.B. 1973. *Democratic Theory: Essays in Retrieval*. Oxford: Oxford University Press.

Tocqueville, Alexis de. 1946. *Democracy in America*. New York: Knopf.

Wood, Ellen Meiksins. 1995. *Democracy against Capitalism*. Cambridge University Press.

Weblinks

Amnesty International
www.amnesty.org/ailib/intcam/femgen/fgm1.htm

Canadians for Direct Democracy
www.npsnet.com/cdd

Canadian Centre for Policy Alternatives
www.policyalternatives.ca/

Democracy Watch
www.dwatch.ca/

THE NDP PLAN TO COPE WITH A RISING NEO-CONSERVATIVE TIDE

CHAPTER 3

MODERN POLITICAL IDEOLOGIES

Objectives

Before there can be any kind of political action or institution, there first has to be a political idea. This is why the political ideas of Western society, beginning with classical Greek civilization, receive so much attention in our study of politics. Typically, students of politics spend a great deal of energy reviewing the origins and arguments of Western political ideologies, especially liberalism, conservatism, socialism, nationalism, and republicanism. In recent years, however, these five different streams of Western political thought have been grouped together under the label *modernist thought*. As products of modernity each of these political ideologies has distinct visions of how society and politics should best be organized. The following chapter examines socialism and other radical ideologies. In this chapter, we explore what is meant by the terms *modernity* and *ideology* and what is the relationship between the two. This chapter starts by outlining the fundamental characteristics of modernity. It then examines its leading ideologies beginning first, and most thoroughly, with liberalism, which has proven to be modernity's most resilient ideology. We then discuss other ideologies that have challenged liberalism's interpretation of modernity. Finally, we examine today's faltering faith in modernity and its implications for the future of these political ideologies.

PETER J. SMITH

Introduction

For centuries, naming something or someone "modern" has been meant as a compliment, as something positive. The modern, especially in the West, was associated with the new, the fashionable and the useful, in contrast to the traditional, which was deemed to be none of these things. Modern political thinking emphasized values such as progress, emancipation, and universality. The strains of modern political thinking described in this chapter assess these and other key values differently. In order to understand the controversies in contemporary political thought, we must first come to grips with what is meant by two terms—*modernity* and *ideology*. Next, we will explore four dominant political ideologies—liberalism, republicanism, conservatism, and nationalism according to three defining elements of ideology—critique, ideal, and agency.

Modernity

MODERNITY IS COMMONLY IDENTIFIED WITH THE KEY IDEAS OF THE Enlightenment period in Europe. This period runs roughly from the mid-seventeenth century to the late nineteenth century. The Enlightenment rested on a dramatic shift in intellectual and popular thinking about the world and the place of humanity in it. This new thinking stressed the importance of reason, progress, emancipation, and universality and formed the foundations of the most powerful ideologies that have shaped the Western world and modern history. The ideologies described in this chapter are all products of modernity even though each has a different assessment of its benefits and liabilities. But what is modernity?

Modernity is most commonly associated with the emergence of capitalism and the nation state in Europe. Beginning in the sixteenth century, European trade expanded nationally and internationally. These years were marked by wars among European powers over which would control trade routes and the riches of the new world. With new abundant resources, expanded markets, and new technologies, these countries also began to industrialize and transform from rural to urban societies. In one process, power shifted from the old nobility to international traders and, later, to industrialists. All these factors laid the foundation for modern forms of political thinking and political organization, particularly the nation state.

Modernity, itself, has four essential features, all of which were relevant to the formation of political ideologies and the debate among them:

1. The rise of capitalism, which changed fundamentally the organization of society and distribution of economic and political power.
2. The formation of the nation state with its key executive, legislative, and judicial institutions that operated within defined territorial boundaries. The state became the dominant organizing feature of political life providing its citizens with political and cultural identities and new expectations about rights and obligations.
3. The rise of new class formations, the middle class (the bourgeoisie) and the working class (the proletariat). With these classes came demands for inclusion into politics and the operation of the institutions of the modern state. Classes

confronted one another and politics increasingly revolved around the distribution of the wealth that capitalism produced.

4. The decline of a religious world view dominated by Christianity and its replacement by a secular, materialist, rationalist culture.

If there was a central idea that emerged from the culture of modernity, it was a belief in the power of reason. Epitomized by the French philosopher, René Descartes (1596–1650), there arose a belief that man (and the emphasis was on men not women) possessed of scientific, calculative reason could not only understand the world but could change it as well. For Enlightenment or modern thinkers this was a profound and revolutionary departure from the assumptions of feudalism, which was guided by fatalism—a belief that man's fate was pre-determined by God. One could do little to change individual lives, or the course of history. However, modernity placed man, not God, at the centre of the world. Man was also the master and possessor of nature. Through reason he could construct a better world. In effect, man could create the type of society and political institutions that he wished to live in and under. Reason, moreover, was a universal phenomenon. All men were capable of reason and could achieve the progress it promised. I use the term *man* deliberately as did the Enlightenment thinkers. Many of them argued that women were not capable of reason. They were tied to the home, to child-bearing and nurturing, and to the dictates of nature. For women, "biology was destiny" and biology prevented them from standing outside their maternal lives to make rational decisions. The exclusion of women from the ranks of rational man and humanity was rarely challenged until the twentieth century.

Modernity brought with it a mood of optimism. Through reason man could be freed from tradition, superstition, ignorance, bondage, and tyranny. Modernist optimism led to a belief that human progress was achievable materially, morally, and politically. Scientific progress would make life easier and more secure for everyone. Moreover, the obvious benefits of modernity, although first felt in Western Europe, would come to embrace the whole world.

Modern Political Ideologies

MODERNITY SPAWNED A HOST OF POLITICAL IDEOLOGIES THAT BOTH challenged and endorsed it. The concept of *ideology* itself sprang from the rationalist, scientific culture of modernity. *Ideologie* was a term invented by a French philosopher, Antoine Destutt de Tracy (1754–1836) who tried to found a "scientific" method of studying the sources of ideas. Tracy believed that ideas were the results of experience and, therefore, it was possible to discover the origins of ideas and explain why different people have different ideas. Tracy and his colleagues, called *ideologues*, hoped that through reason and science, not faith and religion, people could be taught the right ideas—ideas that would lead to a happy and rational society (Ball and Dagger, 6).

Not surprisingly, this movement did not sit well with the traditional elites of France—the Catholic Church and nobility. Napoleon, Emperor of France, striving to gain the support of these elites criticized ideologies and ideologues and linked the terms to what may be described as the "ivory tower" thinking of impractical dreamers out of touch with practical politics. Moreover, Napoleon maintained, ideologies were merely masks that concealed the real subversive goals of his enemies. As a result, ideologies and ideologues came to be depicted in pejorative terms, a connotation that has remained to this day.

While the negative connotation of ideologies persists, for the purposes of this chapter a more neutral interpretation is adopted. Ideologies are an everyday aspect of political life. We all have them. Particularly when challenged by others with differing ideas, our political ideas reveal themselves. However, what do we mean by political ideologies? According to Ball and Dagger, an ideology "is a fairly coherent and comprehensive set of ideas that explains and evaluates social conditions, helps people understand their place in society, and provides a program for social and political action" (1995, 9). Moreover, according to Schwartzmantel, every ideology "contains three elements: critique, ideal, and agency" (1998, 2). As a critique, ideologies tell us what society is like and what is wrong with it, that is, what barriers there are to the realization of a better society (the ideal). For example, the barriers to the ideal for conservatism include radical ideas and change, for nationalism, domination by other nations. By agency we mean a force, an acting subject, capable of transforming society. Each ideology interprets agency differently. For liberalism the acting subject or force is the rational self-interested individual, for republicanism it is the public-spirited citizen, and for nationalism it is the nation. We now turn to four key political ideologies that have (and continue to) organized the politics of the Western world and beyond. Liberalism, republicanism, conservatism, and nationalism will be discussed in terms of ideal, critique, and agency. The following table should assist students in this regard.

TABLE 3.1　*Political Ideologies*

	THE IDEAL	**CRITIQUE**	**AGENCY**
LIBERALISM	Individual freedom to pursue our individual interests, to live our lives as we see fit.	Initially, feudal dependence, tradition, religious conformity. Later, poverty, ignorance, prejudice, and the state.	The rational self-interested individual.
REPUBLICANISM	A self-governing republic with active citizen participation in government.	Kings, princes, despots, the aristocracy. The love of wealth, luxury, and consumption.	The virtuous citizen.
CONSERVATIVISM	A stable, orderly, harmonious, collective, hierarchical society.	Passions, desires, radical ideas and change.	Interdependent members of society.
NATIONALISM	Self-determination, desire for a people, a nation to have its own state.	Domination by other nations, nation states, fear of being left behind by other nation states.	The nation.

Liberalism

The ideologies that first emerged in the modern era took various stances toward modernity. For example, liberalism generally celebrated it, while republicanism both questioned and feared it. In the end, at the latter part of the eighteenth century and in the nineteenth century, liberalism and republicanism reached an uneasy *modus vivendi*, accommodating one another in an uneasy truce. In many countries this truce was embedded in constitutions and in the political institutions of the emerging liberal-democratic state.

At the heart of classic liberalism was a belief in the primacy of the individual and of individual freedom. Liberal freedom was a particular type of freedom: *negative freedom*. By negative freedom, we mean "freedom from," the freedom of the individual to do as he or she wishes without interference from others, whether these be governments, or other private persons (Taylor, 1979). This is a private, personal freedom, a freedom that celebrated the individual pursuit of rational self-interest and happiness. Unlike their eighteenth and nineteenth-century republican counterparts, liberals believed that individuals realized themselves privately, in their personal lives.

Liberalism is the political expression of a commercial and industrial society. More than anything else it was first commercial and then industrial capitalism that was bringing freedom, prosperity, and progress to the world. In particular, it was the market and the individual—rational choices that individuals made within the market—that were affecting progress. It should be underlined, however, that it was only property-owning white males who were afforded freedom of choice.

Liberalism also had a particular view of politics and political institutions. First, the state is a rational instrument necessary to balance and contain self-interest in the private and market spheres. After all, individuals could go too far in the pursuit of their individual freedom and self-interest and thereby harm the interests of others. To prevent this, society required the rule of law applied impartially by the state. This, however, was to be a "minimalist" state. Its interference in private lives and in the market was limited by law and by expectation. The power of government had to be limited by such means as constitutions, which would restrain government in the use of its power. Constitutions attempted to protect individuals from the state and minorities against the power of majorities as well as preserve basic individual freedoms such as freedom of speech, religion, and association. Moreover, individuals had rights to property and individual security that government could not infringe upon and had to protect. Finally, as each individual knew what was best for himself, the state could not impose a uniform vision of "the good life" upon society or the individual.

How then, did liberalism conceive of the relationship between ideal, critique, and agency? As indicated above the ideal was seen as one in which individuals live lives as they see fit without interference. Initially, the primary barriers or obstacles to individual freedom consisted of the restrictions of feudalism, tradition, and religious conformity. Later liberals saw the primary threats to the pursuit of their individual goals as stemming from ignorance, poverty, prejudice, and the state. All liberals shared an unshakable faith in the rational individual as the agent or force capable of transforming society.

Historically, while all liberals shared common basic values, liberalism was not a homogeneous or static creed. In fact, we can identify three distinct cleavages within liberalism:

1. *Classical liberalism,* which dominated from its origins in the seventeenth century to the nineteenth century;

2. *Social liberalism,* which evolved during the latter part of the nineteenth century and became dominant in the twentieth century; and

3. *Neoliberalism,* which became dominant in the closing years of the twentieth century.

Classical liberalism can trace its origins to the English political thinkers, Thomas Hobbes (1588–1679) and John Locke (1632–1704). Hobbes and Locke lived during a period of great turmoil in England in which the established authority of the land-owning aristocracy, Crown, and Church of England were being challenged by a new middle class of gentlemen farmers and merchants, Parliament, and Puritans. Both were **social contract theorists**, that is, both conceived of the origins of government in terms of a contract among free, rational individuals who consent to the establishment of political authority.

Hobbes's most notable work is *Leviathan* (1651). A leviathan is a mythical monster of the sea that rules over other creatures. Because of the turmoil and civil war that erupted in 1642, Hobbes thought the English needed a leviathan. Hobbes maintained that everyone should obey whoever is in power, even an absolutist ruler, as long as that person or persons could maintain order and protect them. To support his argument that the reason for government was to provide order, protection, and security he asked his readers to imagine what life would be like without any ruler. Without a political authority people would live in a **state of nature.** In a state of nature, without a government to enforce rules, individuals would be equal and have a natural right to act as they wished. The problem, in a state of nature, was human nature. Hobbes thought human beings were aggressive, self-interested, and driven by an insatiable desire for power and domination over others. The consequence would be chaos, "a warre of every man against every man" in which life would be "solitary, poore, nasty, brutish, and short" (Hobbes, 1968).

Hobbes believed, that as rational individuals, people sooner or later would realize the necessity of establishing a ruler with sufficient power to enforce peace and security among them. Hobbes thought people could escape the state of nature by means of a social contract in which they would agree to surrender all rights—save the right to defend themselves—to a political authority to rule over them.

Hobbes's conclusion that an all-powerful ruler is needed to create laws and to establish political and social authority cannot be considered liberal. What makes Hobbes's thought liberal is not his conclusion but his basic premises. Hobbes, like later liberals, conceived of individuals as being naturally free, rational, self-interested human beings who create government by means of consent to protect their interests and live lives as they saw fit.

Hobbes's insistence on the need for an all-powerful, indivisible sovereign left him open to criticism. John Locke moderated and made Hobbes's social contract theory more socially acceptable. Like Hobbes, Locke began his argument with the state of nature, a place where everyone was equal and had no authority above them. For Locke, however, the state of nature was not a state of war. In fact, Locke believed that people were generally good and the state of nature, at least in the beginning, was peaceful. Unfortunately, while good, people were not perfect, and the state of nature would not last as some people might try to take advantage of others. Conflict would be the result. Recognizing the "inconveniences" of a state of nature people voluntarily consent to enter into a social contract to establish a society. After society is established people agree to create a government to protect their natural rights of "life, liberty, and property," rights which they possessed in a state of nature and did not surrender once they created society.

Unlike Hobbes, then, it was clearly not Locke's intention to endorse an all-powerful ruler. Rather, he believed that people only consented to create a constitutional or limited government. If government did not protect the life, liberty, and property of its subjects they could remove that government and establish another. Moreover, if a government were overthrown there would be no return to a state of nature, for the social contract is not dissolved, an importance difference from Hobbes. For Locke, the majority (of people of property) can check the power of government for government is sustained by the consent of individuals.

In many ways Locke prepared the way for what became known as representative government. Locke, however, was not a democrat for he limited political participation to landed property owners, a small minority of the population at the time. Moreover, Locke was vague on how government was to be held accountable to the governed.

Stepping into the breach to remedy the limitations of Locke's views on democracy, from a theoretical perspective at least, were the Utilitarians, in particular, Jeremy Bentham (1748–1832), James Mill (1773–1836), and his son, John Stuart Mill (1806–1873). The Utilitarians were acutely aware that although the Industrial Revolution in England had produced a middle class of factory owners and professionals and a large working class, neither class was allowed to vote or sit in the Houses of Parliament. The Utilitarians were also aware that government had to be made more democratic and accountable to the population.

The Utilitarians based their philosophy of government on the **doctrine of utility** which proposed that the standard by which all human action, public and private, should be judged was the "greatest happiness of the greatest number." They believed that all actions were good which provided happiness for the greatest number of people. Moreover, in calculating this happiness, all individuals were equal, the happiness of any one individual was as important as the happiness of any other. Additionally, the Utilitarians believed that individuals were the best judges of what was good for themselves or for their country. From this they drew two conclusions. One, that government had to be accountable to everyone, not just a small minority. This meant everyone had to be allowed to vote. Second, since people knew what was good for themselves the government could best promote the greatest happiness of the greatest number by letting people live as they chose.

While Bentham did not live to see the adoption of many of the political reforms he advocated, other Utilitarians did. The Reform Bill of 1832 lowered property qualifications sufficiently to permit middle-class males the right to vote. In 1867 the working class in Britain received the right to vote but it was not until early in the twentieth century that women were permitted to vote and in other countries it was not until well into the twentieth century that other minorities were granted the right to vote.

Beginning in the nineteenth century, distinct ideological differences began to appear within liberalism. These differences were instrumental in permitting liberalism to adapt to the problems posed by industrial capitalism. These divisions are epitomized by the ambiguities in the thought of John Stuart Mill. Mill began his career as a classic liberal and defender of *laissez-faire* capitalism. Over time, however, Mill developed a much greater sensitivity to the problems that industrial capitalism was creating, for example, economic inequality and large-scale urban poverty. Mill came to advocate some wealth redistribution and became recognized as an early proponent of reform or *social welfare liberalism.*

Social welfare liberalism, unlike classical liberalism, maintained that government was not just a necessary evil, that government should promote individual liberty by ensuring that everyone had an equal opportunity in life. Social welfare liberalism maintains that the basic necessities of life should be provided for those who are truly in need, for those who are unable to provide for themselves through no fault of their own.

Social welfare liberals saw, therefore, the need for a positive state that would provide not only assistance to the poor and the defenseless, but also pensions, public pensions, public hospitals, and much more. Social welfare liberalism prevailed over classical liberalism in the twentieth century in the West. It represented a compromise between Marxist critiques of capitalism and classical liberalism which saw only a small role for government in reducing social inequalities. Social welfare liberalism relied on a capitalist economy but developed social programs to alleviate its most glaring social costs.

By the 1970s, however, the social consensus that underpinned social welfare liberalism began to erode. World economic crises in the mid-1970s and early 1980s increasingly led to large fiscal deficits in liberal democracies and criticisms of the large, bureaucratic welfare state. In addition, demands for state resources, inclusion, and recognition by previously marginalized groups, for example, Aboriginal people, women, and the disabled were met by criticism from groups resisting expansion of the welfare state. Finally, the emergence of economic globalization in the early 1990s undermined social welfare liberalism. Under economic globalization production and markets increasingly spread beyond the confines and control of the nation state. Together, these developments served to promote the emergence of **neoliberalism** in which the market, not the state, becomes not only the primary means of allocating goods and services but also the leading principle guiding individual and collective action. In ascendancy throughout the 1990s, neoliberalism demands a smaller role for the state in the economy, a much reduced welfare function, and privatization of many government services. Although neoliberalism resembles classical liberalism in many respects, it differs in that classical liberalism could claim to be an emancipatory creed struggling against the power of kings and an entrenched landed aristocracy while neoliberalism champions the cause of transnational corporations which are the most powerful standard bearers of the market and economic globalization.

Republicanism

In many ways republicanism was the mirror image of liberalism. As an ideology, republicanism rested upon the views of such influential political thinkers as Aristotle,

Machiavelli, James Harrington, and Rousseau. Like liberalism, republicanism promotes freedom, but "freedom to," not "freedom from." The difference is critical. Positive freedom essentially consists of being one's own master and is associated with exercise of control, the control of one's life, and the collective control over the common life, that is, self-government. Republicanism, which emerged in the modern era at approximately the same time as liberalism, encourages the participation of citizens in the affairs of government. Liberalism has a legal notion of citizenship that grants an individual the right to belong to a community governed by law. In contrast, the republican notion of citizenship is much more robust and active. It locates "freedom and autonomy in the actual public activities of citizenship," that is, public participation in public discussion and decision making (Young, 1989, 178). For republicans, man is a political animal who fulfills himself as a human being by participating in politics and by acting selflessly for the common good. In other words, as citizens we are obligated to transcend our particular, self-interested lives by coming to an agreement on what is good for society as a whole, not just good for ourselves.

It was because of their belief that personal fulfillment came from engagement in politics and the public sphere that republicanism feared the rise of a commercial society. After all, republicans argued, if we devoted too much time to our private lives, to working, producing, and consuming how could individual citizens fulfill their public duties and responsibilities— their public virtue? Republicanism thus feared a liberal, commercial society where the pursuit of one's self-interest was put before the public good. Republicans especially feared that the pursuit of money and material interests would lead to the corruption of citizens and politics thus imperilling self-government.

In terms of ideal, critique, and agency, then, republicans differ from liberals. The republican ideal is a self-governing republic in which virtuous citizens participate actively in the making of decisions. Republicans not only opposed kings, aristocracy, and tyrants but also the individual pursuit of wealth and luxury over the interests of the republic. The acting force or agent of republicanism is the virtuous citizen who is willing to sacrifice for the common good of all. Eighteenth and nineteenth-century republicans, particularly in North America, including Canada, clung to the ideal of an agrarian society of small property owners, neither too rich nor too poor, who had both the time and resources to engage in politics at a local level. As the agrarian world of the farmer slipped away in the late nineteenth and early twentieth centuries, so did the cutting republican critique of capitalism in Canada and the United States.

Another related concern for republicanism was how best to realize republican government. Republicanism was based on the ideal republic of classical antiquity in which citizens (women and slaves excluded) participated directly in the affairs of government. Yet, in a modern society direct participation was impossible. Modern societies were too complex, too large in population and territory to participate directly in government. The introduction of representative government whereby citizens voted for other citizens who made decisions on their behalf was a reluctantly accepted, second best solution for republicans. Where possible republicans favoured a local and decentralized government which was close to the people.

Republicanism saw its most marked impact in the American and French Revolutions but its ideas about self-government, citizenship, participation, and the common good have left their imprint on modern politics in general. Even today where neoliberalism is ascendant, the concerns of eighteenth- and nineteenth-century republicans still find resonance in modern politics. How are we to relate to government—as citizens or as customers? The difference is profound. As citizens we are politically empowered, that is, as citizens we have the right to participate, to a voice in the making of the decisions that affect us. As customers, on the other hand, we are economically empowered by the market only as individual consumers, and have the power of "exit," not voice, such that if we do not like what services are being provided we can (in theory) choose others.

Today, a group of communitarian thinkers have "rediscovered" republicanism and found in it a means of critiquing what they perceive to be the weaknesses of modern liberalism, in particular, liberal individualism. Communitarians argue that modern society possesses an excess of callous, self-interested individualism and hedonistic selfishness that have had profound negative social and personal effects—rampant consumerism, drug use, business greed. In response communitarians remind us that individuals cannot exist outside communities, that our identities as human beings are defined by our membership in a community. Communitarians call for a renewed recognition of the values of community, public participation in decision-making, and commitment to the common good, all of which they claim that liberals overlook. In turn, communitarians have been criticized for being vague on what they mean by community, for ignoring the importance of power, and for their emphasis on social solidarity which neglects the growing diversity in society (Frazer, 1999).

Conservatism

Like liberalism, conservatism too is a creature of modernity and the Enlightenment. Conservatism, however, represents a protest against and a critique of modernity and its ideals of reason, progress, and emancipation. Where liberalism celebrated the rise of a commercial and industrial society, conservatism feared it because it was thought it was leading to social breakdown and disintegration. Conservatism also rejected the use of reason as a means of re-ordering society. In the eyes of conservatives society was being torn apart by the pressures of rapid social change.

To understand why conservatives thought this way one must have an understanding of how they interpreted human nature and envisioned society. For conservatives, reason was not the defining characteristic of human nature. In fact, conservatives believed man was only partially rational. Men were also passionate and possessed irrational drives that could blur clear judgment. Moreover, human nature was a mixture of good and evil. In short, men were highly fallible and imperfect creatures incapable of building a new society on the basis of human reason. The result would be disaster as was clearly evident from the chaos of the French Revolution.

In place of a society constructed upon the ideas of individuality and equality, conservatives presented an alternative vision of society and social change. For conservatives the best form of society was a collective, hierarchical society in which everyone knew their place. In such a community some would rule and the rest would be ruled. In place of freedom, both positive and negative, the conservative cherished order. And, in place of reason, conservatives valued tradition. Finally, conservatives believed that God, not man, was at the centre of things and that there was an objective, moral order that everyone was obliged to follow.

Conservatives distrusted the belief that man was at the centre of things and could re-order society through reason. Society was not an entity to be created and re-created by means of our reason. Moderate conservatives such as Edmund Burke (1729–1797), a British parliamentarian, who accepted, and even defended, commercial society, rejected the use of reason to re-order society. According to Burke, society was a product of history, not reason. It had evolved slowly over the ages and could not be remade in a single stroke. Its institutions possessed a wisdom that no individual possessed. Change was possible but only gradually. Societal continuity was essential. The French Revolution, according to Burke, had led to turmoil and the threat of tyranny where the many, the least able, and not the few, the best, would rule. In political terms, this was a time when the ruling order was being turned upside down.

In brief, conservatives believed in a well-ordered, stable, hierarchical community. However, in the nineteenth century few conservatives wanted to actually turn the clock back to a pre-capitalist era and restore the long-departed medieval world. Like Burke, they believed that capitalism required hierarchy and the moderating effects of tradition to temper modernity's more divisive and atomizing tendencies.

Conservatism had a very different interpretation of the ideal, critique, and agency than did other ideologies. For conservatives the ideal was a stable, orderly, harmonious, hierarchical society that changed slowly over time. Conservatives feared man's passions and desires as well as the radical ideas and rapid change accompanying modernity. The active agent or force in society was the interdependent members of society.

Today, conservatism has moved to a close accommodation with capitalism. In the 1990s, a blend of what are described as neo-conservativism and neoliberalism was evident in the governments of Ralph Klein in Alberta and Mike Harris in Ontario and in the Canadian Alliance Party. Neo-conservatives advocate the preservation of hierarchical institutions outside the state, for example, the patriarchical family and patriarchical churches—institutions which men head and dominate. Neo-conservatives have a vision of society where the father works, the mother stays at home, and which encourages strict standards of morality that oppose, for example, abortion and gay and lesbian rights. While neo-conservatives accept the neoliberal and minimal state intervention in economic matters, they support a state that would intervene to promote their vision of the family and their moral and religious views.

Nationalism

Nationalism is an ambiguous ideology. It is both a product of and a reaction against the Enlightenment and modernity and has proven it can adapt to all ideologies. However, while nationalism has proven to be highly resilient and compatible with all ideologies, it represents a rejection of the liberal ideal of universality. Liberals believed that nationalism and its political embodiment in the nation state was only a passing stage to be ultimately replaced by a universal, rational individualism (liberalism) or the classless society of socialism. Perhaps one of the biggest quandaries of the current era of globalization is that the power of the nation state is perceived as eroding at the same time that a narrower, ethnically based nationalism is flourishing.

What is nationalism? According to Schwartzmantel, nationalism can be defined as "a belief system that prioritizes or gives special significance to the nation as a focus of loyalty" (1998, 134). The nation, in essence, is a particular form of community, with a history, tradition, and identity that its people desire to promote and preserve. Nationalism can have both civic and, more lately, ethnic/linguistic embodiments.

Nationalism, to develop fully, has always demanded political institutions and the national territory of a state. France, Britain, the United States, and Canada are examples of nation states. As the first states, France, Britain, and the United States produced a form of rational, liberal, civic nationalism that included all those living within the territorial boundaries of the nation state regardless of their ethnic origin or mother tongue. More often than not it was the state that promoted and inculcated nationalist ideas and myths throughout society. For example, France, through its educational system, deliberately promoted the rhetoric of patriotism (love of one's country) and the love of the French republic to solidify it as a nation and to legitimize the nation state. Elsewhere, it is obvious how American politicians and government have historically used patriotism as a part of a civic religion to unite Americans as a national community.

While nationalism assumes that each nation deserves its own state, frequently that has not been the case. Canada is an excellent example of a multinational-ethnic state containing people of differing nationalities. Britain is another example of a multinational-ethnic state as are Switzerland and Belgium. Significantly, it is when there is no congruence between nation and state that nationalism has the potential to arise as a political force. For example, the Palestinian movement has struggled for an independent state in the Middle East since 1948.

In the twentieth century another form of nationalism emerged based on ethnicity and language. Nazi Germany, for example, pursued an "irrational" nationalism that stressed emotion, romanticism, and racial and cultural superiority. The result, as we know, was one of the darkest periods of history. Today, ethnic/linguistic nationalism centred around smaller nation states has increased. Nationalism in Quebec is associated with the desire by many Quebecois for an independent state. Britain is facing pressure by Scottish nationalists for greater autonomy. In its extreme form this type of nationalism resulted in the "ethnic cleansing" in the former Yugoslavia in the 1990s.

Whatever differences exist within various types of nationalism, it possesses a common ideal or goal of self-determination in which every nation will have an independent state of its own. Nationalism is often driven by the fear of domination by other nations or nation states or the fear of being left behind by other nation states. In nationalism it is the people or nation that is the transformative force or agent that realizes the dream of an independent nation state.

Modernity and Modern Political Ideologies in Question

IF THE POLITICAL IDEOLOGIES WE HAVE DISCUSSED ARE ESSENTIALLY A DEBATE about modernity, what happens when the essential features of modernity listed earlier in the chapter are called into question? For example, we noted that modernity centred around the rise of first commercial, and then, industrial capitalism. Today, however, industrial capitalism is in decline and a new, post-industrial world view is emerging. Industrial capitalism was predicated on standardization, mass production of goods, and a large industrial workforce (Webster, 1995, 138). Today's economy relies heavily upon smaller and more flexible units of production employing both advanced information systems and an educated workforce and shares little in common with its industrial predecessor (Sigurdson, 1994, 255). Moreover, globalization and the rise of transnational corporations make it difficult to imagine how the emancipation project should be advanced and by whom. Many would argue that the class-based politics of modernity are being replaced by cultural forms of politics based on new social movements (labour being the "old" social movement)—feminist, Aboriginal, environmental, disability-based, gay and lesbian.

Globalization has also called into question the relevance of the modern nation state. How will nationalism and citizenship have any relevance in a world in which national borders are becoming more porous and even disappearing? Finally, the status of the key concept of modernity, reason, has also been put in doubt. Can we continue to use reason to master and control nature? An environmentalist might argue that in attempting to master nature we have harmed it.

The implications of the declining faith in the core features of modernity are profound for the political ideologies constructed around it. Only liberalism in its latest neoliberal manifestation retains faith in rational individualism, and in its belief that it is a universal ideology applicable to all people everywhere. Yet, intellectually speaking, contemporary liberalism is troubled. Today, liberalism appears to have lost its emancipatory vision and is criticized for having problems with the idea of community and for elevating the market as the ultimate end for which all else is sacrificed.

DEBATE BOX

Where Do You Stand?

One of the key questions that has confronted Canadians of every generation is what role government should play in society. Our answer to this question is guided by the values we have. Where, ideologically speaking, do you fall on the following issues? your friends and classmates? your partner and/or parents? What are the key differences? Overall, where do the answers to these questions place you with respect to the four ideologies discussed in this chapter?

- Education, health and welfare programs and services are best provided by: a) governments; b) partnerships of public and private providers; c) private providers only.

- Canada should reinstate the death penalty.

- Both capital and labour should be permitted to move freely around the world with a minimum of state controls.

- If Canada needs more electricity, government engineers should build more dams.

Summary

With modernity in question, its political ideologies would appear to have no future. Is this the case? Clearly, any ideology that purports to have the answer to all of society's problems probably faces a bleak future. There is little doubt that ideologies will have to be more flexible and adapt themselves to the diversity of contemporary society and the contending allegiances of ethnicity, race, religion, gender, and sexual preference.

Moreover, while we may be in a post-industrial society this does not mean that questions about the distribution of wealth, so central to modernity, are irrelevant. Today, with neoliberalism and economic globalization bringing ever wider disparities of wealth it is possible to see the values of equity, fairness, and distributive justice becoming politically potent once again. In addition, the state is not as anemic as many suggest. In an era of burgeoning government surpluses and decreasing debt, states have a much greater capacity to maintain social policies and broad equity concerns. The politics of distribution may not be completely dead.

Finally, with the exception of liberalism, all ideologies recognize the importance of community. In a complex, fragmenting world the desire for community remains stronger than ever. But what type of communities will they be? Will they recognize the importance of social equality? Will they respect national identities and the right to self-determination but not to the exclusion of other identities and ethnic affiliation? Will these be communities in which people have a voice in the matters that affect them? Will human rights and the freedoms of speech and assembly be respected? To these questions no one ideology has the answer but each has critical insights.

Discussion Questions

1. What is modernity? What is a political ideology? How are they related to one another?

2. How do liberalism, republicanism, conservatism, and nationalism differ?

3. How critical is the concept of reason to modern political ideologies? Provide specific examples.

4. What do we mean by "negative" and "positive" freedom? What should the balance be between the two in a liberal-democratic society?

5. What relevance do political ideologies have to contemporary society?

References

Ball, Terence and Dagger, Richard. 1995. *Political Ideologies and the Democratic Ideal.* 2nd edition. New York: Harper Collins.

Frazer, Elizabeth. *The Problems of Communitarian Politics.* Oxford: Oxford University Press, 1999.

Gibbins, Roger and Youngman, Loleen. 1996. *Mindscapes: Political Ideologies Towards the 21st Century.* Toronto: McGraw-Hill Ryerson.

Hobbes, Thomas. *Leviathan.* Edited by C.B. Macpherson: Harmondsworth. Mddx.: Penguin Books, 1968.

Schwartzmantel, John. 1998. *The Age of Ideology: Political Ideologies from the American Revolution to Postmodern Times.* New York: New York University Press.

Sigurdson, Richard. 1994. "Preston Manning and the Politics of Postmodernism in Canada." *Canadian Journal of Political Science. Vol. 27:2.* 249B277.

Taylor, Charles. 1979. "What's Wrong with Negative Liberty?" In *The Idea of Freedom,* ed. Alan Ryan. Oxford: University Press.

Webster, Frank. 1995. *Theories of the Information Society.* London: Routledge.

Young, Iris Marion. 1989. "Polity and Group Difference: A Critique of the Ideal of Universal Citizenship." Ethics. 99 : 2, 25–274. Reprinted in Ronald Beiner, ed. 1995. *Theorizing Citizenship.* Albany: State University of New York.

Further Readings

Ajzenstat, Janet and Smith, Peter. J. eds. 1995. *Canada's Origins: Liberal, Tory, or Republican.* Ottawa: Carleton University Press.

Gibbins, Roger and Youngman, Loleen. 1996. *Mindscapes: Political Ideologies Towards the 21st Century.* Toronto: McGraw-Hill Ryerson.

Schwartzmantel, John. 1998. *The Age of Ideology: Political Ideologies from the American Revolution to Postmodern Times.* New York: New York University Press.

Sigurdson, Richard. 1994. "Preston Manning and the Politics of Postmodernism in Canada." *Canadian Journal of Political Science. Vol. 27:.* 249B277.

Taylor, Charles. 1991. *The Malaise of Modernity.* Concord, Ont.: Anansi Press, Ltd.

Weblinks

Social Science Information Gateway
http://www.sosig.ac.uk/roads/subjectlisting/Worldcat/polideol.html

Stanford Encyclopedia of Philosophy Table of Contents
plato.stanford.edu/contents.html

Political Theory—Yahoo
http://dir.yahoo.com/Social—Science/Political—Science/Political—Theory/

CHAPTER 4

RADICAL IDEOLOGIES

SANDRA REIN

Objectives

One of the quickest ways to disarm someone in political debate is to use the label "ideological" against your opponent. The news media know this and employ the term "ideological" to categorize and de-legitimate "militant" or protest groups. The implication is that to subscribe to a particular ideology is to give way to extremism and to obscure the truth. However, such everyday uses fail to engage the concept of ideology as a systematic study of ideas or to adequately investigate how a variety of social views may be ideological without being the sole property of extremist groups or protest movements. This chapter will introduce ideology as a critical concept in political science, outline its historical development, discuss key radical ideologies of the past two centuries, and finally, highlight why ideology continues to be a key concept in political science.

Introduction

Terry Eagleton's insightful *Ideology: An Introduction* (1990) makes the humorous observation that "[i]deology, like halitosis, is in this sense, what the other person has" (Eagleton, 1990, 2). Eagleton is referring to the pejorative, that is, judgmental, way in which ideology is often invoked in everyday uses. However, as an analytical concept within the social sciences, ideology has a much more textured and nuanced set of meanings. The systematic study and organization of ideas and concepts can be traced back to Aristotle, but the modern usage of the term *ideology* arises from the French Revolution in the late 1700s. First put into print by Destutt de Tracy, ideology was generally understood to mean the study of ideas. At the turn of the nineteenth century a group known as the Ideologues committed themselves to understanding how ideas come to be formed and transmitted in society. The very concept of ideology, however, quickly took on a negative connotation. Ideology came to be seen as a mechanism that obscured reality and created an environment for the spread of radical political ideas. It is also worth noting that early concepts of ideology were much more closely linked with religion than with politics. In a sense, ideology, as a concept, was a product of the Enlightenment, contributing to the modern critique of religion as a mechanism of social control and demonstrating the Enlightenment commitment to rationality. Beliefs and ideas were negatively juxtaposed with the facts, which were discovered through reason and scientific method.

Although the critique of religion was key to early formulations of ideology, the concept was taken up by a variety of political thinkers as they attempted to form a coherent understanding of the relationship of ideas to social organization. In order to understand the importance of ideology for political science today, it is first essential to review the historical approaches that were developed following the model of the Ideologues in post-revolutionary France.

Defining Ideology

AT ITS VERY BASIC ETYMOLOGICAL ROOTS, IDEOLOGY MEANS SIMPLY THE scientific or systematic study of ideas. However, such a definition is far too broad to be useful to political scientists. Attempts to narrow this broad definition have caused scholars to approach the question of the meaning of ideology from within the historical frameworks established by early political theorists, such as Karl Marx and Karl Mannheim. The following sections will examine some key approaches to defining and understanding ideology. The first section, drawing primarily from the work of Karl Marx and subsequent Marxists, defines ideology as a negative concept; that is, as a coherent set of beliefs and ideas that distort social reality and social relationships. The second section examines the work of Karl Mannheim and Clifford Geertz. Their approaches attempt to create neutral categories for understanding ideological thinking. In this regard, the term loses some of its negative connotations. Finally, we review the range of definitions of ideology employed by today's political theorists and ask what the implications are of choosing one definition over another.

Ideology as a Negative Concept

One of the first approaches to understanding ideology that we will discuss was developed by Karl Marx (1818–1883). What makes this approach interesting is that Marxism is also identified as an extremely influential twentieth-century ideology. For Marx, however, ideology was a central consideration in explaining how class inequalities develop and are maintained. Marx argued that the ruling class, or the **bourgeoisie**, in capitalist society is able to consolidate its power through the enforcement of a dominant ideology. In Marxist literature, this dominant ideology, or bourgeois ideology, creates among the working class, or **proletariat**, a false consciousness. Marx did not actually use the term *false consciousness*. This term was later introduced by his colleague and long-time friend, Friedrich Engels. However, Marx's political theory focuses attention on the means through which the working class come to accept and even work for the continuation of oppressive economic and social relations. Marx's answer to the age-old question of why the oppressed support their oppressors was to argue that through the manipulation and promotion of certain ideas by the dominant class (that is, ideology), the oppressed class comes to believe that their position can only be improved by supporting rather than rejecting the system.

Although Marx's formulation may seem quite complicated, in essence it is quite direct and simple. Consider it in this way: Marx argued that the working class lives in circumstances of impoverishment and exploitative working conditions. Rather than revolting against these circumstances, Marx tells us that the working class come to see their only escape through increased dedication to their working environment and the wholesale embrace of capitalism. We can see everyday expressions of Marx's theory when we hear of the "rags to riches" stories of the worker who works hard and finds "just" reward in increased material wealth. The simple message is that class mobility is possible through hard work and submission to the dominant social order.

So, where does false consciousness enter into the equation? Marx argued that ideology is the misrepresentation of the reality of the lives and working conditions of the working class. This misrepresentation is promoted by the ideas espoused and transmitted by the ruling class. As a result, the working class come to adopt ruling-class ideals and, in this sense, adopt the values and ideas that are in their very essence antithetical to the interests of the workers. The ruling class ideology does not fairly represent the realities of working-class life. It is neither in the interest of the proletariat nor does it work to improve working and living conditions. However, for Marx to argue that the ideology is false is not the same as saying that the proletariat is no longer in touch with reality. What his argument does is draw a distinction between the ideas communicated by the ruling class and the conditions under which the majority of the population live. It was Marx's own conclusion that the disparity between the "real" and the "ideological" would cause the working class to organize against the capitalist class and engage in socialist revolution. False consciousness was not an iron cage, forever oppressing the working class, but instead a social process of *increasing* working class consciousness.

Marx was not alone in identifying ideology as a set of ideas that serve to distort reality. Several key political philosophers and sociologists also apply a negative conception of ideology to all forms of political radicalism and social organization. However, these authors also argued that ideology, even as it distorts reality, could provide a positive goal toward which people could organize themselves. In this sense, ideologies remain negative or false representations, but, these representations can motivate people to achieve positive and necessary social change.

Georges Sorel (1847–1922), for example, replaced the word *ideology* with *myth* to indicate that social groups, particularly political movements, develop key myths in order to generate solidarity among members (Sargent, 1996, 9). A committed socialist, Sorel argued that socialism used stories and images to motivate the working class to organize against the bourgeoisie. Sorel did not use the word myth to mean falsity. Instead, Sorel argued that the myth of the General Strike was useful in creating a common goal for the working class. In other words, a strategy of mobilization was implicit within Sorel's work, providing the workers with an organizational means (that is, the General Strike) to oppose conditions of their oppression.

Antonio Gramsci, an Italian communist who was imprisoned by the Italian fascists in the 1930s, also wrote extensively about the political importance of ideology. His idea of hegemony is particularly relevant to this discussion. Gramsci argued that the success of modern rulers and ruling classes was only assured by their ability to establish a hegemonic position in society. By this, he meant that the ruling class must enjoy widespread popular support for its ideas, or what Gramsci would name their world view. Gramsci, however, also argued that no hegemonic project is complete. There is always critical space for groups to challenge the values and consensus being promoted by the ruling class. Gramsci calls these counter-hegemonic movements. Modern-day examples of such counter-hegemonic movements would include the women's movement and the environmental movement. The strength of Gramsci's analysis is that it maintained Marx's original insight about the distorting nature of dominant ideology while drawing attention to the groups and ideas that constantly challenge that hegemony.

Ideology as a Neutral Concept

Karl Mannheim (1893–1947), a turn-of-the-century sociologist and political theorist, agreed with Marx that ideology serves the interests of the ruling class. Nevertheless, he wanted to develop a concept of ideology that better fit his own theory of knowledge. Mannheim proposed that ideology was best studied by looking at the social conditions of those who held specific sets of beliefs.

The approach that Mannheim developed to assess political values and beliefs focused on what he termed the particular and total conceptions of ideology. For Mannheim the *particular* conception of ideology is achieved by examining the beliefs and values held by an individual. The particular conception of ideology holds that our political opponent will distort reality in order to further his or her own interests. This particular conception sees ideology as a more or less conscious attempt to disguise the truth (Mannheim, 1936, 55).

The *total* conception of ideology does not concern itself with individual beliefs or values, but instead focuses on the values and beliefs held by a concrete socio-historical group, such as a social class. The total conception of ideology also investigates the key ideological thought of a specific age (or epoch). In application, Mannheim argued that the total conception is "concerned with the characteristics and composition of the total structure of the mind of the epoch or historical group" (Mannheim, 1936, 56).

Mannheim noted that for both the particular and the total conceptions of ideology "opinions, statements, propositions, and systems of ideas are not taken at their face value but are interpreted in the light of the life-situation of the one who expresses them" (Mannheim, 1936, 56). Thus, in order to develop either a particular or total conception of ideology, Mannheim directs us to always consider the socio-political-historical context of the individual or group holding the belief. This focus on the life-situation and history is integral to Mannheim's larger project of developing a sociology of knowledge.

Mannheim however drew three important distinctions between the concepts of particular and total ideology. First, the particular conception is only concerned with the content of an opponent's assertion. The total conception, in contrast, calls into question the entire world view of the speaker and seeks to locate his or her values as an expression of collective or social life (Mannheim, 1936, 57). Second, the particular conception is exclusively an individual and psychological evaluation of social expression. The total conception, however, moves beyond a psychological evaluation to consider the form (how ideas are expressed) as well as their content (what is being expressed). Finally, the particular conception is evaluated as the single, individual expression of self-interest, whereas the total conception is not concerned with individual motivation, but instead conceptualizes how beliefs function at a social level (Mannheim, 1936, 57).

When Mannheim applied his total and particular conceptions of ideology, he found that individuals become "stuck" within specific historical forms of thinking which he termed *historical political parties.* For Mannheim, political parties were not the organizations that we have come to associate with the term today. Instead, political parties were distinct ways about thinking about the world. Mannheim argued that we can identify five key "political parties" that ideally portray different ideological formations (total conception) throughout history (Mannheim, 1936, 118). The five ideal-types identified by Mannheim are:

1. *Bureaucratic conservatism*—typified by the eighteenth-century nobility in Germany and England. Solutions to problems are seen as administrative rather than political. Society is highly stratified;

2. *Historical conservatism*—best demonstrated by the political thought of Edmund Burke's *Reflections on the Revolution in France.* The historical conservative wants to avoid sudden social upheaval. There is also reverence for tradition and history;

3. *Liberal-democratic bourgeois*—advocates laissez-faire (free market) economics and democratic decision making based on majority rule. Mannheim says that this is the most successful ideology and that it serves the interests of the bourgeoisie well in capitalist society;

4. *Socialist-communist*—advocates social transformation through revolution and ultimately seeks a classless society; and

5. *Fascism*—arises when class forces are disjointed and there is an opportunity for a forceful leader to seize control.

From the development of ideological "ideal-types," Mannheim was able to demonstrate the value of tracing ideas through their historical forms. Mannheim's approach does, however, raise the question of who would be in a unique position to identify either the total or the particular forms of certain beliefs. Put differently, if we can never stand outside an ideology, how can we study its effects? Scientifically, this question was not overlooked by Mannheim, although his answer would be dubbed "elitist" today. Mannheim argued that only intellectuals could observe and reveal the ideological content of social values and beliefs without bias. Intellectuals, Mannheim argued, were in a unique position to study ideology because they did not fit neatly or permanently into any class position.

Building on historical works relating to ideology, anthropologist and social theorist Clifford Geertz is recognized as one of the leading modern commentators on ideology. Geertz wanted to provide a neutral definition of ideology and argued that ideologies only emerge when there is significant social disruption and political dislocation. For Geertz, ideologies play an important role by "filling in" when reality is no longer clear. From Geertz's perspective: "[i]deology emerges, in other words, when political life becomes autonomous of mythic, religious or metaphysical sanctions, and must be charted in more explicit, systematic ways" (Eagleton, 1990, 151). Ideology plays an important social role by providing individuals with a necessary point of reference for making sense of the world around them.

Ideology Today

THE CONCEPT OF IDEOLOGY HAS BEEN A CONSTANT THEME IN THE STUDY OF social and political life. Terry Eagleton's survey of the legion of definitions reveals that more than sixteen different uses are commonly invoked by scholars (Eagleton, 1990, 2). So, how is a student to understand ideology? For Eagleton, and for our purposes in this chapter, the answer is to find the middle ground between the negative conception of ideology and the more neutral approaches. Such an approach to defining ideology is developed as follows. The history of ideology is essentially the competition between what may be called negative representations, which define ideology as myth, illusion, as false consciousness and the more sociological approaches, which explore ideology as the role of ideas in social and political life. The results of straddling these two approaches are what Eagleton calls "lived relations" (Eagleton, 1990, 30) and an "organizing social force" (Eagleton, 1990, 222). Borrowing from Eagleton's analysis, we need to think about ideology as key sets of both those beliefs and values that serve to legitimate a certain social order, the so-called dominant ideology, and those values and beliefs that may be said to oppose or challenge the dominant ideology. There are several important implications that result from using such an approach to ideology. First, people promote and contest dominant ideologies. Second, this definition accepts that ideologies have interested parties who stand to benefit from the adoption of their ideas and that the individuals adopting these ideas may be misled. Finally, this definition of ideology focuses attention on the contestable nature of social ideas. Although we recognize that ideologies play an important role in organizing social stability, they are also the primary mid-wives of social change.

Modern Radical Political Ideologies

IN THIS SECTION WE REVIEW THE KEY COMPONENTS OF MARXISM, SOCIALISM, anarchism, and communism. Each can be considered a radical political ideology and a political movement. Each offers an analysis of the ideas that organize social relations as well as a program of change. In Eagleton's words, each political ideology under discussion here has something to say about "lived relations" and "organizing social forces." However, before proceeding to a discussion of Marxism, a word or two needs to be said about why these particular ideologies are termed "radical."

Much like *ideology*, the term *radical* often suffers from a pejorative connotation. The very use of the word signals to one's audience that whatever follows is extreme and should be, in the name of reasonableness, discounted. However, radical has a more nuanced meaning. Rather than beginning our analysis by prejudging radical ideologies as extremist, we are better served by looking at radical thought as critical social theory. The Latin origin of the term radical is *radic*, meaning root. Radical critiques, thus, are those that propose to go to the root of the problem. All four ideologies under consideration offer a fundamental and thorough critique of various forms of social organization. In this sense, to be radical means to offer significant challenge to the status quo. Social scientists today who draw their analyses from radical political thought, particularly from the Marxist tradition, tend to avoid the pejorative title radical and instead opt for the general name *critical theory*. Nevertheless, the key consideration is always the critique of the status quo and what Marx called the "ruthless criticism of all that exists."

Marxism

Method

Marxist political theory is, first and foremost, distinguished by its method—a dialectical model known as **historical materialism**. It forms a theoretical orientation that traces human history through the lens of how the *means of production* (land, labour, resources; those elements that are necessary to produce material things) have been organized. The way that a society organizes its means of production is called a *mode of production*. Societies founded on particular modes of production are also characterized by specific and predictable antagonistic relationships and political conflicts. Marx associated different modes of production with specific epochs, or stages, in human history. The key stages for Marx included slavery, feudalism, and capitalism. Each epoch is defined by a specific antagonism such as the struggle between owner and slave, lord and serf, and bourgeoisie and proletariat, respectively. Marx argued that the transition to capitalism from feudalism simplified social antagonisms so that the key struggle became the class struggle between the owners of the means of production (the bourgeoisie) and the workers (the proletariat). In Marxist analysis, historical materialism allows us to see human history as a history of class struggle. Marx did not suggest that history unfolds in a predetermined way, but demonstrated that there were real struggles taking place within real historical societies with real historical consequences. That being said, Marx did have an ultimate goal in mind as he traced the history of class struggle. The goal was to outline the conditions under which the proletariat may overcome the bourgeoisie and end class struggle through the formation of communist society.

Wage–Capital Relations

A second distinguishing element of Marxist political theory is its emphasis on wage–capital relations. Marx argued that the transformation from feudal and merchant economies to capitalism created a new relationship between the labourer and the products he or she produces. This new relationship was based on the notion that the labourer independently possesses labour power. Under capitalism, labourers do not produce for themselves, but instead sell their labour to capitalists. In theory, the labourer is free to sell that labour power to whichever capitalist he or she wishes; however, the relationship, as Marx revealed, is one that really deprives the worker of choice. Without employment (that is, the selling of one's labour power) the worker would be unable to purchase food, shelter, clothing, and the other necessities of life. Because of this, workers are forced to work for the capitalist regardless of how bad working conditions may be. Also, because workers are dependent on capitalists, wages can be decreased and working hours increased without the capitalist worrying about losing his or her workforce. It was Marx's theory that the fundamentally unfair relationship between workers and capitalists (the wage–capital relationship) was necessary for the creation and expansion of capitalism. Marx noted: "The process, therefore, that clears the way for the capitalist system can be none other than the process which takes away from the labourer the possession of his means of production; a process that transforms, on the one hand, the social means of subsistence and production into capital, on the other, the immediate producers into wage-labourers" (Marx, 1959, 350).

A crucial element of the wage–capital relation is the concept of surplus value. **Surplus value** represents the underpinnings of capitalism. It represents the ability of the capitalist to earn profit through the labour of others. A capitalist gains surplus value (or profit) by increasing a worker's productivity beyond the break-even point. Surplus value works like this: let's assume that the goods a worker produces in the first six hours of work cover all the capitalist's costs of production (that is, the worker's wages and the materials that are used in manufacturing the item). This means if the worker only works six hours and the capitalist sells everything he or she produced, the capitalist would not make any profit. Of course, Marx rightly noted, capitalists do not want to break even, they want to earn a profit. The only way to earn a profit, then, is to increase the hours of work beyond the break-even point. Now, if the worker produces goods for another two hours after reaching the break-even point, he or she will generate surplus value for the capitalist.

Although it may seem self-evident that the main goal of capitalists is profit, the desire to accumulate profit (or capital) does require a theoretical explanation. Marx argued that capitalists need to accumulate capital because of what he called the **principle of commodification.** Simply put, Marx theorized that capitalism functioned by the value goods have in exchange rather than by their actual use. In capitalist society, items are valued as commodities and these values can be converted into other goods or, as Marx noted, even into political power. According to Marx, commodification means that the value of a good or service is not determined by how useful it is, but instead by the market and exchange.

Commodification effectively reduces all social interaction to a form of market exchange. For workers, Marx noted, commodification reduces the exchange value of labour through low wages and worker exploitation, while increasing the exchange value of commodities.

The inverse relationship between wages and exchange value raised two other important observations for Marx. First, capital, usually in the form of money, can be converted into other types of power, such as political power. The organization of the economy, in other words, has direct consequences for the organization of politics. The idea that capital may express itself in power relationships explains Marx's particular conception of the state as a representative of the interests of capital. This relationship between capital and the state allows capital (the bourgeoisie) to use the state to maintain power. For Marx, the relationship between the accumulation of capital and politics is mutually reinforcing. The mode of production, then, creates the conditions for a political superstructure that consists of ideology, ideas, and institutions that are the product of class struggle. The second issue commodification raises is that capital will increasingly become concentrated in fewer and fewer hands, and, thus, the profits derived from the commodification of society in general will benefit fewer rather than more individuals.

For Marx, the great irony of capitalism was that it held the potential to eradicate human want. Poverty, hunger, and scarcity could be ended through the technological innovations that present themselves in capitalism. Because of increasing concentration of capital, however, the technological means to end scarcity merely serve to further impoverish the worker. A fair and equitable distribution of wealth, Marx argued, would first require the working class to become conscious of their exploitation.

Contradictions and Crises of Capitalism

A fundamental question for Marx was how workers were to become conscious of the class exploitation inherent in capitalism. His answer was that modern capitalism produces fundamental contradictions in the lives of the working class. The first contradiction is that the drive to increase profit leads to an on-going attempt to depress workers' wages. As a result, workers have less money to spend, which reduces the consumption of the very goods they are producing. The second contradiction inherent in capitalism is that over time profits fall because the investment of capital per unit of labour increases (Tucker, 1978, 478). This means that the profit earned per unit of production actually decreases over time. This decrease is due to productivity decreases. These two inherent contradictions of capitalism lead to on-going cyclical crises—the so-called "boom and bust" cycle. Marx argued that the underconsumption of consumer goods by domestic workers necessitates finding new markets. Further, the rising cost of labour forces a search for cheaper sources of labour and production. As Marx and Engels wrote in the *Manifesto of the Communist Party*: "And how does the bourgeoisie get over these crises? On the one hand by enforced destruction of a mass of productive forces; on the other, by the conquest of new markets, and by more thorough exploitation of the old ones" (Marx, 1978, 478).

The global expansion of capitalism, because of the inherent contradictions and crises of the system, leads to a situation in which there is a long-run decrease in the standard of living of all workers. The very fact that capitalism is constantly forced to expand to wider productive and commodity markets encourages an international association among workers which Marx argued is necessary for a proletarian revolution. What remains missing, then, to foment this revolution, is the organization of the workers. Notably, Marx proposes that participation in a revolution among workers will be supported by those members of the ruling class who will also feel compelled to participate. Marx noted: ". . . the whole range of society, assumes such a violent, glaring character, that a small section of the ruling class cuts itself adrift, and joins the revolutionary class, the class that holds the future in its hands" (Marx, 1978, 481). Thus, the end to the alienation, exploitation, and immiseration of the working class is a revolutionary movement led by the proletariat which establishes first socialism (the so-called **dictatorship of the proletariat**) and finally a communist state. For Marx, this state would embody the principle that "the free development of each is the condition for the free development of all" (Marx, 1978, 491).

Marx believed that the only route to social change was through revolution. Although somewhat ambivalent about the necessity of violence to achieve revolutionary transformation, he remained committed throughout his lifetime to providing support to workers' organizations and movements. Marx's revolutionary theory would have significant impact on world-wide revolutionary movements spanning every continent.

Socialism

Historically, socialism as a political ideology predates Marxism, although it is impossible to deny that Marx's writings irrevocably changed socialism. The intellectual heritage of the key ideas of socialism are traced to Rousseau's critique of differences in property ownership, the concept of organic society, and the belief that individuals can aspire to the greater good (Baradat, 1988, 170). Rousseau's ideas were felt throughout revolutionary France. Another important early socialist who found inspiration in the French Revolution was Francis Babeuf (1760–1797). Babeuf advocated an extreme socialism that called for revolutionary transformation and the existence of an elite corps to lead the masses to revolution (Baradat, 1988, 171).

Breaking from its revolutionary roots, socialism coalesced into a coherent set of ideas in the form of what has been termed utopian socialism. This form of socialist thought advocated the public ownership of the means of production, democratic social organizations, and the eradication of all want in society. Robert Owen (1771–1858) is identified as the "father" of utopian socialism. Ironically, Owen was a successful industrial capitalist who embarked on realizing his utopian vision after retiring from business. He was convinced that his factories had been productive because of his ethical treatment of employees. To prove his point, Owen participated in setting up communes on the principles of economic self-sufficiency and democratic decision making. The New Harmony commune, established in 1825 in Indiana, is recognized as one of Owen's most successful attempts at communal living. New Harmony, like all of the communal experiments of the time, ultimately failed because of an inability to be economically independent and to sustain democratic group decision making.

Following utopian socialism, socialist thought was dominated by Marx's influence. Marx proposed that his form of socialism was scientific—drawing on Enlightenment notions of rationality and science. Marx argued that socialism is merely a stage of economic and social development following the demise of capitalism. Although scientific socialism had tremendous impact on the organizational forms of the working class (most notably in the case of the formation of the International Workingmen's Association, known as the First International), Marx's theories quickly became subject to debate leading to significant revision by subsequent socialist thinkers. Two areas of Marxist thought were most hotly contested: the commitment to change through revolution only; and what was perceived as the over-emphasis on economic relationships (economic determinism). The resulting revisionist movement argued that social change could be achieved through evolution rather than revolution. The revisionists also stressed the moral/social values of socialism rather than economics. This was the position taken by Canada's most influential social democratic party—the Co-operative Commonwealth Federation which emerged from the depths of the Great Depression of the 1930s—its manifesto is reprinted below.

The Regina Manifesto
(Programme of the Co-operative Commonwealth Federation,
adopted at First National Convention held at Regina, Sask., July, 1933)

The C.C.F. is a federation of organizations whose purpose is the establishment in Canada, of a Co-operative Commonwealth in which the principles regulating production, distribution and exchange will be the supplying of human needs and not the making of profits.

We aim to replace the present capitalist system, with its inherent injustice and inhumanity, by a social order from which the domination and exploitation of one class by another will be eliminated, in which economic planning will supersede unregulated private enterprise and competition, and in which genuine democratic self-government, based upon economic equality, will be possible.

The present order is marked by glaring inequalities of wealth and opportunity, by chaotic waste and instability; and in an age of plenty it condemns the great mass of the people to poverty and insecurity. Power has become more and more concentrated into the hands of a small irresponsible minority of financiers and industrialists and to their predatory interests the majority are habitually sacrificed. When private profits is the main stimulus to economic effort, our society oscillates between periods of feverish prosperity in which the main benefits go to speculators and profiteers, and of catastrophic depression, in which the common man's normal state of insecurity and hardship is accentuated. We believe that these evils can be removed only in a planned and socialized economy in which our natural resources and the principal means of production and distribution are owned, controlled and operated by the people.

The new social order at which we aim is not one in which individuality will be crushed out by a system of regimentation.

Nor shall we interfere with cultural rights of racial or religious minorities. What we seek is a proper collective organization of our economic resources such as will

continued

make possible a much greater degree of leisure and a much richer individual life for every citizen.

This social and economic transformation can be brought about by political action, through the election of a government inspired by the ideal of a Co-operative Commonwealth and supported by a majority of the people. We do not believe in change by violence. We consider that both the old parties in Canada are the instruments of capitalist interests and cannot serve as agents of social reconstruction, and that whatever the superficial difference between them, they are bound to carry on government in accordance with the dictates of the big business interests who finance them.

Today, socialism remains a vibrant political ideology. While some movements still maintain a link to historical scientific socialism, the more prevalent legacy is apparent among social democratic parties found in Western Europe. Social democracy is characterized by a commitment to universal social programs for citizens, a mixed economy of public and private enterprise, and public taxation to decrease income disparities. In the European Union, social democratic parties continue to be a significant presence on Europe's political landscape. The success of these parties has sustained interest in social democracy, and socialist thinking more generally, proving the on-going relevance of this ideology.

Courtesy of Saskatchewan NDP.

Anarchism

Defined most simply, anarchism is the rejection of hierarchical forms of governance. Yet, this definition fails to capture the rich history of anarchist thought. Anarchism as a political ideology became popular in the early nineteenth century in response to the Industrial Revolution. Since that time, subscribers to anarchist thought have organized in most industrialized countries and have had a significant impact on developing political regimes, particularly in Africa. Generally, anarchist thinking can be divided into two distinct categories: social or collectivist versus individualist anarchism. We will examine each in turn.

Social Anarchism

Pierre Joseph Proudhon (1809–1865) was the first political thinker to call himself an anarchist. Proudhon is best remembered for his answer to the question "What is property?" He replied "Property is theft." Proudhon outlined the key elements of anarchism which would see the eradication of the state and the free and harmonious association of individuals. Specifically, Proudhon advocated the organization of workers into syndicates that would collectively make all decisions about production and collectively share ownership. Proudhon's form of anarchism is often referred to as **anarcho-syndicalism**. Anarchist syndicate experiments did enjoy some short-lived success in Spain between 1936 and 1939. However, these syndicates obtained worker control through violent means, in contrast to Proudhon's non-violent prescription.

One of the best-known anarchists, Mikhail Bakunin (1814–1876), believed that violence was necessary to achieve an anarchist society. Closely associated with social (or communist) anarchism, Bakunin argued that revolution would be achieved by arming the most undesirable elements of the population. Clearly one of the most radical anarchists, Bakunin's legacy is his strong belief in the necessary role of violence in effecting social change. Another well-known anarchist who subscribed to Bakunin's radicalism is Emma Goldman (1869–1940). Goldman carried her anarchist message throughout the United States, the Soviet Union, and Canada. A tireless radical, Goldman was also outspoken on issues concerning women's rights and was particularly active in working for the legalization of contraception for women. Goldman's early anarchism was closely aligned with Bakunin's.

In her later years, however, Goldman became less committed to violent overthrow largely because of the influence of Peter Kropotkin's (1842–1921) thought. Kropotkin argued that society was more likely to progress through cooperation than aggression. Also a communist anarchist, Kropotkin believed that the modern state was "the personification of injustice, oppression, and monopoly." Kropotkin's vision of anarchist society was one of harmony and cooperation. Kropotkin was not convinced that revolutions were the best way to change social organization. He believed that industrial progress and technology would eventually eradicate human want. Once this level of technological advancement had occurred, Kropotkin believed that society would evolve to communism.

Individualist Anarchism

Both anarcho-syndicalism and communist anarchism share a belief that government prevents the free association among individuals and therefore limits personal autonomy and the possibility of cooperative and harmonious social organization. However, there is another strain of anarchist thinking that asserts that individuals should be completely free of social responsibility. Lyman Sargent notes that "[t]he individualist anarchist recognizes nothing above his ego and rebels against all discipline and all authority"(Sargent, 1996, 177). Individualist anarchist thought is historically associated with Max Stirner (1806–1856) who nicely summarizes his political ideology with the slogan "The people are dead. Up with me!"

Stirner represents individualist anarchism at its most extreme. **Libertarianism**, in many ways, represents a softer variant of Stirner's philosophy and continues to have significant impact on contemporary politics, especially in the United States. Libertarianism is closely associated with the work of Robert Nozick, who asserts the "pre-eminent right" of private property. Libertarians reject government intervention in areas of social policy and economic markets, but do see a need for government in a very limited and controlled sense. Threads of libertarian thought run through the rhetoric of political movements and political parties that promise to "down-size government" and to guarantee the "free market." For example, during the 2000 American presidential campaign, George W. Bush frequently asserted that he believed in "the people" and not "government." Indeed, a handful of libertarians typically compete in Canadian federal elections in order to deliver this message.

Communism

Communism, of all the ideologies discussed here, is the most difficult to define. We all have a sense that we know what communism is. We've seen it in its application in the former

Soviet Union, China, Cuba, and the former Yugoslavia. With the demise of the communist regimes in many of these countries, we are also left with the sense that communism is a failed experiment, a political ideology that was "good in theory" but did not work in practice. However, this is a far too simplistic dismissal of the question of what communist ideology consists of and means in application. The "failure" of avowedly communist regimes or the more recent movement towards "democratization" and market liberalization does not speak to the theoretical and ideological concepts that underpin communist theory. In fact, many traditional Marxists were highly critical of the Soviet experiment. As with all political ideologies, there is often a large gap between political ideas and their concrete expression in political actions and institutions.

Marx argued that communism could only be achieved after capitalism and socialism, but actually wrote very little about what communist society would look like. Some ideas, however, are found in his theoretical work. Communist society would involve the public ownership of the means of production (factories, etc.), absolute social equality (that is, a classless society), and the "withering away" of the state. In this sense, communism is very much the melding of scientific socialism and social anarchism. For Marx the communist ethic was embodied in the statement: "from each according to his abilities, to each according to his needs." From Marx's original work on the question of communist society, other Marxists began to develop a more defined picture of communism. Most notably among these thinkers is Lenin (1870–1924). Lenin's concern was to take the theories that Marx espoused and to put them into action. As one of the key leaders of the Russian Revolution, Lenin was in a unique position to further develop communist political thought. Lenin was consumed by two concerns: how capitalism worked internationally, and how to organize a successful revolution. With regard to the latter concern, Lenin developed the notion of the party vanguard. Lenin argued that in order to successfully organize a revolution, it would be necessary to have a well-trained cadre of dedicated individuals who would work tirelessly for the success of the revolution. Following the revolution, the **vanguard** would ensure the nationalization of industry and the dictatorship of the proletariat.

Following Lenin's death in 1924 Joseph Stalin came to power in the Soviet Union. Stalin consolidated his personal authority in the USSR through bloody purges and political intrigue and challenged one of the fundamental precepts of Marxist thought. Marx believed that socialism had to be an international project. Stalin, in contrast, contended that "socialism in one country" was not only possible, but desirable. To this end, Stalin implemented intense industrialization and central planning. Some argue that his policies led inevitably to the demise of the Soviet economy in the 1990s. However, Stalin was not alone in attempting to offer significant revision to Marx's work. In China, Mao Tse-tung, leader of the Chinese revolution, argued that mobilization of the peasants, not workers, was the key to revolutionary success. This also represented a significant shift away from Marxist reliance on the working class as the focal point of revolution. Mao's communist reforms focused on the collectivization of farming as opposed to the Soviet model of speedy industrial development.

This very brief overview of communism leads us to two general conclusions. The first is that communist ideology need not be tied to the projects of the formerly communist countries. In fact, the basic tenets of communism—classless society and public ownership and direction of production—can be separated from those movements that have named themselves communist. Second, a political ideology can espouse a quite different view of social organization than what is achieved in the application. The Soviet Union, Yugoslavia, China, and Cuba each had to adapt and change their political ideologies to face changing domestic and international circumstances.

The Continued Importance of Ideology

THE DISINTEGRATION OF THE SOVIET UNION, LIBERALIZATION IN CHINA, AND democratic reforms throughout the former Eastern block have encouraged some political scientists to talk about the "end of ideology." The implication is that the "triumph" of U.S.-style democracy and the market economy has trumped all thinking about alternative forms of government. This argument is suspect on at least two counts. In the first place, it implies that democratic governments such as those found in Canada or the United States are non-ideological. And in the second place, it denies the continuing influence of radical ideologies on political movements around the globe. As we have already noted, Western Europe seems to be witnessing a resurgence in socialist-influenced politics, and countries in parts of the developing world such as Africa and Central America continue to draw on the insights and programs of previous ideological movements.

The end-of-ideology view also tends to overlook the importance of new and emerging critical movements. Critical political projects such as environmentalism, feminism, racial equality, and gay liberation also draw their organizational forms and critiques from the historical analysis of key radical ideologies. Within feminism, for example, there are strong socialist, Marxist, and anarchist sentiments that are reshaped by a new focus on issues of gender. Returning to Eagleton, for a moment, it is clear that the role of ideology to make sense of our lived experiences and to offer insight into new forms of social organization is likely to be a consistent feature of human social existence. To argue that ideology is no longer a relevant concept is to deny our ability as human beings to contest current social conditions and to think about alternative ways of living.

Summary

The concept of ideology has a rich and varied history. The social science uses of the concept have been drawn from two conflicting influences. The first is the negative conception of ideology as espoused by Marx. The second is a more sociological conception that treats ideology as a neutral but important way to understand societies. Today's use of the concept must find a way between these two influences to provide a definition that reflects both lived experience and potential new social organizational forms. Much of the social critique embodied in Marxism, socialism, and communism draws on the theoretical works of Karl Marx and then attempts a revision to make sense of changing historical situations and to offer an alternative form of social organization. Anarchism offers yet another prescription for an alternative society. Critical ideologies continue to be important to political science as they respond to changing historical circumstances. The key ideologies studied in this chapter continue to have significant impact on emerging social movements today.

Discussion Questions

1. What does it mean to use *ideology* as a neutral concept? Would you agree that it is a neutral concept or would you define it differently?

2. Do you find that your thinking about some issues could be considered ideological? In what ways?

3. Are radical political ideologies desirable? Why or why not?

4. What do you think is the future of socialist or communist movements today?

References

Baradat. Leon. 1988. *Political Ideologies: Their Origins and Impact.* Scarborough: Prentice Hall.

Eagleton, Terry. 1991. *Ideology: an Introduction.* New York: Verso.

Kettler, David, Volker Meja, and Nico Stehr. 1984. *Karl Mannheim.* New York: Tavistock, 1984.

Mannheim, Karl. 1936. *Ideology and Utopia: an Introduction to the Sociology of Knowledge* translated from the German by Louis Wirth and Edward Shils. New York: Harcourt, Brace & World.

Marx, Karl. 1959. *Das Kapital* edited by Friedrich Engels and condensed for modern readers by Serge L. Levitsky. Chicago: Henry Regnery Company.

———. 1978. *The Marx-Engels Reader* edited by Robert C. Tucker. New York: Norton.

Sargent, Lyman Tower. 1996. *Contemporary Political Ideologies: A Comparative Analysis.* New York: ITP.

Further Readings

Anderson, Kevin. 1995. *Lenin, Hegel, and Western Marxism: A Critical Study.* Chicago: University of Illinois Press.

Dunayevskaya, Raya. 1991. *Women's Liberation, and Marx's Philosophy of Revolution,* 2nd edition. Chicago: University of Illinois Press.

Geertz, Clifford. 1973. *The Interpretation of Cultures: Selected Essays.* New York: Basic Books.

Goldman, Emma. 1969. *Anarchism and Other Essays.* New York: Dover Publications.

Gramsci, Antonio. 1971. *Selections from the Prison Notebooks of Antonio Gramsci,* edited and translated by Quintin Hoare and Geoffrey Nowell Smith. London: Lawrence and Wishart.

Lenin, Vladimir Il'ich. 1972. *Collected Work of V. I. Lenin* translated by Clemens Dutt. London: Lawrence and Wishart.

Mao, Tse-tung. 1969. *On Revolution and War* edited with an introduction and notes by M. Rejai. Garden City: Doubleday.

Proudhon, P.-J. (Pierre-Joseph). 1994. *What Is Property?* edited and translated by Donald R. Kelley and Bonnie G. Smith. New York: Cambridge University Press.

Sorel, Georges. 1976. *From Georges Sorel: Essays in Socialism and Philosophy* edited and with an introduction by John L. Stanley and translated by John and Charlotte Stanley. New York: Oxford University Press.

Tucker, Robert C. 1969. *The Marxian Revolutionary Idea.* New York: Norton.

Weblinks

The Vladimir Ilyich Lenin Internet Archive
csf.Colorado.EDU/psn/marx/Other/Lenin/

The Socialist International
www.socialistinternational.org/

Institute for Anarchist Studies
www.flag.blackened.net/ias/

World Socialist Web Site
www.wsws.org/

The Communist Party of Canada
www.communist-party.ca/

The Marx/Engels Internet Archive
ww.csf.colorado.edu/mirrors/marxists.org/

CHAPTER 5

ETHICS AND POLITICS

Objectives

In this chapter we focus on the moral assumptions that underlie the political realm. Moral assumptions guide both our assessments and our criticisms of political claims. In the 2000 federal election, for example, Canadians were asked to choose between two competing sets of values. One stressed the role of the market in providing for the well-being of Canadians, while the other stressed a more active role for the state. The election therefore raised a moral debate between those who believe that the market can provide goods such as health care more efficiently, and those who believe that such basic goods should never be produced for profit.

STELLA GAON

This chapter begins with a discussion of the relationship between ethics and politics. We then provide a working definition of the concept of "ethics," and describe three important approaches to ethics in the history of political thought. We go on to outline prominent moral positions and to map them onto political views. We pay special attention to how the critical concept of reason has influenced political thought and practice during the modern era.

Throughout the chapter we emphasize the importance of making visible the moral assumptions underlying politics. But we also stress the critical point that political interests are served by particular moral claims. The question of whether political interests influence moral perspectives is raised in the context of contemporary challenges to modern moral and political thought. Our conclusion is that it is necessary both to criticize politics on moral grounds and to criticize moral perspectives and approaches on political grounds. The conversation between ethics and politics, in other words, flows in both directions.

Introduction

It is common, today, to think of ethics and politics as two entirely separate spheres. For example, politics is often understood in terms of the mechanics, strategies, and structures of power. The question of ethics, if it arises at all, is often limited to reflection on a politician's or ruler's personal integrity. Ethics is generally understood as a strictly personal matter, one that does not have much bearing on the political realm. Political arguments and decisions, however, are thoroughly saturated with ethical claims, assumptions and beliefs, whether or not these ever become explicit. For instance, should governments support medical developments in the fields of bio-technology and genetic manipulation (such as genetically modified foods and cloning)? Are property rights for music and books desirable in a digital universe? Should there be legal limitations on such fundamental freedoms as free speech in a democratic society—for example, in the case of racist or hate speech? Is it appropriate to impose human rights legislation on other countries through military and economic intervention? These political questions require one to take a particular ethical stance. They have profound moral implications.

The moral issues may well be unanswerable—or perhaps not satisfactorily answerable—in the final analysis. Nonetheless, it is important to bring ethical questions to the fore in political debates, not least because a conflict over ethical beliefs often drives political conflicts. For this reason, it is important to learn when moral assumptions are at work in the political sphere, and to develop arguments that can be used either to contest or defend them.

Defining Ethics

IN ENGLISH USAGE, BOTH *ETHICS* AND *MORALITY* REFER TO A BELIEF OR SET OF beliefs about what one ought to do, how one ought to live, and what ought to be. The word **ethics** comes from the Greek *ethos*, which means the general way of life and customs of a people; an *ethos* encompasses a society's cultural, traditional, religious, social and political norms. The word **morality** is related to the Latin *mores*, which is a synonym for the Greek word *ethos*. *Mores* are customs of a people that are considered socially beneficial. *Mores* sometimes develop into formal laws. The words *ethics* and *morality* may be used interchangeably, although some philosophers distinguish between them for the purposes of a specific theoretical argument.[1]

Ethics is generally broken down into two components: theoretical study and practical application. In its theoretical sense, ethics is a branch of philosophy which involves the study of what is *good* and what *ought* to be. Theoretical ethics is concerned with such questions as whether it is possible to justify moral beliefs with rational arguments, what role community values or traditions should play in ethical deliberation, and what the meaning of happiness and the good life is, and how we might best achieve it.

In its practical sense, ethics refers to the study of particular problems and the attempt to devise solutions to them (Birsch, 1999, 2). Contemporary examples of issues in practical ethics include (among others) the moral and political questions of abortion, euthanasia, cloning and reproductive technologies, legal punishment and the death penalty, world hunger, environmental issues, and the moral treatment of animals. Theoretical and practical ethics may be understood as two sides of the same coin, since people often brings theory or ideas to bear on practical problems and, similarly, practical problems—such as those encountered in the spheres of politics and the law—often inspire further theoretical reflection.

History of Ethics in Political Thought

THE HISTORY OF WESTERN POLITICAL THEORY IS, FUNDAMENTALLY, A HISTORY of on-going moral reflection about how we *ought* to live collectively. This moral reflection includes the consideration of how we should organize ourselves as a society for the maximum good of each person, of what role the state should play in citizens' personal lives, of whether personal or collective goods should take precedence in political deliberation, and of how to judge when political power is being used for morally good ends or is being used unjustly. As soon as we direct these kinds of **normative** questions to the realm of politics, we are drawing on ethics, because we are trying to decide what *ought* to be the case within a particular political context or practice.

Of course, political contexts and practices have changed profoundly over the centuries. Not surprisingly, the nature of theoretical reflection on the question of how we ought to live collectively has changed as well. Despite the vast diversity of ethical and political views, one can map three broad historical tendencies with regard to the foundational moral questions of Western political thought.

Classical Approaches

Ancient Greek philosophers such as Socrates, Plato, and Aristotle represent the *classical* approach to political philosophy. For these thinkers, ethical questions concerning how the individual ought to live, or what qualifies a person as "good" or "just," were fundamentally tied to the question of the just political regime. In other words, the idea was that a properly organized political regime would create conditions in which good citizens would emerge. Indeed, classical conceptions of the just political regime or state are characterized by their inseparability from the question of justice and virtue in the individual.

The ethical and political beliefs of Socrates (c. 470–399 B.C), one of the earliest political philosophers in the history of Western thought, are presented in Plato's early writings. Socrates believed that the only morally worthwhile life is one dedicated to the search for wisdom. This search was to be directed at understanding the principles of justice by which one ought to live, the nature of truth, and the meaning of human excellence in general. For Socrates, as for Plato, virtue is knowledge; thus, the just man[2] is one who seeks truth by relentlessly investigating and interrogating both his own beliefs and those of others. Socrates further believed that just as one can only do wrong if one does not know what is true, so knowing what is true means that one *cannot* do wrong. From this point of view, the just political state appears to be realizable if each citizen dedicates his life to the pursuit of knowledge and wisdom. A collective of virtuous (that is, knowledgeable and wise) citizens would constitute a good political state.

For Plato (c. 427–347 B.C) the moral virtue of the individual was even more important with respect to the just political regime than it was for Socrates. Focusing directly on the regime as a whole, Plato argues in his *Republic* that the only appropriate rulers of the *polis* (city-state) are those who have been trained and carefully educated in philosophy for most of their adult lives. Rulers, Plato argued, must develop the capacity to understand the ultimate "good" by virtue of which all knowledge is possible. This stress on educating the political rulers in philosophy follows from Plato's belief, which he shared with his teacher Socrates, that the search for knowledge constitutes the morally good life. Thus, political justice can only come about when rulers have each achieved an understanding of what is eternal and unchanging. At the same time, however, Plato stressed that it is necessary to create a just state in order to produce morally virtuous citizens, because virtue is achieved when everything is in its rightful place, and only philosophers can know fully what the rightful order is. All others require the "philosopher-kings" to legislate how they ought, morally, to live.

Aristotle (384–322 B.C) also connected the moral virtue of the individual to the political virtue of a just state in this way. He argued in his *Politics* that if one wants to produce a just man, one must make him a citizen of a just state, because people are by nature political animals, not isolated beings. Unlike Plato, however, Aristotle believed that moral goodness depends on one's particular context and on one's relations to others. He argued that hard-and-fast notions of justice such as those Plato tried to formulate were not applicable to the political realm. For Aristotle, virtue is achieved through habit and practice. It cannot be gained simply through study. He therefore argued that the more just the political regime, the more likely it will be that the individual will have opportunities to practise a morally virtuous life. Despite these differences, all classical philosophers see an intrinsic connection between the individual and the state with regard to the foundational moral questions of political life.

Medieval Approaches

The first few centuries A.D. saw Greek philosophizing and faith in pagan gods replaced with Christian doctrine as the authoritative source for all ethical and political questions. In the Western world, Christianity dominated moral and political reflection until well into the fifteenth century, and beyond. Whereas the classical tendency was to answer the foundational ethical questions of political thought with reference to the individual's reasoning capacity and his (or her) relation to the state, the medieval tendency was to answer these questions with reference to the individual's faith and his or her relation to the heavenly realm as described in the holy Christian scriptures.

Two particularly important medieval philosophers who reflect this second tendency are St. Augustine (354–430) and St. Thomas Aquinas (1225–1274). Augustine offers a Platonic approach to political philosophy. He emphasizes the priority and the reality of the ideal heavenly realm, just as Plato had emphasized the reality of the ultimate "*good*." Specifically, Augustine describes the earthly realm—what he calls the "city of man"—as a mere appearance or shadow of the true "city of God." Nonetheless, Augustine believed that political stability was important because it provided a secure context for Christian worship.

In contrast to Augustine, St. Aquinas focuses on the application of reason to what we *do*. Aquinas shares with Aristotle the fundamental belief that it is important to *practise* virtue, not simply to contemplate it. He held that through virtuous acts a person becomes good. Thus, Aquinas argued that political institutions and secular authority can play a central role in the production of virtuous individuals, provided that human laws honour the natural, God-given laws to which we have immediate access. Natural law, for example, inclines all people to act rationally (on the basis of reason), to propagate the species, and to live co-operatively. Human law is only legitimate, in Aquinas's view, to the extent that it corresponds with these self-evident, God-given truths.

Augustine and Aquinas believed that reason plays an important role in the virtuous life. Unlike ancient thinkers, however, they ultimately defer to Christian doctrine for the final word on the moral status of individual acts and political regimes. For both Augustine and Aquinas, perfect justice and virtue are not of this world; they are only realizable in the heavenly realm.

Modern Approaches

The third broad approach to ethics and politics rejects philosophical appeals to religion and tradition. Moreover, in the absence of an active moral role for the state, moral authority has nowhere left to rest but within each individual. In an odd way, therefore, medieval philosophy opened the door to the modernist separation between the individual and the state. For medieval philosophers undermined the ancient belief that the state plays a central role in the production of the morally good man or woman. Morality was seen as a matter between each individual and God. Thus, once virtue was taken out from under the secular authority of those holding political power and placed under the divine providence of God, the way was paved for the modern, individualist approach to ethics and politics.

The modern separation between the individual and the state is commonly understood in terms of a distinction between what is of public interest and what is strictly private. For example, questions of government spending on services such as roads and defence are public matters. Personal beliefs, on the other hand, are considered a private affair. Thus, for modern political philosophers the distinction between public and private parallels the distinction between state and church: religion and morality become questions best left to the individual, while the public, political questions are to be determined on the basis of reason alone. In this sense, the modern era is characterized by a return to Greek **humanism**; this entails, among other things, the belief that what is morally and politically "good" can be judged by humans rather than by God. The human being thus became the foundation of modern philosophical and political thought.

In modernity—beginning with Niccolò Machiavelli (1469–1522) and Thomas Hobbes (1588–1679) through to later modern thinkers such as John Locke (1632–1704), David Hume (1711–1776), and Immanuel Kant (1724–1804)—the virtues of rational self-determination and freedom became guiding moral and political principles. These values replaced both the ancient virtues of citizenship, manliness, and courage, and also the medieval, Christian virtues of charity, humbleness, and faith.

Even today, **autonomy**—the capacity to determine one's *own* goals on a rational basis—is taken as a fundamental moral good. It is applied both to individuals as well as to states in their sovereignty. The modern approach to ethics and politics is characterized by one basic assumption. Since all human beings are at least potentially rational, conceptions of justice that are rationally justified can gain the consent of all citizens. In this approach, private beliefs and cultural differences are considered irrelevant. In this sense, the modern era sharply distinguishes between public and private concerns. In the public realm, the value of self-determination became a new unifying moral principle.

Modern Moral and Political Philosophy

THE HISTORY OF POLITICAL THOUGHT REFLECTS A SERIES OF CHANGES IN THE general understanding of the relationship between ethics and politics. But this is not to say that there has ever been, at any one moment, uniform agreement about what constitutes a truly ethical decision or act. For example, Plato and Aristotle both stressed the state's role in the production of virtuous individuals, but they disagreed about whether a theory or a practice of political justice ought to be emphasized, and about exactly what justice entails. Similarly, Augustine and Aquinas both ranked divine wisdom over political authority. Nonetheless, they took different positions on the question of what moral role the state might still be expected to play. Contemporary moral philosophers who follow in the tradition of Hobbes, Locke, and Kant all accept that human reason is the most reliable authority on matters moral and political. They disagree, however, on what are the specific ethical and political implications of the critical concept of reason. Thus it is possible to identify a number of distinct types of moral arguments within this broad framework.

Consequentialism

One form of rational justification for moral claims is called **consequentialism**. This moral theory suggests that in order to judge the validity of political and moral beliefs, one need consider only the consequences of the action or the decision. **Act utilitarianism** is a common variant of consequentialism. This approach to moral theory stresses the utility likely to result from one's act or choice. In moral theory, "utility" is defined in terms of an increase in pleasure and/or a decrease in pain. As Douglas Birsch explains, act utilitarianism is, "related to the insight that an action is morally bad if it harms someone, whereas it is morally good if it helps or benefits someone" (1999, 31).

Typical representatives of the utilitarian position include Jeremy Bentham (1748–1832), John Stuart Mill (1778–1836) and William James (1842–1910). Bentham believed, for example, that the only meaning of the term *good* is pleasure, and that the only meaning of the term *evil* is pain. He further argued that the moral principle of utility (so defined) could be applied to the sphere of criminal law in two ways. First, he argued that if an act does not cause a calculable injury or harm, it should not be punished. Secondly, he contended that if an act does contribute to harm, the punishment should be determined with a view to providing a harm to the offender that is greater than the pleasure or benefit gained from the criminal act. In this way, the punishment will serve as a deterrent.

Another act utilitarian is the British political philosopher John Stuart Mill, who is best known as a social reformer, particularly with regard to the issue of minority rights. For example, Mill was among the earliest supporters of women's right to vote. His moral philosophy follows the path laid out by Bentham. He argues that in order to know what one ought to do, it is necessary to calculate the greatest good or happiness for the greatest number. Thus, for Mill as for Bentham, the basic moral norm is that one ought to act, and one ought to be motivated to act, so as to maximize utility or pleasure as much as possible. Like all consequentialists, Mill believed that one should rationally calculate the likely consequences of one's actions, and weigh the potential harms in comparison with the potential benefits in order to determine whether an act or decision is ethically good.

The idea that the consequences of actions are of key moral significance, and that consequences can be rationally calculated, has been brought to bear directly on the field of politics in a number of ways. A ground-breaking case in legal jurisprudence provides one salient example. This is the Canadian Supreme Court case *R. v. Oakes.*

David Oakes was arrested and subsequently found guilty of possession of illegal narcotics. According to a section of the Narcotic Control Act then in effect, anyone found guilty of possession was also guilty of trafficking in a narcotic, *unless* he or she could prove otherwise. The trial judge therefore found Oakes guilty of trafficking as well. Oakes appealed the decision to the Supreme Court of Canada on the grounds that the Narcotic Control Act violated his constitutional right to be presumed innocent until proven guilty (s. 11d of the *Charter*). His argument was that while he had been proven guilty of possession, he had not been *proven* guilty of trafficking. He had simply been *presumed* guilty. Oakes argued that in putting the burden on him to prove his innocence, the Narcotic Control Act was making an unconstitutional demand.

The Supreme Court found in Oakes' favour. What was most interesting about this case was that their unanimous ruling set the ground rules for all future cases about when a government is entitled to limit someone's fundamental rights (as laid out in the *Canadian Charter of Rights and Freedoms*), and when they are not. Specifically, the ruling in *Oakes* sets out two tests that the state must satisfy. These tests concern the social good or end at which the legislation is directed, and the means the Government uses to achieve it. The fundamental question laid out in *Regina v. Oakes* is are the means appropriate to the end—particularly when the means limit one of our fundamental Charter rights?

In the *Oakes* case, the purpose of limiting the right to be presumed innocent until proven guilty was to protect society from the dangers associated with drug trafficking. However, the means used to achieve this end had to be legitimate as well. In order to satisfy this second test, the Crown had to answer three questions. First, are the means rational, or are they arbitrary or unfair? Second, do the means used keep the infringement of rights to a bare minimum? In other words, is there a better way of achieving the same social good—one that would not limit a person's or a group's rights to as great an extent? Third, are the means proportional to the ends? The more severe the effects of a legal measure, then the more important the social objective must be.

In David Oakes' case, the Supreme Court ruled that the Crown failed to satisfy the second test.

With respect to the first question, they judged that it is irrational to conclude that someone in possession of only a small quantity of narcotics intends to sell them. In other words, the means used to protect society from the dangers of drug trafficking were not rational. The section of the Narcotic Control Act was therefore ruled unconstitutional. It was subsequently changed. Since these various tests were set out in *R. v. Oakes*, the Crown can only uphold legislation that limits our fundamental rights if it provides good arguments based on these utilitarian principles.

Virtue Ethics and Communitarianism

Virtue ethics shares with all modern moral philosophy the understanding that ethical values must be supported with rational arguments, but in this case the values that are upheld are derived from particular conceptions of the good person, rather than from conceptions of the good act. The theory begins from the basic insight that, "virtues help persons to achieve well-being or live good lives" (Birsch, 1999, 81).

This approach can be traced back to Aristotle, who held that human beings, like all other beings and things, have a distinctive purpose that makes us what we are. Specifically the capacity to reason is what distinguishes human beings from all other animals. Therefore the distinctive form of flourishing that humans can achieve must put this capacity into practice. This means that the intellectual virtues are of primary moral significance with respect to the end or purpose of human life. As Birsch explains, "in virtue ethics the ethical standard will not be a rule or a principle that designates ethical actions but rather *a moral model or ethical ideal of the virtuous person*" (1999, 83; original emphasis).

A derivative of virtue ethics is **communitarianism**. Communitarians believe that ideals of the good life and the virtuous person are culturally specific—each community has a different conception of what virtue is and how we ought to live. Thus, individuals from different communities may have very different understandings of the concepts of the good life and the ethical person. This version of virtue ethics can be traced to the German philosopher Georg Wilhelm Friedrich Hegel (1770–1831), who argued that individual morality is a product of the ethical order, the moral structure of society, in which one lives. Contemporary moral and political theorists Alasdair MacIntyre and Charles Taylor follow in this tradition. They emphasize that any rational principle of justice that distinguishes between what is morally right and what is morally wrong will also embody particular, tradition-based ideas concerning the purpose and meaning of human life.

Taylor argues, for instance, that moral judgments are never strictly rational; principles, values, and beliefs are formed in part by the cultural traditions in which they evolve. Taylor therefore suggests that in order for *different* cultural groups—such as francophone and anglophone Canadians, or Aboriginal peoples and Canadians of European descent—to come to an agreement about principles of justice, there must be a "fusion of horizons" (1994, 67). By this he means that a meeting of cultures necessarily requires the development of a *common* moral horizon. The production of a common ground, in turn, requires all parties to open their own moral standards and social norms to criticism and change. In this way, conflicting conceptions of justice that are based on diverging conceptions of virtue might ultimately be harmonized. Communitarianism, Taylor suggests, is a useful ethical approach to political questions arising from cultural differences in pluralistic societies like Canada's.

Rule-Based Moral Theories

One of the most influential moral theories with regard to contemporary politics is called **deontology**. This liberal, individualist approach to ethics and politics emphasizes the principles or rules upon which one judges or acts. It is strictly a formal, rule-based moral theory: it ignores all substantive questions such as those concerning the consequences of actions, one's relationship to others in a community, or one's commitment to particular traditions or beliefs. Deontologists maintain that the only morally relevant question is whether or not one has acted on the basis of a principle that can be rationally defended.

This theory was most fully developed by the German philosopher Immanuel Kant, who is best known for his formulation of the *categorical imperative.* It states that the only morally right act is one that satisfies the requirement that it would be rational for one to will (agree to, or choose) that one's act become a universal law (Kant 1993, 42). If one can universalize one's act without contradicting oneself, Kant argued, then one's decision is ethically right, because it is rationally justified. It is, therefore, one's moral *duty* to undertake it. If you are planning to vote in an election by mail, for example, and if by mistake you receive two ballots instead of one, what should you do? A deontologist would argue that it is contradictory to take advantage of this situation. For, if everyone did so, the electoral process would no longer work. In other words, since your goal is to have the opportunity to elect the candidate of your choice, it would be counter-productive to act in such a way that, if universalized, your vote would lose any meaning, and cease to count. It would no longer be possible to vote at all. Thus it is your moral duty to destroy the second ballot.

This rule-based approach to moral theory has enormous political currency. Consider the ethical values of equality or basic human rights as expressed in the *Canadian Charter of Rights and Freedoms.* The rights not to be tortured or imprisoned arbitrarily, for example, are upheld in Western democratic countries on principle, or *categorically.* These rights are upheld regardless of what consequences they may have, and regardless of the particular religious beliefs, gender, sexual orientation, cultural traditions, or personal characteristics that distinguish people from one another. For instance, even though there may be completely reliable witnesses to a murder, and even though there is always the risk that the alleged murderer will be found innocent by a jury or released on a technicality, every individual *still* has a right to a fair trial. Individuals are never held in jail automatically, no matter how compelling the evidence. Moreover, this principle can be supported on rational grounds. Specifically, it is argued that it is irrational (or contradictory) to treat one person in one way, while treating someone else in the same situation in a different way— for example, by imprisoning those with certain beliefs or certain histories, but not those with other beliefs or other histories.

Deontological moral theories are universalist in orientation, because they make no exceptions among rational beings. They are also individualist, because they suggest that moral action is something that each person can and should decide on his or her own. In fact, Kant considered that one was not morally virtuous if one was influenced by others. If one relies on culture or tradition for moral norms, for example, one is not acting morally. In formulating his ethical theory in this way, Kant inaugurated a powerful political belief in the universal good of autonomy, or rational *self*-determination.

A common derivative of deontology is *social contract theory*. Social contract theories explain why it is rational for individuals in societies to agree to certain restrictions of their freedom—for example, by following laws, paying taxes, or respecting the property of others. It is rational to agree to such restrictions, philosophers such as Thomas Hobbes argued, because of the physical and psychological security that they provide.

Two contemporary philosophers who follow in the tradition of deontology and social contract theory, respectively, are Jürgen Habermas and John Rawls. Habermas modified Kant's moral theory to accommodate the understanding that not all people share the same political beliefs or interests, even though all may be capable of rational reflection. Habermas (1990) argues that moral and political claims are only legitimate when all parties who are affected by them engage in a rational discussion and come to a rationally based consensus. In Habermas's view, when it comes to moral claims that affect other people, we cannot decide by ourselves.

Social contract theorist John Rawls takes a similar approach, but he devises a different method for establishing the basic principles of justice on which social policy ought to be based. Rawls argued that if we are (hypothetically) forced to choose the fundamental principles of justice from behind a "veil of ignorance" (Rawls 1971)—that is, if we reflect on how these principles would affect us whether we are poor or rich, able-bodied or disabled, female or male, and so on, without knowing anything at all about our identities or our place in the social hierarchy—then any principles that we adopt are likely to be just. In this hypothetical context, no one's interests are privileged over anyone else's.

Habermas and Rawls develop different procedures for determining the moral good, but both are rule-based moral theorists. For both, the most important moral issue is whether the principles that a person or a state acts upon are rationally defensible and universally acceptable.

Contemporary Challenges to Ethical and Political Legitimacy

MORAL REFLECTION ABOUT HOW WE OUGHT TO LIVE COLLECTIVELY HAS ALWAYS changed as a result of political and historical transformations in society, and it continues to change. Indeed, many theorists understand the present moment as one of crisis for the modernist belief in human reason and the promise of freedom that reason once held. The crisis is due, in part, to the rapid technological advancements made during the twentieth century, and to the proliferation of social difference in multicultural societies. But it is due as well to increasing pressure from marginalized groups who previously were silenced: women, disabled people, racial minorities, gays and lesbians, and citizens of countries that have gained independence from colonial empires and states.

This era has been characterized variously as "late modernity" and as the "postmodern condition" (Lyotard 1984). However, it is too early to tell whether it will give rise to a new, distinct tendency in the history of political thought, or what the characteristics of this tendency will be. What is clear is that ethical questions of social organization, of state involvement in citizens' lives, of how to balance individual and collective needs, and of the legitimacy of political power are being asked forcefully and anew. Modern moral beliefs are being questioned from the explicitly political perspectives of Marxism, feminism, anti-racism, post-colonialism, and queer theory. In the process, the rationalist foundations of ethical and political thought have begun to crumble. Indeed, analyses undertaken on the basis of such critical concepts as class, race, physical ability, sex, sexual orientation, and colonialism raise significant questions about whether political stakes underline modern moral thought. In particular, it is argued that the emphasis on universal reason trivializes politically significant differences among people. In so doing, it serves and maintains the interests of privileged social groups. These critiques will undoubtedly give rise to ethical and political perspectives that cannot be foreseen.

DEBATE BOX

What is Equality?

Until 1990, the Western Institute for the Deaf, a private non-profit organization, provided free sign language interpretation services in British Columbia hospitals. These services ceased being provided in 1990 as a result of lack of funds, following the rejection of the Institute's request for financial assistance from the provincial Ministry of Health.

By 1992, Robin Eldridge and John and Linda Warren had all experienced problems within the provincial health care system because of their inability to communicate with health care providers in the absence of interpretation services. These were deaf residents of British Columbia, who all communicated by sign language. They filed an application with the British Columbia Supreme Court. They contended that the absence of interpreters impaired their ability to communicate with their doctors and with other health care providers, and that this increased the risk of misdiagnosis and ineffective treatment (Jackson, 1998). Jackson explains, "for example, Mrs. Warren underwent an emergency delivery of her twin daughters without being able to communicate with the physician or nurses during or after her delivery, because sign language interpretation was not available in the hospital"

(1998, 353–4). Jackson continues, "the appellants claimed that the failure to provide sign language interpretation services under the provincial Medical and Health Care Services Act and Hospital Insurance Act violated their Charter right to equality without discrimination [s. 15(1)] based on physical disability" (1998, 354).

The British Columbia Supreme Court ruled against Eldridge on the grounds that "any inequality which resulted from the fact that the deaf remain responsible for the cost of interpretation services in order to receive equivalent medical services 'exists independently of the legislation and cannot be said in any way to be an effect of the legislation'" (Jackson 1998, 355). In other words, it was judged that the medical acts did not discriminate against the deaf population, because the acts only serve to ensure that no one is charged for medical services, and they ensure this for the deaf and for the hearing alike. Therefore, the inequality at issue has nothing to do with the legislation itself.

This ruling was overturned by the Supreme Court of Canada. The Justices concluded "to argue that governments should be entitled to provide benefits to the general population without ensuring that disadvantaged members of society have the resources to take full advantage of those benefits bespeaks a thin and impoverished vision of s. 15(1) [of the Canadian Charter]. It is belied, more importantly, by the thrust of this Court's equality jurisprudence" (*Eldridge v. B.C.* at 629).

Which court, the British Columbia or the Canadian Supreme Court, made the right moral decision? Were the two courts working with two different moral principles or with the same one? What moral theory or theories best explains each court's ruling? Is the state responsible for disadvantaged citizens in this case?

Summary

This chapter has examined the relationship between ethics and politics, and has shown that the conversation between them flows both ways. We have outlined how answers to basic ethical questions at the root of political thought have changed over time, and how they continue to do so. In particular, we saw how the modern moral emphasis on reason and individualism developed only after the medieval period, once the site of moral authority had shifted to God from the state. With the rejection of appeals to religion and tradition, there arrived the humanism of the modern period, and along with it, the split between the public and the private spheres.

Modern moral theories differ from one another. But they all arise from the understanding that human reason is a fundamental resource for answering moral and political questions. In this chapter, we have seen that consequentialism, virtue ethics, and rule-based moral theories share, to varying degrees, the belief that if moral claims are to be applied to the public realm, they must be grounded on reason. However, recent scholars have questioned whether the critical concept of reason is adequate to address the political issues that face us today. Each moral theory illuminates certain political views; for instance, consequentialism can apply to legal interpretation, communitarianism can support multicultural policies, and rule-based theories can justify universal human rights. But the modernist approach is also limited. It may not be suitable to the politically significant differences between people that have come to the fore. We have shown in this chapter that just as ethical assumptions can inform political claims, so too do political issues inform and challenge moral beliefs. Ethics and politics are always deeply entwined.

Endnotes

[1] For example, the political philosopher Jürgen Habermas uses the term "ethics" to refer specifically to values that are held by individuals privately, based on their personal histories, culture, traditions, and religious beliefs. He uses the term "morality," in contrast, to refer to values that can be supported with rational arguments, and that can be agreed to publicly by all people, regardless of what their culture, their religion, or their personal histories happen to be.

[2] In the *Apology* and the *Crito* — two of Plato's early texts on Socrates — there is not any discussion at all about the capacity of women to pursue the moral life that Socrates describes. The term "citizen," moreover, applies only to free, male adults. Thus the word "himself" should be taken literally

in this and other contexts in which the theorist speaks exclusively about men. Plato presents a more egalitarian view of the relations between the sexes in his later work, the *Republic.*

Discussion Questions

1. Do you think it is possible for people of different cultural backgrounds and religious traditions to agree about what is morally right or wrong?

2. Canada has laws concerning public access to health and education, despite the fact that people disagree about whether these services should be paid for with tax revenues. Do you think the government ought to support the values of health and education by imposing them as public goods, or are decisions about health and education best left to the discretion of private citizens? Why?

3. Is it possible to separate morality from religion as some philosophers suggest, or are all moral claims necessarily linked to religious or spiritual beliefs?

4. Many people argue that Karl Marx was right to notice that capitalism is inherently unfair. Those who take this view believe that liberal moral theory and capitalist economic relations overlook the fact that individuals do not have equal access to property and wealth. They see socialism as a more ethical economic system. Why do you agree or disagree with this view?

References

Beatty, David. 1991. "The End of Law: At Least as We Have Known It." Richard Devlin (ed.), *Canadian Perspectives on Legal Theory.* Toronto: Emond Montgomery Publications Ltd.

Birsch, Douglas. 1999. *Ethical Insights: A Brief Introduction.* Mountain View, CA: Mayfield Publishing.

Eldridge v. B.C., [1997] 3 S.C.R. 624.

Habermas, Jürgen. 1990. *Moral Consciousness and Communicative Action.* Translated by Christian Lenhardt and Shierry Weber Nicholsen. Cambridge, MA: The MIT Press.

Jackman, Martha. 1998. "'Giving Real Effect to Equality:' *Eldridge v. British Columbia (Attorney General)* and *Vriend v. Alberta.*" *Review of Constitutional Studies* IV, 2: 352-371.

Kant, Immanuel. 1993. *Grounding for the Metaphysics of Morals: On a Supposed Right to Lie because of Philanthropic Concerns.* Third Edition. Translated by James Ellington. Indianapolis: Hackett Publishing.

Lyotard, Jean-François. 1984. *The Postmodern Condition: A Report on Knowledge.* Translated by Geoff Bennington and Brian Massumi, forward by Fredric Jameson. Minneapolis: University of Minnesota Press.

Rawls, John. 1971. *A Theory of Justice.* Cambridge, MA: Harvard University Press.

R. v. Oakes, [1986] 1 S.C.R. 103.

Taylor, Charles. 1994. "The Politics of Recognition." Amy Gutmann (ed.), *Multiculturalism: Examining the Politics of Recognition.* Princeton, NJ: Princeton University Press.

Further Readings

Becker, Lawrence and Becker, Charlotte, eds. 1992. *Encyclopedia of Ethics*. New York: Garland.

Card, Claudia. 1990. "Gender and Moral Luck." Owen Flanagan and Amelia Rorty (eds.), *Identity, Character, and Morality: Essays in Moral Psychology*. Cambridge, MA: The MIT Press.

Code, Lorraine. 1988. "Autonomy Reconsidered." *Atlantis* 13, no. 2 (Spring): 27-35.

Dillon, Robin S. 1992. "Care and Respect." E. Browning Cole and S. Coultrap McQuin (eds.), *Explorations in Feminist Ethics: Theory and Practice*. Bloomington: Indiana University Press.

Jacobs, Leslie A. 1997. *An Introduction to Modern Political Philosophy: The Democratic Vision of Politics*. Upper Saddle River, NJ: Prentice-Hall.

Liszka, James Jakób. 1999. *Moral Competence: An Integrated Approach to the Study of Ethics*. Upper Saddle River, NJ: Prentice-Hall.

Lukes. Steven. 1991. *Moral Conflict and Politics*. Oxford: Oxford University Press.

Rest, James. 1984. "The Major Components of Morality." In William M. Kurtines and Jacob L. Gewirtz (eds.), *Morality, Moral Behaviour, and Moral Development*. New York: John Wiley & Sons.

Singer, Peter, ed. 1991. *A Companion to Ethics*. Oxford: Blackwell.

Weblinks

Centre for Practical Ethics, York University
www.yorku.ca/mclaughlin/ethics/ethics.htm

Ethical Updates
http://ethics.acusd.edu/index.html

Kennedy Institute of Ethics
http://guweb.georgetown.edu/kennedy/

Noesis: Philosophical Research On-line
http://noesis.evansville.edu

Philosophy in Cyberspace
http://www-personal.monash.edu.au/~dey/phil/section1.htm

Institutions

Although the exercise of political power and authority is often informal, all modern societies are governed by formal rules and practices exercised through political institutions. In political science institutions are defined as deliberate, formalized, and expected patterns of behaviour. Political institutions are the embodiment of a nation's history of conflict and compromise as well as sites of ongoing political struggles. In this part of the text, we will discover that different countries at different times have had different configurations of political institutions or regime types, ranging from monarchies to dictatorships to liberal democracies. Yet, central to all is the state, an amalgam of political institutions that claims sovereignty over a territorial unit. All states tend to share common political institutions, perhaps most fundamentally, a constitution. Constitutions are the basic blueprint for the daily operation of the state dividing powers among levels of government, across institutions, and between leaders, elected legislators, public administrators, and citizens. The chapters in this section outline how these powers are commonly divided in liberal democracies. We will examine how power is divided between leaders and legislators in parliamentary and presidential systems. Next discussed is the judiciary which decides among competing claims when political actors disagree about who has the right to exercise power and over what areas of daily lives. This section also examines the electoral system which embodies the rules and procedures whereby leaders are chosen; the bureaucracy which is empowered to enforce state laws and regulations; and local government, which is taking on increased importance in the current era. The chapters in this section demonstrate that the core institutions of the state are arenas in which political conflict is contained and managed, rules are made and enforced, and political visions are contested and realized. Institutions, in other words, are the bread and butter of political analysis.

CHAPTER 6

POLITICAL REGIMES

Objectives

Human society, anthropologists inform us, has from its origins been organized into groups so as to secure and distribute the means to life, to ensure survival and reproduction, and to develop and transmit culture. However "primitive" or complex a society, there is a discernible pattern of authority within which decisions are made regarding fundamental activities. The study of those patterns of authority is the essence of political science. **Power** is the capacity to make decisions and **governance** is the organized exercise of that capacity, including the administration of those decisions. Political science has concerned itself with examining power, usually focusing on government—that set of political institutions and structures embodying power. One way it does so is by categorizing and comparing the variety of organized governance experiences that human society has had. While many political scientists use the term *state*, another term applied in the comparative study of governance is *regime*. Critically defining regime and categorizing different types of regime for purposes of political analysis is the subject of this chapter.

FRED JUDSON

Introduction

In the social sciences we in effect observe ourselves. This fact raises different problems of objectivity from those occurring in the natural or physical sciences. As well, political science has been infused with value judgments relating to the philosophical search for the good, the best, or the ideal regime. We need to acknowledge, therefore, the subjective character of regime typologies. This is easily done if we reflect that the wealthy and powerful have not always found democracy to be in their best interests. Neither have the poor and powerless always found democracy to best suit their needs. At some time each group may have preferred some form of monarchic, authoritarian, or revolutionary regime. Such concrete human historical experience alerts us that differing social interests, groups, identities, or classes may hold quite divergent views about specific regime types and have contradictory experiences under those regimes.

Ethnicity, gender, religion, and language are elements of an individual's or a society's culture that are likely to shape political judgments and preferences for regime types. Individual, societal, and cultural values are likely to be present in definitions and comparisons of regime types. These differing bases for making judgments about regimes suggest two possible responses. At the extreme, we might decide to abandon all political analysis, concluding that it cannot be free of bias. On the other hand, we could decide to embrace difference and the great variety of human historical experience—accept that cultural perspective, concrete experience, and interest may well shape our own and others' analysis—and proceed, the objective being understanding and communication.

Finally, we should keep in mind that political science as it is generally studied today also has its own history. Specific historical events and processes have shaped the prevailing thinking about regime types, governance, and the state. These include the relatively recent and mostly European origins of modern *nation states* and the parallel international state system; the emergence and rapid development of *capitalism* in the past two centuries as the dominant economic form; the dual phenomena of *colonialism* and *imperialism,* which accompanied those developments; the recurrence of *revolution* as a mass political phenomenon of the modern historical era; the genesis of the prevailing social sciences in the scientific, cultural, and value orientations of the European Enlightenment; and most recently, the complicated processes of economic globalization.

These are monumental, even epochal processes. They certainly do not encompass, however, the whole of human social experience—past, present, or potential. And thus, to the degree that prevailing social and political science thinking is embedded in these events and processes, it is incomplete. Forceful and articulate voices argue that much of the social sciences is essentially masculinist, patriarchal, elitist, and racist. The point here is that the social sciences have a specific history, making them at times exclusive and subjective, rather than inclusive, objective, value-free, and universally applicable.

Some Foundational Matters

NEARLY A CENTURY AGO, THE GERMAN HISTORICAL SOCIAL SCIENTIST MAX Weber settled on the term *ideal-type* to capture the way we categorize and understand seemingly unique things and events. He certainly was neither alone nor the first to note that we create imaginary models. Plato and Machiavelli, within the Western traditions, immediately come to mind. They helped establish the central place of terms such as democracy, oligarchy, tyranny, and republic in political science. Like them, Weber insisted that the reality of specific experiences of governance would never precisely conform to such ideal-types.

Another of Weber's insights, shared by Karl Marx, was that while ideal-types and terms appear to be static, what they capture is definitely not. Each considered human societies and organized governance structures to be evolving, changing, and regressing, both slowly and rapidly. Weber was concerned with delineating several types of authority that characterize power and governance. He categorized different forms of authority under three broad types—traditional, charismatic, and bureaucratic. Weber also sought to understand each type's developmental aspect, its "laws of motion," as Marx would have put it. Marx focused on how the inherent contradictions of the grand social models of human society he studied— slavery, feudalism, and capitalism—influenced social development and change.

Marx and Weber were nineteenth-century European thinkers. What they have to teach us about the study of regimes in these global, postmodern, and difference-defined times we probably know intuitively or from our diverse cultural perspectives. Regimes, or organized governance experiences, are developmental and dynamic. They can be analyzed and understood historically and they can be compared with other regimes in other societies, with themselves at different points in time, and with ideal-types.

One of the broadest and most flexible of the concepts that Karl Marx developed was that of **social formation**. It conveys the idea that a society is organized economically, politically, and culturally and develops its coherence over time. In this sense, a social formation is a system of interlocking and interacting dimensions. Social formations and systems, in political science, can be understood as both abstract concepts and real social entities which are "greater than the sum of their parts," but are also understood in terms of the relationships among the parts.

Defining the Four Spheres of Regime

How can *regime* be defined, then, so that both its stability and constant change can be captured? The Latin stem *reg-* refers to the verb "to rule," so we know the basic meaning of *regime* is "form of rule" over given spheres of human activity and behaviour, an "organized governance experience." Let us consider that the concept of regime contains four spheres, namely state, society, market, and global insertion. Each sphere is very complex and relates to the other three and to the whole that together they form—in other words, each sphere's dynamics affect and are affected by the others.

State

To understand the first sphere, the **state**, we can think of regime in the way Marx thought of "social formation"—as a social whole, much in the same way that scientists currently conceive of oceans as ecosystems or economists speak of the market. Perhaps the common

FIGURE 6.1   *All regimes contain four spheres*

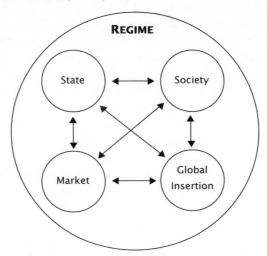

Arrows indicate dynamic interaction

notion of a *country* is closest to regime at such a general level. The world's land and population are presently contained (only the Antarctic land mass and a few islands are not inhabited) in some 160 countries. When we think of countries we are thinking classically of states as sovereign units in the international political system. This means that, at least theoretically, no external authority may prevail over domestic authority. No matter what regime form characterizes that sovereign domestic authority, all states share the attribute of sovereignty. Even though many now question the meaning of sovereignty in light of the striking inequalities among states and the politics of globalization, it remains a vital characteristic of states in the international system.

The domestic dimension of **sovereignty**, the actual exercise of the capacity to make the defining political decisions within a country, remains the critical aspect of the state as a sphere of regimes. The state is also the classic realm of political science inquiry: power and its sources; structures and practices of authority, be they democratic, authoritarian, totalitarian, or revolutionary; and political institutions, such as constitutions, presidencies, legislatures, and political parties, along with their relationships to society. Whatever the characteristics of a regime as a social whole, it is mainly in the state that "who gets what, and how" is determined. Despite the international inequalities of states and border-ignoring globalization dynamics, for several centuries it has been the domestic dimensions of states that most affect the daily lives of citizens and non-citizens alike.

Society

We can deepen our understanding of the state and of regimes as social wholes by considering the second sphere—society. Weber held that the social and cultural composition of a society would largely determine the character of its state, structures of authority, and political institutions. In other words, the country shapes its state. His approach can be called **political sociology**. Greatly simplifying his voluminous studies, we can say that a society of "traditional" values and social classes, such as peasant, rural, and religious Russia before 1917, would most likely have a monarchy. A society in transition to an urban, secular, and capitalist society would likely be in revolt against state forms inherited from feudal, traditional, and aristocratic times. Such a society would either develop a liberal democracy or an industrializing authoritarian state, possibly even a totalitarian police-state. In either case, Weber argued, a large state bureaucracy would arise to administer the economic, social, and political complexities of a modern industrial society. Power contenders in all cases would almost always be elite groups, usually economic elites, but masses (peasants, industrial workers, small merchants and professionals, the poor) could be volatile and decisive political actors.

Marx advocated another approach, called **historical materialism** or political economy. He argued that the most fundamental organized human activity was economic, from hunting and gathering to agriculture to modern industrial production. The production of the means to life, for Marx, was logically prior to society and culture. Humanity's basic political aspect lay in the organization of the labour and material resources involved in that production and the distribution of what was produced. Social classes, such as serfs and landlords or capitalists and workers, derived from the relationship of people to the means of production (land, tools, machines, capital) and their roles in production—the division of labour. For him, the state was the political expression and forceful guarantor of those basic social and economic relationships. Coincidentally, Max Weber defined one of the chief prerogatives of the state as "a monopoly on organized violence." Marx, however, tied this monopoly to the organization of the economy. In class societies, he argued, the dominant social class, such as a landed aristocracy or an industrial bourgeoisie, owned both the means of production and the state. This observation led Marx to claim that "the state is the executive committee of the ruling class."

Market

After more than two centuries of capitalist economic development, with its prodigious increases in production and consumption in the world's richest societies, the importance of the economic dimension for understanding the modern state, society, and regimes is hardly in question. The triumph of capitalism over the great socialist experiments of the twentieth century and the acceleration of capitalist globalization also underline the centrality of the market. Weberian and Marxist approaches in the social sciences find common ground in our third sphere, the market. Considered broadly, the market sphere includes production, exchange, and distribution. Taking a cue from Marx, it includes relations of property and production, particularly who owns the means of production, who finances the processes, who actually produces goods and services, and who takes the profits. Following Weber's insights that a society's priorities are its cultural and political identity, and shaping its public policy agenda, we can characterize most of the world's societies as "market societies." In such societies, to a great degree, the social worth of individuals and their contributions are determined by "market principles," such as ownership, price, income, costs, and supply and demand.

Within this market sphere, both Marxists and Weberians have drawn links between wealth and political power. The market is where production and accumulation of wealth occurs, where the social contours of modern societies take shape, and also where power focuses its attention. The market is the sphere in which a society's economic "model of accumulation" operates, and from which states, like social classes and specific interests, draw their material resources for the exercise of power and the contention for power. Some contemporary social scientists use the phrase "regimes of accumulation" to capture these social, economic, and political aspects of the market sphere. The phrase conveys the sense that market decisions regarding such things as investment, production, and currency values are as important in influencing political decisions as are parliamentary, legislative, executive, and party activities; and elections. Moreover, the link between market and political decisions is inherent. This link can be immediately grasped by noting the political significance, for example, of the Japanese recession of the 1990s, the North American Free Trade Agreement debates in the 1980s and 1990s, the fortunes of the Canadian dollar in recent years, or the Asian meltdown of the late 1990s.

Global Insertion

It is a short mental leap from observations about the market to the fourth sphere necessary for a critical and contemporary conception of regime—global insertion. All countries, their respective societies, states, and markets occupy certain positions in larger international contexts. One context is the international state system examined in the field of international relations, concerned with power distributions and hierarchies among states, foreign policy, war and peace, international organizations, and the nature of sovereignty. Another is the international economic system examined in the field of international political economy, which examines trade and financial transactions among states, comparative economic development and underdevelopment experiences, transnational patterns of production and distribution, and, increasingly, globalization. These two international contexts—the modern state system and the international economy—have constituted a world system since the sixteenth century.

The state system has been shaped by a small number of "great powers" who contend for both regional and global dominance and whose interests and exercise of power determine the "rules" of international politics for all the lesser states. The international system has been conflictual. War, preparation for war, and national security concerns are constant elements of the global system. It is a hierarchical system, reflected in the twentieth century's experience of colonial "possessions," "great" powers, regional powers, client states and satellites, and superpowers and their respective military alliance systems—although a degree of community and equality, based on sovereignty, is also present in global society.

The language of World Systems Theory divides the world's states into *core, periphery* and *semi-periphery*. The familiar terms First and Third World, with socialist countries, particularly China and the Soviet Union until recently comprising a Second World, only partially convey the global structural analysis of World Systems Theory.

The economic dimension of the world system has also been hierarchical, and often marked by domination and exploitation. European colonial acquisition of virtually all the rest of the world was accompanied by capitalist economic development. Simplifying greatly, capitalist economies in the core countries determined the patterns of economic development and underdevelopment in the rest of the world, appropriating resources and labour in a system often called **imperialism**. The crucial political and economic decisions affecting the world's peoples were made by small numbers of people in the ruling classes of core countries. This resulted in dependency—a relationship between core and periphery characterized by unequal exchanges, distorted development, and underdevelopment.

Countries able to improve their position in what political economists call the international division of labour, with some industrialization, increases in productivity, and improvements in quality of life, make up the semi-periphery. In recent decades, some have been termed NICs (Newly Industrializing Countries). The rest, referred to as less-developed, developing, or underdeveloped countries, constitute the periphery.

The three world systems terms capture the political and economic "global insertion" of countries. One of the great discussions in the social sciences today concerns the nature and dynamics of globalization. In terms of our fourth sphere, global insertion, we can consider globalization as the evolution of the world system from the international state and market systems towards an integrated global economy and some kind of post-sovereignty global politics. Several of the essential characteristics of the world system also define the processes of globalization, including great social, political, and economic unevenness among and within countries. Capitalism creates extremes of wealth and poverty even as it includes more of the world's territory and population in a global market system. Politically, a wide variety of states and regime forms are present. Societies are greatly affected by external influences and forces. Relationships of hierarchy and domination, between states and within societies, are present, but so are relations of civility, tolerance, cooperation, community, and solidarity. Altogether, they produce social forces of resistance and struggle, which contribute to change.

In sum, the four spheres allow us to redefine regime. A **regime** is a mode of governance over the organized activity of a social formation within and across its particular configuration of society, state, market, and global insertion. As organized governance across the four spheres, regimes are "modes of accumulation" for a social formation. Society's form and cohesion (its structure) are produced, enforced, and changed. The state is provided its institutions and practices, and is staffed, managed, and shaped. The market sphere has its means and relations of production, property, and distribution provided the conditions they need to proceed and expand. A regime coordinates processes of accumulation within, between, and among the four spheres; in that sense a regime is a system-controller, a "hard drive" for a social formation.

A Classic Regime Typology

THE TWENTIETH CENTURY WAS LIKELY WITNESS TO THE GREATEST VARIETY OF regimes humanity has known, as highly complex and developed societies lived alongside

"Stone Age" communities, as colonialism's end generated an array of post-colonial regimes, as socialist revolutions engaged up to one-third of the global population, as capitalism, science, and technology transformed whole societies while the "development gap" widened, as the planet's population and production surged explosively, as hundreds of wars raged, and as forceful ideologies shaped both domestic and international politics. But if there has been a single dominant raison d'etre for regimes in the twentieth century, it has been the pursuit of economic development and progress within the dynamics of the world system. It is in that larger context that regimes can be thought of as of system-controllers and "modes of accumulation" across the four spheres.

Greatly reducing, we can classify twentieth-century regimes under three broad categories: authoritarian, democratic, and revolutionary. All three have to be understood as ideal-types and as specific human experiences. When we identify characteristics of one category we will recognize that they may also pertain to another. **Authoritarian** regimes are generally thought of as "rule by the few," where force or the threat of force to maintain "order" may be implicit or explicit. **Democratic** regimes are usually considered to be "rule by the many," where force is rarely necessary because the majority accept, benefit from, and support the particular "order" of the society—its economic and political arrangements. **Revolutionary** regimes are those where certain elites, groups, and/or the majority have overthrown the given socio-economic and political order and have undertaken a radical transformation, usually in the name of a dominated and exploited majority.

Authoritarian Governance in the Twentieth Century

By definition, absolutist monarchies are authoritarian, but few such regimes can still be found. Present examples might include Saudi Arabia and Brunei, but most existing monarchies do not "rule" the regimes in their respective countries. Instead, they are constitutional monarchies, with greater or lesser degrees of authority and symbolic importance. There is much more association of authoritarian regimes with a "modern" experience—so-called "late" industrialization. Following Weber, analysts sought to explain ultra-authoritarian regimes, usually called *totalitarian*, in both capitalist and socialist countries, as having emerged from the stresses and crises of "late" modernization and rapid industrial development. The two main cases are Nazi Germany, which had an extreme and elaborated form of fascism, and the Soviet Union under Joseph Stalin. Japan, another "late-industrializing" country, also experienced a militarist, authoritarian, and theocratic regime in the 1930s and 1940s. Some have deemed the People's Republic of China totalitarian, at least for various periods since its establishment in 1949. Many would also include North Korea and Cambodia under the Khmer Rouge.

A number of core countries have had fully authoritarian or semi-authoritarian regimes in the twentieth century, often called *dictatorships*. What might be called the "periphery of the core," countries such as Portugal, Spain, Greece, and Turkey have had such regimes. Specific national versions of authoritarian socialist regimes ruled virtually all of Eastern and Central Europe until the 1990s.

A number of authoritarian regimes, especially in Latin America but also in post–World War II East and Southeast Asia and the Middle East/Persian Gulf, played roles in the global

TABLE 6.1   *The Three Regime Types*

	AUTHORITARIAN	**DEMOCRATIC**	**REVOLUTIONARY**
MAJOR CHARACTERISTICS	rule by the few concentration of power use or threat of force state dominates civil society usually social and economic inequality class struggle controlled	rule by the many through elections constitutional separation of powers consent of the majority degrees of economic redistribution class conflict managed pluralist society	radical transformation of social and political order mass mobilization socialist economic principles class conflict is "official"
EXAMPLES	Latin American dictatorships, 1960s–1980s Indonesia, 1965–1998 Nazi Germany	Germany Costa Rica Canada	Cuba Vietnam early Soviet Union

political, military, and economic strategy of the United States and other core states during the twentieth century. In many cases, it is clear that American policy had a direct hand in the establishment and maintenance of "client" military-dominated authoritarian regimes. The term *bureaucratic-authoritarian* is frequently used to designate several such Latin American regimes of the 1960s to 1980s. But it is not sufficient to reduce these regimes to "sub-fascist client states" or "tools of multi-national corporations," just as European and Third World authoritarian socialist regimes should not simply be considered Soviet "satellites." Authoritarian regimes are shaped by their global insertion but also by the spheres of state, society, and market.

Post-Colonial Authoritarian Regimes

Decolonization after World War II transformed most of Africa, the Middle East, and much of Asia from colonial regimes to sovereign states. Authoritarian regimes have abounded in these post-colonial social formations, though democratic and revolutionary regimes have also been prominent. Various explanations have been advanced for the high incidence of authoritarian regimes in post-colonial countries. These countries, for the most part, were "artificial" creations of colonial powers or of elites created under colonialism. Pluri-national, multi-ethnic, cultural, and religious divisions are more pronounced than in core countries and are simply less manageable. Moreover, the political culture and values required to sustain democracy either do not exist, are underdeveloped, or cannot compete with tradition, religion, ethnic politics, or ideology. Some also argue that authoritarian regimes in post-colonial societies are more convenient for former colonial powers or international capitalism. For others, capitalism as an economic system in the periphery is incomplete, distorted, and externally oriented and thus cannot support civil society and liberal democracy as they developed in the West. Finally, it is argued that absolutist and authoritarian regimes are part of the universal growth process leading to democratic regimes. Such explanations frequently appear in development studies.

As in most broad explanations, each of the above has some proportion of applicability. A deeper understanding of Third World authoritarian regimes would result from considering each regime's engagement with the four spheres of state, society, market, and global insertion. What we can assert is that just as patterns of economic dependency and U.S. power are necessary but not sufficient elements in understanding Latin American authoritarian regimes, the historical experiences of colonialism, insertion into the state system, and international division of labour in the twentieth century are necessary but not sufficient for analysis and understanding of post-colonial regimes in Africa, the Middle East, and Asia. We can also suggest that post-colonial regimes are likely to manifest a greater prominence of so-called "traditional" affinities, values, and identities than are core countries (there are very visible exceptions). These include patron–client and pre-capitalist socio-economic relations, charismatic figures and movements, tribal/clan/family networks reflected in the state and market, patriarchy, strong religiosity, and the prevalence of social divisions based on caste, ethnicity, and language. But we must also be careful here not to fall into "othering" and patronizing—each of the above can be found in core countries as well. We can recognize that Aboriginal peoples, ethnic minorities, disadvantaged social classes, and women have experienced as much (or more) marginalization and repression under Western liberal democracies as have their counterparts under Third World authoritarian regimes.

In many post-colonial social formations, a capitalist "ruling class" lacks the material substance and social cohesion of its counterparts in the core and semi-periphery. With its various factions contending for control of the state apparatus more from a patrimonial perspective than from a hegemonic and inclusive national "regime of accumulation" perspective, such post-colonial elites have been vulnerable to military coups, external intervention, or revolutionary upsurges. In most cases where oil or another commodity is important to the international economy or where the country has geo-strategic importance, either traditional, civilian nationalist, or military elites have struck up working alliances with external actors, that is, multinational corporations and/or core states.

The variety of post-colonial authoritarian regimes is striking. In what is called sub-Saharan Africa, personalist semi-authoritarian regimes often followed the initial post-independence experiences of formal and limited parliamentary or presidentialist democracy. Charismatic figures with leading roles in the independence movement headed presidential and single-party regimes. There were instances in Asia and the Middle East as well. In a number of African countries experiencing wars of national liberation waged by revolutionary movements, the new regimes have had personalist, single-party, and authoritarian elements. Other personalist regimes, more identified with foreign patrons, an opulent life-style, and varying degrees of repression, ruled in countries as diverse as Ivory Coast and the Central African Republic. In cases lacking a single charismatic figure, a series of military individuals or groups managed varieties of authoritarian regimes in some of Africa's richest and poorest countries.

TABLE 6.2   *Variety of Authoritarian Regimes in the Twentieth Century*

	TYPE	**EXAMPLE**
AUTHORITARIAN	totalitarian	Nazi Germany, Stalinist USSR
	fascist	Mussolini's Italy, Spain under Franco
	militarist dictatorship	Chile under Pinochet, Indonesia under Suharto, Burma
	authoritarian socialist	Eastern Europe during the Cold War
	bureaucratic authoritarian	Brazil 1964–1985, Argentina 1976–1982
	personalist	Zaire under Mobutu
	charismatic	Ghana (Nkruma, Rawlings)
	personalist, reformist	Egypt (Nasser)

In the Middle East, several forceful leaders (Nasser, Qaddafi, Asad) emerged in the 1950s and '60s articulating a mix of populist, nationalist, pan-Arab, anti-imperialist, and anti-Israeli messages while also promoting economic development and social responsibility. Their regimes could be considered semi-authoritarian, with varying degrees of repression, perhaps culminating in a fully authoritarian Iraq. Several of the Gulf states were either semi-authoritarian monarchies or oligarchies dominating the oil wealth. At present, several countries have self-denominated Islamic regimes (Iran, Afghanistan, Saudi Arabia, Sudan), each with greater or lesser degrees of authoritarianism (it should be said that Islam is not inherently authoritarian).

Authoritarian post-colonial regimes have characterized South and Southeast Asia, though not exclusively. More than half of Pakistan's political history was of military rule, as has been much of Bangladesh's. Indonesia is only now emerging from over thirty years of personalist, military-backed semi-authoritarianism, while the military has played central roles in Myanmar and Thailand over the decades. The Cold War's global dynamics greatly influenced regime formation in much of the region, ranging from the semi-authoritarian regime of Marcos in the Philippines and the pro-U.S. dictatorships of Indochina to the authoritarian socialist regimes which followed them, reaching the tragic extreme of the Khmer Rouge in Cambodia.

Characterizing Democratic Regimes

Just as there is a continuum of authoritarian regime types reflecting a wide variety of concrete experiences and differences in the four spheres, there is also considerable variation among democratic regimes. In order to have "governance by the many," according to theory relating to the ideal-type of liberal democracy, individual citizens must be endowed with "inalienable" rights which amount to freedom. These rights should also embrace political and civic responsibilities, such as taking part in government. In practice, liberal democratic regimes are much more representative than participatory, with elected parliamentary and executive institutions, and with appointed and merit-based bureaucracies.

Together these bodies manage the apparatus of the state and exercise actual governance, embodying power in and over the civil and market society. The inclusiveness and pluralism of such societies is ostensibly reflected in these regimes.

Liberal democratic regimes, which exist in consolidated form in some thirty or forty countries, presently appear to be the dominant regime type. Large numbers of formerly authoritarian regimes are also in transition to liberal democracies. These are termed newly democratizing regimes. Prominent American social scientists have pointed to the disappearance of most authoritarian socialist regimes, the end of the Cold War, and the decline of many authoritarian capitalist regimes in the Third World as evidence of "the globalization of democracy." A premise of this celebration is that capitalism and democracy are natural and necessary partners. Numerous authoritarian regimes, however, have coexisted with capitalism, in every part of the world. As a harsh Marxist judgment might put it, "for capitalism, democracy if possible, but not necessarily democracy." This very polemical Marxist article of faith contains an insight into a basic tension in liberal democracies. There may be formal, public political democracy and citizen equality in such regimes, but there is not an equivalent economic democracy and equality. Market societies are in fact constructed on the concentration and centralization of property and wealth in private hands, and these regimes tend primarily to promote "ruling class" interests. Historically, this tension has been managed either by force or by the state's appropriation and redistribution of some of the wealth generated by the "free enterprise system." Thus liberal democracies have taken a social democratic form. Here, the state uses instruments such as social assistance to bring the citizenry's social and economic status closer to the political equality all presumably have in liberal democracies.

Many students of liberal democracies have applied the term **corporatism** to the state-directed arrangements between business and labour, and between organized civil society and government that social democratic policy agendas seem to require. They also point to the political functions of such policy and arrangements. In short, the majority accept the "undemocratic" market as legitimate in exchange for a "share" of the wealth that the market produces. Theoretically, the electorate could choose to establish a socialist democracy, as in the 1970 election of Allende in Chile. Such a regime would "resolve" the contradiction by "socializing" the capitalist economy (Allende's government took over significant sectors of the economy, compensating the owners), just as liberal democracy had "socialized" political authority.

Just as critics have considered liberal democracies in the core to be fundamentally "class regimes," they have been skeptical regarding newly democratizing regimes in former "authoritarian capitalist" countries in the Third World. Usually critics associate neoliberal economic policy, trade liberalization, and capitalist globalization, which favour the core economies and periphery/semi-periphery elites, with those post-authoritarian regimes. They argue that formal democracy is in fact accompanied by "savage capitalism" and a deterioration in living standards for the majority. Some, therefore, argue that descriptors such as "oligarchic democracy," "limited democracy," or "dependent democracy" are more accurate terms to describe these regimes. They insist that working-class, peasant, and leftist political movements were crushed or severely weakened by decades of authoritarian regimes and now have no significant role in competitive electoral politics, making the post-authoritarian regimes less pluralist than they seem. Some view the political conditionality of World Bank and International Monetary Fund debt-restructuring and loan policies for Third World countries as an artificial imposition of vacuous democratic processes and institutions. As we did for authoritarian regimes, however, we should consider "democracies-in-transition" across all four spheres of the regime, acknowledging multiple sources of democratic impulses.

The rapid transformation of authoritarian socialist regimes into versions of liberal democracies illustrates this last point. It was not only the "flawed" global insertion of socialist regimes which brought their demise; the other three spheres need to be present in an explanation. The current transitional regimes are characterized according to analysts' emphasis on one or another sphere. For example, some refer to Russia's successive economic crises and the impoverishment of the majority as "Third Worldization." Others focus on patterns of capital accumulation and certain business successes as "primitive capitalist accumulation" or "gangster capitalism." In the formal political realm, the assessment of democracy seems to follow the electoral fortunes of particular political parties and individuals, such as Yeltsin, Zhirinovsky, and Zyuganov as much as it does "efficiency" in governance or public opinion poll results. Fears are expressed about a "return to socialism," virulent nationalism, Russian imperial designs, instability, economic implosion, and even fascism.

It is evident that the transition from authoritarian socialist regimes is fraught with uncertainties. The composite modes of accumulation that comprise a post-socialist regime across the four spheres have been profoundly altered. It is also not clear who constitutes the "ruling class," and the state is often incoherent. The exposure of the majority to the non-democratic aspects of the capitalist market has been abrupt and society has been thrown into decomposition and fragmentation. Global re-insertion, overall, has led to political and economic decline.

TABLE 6.3   *Liberal Democratic Regimes*

	TYPE	**EXAMPLE**
LIBERAL DEMOCRATIC	representative	Canada, United States, India
	social democratic	Sweden
	new democratizing	Chile, Philippines, Mexico, Russia
	corporatist	Germany, France, Japan
	socialist	Chile 1970–73
	oligarchic	Colombia

Revolutionary Regimes

In many respects, the transitions underway in post-socialist regimes match the transformational dynamics expected under revolutionary regimes. There have been democratic (the state sphere), bourgeois/middle class (the society sphere), and capitalist (the market sphere) revolutions in a number of core countries, but not socialist revolutions. Some twentieth-century revolutions (Mexico, China) have combined nationalism with a partial socialism. But generally we associate twentieth-century revolutions with socialism and Marxism, a centrally planned economy and suppression of capitalism, a political monopoly of the Communist Party, and a commitment to the interests of the working class over others.

Failed socialist revolutionary efforts significantly outnumber actual revolutionary regimes, but there are two sets of circumstances that seem to favour the latter—international wars and national liberation struggles. The Bolshevik and Chinese Revolutions emerged from World Wars I and II, respectively. In 1919 significant but unsuccessful attempts at socialist revolutions occurred in Central and Eastern European countries ravaged by war. From the 1930s to the 1970s at least a score of anti-colonial and anti-imperialist struggles in colonized regions of Asia and Africa assumed a Marxist revolutionary character. And dozens of attempts to replicate the Cuban Revolution of 1959 took place throughout Latin America, all considering themselves both anti-imperialist and anti-capitalist. Only one, however, achieved state power—the 1979 Sandinista Revolution in Nicaragua. Very few revolutionary movements have approached power through formal democratic means. The Popular Unity coalition which elected Salvador Allende in Chile in 1970 is a rare example and it was overthrown by a military coup in 1973.

Given that most revolutionary regimes are born out of violence, it is not surprising that many have had strong militaristic, security, and disciplinary elements. Often faced with a hostile international environment, these regimes are usually very defensive. As well, both the course of the struggle and certain ideological foundations, especially Leninism, produce secretiveness and closed political processes. Defending the revolution; confronting capitalist and other domestic opposition; and launching the massive projects of "socialist economic accumulation," especially socialization of commerce, collectivization of agriculture, and rapid industrialization—all these tasks seemed to lead to nothing other than authoritarian regimes. The democratic aspects of socialist revolutions emphasized in many strands of thought were either considered dangerous opportunities for the class enemy, unaffordable luxuries that impeded economic efficiency and the creation of socialist values, or to be postponed until socialism matured into communism.

Strategic dispositions at the end of World War II combined with the Cold War and with war's impact on state, society, and economy in Europe and Eastern Asia to cast different countries into opposing regime types. Liberal democracies were established in Germany and Japan. A dual-authoritarian regime divided Korea, while a socialist and Soviet system prevailed in Eastern Europe. The socialist revolutionary regimes in Eastern Europe experienced Stalinist authoritarian patterns as well as surges of liberalization. Several decades of experiments in what is called "market socialism"; that is, independent working-class organization, loosening of Communist Party monopoly, and pluralist civil society seemed to indicate a regime-type that might in the future be a hybrid of social democracy and democratic socialism. Such an "evolutionary socialist" regime would combine the political processes and institutions of liberal democracy with a majority political culture of socialist values. The centrally planned command economy model would become suppler and

TABLE 6.4   *Selected Examples of Regime Types*

DICTATORSHIP	Nazi Germany, Stalinist USSR, Iraq, Chile 1973–1990
BUREAUCRATIC-AUTHORITARIAN	Brazil, Argenina 1960s–1980s
AUTHORITARIAN-SOCIALIST	USSR, China
LIBERAL DEMOCRACY	Britain, India, South Africa since 1994
SEMI-AUTHORITARIAN	Mexico, Malaysia
ABSOLUTIST-MONARCHY	Brunei, Saudi Arabia
PERSONALIST SEMI-AUTHORITARIAN	Kenya, Ghana
PERSONALIST KLEPTOCRACY	Zaire (Mobutu)
ISLAMIC	Iran, Sudan

more responsive to market principles, permitting small private enterprise, large worker-controlled cooperatives and normalized engagement with fully capitalist economies through trade and investment.

Marxist political strategy, socialist industrialization, and agricultural collectivization held strong appeal for many involved in movements for independence in colonized Asia and Africa. The Soviet Union's rapid industrialization provided an example of how to become developed and enter the realm of progress. The presence of the Soviet Union as a superpower, and to a lesser extent China, with an official anti-colonial and anti-imperialist ideology made them "natural allies" for radical national liberation movements. A number of those movements came to power and affiliated to greater or lesser degrees with the "international socialist community," with trade and aid, arms and advisors becoming integral to their regimes.

While Marxist revolutionary ideology certainly emphasizes internationalism and solidarity, most Third World revolutionary regimes have concentrated more on the spheres of state, society, and market. Replacing the previous regime, trying to transform social and class relations while creating a post-colonial national identity, and establishing a viable socialist economy absorbed the attention and energy of the rather limited number of people undertaking those tasks. These transitions would not have been easy in the best of global circumstances, given the generally limited resources available. Yet, the socio-economic achievements, measured, for example, by degrees of equality, suppression of exploitation, and marked improvements in quality-of-life indices of many Third World revolutionary regimes cannot be discounted.

Future Trends

THE HISTORICAL PREPONDERANCE OF AUTHORITARIAN REGIMES IS STRONGLY contrasted by consolidated and transitional liberal democratic regimes as the century ends.

Liberal democratic regimes also have an important long-term advantage—they have long been the world's richest. Neither type is guaranteed, though revolutionary regimes are more likely to issue from authoritarian than from democratic regimes. The market and society are the more crucial spheres to consider in determining whether transitional democratic regimes in both Third and Second Worlds become consolidated. People are more likely to adopt a revolutionary stance against a repressive authoritarian regime than a democratic one, even if the democracy is limited or corrupt. But the circumstances become more volatile, even for liberal democracies, when economic recession/depression increases marginalization and immiseration, especially when the wealth of the privileged is evident. War, of course, introduces other factors tending towards pre-revolutionary situations.

The normal and expected societal, economic, and ultimately political stresses of democratic transitions, when exacerbated by the unevenness of globalizing capitalist accumulation, are more likely to lead to renewed authoritarian forms than to revolution. Both Marxists and Weberians would agree on that point, but we are also already witnessing some other regime outcomes. In parts of Western Africa and in Somalia in the 1990s it is possible to speak of non-regimes or "vacated" regimes. In some situations of humanitarian disasters, such as war, genocide, and famine, there have been temporary but functional United Nations peacekeeping regimes, non-governmental organization aid regimes, or proxy regimes operated by a militarily intervening neighbour. In a very real sense, these are forms of transnationalized regimes.

The manifold processes we call economic globalization also hold regime implications. Whether in Export Processing Zones or in countries where huge multinational corporations are the most important economic and political actors, there is a semblance of corporate feudalism, much like the "banana republics" of the early twentieth century, which operated like fruit company fiefdoms. And with the evident power of finance capital, currency markets, banks, and international financial institutions to affect government's borrowing, debt-restructuring, and budgets, we have in effect yet another realm of transnationalized governance.

None of these transnationalized forms amounts to a full regime across the four spheres, yet clearly sovereignty is affected by such governance. In many instances, we could speak of layered regimes, some exercising governance over single countries, some local, regional and national, and others transnationalized. Layered experiences in fact are not limited to poor, peripheral, or transitional regimes. Richer or larger countries, however, are generally better able to resist the transnationalization and layering of governance across their four spheres.

Summary

In this chapter we have sought to broaden the definition of regime as a basic concept employed in comparative studies of governance. The four spheres of a country that regimes control and coordinate in varying degrees are the state, society, market, and global insertion. In presenting the typology of regimes in the twentieth century, it is clear that attributes of one regime-type are often found in another. We should expect to continue observing that in concrete cases. For example, democratic aspects of authoritarian regimes should not be ignored. Similarly, many democratic regimes have manifested authoritarian features. It is helpful to think of concrete regimes as composites or hybrids, both unique and comparable within a typology. We might even begin to consider a category of composite or hybrid regimes. We have seen, for example, that both authoritarian and liberal democratic regimes in capitalist countries employ corporatist arrangements to manage business/labour relations and public policy. We have also seen some convergence of social democracy and democratic socialism, though perhaps more in theory than in practice. And some revolutionary regimes have engaged with democratic pluralism and experimented with "market socialism." At present, as the processes of globalization accelerate and affect all regimes, difference in the world is both expanding and contracting; thus we should expect as much regime diversity in the future as the twentieth century exhibited and more regime composites.

Discussion Questions

1. Contrast the Marxist and Weberian approaches in the social sciences.
2. Select a country with which you are familiar and briefly characterize its spheres of state, society, market, and global insertion.
3. What do you think will be the impact of globalization on our current typology of regimes?
4. Why have authoritarian regime forms been so common in the twentieth century?
5. What factors make democratic regimes likely in post-colonial countries?
6. Where do you consider revolutions possible in the twenty-first century? Why?

Further Readings

Brinton, Crane. 1952. *The Anatomy of Revolution.* New York: Prentice-Hall.

Cox, Robert W. 1987. *Production, Power, and World Order : Social Forces in the Making of History.* New York: Columbia University Press.

Hobsbawm, E. J. 1994. *The Age of Extremes: A History of the World, 1914-1991.* New York: Pantheon Books.

Kuhn, Thomas S.1970. *The Structure of Scientific Revolutions.* Chicago: University of Chicago Press.

Macpherson, C. B. 1977. *The Life and Times of Liberal Democracy.* Oxford; New York: Oxford University Press.

Marx, Karl. 1967. *The Communist Manifesto* with an introduction and notes by A. J. P. Taylor. Harmondsworth: Penguin Books.

Wallerstein, Immanuel Maurice. 1974. *The Modern World-System.* New York: Academic Press.

Weber, Max. 1949. *Max Weber on the Methodology of the Social Sciences* translated and edited by Edward A. Shils and Henry A. Finch; foreword by Edward A. Shils. Glencoe: Free Press.

Weblinks

Comparative Politics Online: Internet Resources
www.hauss.politics.wadsworth.com/default.html

Comparative Politics/International Relations
www.uark.edu/plscinfo/comp.html

U.S. State Department Background Notes
www.state.gov/www/background_notes/index.html

IANWeb Resources—National Governments
www.pitt.edu/~ian/resource/national.htm

CHAPTER 7

THE MODERN STATE

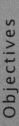

Objectives

The state is the core concept in political science. The concept is used to identify where the formal and institutional terrain of politics begins and ends. There have been many diverse kinds of states in recorded history, ranging from the early Greek city state to the modern liberal democratic state. All states, however, perform similar tasks such as making and implementing political decisions and protecting communities from internal and external threats.

LOIS HARDER

This chapter explores the role of the modern state. It traces its lineage back to sixteenth-century Western Europe. We will discuss how the process of governing is divided among the modern state's primary political institutions. These are the legislature, the executive, the bureaucracy, and the judiciary. We will then assess four models—the pluralist, elite, Marxist, and autonomous models—that try to explain why the state operates as it does. Finally, the chapter will examine three different variations of the modern liberal democratic state which have governed Western societies for the past two centuries.

Introduction

The term *the state* often conjures a dark and foreboding image. China, Iran, the former Soviet Union, or Cuba might come to mind as places where the state has been an overwhelming force in people's daily lives, controlling, among other things, the workplace, the market, and private matters such as worship and sexuality. Images of long lines of consumers in Moscow supermarkets greeted by empty shelves, or the dilapidated buildings and potholed streets of Havana have often been used to illustrate the failure of the state to provide the necessities of life. The state has also fallen under intense scrutiny in Western industrialized countries. Voters have become concerned about the condition of national finances as well as the quality of state-funded social programs. Some argue that the taxes raised to pay for these programs are a drag on the global competitiveness of corporations and a deterrent to investment and job creation. Yet even as governments in communist regimes reorganize themselves to incorporate a greater role for the market and Western governments privatize public services, the state persists as a fundamental vehicle for the organization of social life.

All societies, from the most simple to the most complex, have organized some way to govern themselves. History has witnessed many experiments in government and many different kinds of states. Some have been efficient and enduring while others have been decided disasters. States have been a pervasive fact of our collective political history. Their sheer number and variety, however, evade a simple definition. The political sociologist, Max Weber, described the state as something that can "successfully claim the monopoly of the legitimate use of physical force within a given territory" (1947, 154). Others make the rather circular argument that the state is the other side of civil society. The state is thus contrasted to those areas of social life—the domestic world, the economic sphere, and cultural activities—organized by private and voluntary arrangements, individuals, and groups. (Held, 1996, 57). More tangibly, the modern state is defined by a number of common characteristics. All modern states are nation states, or, as some prefer to call them, national states. They have a fixed geographic territory. States also have a monopoly on legitimate means of force within that territory. Only they can organize legally sanctioned standing armies and police forces. Finally, all national states have an institutional structure, "distinct from the ruler and ruled" which has supreme authority over a territory. States, in other words, have sovereignty (Held, 1996, 71).

Functions of the State

AFTER RECOGNIZING THE MODERN STATE'S TERRITORIALITY AND SOVEREIGNTY, political scientists typically study the state in terms of what it does—its functions. The most important among these are its legislative, executive, administrative, and judicial functions. Different kinds of states organize these four functions in different ways.

The Legislative Function

Generally speaking, the legislative function of the state is concerned with the making of laws. Who makes the laws, what areas of social life are open to law making, and how the process of law making will occur are all dimensions of the legislative function. Depending on the country and its structure of governance, the legislative function may be undertaken by people formally elected as legislators, although the executive and the bureaucracy also play an influential role in law making. For the purposes of this discussion, however, it should be noted that, in a congressional model of government such as that of the United States, the legislature (or Congress) plays an active role in the legislative process. By contrast, in parliamentary systems of government such as those of Canada, the United Kingdom, Australia, and New Zealand, the initiation and formulation of legislation is largely undertaken by the cabinet and the prime minister—that is the executive—while the legislature serves an overseeing and approval function.

The Executive Function

The role of a state's executive is to implement the laws passed by legislators. Members of cabinet in both parliamentary and congressional models of government oversee the implementation process within specific areas of jurisdiction. They set the policy agenda, determining which issues will command the most attention. This function has been referred to as *steering* (Osborne, 1992). The majority of executive functions, however, are undertaken by non-elected officials. In this regard we might think of the offices and agencies we typically recognize as the bureaucracy. Unlike the elected politicians or political appointments who make up cabinet and are expected to steer, the role of the bureaucracy is to *row* (Osborne, 1992). Their job is not to set the overall policy direction, but to provide the means by which that policy direction can be achieved.

Clearly one of the important functions of the executive is to enforce laws. Hence, the police and various regulative agents such as health inspectors, environmental regulators, and securities commissioners are included within the executive branch of the state. In addition, a state's executive is involved in the delivery of services that are outlined in law and in providing the structures through which law and policy can be enacted. Here we might think of the operations of Canada Customs and Revenue Agency, the Student Finance Board, or the Land Titles office.

The offices we most centrally associate with the executive are those of the president or prime minister. This is the site of final accountability—where the buck ultimately stops. Each country selects and defines the role of its chief executive in different ways but generally, the individual who holds this seat is the primary spokesperson for the government. Further, a president or prime minister serves an important symbolic function as the highest ranking representative of the country in international forums.

The Administrative Function

In simple terms, the act of administering is one of making distinct entities work toward a set of common goals. Coordination is central to successful administration. The governance of society is a highly complex administrative task, in terms of the relationships both among the state, citizens, organizations, and corporate entities and within the myriad offices of the state itself. It should not be surprising then, that administration is a key function of the state. It is made more complex in a democratic society by the demand for accountability. As citizens, we want to know how decisions are made and why things are done as they are. This demand for knowledge requires that the trail of decision making be easily followed.

The people who perform the state's administrative function are known as civil servants. They are expected to provide politicians with objective information regarding a range of policy options, enabling them to make the best possible decision. They are also expected to operate without regard for political considerations and hence, people employed as civil servants do not, generally, lose their jobs when a new government is elected to office. In order to ensure the non-partisan character of civil servants, many countries impose strict limits on the political involvement of state employees. In the United States for example, civil servants are not allowed to run for public office or to attend political conventions as delegates. In Canada, by contrast, civil servants can run for office, but only if they take a leave of absence from their jobs. Additionally, positions within the civil service are to be awarded on the basis of merit rather than patronage (political affiliation) or nepotism (personal connections). An extensive examination process is central to the selection process.

The Judicial Function

The fourth function integral to the state is adjudication. Laws are not always precise and hence there may be differing views as to if and how they should be enforced. It is the state's role to undertake this process of determining whether actions fit within the purview of the law. While the largest share of this function is undertaken by a country's court system, judicial functions may also be undertaken in less formal settings with less punitive outcomes. Some of these settings might include human rights commissions, the office of the ombudsman, and bureaucratic appeals processes.

The state is also responsible for ensuring that the "rule of law" is upheld. Effectively, the rule of law refers to the conditions that must exist for a law to be justified. Certain procedures must be followed in the development of law in order for it to be considered valid; the punishment for breaking a law must be the same for all people; and laws must apply to everyone equally, regardless of their position within society.

The issue of the impartiality of the law was tested in Chile when an appeals court ruled that former president Augusto Pinochet should be stripped of his immunity for human rights abuses that occurred during his regime. Although Pinochet had attempted to protect himself from prosecution by passing legislation granting amnesty to those who had been responsible for the torture and death of thousands of Chileans during the 1970s, the Chilean court, under considerable pressure from Spain and the international community, ruled that it was illegal for the former leader to put himself above the law.

So far we have outlined the basic functions of the state. However, knowing that all states fulfill legislative, executive, administrative, and judicial functions and that these functions are outlined within constitutions does not tell us much about how power operates within states nor about how that operation of power may be altered over time. In order to begin exploring these questions we must first understand how the concept of the state differs from the concepts of government and nation.

State and Government

ONE WAY TO THINK ABOUT THE DIFFERENCE BETWEEN STATE AND GOVERNMENT is to imagine a car and its driver. The car is analogous to the state while the driver is analogous to government. All cars have certain components that are required for them to run. These components may be organized in a variety of ways and may be more or less powerful depending on the car's design. Similarly, all states perform certain basic functions such as maintaining the rules through which people interact, though some states may do this more actively than others. Now obviously a driver is essential if the car is to move, but there is no requirement that the driver always be the same. Different drivers may treat the car differently and may choose to steer the vehicle in different paths. They may be more active or passive, but there are limits as to what the machine itself will bear.

Consider the replacement of one political party by another within a modern liberal democracy. A **liberal democracy** is the system of government in which citizens elect representatives in periodic elections held at regular intervals. When a new party is elected to form the government, voters have chosen to alter the leadership or policy orientation of the government by selecting a party that will drive the state differently. The offices of the state remain largely the same. The office of president or prime minister remains as do cabinet portfolios in finance, transportation, health, and justice. In other words, the offices of the state persist despite the change in government, although the policies pursued by these departments may be altered.

Usually then, the election of a new government does not signal a change in the principal institutions of the modern state. However, over time, the state too, may be transformed in response to political struggle, altered circumstances, and new ideas. We will discuss changes in state form in a later section of this chapter. It should also be noted, as the analogy suggests, that just as there are different models of cars, there are different models of the state—totalitarian, authoritarian, and liberal democratic. Even among liberal democracies, some states are more interventionist than others.

Perhaps one of the most well-known examples for Canadians is the difference between the American and Canadian state with regard to the provision of health care. In Canada health care is treated as a public good, available to all citizens regardless of financial status. The state places limits on what doctors can charge for certain procedures and determines which procedures will be paid for by the public purse. In the United States by contrast, except for the very old or very poor, medical services must be purchased through the market. If you, as an individual or through medical insurance, cannot afford to pay the fee required, you cannot obtain the service. When Bill Clinton attempted to reform the health care system in the United States so that the state would play a greater role in ensuring that more citizens received adequate medical treatment, his initiatives were thwarted by groups who argued that the expansion of the state into the realm of the provision of medical services was unwarranted.

Why is it that states differ with regard to their particular configurations of functions, levels of interventionism, and styles of governance? In large part, the answer to this question rests in historical circumstances and political struggle. If we are to understand a particular state we must investigate what and who is important to that jurisdiction and how that importance is achieved, maintained, and transformed.

State and Nation

ANOTHER DISTINCTION THAT MUST BE MADE IF WE ARE TO UNDERSTAND THE meaning of the *state* is how it differs from the concept of *nation*. The state, as discussed above, is a legal entity that performs the core functions of governance over a distinct and bounded territory. The concept of nation is more difficult to define. A **nation** is composed of individuals who identify with each other on the basis of common history, language, culture, and religion. In the early period of state formation, the boundaries of state and nation tended to overlap, thereby shaping strong nationalist sentiments. Nationalism advances the idea that all nations have the right to form their own state, the right to self-governance. However, few states are nation states in the sense of being ethnically homogeneous. The construction of empires, conquest, colonialism, wars, natural disasters, economic crises, to name a few factors, have resulted in both massive relocations of people and the redrawing of boundaries. Most states incorporate different groups of people or nations. Further, this shifting and redrawing of boundaries has meant that several groups of peoples who identify with a particular ethnicity, religion, language, set of traditions, and common descent and hence constitute a nation, may exist within a state or between states. The concept of the state, then, is one that concerns boundaries and territory as well as administration. The people who are entitled to live within those boundaries are its citizens (with some important exceptions) who may or may not share a common identity.

The collapse of the Soviet Union in 1989 into its component republics has seen a resurgence of nationalist struggles in which ethnic communities are attempting to reassert a state structure that corresponds to a national identity. Similarly, in Canada, many Quebeckers consider themselves to be a separate nation and thus desire a new state, independent from the larger federation. In the cases of various Eastern European countries and Quebec, however, we also see the difficulties of realizing the correspondence between nation and state. Even within relatively contained geographical areas many ethnic groups may be found whose members desire representation within the state. Their success in securing representation will depend on the political context in which it is asserted. The phenomenon of "ethnic cleansing," or the forced removal of minority groups from a region, indicates one particularly challenging political atmosphere in which to press for representation. The state, then, denotes a particular physical area and the body recognized by the international community as responsible for its governance. The vast majority of states are multinational, incorporating a variety of ethnicities and cultures. Thus, now more than ever, it is more appropriate to speak of the *national state* rather than the nation state.

Theories of the State

UP TO THIS POINT WE HAVE DISCUSSED THE STATE IN GENERAL TERMS. However, if we are to appreciate why political scientists pose particular questions and frame the answers in particular ways, it is important to have some insight into their assumptions regarding how the state organizes power and how it is affected by the exercise of power. There are many ways of describing this relationship between power and the state, some more sophisticated than others.

In essence, a theory of the state is a model that sets out, in abstract terms, how the offices of the state operate and interact with society. For as Ralph Miliband observes, "a theory of the state is also a theory of society—of the distribution of power in that society" (1973, 4). Although such a theory represents generalizations and is more simplistic than reality, it is, nonetheless, important to both political scientists and to citizens. For political scientists, theories of the state help to explain how policies come to be, who has power, and how it will be exercised. For citizens, theories of the state help us to better understand the constraints and possibilities of influencing public policy. For the purposes of this introduction we will limit ourselves to four main theories.

Pluralism

The pluralist approach to the state is generally regarded as the "common sense" understanding of how power operates in modern societies. According to the pluralists, society is composed of individuals belonging to different groups that, in turn, assert various, and often competing, demands on the state. The offices and agencies of the state are responsive to whichever group manages to command sufficient resources to make its demands known to state agents and to persuade those agents that the concerns of the group are worthy of the state's attention. While money is undoubtedly the most significant of these resources, the force of numbers, charm, contacts, organizational sophistication, a shared social background between the group's spokespeople and decision makers, the justness of the demand, among other factors, may also serve to advance the cause of a particular group.

The process of policy making from a pluralist perspective is one in which bureaucrats and elected representatives are open to the demands of various constituencies and see their obligation as reflecting the will of the people. State officials act as neutral arbiters among competing interests, attempting to assess policy proposals according to their relative benefit to the populace at large.

Of course, not every citizen cares equally about every issue. It makes sense, then, that people with specific concerns would come together to advance their cause. Further, an individual's membership in a group is often temporary—lasting only as long as a cause has meaning for that individual or until the issue is satisfactorily addressed by the state. The political arena then, is populated by an ever-changing cast of characters. Politics is fluid and competition between groups is what fuels the system. This competition, however, is not to challenge the system itself. When that possibility emerges, the state intervenes to reinforce the rules governing the interaction between groups (Young, 1990).

Many have argued that the pluralist notion of the state is idealistic and inaccurate. Pluralists are relatively unconcerned by the observation that the groups with power are generally the same over time and that the majority of state policies have a tendency to favour groups that already have power at the expense of those who do not. Nonetheless, the pluralist notion is important to bear in mind because it sets the standard according to which the democratic character of the state is judged, that is, the extent to which the state actually is responsive to a range of groups within society. Moreover, the integrity of liberal democracies relies on the presumption that all citizens can have a role in shaping policy.

Elite Theory

Elite theorists attempt to address some shortcomings of the pluralist view of the state. They understand society as divided into two groups—a small group composed of the leadership of key segments of society such as industry, government, the military, the media, and organized labour and the much larger group populated by the undifferentiated masses. These thinkers observe that the policies of liberal democratic states are regularly shaped to benefit the interests of elite groups within a society. Moreover the members of these elites are linked through similar class backgrounds, bonds of kinship, education, membership in social clubs, and participation in similar activities. According to elite theorists then, state policies are the product of competing, or possibly cooperating, elite groups interacting with government officials drawn from similar backgrounds. Sociologist C. Wright Mills' idea of a military-industrial complex is an example of elite theory. The military-industrial complex refers to the idea that key leaders from the military and national industry coordinated their efforts in order to persuade decision makers to implement policies and allocate resources that would benefit the defence industry.

Elite theorists view state policy making as the product of exclusive, country club-type interactions. Certainly the exposés of Canada's elite written by authors such as Peter Newman, Linda McQuaig, and John Sawatsky and more scholarly treatments undertaken by John Porter and Wallace Clement appear to confirm the claims of elite theory. These authors demonstrate the intimate links between the business and political elite in Canada. The familial ties between the head of Power Corp., one of the largest business holdings in Canada, and the leadership of the Liberal Party is just one example of this type of relationship. Of course, the upper echelons of power are not completely closed to newcomers. As John Porter observed, however, the bonds between elites are significant and should cast doubt on the view that opportunities for success are equally available to all Canadians (Porter, 1965, 557).

Elite theorists have been rightly criticized for disregarding the democratic process. Elections, in their view, represent little more than switching one political elite for another. Moreover, in most countries, but particularly in Canada and the United States, there is very little difference among the leaders of the major political parties. In fact, one of the most persuasive arguments for the remarkably low voter turnout in American elections is that people anticipate little substantive difference to their lives as a result of the party affiliation of the representatives for whom they vote. Indeed, this was the central message of Ralph Nader's 2000 presidential campaign. It is easy to be sympathetic to this view, but it may oversimplify the situation. Public will can successfully resist the wishes of unified elites, as demonstrated by the collapse of the Milosevic regime in 2000. Closer to home, a significant example of this expression of the public will over the wishes of elites can be seen in the defeat of the Charlottetown Accord in a national referendum in 1992. Although all of Canada's political elites and its major political parties (with the exception of Reform) supported the Accord and invested considerable resources in the attempt to persuade Canadians to ratify it, the Canadian public voted against the deal.

Elite theorists also have difficulty explaining those moments in the political process in which non-elite groups are successful in persuading state agents and government officials to adopt policies antithetical to the interests of powerful elites. A recent example can be seen in the success of grassroots efforts to persuade countries to ban the use of land mines. Although many governments, including that of the United States, initially rejected the initiative under pressure from vested interests in the military, public pressure eventually succeeded in overwhelming these objections. While elite theorists might argue that these cases represent the exceptions that prove the rule, such a view circumscribes our understanding of significant political activism and, hence, provides only incomplete explanations as to why the state operates as it does.

Marxist Views on the State

Theorists inspired by Karl Marx have devoted the greatest energy to understanding the state. It would be incorrect to assume, however, that this affinity between Marxists and state theory is directly related to the central role of the state in the communist regimes that emerged and collapsed in the twentieth century. In fact, Marxist theorists have concerned themselves primarily with understanding the state as it functions within capitalist societies, and in particular, within liberal democracies.

In its crudest form, Marxist theory argues that the dynamics of society are driven by the tension between two dominant classes—the bourgeoisie, which controls business and finance, and the proletariat, or the workers. The policies of the liberal democratic state function to ensure that the interests of the bourgeoisie (or capital) are central to the policy-making process. Since the business community frequently articulates its unhappiness with government, this understanding of the state seems strangely at odds with our commonsense notions of the relationship between capital and the state. Yet we should not dismiss this claim too abruptly. As these theorists have observed, the integrity of a government within a capitalist society depends chiefly on its capacity to ensure prosperity through the smooth functioning of the market. If the economy is growing, citizens will be employed, businesses will be generating profits, and governments will be able to extract revenue through taxation in order to fund the programs and services necessary to sustain the country and, more immediately, to achieve re-election.

James O'Connor argues that the state has two central functions—accumulation and legitimation—and that there is an essential tension between them. On the one hand, agencies of the state need to concern themselves with facilitating conditions that are advantageous to the business community—low corporate tax rates, low wages, relatively weak environmental regulations, and strict laws limiting workplace organization—in order to ensure high levels of profitability and tax revenue. This is what is meant by *accumulation*. On the other hand, in order to achieve re-election, governments must also be responsive to the demands of citizens and provide services that will justify a government's continued tenure in office as well as the private accumulation of capital. This is what is meant by *legitimation*. As long as a relatively consistent level of growth is sustained, liberal democratic states are capable of maintaining a balance between these two functions. However, in times of economic crisis, or when capital perceives that state activities are cutting into profit margins, the potential for crisis emerges (O'Connor, 1973).

A further embellishment to the legitimation and accumulation theory is that the process of legitimation often works in the long-term interests of capital. Although businesspeople may assert that laws such as workers' compensation, minimum wages, public health care, education, and restrictions on working time are an impediment to profitability, it can also be argued that such regulations help to ensure the health of workers as well as their capacity to buy goods in the marketplace. By addressing the well-being of workers then, the state is not only exercising its legitimation function, it is also providing for the long-term interests of capital thereby also fulfilling its accumulation function.

There are a number of factors that serve to complicate this picture of the state. None of its elements—the state, capital, or citizens—"is a coherent and unified body." The interests of one group of capitalists may not be shared by another group. Finance capitalists, those businesspeople who make their profit through currency exchange and speculation in international stock and bond trading, may see their interests served through a trading regime that is relatively unregulated. They would prefer an environment in which financiers are able to move their money across borders with few restrictions imposed by the states in which they are trading. Industrial capitalists, by contrast, might prefer relatively high levels of government intervention in order to protect domestic goods from foreign competition and ensure secure domestic markets (Helleiner, 1994).

Further, the state itself is a highly differentiated body. It is composed of a myriad of offices and agencies with a disparate collection of constituents receiving and demanding services. The actions of the state are often contradictory, inconsistent, and even incoherent. Moreover, some parts of the state are in active competition with one another for scarce resources. In the aftermath of the Cold War, for example, defence ministries have regularly found themselves under attack from social service departments who view assistance to the poor, health, and education as more appropriate spending priorities. To see the state as operating solely in the interests of capital is a claim in need of some qualification.

The State as Autonomous

Some scholars argue that the state is relatively autonomous from the demands of capital, or, more broadly, from any group of interests in society (Skocpol, 1985; Block, 1987). Many of the theorists who fall into this category have some link to the Marxist tradition. The observation that state agents have their own agendas, however, is a view also shared by other political thinkers including elite theorists and political conservatives. According to the latter group of thinkers, the fact that state agents are answerable to an assortment of interests including their political masters, the people they serve directly, the electorate more broadly, the public good, and their own ambitions and goals means that the interests of capital are not necessarily foregrounded in their activities. Moreover, the state, in responding to the demands of various groups of claims-makers, may articulate a distinct vision of how best to organize power, though, as noted above, this vision is not necessarily a coherent one.

But why does it matter if the state is autonomous from capitalist interests? For those interested in a radical transformation of the capitalist system, the possibility that the state is autonomous means that interests other than those of capital might become dominant in the decision-making process.

By contrast, for those more sympathetic to capitalism, the perception that the state is autonomous, working according to its own motivations and objectives, serves as a justification for the diminishment of the state. According to this view, public employees are not seen as working for the public good, but rather for their own selfish ambitions. It is asserted that civil servants are constantly seeking to expand their range of influence and, subsequently, the purview of the state. The state is not understood as a reflection of the society it governs, but rather as an independent entity ever-susceptible to the pursuit of objectives that may thwart economic growth and the success of capital or may engage in the "social engineering" of its citizens. It follows, then, that the growth of the state must be checked in order to ensure the health of capital and to safeguard individual freedom.

Variations on the Liberal Democratic State

EARLIER IN THIS CHAPTER WE EXPLORED THE ANALOGY BETWEEN CAR AND STATE, driver and government. Within the context of that discussion it was asserted that drivers may change but the structure of the car remains more or less the same. Over time, however, the vehicle's structure is subject to innovation and redesign in response to new demands and conditions in which it must operate. Similarly, the form of the state has also undergone transformations. Revolutions represent the most dramatic method of altering the form of the state, shifting dictatorships to democracies as in the case of the former Soviet republics, and democracies to dictatorships as occurred in Guatemala in 1956 and Chile in 1973. Less radically, modern liberal-democratic states also evolve and transform. These changes in state form are significant because they reflect a re-ordering or re-balancing of power within society and, as such, indicate the parameters framing citizen participation in their own governance. For the purposes of this introduction we will examine three liberal democratic state forms that have been implemented in western liberal democracies. These include the night watchman or minimalist state, which saw its most profound incarnation in Britain during the period of the industrial revolution; the welfare state, which prevailed, in varying degrees within all Western liberal democracies in the period between the 1930s and the early 1970s; and the neoliberal state, which is currently in the process of being embraced, again with numerous variations, on a global scale.

The Night Watchman State

It is not surprising that Marx, writing in the mid-nineteenth century during Britain's industrial revolution, would assert that the state was nothing more than "an executive committee of the whole bourgeoisie." He was arguing that the state operated solely in the interests of capital. During this period, participation in elections and the holding of public office was limited to property owners who had little compulsion to consider the interests of the majority of the population. Due to the unprecedented level of technological development occurring during this period, the production of goods increased at an astounding rate and industrialists were enriched accordingly. Agents of the state and elected representatives, most of whom were part-time politicians and full-time businessmen, saw their role as facilitating economic growth, primarily by allowing the market to function in as unencumbered a fashion as possible. In practice this meant intervening as little as possible in the economy while upholding the laws of property, contract, weight and measurement, and serving as a lender of last resort.

On the surface the night watchman state appears passive, but its effects on the majority of people were profound. In the absence of any regulation of the conditions of work and the length of the working day, business owners required their employees to labour for long periods of time in dangerous environments. Further, poor laws were implemented which, rather than providing the jobless with a means of subsistence, subjected them to increased misery. The rationale behind this treatment was to make the condition of unemployment so terrible that people would be willing to labour under undesirable circumstances in order to avoid the even more horrendous conditions of the poor house. By refusing to play a role in regulating the workplace, the state appeared to be acting passively. However, for the majority of the population, this passivity had significant consequences in terms of their health and their independence. While business owners enjoyed an impressive level of personal liberty, such was not the case for the vast majority of the population—the workers.

This minimalist approach to the regulation of business, and the consequent distance between the rhetoric of equality, liberty, and solidarity that imbued the liberal democratic tradition and the real conditions of life for the majority of people could not be maintained indefinitely. It became increasingly apparent that the long-term success of capitalism was not being well served through employment practices that regularly left workers debilitated and, hence, unable to provide for themselves. To persist with such practices would mean that either factories would run out of workers or that workers would become so disillusioned or angered by their ill-treatment that they would organize to overthrow their employers and perhaps the state as well. Moreover, as governments were increasingly pressured to broaden the electorate on the basis of the contribution that non-property holders were making to the growth of the economy, politicians were compelled to address the demands of workers as well as owners in order to secure their re-election. It would take the Great Depression of the 1930s, however, before sufficient support for a more interventionist role for the liberal democratic state was achieved.

The Welfare State

The economic crisis that gripped the world in the aftermath of the American stock market crash in October 1929 represented a dramatic challenge to the existing economic and political order. The breadth of the collapse cast so many workers into the ranks of the unemployed that it was no longer possible to blame individuals and their moral weaknesses for their inability to find work. It was clear that some action on the part of the state would have to be undertaken in order to prevent people from perishing and to salvage failing capitalist economies. It was during this period that social welfare and unemployment insurance programs began to be implemented and legislation that facilitated greater workplace organization by trade unions was put into place. It should be noted, however, that these initiatives, particularly in Canada and the United States, were rather tentative in their initial stages. In fact, it was only after the Second World War that the policies and programs of the welfare state were elaborated.

The devastation wrought by the war to the economies of Europe and Japan and the sacrifice of so many soldiers' and civilians' lives were powerful catalysts for a rethinking of the role of the state within society. It was clear that an active state would be necessary to rebuild war-torn countries. Further, the enfranchisement of virtually the entire adult population of most Western countries meant that the interests of a broad range of the population would have to be incorporated within the decision-making process.[1] It was under these conditions that the welfare state realized its fullest expression.

Wanting to prevent further economic dislocations, governments in western industrialized countries attempted to regulate their economies through the taxing and spending, or fiscal, policies first advocated by the British economist John Maynard Keynes. Keynes and the governments that took up his ideas wanted to balance out the boom and bust cycles that are characteristic of capitalist economies in order to maintain a steady level of growth and prevent economic and social crises. Rather than leaving the market to sort itself out on its own, Keynesianism promoted state intervention through fiscal and monetary policy instruments. In times of economic downturn governments would use their capacity to borrow on international markets as well as the revenues generated during times of growth to inject funds into the economy. Make-work projects such as bridge and road construction and other public works initiatives as well as unemployment insurance and social assistance payments would ensure that people had money to spend, and hence, would continue to purchase goods, maintain demand, and fuel production. In order to offset the deficits created during periods of economic downturn, the state would extract surplus funds during periods of economic growth, thereby creating a balanced budget over the long term.

As it turned out, governments proved to be adept at spending but rather less able to save for rainy days. For most of the period between the end of the Second World War and the late 1960s this was not a serious concern since the level of growth achieved by Western economies was unprecedented. The growth of welfare state programs was readily financed through the subsequent growth in personal and corporate income taxes. Postwar economic growth began to decline, however, in the 1970s. This situation was the result of a variety of factors including the decreased competitiveness of the American economy, the rebirth of

Japanese and European economies, inflation created by the Vietnam war, and, most importantly, the oil shocks. The ability of the state to regulate the economy became the focus of political debate, largely because inflation and unemployment were growing in tandem. Termed "stagflation," this development was contrary to the predictions of Keynes. It is a testament to the success of Keynesianism in realigning our thinking about the role of the state in the economy that we continue to locate the blame for poor economic performance at the doors of the state, rather than seeing the dynamics of the market as making the central contribution to economic health.

The welfare state is also associated with a variety of universal social programs including public education, health care, child care, and wage replacement programs such as unemployment insurance, old age pensions, maternity benefits, and social assistance. Of course, not every country offered the same range of services nor were services equally generous across national borders. In the Anglo-American democracies of Canada, Great Britain, the United States, and Australia, for example, many social programs were not universally available to all citizens. Those with adequate incomes might be required to purchase services through the market rather than relying on the state. Other services, particularly public education, would be available to all citizens regardless of income. With regard to services provided on an income, or means-tested, basis, citizens who could not afford to purchase services in the market were subject to the inquiries and regulations of state officials in order to prove their need and establish their worthiness. Often this relationship between citizen and social worker could be quite paternalistic. It is not surprising then, that as the economic interventionism of the welfare state came into question, so too did the interventionism of state agents in the lives of citizens.

Perhaps the greatest promise of the welfare state lay in its presumption that all citizens should be able to maintain a minimum standard of living—that there should be some rough equality, if not in terms of outcome then certainly in terms of opportunity. Initially this equality was to be realized among members of the working class. White male industrial workers and their families, in particular, were the object of these ambitions. Yet many other groups were also interested in taking advantage of the opportunities promised by the welfare state. Hence, the postwar period is marked by the struggles of various groups. The Civil Rights movement, Aboriginal peoples, women, the disabled, and youth demanded that the state include their concerns and perspectives within the policy-making process. These growing demands on state resources by groups previously marginalized within the economy and political process were perceived as a threat by the established order whose members had long benefited from those exclusionary practices. In addition to the economic crisis and the criticism of the welfare state's methods of service provision then, the welfare state was subject to criticism from groups who viewed the broadening of the welfare state's constituency as an unwarranted drain on increasingly limited resources. Some argued that these demands were overloading the state, leading to a crisis in governability, while others viewed them as a distraction from the more fundamental role of the state of ensuring the smooth functioning of the market.

As these criticisms intensified and various Western industrialized countries elected governments that reflected support for a rethinking of the welfare state, it underwent a profound crisis from which it is now emerging. Although certain elements of the welfare state persist in the state form prevalent in liberal democracies today, it would appear that a new arrangement between state and society is in the process of being consolidated. This new state form has been named the neoliberal state.

The Neoliberal State

The central concern of the agencies of the neoliberal state is to expand the terrain of the free market through cutbacks in social spending, the deregulation of industry, and the privatization of public services (Yeatman, 1994). This objective is reminiscent of that of the night watchman state of nineteenth-century Britain. The current neoliberal state, however, emerges amidst the increased complexity of late twentieth-century societies, the historical experience of the welfare state, and popular expectations regarding the accountability of democratically elected governments. The welfare state both made the promise of equality and incorporated an ever-broadening circle of legitimate claims-makers within the purview of policy making. In the process it created expectations of openness among those who might wish to challenge the new state form. The neoliberal state's emphasis on the primacy of the market, however, has closed many familiar avenues for groups to challenge its policy objectives. It is in this context that we hear disparagements of "special interests" (Brodie, 1995) and the frequent invocation of the bogie of "political correctness." It has become increasingly unpopular to make demands on the state. Instead, we, as individuals, are expected to look out for ourselves.

The emergence of the neoliberal state form reflects the belief that the power of the state has extended too far with deleterious consequences for the market and for individual freedom. According to its proponents, power would be better organized on the basis of the informal networks of the family, community, and market with the state limiting its role to ensuring suitable conditions for economic growth. Neoliberals assert that the national state should divest itself of those functions that impede the market's operation, particularly those that consume the greatest share of tax revenue, as well as state functions that attract political controversy. Governments at the regional level, but especially the local level, are viewed as more appropriate sites for political struggle, since the impact of such disputes can be confined within a limited geographic region (Kristol in Devigne, 1994).

Another significant motivation behind the push for the neoliberal state is the desire to accommodate the global mobility of capital, particularly financial capital. In the attempt to address the problem of overproduction and declining profitability that contributed to the demise of the welfare state, large corporations began to shift their operations beyond their home countries. Subsequently a global marketplace has been created in which states compete with each other to attract and maintain increasingly mobile capital. In order to succeed in this process, many governments have chosen to reorient the state structures they administer so as to create an appealing environment for investors. While such an environment may be created through a highly educated and skilled workforce, a healthy population, a safe physical environment, and an efficient and effective infrastructure, such an approach requires high levels of public expenditure. Rather than making these investments, many governments have chosen, instead, to promote a low-wage workforce,

DEBATE BOX

Universal vs. Private Health Care

Canadians have regarded public health care as a key benefit provided by the state. In recent years, however, the federal government has provided less money to the provinces to fund health services, and provincial governments have also reduced health care spending in order to balance their budgets. As a result, health services are under increasing strain throughout the country. The media frequently report lengthy waits for cancer treatment and joint replacements, provide images of patients lining hospital corridors, and recount crises in emergency rooms where ambulances are turned away. As governments seek solutions, the possibility of allowing private clinics to provide services to people who are willing to pay for them directly has been raised. Proponents of this view argue that private clinics will help to diminish the strain on the public system and thus everyone, rich and poor, will receive care more quickly. Opponents argue, however, that by allowing private clinics, governments will create a two-tiered system in which the rich will be able to receive better care and receive it faster than those who cannot afford to jump to the front of the line. They observe that there are only a fixed number of health care providers in the system and that private clinics will do nothing to address this problem.

What role should the state play in providing for the health of citizens? Should it be possible to profit by providing health services to the sick? Are some kinds of health services better provided by the state than by the market?

minimum levels of regulation, and low taxes, especially for the corporate sector. Not surprisingly, levels of public service provision have been reduced accordingly. The degree of citizen participation in governance has also been reduced. International trade agreements such as the North American Free Trade Agreement and the proposed Multilateral Agreement on Investment limit the range of policies available to governments. Proposals that might be perceived as infringing on profitability or protecting the domestic economy are open to challenge from other countries.

In terms of the organization of power within a society governed by a neoliberal state, then, those people and groups employed within the management ranks and the highly skilled trades and professions integral to mobilizing capital command substantial influence. Those employed to serve them or who continue to labour in declining industries face a much less certain economic future. Moreover, the capacity of citizens to influence their national governments has also been reduced, both in terms of opportunities and avenues of appeal and in terms of the social acceptability of organized dissent.

Summary

This chapter has demonstrated that the state is both constant in its enforcement and reflection of the power dynamics at work within a given society and adaptable to the historical circumstances in which it is situated. Although the state is often perceived as monolithic and impenetrable, a long-term view reveals that the institutions and functions of the state change considerably over time.

This introduction to the state has attempted to provide a sense of the breadth of this topic and a sampling of some of the more well-known approaches to its study. Before we could consider the various theories of the state and transformations in the form of the liberal democratic state, it was necessary to clarify the distinction between state and government and state and nation. The car and driver analogy served to elaborate the former distinction, while the difference between state and nation was described with reference to territory and legal relationships as opposed to a sense of shared identity. All states, regardless of whether they are liberal democracies or dictatorships, capitalist, command, or barter economies, must fulfill legislative, executive, administrative, and judicial functions. How these functions are fulfilled, however, depends on the specific political system and the character of a particular government.

Context is also central to the consideration of theories of the state and state forms. In order to test the applicability of abstract theories we need to set them against the operation of existing states. Moreover, while a portion of a theory may have relevance, other assertions may detract from its applicability. Finally, the transformation of the liberal democratic state from night watchman through welfare to a neoliberal form demonstrates the dynamic character of the relationship between the state and the society it governs. The state is not fixed in time but is reformed through political struggle and altered circumstances.

The fact that scholars propose varying interpretations of the operation of power within the state and between state and society points to the difficulties inherent in making sense of the process of governance. It would be a mistake, however, to view these difficulties with dismay or disgruntlement. More positively, the study of the state should be viewed as a rich field of inquiry, and one which, in all its complexity, is an essential component of the study of politics.

Endnotes

[1] In Canada, however, people of Asian and south Asian descent could not vote until 1948, and Aboriginal peoples were not enfranchised until 1960.

Discussion Questions

1. What are the primary functions of the state and how do they relate to each other?

2. Each theory of the state reveals assumptions regarding the appropriate arrangement of power within society and the place that the state should occupy in expressing and ordering that power. Which of these views, if any, reflect your own experience of state agencies?

3. As you read the newspaper today, did any one of the state theories suggest a framework for understanding the actions of the state, particular social groups, or capital? How might these theories be honed to more appropriately reflect the dynamics of power at play within a contemporary political event?

4. Is it fair to say that our national state is undergoing a change in its form? What evidence can you produce to support your claim?

References

Brodie, Janine. 1995. *Politics at the Margins: Restructuring and the Canadian Women's Movement.* Halifax: Fernwood.

Held, David. 1996. "The Development of the Modern State." In Stuart Hall, David Held, Don Hubert and Kenneth Thompson, eds. *Modernity.* London: Blackwell.

Miliband, Ralph. 1973. *The State in Capitalist Society.* London: Quartet Books.

O'Connor, James. 1975. *The Fiscal Crisis of the State.* New York: St. Martin's Press.

Osborne, David. 1992. *Reinventing Government: How the Entrepreneurial Spirit is Transforming the Public Sector.* Reading, Mass.: Addison-Wesley Publishing.

Porter, John. 1965. *The Vertical Mosaic.* Toronto: University of Toronto Press.

Weber, Max. 1947. *The Theory of Social and Economic Organization.* New York: Free Press.

Yeatman, Anna. 1994. *Postmodern Revisionings of the Political.* London: Routledge.

Young, Iris Marion. 1990. *Justice and the Politics of Difference.* Princeton: Princeton University Press.

Further Readings

Pierson, Christopher. 1998. *The Modern State.* London: Routledge.

Held, David. 1989. *Political Theory and the Modern State: Essays on State, Power and Democracy.* Stanford: Stanford University Press, 1989.

Jessop, Bob. 1992. *State Theory: Putting the Capitalist State in its Place.* Cambridge: Polity Press.

Weblinks

Political Resources on the Net
www.yorku.ca/research/ionline/politicaltheory.html
www.sosig.ac.uk/politics
http://polisci.nelson.com/nations.html
www.gc.ca

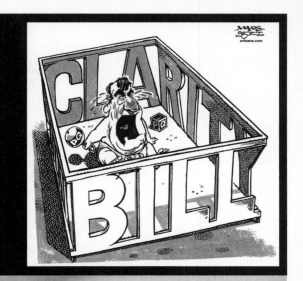

CHAPTER 8

CONSTITUTIONS

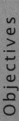

Constitutions provide the blueprints for modern government. In this chapter, we will discuss how constitutions ensure that the rule of law is the fundamental principle structuring the operations of governments in liberal democracies. We will also consider what the evolution and resolution of constitutional debates tell us about a country's politics. We will explore the difference between political systems governed by written and unwritten constitutions as well as the critical role played by constitutional conventions in the political life of both kinds of systems. We will discuss how constitutions may or may not divide sovereignty between national and regional governments and how constitutions are changed. We end by taking a critical look at the idea that written constitutions are crucial to the protection of the rights of citizens.

IAN URQUHART

Introduction

We start our look at constitutions by travelling to south Florida and then to Washington D. C. The trip to south Florida takes us to Cooper City, a small community known more for its quiet residential neighbourhoods than for its relevance to introductory discussions of constitutions. Cooper City finds its way into this tale because of some rather extraordinary events which took place there in 1998. In the summer of 1998 the people of Cooper City were shocked to learn that public corruption infected the city's building inspection department. Building inspectors were demanding payoffs in return for favourable inspection reports.

Political scandal of a different type and magnitude gripped Washington in the summer of 1998. There, Independent Counsel Kenneth Starr investigated allegations that then-President Clinton had committed two federal crimes—lying under oath and obstructing justice. Starr subpoenaed President Clinton to appear before a federal grand jury and answer questions about the President's relationship with Monica Lewinsky, the now-famous White House intern.

What do these stories have in common? How are they related to constitutions? The link between these stories and constitutions is provided by "**the rule of law,**" a fundamental concept or principle in all liberal democracies. According to this principle, all of a country's citizens are governed by a single set of legal rules. These rules are applied equally and impartially to all. The power government officials wield in liberal democracies is neither arbitrary nor capricious. Instead, their authority springs from legal rules that constrain as well as empower their behaviour and activities. When the rule of law is upheld in Cooper City, a builder's ability to earn a living does not depend on being able to pay a bribe. Instead, it hinges on the ability to satisfy the relevant rules and regulations.

In the case of President Clinton, Starr's subpoena raised the issue of whether or not a President enjoys absolute immunity from the ordinary criminal law process while holding office. The President's opponents claimed that Clinton's behaviour throughout the Paula Jones and Monica Lewinsky affairs demonstrated that he was trying to use the power and prestige of the Oval Office to avoid a fundamental condition of the rule of law. The condition is that all citizens are subordinate to the law, regardless of wealth, social status, or political position.

The importance of the rule of law does not mean, however, that politics cannot survive, even thrive, without it. Max Weber, the famous sociologist, emphasized that systems of authority do not have to be based upon legal rules. They may also be based upon the foundations of charisma and tradition. But, where political life is based on a body of legal authority it is virtually always the case that we will find a constitution at its head. In societies governed by the rule of law a constitution stands out as the most important source of legal authority. A constitution's overarching importance arises from the fact that its provisions regulate the fundamental operations of the political system and the relationships between the system's key political institutions. Constitutions offer us basic information about the rules of the political game, who is allowed to play, and who is likely to play starring and supporting roles.

A glance at the American constitution illustrates this point. Its first three articles clearly delineate the division of powers among the legislature, the executive, and the judiciary.

The first Article prescribes that the legislative power in the United States is vested in the House of Representatives and the Senate. It goes on to outline the structure and powers of these institutions, the qualifications needed to run for electoral office, and the timing of elections. What powers does the president have? Who can run for president? Questions like these are answered in the second Article's discussion of the executive powers of the presidency. What are the responsibilities of the American court system? The answer to this question begins in Article III.

Not all written constitutions offer, however, good guidance to how a political system operates or the values it respects. The constitutions of authoritarian regimes such as the former Soviet Union's, for example, may trumpet the importance of rights such as freedom of speech, assembly, the press, and religion; but, in reality, these constitutional promises are empty. In liberal democracies too, political practice may stray from the expectations raised by written constitutional documents. Sometimes, as discussed later in this chapter, constitutional conventions are responsible for such departures. On other occasions, in liberal democracies, claims that political practice does not respect constitutional guarantees are qualitatively very different from the situations encountered in authoritarian regimes. They are best seen not as the absolute rejection of core constitutional values (e.g., freedom of speech or equality), but rather as part of an important debate about the spheres of our lives in which these constitutional rights should govern behaviour.

Constitutions as Barometers of Political Conflict

CONSTITUTIONS SHOULD BE STUDIED FOR REASONS OTHER THAN FOR WHAT they tell us about how the political process operates. Constitutions bear examination for what they reveal about the nature of political conflict and the balance of political power in the countries we study. The evolution of constitutional documents and debates also tells us a great deal about the sorts of changes occurring in a society.

The drafting of the United States Constitution is instructive here. Shortly after the Declaration of Independence (1776) the thirteen states drafted the Articles of Confederation. The Articles underlined emphatically that the War of Independence was a war against tyranny and for liberty. The revolutionaries had no desire to replace the British despot with a strong American central government that also could pose a threat to their liberty. In the Articles, the states guarded their sovereignty very jealously and ensured that the national government would be a weak and secondary level of government. Events during the subsequent decade suggested that hamstringing the national government was a serious constitutional error. An enfeebled national government was unable to maintain civil and economic order in the new Republic. Shays' Rebellion of 1786 supplies the exclamation mark for this observation. Disgruntled farmers, many of them veterans of the Revolutionary War, marched against a Massachusetts courthouse to stop farm foreclosures. When twelve of the thirteen states refused to give Washington financial aid, the national government was powerless to respond. Although the Massachusetts militia ultimately quelled the rebellion this event stood as an important sign that the United States government could not guarantee that it could preserve order or protect property.

These concerns provided the fuel for many of the debates during and following the Constitutional Convention of 1787. A strong national government was needed to ensure that the masses would not threaten the property of the rich or the order of America. The success of wealthy economic interests in securing a stronger national government is seen in various sections of the United States Constitution. Among other provisions, Article I outlines the military and commercial responsibilities entrusted to the national government. For example, Congress would issue all money in the United States, regulate interstate commerce, and raise an Army and Navy. The states could not pass laws excusing their citizens from paying their debts.

Canada's Constitution Act of 1867 provides a similar snapshot of the significant political conflicts that shaped Canada's formation. A number of the provisions in the British North America Act of 1867 (renamed the Constitution Act 1867 by the constitutional patriation exercise of 1982) may be traced to the importance of the English/French tensions in the colonial politics of British North America. The political importance of "les Canadiens," the French-speaking population centred in Quebec (then called Lower Canada), forced reluctant English-speaking politicians to accept a federal rather than a unitary, political system. Powers such as education and property/civil rights were regarded as essential to the preservation of Catholicism and the French language and culture in Quebec. Consequently, they were entrusted to the provincial governments. Features of the Canadian parliamentary structure also testify to the importance of the French/English cleavage in the struggle to unite the British North American colonies into one country. In the House of Commons, Quebec was guaranteed 65 seats, the same number of seats it claimed in the pre-Confederation legislative assembly. If Quebec's population fell, the province's political representation in the Commons would not fall below this minimum number. Quebec's representation in the Senate, the upper chamber in the Canadian Parliament, was equal to that enjoyed by the more populous province of Ontario.

The evolution of constitutions, like their creation, is also a valuable indicator of underlying political currents in societies. Throughout British history, a number of constitutional developments have signalled how power has shifted between competing political actors. For example, the Reform Act of 1832 is one such signpost. The Reform Act signalled an important shift in the balance of power in Parliament; it marked the arrival of the British middle classes as a significant political force in national politics. The Reform Act effectively wrested power out of the hands of the king and a small number of landowners and thrust it into the eager hands of members of the middle class elected to the House of Commons. The control of Britain's destiny passed effectively from the king and aristocracy to the emerging middle class and the House of Commons.

The performance of Tony Blair's Labour government since it came to power in 1997 provides another example. Labour's manifesto pushed the United Kingdom onto a radical path of constitutional change. Devolution of power from Westminster to a Scottish Parliament elected in May 1999 was one of the Blair government's changes to the British Constitution. Another significant constitutional change came in the shape of the Human Rights Act, a law incorporating the rights and freedoms outlined in the European Convention on Human

Rights into British law. Finally, the Blair government tackled the House of Lords. First, it eliminated the right of roughly 90 percent of the hereditary peers to sit and vote in the House of Lords. Second, the government appointed a Royal Commission to examine the roles, functions, and composition of the second chamber. Taken together, these measures will bring a dizzying amount of constitutional change to Britain. These current and anticipated changes also reflect shifting balances in British politics and public opinion. They represent responses to the important political pressures emanating from Scottish nationalism and from segments of public opinion which believe that individual rights are better secured by written constitutions than by the laws of legislatures. The Human Rights Act also reflects international pressures on Britain to bring its governmental processes closer in line with those of its partners in the European Union (EU).

Amendments to the United States Constitution tell a similar story. They testify to how emerging political conflicts modified the political consensus forged in the Constitution. The American Bill of Rights of 1791—the first ten amendments to the Constitution— harked back to the American Revolution's emphasis on individual liberty. The Constitution drafted at the Constitutional Convention of 1787 lacked an explicit commitment to protect individual freedoms. Those who feared that a strengthened national government would be emboldened enough to try on the robes of the English king demanded the addition of a list of guaranteed freedoms.

The history of subsequent amendments to the Constitution in part may be used to gauge the importance of battles over the importance and meaning of political equality to American politics. One of the constitutional consequences of the conflicts leading to the Civil War of the 1860s was the adoption of three amendments, the Thirteenth to the Fifteenth, that promoted the political equality of blacks. The Thirteenth Amendment prohibited slavery and involuntary servitude. Part of the Fourteenth Amendment also sought to protect recently freed black slaves. All persons born or naturalized in the United States—recently freed slaves included—were citizens of the United States and the state they lived in. States were prohibited from abridging the privileges or immunities of citizens of the United States, from depriving any person of life, liberty, or property without due process and from denying people the equal protection of the laws. The Fifteenth Amendment stipulated that the voting rights of American citizens could not be taken away or restricted due to "race, color, or previous condition of servitude." Expanding the boundaries of political equality also inspired several twentieth-century amendments, including the Seventeenth (popular election of Senators), the Nineteenth (granting women the right to vote), the Twenty-fourth (supporting the right to vote even if taxes are unpaid), and the Twenty-sixth (reducing the voting age to eighteen).

Written or Unwritten Constitutions and the Importance of Conventions

One of the key distinctions made in the study of constitutions is between *written* and *unwritten* constitutions. The United States Constitution, the longest living written constitution, stands as the classic example of a written constitution. In that one document you will find most of the information needed to understand the basic structure of political institutions and the logic of the American political process, in particular, the division of power among the three branches of government. A second defining feature of the written constitution, the type of constitution that most nations have adopted, is that it is an extraordinary legal document. It carries much more interpretive importance and weight than the ordinary laws that flow out of the corridors of Congress. In the United States Constitution, for example, the document's overarching importance is outlined in Article VI. There, the Constitution is identified as "the supreme law of the land." As such, it takes precedence over any state constitution or state law. All law, federal or state, must correspond to the provisions and principles of the American Constitution as interpreted by the Supreme Court.

When the written portion of the Canadian Constitution was enlarged in 1982 an even more explicit statement of the Constitution's importance was included. After following the American example by identifying the Constitution as "the supreme law of Canada" Section 52 of the Constitution Act (1982) went on to point out that "any law that is inconsistent with the provisions of the Constitution is, to the extent of the inconsistency, of no force or effect."

Britain is generally regarded as offering the classic example of a country guided by an unwritten constitution. But, the label "unwritten" is quite misleading. It really means that the British Constitution, unlike its American counterpart, cannot be found primarily within the confines of one document called "The Constitution." In fact, the unwritten British Constitution is made up, in part, of many written laws. Some were passed by English kings and others by English parliaments. The Magna Carta, signed by King John in 1215 and modified by Parliament in 1297, is one of the written foundations of Britain's unwritten Constitution. The Magna Carta was a product of a rebellion by English noblemen who believed King John was abusing his powers, especially by taxing them too severely. The Magna Carta limited the monarch's power and protected the English lords from royal authority.

A fundamental modern guarantee of all Anglo-American democracies is that a person may not lose life, liberty, or property without a trial by one's peers. This guarantee can also be traced back to the Magna Carta. Nearly five hundred years later, the struggle between a Protestant parliament and a Catholic king (James II) led to limitations on royal authority contained in The English Bill of Rights of 1689. It is an ordinary piece of parliamentary legislation and could be repealed by a simple majority vote in any parliament. Nonetheless, the English Bill of Rights established that only parliament, not the king, could suspend laws, raise taxes, and approve the raising of an army. It stands as another important written element of the British constitution.

The insistence on calling the British constitution "unwritten," rather than say, uncodified, is best defended by pointing out that many of its most significant and well-accepted elements do not rest in written laws at all. They exist as constitutional conventions. **Constitutional conventions** may be regarded as extra-legal constitutional rules; rules without a foundation in the law. Because they lack a basis in law they cannot be enforced by the courts. Their extra-legal nature does not mean, as one might think, they are less important than laws. In 1981, for example, the Supreme Court of Canada was asked whether the Canadian government could ignore the constitutional convention that the approval of the national government and a substantial number of provinces was needed to amend the constitution. A majority of the Supreme Court answered that "some conventions may be more important than some laws. Their importance depends on that of the value or principle which they are meant to safeguard."

The types of conventions that have become most important are conventions that effectively transfer de facto power from one authority or one actor to another. In Britain, for example, the queen has the legal prerogative to refuse to give Royal Assent to any legislation passed by her Parliament. Without Royal Assent, the bills passed by Parliament cannot become laws. Use your imagination for a moment. Suppose that the queen had objected to the Labour government's Scotland Act, the law that gave some of the British Parliament's powers to a Scottish Parliament. She had the legal power to refuse to give the assent needed for this bill to become law. But, there is a convention in British politics that the Monarch will not refuse to assent to a piece of legislation passed by a majority in Parliament. What we have here is the type of clash identified above by the Supreme Court of Canada—a clash revolving around the importance of the value of representative democracy. In a country where the legitimacy of electoral politics is unshakable, it is unthinkable that a monarch who sits on the throne due to an accident of birth would frustrate an elected and publicly accountable Parliament. Because of its democratic pedigree, the convention that the queen always grants her assent when it is requested trumps the legal possibility that Royal assent may be withheld. While the queen continues to hold this de jure power, the de facto power to say yea or nay to legislation has been passed to the prime minister and a parliamentary majority.

The importance of conventions to political practice in Britain or Canada, a parliamentary democracy with a British pedigree, may also be demonstrated by considering their most important political office—the office of the prime minister. The position of prime minister only exists by convention. It was never created by a constitutional document or by a piece of parliamentary legislation. The same could be said of the cabinet, the de facto decision-making body headed by the prime minister, or the accepted practice that the leader of the party which receives the most votes in an election is asked to form a government. These are all conventions of British-style politics; they are non-legal rules. They are nonetheless fundamental elements of constitutional systems which are based upon British practices.

Conventions also may play an important role in the political life of nations governed primarily by written constitutions. In American politics, for example, the importance of **judicial review** is an American constitutional convention rather than a feature of the written constitution. Article III of the United States Constitution outlines the judicial power of the American courts. Nowhere does this Article of the Constitution stipulate that the courts have the authority to declare congressional legislation to be unconstitutional or to declare that the behaviour of officials violates the Constitution. In *Marbury v. Madison*, a famous case decided in 1803, Chief Justice John Marshall argued that Article III's language gave the courts the power of judicial review and the authority to strike down any law the courts felt violated the Constitution. The United States Congress acquiesced and an important convention was added to American government and politics.

Constitutional Change

WHY SHOULD ANYONE PAY ATTENTION TO THIS DISTINCTION BETWEEN WRITTEN and unwritten constitutions? One reason this distinction is valuable concerns the possibility of constitutional change. Written constitutions are notoriously difficult to amend. Since written constitutions are supposed to reflect the fundamental and enduring values of their host societies, constitutional amendments usually require extraordinary majorities. If a constitution is to be amended, the proposed change must be welcomed by a broad consensus in the society.

The United States Constitution and the Canadian Constitution Act (1982) illustrate this point about extraordinary majorities. Generally speaking, an amendment to the American Constitution must be passed by a two-thirds majority in both the House of Representatives and the Senate. The amendment must also be passed by three-quarters of the states (38 of 50). There are two qualifications to this general formula. Any state can veto an amendment depriving it of equal representation in the Senate. Also, the American Constitution may be amended by a national constitutional convention. This convention can only be called if two-thirds of the states agree and, like the general amending formula, three-quarters of the states would have to ratify the amendment. The Constitution is silent on the questions of the number of delegates to this convention and how they would be chosen.

The Canadian amending formula is more complicated. Some items of the Canadian system of government, such as the composition of the Supreme Court or the amending formula itself, require the unanimous consent of the national legislature and all of the provincial legislatures. According to the general amending formula, a formula which applies to subjects such as the powers of the Senate, the method of selecting senators, and the establishment of new provinces, a constitutional amendment requires the agreement of the national Parliament and the legislatures of at least two-thirds of the provinces (7 of 10) which have at least fifty percent of the total provincial population. As in the United States, the formal requirements for constitutional amendment in Canada constitute a substantial hurdle to change.

The situation with respect to unwritten constitutions is significantly different. Since the constitution does not live in one document a formal amending formula is nowhere to be found. Rather than facing the rigidity of a formal formula, advocates of constitutional change face a far more flexible environment. For decades, this flexibility was "academic" in the pejorative sense of the word—it did not seem to have much bearing on daily life. However, the path taken by the Blair government in Britain changed that. Two laws, the Scotland Act and the Human Rights Act, plus the serious interest in changing the House of Lords as well as the electoral system, led the *Times of London* to conclude: "Constitutional reform is changing the way Britain is governed in much more radical ways than is generally appreciated."[1] The flexibility of the unwritten constitution is a key contributor to this situation. Without that flexibility, these radical changes would be much more difficult— perhaps impossible—to realize.

But should Canadians *want* that kind of flexibility? In the first place, since the Blair changes are all taking place through individual pieces of legislation some worry that this approach to constitutional change is not as comprehensive or as well thought out as it should be. In other words, should constitutional change be a piecemeal process or a coherent and encompassing one? The flexibility afforded by unwritten constitutions also raises important issues about democracy. If constitutions should reflect a political consensus in society, is it wise or desirable for the constitution to be changed by the party that holds a parliamentary majority? Blair's Labour government, for example, only received 44 percent of the vote. Should fundamental changes to a constitution not be subject to a wide-ranging public debate—a more inclusive debate than these pieces of legislation saw when they were debated within the walls of the Parliament at Westminster?

Unitary or Federal?

ANOTHER IMPORTANT FEATURE OF CONSTITUTIONS IS THAT THEY SPECIFY HOW jurisdictional power will be divided among national and subnational governments, if at all. In other words, the constitution sets out the rules for both unitary and federal systems. What do we mean when we say that a constitution is federal? The term *federal* refers to how sovereignty or ultimate governing authority is arranged between the different governments ruling over a shared territory. A **federal constitution** divides sovereignty between a national government and subnational governments (states in the United States, provinces in Canada). In some policy areas, the national government will have the constitutional authority to act or to exercise sovereignty; in other areas, this sovereignty will rest with the regional governments. In the American Constitution, for example, the power to issue money, to regulate interstate commerce or to sign foreign treaties are exclusively national powers. State laws intruding upon these areas of governing are unconstitutional. In Canada, commercial fishing is vitally important to the people who live in the Atlantic provinces but the constitution assigns power over the fisheries to the national government. Therefore, the province of Newfoundland cannot pass legislation regarding who may fish or how many fish may be taken off its shores. Education, on the other hand, is an area of provincial jurisdiction and the national government cannot legislate the content of the curriculum taught in Canadian classrooms.

The way this sovereignty is divided between the two levels of government is generally a good indicator of whether the federation is centralized or decentralized. If most of a country's sovereignty rests with the national government the political system is centralized; if most of a country's sovereignty rests with subnational governments the political system is decentralized. In the United States, the federal system generally has evolved in a centralist direction. In Canada, the federal system today is much more decentralized than had been intended by the Fathers of Confederation.

The idea of sovereignty offers a useful means to distinguish between federal and unitary constitutional systems. In a system governed by a **unitary constitution**, all governmental sovereignty rests in the national government. Although subnational governments may exist in a unitary state, those governments are empowered to govern by the national government. The national government gives them the authority to act; the subnational governments do not enjoy their own constitutionally entrenched and protected source of authority. We can illustrate this point by looking once again to recent developments in Britain. When the Scottish Parliament was elected in 1999 it was empowered to legislate on matters such as education, health, and local government. It was also allowed to vary the income tax Scots pay by a very small amount—a so-called "Tartan Tax." These powers were given to the Scottish Parliament by the British Parliament, not by the constitution. The British Parliament retains the power to modify the Scottish Parliament's basket of powers in any way it wishes. Strong Scottish nationalists abhor this element of the devolution arrangement for it underlines the fact that the face of constitutional government in Britain will still be a unitary one.

Rights and Constitutions

JUST AS FEDERAL CONSTITUTIONS LIMIT THE LEGAL AUTHORITY OF governments vis-à-vis each other, constitutions may also limit the legal authority of governments vis-à-vis their citizens. This is one of the most important and controversial functions of constitutions. In the United States, the sovereignty of the government over its citizens is limited by The Bill of Rights and other amendments to the Constitution. In Canada, the Charter of Rights and Freedoms plays the same role. The Canadian Charter, with its regime of constitutionally entrenched rights, was not added to the Canadian constitution until 1982. Part of the drive to incorporate a written Charter into the Canadian constitution developed out of a major shortcoming of the Canadian Bill of Rights (1960). While the Supreme Court decided in the case of *R. v. Drybones* that the Bill of Rights took precedence over federal laws which were inconsistent with its provisions, the Bill of Rights was only an ordinary piece of federal legislation. This meant that its guarantees did not apply at all to the activities of the provincial governments.

Viewers of American television crime dramas are familiar with the Miranda warning that American law enforcement officers are required to give to suspected criminals who are in police custody and will be interrogated. The requirement to warn suspects that they have the right to remain silent and to consult a lawyer arose from the case of *Miranda v. Arizona*. In that case, the Supreme Court overturned the conviction of a confessed kidnapper and rapist because the police violated Miranda's Fifth Amendment right not to be compelled to make self-incriminating statements. This Fifth Amendment protection exemplifies **negative rights**—rights individuals have against being interfered with by other actors such as government. In the context of the government–citizen relationship, negative rights protect people from government interference.

The rights guarantees found in written constitutions may also exist as so-called **positive rights**—rights which require government intervention in order to be realized. The minority-language educational rights outlined in Section 23 of the Canadian Charter of Rights and Freedoms illustrate this alternative form of rights guarantee. This section stipulates that, where the numbers of children warrant, Canadian citizens have the right to have minority language (English/French) education and educational facilities provided and paid for by the government.

Constitutional guarantees of rights are controversial for many reasons. The Miranda case raised one of the controversies associated with legal rights. Respecting individual rights occasionally may mean that the guilty escape punishment because their rights were violated somewhere in the criminal justice system. For some, constitutional rights are controversial because the job of interpreting what constitutionally appropriate behaviour looks like is turned over to the courts. Critics of judicial review on both sides of the United States–Canada border worry that judges will hijack the constitution and fill its language with meanings that were never intended by the framers of the constitution. Moreover, judges are not elected and thus are distanced from the test of democratic accountability.

Courts and Legislatures

IMPORTANT AS THESE CONTROVERSIES ARE, I WOULD LIKE TO FOCUS ON A developing mythology, particularly significant in Canada, about constitutional rights. The core of the mythology is that judges, through judicial review, further rights while politicians and public servants, through their laws and actions, restrict rights. This is a dangerous caricature. It exaggerates the rights-protecting nature of the judiciary and undervalues the extent to which legislatures may also be important champions of the rights and well-being of citizens.

This perspective draws much of its strength from how the Charter of Rights and Freedoms was marketed to Canadians during the 1980–81 debates over constitutional renewal. The Charter would protect Canadians from government. It was portrayed as a bill of rights which would protect individual Canadians from unfair treatment by any Canadian government.

There are a couple of important fallacies in this outlook on rights, courts, and legislatures. One fallacy lies in the message that the Charter simply protects the rights of individuals against the state. While this is sometimes true it is a very simplistic view of the Charter. It would be more accurate to add that when the courts interpret the Charter they may instead protect the rights of a certain group of individuals at the expense of another group or category of individuals. In other words, individuals or groups of similar individuals both win and lose in some Charter decisions. Judicial review of the Charter may involve considerably more than upholding the rights of the individual against the government.

This general point that significant Charter decisions may pit some citizens against other citizens was illustrated dramatically in a case decided by the Supreme Court of Canada in 1991, *R. v. Seaboyer*. The case of Seaboyer struck down Canada's rape-shield law. The rape-shield law, passed by the federal Parliament in 1983, was designed to abolish some old common-law rules that permitted evidence of a rape victim's sexual conduct to be heard by a jury, irrespective of whether or not the evidence was relevant to the case at hand. Defence lawyers in rape trials would grill the victim of a rape in an effort to convince the jury that she was unchaste, had probably consented to the alleged assault, and therefore was not a credible witness. The rape-shield law, which permitted such evidence in only limited circumstances, was also designed to encourage the reporting of sexual assaults and to protect the victim's privacy.

Seaboyer was charged with sexually assaulting a woman he had been drinking with in a bar. The judge in his trial, following the provisions of the rape-shield law, refused to let Seaboyer's lawyer question the complainant about her sexual conduct on other occasions. Seaboyer's attorney hoped to link bruises on the woman that the Crown had entered into evidence

DEBATE BOX

Freedom of Expression, Child Pornography, and Section 33 or Should Possession of Child Pornography be Protected by Freedom of Expression?

In 1995 and 1996 Canada Customs and the RCMP seized computer disks, books, other writings, and photographs from John Robin Sharpe. In the opinion of the Crown, these materials constituted child pornography as defined by section 163.1 (1) of the Criminal Code of Canada. Four charges were laid against Sharpe—two for the possession of child pornography and two for possession with the purpose of distribution or sale. Under section 163.1 (3) of the Criminal Code, the possession of child pornography for the purpose of distribution or sale may be punished by a term of not more than ten years in jail; under section 163.1 (4) simple possession is punishable by a term of not more than five years.

Before Sharpe's trial began, the Honourable Mr. Justice Shaw of the British Columbia Supreme Court was asked to rule on the constitutionality of several provisions of section 163.1. Sharpe claimed that part of the definition of child pornography [section 163.1 (1)(b)] as well as criminalizing the possession of child pornography [section 163.1 (4)] violated several fundamental freedoms outlined in the Canadian Charter as well as the Charter's equality guarantees. Mr. Justice Shaw agreed with part of Sharpe's submission. The judge concluded that, while child pornography may be harmful, there is no evidence that it causes a significant increase in danger to children. He wrote: "The intrusion into freedom of expression and the right to privacy is so profound that it is not outweighed by the limited beneficial effects of the prohibition." Sharpe's fundamental "freedom of thought, belief, opinion and expression" had been violated by criminalizing the possession of child pornography. Justice Shaw dismissed the possession counts against Sharpe (he could still be tried on the two counts of possession for the purpose of distribution or sale).

The public was outraged over Justice Shaw's ruling. It took no comfort from the B. C. Court of Appeal's subsequent decision to uphold his ruling. There, Madam Justice Southin concluded "that legislation which makes simple possession of expressive materials a crime can never be a reasonable limit in a free and democratic society. Such legislation bears the hallmark of tyranny." In the majority opinion of the court, the definition of child pornography was too broad. The Court of Appeal's decision was appealed to the Supreme Court of Canada where arguments were heard in January 2000.

In Parliament, all of the opposition parties and a significant minority of the Liberal party called on the Liberal government to use the notwithstanding clause to reinstate the possession provisions in the Criminal Code. Justice Minister Anne McLellan rejected these demands. She said that it was her duty to defend the legislation, not by invoking Section 33, but rather by appealing the ruling vigorously in the courts. In her view, it was premature to consider using Section 33 until after the Supreme Court had ruled on the case.

In January 2001, the Supreme Court upheld most of the law, with two exceptions. The first concerned material created privately, such as journals or drawings, that was not intended for distribution. The second ruled that it was permissible to possess videos for private use as long as the material did not depict unlawful sexual activity. Such materials, in the Court's opinion, "raise little or no risk of harm to children." But the Supreme Court was divided in its decision. Three judges would have upheld the law in its entirety, allowing the possession of no material that "degraded or dehumanized" children.

In light of this difference of opinion, should parliament use Section 33 to uphold the law in its entirety?

with other acts of sexual intercourse. Seaboyer's lawyer took the case to the Supreme Court.

At the Supreme Court level, Justice Beverly McLachlin, writing for a majority of the Court, found that the rape-shield law violated the accused's right under section 11(d) of the Charter to a fair trial. In McLachlin's opinion, there was "the real risk that an innocent person may be convicted." At one level, this decision fits the individual versus the state framework well. An individual who was treated harshly by a national law had his rights upheld by the courts. However, if we peel the decision back to another level we can also see that the state's law existed to protect the rights or the interests of a vulnerable group in society; the victims of sexual assault. At this level, the decision was one where the interests of one category of individuals (those accused of sexual assault) were protected at the expense of the interests of others (the victims of sexual assault). Court battles over whether laws violate the Charter may well be battles between classes of individuals and not simply battles between individuals and the state.

The Seaboyer case also allows us to argue that the core of the constitutional rights mythology, that courts further rights and legislatures restrict rights, is fallacious. The example of Seaboyer shows that the reality may be far more complicated. Government legislation actually protects or furthers the rights or interests of particular constituencies. Through legislation such as the rape-shield law, governments may improve the position in our society of vulnerable or disadvantaged groups.

Summary

In this chapter we have sketched out the important roles which constitutions play in liberal democracies. They establish the essential rules of political competition. They define the relationships among a country's key political actors. In this respect, they may or may not divide sovereignty between different levels of government and stipulate the sorts of protections and duties citizens can expect from their governments. We have also argued that constitutions are focal points for political conflict. For centuries, political actors have regarded constitutional provisions as key political resources, an outlook which is bound to flourish in the twenty-first century.

Endnotes

1 "The oracle of Westminster," *The Times (London)*, 27 July 1998.

Discussion Questions

1. If you were given the job of drafting a constitution for a new country, would you require extraordinary majorities in the constitutional amendment formula?

2. "Political practices which evolved out of conventions are probably more secure than practices which are entrenched in a written constitution." Would you agree with this statement? Why?

3. Do you believe that individual rights are best protected by entrenching them in a written constitution?

Further Readings

Bagehot, Walter. 1963. *The English Constitution.* London: Collins.

Cairns, Alan C. 1995. *Reconfigurations: Canadian Citizenship and Constitutional Change.* Toronto: McClelland and Stewart.

Rossiter, Clinton. ed. 1961. *The Federalist Papers.* New York: Mentor.

Russell, Peter H. 1991. "Standing Up for Notwithstanding," *Alberta Law Review, 293.*

——————— 1992. *Constitutional Odyssey: Can Canadians Be a Sovereign People?* Toronto: University of Toronto Press.

Whyte, J. D. 1990. "On Not Standing for Notwithstanding," *Alberta Law Review, 347.*

Weblinks

Centre for Constitutional Studies
www.law.ualberta.ca/centres/ccs

Solon Law Archive: Canadian Constitutional Documents
http://www.solon.org

Kingwood College Library: Constitutions of the World
http://www.nhmccd.cc.tx.us/contracts/lrc/kc/constitutions-subject.html

CHAPTER 9

LEGISLATURES AND EXECUTIVES

Objectives

Legislatures and executives rarely excite students of political science in the same way that compelling political issues such as war and peace, abortion, and civil rights do. Legislatures and executives are, however, critical political institutions and vital to understanding political decision making and political power in almost all countries. The elected and appointed representatives who sit in these institutions are at the centre of decision making in democratic systems.

BRENDA O'NEILL

This chapter describes the two most prevalent democratic political systems currently found in the world—the presidential and parliamentary political systems. These two systems differ significantly in their organization of the relationship between the executive and legislative branches of government. The chapter next provides a closer examination of the legislature and the executive. The functions and structures of these two institutions are outlined in an effort to better understand how they undertake their assigned responsibilities. Finally, the chapter discusses the weakening of the power of legislatures relative to executives that has occurred in most democracies. The "decline of legislatures" is considered by many as a negative development in democratic systems.

Introduction

The power vested in legislatures and executives is often celebrated as a measure of democratic decision making. This power, however, actually reflects a loss of power to citizens. Legislatures and executives are the key institutions of **representative** or **indirect democracy**. In this type of democratic system a small number of elected representatives make political decisions on behalf of all citizens. While all citizens have the right to vote during periodic elections in which representatives are chosen, elections are extremely limited in their ability to control the power accorded these representatives. And as the 2000 American presidential election race made clear, there are no guarantees that votes always determine electoral outcomes.

In that race, challenges to the voting process (who hasn't now heard of a dimpled chad?) and to the procedures employed to count disputed ballots led to a dizzying debate regarding which political institution possessed the legal authority to decide the election's outcome in the state: the Florida Secretary of State, the Florida Supreme Court, the Florida legislature or the U.S. Supreme Court. Many observers were previously unaware of the existence of the electoral college and its function in presidential elections. And fewer still knew of the role that state legislatures had historically played, and possibly could still play, in selecting the members of the electoral college, a power granted in Article II of the American Constitution. The ability of the state legislature to select an electoral college, of the Secretary of State to certify the results of votes cast in an election, and of the courts to interpret electoral and constitutional law were all directly relevant to the outcome of the presidential election race, quite apart from the ballots cast by individual Americans.

"None are more conscious of the vital limits on judicial authority than are the members of this court, and none stand more in admiration of the constitution's design to leave the selection of the president to the people, through their legislatures, and to the political sphere. When contending parties invoke the process of the courts, however, it becomes our unsought responsibility to resolve the federal and constitutional issues the judicial system has been forced to confront" (United States Supreme Court, *Bush v. Gore*, December 2000). The U.S. Supreme Court ruling in the dispute over the Florida election recount seems to suggest that it was an unwilling yet key participant in the process. Many others argued that the Supreme Court should not have ruled on the issue because in doing so it undermined the authority of the Florida Supreme Court. That court had previously ruled on the case and, since US states hold responsibility for electoral law, overturning its decision was tantamount to infringing on states' rights. Others, however, argued that the courts had no legitimate basis for intervening; electoral law, as established by each state, provided a clear basis for appeals which the courts were essentially violating. Yet partisanship (often referred to as bi-partisanship) was explicit in many of the decisions that were made by members of the executive and legislature. Finally, the Gore camp rhetoric focused on the need to "let every vote be counted"—but *shouldn't* ballots actually play some part in determining the winner? Who should decide the outcome of contested elections?

Most of us have heard something about the three branches of government and their functions. The legislative branch makes laws, the executive branch puts these laws into action, and the judicial branch of government resolves conflict over laws. More formally these are called the legislative, executive, and adjudicative functions of government. This description, however, is tremendously simplistic. In reality, the lines of responsibility over-lap across the three institutions. Additionally in most systems the effective role of each institution differs somewhat from the formal one normally assigned to it in the constitu-tion, if one is assigned at all. Over time political institutions adopt roles that can differ significantly from those originally intended, either by specific intent or merely for practical reasons. In Canada, for example, the adoption of the Charter of Rights and Freedoms in 1982 gave the courts far more freedom in influencing the making of laws, a responsibility formally assigned to the legislature in the Constitution Act of 1982. This chapter adopts a focus that will clarify the relationship between legislatures and executives. As such, dem-ocratic countries will be categorized in one of two possible ways, as either parliamentary or presidential, a distinction based on the legislative-executive relationship.

Parliamentary and Presidential Systems

THE PARLIAMENTARY SYSTEM, ALTERNATIVELY REFERRED TO AS THE "WESTMINSTER model" or cabinet government, has its oldest example in the United Kingdom. It is also the model adopted by many Commonwealth countries including Canada. The legislative and executive branches in this system are fused. The result is an executive normally accorded a significant degree of freedom in directing the state. Alternatively, the United States provides the oldest and most distinct example of the presidential system of government. Also referred to as the congressional system, it has been copied in various forms in many of the world's countries. The division of power in a **presidential system** between the two main branches of government normally results in an executive that has a weaker ability to govern independently of the legislature than that enjoyed by its equal in parliamentary systems. These two models of government dominate in the world's states. Approximately 38 percent have chosen to follow the parliamentary model while another 54 percent follow the presidential model. The majority of countries adopting the presidential model have done so recently, often following the transition from authoritarian or military rule. The long-term stability of these regimes may be in some doubt (Derbyshire and Derbyshire, 1996, 39). Other democratic states have adopted a mixed, or dual, system that combines particular elements of the parliamentary and presidential systems. The best known example of the mixed system is currently found in France.

There are three fundamental differences between presidential and parliamentary systems:

1. The fusion of political power versus the separation of powers;

2. The existence versus absence of the principle of responsible government; and

3. Distinct versus combined heads of state and government.

Fusion versus Separation of Power

A key difference between a parliamentary and a presidential system is the division of powers between the legislative and executive branches. In presidential systems power is separated, as contrasted with the fusion of power found in parliamentary systems (see Figure 9.1). The presidential system's **separation of powers** reflects an explicit attempt to control the abuse of governmental power. The presidential system of government attempts to do this by assigning distinct powers to each of the legislative and executive branches in the hope that a balancing of powers will restrict the ability of one branch to dominate the other. In addition, each branch is accorded varying powers of review over decisions taken by the other. These checks and balances are intended to prevent either branch from abusing its power. As James Madison argued in the Federal Paper no. 47, "The accumulation of all powers, legislative, executive, and judiciary, in the same hands, whether of one, a few, or many . . . may justly be pronounced the very definition of tyranny" (Hamilton et al., 1961, 301).

In addition to divided responsibilities and the power of review, neither branch's security of tenure is dependent on the other. This allows each institution the freedom to act without fear of repercussion. The ability to impeach the leader of the executive provides the only exception to this rule. The legislative branch possesses the power to remove the president (the leader of the executive) but only for specific abuses of power and only after having met certain stringent requirements. Most recently, for example, the actions of American ex-president Bill Clinton fuelled discussions regarding the definition of "other high crimes and misdemeanors," terminology that appears in the Constitution of the United States. According to that document, if the president is found to have engaged in such activities then Congress has the power to begin the impeachment process. If President Clinton's actions had included obstruction of justice and perjury, both of which constitute grounds for criminal prosecution and as such would seem to meet constitutional criteria, then impeachment would have been a likely result. The separation of powers also extends to a separation of structures. Those elected or appointed to one branch cannot simultaneously hold positions in the other. Allowing for such a possibility would mean that government members were responsible for "checking" themselves, an unacceptable situation.

The United States provides the clearest example of the presidential model. In this system, Congress (the legislative branch of government that includes the House of Representatives and the Senate) is granted formal legislative power over the president. The office of the president is one element of the executive branch of government that also includes the cabinet, and both executive and administrative offices. Only Congress can introduce, debate, modify, and pass legislation. The president, however, possesses veto powers of various strengths that provide the ability to curb Congress' legislative strength. The president generally enjoys freedom in the implementation and administration of policy. He or she has the power to appoint a cabinet; draft the budget; appoint individuals to a number of powerful political positions, including judicial and administrative positions; and control the government's administration and bureaucracy. Yet this executive power is not absolute. Congress is granted powers such as the ability to review and reject various presidential appointments, as well as the presidential budget.

This separation of powers is alternatively referred to as a sharing of power since the two branches of government must cooperate in order to ensure the smooth functioning of the legislative and policy processes. When the president wishes to pass a piece a legislation in Congress, he or she must initially convince a member of Congress to introduce the bill, and

FIGURE 9.1 *Parliamentary and Presidential Systems*

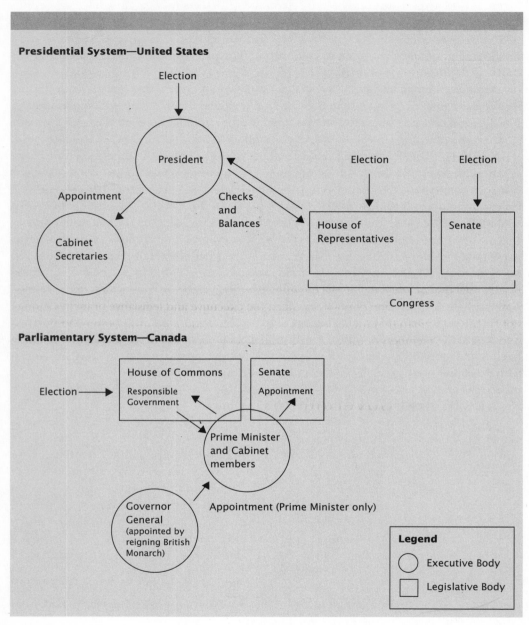

Presidential System—United States

Election

President

Appointment

Checks and Balances

Cabinet Secretaries

Election

Election

House of Representatives

Senate

Congress

Parliamentary System—Canada

Election

House of Commons

Responsible Government

Senate

Appointment

Prime Minister and Cabinet members

Governor General (appointed by reigning British Monarch)

Appointment (Prime Minister only)

Legend

◯ Executive Body

☐ Legislative Body

then subsequently generate significant support among members of Congress to see the bill pass. This latter requirement involves much concerted effort on the part of the White House staff since members of Congress do not normally vote along party lines. Bargaining and compromise are required to secure members' votes on individual bills. The U.S. president is often considered to be one of the most powerful politicians in the world, but on the domestic political scene presidential power is significantly checked by that of Congress.

The separation of powers in the presidential system of government contrasts sharply with its fusion in the parliamentary system. The term **fusion of power** refers to the integration of the executive and legislative branches. In practice this means that members of the executive branch, including the prime minister and members of his or her cabinet, are chosen from within the legislature. The executive draws its power directly from its position within the legislature and only indirectly from election by the people. The point comes across clearly in the manner in which the executive is chosen. The leader of the executive is normally the leader of the party that wins the most seats in the legislative assembly as a result of election. The leader then appoints as ministers a select number of individuals from within the governing party **caucus**, collectively referred to as *cabinet*. The executive is composed of a handful of members chosen from the largest, and often the majority, party in the legislature. A **majority government** exists when the governing party commands a majority of seats in the legislature. **Minority governments** are those in which the governing party holds more seats that any other party in the legislature but not a majority of all legislative seats. Citizens do not elect members of the executive as is the case in the presidential system. Instead they elect members of the legislature from which the executive is then selected. The fusion of power between the executive and legislative branches should not be taken to mean that the legislature and executive share political power. Despite the selection of the members of the executive from among members of the legislature, political power is held almost exclusively by the executive. It is nevertheless responsible to the legislature for the manner in which it exercises that power.

Responsible Government

The executive's ability to remain in power in the parliamentary system, before having reached some maximum tenure as set by law, depends directly on its ability to maintain the confidence of the legislative chamber from which it is drawn. This principle is referred to as **responsible government**. This legislative check is intended to limit potential abuses of executive power. No similar convention exists in the presidential system since abuses of power are held in check by the division of power between the two branches. Legislative votes are the yardstick employed to measure the degree of confidence held in the executive branch. The executive is said to hold the confidence of the legislature if it can secure a majority of votes on key pieces of legislation that come up for vote in the assembly. The most important vote that occurs in the legislative assembly is the **vote of no confidence**. To lose such a vote implies that the executive no longer has the support of the legislature, the body directly elected to represent the citizenry. Symbolically, then, the loss suggests that the people no longer consent to government by the particular executive in question. Under these circumstances, it is expected that the executive will step down and call an election.

The legislative check over executive power may at first glance seem tremendous. The reality, however, is that party discipline has weakened the power of the legislature over the executive because it requires a party's legislative caucus to vote collectively on legislation.

The convention was adopted as a natural response to the principle of responsible government. If a defeat of a key government bill leads to the death of a government, then smart governments will make sure that they secure enough votes to pass key bills. There are infrequent occasions when legislators are allowed to vote independently from the party position. These free votes usually involve matters of individual conscience or religious belief, such as abortion or capital punishment.

The concentration of power in executive hands explains why the system is sometimes referred to as "executive government." Critics of the parliamentary system point to the real potential for executive abuse of power, particularly in light of the weakening of legislative control. But as its supporters are quick to point out, this disadvantage is offset by the increased executive effectiveness resulting from the concentration of power. Unlike the presidential system, the parliamentary system allows the chief executive to easily legislate and implement policy agendas, particularly when supported by a majority government.

Heads of State and Government

A final difference between the parliamentary and presidential systems exists in each system's treatment of the positions of the **head of state** and **head of government**. In parliamentary systems, the positions are divided and held by different individuals. In presidential systems, one individual, the president, is head of both state and government. Head of state is a position that symbolizes the history and continuity of the state and its institutions, contrasted with the temporary nature of individual governments. Individuals appointed, elected, or inheriting these positions normally hold them for a longer period than the more transient governments of the day. In Britain, Queen Elizabeth II has held the position of head of state since 1953 and ten prime ministers have come and gone since her coronation. The head of state (in Canada, the governor general) is rarely granted any effective political powers and normally assumes only ceremonial responsibilities such as greeting dignitaries, providing assent to legislation, selecting the head of government, dissolving parliaments, and calling elections. The head of government, the prime minister in parliamentary systems, in contrast, holds effective power.

The combination of the positions of head of state and head of government in one individual, the leader of the executive, in the presidential system reflects an explicit rejection of the power of royal prerogative once vested in the British Crown. The symbolism in the uniting of the two positions is clear. It implies that the powers of the state and government are vested in the people, and only the people, and there exists no power above or beyond that of their elected representatives. In contrast, their separation in the parliamentary system reflects the traditional belief that the power of the state is vested in the sovereign, and carried out by the government in its name.

Legislative Assemblies

THE TRADITION OF THE DEMOCRATICALLY ELECTED ASSEMBLY IS LENGTHY. THE MODEL of **direct democracy** in ancient Greece allowed all citizens, which at the time meant a select number of males, to engage directly in political decision making through participation in the assembly, its legislative body. Modern states are now much larger, and engaging all citizens in effective state decision making is impossible. Representative democracy has become an acceptable alternative allowing citizens to vote democratically for a limited number of people who, in turn, sit as their representatives in legislative institutions. Even non-democratic states go to great pains to set up albeit impotent puppet assemblies, as key symbols of democracy, in attempts to gain the appearance of respectability. At present all but seven of the world's 192 states have an active assembly, variously named the House of Commons, the House of Representatives, the National Assembly, Parliament, Congress, the Senate and so on.

The key responsibility of legislatures is to pass laws or rules under which countries are governed. The Latin root of the word *legislate* is "to bring law." Representative democracy requires that laws be approved by a democratically elected legislative assembly, composed of the citizens' representatives. Some pieces of legislation are undoubtedly more important than others. The budget is a primary example. In Canada, the House of Commons' **power of the purse** is such that the executive's budget requires Commons' approval and, by convention, the failure to win this approval results in the defeat of the government.

If legislatures once dominated the legislative process, it is now the case that most legislatures play only a secondary legislative role. For the most part, legislation is introduced by the executive, the legislature reviews it, possibly modifies it (without changing the substance of the bill), and then approves it. The legislature's key role in this process consists primarily of legitimization. The approval of the citizens of the state, at least through their representatives, of the laws under which their actions will be bound grants authority to those laws. One exception to this generalization is the U.S. Congress, which continues to play an important role in the legislative process, although its approval of legislation also provides the stamp of legitimacy.

Tied to the responsibility to legislate is the important role of deliberation in the legislature. John Stuart Mill called the legislature the "the Congress of Opinions; an arena in which not only the opinion of the nation, but that of every section of it, . . . can produce itself in full light and challenge discussion" (1948, 172). Indeed, the title of the first modern legislature, the British parliament, comes from the French word *parler*, meaning "to talk." Open debate occurs in a number of legislative settings, including Oral Question Period in parliamentary systems, which grants the opposition the right to a response from government to questions posed in the assembly. Regular debate also occurs at various stages in the legislative life of a bill in both the legislature and in legislative committees. These opportunities provide legislators with a means of challenging executive actions and decisions, of discussing the merits and weaknesses of legislative proposals, and of raising the general and particular concerns of their constituents.

Individual legislators are every citizen's link to their government and as such, the voices of the people reside in their representatives. The effectiveness of legislative assemblies is, as a result, also measured by the degree to which legislators "represent" the interests of all citizens. The concept of representation is nevertheless a difficult one to pin down. For instance, legislators' responsibility to "represent" can mean that they voice either their constituents' interests, the interests of the party they were elected to represent, the interests of the country as a whole, or their individual conscience (Pitkin, 1967). The particular concept of representation adopted by legislators will depend in part on the type of system in which they find themselves but also on the existing political culture. In parliamentary systems, it is quite likely that party will be an important factor in determining how legislators decide to vote, but their voting behaviour in the privacy of caucus meetings is very likely to be governed by other considerations. The United States' Congress, given its lack of party discipline, would at first glance appear to be the model for the clear representation of constituents' interests. However, the strength of PACs (Political Action Committees), organizations that provide significant funds for congressional election campaigns, means that legislators are very often more heavily influenced by interest groups in the legislative process than they are by the interests of their constituents. Party discipline in the Canadian House of Commons is often argued to severely weaken the ability of members of Parliament to vote on their constituents' behalf, but as the American case demonstrates, the lack of party discipline does not necessarily translate into a stronger voice for citizens.

Structure of Legislatures

Legislatures are composed of either one (**unicameral**) or two (**bicameral**) houses. Canada provides examples of both. At the federal level, the House of Commons and the Senate make up the legislative branch. Alternatively, each provincial legislature consists of a single house, accorded a variety of titles across the provinces. The terminology employed to describe the two legislative institutions in bicameral states varies but normally the lower house, or chamber, is the primary legislative body, and the upper, or second, chamber is secondary in the legislative process. In Canada, the House of Commons is the lower chamber and the Senate is the upper. Only a third of the world's assemblies are bicameral, reflecting an unwillingness to divide legislative power between two institutions and increase the potential for deadlock or disagreement between the two bodies (Derbyshire and Derbyshire, 1996, 58).

One of the most common rationales for adopting bicameralism is the belief that a second chamber, composed of individuals representing different interests than in the lower chamber, provides a mechanism for considered review of decisions emanating from the other chamber. This function has been described as "sober second thought" with reference to the Senate in Canada. Another rationale for dividing legislative power is the perceived need for special group representation in the assembly, including cultural, social, and regional. In fact 79 percent of existing **federal states**, in which sovereignty is constitutionally divided between two or more governments, are bicameral since the upper chamber provides representation of constituent governments' interests within the institutions of the national government. The regional basis of representation reflects itself in the selection principle adopted by upper houses in federal systems: not **representation by population**, as in the lower house, but rather representation by region. In the U.S. Senate, for example, two representatives are chosen from each state, in spite of the vast differences in populations across them.

Executives

LEGISLATURES ENJOY A LONG HISTORY, BUT EXECUTIVES HAVE BEEN WITH US since long before the idea of popular sovereignty gained support. The label *executive* emphasizes the function of the institution, that is, to execute laws and put them into action. But their functions in the political systems are more central than conveyed by their title. According to one political scientist, "executives are the nerve centers of the governmental process" (Blondel, 1972, 117). We normally associate the term *government* with the particular leaders of the executive branch—the prime minister in parliamentary systems and the president in presidential systems. But the executive includes a number of other political actors and offices. A useful distinction can be drawn between the political executive—those politicians who happen to be in power and their personal advisors—and the permanent executive, commonly referred to as the political bureaucracy, a majority of whom retain their positions in spite of changes in government.

The primary function of the executive branch is the day-to-day direction of the state involving both policy formulation and the implementation and administration of legislation. This role, akin to that assumed by chief executive officers of large business organizations, is a particularly demanding one given the sheer size of the government "enterprise." One element alone, the administration of departments in modern governments, is a formidable task given the tremendous growth in the scope of government activity in recent decades. In addition to responsibility for roads, defence, mail, and currency, governments are also likely to be involved in such diverse fields as space exploration, telecommunications, and the delivery of health services. And despite recent periods of government restraint, the smooth functioning of these numerous government programs and the effective delivery of services continue to require a large government bureaucracy.

In addition to responsibility for the administration of programs and services, the executive branch has increasingly assumed responsibility for formulating much of the legislation introduced in legislatures as part of its policy agenda. Part of this shift in responsibility from the legislature to the executive branch stems from the increasing complexity of policy issues and other pressures. The executive is aided in the execution of this role by both political advisors and the large governmental bureaucracy responsible to it. One can imagine the executive branch as a pyramid: the political executive sitting at the top of the pyramid and their advisors and the bureaucracy directly below them. The shape of the pyramid, whether short or tall, depends on the nature of the political system as well as the particular leadership style of its chief executives. While some leaders prefer a more collective decision-making process (short pyramid), others prefer less democratic decision-making styles (tall pyramid). Policy advice filters its way up through the pyramid for executive review and is then directed to the legislature to begin life as a bill.

The executive branch assumes a number of additional responsibilities. First, the political executive is often charged with selecting and appointing individuals to a number of government positions, such as judges in the country's courts and ambassadors abroad. In the United States, for example, over two thousand appointments are the responsibility of the White House (Welch et al., 1995, 339). Symbolic and ceremonial functions, ranging from presenting medals of honour to phoning the winners of the Super Bowl are additional responsibilities, acts important for the leadership they convey and their role in unifying citizens around common symbols. And the leader of the political executive also serves as a chief diplomat for the state in international settings. The recent trends to globalization and the removal of trade barriers make this role particularly important. At critical times, such as upon the declaration of war, the importance of this role cannot be overstated. Lastly, the political executive is normally charged with those responsibilities seen as most important for "the well-being of its citizens" and "of prime importance to the nation" (Blondel, 1972, 124). Protection of the state's borders and its sovereignty figure prominently in this role and the executive branch is normally charged with responsibility for the military and for foreign affairs.

Structure of Executives

The structure of the executive branch varies greatly between parliamentary and presidential systems, and so a description of each system is required. In the American presidential system, the chief executive is wholly responsible for the administration of the state. The president is directly responsible to the electorate. Cabinet secretaries, each with a responsibility for a government department, are appointed at the discretion of the president, and are responsible only to the president. They assume primary responsibility for the administration of the governmental bureaucracy. Cabinet secretaries do not, as a rule, meet formally to discuss policy issues or to advise the president on legislative initiatives. Instead, two offices dominate in providing such policy direction. These are the White House Staff and the Executive Offices. The political nature of appointments to these offices means that a change in government results in wholesale turnover in their personnel. The White House Staff are the president's personal advisors with such responsibilities as preparing the president's calendar and assessing his or her political fortune. Alternatively, the Executive Offices assume primary responsibility for policy development and provide key presidential advice in various policy areas. One such office, the Office of Management and Budget, is instrumental in drafting the presidential budget. And since the separation of powers in the presidential system restricts the executive's control of the legislative agenda, these offices play an important part in generating support for presidential legislative initiatives in Congress, an oftentimes difficult task requiring much bargaining and compromise.

In contrast, the Canadian parliamentary executive is divided between the head of state and the head of government. The governor general, appointed by the queen on the advice of the prime minister, acts as the Crown's representative. As we have seen, however, the position is a formal and symbolic one enjoying little effective political power. Instead, responsibility for policy development and the administration of the state is shared by the prime minister and cabinet, who in turn are responsible to the House of Commons through the principle of responsible government. The prime minister, however, as leader of the party in power and for other reasons, assumes a leadership position within cabinet and has been appropriately called "first among equals." Cabinet members, it will be remembered, are selected by the prime minister from among the party's governmental caucus and each cabinet member undertakes two functions. A member of cabinet both develops government policy and acts alone as political head of an administrative department. The principle of

individual ministerial responsibility requires that cabinet members assume responsibility for leading their departments, defending them in the legislature, and if necessary, resigning in the face of a major administrative blunder. Cabinet ministers have political staff to provide them with policy advice. Nevertheless, **deputy ministers,** members of the non-elected bureaucracy and administrative heads of government departments, have increasingly been called upon to provide their ministers with policy advice.

The Decline of Legislatures

Legislatures stand as the symbol of democracy, and serve as a vehicle for the representation and articulation of citizens' interests. They were originally granted powers and responsibilities intended to provide a means of controlling the use of arbitrary political power and for ensuring that political decisions were made with the consent of the majority. The Boston Tea Party's slogan was, after all, "no taxation without representation." Many continue to believe that the most important work of government continues to take place on the floor of legislative assemblies. But in most democratic systems their power has not increased in concert with that of the executive branch. Indeed, the power of legislatures has been partly supplanted by that of executives. Although the trend is less evident in the case of the American Congress, everywhere legislatures have declined in importance relative to the executive branch of government. While the legislature's remaining functions are integral for democratic governance and generate sufficient work to require that legislators work full rather than part-time, legislatures only currently debate the merits and faults of legislation brought before them by the executive and tinker with the wording of those proposals. They provide little in the way of legislative initiatives, and rarely dominate the legislative agenda. As such, the approval of the citizens' representatives of the laws by which they are governed has become little more than a rubber stamp.

Lord Bryce argued that legislatures were in decline in the 1920s. Their decline, however, has accelerated recently because of several factors. In the first instance, the legislative function was assigned to representative assemblies at a time when laws were less complex and concerned fewer policy areas than those of today. The increased social and economic roles assumed by governments in the nineteenth century and the speed with which many of these decisions have to be made has meant that executives are well placed to take over much of the responsibility for law making. The executive can develop laws more quickly than the larger, more cumbersome legislature and has at its disposal a sophisticated and experienced network of institutions providing it with superior policy research capabilities.

The decline of legislatures is also the direct result of the increased presence of other institutions in the political system. The media now provide an accessible forum for citizens to learn about important political issues and debates. This role once was accorded to the legislature and individual legislators. "Citizens can now hear and see speakers and debates and discussions on political and social questions which may seem to them to be more interesting and persuasive, less concerned with the arid controversies of party warfare, than what is provided by the speeches of legislators, inside or outside their chambers" (Wheare, 1969, 173–4). Interest groups and professional associations have also become increasingly involved in representing their members' interests in the political arena, and have done so rather successfully. Citizens are thus provided with an alternative forum for airing their grievances, which further diminishes the importance of legislators and their institutions. Moreover these groups are very likely to target the executive and the bureaucracy for bringing about change, and, in the process, completely bypass the legislature. The result is that legislatures are no longer as critical as they once were to the democratic decision-making process.

Summary

Legislatures and executives constitute the primary institutions of political decision making in democracies. Parliamentary systems concentrate power in the hands of the executive, providing for effective government, while requiring that executives maintain the confidence of the legislative branch. Presidential systems divide power between the legislative and executive branches and provide each with effective checks for controlling the other. One system employs responsible government and the other adopts checks and balances. Despite such divergent foundations, these two institutions nevertheless perform similar functions across systems. Legislatures approve laws, represent citizens' interests in the political system, and provide supervision and review of executive action. The executive branch is charged with overseeing the day-to-day administration of the system, control of the policy agenda, protection of state sovereignty, as well as a number of ceremonial and symbolic duties. And while the legislature was originally intended as a key element in the democratic process, necessity and the growth of competing institutions have weakened its position relative to that of the executive. Yet both remain key decision-making actors in democratic political systems.

Discussion Questions

1. What factors are most important in the decision regarding the type of institutional structure to adopt in any system? What questions would need answering before you could decide on a unicameral versus bicameral legislature, a presidential versus a parliamentary system?

2. Which element is more valuable to a political system: effective checks on the abuse of power or the ability to successfully implement a policy agenda? Why?

3. If party discipline were dropped as a principle in parliamentary legislatures, what might be the likely consequences?

4. What might legislatures do to reinvent themselves in order to increase their role in the legislative process and their relevance in the political process?

References

Bardes, Barbara, Mack C. Shelley II and Steffen W. Schmidt. 1992. *American Government and Politics Today: The Essentials*. New York, NY: West Publishing Co.

Blondel, Jean. 1972. *Comparing Political Systems.* New York, NY: Praeger Publishers.

Bryce, Lord. 1921. *Modern Democracies.* London, UK: Macmillan.

Derbyshire, J. Denis and Ian Derbyshire. 1996. *Political Systems of the World.* New York, NY: St. Martin's Press.

Hamilton, Alexander, James Madison and John Jay. 1961. *The Federalist Papers.* Scarborough, ON: New American Library of World Literature Inc.

Mill, J.S. 1948. "Considerations on Representative Government." In R.B. McCallum, ed. *On Liberty and Considerations of Representative Government.* London: Basil Blackwell & Mott Ltd.

Pitkin, Hanna. 1967. *The Concept of Representation.* Berkeley, CA: University of California Press.

Welch, Susan, John Gruhl, Michael Steinman, John Comer, Margery M. Ambrosius and Susan Rigdon. 1995. *Understanding American Government, 3rd edition.* New York, NY: West Publishing Company.

Wheare, K.C. 1969. "The Decline of Legislatures?" In J. Blondel, ed. *Comparative Government.* Garden City, NY: Doubleday and Company.

Further Readings

Lijphart, Arend ed. 1992. *Parliamentary versus Presidential Government.* Toronto, ON: Oxford University Press.

Jackson, Robert J. and Michael M. Atkinson. 1980. *The Canadian Legislative System,* 2nd ed., Toronto, ON: Macmillan.

Neustad, Richard E. 1990. *Presidential Power and the Modern Presidents.* New York, NY: The Free Press.

Weaver, R. Kent and Bert A. Rockman eds. 1993. *Do Institutions Matter? Government Capabilities in the United States and Abroad.* Washington, D.C.: The Brookings Institution.

Weblinks

Government of Canada
canada.gc.ca

U.S. House of Representatives
www.house.gov/

U.S. Senate
www.senate.gov/

The White House
www.whitehouse.gov

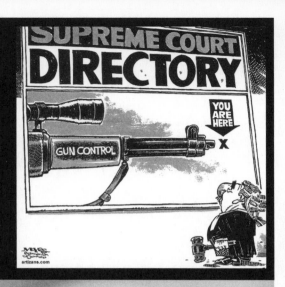

CHAPTER 10

THE JUDICIARY

DAVID SCHNEIDERMAN

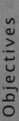

Objectives

The judiciary may be one of the least obvious and most misunderstood components of liberal democracies. Yet they continue to gain increasing power and influence—some would say at the expense of democratic politics generally. In this chapter, we focus on the judicial role in the political life of Western democracies. First, we trace the origins and rise of judicial review in the English-speaking world and examine the political theory that arose to explain the need for an independent and impartial judiciary. Having traced the origins of judicial authority, we next review how that power is exercised. Judges have developed a variety of techniques to guide their work so that their decisions are not simply the result of their political preferences. We examine these techniques of **constitutional interpretation** that attempt to constrain judicial decision making. Lastly, we examine institutional solutions that keep the judicial role in check. Two such solutions are reviewed—the possibility of constitutional amendment and, a particularly Canadian solution, the **notwithstanding clause**.

Introduction

Judge Learned Hand of the United States Court of Appeals concluded in his 1944 essay "The Contribution of an Independent Judiciary to Civilization" that an independent judiciary could not reasonably be expected to play any significant role in the preservation of political society. In Hand's assessment:

> A society so riven that the spirit of moderation is gone, no court *can* save; ... a society where the spirit flourishes, no court *need* save; . . . in a society which evades its responsibility by thrusting upon the courts the nurture of that spirit, that spirit in the end will perish (Hand, 1952, 181).

Judges, however, are increasingly called upon to resolve all sorts of controversies over which there may be deep division in society. In Canada, for instance, the Supreme Court was asked to rule whether the province of Quebec could remove itself unilaterally from the Canadian constitutional framework. In the new Republic of South Africa, the judiciary decided whether the death penalty was permissible under the new South African Constitution. The judiciary in countries with written constitutions, such as Canada, the United States, and Germany, are oftentimes asked to consider whether such socially divisive issues as access to abortion, medically assisted suicide, and the promotion of hatred against minority groups are constitutionally protected rights.

In so doing, courts are usually asked to scrutinize legislative choices made by democratically elected legislatures. The judiciary review government action for the constitutional correctness of choices the people's representatives have made. Whenever political power is being exercised, the principle of democracy insists that political authority be accountable to the public. Citizens are expected to control the exercise of political power. If citizens do not like how that power is exercised, they can vote, organize, and lobby to ensure that decision makers change their minds or are otherwise replaced. If citizens do not like how the judiciary are performing their role, however, citizens can do little, for the judiciary are not accountable to any democratically elected institution. They hold their jobs on "good behaviour" until, depending on the country, retirement age or for life. They cannot be easily removed. Why then do citizens in modern democracies empower unelected, unaccountable judges to invalidate decisions made by democratically accountable legislators?

In constitutional democracies, the judiciary are considered the guardians of the constitution. They are a check on what is called the **tyranny of the majority**. Judges have the power of **judicial review**, the constitutional authority to review legislative and executive acts for their consistency with foundational constitutional text. This power is seen to enhance the practice of democracy. As constitutions limit what governments can do, the judiciary oversee the operations of government so as to ensure governments do not exceed those limits. In those instances where a citizen, group of citizens, or business interest feel aggrieved by a government act and believe that the act is beyond the constitutional capacity of government, judges are called upon to resolve the dispute. For instance, a citizen might claim that a fundamental freedom, such as freedom of expression, has been abridged. Another might claim that a provincial government is enacting legislation that more properly belongs within the authority of the federal government. In most of these disputes, the judiciary are asked to apply constitutional text to specific controversies. Yet most constitutions are not so clear that they provide obvious answers to many of the disputes judges are asked to resolve. Numerous constitutional provisions, such as the freedom of expression, are drafted in broad and vague language. In a case where there are conflicting interpretations and outcomes, why should judicial opinions be preferred to those of democratically elected representatives?

The judiciary have the legal expertise to help resolve some of the disputes between individuals and those between individuals and the state. Judges also have a wealth of experience supervising the administration of criminal justice so as to ensure that the innocent are not wrongly convicted of a criminal offence. But the judiciary also have a relationship to the larger structures of political life. If we examine the judicial record from a number of critical perspectives, such as those of class, gender, or race, we will find that the judiciary often reflect the dominant values of the society of which they are a part. Class analysis reveals that judicial decision making has been implicated in the rise of the British and American capitalist economies (Thompson, 1975). Feminist critique shows that judges often reinforce a particularly male view of the world, in which the public and the private are rigidly divided to the disadvantage of women (MacKinnon, 1989, 163). Critical race studies show that the judiciary often have protected the interests of the white majority over those of racial minorities (Spann, 5).

The whole story of how the judiciary act as they do cannot be told using these critical methods of analysis alone. The idea of the supremacy of the law, or the **rule of law**, enforced by judges is central to the organization of contemporary political life. The societal consensus that we are governed by law and legal rules, and that no one is above the law, helps to ensure political continuity and peaceful social change. No matter how far the exercise of legal power departs from the myth that "the law is blind," the legal ideals of liberty, equality, impartiality, and procedural fairness are foundational to the organization of democratic government (Thompson, 1975). These principles provide important resources to resist political authority both in modern democracies and in authoritarian political societies. The role of the judiciary as guardians of these principles remains, then, an important element in modern day political life.

Origins of an Independent Judiciary

POLITICAL AUTHORITY IS NORMALLY UNDERSTOOD TO BE DIVIDED AMONG THREE types of power: legislative, executive, and judicial. Executive power is ordinarily concerned with execution of laws, public security and foreign affairs; legislative power with the making of laws; and judicial power with the administration of the civil and criminal law. This division of labour is represented by the idea of a constitutional regime with a **separation of powers**. When we speak of the *judiciary*, then, we understand this to mean the institutional apparatus of the state concerned with the interpretation and enforcement of the laws enacted by the legislature and as applied by the executive.

There was a time, however, when the legislative and judicial functions were not so clearly separated, in theory or practice. In the middle ages, the British parliament was both court and legislature. The "High Court of Parliament" performed both judicial and legislative functions. It interpreted and enforced existing law and made new law. Over time, the judicial and legislative powers gradually became separated. Legal advisors to the king became experts trained in the *reason* and *custom* of the law. The king and his council, in contrast, were experts in matters of state (McIlwain, 1910, 31). The judiciary were the keepers of the **common law**, that cumulative body of custom and judge-made law which secured the liberty and happiness of the people of the realm and which was "common" to all of its people.

Written documents, such as royal proclamations and statutes, came to take on a greater significance under the judiciary. The *Magna Carta* (1215), for instance, amounted to a concession by the king not to disturb feudal privileges exercised by the nobility. This was hardly a concession conducive to the liberty of the vast majority of the king's subjects. But it took on significance as a document that protected and promoted the liberty of all free men. Judicial use of the *Magna Carta* provides us with an early example of the practice of judicial review. The *Magna Carta* became transformed, in this way, into a foundational document protecting the rights and liberties not just of the nobility, but of everyone (McIlwain, 1910, 54–55).

The Rise of Judicial Review

WITH AN IDENTIFIABLE CORE OF FUNDAMENTAL RIGHTS FOUNDED UPON REASON and experience, namely the common and statute law, what was the institution best capable of enforcing those rights? Lord Coke is usually credited with having articulated the modern doctrine of judicial review. In *Dr. Bonham's Case* (1610), Bonham was punished by the London College of Physicians for practising medicine in London without a licence. The college was the self-governing authority of the medical profession established by statute. Bonham himself was medically trained but practised without a license and so was found guilty of the offence by the college. As punishment, Bonham was fined, yet the college chose to collect half of the fine for its own use. Lord Coke, Chief Justice of the Court of Common Pleas, declared that it was beyond the capacity of the college to punish Bonham. No person, Coke ruled, is entitled to be judge in their own case. In other words, a person could not be expected to objectively judge a dispute in which that person had an interest in the outcome. Here, the college had an interest by way of receiving one half of the fine imposed on Bonham. It was a principle of the common law of England that one could not be judge in one's own cause and this principle could be used to confine the statutory power granted to the college.

This is the main conclusion reached by Lord Coke, but it is not the reason for the decision's fame. Lord Coke followed this conclusion with the statement that: "the common law will controul [sic] acts of Parliament and sometimes adjudge them to be utterly void" when they are "against common right and reason, or repugnant, or impossible to be performed." At the time these words were uttered, judicial and legislative functions were fused in the High Court of Parliament. Coke was not an advocate of the separation of powers. Rather, he advocated that parliament exercise its functions under the controlling authority of the common law (Corwin, 1955, 55–57). Coke was pleading for the supremacy of law, not as interpreted by judges, but as interpreted by parliament.

Modern readers understand Coke as saying that the judiciary should be supreme over parliament. We should be careful not to impose contemporary understandings on times long past. Nevertheless, the idea of the supremacy of law was so threatening to King James 1 that he removed Coke in 1616. King James is reported to have earlier said that, if the law was founded upon reason, "he and others had reason as well as judges" (Maitland, 1919, 268). In those days, there was no security of tenure for judges. They could be removed at the king's pleasure. Security of tenure was only achieved by the *Act of Settlement* (1701) which declared that judges were entitled to hold their positions during "good behaviour." Judges could be dismissed only by a joint address from the House of Lords and the House of Commons.

Coke's idea of the supremacy of law did take hold in England, but it was eclipsed by the doctrine of *Parliamentary Supremacy.* Sir William Blackstone, the author of a famous legal treatise read by all eighteenth and nineteenth century lawyers, declared that parliament could "do everything that was not naturally impossible. . . what they do, no authority on earth can undo" (Blackstone, 1979, 156). Coke himself was to admit that parliament was the supreme authority. This seems to contradict the idea of the supremacy of law. One way of resolving this conflict is to admit that, even if parliament is supreme, it can only speak through acts of parliament. These statutes could then come under the supervision of the judiciary. This is an aspect of the English idea of the **rule of law** (Dicey, 1908, 409). The judiciary could supervise parliament's law-making function in the interpretation and application of the law to particular disputes that came before them.

Alexander Hamilton, one of the U.S. constitution's framers, recognized that the judiciary could act as an intermediate institution between the legislature and the people, so as to keep the legislature "within the limits assigned to their authority." Hamilton's arguments in support of ratification of the new U.S. constitution were compiled in 1788 with those of James Madison and John Jay in the *Federalist Papers*. Of the three branches of government, Hamilton argued, the judiciary would be the "least dangerous to the political rights of the constitution." This was because the judiciary only heard disputes that came before them and had no authority to initiate those disputes or to make new laws. The judiciary, Hamilton wrote, "has no influence over the sword or the purse"; unlike the executive and legislative branches, they have "neither Force nor Will [but] merely judgement" (Hamilton, 1961, No.78).

Hamilton also suggested in the *Federalist Papers* that, in the event of an irreconcilable conflict between the judiciary and the legislature, the judiciary would prevail. The constitution would be preferred over any mere statute. The intentions of the people, as reflected in the constitution, were more important than the intentions of temporary, elected political representatives.

But what if there were differences of opinion over the meaning of the constitution? Whose will would prevail in such a conflict? The case of *Marbury v. Madison* (1803) appears to provides one answer to this question. The case concerned a political skirmish over the appointment of Marbury as justice of the peace, a minor judicial office. The dispute was transformed by Marshall's judicial skill into a case of some constitutional significance. What happens when an Act of Congress is repugnant to the Constitution, asked John Marshall, Chief Justice of the United States Supreme Court? The constitution, he concluded, was the superior law. A written constitution establishes the limits of government action. It was the responsibility of the judicial branch to police those jurisdictional boundaries and to declare legislative acts beyond constitutional limits as void. Marshall did not, however, rule that judicial views would take precedence over political ones. As coordinate branches of government, Marshall was careful not to declare judicial review as the final arbiter in constitutional disputes. The decision in *Marbury*, nevertheless, has come to be understood as giving expression to the idea of judicial finality: that the constitution is what the judges say it is.

Two other features of the decision in *Marbury v. Madison* stand out, for they help us to identify two of the rationales for the practice of judicial review. The first is Marshall's belief that the source of judicial review can be found in the constitution itself. It is a form of "higher law." In a constitutional democracy, it is the people themselves who authorize judges to act as guardians of the constitution. Therefore, in any conflict between the constitution and the action of a legislative majority, the constitution will prevail. In his *Second Treatise on Government,* John Locke had shown that, with their express or tacit consent, the people were the ultimate source of constitutional power (Locke, 1988). According to this consent-based account of judicial review, it is the power of the people that gives judicial authority its legitimacy (Ackerman, 1991).

The second important feature is the idea that written constitutions require review by judges. Written constitutions may divide authority between two different levels of government, as they do in the federal regimes of Canada, the United States, and Australia. Written constitutions may also enumerate rights that limit the capacity of any legislative majority, whether national or subnational. The Canadian Charter of Rights and Freedoms as well as the first ten amendments to the U.S. Constitution of 1787, called the Bill of Rights, are examples of this. Written constitutions are considered "rigid" documents. As they are difficult to amend, it is argued that supervision by independent and impartial arbiters is necessary to allow for change and growth (Ackerman, 1991). This is in contrast to "flexible" constitutions (as the British constitution used to be considered by writers such as Blackstone) that can "make and unmake" any law. Both federalism and rights, as fundamental features of some written constitutions, call for policing by the judiciary. This is a version of a text-based argument for judicial review. Judges simply enforce the textual limits to legislative authority, whether jurisdictional or rights-based, as set out in written constitutions.

Modern Approaches to Judicial Review

RESORTING TO "THE PEOPLE" AS THE ULTIMATE SOURCE OF JUDICIAL REVIEW becomes a difficult idea to defend when the original act of constitution making took place long ago. The exclusion of large segments of the public, such as women and racial and ethnic minorities, from an original constitutional consensus makes less legitimate in the modern day commitments made in generations past. Some of the problems of time are overcome by the use in constitutional text of terms that are broad in scope and seemingly timeless. The problem is that these broad and abstract terms have no precise legal meaning or, if they did at one time, the meaning of those words has changed. Terms such as *freedom, liberty,* and *equality* appeal to the fundamental basic values in liberal democracies. But they are not always the clearest terms to guide the judiciary in their work of constitutional interpretation. What we have called text-based arguments, then, do not provide judges with sufficient guidance to separate law from ordinary power politics.

As government functions have become more complex, the supervisory role of the judiciary has become even more difficult to justify. Governments perform a myriad of complex functions, and they are supported by bureaucrats with scientific knowledge and technical expertise which judges do not have. Legislation, in turn, has become more specialized, intervening in the private market place and in daily life in multiple ways that would be unimaginable to generations past. Constitutional designs of the past seem out of step with the times and judicial review of these provisions anachronistic. The judicial power to override the will of the legislature, in these circumstances, seems less justifiable than it may have been in the past.

The fundamental rules of the common law and of written constitutions are intended to control the future. Yet, in order to perform their review function, judges are required to look to past decisions, also called **precedent**, for guidance and instruction. In this way, judicial review is a backward-looking and largely conservative task. Judicial personalities, moreover, are generally male, trained in elite educational colleges, having achieved distinction in the private practice of law usually for a wealthy clientele. They are generally "persons of a conservative disposition" (Dicey, 1948, 364), and "curiously timid about innovations" (Hand, 1952, 175). Though there is currently more diversity on the bench and reform in some appointment processes, contemporary judicial biographies suggest things have not changed much. In a 1987 survey of Canadian elite opinion, Sniderman and his colleagues conclude that legal elites consistently hold the most conservative views on social policy issues. The ideological thrust of the legal elites they surveyed was decidedly conservative on the ethics of redistribution and the role of government in social policy (Sniderman et al., 1996, 122–130).

This worry about the judicial role in controlling legislative action is underscored by the series of cases decided by the United States Supreme Court in the late-nineteenth and early-twentieth century. This is the period known as the "Lochner era," named after the period's most famous judicial decision. In the case of *Lochner v. New York* (1905) the Supreme Court ruled constitutionally invalid a New York State law which limited the hours of bakery workers to eight hours a day. The court was of the view that there was no rational basis for the belief that the health of bakery workers would be promoted by limiting their hours of work to eight hours a day. The New York statute, the court concluded, was a constitutionally impermissible attempt to interfere with the freedom of contract of workers and their employers. A number of important legislative initiatives in this period were frustrated by this type of judicial reasoning.

The judiciary not only protect economic liberties. They can also protect the rights of the criminally accused or the human rights of vulnerable minorities distinguished by race, religion, or sexual orientation. For instance, in the classic case of *Brown v. Board of Education* (1954), the U.S. Supreme Court ordered the desegregation of public schools in the southern United States. Southern states were required to open previously all-white school facilities to black school children (Tushnet, 1994). In the case of *Delgamuukw* (1997), the Supreme Court of Canada found that aboriginal people in British Columbia had an existing title to traditional aboriginal lands. And in the case of *Vriend* (1998), the Canadian Supreme Court required that gays and lesbians be protected from discrimination under Alberta's Human Rights Code.

These examples of judicial supervision in the interests of minority groups suggest a third argument to justify the authority of judges to overrule legislatures. Judicial review acts as a check on flaws in the operation of the political process. According to this process theory argument, the judiciary police the political process to ensure broad participation in the processes of representative government. Judicial protection of minorities is justified because it ensures the fair representation of minority interests by government. It is the role of the judiciary to remove these blockages in the way of fair and free democratic participation (Ely, 1980, 101–03). Patrick Monahan has advocated the application of this democratic approach in the Canadian context. He argues, for instance, that restrictions on third party advertising during election campaigns (advertising that is not generated by an official political party or candidate) should be permissible under the Charter of Rights and Freedoms. These restrictions promote equal access to the political process and reinforce democratic values by ensuring that "no one political perspective is permitted to drown out competing messages in the electoral marketplace" (Monahan, 1987, 134).

Some conservatives argue the judiciary are usurping the role of elected legislatures, in effect, becoming the captive of a "Court Party"—groups of Canadians who secure through constitutional litigation the type of legal reforms they could not achieve through the democratic process (Morton and Knopff, 2000). These authors argue that judges are susceptible to the claims of well-organized interest groups by reason of the influence of law teachers and their students, some of whom go on to "clerk" for appellate judges for one year by assisting in the research and writing of judicial opinions.

If we accept that judicial review is a legitimate institution in modern democratic states, it still does not explain how that power should be exercised by judges. The results in constitutional cases, concerning some of the most contentious issues in political life, must not reflect merely the personal views of judges or the consequence of pressure placed on judges by well-organized groups. Judicial decision making must have a more objective basis if it is to be legitimate. So as to justify rule by the judiciary, judges have developed a number of approaches to the interpretation of constitutional text (Bobbit, 1982). We have already reviewed some of these, such as the textual and the process-based approaches. These techniques help us to understand the basic ways that judges think about constitutional law. They also reveal how judges perceive their own role in the larger system of government of which they are a part. These approaches have been documented elsewhere by the U.S. constitutional writer Phillip Bobbit (1982) and they are presented here in slightly modified form with the addition of a couple of newer approaches.

History

"Judges need only determine what the framers of the constitution intended." This is the approach preferred by many American conservatives. In order to avoid the imposition of personal values in constitutional interpretation, judges are required to interpret the constitution as it was intended by its framers. In other words, the judiciary must look to history in order to ascertain the original understanding of the framers of the constitution (Bork, 1990).

There are numerous difficulties with this approach. It is often difficult to discern exactly what framers intended. The documentary evidence may be scanty, unclear, and even contradictory. It may also be difficult to identify the "framers," particularly if they met in an assembly. Lastly, it could well be that the original intention was to have judges do their work unconstrained by the understandings of specific framers. There is good reason to believe that this was the intent of the framers of the Canadian Charter of Rights and Freedoms (Schneiderman, 1991, 572).

Precedent

"Constitutional cases are determined by prior judicial decisions." Resort to precedent is a common feature of constitutional interpretation in the English-speaking world. In order to ensure stability and continuity in the constitutional order, judges are loathe to reverse or overrule decisions made by courts in earlier times. The doctrine of precedent prevents judges from too quickly upsetting settled rules and expectations.

There will be many occasions, however, when earlier decisions provide no conclusive or helpful answer to a contemporary constitutional question. Earlier judges may have developed principles of law too abstract to provide answers to new concrete questions. What if the earlier decision is just plain wrong, or what if a contemporary reading of the constitution suggests a different answer? In response to the reality that understandings of the constitution may change over time, judges have developed the idea of progressive interpretation. This technique recognizes that constitutions can grow, like a "living tree," and that judges must on occasion overrule or ignore precedent.

And so, while precedent is often a recurring constraint on judicial review, it may or may not provide helpful answers, and is itself open to interpretation and manipulation by the judiciary.

Text

"Judges need only refer to constitutional text in order to resolve constitutional questions." In this interpretive mode, the judiciary are expected to refer to the text of the constitution, not as the framers may have intended the text to be understood, but in light of contemporary understandings. Textual interpretation is a predominant mode of interpretation and the approach of first resort for many judges. The text, however, often provides guidance only at the start of any constitutional analysis.

The vagueness or "indeterminacy" of constitutional text means that the answers to many constitutional questions are often not apparent from the text alone. There are, admittedly, degrees of indeterminacy in constitutional text. Some provisions are quite clear. The Canadian Charter of Rights and Freedoms section 5 provides, for instance, that there "shall be a sitting of Parliament . . . at least once every twelve months." This is reasonably clear text. Other provisions are not so clear. For instance, according to section 8 of the Charter, "everyone has the right to be secure against unreasonable search and seizure." What is a reasonable search and seizure is not so self-evident. This requires filling out by the judiciary.

Structure

"Judges must identify the overall structural objectives of the constitution." This approach requires the judiciary to find the values underlying the constitutional document considered as a whole. It views the constitution as providing a framework for the practice of a certain form of politics. It seeks, in other words, a political theory of the constitution and looks at the purpose of the whole structure of the constitution. It is this structure that helps to determine the outcome in specific cases. The argument that judicial review reinforces democratic processes is one example of this kind of structural reading.

In order to apply structural reasoning, judges need more than what constitutional texts alone provide. Judges must identify the theory that underlies the constitution. They may look to the framer's theory or contemporary understandings. Often, there are two or three conflicting underlying frameworks. Moreover, even if a single unifying theme is identifiable, it may be so general as to be of little assistance to the judiciary in deciding concrete cases.

Democratic Process

" Judges interpret constitutional rights so as to ensure fairness and to remove blockages in the democratic process." This is the process-based rationale for judicial review under constitutions famously advanced by John Hart Ely. It is intended to reinforce the representative nature of the democratic process by ensuring full opportunity for all to participate in the process by which substantive values are "identified and accommodated" (Ely, 1980, 77). The interests most likely to be blocked or not accommodated by the democratic process are those of "discrete and insular minorities"—this is the language of U.S. Supreme Court Justice Stone in the *Carolene Products* case (1938). Laws that prejudice racial and other minorities are highly suspect under this approach. The legislative process giving rise to such laws are presumed to have failed to take into account the interests of those who have little or no voice in the law-making process.

Judicial review is here intended to reinforce the democratic process, leaving to elected legislators the determination of what substantive legislative goals to pursue. This is an attractive account of the judicial review function under constitutions for it attempts to reconcile that function with democratic and representative institutions of government. While this approach renders judicial review more legitimate, it also significantly narrows the scope of the judicial role. This approach does not justify, for instance, constitutional limitations that are not connected to the democratic process, such as the procedural protections of the criminally accused or of constitutional rights, such as those associated with Aboriginal self-government.

Balancing

" Judges must weigh constitutional rights against state interests." Rather than relying on any single criterion to guide the judiciary in constitutional interpretation, perhaps the better approach is to balance the interests at stake in any particular dispute. Constitutional disputes often pit individual claims against social interests advanced by legislation. The task of the judiciary in these cases is to weigh the individual against the social interest and decide which should take precedence.

In these cases, however, we must ask whether the judiciary are competent to weigh these social interests. Balancing draws the judiciary into areas of expertise far beyond that ordinarily expected of legally trained judges. Anxious about this problem of judicial competence, Justice La Forest, formerly of the Supreme Court of Canada, has argued that the best tactic is to defer to social interests whenever the legislature can show that it had a "reasonable basis" to conclude that it must impair individual rights. The government must also show that it has impaired those rights as little as possible (La Forest, 1996, 147).

Some observers have pointed out that balancing compromises the supremacy of the constitution. There is nothing in the Canadian Charter of Rights and Freedoms, for instance, that instructs the judiciary to weigh interests or engage in a cost-benefit analysis. It simply is inappropriate to weigh non-constitutional values equally against constitutionally recognized rights (Beatty, 1995, 89). Yet another concern is that judges are provided little guidance about when to prefer individual over societal values (Bakan, 1997, 31).

Morals

" Judges must identify the moral principles underlying constitutional rights." A moral reading of the constitution, a position usually associated with the legal philosopher Ronald Dworkin, admits that constitutional rights are drafted in the most general way possible. The framers who drafted those clauses intended for them to be read in their most natural sense, as referring to abstract moral principles that limit government power. It is the task of the judge to identify the best conception of those moral principles that are most consistent with the structural design of the constitution (Dworkin, 1996).

Judges are not asked to read their own personal morality into the constitutional text, but instead to identify the moral principles most consistent with the constitution. The political morality underlying the constitution, however, is not usually so clearly stated as to be uncontroversial. There may be no consensus about what that moral philosophy is or how it may have changed over time (Tushnet, 1988, 140-41). Moreover, no one moral philosophy provides sufficient guidance to judges for them to answer the specific constitutional problems they are asked to solve. Again, we must ask why judges in particular are in the best position to identify those underlying moral principles.

Purpose

" Judges must identify the purpose underlying each constitutional right." This is the preferred approach of the judiciary in Canada and South Africa (*Oakes* [1986]; *De Klerk* [1995]). Judicial discretion is constrained by ascertaining the purpose or objective underlying each protected right. The purpose is found by looking to the history of the right in question, other rights guaranteed in the constitution, the "larger objects" of the constitution, and the country's philosophical and political tradition.

It is difficult for the purposive approach to live up to its billing. It does not confine, in any meaningful way, judicial interpretation. The historical origins of rights and freedoms, and the political and philosophical values underlying the constitutional system, are not matters upon which all are agreed. The variety of sources that inform the purposive approach are contestable and so provide judges with little guidance or constraint (Bakan, 1997, 24).

Justification

"Limitations of rights and freedoms require convincing justification by government to the satisfaction of the judiciary." This approach is often invoked in combination with the purposive approach, as in Canada (*Oakes* [1986]). It has also been adopted in South Africa, where the new constitution has been described as "a bridge away from the culture of authority" to a "culture of justification" (Mureinik, 1994, 32). Judges first identify the purposes underlying the right or freedom in order to determine whether constitutional rights have been infringed. Next, governments justify that infringement to the satisfaction of the judiciary. Legislators may be required to prove that the public interest served by an infringement is of sufficient importance to warrant overriding constitutional rights and that the method (or means) chosen is the least oppressive. Strict scrutiny of the means used gives due weight to the fact that these are constitutional values that judges are enforcing. This standard of justification, it is argued, provides neutral and objective criteria for judges engaged in constitutional interpretation (Beatty, 1997, 150).

To the extent that the justification approach calls for balancing individual rights against societal interests, it exhibits the same problems we noted in our discussion of balancing. The second limb of the justification approach instructs judges to strike down laws whenever legislators choose methods that go too far in restricting rights. The problem is, it can often be shown that some other method will achieve the same objective. Justice Harry Blackmun of the United States Supreme Court wrote that "a judge would be unimaginative indeed if he could not come up with something less 'drastic' or a little 'less restrictive' in almost any situation" (Hogg, 1998, 726).

Institutional Solutions

SOME COMMENTATORS HAVE CONCLUDED THAT NO ONE OF THE INTERPRETIVE techniques we have reviewed fulfills the promise of sufficiently constraining the judiciary in the conduct of judicial review. Are there other alternatives?

Here we consider what might be called institutional solutions. These solutions provide a safety valve for the democratic process in the case of severe disagreement with the judiciary. One institutional solution, in those countries with a written constitution, is constitutional amendment—by changing the text of the written constitution. Constitutions, however, are intended to last for generations, and as the Canadian experience underscores, are difficult to amend.

A more manageable institutional solution that has been developed in Canada is to allow legislatures to override constitutional rights by invoking the **notwithstanding clause**. This clause enables provincial legislatures and the federal parliament to override most rights and freedoms notwithstanding their constitutional status. The clause recognizes that the democratic process will be the ultimate arbiter in constitutional disputes. A law that limits Charter rights can be protected from a declaration of constitutional invalidity for renewable five-year periods. All that is required is a resolution from the legislature or parliament by simple majority vote.

Resort to this institutional solution, however, brings us back to the central problem of political authority that was seemingly solved by the separation of powers. If legislative power is not separated from judicial power, then citizens are vulnerable to the overriding power of a legislative majority.

DEBATE BOX

Quebec's right to Separate

In 1994 the Parti Québécois won a majority in the Quebec Assembly under the leadership of Jacques Parizeau. The new government promised the Quebec electorate a second referendum on sovereignty. The first referendum had been defeated in May, 1980 by a margin of twenty percent. In the second referendum, held on October 30, 1995, Quebecers voted against sovereignty by the narrowest of margins—one percent. Clearly shaken by the prospect of another referendum and the breakup of Canada, in September 1996 the federal government asked the Supreme Court of Canada whether Quebec had the legal right to separate from Canada unilaterally. Three questions were placed before the Supreme Court.

1. Under the Constitution of Canada, can the National Assembly, legislature, or government of Quebec effect the secession of Quebec from Canada unilaterally?

2. Does international law give the National Assembly, legislature, or government of Quebec the right to effect the secession of Quebec from Canada unilaterally? In this regard, is there a right to self-determination under international law that would give the National Assembly, legislature, or government of Quebec the right to effect the secession of Quebec from Canada unilaterally?

3. In the event of a conflict between domestic and international law on the right of the National Assembly, legislature, or government of Quebec to effect the secession of Quebec from Canada unilater-

ally, which would take precedence in Canada?

Below are the excerpts from the Supreme Court decision which was rendered on Thursday, August 20, 1998.

On Question 1, the Supreme Court argued:

The Court in this Reference is required to consider whether Quebec has a right to unilateral secession. Arguments in support of the existence of such a right were primarily based on the principle of democracy. Democracy, however, means more than simple majority rule. Constitutional jurisprudence shows that democracy exists in the larger context of other constitutional values. Since Confederation, the people of the provinces and territories have created close ties of interdependence (economic, social, political and cultural) based on shared values that include federalism, democracy, constitutionalism and the rule of law, and respect for minorities. A democratic decision of Quebecers in favour of secession would put those relationships at risk. The Constitution vouchsafes order and stability, and accordingly secession of a province "under the Constitution" could not be achieved unilaterally, that is, without principled negotiation with other participants in Confederation within the existing constitutional framework.

Our democratic institutions necessarily accommodate a continuous process of discussion and evolution, which is reflected in the constitutional right of each participant in the federation to initiate constitutional change. This right implies a reciprocal duty on the other participants to engage in discussions to address any legitimate initiative to change the constitutional order. A clear majority vote in Quebec on a clear question in favour of secession would confer democratic legitimacy on the secession initiative which all of the other participants in Confederation would have to recognize.

Quebec could not, despite a clear referendum result, purport to invoke a right of self-determination to dictate the terms of a proposed secession to the other parties to the federation. The democratic vote, by however strong a majority, would have no legal effect on its own and could not push aside the principles of federalism and the rule of law, the rights of individuals and minorities, or the operation of democracy in the other provinces or in Canada as a whole. Democratic rights under the Constitution cannot be divorced from constitutional obligations. Nor, however, can the reverse proposition be accepted: the continued existence and operation of the Canadian constitutional order could not be indifferent to a clear expression of a clear majority of Quebecers that they no longer wish to remain in Canada. The other provinces and the federal government would have no basis to deny the right of the government of Quebec to pursue secession should a clear majority of the people of Quebec choose that goal, so long as in doing so, Quebec respects the rights of others. The negotiations that followed such a vote would address the potential act of secession as well as its possible terms should in fact secession proceed. There would be no conclusions predetermined by law on any issue. Negotiations would need to address the interests of the other provinces, the federal government and Quebec and indeed the rights of all Canadians both within and outside Quebec, and specifically the rights of minorities.

On Question 2:

The Court was also required to consider whether a right to unilateral secession exists under international law. Some supporting an affirmative answer did so on the basis of the recognized right to self-determination that belongs to all "peoples." Although much of the Quebec population certainly shares many of the characteristics of a people, it is not necessary to decide the "people" issue because, whatever may be the correct determination of this issue in the context of Quebec, a right to secession only arises under the principle of self-determination of people at international law where "a people" is governed as part of a colonial empire; where "a people" is subject to alien subjugation, domination or exploitation; and possibly where "a people" is denied any meaningful exercise of its right to self-determination within the state of which it forms a part. In other circumstances, peoples are expected to achieve self-determination within the framework of their existing state. A state whose government represents the whole of the people or peoples resident within its territory, on a basis of equality and without discrimination, and respects the principles of self-determination in its internal arrangements, is entitled to maintain its territorial integrity under international law and to have that territorial integrity recognized by other states. Quebec does not meet the threshold of a colonial people or an oppressed people, nor can it be suggested that Quebecers have been denied meaningful access to government to pursue their political, economic, cultural and social development. In the circumstances, the

"National Assembly, the legislature or the government of Quebec" do not enjoy a right under international law to effect the secession of Quebec from Canada unilaterally.

Finally, on Question 3, the Supreme Court answered that:

In view of the answers to Questions 1 and 2, there is no conflict between domestic and international law to be addressed in the context of this reference.

Do you agree with the Supreme Court's decision? How much of a majority would Quebec need to initiate negotiations on secession? What would be negotiated? What would be the outcome if either Quebec or the rest of Canada refused to negotiate?

Summary

We have reviewed the origins of an independent and impartial judiciary and the rise of judicial review as a check on the will of legislators in representative democracies. We have reviewed some of the justifications offered to support the idea that judges are empowered to overrule government choices. They include various techniques that have been developed over time to ensure that, in the course of interpreting the constitution, judicial rulings do not simply reflect judicial political preferences. Lastly, we have reviewed institutional solutions to the practice of judicial review in modern democracies.

Let us return now to the quote from Judge Learned Hand with which we began this chapter. Judge Hand warned us to not place too much emphasis on judicial review as a means of preserving political society. Judicial review cannot save a society where the "spirit of moderation" has been lost, he wrote. By a society that has lost the spirit of moderation, he means a society where citizens press political advantage to the fullest, where one side cannot "understand and respect the other side," and where there is no "unity between all citizens" (Hand, 1952, 181). Hand also tells us that, in those societies where the spirit of moderation flourishes, there is little that society needs from the judiciary.

We could conclude that, as no one society has captured fully that spirit of moderation, we will continue to be in need of a judiciary to oversee government action. But Learned Hand was not providing here a justification for the practice of judicial review—Hand was one judge who did not want to give the "last word" to the judiciary (Hand, 1952, 181). Instead, he probably meant to suggest that we should aspire to be the society he describes. In the process of governing, we might come to regard concern for others as we regard our own concerns. In other words, he was suggesting that we consider our constitutional commitments to equality and liberty as operational ideals; that we take these values seriously in our activities as a self-governing polity; and that we interpret those commitments in their best light and to the fullest advantage of all (West, 1994). In such a political society, Hand would agree, judicial oversight would be superfluous.

Discussion Questions

1. Do you agree that individual liberty is advanced by having an independent judiciary?

2. Do you think the public are concerned that the judiciary have the power to declare that laws enacted by the legislature are invalid by reason of the constitution?

3. Do judges simply reflect the dominant viewpoints held by society-at-large? If so, are they really a check on the majority?

4. Do you think that any of the techniques of interpretation constrain judges so that their judgments simply do not follow from their political beliefs?

5. Can you imagine other kinds of institutional solutions to the problem of judicial review? Can you imagine a political regime in which judges would not be able to overrule majority wishes? Would you want to live under such a regime?

References

Ackerman, Bruce. 1991. *We the People: Foundations,* vol. 1. Cambridge: Harvard University Press.

Bakan, Joel. 1997. *Just Words: Constitutional Rights and Social Wrongs.* Toronto: University of Toronto Press.

Blackstone, William. 1979. *Commentaries on the Laws of England,* Volume 1. Chicago: Chicago University Press [facsimile of first edition 1765B1769].

Beatty, David. 1995. *Constitutional Law in Theory and Practice.* Toronto: University of Toronto Press.

Bobbit, Philip. 1982. *Constitutional Fate: Theory of the Constitution.* New York: Oxford University Press.

Bork, Robert. 1990. *The Tempting of America: The Political Seduction of the Law.* New York: The Free Press.

Corwin, Edward S. 1955. *The "Higher Law" Background of American Constitutional Law.* Ithaca: Cornell University Press.

Dicey, A.V. 1908. *Introduction to the Study of the Law of the Constitution,* 7th ed. London: Macmillan and Co.

Dicey, A.V. 1948. *Lectures of the Relation Between Law and Public Opinion in England During the Nineteenth Century,* 2nd ed. London: Macmillan and Co.

Dworkin, Ronald. 1996. *Freedom's Law: The Moral Reading of the American Constitution.* Cambridge: Harvard University Press.

Ely, John Hart. 1980. *Democracy and Distrust: A Theory of Judicial Review.* Cambridge: Harvard University Press.

Hamilton, Alexander, James Madison and John Jay. 1961. *The Federalist Papers,* ed. by C. Rossiter. New York: New American Library.

Hand, Learned. 1952. *The Spirit of Liberty: Papers and Addresses of Learned Hand,* ed. by I. Dillard. New York. Alfred A. Knopf.

Hogg, Peter W. 1998. *Constitutional Law of Canada.* Student Edition. Scarborough: Carswell.

La Forest, G.V. Hon. 1992. "The Balancing of Interests Under the Charter" *National Journal of Constitutional Law* 2: 133B162.

Locke, John. 1988. *Two Treatises of Government.* ed. by Peter Laslett. Cambridge: Cambridge University Press.

MacKinnon, Catherine. 1989. *Toward a Feminist Theory of the State.* Cambridge: Harvard University Press.

Maitland, F.W. 1919. *The Constitutional History of England.* Cambridge: Cambridge University Press.

McIlwain, C.H. 1910. *The High Court of Parliament and its Supremacy.* New Haven: Yale University Press.

Monahan, Patrick. 1987. *Politics and the Constitution: The Charter, Federalism and the Supreme Court of Canada.* Toronto: Carswell.

Morton F.L. and Rainer Knopff. 2000. *The Charter Revolution and the Court Party.* Peterborough: Broadview Press.

Mureinik, Etienne. 1994. "A Bridge to Where? Introducing the Interim Bill of Rights" 10 South African Journal on Human Rights 31.

Schneiderman, David. 1991. "Taking Documents Seriously" 2 Supreme Court Law Review (2d) 555.

Sniderman, Paul M., Joseph E. Fletcher, Peter H. Russell and Philip E. Tetlock. 1996. *The Clash of Rights: Liberty, Equality, and Legitimacy in a Pluralist Democracy.* New Haven: Yale University Press.

Spann, Girardeau A. 1993. *Race Against the Court: The Supreme Court and Minorities in Contemporary America.* New York: New York University Press.

Thompson, Edward P. 1975. *Whigs and Hunters: The Origin of the Black Act.* New York: Pantheon Books.

Tushnet Mark V. 1988. *Red, White, and Blue: A Critical Analysis of Constitutional Law.* Cambridge: Harvard University Press.

Tushnet, Mark V. 1994. *Making Civil Rights Law: Thurgood Marshall and the Supreme Court, 1936–1961.* New York: Oxford University Press.

Amendment. Durham: Duke University Press.

Cases

Brown v. Board of Education, 347 United States Reports 483 (1954).

United States v. *Carolene Products Co.,* 304 United States Reports 144 (1938).

Dr. Bonham's Case, (1610) 8 Coke Reports 114a.

Edwards v. Attorney General of Canada, [1930] Appeal Cases 123.

Lochner v. New York, 198 United States Reports 45 (1905).

Marbury v. Madison, 5 United States Reports 137 (1803).

R. v. Delgamuukw, [1997] 3 Supreme Court Reports 1010.

R. v. Oakes, [1986] 1 Supreme Court Reports 103.

Reference re: Secession of Quebec, (1998) 161 Dominion Law Reports (4th) 385.

S. v. Makwanyane, 1995 (3) South African Law Reports 391.

Vriend v. Alberta, (1998) 156 Dominion Law Reports (4th) 385.

Further Readings

Bakan, Joel. 1997. *Just Words: Constitutional Rights and Social Wrongs.* Toronto: University of Toronto Press.

Hogg, Peter W. 1998. *Constitutional Law of Canada.* Student edition. Scarborough: Carswell.

Morton, F. L. and Rainer Knopff. 2000. *The Charter Revolution and the Court Party.* Peterborough: Broadview Press.

Weblinks

Canadian Constitutional Documents
www.solon.org/Constitutions/Canada/English/

Centre for Constitutional Studies
www.law.ualberta.ca/centres/ccs/

Constitutional Studies Web Page
www.law.utoronto.ca/conlit/conlit1.htm

Supreme Court of Canada / Cour suprème du Canada
www.scc—csc.gc.ca/

Supreme Court of Canada Decisions
www.lexum.umontreal.ca/csc—scc/

United States Supreme Court Decisions
supct.law.cornell.edu/supct/
www.findlaw.com/casecode/supreme.html

United States Supreme Court Multimedia Database
http://oyez.nwu.edu/

Constitutional Court of South Africa Decisions
www.concourt.gov.za/

Constitutions of the World
www.richmond.edu/~jpjones/confinder/
http://www.psr.keele.ac.uk/const.htm
http://www.uni—wuerzburg.de/law/index.html

J. PAUL
JOHNSTON
and
HAROLD J.
JANSEN

CHAPTER 11

ELECTIONS AND ELECTORAL SYSTEMS

Objectives

When most people think about politics, elections come immediately to mind. As Katz puts it, "Elections are the defining institutions of modern democracy" (1997, 3). Yet, the manner in which elections are used in contemporary democracies and the impact they have on the quality of democracy achieved are controversial matters. Contemporary elections are large-scale, highly complex, collective events and many smaller, more specific events take place within their purview. Elections reflect the extent to which democracy requires the sometimes difficult coordination of many organizations, groups, and individuals in arriving at "government by consent."

Often the formal aspects of the conduct of elections, and the provisions set out in the **electoral system**, are not well understood by citizens, and in this chapter, we attempt to redress this situation. We first consider the role elections play in modern politics, noting how they have been differently employed in constitutions to implement democratic and republican principles of governance. Next, we set out the notion of an electoral system and describe its basic components and purposes. This is followed by a discussion that contrasts the two main kinds of electoral systems in use—those based on majority rule and those based on the proportional representation (PR) of different groups and interests in a society. The strengths and weaknesses of these two systems are assessed and a brief discussion of an increasingly popular alternative to them— "mixed" electoral systems—follows. Finally, we consider the properties that seem most desirable in electoral systems and the general issue of electoral reforms aimed at achieving the promise that democratic politics holds out to citizens everywhere.

Introduction

Among the different mechanisms that link citizens to the governing process in contemporary democracies, elections are the most prominent and most extensive in impact. Indeed, modern elections play an important role in establishing and maintaining representative democracy. Their primary function is to provide a means of selecting those who will hold high public office and exercise the authority attached to such positions. While there are a number of ways this could be done, elections offer a means that extends participation to a broad segment of the citizenry. They also carry out the transfer of control of such offices from one subset of the activist political elite to another in a (usually) peaceful manner. In both respects, their use attests that governing takes place by the consent of those governed.

When conducted in a free and fair manner, elections produce open competition among office-seekers and ideas, giving citizens a range of choices in deciding who is best suited to govern and what ideas should prevail in the governing process. Elections provide a public forum in which any citizen can draw attention to important issues and raise questions about how these have been dealt with, if at all, by current officials. In this regard, elections offer a means of assessing the support that prospective leaders and their policies have among the citizenry.

Electing public officials also extends representation in the councils of government to those participating in making those choices and their dependents. In a sense, popularly elected public officials become the agents of the electors. Moreover, the duties attached to those public offices that are made elective generally include the representation of the interests and concerns of residents in the jurisdictions they serve. Democratic norms make such public officials accountable to those they govern by requiring them to renew their authorization in subsequent elections. Thus, when used on a regular, periodic basis to fill offices, elections provide both a formal means of renewing authorization and a context in which officials show accountability for their performance. In a recent effort to set principles and measures for performing an audit of democratic performance, David Beetham identifies the principle of popular control with that of political equality, as the "guiding thread" of that work, further underscoring the importance of elections (Beetham, 1999, 27–30).

Apart from these largely institutional functions, elections also provide certain benefits to citizens on an individual basis. For example, they provide a context in which people can participate in the democratic political process, giving expression to their sense of civic responsibility. Elections play an educational role, informing people about the issues and problems of the day, the solutions that current and prospective leaders and activists propose, and the controversies involved in proposed remedies. They provide opportunities for citizens to debate political issues, to become involved in partisan organizations, work on campaigns, and even become candidates for elected office. And, in so doing, elections offer citizens a chance to acquire skills useful in participating more generally in the political process.

Elections also contribute to the legitimacy of those elected, the policy agendas they advocate, the governmental actions they assume, or the criticisms they might levy against such actions. To the extent that the conduct of elections serves the purposes indicated above, the legitimacy of the electoral process is enhanced. In turn, the value of the role it plays in the wider political process is affirmed, and the claims on public office of the victors in elections are legitimized. To the extent that such support and stability leads government to meet the needs of the citizenry more effectively and addresses their concerns in open, fair, and considerate fashion, the promise that democracy offers is fulfilled.

More than any other political institution, elections symbolize that promise. This has not always been so. Though elections have long been used, Arend Lijphart tells us that "Democracy is a recent and rare phenomenon," adding "(n)ot a single democratic government can be found in the nineteenth century," though he observes that "its growth in the twentieth century has been spectacular," (1984, 37). At the beginning of the twenty-first century, elections are widely used in nations where the political traditions from which modern democracy evolved are less entrenched.

There is considerable debate regarding the extent to which elections in such countries link governments to their citizens in ways that make democracy a real enterprise. In some, "free" elections are no more than plebiscites ratifying government-nominated candidates. In others, corruption and restrictions on candidacy make "free choice" and legitimate opposition a sham. Similarly, crass manipulation of the electoral process by elites, intimidation, and the likelihood that elected officials may never be allowed to take up their positions undermine efforts to establish democracy in meaningful terms (Harrop and Miller, 1987). In these instances, elections primarily serve a ritual function, providing only a surface impression of democracy.

This debate is also taking place in the established liberal democracies of the founding tradition (see Ginsberg, 1982). Its skepticism extends beyond scholarly circles to include both the so-called "chattering classes"—the media and academics—and a significant portion of the citizenry. The role elections are thought to play is under intense scrutiny in some quarters and the democratic promise they offer is increasingly questioned. Understanding the source of that promise, as well as the skepticism about its realization, begins with a fuller appreciation of how constitutional design and electoral systems shape the role of elections and the success they enjoy in making democracy a reality.

Constitutional Design and the Electoral Process

CONSTITUTIONS ESTABLISH THE ROLE THAT ELECTIONS PLAY IN THE POLITICS of a nation (Rose, 1983). For example, by designating that certain political offices are elective, they establish the democratic principle in the legal and institutional framework of government. Those basic rights required to conduct elections freely and fairly are usually specified in a nation's constitution, along with other rights reflecting freedoms of belief, expression, and association.

The number and type of offices made elective has sometimes been taken as a measure of the extent to which the democratic principle is observed. All nations professing to be democratic choose the members of their primary legislative councils by direct election, although the second chamber of a bicameral legislature is often not elective. Canadian senators, for example, are appointed by the prime minister and can remain in office until they reach the age of seventy-five. See Table 11.1 for the 170 nations with a working national assembly.[1] The majority of democracies also provide for the direct election of the chief political executive office, usually a president (see Table 11.1). These are the only two national-level governmental offices filled through popular elections in most nations.[2] Even then, notable differences still exist across regime types and geographic regions, as Table 11.1 indicates.

For example, consider the differences between Canada and the United States. The American president is directly elected, but Canada's prime minister is not. On the other hand, the prime minister must be an elected member of Canada's House of Commons and, by convention, so must those holding Cabinet positions. In the United States, the president appoints the members of the Cabinet and both they and the president are expressly precluded from being simultaneously members of the Congress. American voters can hold their president directly responsible for his or her performance, whereas Canadian voters can exercise popular control over their prime minister only by threatening the majority standing of his or her party in the Commons. And while Canadian cabinet ministers are directly accountable through the electoral process, unlike their American counterparts, it is only the local constituents of a Canadian cabinet minister who can exercise that popular control. In both instances, institutional arrangements make holding executive officers popularly accountable more complicated than democratic rhetoric suggests.

That effort is also made more difficult in presidential/congressional systems by the ways in which the separation of powers between the executive and legislative branches force those controlling one branch to share control over the policy process with those controlling the other. If opposing partisan camps dominate the two branches, outright competition develops. This often leads to what Americans call "gridlock," wherein one popularly elected branch of government can block the policy agenda of the other branch whose members can claim equal legitimacy to set policy based on their elective status. This makes it difficult to hold those in either branch responsible for failing to fulfill their promises. Such situations do not arise in parliamentary systems. However, the exercise of popular control is so indirect and requires such complex nation-wide coordination that the elective status of officials offers little leverage over them. As a result, where one aspect of constitutional design—making offices elective—creates the opportunity for popular control over governments, another aspect—how power is distributed across offices and institutions—may limit its effective exercise.

Constitutional design is also reflected in the structure of the national assembly. It can be unicameral or bicameral. Bicameral legislatures mirror the opportunities and problems arising from establishing a separation of powers. They can enhance or limit the quality of representation made available through making offices elective and the popular control the electoral process offers. Frequently, the members of one chamber are appointed or,

TABLE 11.1   *Regional Differences in the Scope of the Elective Principle*
[N = 170 nations]

REGION	NUMBER OF NATIONS	DEMOCRACY: POLITICAL RIGHTS[1]		FORM OF GOVERNMENT (% OF REGION N)		DIRECTLY ELECTED PRESIDENT		BICAMERAL NATIONAL ASSEMBLY	ELECTED NATIONAL CHAMBER	
		7-6	1-2	MONARCHIES	REPUBLICS	%	N	%	%	N
Anglo-America	6	6	0	67	33	100	2	83	60	5
Scandinavia	5	5	0	60	40	100	2	0	—	—
Western Europe	16	16	0	38	63	30	10	50	50	8
Eastern Europe	12	5	2	0	100	50	12	50	67	6
Former USSR[2]	15	1	5	0	100	93	15	33	40	5
Africa	40	10	16	7	93	87	37	30	25	12
Middle East[3]	11	2	5	18	82	56	9	69	0	1
Asia	20	4	6	30	70	43	14	35	43	7
Pacific Oceania	12	10	0	42	58	29	7	20	50	2
Caribbean	13	9	1	62	38	40	5	69	22	9
Central America	8	3	0	12	88	100	7	25	50	2
South America	12	7	0	0	100	92	12	67	75	8

SOURCE: Inter-Parliamentary Union PARLINE Database, information about forms of government and direct election of presidents taken from Blais, Massicotte and Dobrzynska (1997), Appendix: 453–55. Freedom House Ratings of Democracy: Political Rights taken from Blais and Massicotte (1997) Appendix A: 118-24.

[1] High rating is "7–6," low rating is "1-2". The original Freedom House ratings use a seven-point format with "1" as the highest rating and "7" as the lowest. Blais and Massicotte convert these to a "0.0 – 1.0" seven point scale with "1.0" as the highest rating.
[2] The "Former USSR" grouping includes Armenia, Azerbaijan, Belarus, Estonia, Georgia, Kazakhstan, Kyrgystan, Latvia, Lithuania, Moldova, Russian Federation, Tajikistan, Turkmenistan, Ukraine, and Uzbekistan.
[3] Cyprus, Egypt and Israel are included in the Middle East grouping with Iran, Iraq, Jordan, Kuwait, Lebanon, Syria, Turkey, and Yemen.

at best, indirectly elected by elective officials in some other part of government. The basis on which representation is distributed to organizations, groups, or individuals may also differ across the two chambers with important consequences. Representation in one chamber might reflect regional interests or those of particular economic, cultural, ethnic, or linguistic segments of the population, whereas the other might serve as a forum for expressing broad majority "consent." If the members of each chamber are directly elected, the electoral rules may differ in ways that affect the outcomes and alter the role the electoral process plays, structuring electoral competition differently in each case. Here, whether government is organized on a federal or a unitary basis also becomes relevant. Federalism is typically adopted to accommodate regional differences, which are usually reflected in the creation of a second chamber in which regional concerns and governments are specifically represented. In the United States, for example, each state, regardless of population size, elects two senators. The prevalence of bicameral national assemblies is indicated in Table 11.1.

Election Laws and Electoral Systems

LAWS GOVERN ALMOST EVERY ASPECT OF ORGANIZING AND CONDUCTING AN election. Their content ranges from constitutional provisions requiring the election of public officials to regulations that set voting hours. Fortunately, it is sufficient for our purposes to group these laws into four broad categories and discuss them in terms of the main functions each serves in the electoral process. We will also develop an understanding of the concept of an "electoral system."

The first category covers definition of **constituencies**. It identifies those "constituents" on whose behalf an elected official acts, indicates how they attain that status, and the procedures involved in establishing it. This varies across different kinds of elective office. Executive officers in national governments typically act on behalf of all citizens. In contrast, representation in a national assembly is usually extended to separate groups of citizens by setting out territorial districts or "constituencies," then assigning each district one or more elected representatives. The number of representatives assigned is called the constituency's "**district magnitude,**" one of the most important aspects of constituency definition. Where the entire nation serves as a single district, its magnitude equals the size of the assembly. Only those members of the assembly assigned to a particular electoral district formally represent residents in that district and only electors in that district can vote to choose them. This is so even though each member of a national assembly represents the whole nation, not just their particular constituency, when acting jointly with other members in carrying out their duties. It underscores the problems of coordination involved in voters exercising popular control over governments.

This "local vs. national" contrast is also reflected in the notion of district magnitude. At one extreme are those nations that create single-member districts (SMDs), electing one representative for each district. Canada, the United States, the United Kingdom, and several Commonwealth countries are examples. At the other extreme are electoral systems that treat the entire nation as one district. Israelis elect their 120 member Knesset to represent the nation as a whole, with the entire country serving as one district. Nations that adopt a majoritarian electoral system generally use SMDs, though sometimes they employ dual or multimember ones. Nations employing proportional representation invariably use multimember districts.[3]

Deciding how and on what basis to divide up representation in legislative bodies is known as apportionment. *Malapportionment* is the overrepresentation of one interest or group at the expense of another. Here, geography often plays an important role. People have to reside somewhere, so that becomes a convenient basis for grouping them together. It is sometimes overlooked that every nation uses territorially defined districts at some level in extending representation. A common practice is to divide the larger community into a number of smaller territorial districts and then assign one or more members of the assembly to represent each of these districts. Setting the boundaries is simply called **districting.** Drawing them in ways that deliberately create an advantage for some group, or cause disadvantage to another is known as **gerrymandering**.

Typically, the allocation of representation to various parts of a nation is a controversial matter. To ensure fairness, a formal procedure for allocating representation is established that apportions representation to different groups of citizens, usually in terms of geographically defined districts. It also sets out various criteria to be used in defining the boundaries of these districts. In Canada, for example, seats in the House of Commons are first assigned to the different provinces and territories in numbers roughly proportional to their populations. In other words, the creation of constituencies reflects the principle of **"representation by population."** Under this principle, equal representation is best achieved by setting boundaries that group together roughly equal numbers of citizens, but with latitude to accommodate other concerns, such as local communities of interests and the efficient delivery of a representative's services. Though such criteria are intended to produce effective representation, fairly shared among the citizens of a province, this is not easily achieved. For example, a remote area with a sparse population may be given the same representation as a densely populated urban district, violating the "rep by pop" principle. This is done to take account of difficulties the remoteness of the area is alleged to create in providing effective and efficient representation. Sometimes seats are reserved for a group whose members warrant special recognition to guarantee representation, as is done for New Zealand's Aboriginal Maori people. These tasks are carried out by different bodies in different nations, though the practice of setting up politically independent commissions to do them has become more common lately. In Canada, such commissions are established in each province to set out the boundaries of the districts contained within its boundary.

A second broad set of election laws defines who can participate in the electoral process, their capacities, and activities. One subset indicates the suffrage requirements persons must meet in order to be eligible to vote in elections. Such laws govern the extension of the **franchise** to wider segments of the citizenry. Another subset of laws included here specify candidacy criteria that one must satisfy to stand for election, plus those rules and administrative procedures to be followed in declaring and pursuing their candidacy. These include regulations about nomination procedures and endorsements, campaign finance and expenditures, access to and use of the mass media, and fair campaign practices. Broadly speaking, these laws address access to the electoral process of candidates, of voters, and of campaign activists.

Choices voters can make in casting their ballot and how they are to be expressed are the focus of the third broad category of election laws. These essentially specify the form ballots can take (ballot structure). Are voters to choose between political parties or among candidates? If the latter, do they choose among individual candidates or lists of candidates in some fixed order of priority (slates) set out by party leaders? If party list ballots are used, do they allow voters to indicate preferences within a given list or to distribute votes over several different lists (panachage)? Are voters to make simple choices among the candidates or parties (a **categorical ballot**) and, if so, how many choices? Or, are they asked to rank order (some of) the candidates, indicating their relative acceptability to the voter (an **ordinal** or **preferential ballot**)? In some instances, two or more parties can endorse a candidate and then have their vote totals combined in support of him or her in the final count (a **fused ballot**). In some proportional representation systems, parties must amass a specified minimum number of votes (a formal threshold) before they can participate in the proportional allocation of votes.

Our final category sets out rules that apply to counting the valid votes, combining and/or comparing vote totals for different parties or candidates, and determining the winner. In short, they provide the details of the electoral formula that is applied to translate a distribution of vote totals across a set of candidates or parties into a distribution of seats won by those who met the standard set by the formula. Sometimes more than one level or "tier" of districts is set out and a different kind of formula applied for the higher tier(s), usually to "fine tune" the proportionality of seat allocations. Typically, the standard set specifies a quota of votes or some proportion of the valid vote cast that one must amass in order to win a position. The decision rule applied may be that one must win more votes than any other competitor (a *plurality rule*) or at least one vote more than the sum of the votes other competitors won (a *simple majority rule*). The electoral formulae comprising one broad family of formulae are designed to distribute seats in an assembly to parties in shares that approximate as closely as possible the share of the total valid vote that each party gained. These are called *proportional representation formulae*, and they come in an almost bewildering variety of forms.

The entire set of rules, procedures, and institutional arrangements that governs how the electoral process is organized and conducted and shapes its outcomes, is known as an **electoral system**. Each time we change one of its component parts, we create a new electoral system (Lijphart, 1994, 13); hence, the variety available is potentially enormous. Different classification systems have been suggested, but the most common practice has been to group them into the two broad families: *majoritarian electoral systems* and *proportional representation systems*.

Majoritarian Electoral Systems

In *majoritarian* systems, elections are primarily meant to provide popular support for governments and legitimize their claim to govern. This is best accomplished when they can claim to have the support of a majority of the voters, i.e., that "majority rule" prevails. Yet, whenever there are more than two candidates or parties competing, it is possible, even likely, that none will gain a majority of the votes and the election will prove indecisive. One option here is to hold another "run-off" election a short time later between the top two candidates in the earlier election, thereby ensuring a majority decision. A variant of this procedure uses a preferential ballot in the first election, then drops the least popular candidate and transfers his or her votes to other candidates according to the second preferences indicated, repeating the process until someone has a majority of the votes. Originally known as the *alternative vote*, it is now called *instant run-off voting* in the United States and Britain where it is currently enjoying renewed interest among the reform-minded. The members of the first chamber of Australia's parliament are elected by this procedure. It was also used in Canada to elect the rural members of the provincial legislative assemblies in Alberta and Manitoba from 1924 to 1955 (Jansen, 1998).

Converting to a **plurality system** is a more common remedy for the potential indecisiveness of the majority formula. Here, the winners are those candidates or parties that receive more votes than any other opponent does. The plurality rule is most commonly combined with single member districts and a **simple candidate ballot,** creating the *first-past-the-post* electoral system (FPTP). Originating in Britain and still employed there, the FPTP system is primarily used in countries that share the British political tradition, such as Canada and the United States. Among the nations surveyed in Table 11.1, 47 use it to choose the members of their unicameral national assembly; another 32 employ it to elect the lower chamber in bicameral assemblies and 17 apply it in choosing members of the upper chamber (see also Blais and Massicotte, 1997, 111). Plurality systems are also commonly used in presidential elections (Blais, Massicotte, and Dobrzynska, 447).

The plurality formula encourages two-party competition in elections, especially when coupled with single-member districts as in FPTP. People who might otherwise vote for parties that have little chance of winning presumably are persuaded to switch their support to a more viable party. Ultimately, all minor party support shifts to one of the two main competitors and a two-party system is produced. This, in turn, leads to majority outcomes. Consequently, proponents argue that plurality systems lead to more stable and decisive government. They also note that accountability is clearer and more direct under FPTP since each district has only one representative and can choose to reward or punish that official as fits their judgment of his or her performance in office. Indeed, this is often cited as FPTP's strongest and most attractive feature. Opponents counter that it encourages insincere, tactical voting that gives a misleading impression of true voter preferences and, in the long run, reduces the choice available to two very similar, centrist parties or candidates.

Several serious problems can arise from using a plurality formula. The least of these is that it is almost impossible to predict what a winning vote will be, as that varies with the number of candidates and the distribution of votes. Like the majority rule, a plurality formula also discriminates against minorities or small parties, unless their vote is sufficiently concentrated in a few districts to allow them to attain pluralities. Moreover, where local concentration of a minority does allow it to gain plurality victories, the result can create striking regional discrepancies between vote shares and seat shares won. This can give a misleading impression of the degree to which regional differences divide a country, thereby intensifying those tensions actually present. Canada presents perhaps the most graphic, long-standing example of such an impact, most recently seen in the results of the 2000 federal election displayed in Table 11.2.

DEBATE BOX

Should Canada Adopt a PR Electoral System?

Compare the Canadian election results to the use of a proportional system in the table below. The column "2000" shows the actual distribution of seat shares of the major parties as a result of Canada's first-past-the-post plurality electoral system. The column "PR" shows what the seat shares would have been if Canada had a proportional representation system.

In what ways would a PR system have changed the federal election results? Would the results from the PR system have been preferable? Why? Why not? Should Canada adopt a PR electoral system? Why? Why not?

TABLE 11.2   Distribution of seats in the 2000 Canadian general election under a hypothetical proportional representation electoral system* [entries are number of seats won by each party]

PROVINCE	LIBERAL		CANADIAN ALLIANCE		PROGRESSIVE CONSERVATIVES		BLOC QUEBECOIS		NEW DEMOCRATS		OTHER	
POLITICAL PARTIES	2000	PR	2000	PR	2000	PR	2000	PR	2000	PR	2000	PR
Atlantic Region	19	13	–	3	9	11	–	–	4	5	–	–
Quebec	36	34	–	5	1	4	38	30	–	1	–	1
Ontario	100	53	2	25	–	15	–	–	1	9	–	1
Prairies	7	8	14	11	1	3	–	–	6	7	–	–
Rockies/Pacific	7	16	50	33	1	5	–	–	2	5	–	1
Territories	3	3	–	–	–	–	–	–	–	–	–	–
Totals	**172**	**127**	**66**	**77**	**12**	**37**	**38**	**30**	**13**	**27**	**0**	**3**

Note*: PR projections based on unofficial vote totals from Elections Canada's website and assume that each province serves as a single at-large district, a party-list ballot is used, and no legal threshold is imposed. A largest remainder formula with a Droop quota is applied. Results calculated by Harold J. Jansen, Department of Political Science, University of Lethbridge.

Green Party: 2 seats (Ontario, British Columbia); Marijuana Party: 1 seat (Quebec).

Prairies: Manitoba and Saskatchewan; Rockies/Pacific :Alberta and British Columbia

Another problem is perhaps even more serious from a democratic perspective: the winning total in a plurality system can be a rather small share of the overall vote. For example, in the 1997 Canadian federal election, a Manitoba district was won with just over 28 percent of the vote. Where there are 11 candidates and a near-uniform distribution of votes, for example, an office could be won with as little as 10 percent of the vote cast. Thus, more votes are "wasted" (cast either for losing candidates or in excess of the minimum number required to win the position) and more voters are left "unrepresented" (having voted for parties that won no seats) in plurality elections than under any other system. This is dramatically illustrated by the results of the Canadian federal elections held in 1993, 1997, and 2000. If one sums the votes gained by all the winning candidates on the government side in each of the first two elections they make up only 30.8 percent and 25.9 percent, respectively, of the total valid vote cast on each occasion. These are voters whose votes actually "counted" in that *they* decided who would govern in each instance. In both elections, a single-party majority government was produced, though far less than a majority of voters supported it. In fact, when one factors in the spoiled ballots and the turnout rates in those elections, about one-fifth of the electorate was able to determine which party would form the government. The majority rule justification of plurality systems pales in the face of such results. Creating such manufactured majorities by awarding an unearned majority of seats to the leading party is probably the plurality formula's most serious weakness from a democratic perspective. However, proponents of the plurality rule see this as a positive feature, one that produces stable "majority government." Indeed, most of the single-party majority governments formed in nations using an FPTP system have been manufactured by its use (Lijphart, 1994, 98; 1999, 166). Such results have occurred in more than half (thirteen) of the last twenty-four federal elections in Canada, including the three most recent elections (1993,1997, and 2000), with minority governments being formed on eight other occasions. In Britain, this has happened in twelve of the last twenty parliamentary elections, with either a minority or coalition government resulting in four others.

Another feature of the plurality rule is its tendency to amplify small changes in the vote share of candidates from one election to the next in competitive districts to create large changes in seat shares. Proponents see this as indicating that a plurality rule is more responsive to changes in voters' preferences over time, something they view as a positive feature. Opponents point out that this can effectively allow a relatively small "rogue" segment of the electorate to dictate sweeping policy changes not desired by the large majority of voters who voted according to their traditional preferences. They note that it can be a source of serious instability when an electorate is badly split over some matter on a continuing basis that allows such a volatile minority segment to determine which side prevails based on its limited interests or short-term preferences. This weakness and the other problems arising from the use of majoritarian electoral systems lead others to endorse the other great principle widely used to organize the electoral process: proportional representation.

Proportional Representation Systems

Those who prefer proportional representation systems believe that the main purpose of elections is to represent accurately the diverse interests and opinions in the electorate.

They argue that the share of seats a party wins should be as closely equal to the share of votes it won as is mathematically possible. They also argue that assigning seats in proportion to the share of the total vote won by a party gives representation to almost all voters. Any party that wins a vote share equal to one or more multiples of a predetermined quota should be awarded a number of seats equal to that number. Obviously, this requires the use of multi-member districts.

Proportional representation systems come in two forms. One uses relatively large district magnitudes and a **party-list ballot**. In each district every party supplies a slate of candidates and voters choose among the several party lists. Seats won by a party are assigned to individual candidates in the order they appear on their party's list, so the party officials decide who will be chosen to represent its supporters. Candidates ranked high on the list are virtually assured election. In most cases, voters simply vote for a whole party list, but in several nations they can also choose among candidates on a party list and, by so doing, alter the rankings party officials set out. In Switzerland, voters can even choose candidates from different parties' lists (panachage)**,** thereby making the process more candidate-centred.

Votes cast for the different lists are totalled separately in each district and seats are assigned to parties by either a divisor or a quota procedure. In each instance the procedure essentially establishes the "price" or "cost" of a seat, expressed in votes. Under the divisor methods, this price changes to reflect the portion of its vote total a party has already "spent" in acquiring seats, inasmuch as the divisors change to reflect the number of seats won (seats are assigned one at a time, sequentially). Each party's quotient indicates how many votes it has available to "bid" for a remaining seat, with the seat being won by the highest "bid." Under a quota procedure the total number of valid votes cast is divided by the number of seats assigned to its district. This sets a quota of votes that must be won to gain a seat that remains fixed for the entire allocation process. To determine how many seats a party has won, one divides its valid vote total by this quota.

The second type of PR, the **single transferable vote** (STV) or Hare System, is only used to elect the Irish Dail, the Australian Senate, Malta's House of Representatives, and the Belfast Assembly in Northern Ireland. It is currently of renewed interest to American advocates of electoral reform under a new label—*choice voting.* In contrast to party-list PR systems, voters choose among candidates, not parties. They rank the candidates in preference and votes are then transferred among candidates based on these rankings in a manner similar to the alternative vote, except multi-member districts are used and a vote quota is established that one must attain to win a seat. Here, votes winners attain beyond the required quota are also transferred according to lower preferences, in addition to those from "dropped" candidates. This counting and vote transfer procedure is rather complex and can involve many rounds of transfers and new counts when the number of seats allocated is large, so the district magnitude is usually kept quite small for STV elections. Doing so makes it more conservative in awarding seats to small splinter parties, which some of its proponents find attractive. Following the First World War it was used for local elections in several cities and towns in Western Canada and in various parts of the United States. It is still used for municipal elections in Cambridge, Massachusetts. From the early 1920s to 1955, the members of the provincial assemblies in Alberta and Manitoba who represented Calgary, Edmonton, and Winnipeg, respectively, were also chosen by STV (Johnston, 1992; Jansen, 1998). More recently, it has been suggested for use in electing members of the Canadian Senate, should reform be made.

All electoral systems award a "bonus" of seats to the leading party and penalize small parties, demonstrating that none is completely unbiased in allocating seats (Rae, 1971, 69–72). However, the difference between parties' seat shares and vote shares tends to be quite small in PR systems, thus confirming its supporters' claims about PR's fairness. In his recent survey of 36 democracies, Lijphart reports that the average disproportionality occurring in PR systems ranged from 1.30% (Netherlands) to 14.41% (Venezuela) with a median value of 3.25% (Italy), and the three highest values (all greater than 10.5%) were in nations with an elected president. By contrast, in majoritarian systems the range extended from 5.03% (Japan's SNTV system) to 21.08% (France), with a median value of 11.74% in Botswana (Lijphart, 199, 162).

The most important factor leading to these results is the district magnitude. One can hardly divide one seat proportionally among several parties or candidates, so PR systems require using multi-member districts, the magnitudes of which typically vary across the districts in a nation. Moreover, the district magnitude plays a key role in determining the "fit" between vote shares and seat shares, since it defines the implicit "threshold" in vote quotas that a party must surpass to win a given number of seats. The more seats a district has, the lower that threshold becomes. Thus, small parties are more likely to win seats and it becomes easier to match vote shares and seat shares more precisely for all parties. However, this principle works in reverse fashion for plurality and majority systems. In these systems, when more than one seat is contested in a district, voters are usually allowed to cast as many votes as there are seats to be filled. If five seats are assigned and four parties run slates of candidates, a party that can attract a dominant plurality of the electorate, say thirty-five percent, can win all five seats if each supporter votes for all of its candidates and only them. Thus, the "winner-take-all" feature of such electoral systems magnifies the disparity between vote shares and seat shares they produce. In contrast, where PR formulas are coupled with high district magnitudes parliamentary representation generally mirrors the diversity of interests and viewpoints in the electorate quite accurately.

Opinions are mixed on the benefits of achieving such accuracy of representation. Women and members of minorities who tend to get fairer representation under PR (Rule, 1987) see it as correcting a bias that generally works against them. Opponents of PR argue that it encourages a proliferation of minor parties by granting representation to parties that gain only minuscule support from the electorate, and view it as source of political instability, especially when it advantages fringe or extremist parties. They believe it encourages a splintering of party support rather than moderating the partisan divisions already present, producing unstable coalition governments. They cite the former Weimar Republic, postwar Italy, and Israel as examples. These are extreme cases, though. In rebuttal, one can cite Switzerland, the Scandinavian countries, and Germany (where PR is used in a mixed system) as nations that have used PR in conjunction with relatively high district magnitudes without producing the negative results that its opponents cite. Given what is now known about electoral system design, the use of formal thresholds, smaller district magnitudes, and more punitive formulae can often lessen or prevent formation of splinter parties or "nuisance" parties of the kind that trouble critics. Hence, such criticisms have lost much of their relevance.

Nevertheless, since seats are shared over a number of parties it is seldom that a single party gains a majority of the seats and can form a government. Thus, coalition governments tend to be the rule in most PR systems. Coalition governments are not necessarily unstable, however. Often these coalitions are quite broadly inclusive and produce very stable governments. Moreover, one can argue that single-party governments formed by the "catch-all" brokerage parties that prevail in majoritarian systems are, in a sense, "coalitions" of an informal kind formed in advance of the election, but with no clear rules about the division of the "spoils" should they win. This yields its own kind of uncertainty about policy directions. Yet, the argument about uncertainties arising from the post-electoral formation of governments in PR systems still carries considerable force with many observers, as does that concerning the problem of assigning responsibility where a district has many elected representatives.

Finally, PR systems *do* seem to increase citizen participation in elections. Cross-national studies show that countries using PR report higher levels of voter turnout than those using a plurality system. Andre Blais and Ken Carty suggest three reasons this happens (1990, 167). By improving the fit between vote shares and seat shares, PR systems make voters feel their vote makes a difference. This makes elections more competitive under PR systems, leading parties to campaign more widely which, in turn, increases voter turnout. Finally, proportional representation also encourages more parties to compete, thereby increasing the likelihood that voters will find parties with which they can agree and representation will become more inclusive.

The Emergence of Mixed Electoral Systems

In recent decades, the debate over the merits of majoritarian versus PR systems has led electoral reform advocates to combine elements of both plurality and proportional representation systems in the hope of achieving the best features of each, thereby creating **mixed-member proportional systems (MMP)**.[2] The best-known example involves the procedure used to elect Germany's lower chamber, the Bundestag, adopted in 1949 and continued to present times with some modifications. However, such systems have been in use since 1906 (Massicotte and Blais, 1999, 343) and one variant was used for provincial elections in Alberta and Manitoba from the 1920s through 1955 (Johnston, 1992; Jansen, 1998).

The most commonly used MMP design employs two tiers of districts—one consisting of single-member primary districts chosen by a plurality or majority formula and a secondary tier composed of either a single national pool of seats or several regionally defined pools, which are allocated by a PR formula. How many seats are allocated under each formula is seemingly a crucial factor in how such systems work, but the relative proportions vary quite widely in existing systems, with the PR component ranging between 10 and 90 percent (Massicotte and Blais, 1999). With such variation, coupled with a wide variety of formulae, any attempt to predict or generalize about the performance of such systems is quite risky. The intent behind their adoption seems to be to combine "the accountability strengths of plurality rule in single-member constituencies with the offsetting proportional qualities of regional and national lists" (Dunleavy and Margetts, 1995, 27). However, they also combine the FPTP tendency to reward territorially concentrated minorities disproportionately with PR's tendency to encourage splinter parties where a large magnitude nation-wide district is employed. As Kent Weaver (1999) has noted in arguing against the adoption of a German-style MMP system in Canada, MMP "tends to stimulate parties along whatever cleavage lines are most salient in a society" (81) and in so doing provides "too much of some good things" (79).

Mixed systems offering variants of this model recently adopted in New Zealand, Italy, and Japan provide the basis for electing the newly formed Scottish Parliament and Welsh National Assembly for both proposals made by the Jenkins Commission regarding reform of Britain's electoral system. Unicameral national assemblies in twenty-one nations are now elected by mixed systems and MMP is used to choose the lower chamber in another nine countries (Massicotte and Blais, 1999, 345). It is also the most commonly mentioned option put forward by those seeking reform of the Canadian federal electoral system (Milner, 1999).

Summary

Early in this chapter we discussed Arend Lijphart's observation that democratic government in any true sense has been limited to the twentieth century. That conclusion rests on the fact that national elections conducted on a near-universal franchise did not occur in most nations before that time. In this regard, elections are, indeed, the "defining institutions" of modern democracy. They provide that linkage between citizens and members of the political elite that forces the latter to pay attention to the needs and concerns of the electorate. The mediation electoral systems provide shapes the focus of electoral competition in a number of important respects. While the basic choice remains that between majoritarian and proportional representation schemes, research on the workings of electoral systems in different societies and competitive circumstances has yielded a better understanding of which features can be most easily manipulated to produce specific desired results (Taagepera and Shugart, 1989, 236). Such knowledge provides a basis for more prudent reforms in the future, though the differences in basic political philosophy that divide proponents of the two main forms of electoral systems will likely remain.

Andre Blais has argued that in implementing and mediating operation of the electoral process, a well-functioning electoral system should meet certain criteria. It should ensure that the voting system is simple enough for voters to understand (in contrast to the controversial "butterfly ballot" used in Florida's Miami/ Dade County election which badly confused many voters in the November 2000 U.S. presidential elections), yet still capable of accurately reflecting their preferences. It should also ensure that each person's vote counts equally. It should produce elected officials and governments that are broadly representative of the electorate's interests and concerns and not systematically biased against certain groups or interests. And, finally, it should produce public officials and governments that are accommodating to citizens, effective in governing, and easily accountable to voters (Blais, 1999). As we have noted throughout this chapter, many other factors influence the degree to which these criteria are met. Still, if we can achieve electoral rules and procedures that produce elections that are fairly conducted and representative of the voters' preferences, then we will be well on our way to confirming that elections are, as Katz told us, the defining institutions of modern democracy.

Endnotes

[1] The exact number seems to fluctuate almost weekly. The number we report is based on information taken from the Inter-Parliamentary Union's PARLINE database (www.ipu.org/parline). Unless otherwise noted, all data cited in this chapter come from this source, supplemented by information from Katz (1997), Blais and Massicotte (1996, 1997) and Blais, Massicotte and Dobrzynska (1997) or, in the case of Canadian election results, from the official reports of Canada's Chief Electoral Officer.

[2] We agree with and adopt the criteria Massicotte and Blais (1999) propose for identifying mixed systems: (a) that they must combine formulas drawn from the opposing majoritarian/plurality and PR families in the choice of an assembly and (b) that at least five per cent of the assembly's members must be chosen by least used of the two formulas. Hence, nations like Switzerland, where the use of a few single-member districts representing half-cantons leads to application of a majoritarian formula within a system that uses PR for the overwhelmingly majority of seats, are not classified as "mixed systems."

Discussion Questions

1. Discuss the role that constitutions play in determining the extent to which elections decide who governs.

2. Are there political contexts in which the strong control that majoritarian electoral institutions provide a dominant plurality or majority is as harmful as the fragmentation and instability that PR systems can foster? What issues are relevant in evaluating these two scenarios?

3. What aspects of electoral systems seem to be most influential in shaping electoral competition and voter participation and in what ways do they affect those matters?

4. Discuss the impact that adoption of a mixed-member proportional (MMP) electoral system for choosing the members of the Canadian House of Commons might have on the current regional fragmentation of party competition in Canada.

5. Should Canadians be allowed to cast two ballots in federal elections: one to choose their local MP and the second to indicate which party they would like to see form the government? What impact do you think the adoption of this practice would have on the conduct of government and on party competition?

References

Beetham, David. 1994."Key Principles and Indices for a Democratic Audit". In David Beetham (ed.). *Defining and Measuring Democracy*. Thousand Oaks, CA: Sage Publications, 1994.

Blais, Andre. 1999. "Criteria for Assessing Electoral Systems," *Electoral Insight, 1*: 3-6.

Blais, Andre and Ken Carty. 1990. "Does Proportional Representation Foster Voter Turnout?" *European Journal of Political Research. 18*, 167–181.

————— . 1997. "Electoral formulas: A macroscopic perspective." *European Journal of Political Research. 32,* 107–29.

Blais, Andre, Louis Massicotte and Agnieszka Dobrzynska. 1997. "Direct Presidential Elections: A World Summary." *Electoral Studies. 16,* 441–55.

Butler, David. 1983. "Variants of the Westminster Model." In Vernon Bogdanor and David Butler (eds.), *Democracy and Elections: Electoral Systems and their Consequences* (pp. 46–61). Cambridge: Cambridge University Press.

Cox, Gary W. 1997. *Making Votes Count: Strategic Coordination in the World's Electoral Systems.* New York: Cambridge University Press.

Dunleavy, Patrick and Helen Margetts. 1995. "Understanding the Dynamics of Electoral Reform." *International Political Science Review. 16:* 9–29.

Ginsberg, Benjamin. 1982. *The Consequences of Consent.* Reading, MA: Addison-Wesley.

Harrop, Martin and William L. Miller. (1987). *Elections and Voters: A Comparative Introduction.* London: Macmillan Education, Ltd.

Hazan, Reuven Y. 1997. "Three Levels of Elections in Israel." *Representation. 34,* 240–49.

Jansen, Harold J. 1998. *The Single Transferable Vote in Alberta and Manitoba.* Unpublished doctoral dissertation. University of Alberta. Edmonton, Alberta, Canada.

Johnston, J. Paul. 1992. *The use of the Single Transferable Vote in Alberta provincial elections, 1924-1955.* Paper presented at the Annual Meeting of the American Political Science Association, Chicago, IL

Johnston, J. Paul and Harvey E. Pasis, (Eds.), 1990. *Representation and Electoral Systems: Canadian Perspectives.* Scarborough, Ont: Prentice-Hall Canada.

————— 1997. *Democracy and Elections.* New York: Oxford University Press.

Lijphart, Arend. 1984. *Democracies: Patterns of Majoritarian and Consensus Government in Twenty-One Countries.* New Haven: Yale University Press.

————— 1994. *Electoral Systems and Party Systems.* New York: Oxford University Press.

————— . 1999. *Patterns of Democracy.* New Haven. Yale University Press.

Massicotte, Louis and Andre Blais. "Mixed electoral systems: a conceptual and empirical survey." *Electoral Studies, 18:* 341-66.

Rae, Douglas W. 1971. *The Political Consequences of Electoral Laws.* 2nd. ed. New Haven: Yale University Press.

Rose, Richard. 1983. "Elections and Electoral Systems: Choice and Alternatives." In Vernon Bogdanor and David Butler eds., *Democracy and Elections: Electoral Systems and their Consequences (20–45).* Cambridge: Cambridge University Press.

Rule, Wilma. 1987. "Electoral Systems, Contextual Factors and Women's Opportunity for Election to Parliament in Twenty-Three Democracies." *Western Political Quarterly. 40,* 477–498.

Taagepera, Rein and Matthew Soberg Shugart. 1989. *Seats and Votes: The Effects and Determinants of Electoral Systems.* New Haven: Yale University Press.

Taylor, Peter J. and Arend Lijphart. 1985. "Proportional Tenure vs Proportional Representation: Introducing a New Debate," *European Journal of Political Research. 13,* 387–399

Weaver, Kent. 1999. "MMP is Too Much of Some Good Things." In Henry Milner (ed.) *Making Every Vote Count: Reassessing Canada's Electoral System.* Peterborough, Ont.: Broadview Press.

Further Readings

Cox, Gary W. 1997. *Making Votes Count: Strategic Coordination in the World's Electoral Systems.* Cambridge: Cambridge University Press.

Harrop, Martin and William L. Miller. 1987. *Elections and Voters: A Comparative Introduction.* New York: New Amsterdam Books.

Johnston, J. Paul and Harvey E. Pasis, eds.1990. *Representation and Electoral Systems: Canadian Perspectives.* Scarborough: Prentice-Hall.

Katz, Richard S. 1997. *Democracy and Elections.* Oxford: Oxford University Press.

LeDuc, Lawrence, Richard G. Niemi and Pippa Norris, eds. 1996. *Comparing Democracies: Elections and Voting in Global Perspective.* Thousand Oaks, CA: Sage Publications.

Lijphart, Arend. 1994. *Electoral Systems and Party Systems.* Oxford: Oxford University Press.

Taagepera, Rein and Matthew Soberg Shugart. 1989. *Seats and Votes: The Effects and Determinants of Electoral Systems.* New Haven: Yale University Press.

Weblinks

Canadian Elections on the Internet
www.library.ubc.ca/poli/cpwebe.html

Elections Canada
www.elections.ca

Inter-Parliamentary Union
www.ipu.org

Proportional Representation Library
mtholyoke.edu/acad/polit/damy/prlib.htm

Elections Around the World
www.agora.stm.it/elections/election.htm

Administration and Cost of Elections (ACE) Project
www.aeproject.org

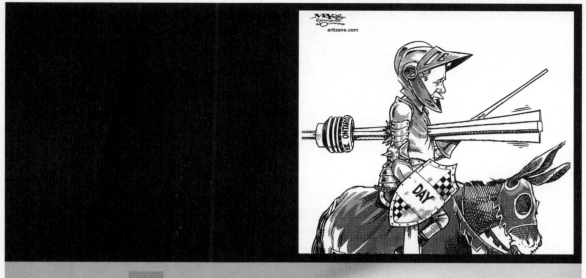

CHAPTER 12

POLITICAL PARTIES AND PARTY SYSTEMS

Objectives

Probably the first things that come to mind when thinking about politics in democratic political systems are political parties. Many citizens identify themselves as being affiliated with a party, even if they do not hold a formal membership. We identify others as being, for example, Liberals or Alliance; or Democrats or Republicans. These labels, in turn, act as a political short-hand, revealing political predispositions and leadership preferences. When citizens exercise their right to vote they almost always cast their ballot for a political party or for someone who stands as a party candidate.

DAVID STEWART

In this chapter, we take a critical look at political parties. We begin with the questions "What are political parties?" and "What do they do?" We assess whether parties actually perform the tasks generally assigned to them. Finally, the chapter describes different kinds of political parties and party systems.

Introduction

Almost a decade ago, the Royal Commission on Electoral Reform and Party Financing celebrated the role of political parties in Canadian politics. Political parties, it noted, "give voters meaningful choices, both in the direct election of their individual Member of Parliament and in the indirect election of a government" (Canada, 1991, 207).

Many citizens, in Canada and elsewhere, however, do not share this optimistic endorsement. A research study for the same Royal Commission discovered that most Canadians believe:

- Government doesn't care what ordinary people think;
- Those elected to parliament soon lose touch with the people;
- Most politicians make promises they have no intention of fulfilling;
- MPs make a lot of money misusing their offices; and
- Parties confuse issues rather than provide a clear choice (Blais and Gidengil, 1991, 14, 42, 79).

Citizens are not alone in this negative attitude towards political parties. Some academic critics suggest that parties give a rather false sense of confidence in the vitality of democracy. Lyon, for instance, uses a supermarket analogy to critique parties. In his evocative analogy, citizens are like consumers who upon entering a grocery store are presented with a choice among a number of shopping carts (parties) and on the basis of the choices they make are expected to believe they control the grocery industry (1996, 533–534). In reality there is much overlap in the content of the carts, consumers must take the entire cart and not pick and choose, may not be able to see all items, and each cart will contain items the consumers do not want. And, unlike stores, parties allow no refunds or exchanges. How well founded are these criticisms? We will begin to answer these questions by exploring what political parties are and what they do.

What Are Political Parties?

COMPARED TO CONSTITUTIONS, EXECUTIVES, AND BUREAUCRACIES, POLITICAL parties are relatively recent political inventions. Political parties find their origin in legislative assemblies filled with aristocrats who were elected by male property owners. Over time, these elites formed relatively stable political coalitions or legislative factions as they are sometimes called. These factions provided the foundations for the first organized political parties, which developed in the late eighteenth and nineteenth centuries in the United States and Western Europe. Political parties really began to assume their central role in democratic politics, however, when the voting franchise was extended to non–property owning men and later to women. Groups of legislators organized themselves into political parties to attract support from new voters. As well, new parties originating outside the legislature were formed with support from new voters, often in the trade union movement, who were suspicious of the existing legislators who had not exactly expedited their acquisition of the right to vote. These two paths, intra and extra legislative, continue to be the major routes of party origin. Some parties emerge to represent groups in society who feel that the existing parties are not paying sufficient attention to their issues. Others emerge as a fragmentation of existing legislative parties which occurs when certain legislators leave the party for which they were elected and form another party. In Canada the former Reform party was an example of the former while the Bloc Quebecois exemplifies the latter.

The British philosopher and parliamentarian Edmund Burke supplied one of the first definitions of a party. In his words: "[a] party is a body of men united, for promoting by their joint endeavours the national interest, upon some particular principle in which they are all agreed." This definition has been challenged both for its exclusion of women and for linking party so explicitly with principle or ideology. Other analysts define political parties primarily in terms of their quest to win elections. In one of the most commonly accepted contemporary definitions, La Palombara and Weiner define a political party as a "formal organization whose self conscious, primary purpose is to place and maintain in public office persons who will control, alone or in coalitions, the machinery of government" (1966, 6). While this definition may capture the American Republican–Democrat battle quite well, its universal application is more problematic. It fails to deal with parties that, rather than seek office, merely wish to educate the electorate and/or influence public policy. A modified definition advanced by Sartori escapes this difficulty. He defines party as "any political group that presents at elections and is capable of placing through elections, candidates for public office" (1976).

What Do They Do?

THE LITERATURE ON PARTIES IS IN GENERAL AGREEMENT AS TO WHAT PARTIES do, or are supposed to do. They are supposed to structure the vote into competing camps, make voting easier for the average citizen by nominating, supporting, and publicizing their candidates for elected office. Political parties are supposed to integrate and mobilize citizens into the political system. In other words, political parties help citizens identify with and participate in politics. They also help supply many of the individuals who occupy the institutional positions of governmental authority. Party membership is effectively a precondition for holding elected political office. As well, parties recruit political leaders. They provide the pool from which leaders come, provide training for potential leaders, and actively seek out qualified individuals. Another obvious function is policy making and negotiating consensus on divisive political issues. This involves placing issues on the public agenda, resolving the competing interests of societal groups, hearing and judging the demands and ideas of various groups, and giving formal expression to the ideas they accept. Finally, parties have a communication function; that is, they spread political information.

These roles are clearly critical to the democratic and governmental processes. How successfully do parties currently perform these roles? In general, the conclusion is that parties no longer perform all of these functions effectively. In particular, the role of parties in policy making has been largely lost to executives and bureaucracies while the ability of parties to aggregate interests is lessened by, among other things, the increasing involvement of citizens in new social movements, such as the feminist and environmental movements.

With respect to integration and mobilization, it is clear that the vast majority of voters do not participate in politics as members of parties. The proportion of party members among the electorate is generally pegged at less than five percent. In the leadership elections held in Canada by the Conservative party in 1998 and the Alliance party in 2000, the number of people who voted was less than five percent of the number who voted for the Conservatives and Reform in the 1997 election.

The nature of contemporary journalism has further diminished the role of political parties. Parties have lost their role in the communication and explanation of ideas and policies. Public opinion is now shaped and articulated more by the media than it is by parties. Party actions and the political agenda are now as much dictated by the media as by political leaders and party strategists.

Finally, innovations in technology such as the development of polling have mitigated the need for strong party organizations with large memberships. Leaders and their personal entourages have no need for their party to make them aware of grassroots public opinion on specific issues, or to identify which issues are of most concern. Local party activists and elected politicians who are the most prominent members of parties are of limited utility. Public relations consultants, the so-called "spin doctors," and pollsters have displaced party members and activists in this area.

Nonetheless, it would be a mistake to conclude that parties no longer have important roles to play. Parties continue to perform some of their functions well and voters, despite some negative opinions, focus on parties during elections. With few exceptions, voters restrict themselves to electing representatives of parties to legislatures. As the previously cited Canadian Royal Commission on parties and elections noted "Among the fundamental activities performed by parties is the selection and recruitment of candidates for elected office, the selection of political leaders and the organization of electoral competition" (Canada, 1991, 207). These are central roles in a democratic system.

Democracy Within Parties

With the primary functions of parties situated in the organization of government and the provision of representatives, the organization of parties becomes of interest to students of democracy. In the early part of this century Boss Tweed, one of the infamous "Bosses" of the American Democratic party, stated "I don't care who does the electing so long as I can do the nominating." His comment points out the importance of internal party democracy. The choices parties make with respect to leadership and local candidates effectively set the menu for citizens in general elections. The processes through which parties choose their candidates and leaders are thus important subjects for analysis.

In his classic study of political parties, Maurice Duverger argued that there were two types of party organization—*Cadre* and *Mass* (1954). Each type had different origins, different internal democratic norms, and different connections with the electorate. The cadre–mass distinction is still relevant to the study of most parties. According to Duverger, cadre parties were generally formed within legislative assemblies by a grouping of notables to compete in elections. These parties generally have a small formal membership and tend to come alive only at election time or during a party leadership contest. The elected caucus and the party leader dominate the party. Very little of a cadre party's finances come from its members. Instead, it relies on private and corporate donations. Finally, cadre parties tend to present themselves in pragmatic rather than ideological clothing. In Canada, the Liberal and Progressive Conservative parties are typically characterized as cadre parties.

In contrast, a mass party possesses a larger membership and actively recruits members. Joining the party is meaningful, often involving shared political values or some kind of pledge to follow party regulations and support the party. Generally there are formal mechanisms for admission and a sizeable amount of financial support comes from members. Mass parties place a higher priority on policy making and, in theory, party conventions decide policy which is binding on the leader and the caucus. In Canada, the New Democratic and Allianace parties most closely fit the mass party model. For example, the constitution of the Alliance party declares explicitly that "the leader and the caucus are bound by the principles and policies as declared by the members of the Alliance."

There are thus major distinctions between cadre and mass parties with respect to the size and power of the membership, finance, and policy making. However, these distinctions have been to some extent blurred. In particular, questions regarding the role of members and party financing led Katz and Mair to describe a new form of party organization which they term the "cartel" party (1995). These parties finance themselves via state subventions whether through the rebates provided by electoral financing legislation or by individual donations which are tax-deductible. In the process, the party hierarchy possesses significant autonomy from grassroots party activists.

This autonomy is significant since it is through the party on the ground (the party membership and organization) that citizens have opportunities to participate in partisan politics. At a basic level, the local or constituency organization helps the party campaign and compete in elections. In constituency battles the organization helps to identify party supporters and get them out to vote. These tasks involve the distribution of literature, canvassing, and the transportation of sympathetic voters to the polls. Even in cartel parties, these functions continue to be carried out by party activists. However, given the focus that contemporary politics places on leaders and on reaching voters through television, these actions have only a minor impact.

Candidate Selection

More importantly, the party organization chooses candidates for elected office. Indeed, some have suggested that "the selection of candidates is the only area of party activity where ordinary members can expect to have a decisive voice" (Gallagher, 1988, 273). Voters are largely limited to choosing their representatives from the choices offered up by parties; in fact, candidates who do not represent parties, usually referred to as independents, have virtually no chance of election.

One of the most common methods of candidate selection is to allow local constituency associations to choose the candidate for their riding. Typically this involves a party election in which all local party members who have paid their membership dues are eligible to vote. However, in some cases party leaders possess the power to veto candidates and at times central organizations may screen the candidate pool. The Canadian Alliance party requires all potential candidates to undergo a pre-screening process before a nomination meeting is held. The Liberal party gives its leader the power to bypass local nominations and directly appoint a number of candidates. In recent elections this has been used to protect some incumbents from challenges, to ensure the nomination of "star" candidates and to increase the number of women candidates. Canada's electoral law gives the leader of every party the power to veto any candidacy regardless of the outcome of the constituency election. Still, the vast majority of candidates are selected by a local meeting of all party members who desire to participate.

Another selection method restricts the decision to a tiny percentage of the members. For example in the major British parties "the selection is made by a convention-like body representing local members . . . from a shortlist drawn up by committee" (Gallagher, 1988, 240). Similarly, party committees select most of the candidates for parties in countries such as Ireland, Germany, and Australia. In a handful of cases the power to select candidates is in even fewer hands. Generally, these fewer hands are those of the party's national executive. Ordinary members, in parties such as the French UDF (Union for French Democracy) and RPR (Rally for the Republic), are left with little voice in candidate selection.

In the United States, the selection of candidates is heavily regulated by law. Each of the fifty states organizes primaries for each party in which all voters who register themselves as supporters of a particular party are eligible to vote. The rules governing these primary elections vary from state to state and it is difficult to generalize about the process. Nonetheless, decisions regarding party candidates have been removed from the control of party activists and devolved even further to voters.

Leadership Selection

American presidential nominees are chosen in the same direct primaries that elect candidates. Although their nomination is confirmed in a convention, such conventions have become a forum for ratification rather than selection. Party regulars thus have a very limited role in determining who will head their party's ticket. Instead, voters make such choices and party activists lack a privileged voice (DiClerico and Uslaner, 1984). Thus the American leadership selection process demonstrates the ultimate devaluation of party membership. Of course, American parties are somewhat distinct in that they do not have leaders in the same way that parties in other countries do. Instead they have presidential candidates who, despite serving as the titular heads of their parties, exercise virtually no control over the party or other candidates.

In contrast to the American system, some parties make no pretense of directly involving even their membership in the choice of a leader. In these parties participation in the selection of leaders is restricted to elected members of legislatures. In certain cases the caucus has the sole voice in determining who the leader will be, while in others it simply has a disproportionate voice. In the most extreme example, the leader could be deposed at any meeting of the caucus. The caucus can in fact depose leaders who have received popular mandates from the electorate. Former British Prime Minister Margaret Thatcher and former Australian Prime Minister Robert Hawke were both overthrown by their caucus in spite of electoral success.

Most parties have moved away from caucus selection and use party leadership conventions. Here delegates representing ordinary party members join elected party and public officials to choose the leader. In this process, a party's legislative caucus has a limited voice and the leader possesses a clear independence from his or her legislative colleagues. The leader of such a party enjoys greater security of tenure and can be removed unwillingly only at another convention. Although conventions involve rank and file party members in the party's most important choice, they have come in for a good deal of criticism.

In the Canadian context, these critiques have involved questions ranging from the competence of ordinary members to select the nation's leaders to concerns that the process is not democratic enough (Perlin, 1991). Concerns regarding the absence of democracy in leadership elections now dominate.

Critiques of conventions on this basis note that the election of leaders typically involves only a small percentage of the party membership and is subject to manipulation. At these gatherings, the party elite, especially the elected representatives, make up a significant portion of the assembly who attempt to influence the votes of ordinary delegates by virtue of their eloquence, or standing, or popularity. Ordinary party members look up to and are often in awe of elected representatives who can thus psychologically manipulate members by offering their opinion. Participation in party conventions is also affected by manipulation of selection meetings. If delegates are to be chosen at local meetings, the timing and location of these meetings is critical. Both timing and location are easily subject to the manipulation of party elites. Such elites can also organize the "packing" of such meetings and arrange to have prominent figures or community leaders present to offer their opinions on what should be done. The financial resources necessary to participate in such congresses also disadvantage ordinary party members. Travelling to a party congress is expensive and not all party members are able to afford the outlays required. They are thus excluded from taking part in the final selection of the leader or in policy debates at party assemblies.

These concerns about conventions are not new. Duverger criticized the very nature of "delegation." He believed that delegation ensured that the bulk of the membership was denied an explicit choice in choosing the leader. In his words, "indirect representation is an admirable means of banishing democracy while pretending to apply it" (1954, 140). Further, the "mentality of the delegates is never the same as that of those who delegate them, with the result that every additional stage of delegation increases a little more the gap between the will of the base and the decision of the apex. The election of the leaders of a party by a small group of delegates is not the same in character as their direct election by the mass of the members" (1954, 140).

Most Canadian parties have responded to these concerns by moving away from convention selections to choose their leaders towards direct election by all party members. As the Canadian Royal Commission of Electoral Reform and Party Financing explained, "Advocates of direct election argue this approach is more democratic because it limits the influence of the party establishment over the selection of leaders and gives more influence to rank-and-file members. Direct election of party leaders may also reduce the opportunities for abuse of membership rules" (Canada, 1991, 280). Such elections allow all rank-and-file members of the party in good standing to vote directly for the leader. These elections remain distinct from American primaries in that they are restricted to those who hold party memberships and are not regulated by law.

The leaders of four Canadian parties were chosen by processes that involved some form of universal ballot and most Canadian citizens are now governed at the provincial level by premiers chosen in elections in which all party members were eligible to vote. Among federal parties, only the Liberal party has not chosen its federal leader through an election process that gave every member a direct vote for the party leader and even it has committed itself to a new process for the selection of its next leader.

Concerns exist about the effect such a change will have on Canada's parties (Courtney, 1995). Universal ballots render parties susceptible to penetration by opponents who wish to see the party choose an ineffective leader. And, even among party loyalists, primary voters are less likely than delegates to possess extensive backgrounds in the party and a strong record of service to the party. Primary voters are also unable to immerse themselves in the campaign in the manner open to delegates. Ordinary party members may have a more direct voice in the choice of a leader, but the meaning of membership in a party may be devalued.

Policy Making

The final role for party organization is policy making. Parties devote a considerable amount of time to internal discussions of policy and to the construction of electoral platforms or manifestos. Ideally, parties democratically arrive at policy positions, present these positions clearly to voters in elections, and, if elected, implement such policies. In reality, few parties allow ordinary members a decisive voice in policy. Most parties hold policy conventions where they debate and approve policy resolutions but the degree to which parties in election campaigns or in government are bound by such resolutions is questionable. As Gallagher notes "the relationship between formal policy and what the party's ministers do when in office may be hazy" (1988, 273). Party policy, let alone government policy, may not reflect grassroots beliefs. This disparity helps explain why so many Canadians believe that parties confuse issues, make promises they have no intention of fulfilling, and don't care about the views of ordinary citizens (Blais and Gidengil, 1991).

Party Types

DESPITE MANY SIMILARITIES IN ORGANIZATION, IT IS POSSIBLE TO DISTINGUISH parties by their approach to politics. The most common type of party is the **pragmatic party** sometimes referred to as a "catch all" party or as a "rational–efficient" party. This is a non-doctrinaire party that competes strategically for public office and largely reflects the public image of its leader. This type of party is concerned with winning elections—the main thing is to win—and gears its campaigns not to doctrinal beliefs, but to programs it believes will most likely lead to victory.

When two such parties compete, there is usually overlapping of proposals and borrowing of each other's ideas. Such parties are criticized for having no principles, moving with the wind, and attempting to be all things to all people. Competition between such parties has been described as conflict without principles, or simply a battle of ins versus outs. However, defenders of such parties note that similarity of policy and campaign may simply indicate the preferences of the majority of voters. As well, it can be argued that to seek to maximize your votes does not mean that you do not have any principles, but rather that you have reached the conclusion that your principles cannot be advanced without power. Finally, one may argue that it is not so much that these parties do not have views, but that they are selective in emphasizing their views and defer to the wishes and views of the electorate. A former Canadian Liberal cabinet minister captured the essence of policy in a pragmatic party quite aptly when he wrote that Canadian parties are "inclined to gauge policies and administration primarily in the light of their effect on the voting proclivities of the population, and to assess their value in terms of electoral success or failure, rather than on any other considerations" (Power, 1966).

It is possible to identify a slight contradiction between the overarching desire of pragmatic parties to win and a desire to include something for everyone. Alienating groups of voters for short-term electoral success can have negative long-term consequences. Nonetheless, if the main thing is to win, there is always the possibility that a pragmatic party may try to string together a *minimum winning coalition.*

One variant of a pragmatic party explicitly rejects such a strategy. This is a **brokerage** party, which seeks to aggregate and reconcile differing interests in society and does not reflect divisive religious, ethnic, or regional differences of citizens. Such a party focuses on the reconciliation of the widely scattered interests and aims of a number of regions or groups. Such parties attempt to moderate politics, to minimize differences by down-playing serious ethnic, linguistic, or regional divisions. They do not try to exploit such advantages as they may enjoy among particular groups in the population to the exclusion of more general appeals.[4]

The second major type of party is the **doctrinal party**, also called *ideological* or *programmatic.* This type of party seeks to advance its values and policies and does not view electoral office as an end in itself. Significantly more emphasis is placed on ideological consistency than on attaining government office. Ideology is more important than electoral success. Ideally, competing parties of this type would present lists of different policies and let voters take them or leave them. The advantages of such a party are clear; it is principled and consistently tries to advance its views. However, these parties can be criticized for inflexibility, putting doctrine ahead of voters' desires, and not changing policies to keep up with public opinion. Doctrinal parties suffer from a clear competitive disadvantage when their opponents are pragmatic. The pragmatic parties are generally willing to accept electorally popular policies advanced by doctrinal parties and present them to voters as their own. Few parties are purely doctrinal, but the presence of a significant internal debate over whether the party should compromise its policies for electoral success is an indication that the doctrinal label fits.

There is a third type of party that differs from pragmatic and doctrinal parties on one critical dimension. Pragmatic parties exist to win elections and doctrinal parties want to win elections. However, some parties do not have electoral victory as a major goal. These parties can be called **interest parties**. These parties generally represent a particular interest within society (for example a sector of the economy, a region, or a specific concern such as environmental protection). Their main concern is advancing the interest they represent, not participating in governments. Such a party participates in elections directly but does not make a full attempt to win power. Instead, the focus is more on convincing the public and other parties to take their concerns more seriously.[5] The campaign of Green party candidate Ralph Nader for the American presidency in 2000 provides an example of such a party at work. In Canada it is possible to place the Christian Heritage party and the Green party in this category. In the 2000 federal election, numerous candidates ran for the Marijuana party. Its platform had only two elements—the decriminalization of marijuana use and proportional representation. Its leader promised that the party would disappear once these two policy objectives were met.

There are two other types of parties that are distinctive enough to receive some special attention. The **personal party**, which is founded around a single influential leader, has little presence beyond its leader. In order to survive, most of these parties become pragmatic or doctrinal. Otherwise they cannot survive the death of the leader. Finally, there is the **movement party**. This is a party that begins as a political movement largely pursuing non-electoral goals, and evolves into a party. Examples are movements for national independence that operate outside normal political systems in their quest. However, once national independence is achieved these parties generally transform into other types. A movement party is essentially transitory. The African National Congress in South Africa is a good contemporary example of such a party.

Electoral Support

PARTIES DIFFER IN THEIR APPROACH TO POLITICS, THEIR ORGANIZATION, AND the degree of internal democracy they possess. They also differ with respect to electoral support. Much has been written about the recent weakening of long-term loyalties to political parties among particular groups and the increasing volatility among voters (Dalton, Flanagan and Beck, 1984, 450). Parties cannot count on the same solid base of support among voters they could twenty-five years ago and many new parties are experiencing electoral success. These changes have enhanced the role of issue positions and leadership images in elections, but still, almost all parties in a competitive situation (even pragmatic parties) draw disproportionate support from particular groups in society. These enduring bases of support reveal a good deal about a party's history as well as the interests and issues which divide the electorate.

Historically, socioeconomic divisions were regarded as the most important divisions among voters. Sometimes called "class politics," this division usually reflects the nature of politics as a battle between the working class and the middle class. Party politics becomes premised on somewhat different views regarding private ownership, the role of government in economic planning, social welfare, and the redistribution of wealth. Western European politics has been predominantly structured by class politics since the emergence of socialist and social democratic parties at the turn of the twentieth century.

Religious divisions are often important in distinguishing one party's support base from another's. Many countries reveal historical patterns in which different religious groups have ties to different parties. Members of particular religious groups are more likely to support one party than another. Partisan differences of this sort are often based as much on history as on contemporary disagreements. Divisions on this basis can be based on clear religious differences (Christian or non-Christian, Muslim or non-Muslim) more sectoral divisions (Protestant or Catholic, Sunni or Shiite), or divisions between those for whom religion is important and those for whom it is not. In Canada the Liberal party has drawn disproportionate support from Roman Catholics while the Progressive Conservative party has received more support from Protestants.

Cultural, linguistic, or ethnic divisions between communities are also frequent sources of party division, as are regional differences. It is not uncommon to find that the electoral support for parties differs widely by region or that certain parties have difficulty attracting support from certain linguistic or ethnic groups. Similar urban–rural divisions in support often exist as well. In Canada such divisions clearly underlie election results. Quebec, which simultaneously illustrates cultural, linguistic, ethnic, and regional dimensions, delivered half of its seats in 2000 to the Bloc Quebecois, a party that does not contest elections elsewhere in the country. Quebec's distinct patterns of electoral support extend far beyond the Bloc. For most of this century solid support for the Liberal party from Quebec voters kept the party in power. In more clearly regional terms, the Western provinces have provided the launching pad for a number of new parties such as the CCF–NDP, Social Credit, and Reform. This phenomenon is not peculiar to Canada. For most of this century, the Southern American states were as steadfast in their support for the Democratic party as Quebec was for the Liberals. And in Britain, a strong Labour presence in parliament was assured by its support in Northern England, Scotland, and Wales.

More recently gender has emerged as a factor which differentiates parties with respect to electoral support. A fairly consistent trend is evident on this basis as women generally seem to be more inclined to support parties of the "left." Among Canadian parties, polls indicate that the Alliance receives much more support from men than it does from women.

DEBATE BOX

Divided We Stand?

In the early fall of 2000, shortly after the death of former Liberal Prime Minister Pierre Trudeau, Jean Chrétien called a federal election for November 27. The Liberal Party had a strong lead in public opinion polls but it had served only three years of its possible five-year mandate. Opposition party leaders accused the prime minister of arrogance, arguing that Canadians were being called to the polls for no other reason than to ensure Chrétien a third mandate—a record not surpassed since the early days of Confederation.

The 2000 campaign also marked the entry of a new federal party (in name, at least) into the electoral fray. After the 1997 campaign, it became apparent that the Reform party had to reach beyond its support base in Western Canada in order to win a majority of seats to form the government. Preston Manning, the Reform founder and leader, started a campaign to "Unite the Right" under the umbrella of a new party that would appeal to voters across Canada, especially those in Ontario. The Alliance Party of Canada, a new party with a new leader, Stockwell Day, was launched in the summer of 2000. As the campaign unfolded, few issues caught the public imagination. Instead, commentators remarked that it was one of the dirtiest campaigns in recent memory. Chrétien and Day took many personal shots at one another, while public opinion polls showed that almost one-half of Canadians trusted neither of the party leaders.

In the end, however, Chrétien's gamble paid off. The Liberals gained a third mandate with an even stronger majority than before while the Alliance party failed to make any significant breakthrough beyond its Western support base. The Bloc Québecois, while somewhat diminished, remained a force to contend with in Quebec. The Progressive Conservatives and the New Democratic Party managed to maintain official party status—but just barely.

The 2000 campaign, however, reinforced two disturbing trends that have characterized federal campaigns in the past decade. First, only 63 percent of registered Canadians voted—the lowest voter turnout ever in a federal election. Second, party support was deeply fractured by region as Table 12.1 shows. The governing Liberal party gained 78 percent of its seats from Ontario alone while fully 97 percent of the Alliance party support came from the provinces west of Ontario.

What are the factors that contribute to the regional polarization of party support in Canada? Does it matter that the governing party has only a handful of elected representatives in the vibrant and affluent provinces that make up the Canadian West? Is the role of the Official Opposition compromised because the Alliance party finds its support only in the West? What can the federal parties do to broaden their appeal to all Canadians and all regions in the next federal election?

TABLE 12.1   *Party Support by Region, 2000 Election*

	North	West	Ontario	Quebec	East
Number of Seats	3	88	103	75	32
Liberal	100%	16%	97%	50%	59%
Alliance	—	73%	2%	—	—
Bloc	—	—	—	50%	—
NDP	—	10%	—	—	13%
PC	—	3%	—	—	28%

Party Systems

THUS FAR WE HAVE DISCUSSED PARTIES AS INDIVIDUAL ENTITIES. HOWEVER, parties do not exist in isolation from each other or in isolation from the state which establishes the parameters within which parties function. The actions and electoral fortunes of one party influence others. Identifying the party system in a given polity provides insight into the nature of political competition. Therefore it is useful to conclude by examining the relationship between parties as measured by the party system. The term *party system* refers to the relationships between parties, and maps the parties that are important in a given system. The most common method of analyzing party systems is numeric—counting the number of parties.

The basic distinction in party systems rests between the two-party (Anglo–American model) and the more common multi-party system. In the Anglo-American model only two parties participate in governments and coalition governments are rare. The Anglo–American model is demonstrated by the Republican–Democrat duopoly in the United States and the Conservative–Labour alternation in Britain. There are no pure two-party systems; even in the United States, where only Republicans and Democrats enjoy electoral success, there are lots of parties. However, the fact that more than a dozen parties contest presidential elections presents a misleading portrait of the American political system. In multi-party systems, coalition governments are the norm and more than three parties are regularly represented in the legislature. Over time most of these parties have a realistic chance of participating in government. Traditionally, the two-party system has been praised for its political stability and its ability to produce single-party majority governments. Parties in such a system tend to be pragmatic. As Blondel (1968) has shown, this simple dichotomy of party systems does not fully capture the nature of party competition in liberal democracies. There are a number of variations that offer a more precise picture.

The first is the one party dominant system. In this system there is, of course, more than one party contesting elections, but only one party is capable of winning and only one party is in a position to compete for the majority of seats. Defeat of the dominant party is possible but unlikely. The current Canadian party system fits into this category. Five parties are represented in the Canadian House of Commons, but one party, the Liberals, clearly outdistances the others in seats and popular support. For instance in the 2000 election the Liberals received 41 percent of the votes cast while its major opponent, the Alliance, garnered 25 percent. One hundred and seventy-three Liberals were elected compared to only 66 for the strongest opposition party. One-party dominance is also demonstrated by longevity in office. In the twentieth century the Liberals held power almost 70 percent of the time.

The two-and-a-half party system is a variant of the classic two-party model. In such a system, in addition to the two large parties there is a considerably smaller party (or parties) which nonetheless has the potential to play a significant political role. The smaller parties are unable to challenge the dominance of the two bigger parties, but when neither of the two big parties can form a majority government, the smaller parties affect the composition of the executive. States such as Germany and Australia are placed in this category. Canada also was characterized as a two-and-a-half party system in the 1960s and 1970s. Then, more than 90 percent of federal voters supported either the Liberal Party, the Progressive Conservative Party, or the New Democratic Party.

As discussed above, multi-party systems involve a much larger number of parties and these systems are usually marked by coalition governments and the presence of a number of parties on the opposition benches. Multi-party systems can be divided into polarized and non-polarized systems (Sartori, 1976). The multi-party non-polarized systems typically involve only a few parties and each of these parties has the capability of participating in government. The legislature coalesces into a group of parties participating in government and usually only one large grouping of parties opposed to the governing coalition. The party systems in the Scandinavian countries fit into this category. In contrast, polarized systems tend to be marked by bilateral oppositions and parties which lack coalition potential. The presence of bilateral opposition is indicated by an inability of all opposition parties to cooperate in opposing the government. Disagreements among opposition parties are as strong as the disagreements with the governing coalition. The absence of coalition potential is marked by parties that cannot attract support from other parties. A contemporary example of such a party is the French National Front. More historically the electorally strong Italian Communist party was one which other major parties would not consider as a coalition partner but which nonetheless affected the conduct of government and elections.

Summary

Our review of political parties has looked at definitions of parties and at what parties are supposed to do. We have examined the ability of parties to carry out their supposed tasks and concluded that although they experience difficulties in performing many of them, the tasks they do perform are central to democratic politics. We have seen that parties differ from one another in their origin, organization, manifestations of internal democracy, type, and electoral support. Each of these differences tells us something about the individual party and about the political system in which it is successful. As well, parties exist in a variety of different party systems that vary between countries and over time.

An examination of political parties and the way they operate challenges simple interpretations of democracy. Most citizens participate in politics predominantly through elections in which their choices are effectively restricted to the options parties place before them. Contrary to much political rhetoric, parties are not completely responsive to public opinion and involvement in parties does not guarantee citizens opportunities to influence public policy. Political parties do not merely respond to the wishes of voters, they attempt to influence the wishes voters express and focus the political agenda on issues that work to their advantage. Although the hard work of party activists does not enable them to fully control their party, involvement with parties does offer the only chance to hold government office and affords opportunities to interact with decision makers. It is the parties themselves that determine the rules under which elections take place, the ways in which money can be raised and spent, and how votes are translated into seats. Parties exert a measure of control over their own electoral fortunes. It is somewhat ironic that contemporary democracy depends on parties whose internal democracy is questionable. Like sausages, the internal operations of parties should not be examined closely by those who wish to enthusiastically enjoy the product.

Discussion Questions

1. Is citizen dissatisfaction with parties justified? Why or why not?

2. Is it better to leave the choice of party leaders to an informed elite who will make "more competent" judgments, or is it better to broaden participation?

3. How would you classify the parties in Canada with respect to their approach to politics?

4. Does the contribution pragmatic parties make to stability by endeavouring to include something for everyone outweigh the clearer choices offered voters by doctrinal and interest parties?

5. Where do the major parties in Canada have their primary support bases? How do you account for this?

6. How would you describe the party system in Canada? Has it changed recently?

References

Blais, Andre and Elizabeth Gidengil 1991. *Making Representative Democracy Work: The Views of Canadians.* Dundurn Press.

Blondel, Jean. 1968. "Party Systems and Patterns of Government in Western Democracies." *Canadian Journal of Political Science, 1.*

Canada, Royal Commission on Electoral Reform and Party Financing. 1991. *Reforming Electoral Democracy. Volume 1*, Ottawa.

Courtney, John. 1995. *Do Conventions Matter?* Montreal: McGill-Queens.

Dalton, Russell, Scott Flanagan, and Paul Allen Beck. 1984. "Political Forces and Partisan Change." In *Electoral Change in Advanced Industrial Democracies*, eds. Russell Dalton, Scott Flanagan, and Paul Allen Beck. Princeton: Princeton University Press.

DiClerico, Robert and Eric Uslaner. 1984. *Few Are Chosen: Problems in Presidential Selection.* New York: McGraw-Hill.

Duverger, Maurice. 1954. *Political Parties.* London: Methuen.

Gallagher, Michael. 1988. "Conclusion." In *Candidate Selection in Comparative Perspective: The Secret Garden of Politics*, ed. Micahel Gallagher. London: Sage.

Katz, Richard S. and Peter Mair. 1995. "Changing Models of Party Organization and Party Democracy: The Emergence of the Cartel Party." *Party Politics, 1.*

LaPalmobara, Joseph and Myron Weiner. 1966. "The Origin and Development of Political Parties." In *Political Parties and Political Development*, eds. Joseph LaPalombara and Myron Weiner. Princeton: Princeton University Press.

Lijphart, Arend. 1977. *Democracy in Plural Societies.* New Haven: Yale University Press.

Lyon, Vaughn. 1996. "Parties and Democracy: A Critical View." In *Canadian Parties in Transition*, eds. A. Brian Tanguay and Alain G. Gagnon. Toronto: Nelson.

Perlin, George. 1991. "Leadership Selection in the PC and Liberal Parties: Assessing the Need for Reform." In *Party Politics in Canada*, ed. Hugh Thorburn. Scarborough: Prentice Hall.

Power, C.G. 1966. *A Party Politician.* Toronto: Macmillan.

Sartori, Giovanni. 1976. *Parties and Party Systems: A Framework for Analysis.* Cambridge: Cambridge University Press.

Tanguay, A. Brian and Alain G. Gagnon eds. 1996. *Canadian Parties in Transition.* Toronto: Nelson.

Thorburn, Hugh (ed.), *Party Politics in Canada.* 1996. Scarborough: Prentice Hall.

Further Readings

Duverger, Maurice. 1954. *Political Parties.* London: Methuen.

Gallagher, Michael ed. 1988. *Candidate Selection in Comparative Perspective: Th Garden of Politics.* London: Sage.

Sartori, Giovanni. 1976. *Parties and Party Systems: A Framework for Analysis.* Cambridge: Cambridge University Press.

Tanguay, A. Brian and Alain G. Gagnon eds. 1996. *Canadian Parties in Transition.* Toronto: Nelson.

Thorburn, Hugh (ed.), *Party Politics in Canada.* 1996. Scarborough: Prentice Hall.

Weblinks

Democratic Party (USA)
www.democrats.org/

Republican Party (USA)
www.rnc.org/

Green Party (USA)
www.greenparty.org/

Bloc Québécois (Canada)
blocquebecois.org/

Liberal Party (Canada)
www.liberal.ca/

New Democratic Party (Canada)
www.ndp.ca/

Progressive Conservative Party (Canada)
www.pcparty.ca/

Canadian Reform Conservative Alliance (Canada)
www.canadianalliance.ca/

CHAPTER **13**

THE CIVIL SERVICE

Objectives

This chapter explores the critical issues spawned by the growth of powerful civil services in democratic countries. The civil service was initially conceived as an administrative machine whose role was to implement political decisions. But this view seems naive in today's complex world. The civil service plays a central role in policy making and policy implementation. How do democratic societies then reconcile the tensions between the imperatives of democracy and the necessities of effective public management? This chapter probes how the civil service is held accountable to politicians. Next, it details new ideas about public management which argue that the civil service must be managed like a private firm. The chapter concludes by asking whether the civil service as we have come to know it will survive this fundamental reinvention of democratic government.

ALLAN TUPPER

Introduction

Consider the following three major political issues which arose in 2000. First, a substantial debate erupted over the quality of municipal water supply in Ontario and other parts of Canada. The debate was spurred by the tragic deaths of seven residents of Walkerton, Ontario and the serious illness of hundreds of others who were infected by deadly *e coli* bacteria in their tap water. The events at Walkerton raised complex issues about the quality of public administration in Ontario, the impact of government expenditure restraint on public service, and the obligations of public servants and politicians to citizens. A second controversy erupted when a privately owned transport ship carrying substantial weaponry for the Canadian Armed Forces became embroiled in a legal dispute and refused to dock in Canada. The situation required armed intervention by the Canadian navy. How dependent are Canadian governments on services provided by contract? Can vital services really be delivered this way? Why don't the Canadian Armed Forces have their own transport ships? A third major controversy arose when the chronically controversial federal department of Human Resources (HRDC) was found to have access, without Canadians' consent, to large amounts of personal information. The Department argued that it required data to develop effective social policies for the knowledge economy.

What do these three issues have in common? First, each involves civil servants. In the Walkerton tragedy, civil servants were key players at the municipal and provincial levels. They ran the water system, inspected it, and established and enforced standards. They did so in conjunction with public health workers, police, and government scientists. In the armed forces case, soldiers were on board the transport ship. They were crucial actors in reclaiming the military equipment. Government lawyers and diplomats in Ottawa and Washington resolved the matter. And at Human Resources, civil servants were involved in policy making and were prime users and suppliers of confidential personal information. Each case reveals civil servants at the heart of an important controversy. Second, the cases show the complexity of the modern public sector. The tragedy at Walkerton revealed, probably for the first time to many Canadians, the considerable complexity of public administration as it is now widely undertaken. The provision of water, an activity citizens seldom consider carefully, was shown to involve a plethora of municipal, provincial, not-for-profit and profit-seeking organizations. The armed forces case shows that matters of national defence also embrace a whole range of government and private agencies. And the Human Resources case revealed to many Canadians an obvious abuse of confidential information. How much nominally confidential information is shared, via computer data banks, between government agencies? Can health insurance companies and employers also have access? Can the data be sold?

Two themes dominate our exploration of the civil service and public management. First, the civil service is a powerful institution. It exerts influence by participating in the setting of the policy agenda, both by implementing policy and by making regulations that shape society. As this chapter explains, these critical roles pose complex and controversial questions about democracy, representation, and accountability. The second theme is that the civil service is being fundamentally altered by new ideas which require that governments be "run like businesses." "New public management" embraces changing ideas about the role of government and the civil service itself. The civil service, traditionally seen as a staid and distant institution is at the heart of a complex debate about the impact of technological innovation, economic restructuring, and international economic changes. In this vein, a critical question, not yet answered, arises. In whose interest is government being reinvented?

Serious students of political science must understand the dynamics, policy influence, and structures of the civil service. But an alert awareness of civil service power serves more than intellectual purposes. Citizens are very likely to engage the political system through contact with a civil servant. Civil servants implement policies that influence our daily lives. They deal with interest groups, politicians, and, in a federal state or in the international arena, other governments. The civil service, even in an era of downsizing, is a huge institution. It is involved in all important and routine operations of modern government. At the same time, it is complex and difficult to understand. It is a force to be reckoned with.

Politics and the Administrative State

EARLIER IN THE TWENTIETH CENTURY, THE RELATIONSHIP BETWEEN BUREAUCRACY and democracy was explained by the **politics–administration dichotomy**. This awkward term means something simple—policy-making and policy implementation are separate and distinct activities. Elected politicians make policy. Appointed civil servants impartially implement it. The further notion is that policy choices embody complex tradeoffs between competing values and interests. Administration, on the other hand, is thought to be a process that, while often complex, is essentially a technical one.

The dichotomy is a poor reflection of reality. Civil servants are extensively involved in policy making. They have the knowledge of past practice, the technical skills and the time to prepare detailed policy proposals for busy governments. Policy making and policy implementation are now seen as intertwined, not separate, activities. Policy is often made by tight alliances between politicians, interest groups, and senior civil servants. Civil service power in policy making is substantial in a country such as Canada where national political parties have no independent policy-making capacity and where election platforms are weak on policy detail. Moreover, the contending parties seldom differ fundamentally about the role of government. Once elected, governments must therefore put flesh on the bones of their platforms. Senior civil servants are key in the policy-making process.

Senior civil servants are expected to give advice that is broadly political. They exercise influence when they analyze the possible response of interest groups and/or other governments to a proposed policy or a change in existing policy. This role led one British writer to describe senior civil servants in Britain in the following way: "The ability to give policy advice took precedence over the qualities of management. The mandarin elite was both anonymous and neutral, in the party political sense. Its role was to be that of the political chameleon; its members were to have the acrobatic qualities necessary to turn political somersaults" (Greenaway, 1991).

The active policy role of the senior civil service rests uneasily with democratic ideals. Concern is often expressed that the civil service has its own "agenda" and gets overly comfortable with governments especially when one political party forms the government for a long time. New governments or governments determined to change policy are often apprehensive about the loyalty of the civil service. In Canada, the federal Conservative party under Prime Ministers Diefenbaker, Clark, and Mulroney worried about the loyalty of the senior civil service who they thought were Liberals at heart. In each instance, a good working relationship was established without undue disruption or dismissal of senior officials. Conservative provincial governments in Ontario and Alberta have stressed the need to put politicians back in charge of decision making.

A change of government in Canada rarely brings dramatic changes in the composition of the senior civil service. This contrasts with the United States, where many senior civil servants are the personal appointees of the president and serve only at his or her discretion. Senior civil servants in the United States are often drawn from the private sector, not the civil service itself. They serve only as long as the president who appoints them is in office. The civil service is not their career. Canadian governments have opted for a senior civil service that is in principle permanent, non-partisan, and anonymous. As characterized in the popular British television show, "Yes Minister," politicians walk a tightrope when dealing with an influential civil service. On one hand, politicians need the cooperation of the senior civil service. On the other hand, efforts to staff the senior civil service with loyalists are criticized for "politicizing" the civil service and robbing it of necessary expertise and neutrality (Whitaker, 1995).

Civil services are the instruments, par excellence, of policy implementation. A civil servant, not a politician, adjudicates student loan applications. Customs agents at border crossings decide who enters Canada. Officials at the Canada Customs and Revenue Agency assess our tax forms. But the implementation of policy can be a complex, contentious process. Civil servants have discretion in how they decide cases. As Stephen Brooks puts it: "Policy implementation is the role of the bureaucracy. It is not, however, an automatic process of converting legislative decisions into action. Unelected officials often wield enormous discretion in applying laws and administering programmes." (Brooks, 1996, 165). Civil service resistance to political leaders can be subtle, hard to detect, and hard to change.

Another distinct role for civil servants is rule making. Modern laws are cast in general terms. They outline principles and desired outcomes and then delegate day-to-day administration to the government and to the civil service. The civil service generates the detailed regulations that make laws come to life when applied in particular cases. Consider, for example, the considerable discretion enjoyed by police officers and customs agents in the performance of their daily duties. In undertaking this role, public servants influence our lives in very specific ways. Civil service rule making is especially important because governments seldom examine carefully the content of regulations and how they are applied. They have neither the time nor the expertise to do so.

The Organization of Government

IN CANADA AND OTHER COUNTRIES, THE CIVIL SERVICE IS ORGANIZED INTO many different organizational forms each with distinctive responsibilities and relationships with governments. In Canada, important public activities are administered by departments of government whose hallmark is direct control by a cabinet minister. At the federal level, the departments of Justice and National Defence symbolize basic roles of government—the provision of a legal framework and the defence of citizens and territory. Such departments as Agriculture and Industry deal with specific sectors of the economy. Indian Affairs and Veterans Affairs serve particular groups of citizens. The Department of Finance provides economic analysis and as already noted, wields great influence. Other departments such as Health, Environment, and Natural Resources deal with particular policy sectors.

Unlike departments, some important government agencies are independent from direct political control. They are at an "arm's length" from cabinet. The Canadian Radio-television and Telecommunications Commission (CRTC) is an important example of an independent, regulatory agency. It makes significant decisions about Canadian content in media, about the rates for cable television and phone service, and about which radio and television stations are licensed to operate. The CRTC enjoys considerable independence from the government and from parliament. In Alberta, a regulatory body, the Energy and Utilities Board, exercises extensive influence over the prices paid for power and over the terms and conditions under which important resource developments can proceed. Like the CRTC, the government establishes its broad mandate but is not involved in day-to-day operating decisions.

Crown corporations are another type of independent agency. Since Confederation, Canadian governments have owned businesses. In the twentieth century, such enterprises became known as Crown corporations; in other countries they are called government or public corporations. Crown corporations represent governments' efforts to supplement the market economy and to shape economic development. For much of the twentieth century, important companies such as the Canadian National Railway, Air Canada, and Petro-Canada were owned by the federal government. Provincial governments also own major firms. Ontario Hydro and Hydro Quebec are prime examples. In the last two decades, governments have "privatized" many Crown corporations including Air Canada, Canadian National, and Petro-Canada. This process has been controversial as critics have argued that governments have given up an important mechanism to control their domestic economies in the face of global economic change. Supporters of privatization discount this argument and contend that many Crown corporations are products of an earlier period in Canadian political economy and that they have outlived their original rationales. Regardless of this complex debate, Crown corporations are still important parts of the economy. As organizations, they operate according to a distinct philosophy. They are free from government interference in their day-to-day activities. Crown corporations, if they are to compete, are said to need freedom of action in their operations. Governments set the overall policy framework, appoint a board of directors, and monitor progress.

Public management theory now claims that many government services and programs can be better delivered by private firms and/or non-profit agencies. Its adherents believe that government departments should establish the policy framework but need not actually deliver services to citizens. This view is embodied in the idea of *alternative service delivery*. This usually means that government becomes a "partner" with non-governmental organizations who actually deal with citizens. For example, many government programs for Aboriginal people are delivered through complex relationships between federal, provincial, and Aboriginal governments as well as firms and not-for-profit agencies. Another very interesting example is Literacy New Brunswick, an organization established by the government of New Brunswick to find new ways to confront the problem of illiteracy (Ferguson, 1997). Literacy New Brunswick is a non-profit agency, independent of government, and run by a private-sector board of directors. Its task is to find new solutions to the problem of illiteracy through the establishment of partnerships between governments, business, schools, and citizen groups. Even universities, allegedly bastions of quiet reflection, routinely embrace partnerships for the acquisition of equipment, the undertaking of research, and even the construction and renovation of buildings. Critics worry that such partnerships undervalue the role of government and the importance of accountability as a democratic value.

Government organization is a political matter, not a technical issue. Skillful governments use organization to political advantage. They regroup departments, for example, to reflect new policy priorities. A good example of this is the federal government's establishment of a Department of Human Resource Development, which was established to bring an integrated federal approach to policy development in the complex field of human resource development. In turn, human resource development is related to the now widely held view that "human capital" (a well-educated, healthy work force) is essential to economic progress in a period of rapid technological change. Governments also use independent agencies to confer policy power on interest groups and to shield them from public debate. They change organizations to weaken the power of some interests and to enhance that of others. As two American scholars argue, government organization is about "power, politics, and position" (Seidman and Gilmour, 1986).

Representative Bureaucracy and Democratic Government

DEMOCRATIC GOVERNMENTS NOW ACCEPT THE IDEA THAT THE CIVIL SERVICE must be staffed on the basis of merit. But merit is a hotly debated topic. Nonetheless, whatever problems there may be with a merit system, it at least means that all citizens should have a chance to gain public employment and that successful applicants for government employment must have the skills required to do the job at hand. It stands in stark contrast to earlier periods when civil service positions were almost exclusively allocated on the basis of political patronage and as rewards for service to a political party.

The ideal of a merit civil service is partially challenged by the competing notion of representative bureaucracy. **Representative bureaucracy** asserts that a civil service must reflect the major social groups in society in its ranks. Such a civil service, it is argued, is an end in itself as well as a means to the end of good government. This is so because a representative civil service will allegedly represent the diversity of the society and reflect specific and competing needs in its policy making. This view of the civil service has a long intellectual tradition that predates arguments about "affirmative action" and "employment equity." The Canadian civil service now boasts a range of policies and procedures designed to recruit and advance such underrepresented groups as women, visible minorities, and Aboriginal and disabled persons.

In Canada the idea of representative bureaucracy assumed national significance when Prime Minister Trudeau was elected in 1968. Trudeau had a distinct vision of Canada and how it should operate if Quebec nationalism was to be tamed. He believed that federal government institutions had to be transformed to reflect Canada's bilingual and bicultural essence. Essentially, Trudeau wanted two things—that francophones be better integrated into all levels of the civil service and that the federal civil service have the capacity to serve Canadians in both official languages. A bilingual federal public service is part of the Trudeau legacy.

As Canada has changed, so too has the debate about representation in the civil service. Aboriginal peoples, women, the disabled, and "visible minorities" now argue that they are underrepresented, especially in the senior civil service. Women's issues received an extended treatment in a 1990 federal task force report that painted a gloomy picture of subtle and overt discrimination against female employees (Canada, 1990). In response, Ottawa has undertaken "employment equity" initiatives. In contrast to the American experience with "affirmative action," the federal government has avoided quotas and preferential hiring practices. Instead, it has tried to change the "climate" and to persuade underrepresented groups to see federal employment as an option. Such a "go slow" approach reduces conflict but also leads to slower progress in achieving a more representative civil service.

Early in the new millennium, the future of employment equity in Canada is unclear. Some governments, notably the Harris Conservatives in Ontario, have reduced substantially their commitment to employment equity and have, in the eyes of equity advocates, radically weakened the province's capacity to promote social justice. On the other hand, civic governments, presiding over large, racially divided cities, face pressures to ensure that police and other "front line" civil servants represent and understand a changing citizenry.

Who Controls the Civil Service?

THE CIVIL SERVICE IS PRIMARILY CONSTRAINED BY OTHER POLITICAL INSTITUTIONS. Parliament has a duty to review and to debate the quality of administration. In Canada, the principle of "individual ministerial responsibility" asserts that a minister is publicly responsible for the decisions of his or her department. This principle establishes a point of accountability. It also allows the civil service to remain anonymous as only the minister defends decisions in public. Such anonymity allows for an easy transition if governments change—the senior civil service is not publicly identified with the policies of the previous government.

Governments also have "central agencies" that scrutinize the activities of other government departments. In Canada, the Privy Council Office is a powerful central agency that reviews other departments' proposals for their "fit" with government priorities. Its head, the Clerk of the Privy Council, is the senior federal civil servant. The Treasury Board Secretariat is a central agency whose role is that of a general manager. It establishes administrative practices for the entire federal government. The rise of strong central agencies highlights an irony—governments establish bureaucracies to check the bureaucracy. Finally, courts have some capacity to review the decisions of civil servants and, under some circumstances, to reverse them.

These controls are not entirely effective. Parliament shows little interest in scrutinizing the complex activities of the civil service. Spectacular maladministration may be the subject of question period but rigorous follow up is rare. The principle of ministerial responsibility is often seen as a reflection of a simpler period and as a device that shields civil servants from scrutiny. Critics mock the idea that a single person can be responsible for the activities of thousands of civil servants, many of whom work far from Ottawa. Central agencies assist governments in controlling the civil service. But they too are small compared to most departments, without substantial budgets, and limited in the sorts of thorough reviews they can undertake. Moreover, who controls the so-called "superbureaucrats" who staff the central agencies? Finally, judicial review of administrative decisions is a slow, expensive procedure that is not readily available to citizens. Many issues of maladministration do not involve large matters of principle or money and for these reasons do not make legal processes attractive. Are you likely to take legal action because a civil servant has been slow, by your standards, in assessing your student loan application? Moreover, courts are often more interested in the procedures employed in government decision making than in the content of decisions themselves. This narrow view makes judicial review even less effective.

Governments use many other devices to keep the civil service responsive to political direction and fair in its dealing with the public. Provincial governments have ombudsmen. An **ombudsman** is an officer of the legislature whose role is to handle citizens' complaints about civil service wrongdoing. Ombudsmen examine decisions to see if they are fair and sensible. The government of Canada has opted for several specialized ombudsmen. It has an information and privacy commissioner, an ombudsman for prisoners and most recently, an ombudsman for the Canadian Armed Forces. The Canadian Human Rights Commission is a quasi-judicial federal agency with powers to investigate complaints of discrimination and wrong-doing. In a hotly debated "pay equity" decision in 1998, it ruled that the Government of Canada had seriously undervalued the work of many female employees and that the government owed them billions of dollars of back pay. Although an intense controversy continues about the meaning of pay equity itself, the federal government has begun to compensate its female employees.

Another important check on the civil service is the Auditor General who is an officer of parliament charged with ensuring the honesty and efficiency of government spending. In recent years, the Auditor General's office has expanded the range of its investigations to include the quality of management processes, the rigour of program evaluation, and the appropriateness, not merely the efficiency, of some federal programs. Considerable debate has ensued about the techniques employed to evaluate the "success" of government programs and the capacity of Auditors General to do this sort of work. The Auditor General's annual report documents horror stories of waste and mismanagement that generate considerable media attention. Government departments take criticism by the Auditor General very seriously even though they often disagree with the conclusions reached.

Freedom of Information legislation (sometimes called Access to Information) also allows for scrutiny of the civil service. Until recently, Canadian governments tightly controlled information about their activities and released it only on their terms. Freedom of Information laws have changed this situation. These laws establish the principle that citizens have a right of access to government information and documents. Such access is not absolute— governments retain considerable amounts of information and dispense it as they see fit.

Access to information laws nevertheless give citizens a new resource in dealing with governments. Finally, media, especially television, frequently publicize civil service wrongdoings. Negative media coverage may lead to the reversal of specific decisions and occasionally to policy changes. But media activities are sporadic, undertaken at the media's discretion, and often geared to business imperatives.

The New Public Management: Issues and Challenges

DEMOCRATIC GOVERNMENT IS CHANGING IN RESPONSE TO COMPUTER TECHNOLOGY, new roles for government, and changes in the world economy. Modern civil services have been profoundly affected by these forces. A "new public management" has emerged that alters the relationships between the civil service, governments, citizens, and the private sector. The civil service has arguably changed more dramatically, and with less debate, than other political institutions and even the private sector. Traditional assumptions about the civil service are rapidly being replaced by the idea that governments should be "run like businesses." This idea has often informed public management in the past, especially in the United States. But seldom has it been so widely accepted as a basis for civil service reform.

"New public management" is a complex set of ideas, civil service reforms, and management processes. At its core, new public management has the following dimensions:

- The civil service, like large private firms, must strive to achieve clearly defined "results."
- Efforts must be made to fully understand the interconnectedness of organizations.
- Traditional distinctions between public and private sectors, between governments and civil society are exaggerated. Spheres of society are interdependent. Above all else, government organizations must understand and celebrate interdependence. They cannot operate in "silos" and in isolation from other sectors of society.
- Civil service performance must be measured by quantifiable indicators called "performance indicators." The civil service must define its "core" mission and establish "business plans" to achieve its goals.
- Civil servants must be "entrepreneurial." They should feel "empowered" to take risks and to be innovative. Classical, hierarchical, control-oriented bureaucracies are outmoded in this environment. Civil servants must be fully prepared to change with the times. Past practice should seldom guide their approach to policy making and service delivery.
- Civil servants must be more attuned to the needs of the citizens. Citizens should be seen as "customers" or "clients" of government agencies.
- Governments should "steer," not "row." The civil service should work with politicians to establish policies and create a framework for action. But where possible, government services should be delivered by private and/or not-for-profit firms that are said to be more "efficient" and responsive to consumer preferences. At

the very least, public services must be "reengineered" to embrace new approaches to service delivery.

- Civil servants must understand the imperatives of a bottom line. They must be skilled in cost cutting and the management of restraint.
- Senior civil servants should shift their priorities from policy advice to general management.

These ideas reflect strands of economic theory, business management ideas about "re-engineering" corporations, the concept of economic "globalization," and the impact of computer technology. The present emphasis on service quality is heavily shaped by the "customer service revolution" in retail industries. For some observers, new public management is the public-sector equivalent of the sweeping changes that occurred in the private sector during the 1980s. For others, it provides ways to increase governments' responsiveness to citizens. Advocates of new public management frequently assert that individual civil servants are intelligent and well motivated. They are hamstrung, however, by rule-bound government bureaucracies that force rigid behaviour. Still others see new public management as a source of new ideas in an era of budget cutting. New management principles will allow the civil service to do "more with less." Seen together, these ideas offer democratic citizens a modern utopia—a civil service that delivers the benefits of active government without the impediment of a threatening, inefficient bureaucracy.

Two commonly held views about new public management require comment. First, some critics see new public management as a fad, another float in the never ending parade of "fix-all" management theories. This view should be treated with skepticism. New public management principles have been implemented throughout the democratic world. They cannot be dismissed as passing fancies. Second, critics of new public management see it as the ideological handmaiden of neoliberal governments determined to weaken government and to strengthen business control over society. New public management sugarcoats a dismantling of democratic government. This generalization should also be approached cautiously. Governments of differing ideologies have embraced new public management. In Canada, for example, the Klein Conservatives in Alberta, the NDP government of Saskatchewan, the Harris Conservatives in Ontario, and the Parti Quebecois government in Quebec are all apostles of new public management.

New public management has sparked criticism and debate within governments, between experts, and at the level of the electorate. This debate is complex but several strands are summarized here:

- Citizens are not "customers" of government. In a democracy, citizens have complex rights and obligations. Their relationship to government is demeaned by the superficial idea of citizen as customer.
- New public management is naive about the differences between governments and business. Government policies embody complex value choices and tradeoffs. They must respond to competing definitions of the public interest and they must operate under strict rules of disclosure, openness, and accountability. Firms face no such issues or constraints.

- Markets have their drawbacks as well as their benefits. In fact, much government activity tries to shelter society from the excesses of market capitalism. An effective democracy requires a balance between the market economy and government intervention through an accountable civil service.

- New public management is preoccupied with measuring results. But the impact of public policies on society is an extraordinarily complex issue. How can results be measured when no consensus exists about the goals of many public policies? In an analysis of this issue, Henry Mintzberg discusses an example—the "success rate" of liver transplant surgery (Mintzberg: 1996). His example shows how nurses, surgeons, and administrators differ deeply about the definition, let alone measurement, of "success." Think about this example and then think about the health care system, the penal system, or the educational system as totalities. What is your definition of success?

- New public management may not simplify government. Critics worry that the civil service is becoming fragmented and more difficult to control. What will happen as governments move into partnerships with private firms who deliver services to citizens on terms negotiated with governments? Who will be accountable when problems arise? Who runs the partnerships?

- New public management's stress on entrepreneurial behaviour in the civil service can lead to serious ethical problems. Civil servants are bombarded with mixed messages about serving the government, their "customers," the "bottom line," and the public interest. In Canada in 1998, an excellent illustration of these tensions occurred when scientists at Health Canada claimed they had been pressured by superiors to approve various drugs for commercial use in the face of scientific worries about the drugs' overall effectiveness and possible serious side effects. Whose interests was Health Canada pursuing—the health needs of Canadian citizens or the commercial needs of the drug manufacturers? Whose values should prevail when conflict occurs between competing interests? (Doig, 1993)

DEBATE BOX

The Tragedy of Walkerton: Bad Luck or Structural Flaws in Government?

The tragic events in Walkerton, Ontario where residents were poisoned by their municipal water supply raise troubling questions. Was the tragedy the result of misjudgment and lack of attention on the part of provincial regulators and municipal officials? Or was it symptomatic of a deeper malaise?

Does Walkerton represent the impact of "new public management" in practice? Is it an example of an administrative system that entails inadequate funding, improper definition of roles and responsibilities, and an excessive number of public and quasi-public actors with unclear roles? Is Walkerton simply a horrible aberration? Or has government restraint and administrative restructuring imperiled the quality of public administration in general? Would a "traditional" government bureaucracy, however defined, have responded better and/or differently? Can you envision reforms?

Summary

Two themes dominate this chapter. First, the civil service is a powerful force in government. It houses the expertise required for effective policy making. It is a key force in shaping new policies, in implementing policy, and in making legislation come to life in everyday situations. Politicians nominally direct the civil service. In reality, they negotiate with it. Second, economic and social changes have given rise to a new understanding of the civil service. "New public management" envisions the civil service as a goal-driven institution whose behaviour should be like that of a large firm.

Can new public management really live up to its claims? Advocates of new public management see their ideas as correctives to the excesses of the modern bureaucratic state. In one sense, the most ardent advocates offer citizens a utopia—the benefits of active government without the obstacle of an inefficient over-bearing civil service. But is the civil service really the "problem" that many citizens and politicians believe it to be? In an insightful analysis of the contemporary American scene, Kenneth J. Meier argues that the civil service is wrongly defined as the source of many political and economic problems. He believes that the civil service is functioning effectively but sees serious problems in the legislative and executive branches and in the party system. Media-driven politicians surround themselves with partisan loyalists who engage in superficial policy analysis aimed at short-run political popularity. Modern politics is a perpetual election campaign. Governments' short-sighted policies fail and public cynicism increases. In Canada, a similar analysis has been provided by Donald Savoie. His argument is that the prime minister has become too powerful, civil servants are wrongly blamed for all sorts of woes, and policy-making is driven by short-sighted appeals to public opinion and image creation (Savoie, 1999).

While some advocate the benefits of the new public management, others emphasize the positive impact of new computer technologies and the great potential in "on-line" service delivery. Citizens will be spared lineups and delays. Governments can group their services more easily, thereby offering "single window service." On the other hand, many government services are complex and cannot easily be delivered on line. And it is not obvious that impersonal, computer-delivered services are, in any deep way, superior to those provided in person. In so far as policy making is concerned, the Internet provides civil servants with access to vast amounts of information. But this information still has to be distilled, reflected upon, and made coherent.

In the early twenty-first century, Canadians will likely see new programs and increased public expenditures in social policy and health care. The "post-deficit" world raises two paramount questions for the civil service. First, after a decade of downsizing, does the civil service have the policy capacity, the depth of knowledge, and the experience required to mount innovative new programs? This concern is reflected in worries about a "brain drain" of senior civil servants to the private sector where remuneration is much higher. Second, has "new public management" so changed the relationship between civil servants, governments, and citizens that policy innovation will be difficult? Is the civil service like a faucet that can be turned on or off depending on the circumstances? Or is it more like Humpty Dumpty—has it changed so profoundly in its philosophy and structure that, once broken, it cannot easily be reassembled?

Discussion Questions

1. Can the civil service be run like a business? Should it be?

2. Do you agree with the idea of a "representative civil service"? How should it be achieved?

3. What issues do modern computer technologies raise for the power and control of the civil service and the quality of democracy?

4. Does the term "permanent politician" aptly describe the role of the senior civil servant?

5. In your opinion, how effective are the existing controls and influences over the Canadian civil service?

References

Brooks, Stephen. 1996. *Canadian Democracy: An Introduction, second edition.* Toronto: Oxford University Press.

Doig, Alan. 1993. "Mixed Signals? Public Sector Change and the Proper Conduct of Government Business." *Public Administration 73*, 191-212.

Ferguson, David. 1997. "Literacy in Your Own Backyard: The Challenge in New Brunswick." In Robin Ford and David Zussman (eds.) *Alternative Service Delivery: Sharing Governance in Canada.* Toronto: Institute of Public Administration of Canada, 205-208.

Greenaway, John. 1991. "Having the Bun and Halfpenny: Can Old Public Service Ethics Survive in the New Whitehall?" *Public Administration 73*, 357-374.

Meier, Kenneth J. 1997. "Bureaucracy and Democracy: The Case for More Bureaucracy and Less Democracy." *Public Administration Review 57*, 193-199.

Mintzberg, Henry. 1996. "Managing Government: Governing Management." *Harvard Business Review May-June*, 75-83.

Prince, Michael. 1998. "New Mandate, New Money, New Politics: Federal Budgeting in the Post-Deficit Era." In Leslie A. Pal, ed., *How Ottawa Spends, 1998-99.* Toronto: Oxford University Press, 31-55.

Savoie, Donald J. 2000. "The Rise of Court Government in Canada," *Canadian Journal of Political Science, 32*, 635-664.

Seidman, Harold and R. Gilmour. 1986. *Politics, Position and Power, fourth edition.* New York: Oxford University Press.

Tupper, Allan. 1994. "The Civil Service." In T.C. Pocklington, ed., *Representative Democracy: An Introduction to Politics and Government.* Toronto: Harcourt and Brace, 239-274.

Whitaker, Reg. 1995. "Politicians and Bureaucrats in the Policy Process." In M.S. Whittington and Glen Williams, eds., *Canadian Politics in the 1990s.* Toronto: Nelson Canada, 424-440.

Further Readings

Osborne, David and Peter Plastirk. 1997. *Banishing Bureaucracy: The Five Strategies for Reinventing Government*. Reading, Mass.: Addison-Wesley.

Pal, Leslie A. (ed.). 1998. *How Ottawa Spends, 1998-99: Balancing Act: The Post Deficit Mandate*. Toronto: Oxford University Press.

Peters. B. Guy and Savoie, D.J. (eds.). 1998. *Taking Stock: Assessing Public Sector Reforms*. Montreal: McGill-Queen's University Press.

Thompson, Dennis F. 1987. *Political Ethics and Public Office*. Cambridge Mass.: Harvard University Press.

Wilson, James Q. 1989. *Bureaucracy: What Government Agencies Do and Why They Do It*. New York: Basic Books.

Weblinks

Alliance for Redesigning Government
www.alliance.napawash.org/alliance/index.html

Canadian Policy Research Networks
www.cprn.com/

Public Service Alliance of Canada
www.psac.com/Homeeng.htm

The Public Policy Forum
www.ppforum.com/

Institute for Research on Public Policy
www.irpp.org/

The Canadian Centre for Policy Alternatives
www.policyalternatives.ca/

CHAPTER 14

LOCAL GOVERNMENT AND POLITICS

JAMES
LIGHTBODY

Objectives

In this chapter we explore the critical issues that define local politics and political participation. Local politics—the governing of cities, villages, towns and municipalities, and their school districts—is often considered of little importance. Local governments, however, directly deliver some of the most tangible public goods of the modern state. Politics and citizenship have little meaning unless citizens have water and sewerage, roads and walkways, fire and police, recreation, and the privacy that ensues from effective town planning.

This chapter discusses how local governments were initially conceived by some as the most appropriate site to nurture democracy and meaningful links between citizens and government. Currently, the alleged decline in the importance of national governments in a globalizing era and the rise of world cities has led to a renewed call for a revitalized local democratic tradition. We will assess several of the themes and debates posed by local government and politics. In particular, we will explore the persistent tension in central—local government relations, agenda-setting at the local level, fiscal austerity and ethical behaviours in local politics and, finally, the interface between local communities and the emerging world economy.

Introduction

It is sometimes useful to distinguish "municipal" from "local" government. The first describes the politics of towns, cities, municipalities; the latter term is more generic and broad enough to include school divisions, library boards, health districts, planning or police commissions, and so on, some of which may be elected while many others are not. A great deal of what political science has to say about political power, both in abstract and applied terms, has come from studies of local politics. It is often understood either as the foundation for democratic politics or as a microcosm of larger political processes. Paradoxically, most people do not consider the politics of municipal government to be as important as that associated with geographically larger governing units. Voter turnout in Canada, for example, is consistently lower in municipal than in provincial or federal elections.

Local government is sometimes referred to as "low" politics in contrast with the "high" politics of national government and its responsibilities for national security as well as fiscal, social, and economic policy. The idea that local politics is less important is hard to sustain however. What low politics is about is our daily lives, our schools, our work, and our communities.

Urbanization and Local Government

OFTEN THERE IS A TENSION BETWEEN MUNICIPAL AND CENTRAL GOVERNMENT political agendas. Central governments may impose rules for local administration that thwart genuine local democracy, limit local revenues, and direct local expenditures. International evidence, however, increasingly suggests that local communities and local community choices are increasingly important to effective performance in the global economy. They are as central to growing national economies as is nurturing the health of wider democratic governing.

Democracy is a disputed political concept. Some equate it solely with the selection of political leaders through periodic elections. The idea of local democracy implies more— it implies the direct, open, free, and meaningful involvement of women and men in the debate and resolution of policies directly impinging on daily life. In most countries, citizen involvement rarely measures up to this ideal. Studies indicate that in Britain, for example, only about fifty thousand people in a population of 44 million are deeply involved in local and national government as political and administrative elites (Lightbody, 1995, 19). Canadian studies reveal a similarly low level of engagement and probably well under five percent of us choose the gladiatorial toil of direct political activity (Higgins, 1986, 261–263). The obvious distance between ordinary citizens and the business of their own governing between elections is a reflection of a time when individuals are openly cynical towards those who hold public office, those who report their activities, and any other traditional hierarchy of authority be it public or private (Zussman, 1997; Graham and Phillips, 1997).

Despite their widespread disregard for local political institutions, most Canadians reside in the urban metropolis, officially designated as Census Metropolitan Areas (CMAs). A CMA is defined as a built-up urban core, plus its proximate commuter-shed, of 100 000 and more population. Some scholars now refer to these central city and commuting suburb systems as city-regions, a term more in vogue in the international community. By the last census in Canada, 22.4 million (or 78 percent) of our citizens were living in 25 of these CMAs. Canada has become one of the most urbanized countries in the world. The population movement from farm to city occurred with such rapidity following the Second World War that both governing and many other social institutions of the city have yet to adapt completely or well. For instance, in 1996, the ten largest of these districts were governed by just under 300 municipalities quite exclusive of schools boards, hospital districts, and the numerous other agencies of the modern state.

In many ways, the governing of large urban centres through multiple smaller municipalities encourages small town politics within the larger socio-economic city. Such practices are partially reinforced by the fiscal self-interest of legally entrenched suburbs and their elected councillors, and partly by nostalgia-driven anxieties of suburban residents that their communities will be subsumed in big city uniformities. Regardless, there are policy consequences. Without an area-wide government, it is always the region whose interest is sacrificed at any bargaining table. The finding of area-wide solutions has not proven to be an easy policy task.

Evolution of Central–Local Relations

CANADIANS ARE CITIZENS OF THREE OFFICIAL LEVELS OF AUTHORITY—THE municipal, provincial, and federal. Similar to the provincial–federal conflicts so characteristic of Canadian politics, there is built into the intergovernmental context a historic conflict between two aspects of local government. These are the administration of the policy objectives of provincial and federal governments versus those reflecting local priorities and control. Over time this has led to heightened local sensitivity over the extent to which municipal citizens possess the defining authority when it is pitted against the national, regional, or provincial economic, social, and political agendas for which the same citizens, presumably, have also voted. Central–local tensions are an ongoing fact of life for municipal governing.

The roots of democratic local government in Canada can be found in the larger struggle for responsible government over 150 years ago. The 1849 Municipal Corporations Act followed directly from the rebellion a decade earlier. It set out the general structure of Upper Canada's, now Ontario's, municipalities. If measured by local autonomy and control, it was a considerable advance beyond what then existed in England and the American states. Still existing in its essentials, this 1849 Act reflected the conclusion of Lord Durham's Report (1839) that the "main cause" of the Rebellion had been the absence of citizen control over local affairs. Durham, nicknamed "Radical Jack" for his drafting and support of the Reform Bill in England, and sent to Canada as a reward, wrote this in his 1839 Report: "The establishment of municipal institutions for the whole country should be made a part of every colonial constitution. . . ." Still, the authority of the crown would be needed to keep an eye on what in time would come to be called provincial authorities "until the people should become alive, as most assuredly they almost immediately would be, to the necessity of protecting their local privileges." It is not at all clear that we have yet done so even as the general prerogatives of the Crown quickly dissipated.

The Durham recommendations were adopted by central authorities as a way to incorporate municipalities and to construct local public works through the use of local taxation on property assessment. Any hope and optimism in direct local democracy initiated by the thoughts and writings of Durham and his successor Lord Sydenham were displaced by cynical cunning to force local self-reliance as a means to relieve the central purse of responsibility for "purely local" undertakings. Central authorities in any case kept the power, then and now, to restrain local spending initiatives on the pretext of protecting the "credit" of local governments, which is another way to say safeguarding the property of wealthy men from local taxation. In this context, the 1990s practice of downloading responsibility for provincial programs onto local governments has solid precedent. What the phrase "downloading" means, in plain language, is the assigning of spending responsibilities to local governments without also providing them with new sources of taxation or other revenue. Buck-passing is another accurate descriptive term. The struggle over who does what to whom when, and why, and who pays, always lies at the very heart of any pattern of central–local relations, and of democratic politics itself.

On the prairies, allowing settlers to use local initiative to create municipalities along Ontario's lines failed precisely because of shrewd suspicions of exactly these same motivations, and an appreciation that new governments would mean new taxes. Once the structures were forced upon them by provincial governments in the early part of the twentieth century however, residents quickly took to them, like ducks to water, for purposes of schooling, public health, and roads. S.M. Lipset, in his *Agrarian Socialism*, once noted that in Saskatchewan in the 1950s local offices in school boards, municipalities, hospital and other districts, and cooperatives, meant that "there is one position available for every two or three farmers." About 15 percent of the rural population held elective posts exclusive of church, community organizations, fraternal lodges, and the like.

Another current issue in central–local relations is the question of how best to govern large metropolitan areas. This question of appropriate institutions has persistently befuddled central governments. Local governing structures that are more or less congruent with their respective urban regions must somehow be sustained. Yet the inexorable growth through urbanization has blurred the once neat separations between city cores and their suburbs. The idea of area-wide governments, however necessary, faces serious resistance. City suburbs, for example, want to maintain their municipal boundaries as a way to keep taxes lower than in the urban central city, and local services such as policing and recreation more responsive to their control.

It was Niccolo Machiavelli who once shrewdly noted that in the practice of politics there is no constituency for change and this is nowhere more the case than in struggles to integrate the multiple jurisdictions of metropolitan areas. Hence the creation of area-wide governments requires either very tough partisan calculations or, sometimes, more purely ideological ones, by a central government. In England, the Conservative government abolished area-wide government in London (and six other metropolitan centres) in 1986 only to have Labour reinstitute it for London in 1998. In Canada, Toronto's communities were amalgamated into one city in 1997 despite fierce opposition. In 2000, also despite fierce opposition, Montreal moved to amalgamate into "One Island One City." Halifax, Winnipeg and Calgary also have one government for the metropolitan area.

Other large CMAs in Canada and elsewhere have yet to see a reform of their municipal government organization to match the realities of the contemporary city. The United States has about 120 local governments in each census metropolis; Pittsburgh has 323, New York has 1787. Communities such as these are ripe for municipal reorganization but it does not develop easily. To be resolved always are problems that require area-wide coordination (water, transit, freeways), policies equalizing tax rates and service costs and questions essentially affixing accountability for what has been accomplished. Or not. Beneath all this, though, is the fundamental concern that cities in the demographic sense, without governments, face serious impediments to longer term economic growth, fairness in social development, and effective governing.

Setting the Agenda

OUR POLITICAL LEGACY IS ONE OF REPRESENTATIVE DEMOCRACY. SIMILAR TO THE United States, Canada's early steps towards local democratic accountability were cast in the struggle against arbitrary authority. But the style and forms of local "administration" were quickly removed from these inklings of direct grassroots control. At higher levels of government the idea of democratic accountability was gradually merged with party politics. In its most idealized form, citizens voted for party platforms and leaders who, in turn, were held accountable through periodic elections. Unlike provincial or federal politics, or municipal politics throughout most of the world, North American community leaders have tried to insulate their municipal politics from party competition. When pressed for an explanation as to why this is so, the typical response is that what local governments do is not suited to partisan division ("there is no Liberal way to pave a street") and that political parties inevitably lead to the grossest corruptions and patronage abuses. Regardless, the argument that the politics of cities that do have purely local parties such as Montreal or Vancouver is any more corrupt than nonpartisan systems would be difficult to sustain.

The political reality is that the non-party council is a political realm in which it is, at one and the same time, both easier and more difficult for those in administrative positions to implement public policy. It is more difficult because councillors are absolute independents elected, in their minds, on the basis of their individual worth. Certainly the mayor is not empowered for, in Canada, this person is only the head of council, not in any sense a CEO, and can promise no victory for any council vote with any degree of certainty. In most provinces, while the head of council is not absolutely symbolic as in Britain, neither is the position that of the strong corporate chief as in many major American cities.

Each issue, every policy choice, all budget votes, any internal reorganization is "up for grabs" for that 50 percent, plus one, voting majority of councillors. Councillors who are nonpartisan have been found to be less able to say "no" to organized interests and new citizen movements than are those operating where local parties control the agenda as is usual in Britain or the United States. In American cities, for instance, the presence of a stong party organization at city hall is consistent with both lower expenditure levels and less expenditure growth when contrasted with those cities whose politics are clientelist in nature (Clark, 1994, 92-99). In the absence of effective party leadership and a strong mayor, skilled administrators engage in behind-the-scenes political behaviour. They must lobby their councils, promote their programs, build citizen alliances with clientele groups and, not uncommonly, sabotage whatever damage they perceive council to have done by either whimsy or intent. It is also more difficult for the administrator because the smarter councillor knows that public recognition of his or her name is a guarantee of reelection (Canadian incumbents enjoy an 80 percent reelection rate) and they seek out clear headlines in whatever media becomes available. To put it another way, the individual election horizon of councillors focuses them on what is newsworthy at the expense of longer-term program considerations.

The administrator's job is easier in some measure because of this political drift. Put plainly, in the usual course of events few councillors are ever elected to make radical program shifts, and it is simpler to make incremental changes to what has worked in past than to rock the boat dramatically. This behaviour is implicitly reinforced by the constitutional position of Canadian local government, as provincial subordinates, in which what is not explicitly permitted is probably neither legal nor constitutional. So, at the heart of the Canadian municipal practice is the shared belief all round that what has worked adequately in past is likely to at least work adequately in the foreseen future. And, everyone's job is secure.

It is fair to say that elections under *nonpartisanship* disguise a real politics of myopia. At the heart of the anti-party vision is a peppy boosterism that, in its essentials, requires unbridled support for a community's sustained growth as assessed in commercial terms. For those subscribing to this kind of fertility measure of success the role of local government is clear. It is to support expansion of the community's entrepreneurs at the expense of any and all other objectives whether they be social, cultural or environmental. These advocates like to build things (arenas, museums, and roads) and tirelessly promote the community to external business leaders. World status is sometimes even believed to be conferred by the hosting of major athletic exhibitions such as the Olympics.

To be sustained, successful politics under nonpartisanship requires three conditions. There must be a tradition of antipartyism locally. Second, social and economic divisions that do exist in the community must be weakened as links to political involvement for municipal purposes. And, local elites must share in a broad common consensus over political ends. Under these conditions otherwise partisan or ideological issues become only managerial problems. Indeed, depoliticizing the city lies at the heart of transforming politics into administration. Such circumstances render political parties irrelevant for they stand in the way of good administrative efficiency.

Purely local parties with no open links to Canada's major political parties do emerge from time to time. They are *cadre* in style, which means that their activities and personnel are focussed on electoral success rather than platforms and political ideas. The platform vision of their local notables standing as candidates becomes some variant of "common sense" or "good government." The fact that few other candidates ever stand for idiocy and bad government does not detract from the apparent salience of this message. One grand Canadian example of such party-like behaviour is the Civic Nonpartisan Association of Vancouver which has dominated city hall in that city, on and off, for over 60 years. The irony of the name of this party has never handicapped any of its adherents.

Canada's approximately 4500 local governments are governed by about 35 000 locally elected and usually nonpartisan councillors. Since by definition, the existence of council seats creates openings for participants, around 2000 local councillors have found the time to oversee the operations of the 290 governments of Canada's ten largest census metropolitan areas. Whether our city-regions today really need so many politicians is very much a debatable proposition. In his observations of the British foreign service, C. Northcote Parkinson noted that those who had nothing very important to do tended to view as being of utmost importance that which they did. Canada's local councillors all know that they do important works.

Bureaucrats and Other Interests

LOCAL COUNCILLORS HAVE A TENDENCY TO SHORT-TERM PLANNING ENGENDERED by their fixed and usually short terms in office. This is reinforced by the whimsy often attending the conditions attached to revenues which local governments receive from more senior levels of government. Many councils' budget decisions are also dictated by quasi-independent agencies such as school boards, police commissions, library boards, parks and planning authorities, over whom they have little leverage. Finally, the lack of political cohesion on council because of nonpartisanship, reinforced by the relative powerlessness of the mayor or reeve, renders policy coordination across any range of activities very difficult.

The classic management form for most small town and rural councils today, inherited from the British, is the council with standing committees. That is, each major department or area of municipal business (parks and recreation for instance) is to be "supervised" by a committee of the councillors themselves. In simpler times this tended to be good enough. But today, more complex (and more urban) municipalities have usually turned to some style of Executive Committee, or a part of council, chaired by the mayor and sometimes including the heads of standing committees, intended to coordinate municipal business and to give some limited political direction to its activities.

Not all of the business of local government, however, is placed in the hands of elected public officials. American business reformers at the beginning of the twentieth century tried to apply the model of the private corporation to city hall. Like a board of directors, councillors would devise "policy" and a professional administrator, a city manager, could then execute its "administration." Naturally there would be no "politics" involved in any of this (i.e., nonpartisanship), and city governing was to be forced to emulate business planning. These methods took root quickly in Canada, and some variant of city management is the dominant municipal form today.

Superficially, much of what local government undertakes does seem like a business operation, but it is never easy to separate the policy from a public business choice. For instance, does the reasonable business expectation that users should pay for operating a public swimming pool not close its doors to residents with lower incomes? Business accepts that not everyone can afford to shop at the GAP; the public policy for pools cannot. Successful municipal managers quickly become sensitized to the expectations of their departmental clientele and mesh these with the political requirements of councillors.

In this process, institutionalized pressure groups such as the local Chamber of Commerce, developers' cartels or even well-established neighbourhood residents' groups become the legitimate voices for sectors in the population. These stable, polished, continuous professional lobbies are consulted in advance of policy change, work behind the scenes with bureaucrats to accomplish policy adaptations, and have their official members appointed to administrative boards and agencies. Generally, they influence the public to inspire the elected office-holder through longer-term media management. Effective administrators have even been known to encourage the emergence of such groups to lobby on behalf of their stake in the local budget. These are the traditional stakeholders whose long-standing control over city hall purse-strings is now so frequently the target for more issue-specific new social movements.

Public Finance

LOCAL GOVERNMENT IS IMPORTANT AS MEASURED BY BUDGETS. IN THE UK, LOCAL spending equalled about 25 percent of all state spending by the 1990s—about 9 percent of GNP. In Canada, in 1998, spending on goods and services by government level was $64 billion by municipalities, $103 billion by the ten provinces and $38 billion by the federal government. Low politics, indeed.

The one solid opportunity for citizens to evaluate the overall operation of any municipality lies in the annual budget. All policy comes out in this wash. Municipal councils are not, by law, permitted to run a deficit on current expenditures such as operating the library or transit system although they may borrow for capital works such as building the libraries or roadways. Most of the rest of the budget is set out for them by either central governments or past policy commitments.

Specific and general purpose grants from central governments constitute about half of any given local government's revenues. These are conditional grants. What is meant here is that one level of government (with superior taxing resources) will support the programs of another if certain conditions are met and if the potential recipient signs up. So, local governments are controlled through the regulations necessary to gain the central government's money. Although the concept of a tax on the value of real property for local spending purposes originated in the middle ages it has not grown with policy expectations over time. Local own-source revenues are no longer coincident with expenditure requirements. Until recently in England, for example, one-fifth of the local budget came from fines, fees, licenses, and charges; two-fifths from central grants; and only one-third from property rates.

Internal choices may often clash with external funding requirements. Of the nearly $30 billion transferred to local governments in Canada from other levels, 98 percent is from the provinces and just under 90 percent of that amount has conditions attached. Grants with program conditions are a concept inherited from the nineteenth century (the UK has had such since 1835) and will undoubtedly be sustained in the twenty-first. This means that local priorities are to be set elsewhere. Just under two-thirds of federal funds are untied general grants with no conditions, but the ratio of tied funding to general grants, provincial to local, is nine to one. Today in Canada, less than 50 percent of local government revenues derive from the general property tax. Less than one percent comes from permits and licenses so the purpose of these last is clearly control and regulation, not revenue generation.

Traditional interest groups are probably at their most clever when it comes to lobbying for a share of the public purse, usually as the established clientele of various civic departments. As has been noted, nonpartisan councillors apply "common sense" to their decisions, which is only, of course, each person's own best judgment applied. The careful observer will note that ward-healing, or satisfying direct demands for local services from their own constituents, crops up when councillors sensibly spend tax money to raise their personal reputations in their wards. Since the local government budget is divided along three basic dimensions, between hard (pipes and roads) and soft services; between capital and operating; and between what is mandatory (required by provincial government statutes) and what is permitted, councillors are limited in personal gratification to those realms that fall under the latter part of all three categories. In short, they build recreational monuments and provide symbolic names for parks, and they cut deals to ensure that each of them has been fairly served.

Fiscal austerity for local governments is a relatively new global phenomenon. What is newest is the incapacity of central governments to fund longstanding initiatives and the concomitant decision to require municipalities to pay a greater portion. Clearly said, central governments have enticed localities into programs with conditional grants and are now reneging on their share. This is why reliance on the property tax as a source of revenue rose, as a proportion of total municipal income in Canada, from 40 to 50 percent in the decade from 1986 to 1996. The "reinventing government" discussions of today's newspapers disguise a tactic known at the time of the 1849 Baldwin Act in Canada. That is, to initiate decentralization, masked as local autonomy, is to tap into new sources of local fund-raising. Of necessity local government administrators have become imaginatively innovative.

New Social Movements and Their City Hall Agendas

THE TERM "DEMOCRATIC DEFICIT" HAS BEEN EMPLOYED TO DESCRIBE THE demonstrated lack of trust shared by many Canadians in their politicians and political institutions. This fuels a collective sense that ordinary citizens no longer have reasonable means to influence public policy choices. The apparently calculated and continuous manipulation of participation at all governing levels, from the process of elections and public hearings to board and agency appointments, has produced extensive cynicism in response. Survey evidence suggests that this gap appears most bitterly felt in the local government realm with many citizens, if not most, unwilling to place any ongoing trust in the judgments of either the very neighbours who elected them or whom they have elected.

These views are coincident with recent studies across the industrialized democracies that have uncovered the growth of a new local political culture and innovative leaders who have been labelled "fiscal populists" (Clark, 1994, 21–78). What has been found is that the classic left–right dimension has shifted as the left grows to stand for social issues rather than state economic intervention. This means that social and fiscal issues are distinguished; a political leader's stance on one cannot be inferred from a position on the other. Marxist mayors have privatized garbage collection; conservatives have supported same-sex benefits for civic employees and stringent privacy laws. With change in the public's policy awareness of social causes (e.g., on environmental issues) the appearance of new stakeholders leads to new social movements. More precise, short-term, dramatic, and demonstrable outcomes are demanded by citizens with the time and affluence to command the short attention spans of those in full-time public life. Many of these newly informed attitudes have been sculpted in the suburbs of the city-region. In the United States today, where Democrats win the cities and Republicans are predominant in the rural areas, the "Soccer Mom" has become a metaphor for the crucial swing vote, based on gender and located in the suburbs. In Canada, the "905 vote" (that being the area code for Toronto's suburban ring from Niagara Falls around to Oshawa) sustained both Harris Conservative party majorities. And, in both instances, the new focus is on life-style issues.

Some of these attitudes have spilled into green takes on the neighbourhood beautiful with the frequent consequence of balkanizing the city. Such neighbourhood control and constraints exerted by specific interests have fragmented decision possibilities. In the late 1960s, at the height of the third period reform wave, NIMBY (Not In My Back Yard) movements marked the high-water point of citizen struggles with traditional hierarchical structures in city politics throughout North America. In Canada, similar behaviour found vivid expression in the heated arguments against the Toronto "megacity" amalgamation. Here, the traditional opposition of suburban councillors was joined in alliance against change by groups representing specific issue areas in the city centre who had established a working policy arrangement with their own council under a "new localism" veneer. The only real substance and unifying element across the coalition was, as Machiavelli warned, no change.

The broader matter in the emergence of these new elites is the lowered relevance of old community power discussions in the social sciences. The new populism of the 1990s, which can mobilize people very quickly by electronic means, cuts through old class divisions to focus on the individual. It has thus overcome structural relationships with organized groups and their self-perpetuating leaderships. So, being out of the policy "loop" in this private sense, citizens have come to view themselves as being out of the public loop entirely. Who is "in the loop" is irrelevant if only a small band of gladiators perseveres. This scenario is abetted by the actual shrinking of the state which has produced a growing individual responsibility of necessity. Now unwilling or unable to turn to state mechanisms for broader economic purposes, the collective sense of community has moved into issues directly impinging on life choices. Nudged by state downsizing and complemented by new patterns for non-manipulative participation (i.e., the Internet), new elites and movements do seem prepared and able to enter, and quickly exit, the government policy world that is most at first hand—the local.

Ethical Behaviours in an Oft-Troubled Landscape

ALL OF THE ABOVE SET THE STAGE FOR CONTEMPORARY CONCERNS WITH THE practical ethics of municipal politics which can only be introduced here. These matters assume two dimensions, the more traditional of which concerns the individual as public

DEBATE BOX

You Are Mayor

As mayor of Sylvana, a small city some distance from the metropolitan centres in Western Canada, you are well aware of the residents' strong connections to both their farming past and to friends and families still directly engaged in agriculture. Certainly the community's leading citizens are mostly people who own smaller businesses and are anxious to sustain good relations with their rural customers.

These community leaders have recently fought successfully to prevent the rail line's abandonment and shutdown of the grain elevator operation. Additionally the city's economic development committee has just persuaded Zapp Chemicals, which had looked closely at several alternative sites, to locate its central warehousing and distribution centre for the prairies (and 28 new jobs) in Sylvana. The only action now required of city council is to rezone several blocks for industrial purposes.

But a political problem has suddenly emerged. Long-time resident Ms. Sara Lynx, who clearly spends even more time on the Internet than she does on civic issues, has organized a community movement in support of a complete ban on the use of pesticides within city limits. She argues that a number of Canadian cities such as Halifax, Calgary, and Ottawa have already greatly cut back on their pesticide use based on growing evidence that their use may be linked to health problems and learning disorders in children. These findings are supported by research released in August 2000 by the nonprofit Canadian Institute of Child Health. And, in its report on pesticides in May 2000, the House of Commons Standing Committee on the Environment noted that there are over 7000 registered pesticides with over 500 active ingredients deployed in Canada. Ms. Lynx has filed copies of these documents with the city clerk, and is organizing a petition drive.

Your city solicitor has urged cautious study before acting, noting that a recent review of amendments to Ontario's Child and Family Services Act outlines the possibility that "persons having charge of a child" can be so construed that if neurological damage is traceable to a permitted usage of pesticides such as chlorpyrifos, then that permission may mean that the city could be held liable for environmental child abuse. Of course the solicitor always advises caution.

The Western Crop Protection Association, which represents pesticide manufacturers, retailers, and distributors, has sent out a detailed letter indicating that their members monitored studies of public health and child development with great care, and that voluntary withdrawals of products thought harmful would be quickly done, just as Dursban was taken off the shelves in the United States in July 2000. A company official has told you in confidence that the bylaw's passage would be considered an attack on his company's integrity and that they could easily locate elsewhere.

You consider your fellow councillors to be persons of integrity, thoughtful parents, and highly protective of their community's well-being. They are also merchants. One councillor has already told you that the city needs the employment and the businesses need those customers' new purchasing power. She does remark, however, that whenever she has noticed a lawn pesticide truck in her neighbourhood in past, "it has always been enough to close the windows and keep the kids inside for a time."

As head of council your leadership has been persuasive in the past. What actions should you now propose?

official. At this micro level, over the years people involved in local government have often found themselves compromised by smudging the line between personal aggrandizement and the public interest in land development. This is because the public business of local government almost always relates to the value of property in one way or another. The sorcery of roadway, water, and sewerage connections transmutes mud into subdivisions.

This behaviour often takes the form of honest graft, which fuelled the private treasuries of American boss, or machine, politics in the 1830s to 1930s. In the words of Boss Plunkitt of Tammany Hall, "I seen my opportunities and I took 'em." In short, prior knowledge of a local government's plans to develop, gained through holding a public office, permits an official (or friends and family) to benefit by acquiring properties advantageously. Such less-than-benign omissions of propriety with property have permitted some pretty impressive avoidance of personal poverty of which one prominent Canadian example was Edmonton's Mayor Bill Hawrelak. To remedy this scrofulous but generally petty larceny, stringent conflict-of-interest rules have been adopted in most large urban centres; their precise application is still more problematic for the several thousand jurisdictions outside them (Lightbody, 1994, 205–210).

Some issues that are system-wide have continued as subject for public debate (Lightbody, 1995, 302–304). For example, consideration of the bias in local electoral systems reminds us that, unlike the world of high politics, local councillors usually, within the broad frame of provincial law, design their own rules for wards and voting. In any reorganization, the common sense applied has thus been "If it ain't broke why fix it?" It isn't broke, clearly, if the system worked to elect those presently in office. The rules governing who might contribute in elections, and how much, and whether this is publicly reported, are also still very loose in municipalities across this country.

More recently in the spotlight have been systemic questions with respect to, among other matters, who exercises final authority when making tough fiscal choices and who must be consulted. New stakeholders also define new stakes; in environmental matters private rights clash with newly defined collective goods. Many scholars have alerted us to policy issues of inclusion which inevitably follow the growing multicultural diversity of metropolitan areas. New cultures may expect affirmative actions to reduce unacknowledged glass ceilings for instance. Elements of personal privacy and property rights may have to be subordinated to the wider demands of better community planning. Neither tolerance nor understanding can be legislated of course and it will be local governments which stand in the front lines of removing the stumbling blocks that lack of patience will produce. The local state is under pressure and in flux. The good news is that its institutions are infinitely more flexible than central governing operations.

Summary

Over the past two decades one interesting new development in local government has been the emergence of a loosely linked global network of "world cities." Cities in this situation have elaborated quasi-autonomous economic, social, and political links with communities abroad that either subordinate, or bypass entirely, existing national and sub-state regional government institutions. This is what some authorities now recognize when they speak of new international opportunity structures, transnational capital movements, and globalization. These cities have increasingly begun to evaluate their performance in comparison with their major international trading partners and competitors, not necessarily with other centres in their own countries. In some analyses, the national state seems only able to facilitate while it is dominant local communities that initiate and implement.

Canada has three such internationalized urban centres—Vancouver, Toronto, Montreal—and another (Calgary) evidently in the wings. For such international exposure to happen requires a complex series of relationships which includes, at a minimum, a cosmopolitan population, international transportation and telecommunications links with their concomitant trading patterns, a local presence of world financial institutions (and such local institutions working abroad), significant social interactions with multiple foreign organizations and associations (students, tourism, cultural exchanges), and independently initiated formal public and private cooperative agreements with other world communities. Such cities often host international sports events, cultural festivals and exhibitions, will have established twinning agreements or strategic links with other countries' major cities and, in some instances, have begun to develop their own foreign policies (e.g., strategies as to where to invest, with whom to trade).

It is partly in this context that some writers have gone so far as to forecast the general decline of the traditional nation-state (Gibbins, Youngman, 1996, 271–290). Certainly, during the forthcoming "tempest of uncertainty" through the transitional period to the new world economy, elites rooted in knowledge will be easily and electronically able to transcend national borders. It is entirely probable that they will discover that their common interests lie not with those citizens without such education and access at home but with their own knowledge compatriots abroad. Their shared, and urban, culture will be that we have discussed above.

In some developing countries the prospect of enhanced world status (and the prospect for resulting economic growth) may mitigate oppressive state practices and open doors, at least municipally, for local citizens. Knowledge networks mobilized will rapidly apply targeted sanctions otherwise. In the more industrialized world, the existence of world cities means the low politics of city policy-making simply becomes more complex; even the simple choices (roads and sewers, protection and social services) become lumbered with important normative dimensions. For instance, what is the public consequence of privatizing the enforcement of environmental standards to quasi-autonomous non-governmental agencies? In short, who ensures potable water?

The new urbanism now operates with more information and yet less certainty of outcome. Even if you build "it" they may not come! This is as true for the stadia and convention centres in the developed world's cities as it is for forms of decentralized but non-democratic local administration elsewhere. This is so because globalization, ironically, also means localism and the most legitimate expression of local community comes through democratic means. Citizenship means influence, influence requires direct participation, and direct involvement is most likely to emerge when making choices whose outcomes have an immediate impact on daily lives. So in the times ahead, traditional nation-states may come to be downsized to hollow spheres of patriotism, but the corollary is that the spark of democratic opportunity that lies at the epicentre of local governing will thrive.

Discussion Questions

1. How is local government important to national and global economies?
2. Are you interested in local politics? Why or why not?
3. How would you rate your local democracy? Why is it, or is it not, effective?
4. What are some local political decisions that directly affect you?
5. In an era of globalization, do you expect local politics to become more or less important? Explain why.

References

Clark, Terry Nichols, ed. 1994. *Urban Innovation: Creative Strategies for Turbulent Times.* Thousand Oaks, Calif: Sage.

Gibbins, Roger and Loleen Youngman. 1996. *Mindscapes: Political Ideologies Towards the 21st Century.* Toronto: McGraw-Hill, Ryerson.

Graham, Katherine A., Susan D. Phillips, Allan M. Maslove. 1998. *Urban Governance in Canada: Representation, Resources and Restructuring.* Toronto: Harcourt, Brace.

Graham, Katherine A. and Susan D.Phillips. 1997. "Citizen engagement: beyond the customer revolution," *Canadian Public Administration*, XXXX, 2 Summer), 255-273.

Higgins, Donald, J. H. 1986. *Local and Urban Politics in Canada.* Toronto: Gage.

Hobson, Paul A.R. and France St-Hilaire. eds. 1997. *Urban Governance and Finance: A Question of Who Does What.* Montreal: Institute for Research on Public Policy.

Lightbody, James, ed. 1995. *Canadian Metropolitics: Governing Our Cities.* Toronto: Copp, Clark.

Lightbody, James. 1994. "Cities: "the dilemmas on our doorsteps," in John Langford and Allan Tupper, eds. *Corruption, Character & Conduct: Essays on Canadian Government Ethics.* Toronto: Oxford University Press, 197-216.

Tindal, C. Richard and S. Nobes Tindal. 2000. *Local Government in Canada.* 5th edition. Toronto: ITP Nelson.

Zussman, David. 1997. "Do citizens trust their governments?" *Canadian Public Administration*, XXXX, 2 (Summer), 234-254.

Further Readings

Graham, Katherine A., Susan D. Phillips, Allan M. Maslove. 1998. *Urban Governance in Canada: Representation, Resources and Restructuring.* Toronto: Harcourt, Brace.

Lightbody, James, ed. 1995. *Canadian Metropolitics: Governing Our Cities.* Toronto: Copp, Clark.

Zussman, David. 1997. "Do citizens trust their governments?" *Canadian Public Administration*, XXXX, 2 (Summer), 234-254.

Weblinks

International Union of Local Authorities
www.iula.org

Institute for the Study of Civic Values
www.libertynet.org/edcivic/iscvhome.html

Federation of Canadian Municipalities
www.fcm.ca/

The Brookings Institution Center on Urban and Metropolitan Policy
www.brook.edu/es/urban/urban.htm

Political Influence

T his section examines some of the most important actors, outside the formal institutions of the state, who influence the course of political events. These political actors compete for power and advantage within a political context that includes different ideas and institutions. In this section, we begin by exploring different understandings of culture, community, and identity. These broad themes form the political terrain for the most basic unit of politics in liberal democracies—the citizen. Citizenship is much more than formal membership in a state. Over time, our understanding of who can be a citizen and of the rights that citizens can claim from the state have changed dramatically.

Globalization challenges many of our accepted notions of citizenship as ever-larger numbers of people move across borders or, as refugees, become stateless persons. Citizens may attempt to influence the state on their own but most frequently join together with other like-minded citizens, within a political party organization or interest group. Political parties take on many different forms but most are geared toward gaining political influence by electing members to political office. Interest groups, in contrast, attempt to have their policy preferences met by influencing the decisions of elected politicians and public administrators.

Currently, many political scientists argue that political parties have become less important than interest groups as a means for citizens to influence government decision making. An important recent development has been the growth in numbers and influence of new social movements and global civil society movements who focus their energies on issues that political parties and established interest groups have not adequately addressed in the past, such as gender and sexuality, or on issues that transcend the national boundaries, such as the global environment and human rights. Citizens mobilize behind many vehicles for political influence, but not all citizens share the same capacity to influence political affairs. Gender, ethnicity, and class are also critical in determining who plays and, importantly, who wins in the game of politics.

"THIS IS INTERESTING. IT'S A CONCEPTUAL PIECE CALLED 'REFLECTIONS OF A FOOL AND HIS MONEY BEING PARTED.'"

CHAPTER 15

CULTURE, DIVERSITY, AND GLOBALIZATION

Overview

Culture is a contentious and critical political concept. The purpose of this chapter is to explore why culture is important in the study of politics. The chapter introduces the ways that culture and politics are linked and provides an overview of three distinct approaches to the study of culture and politics. These are the *political culture, cultural studies*, and *cultural identities* approaches. All three of these approaches traditionally examine politics and culture within the boundaries of a given state or country. However, the current period of globalization, coupled with the increasing diversity of national populations, suggests that we develop a new perspective on culture. In order to come to grips with the relationship between culture and politics in the twenty-first century, political scientists increasingly need to consider the implications of ideas, images, and especially people rapidly criss-crossing state borders.

YASMEEN
ABU-LABAN

Introduction

What does *culture* mean? Typically, the word refers to art, music, literature, and painting. Some distinguish between the "high culture" of classical composers such as Mozart or the plays of William Shakespeare, and today's "popular culture" forms, such as the rock music of Madonna, or the animated television show "The Simpsons." Even if there were agreement that modern cartoons and Shakespearean sonnets are both culture, does culture extend beyond the arts? What about language, religion, sports, or advertising? Are we referring only to the arts when we connect the word *culture* with collectivities of varied sizes, as seen in phrases such as "Western culture," "American culture," or "youth culture"?

Culture has been a notoriously contentious concept. While there are, quite literally, hundreds of definitions that have been offered for the word (Chilcote, 1994, 178), social scientists generally agree that culture is something broader than just the arts, and define **culture** simply as a shared way of life. Culture is not the property of an individual, but rather is collective. Culture includes language, customs and manners, dress, rituals, behavioural conventions, and religion and other systems of belief (Jary and Jary, 1991, 101–103). Precisely because culture is collective, a human creation and inherited, it is of interest to those who study human social and political life. Indeed, the link between culture, cultural differences, and politics has puzzled students of politics throughout the centuries (Almond, 1980).

The Significance of Culture to the Study of Politics

IN THE POST–WORLD WAR II PERIOD, CULTURE HAS BEEN VIEWED AS SIGNIFICANT to the study of politics for three reasons. One reason has been that culture helps to describe and explain the differences between states, including the kinds of policies they may adopt. For example, although Canada and the United States share a border, and both are countries with a high standard of living, Canada has a universal health care program and the United States does not. Moreover, in Canada, the number of government Crown corporations (in areas such as broadcasting, transportation, and electricity) is greater than in the United States. It has been argued that such contrasting characteristics can be explained by Canadian and American cultural differences. For example, Seymour Martin Lipset (1990) argues that Canadians are more trusting of government, have a more collective orientation, and are less individualistic than their neighbours below the forty-ninth parallel.

A second reason that those studying politics are interested in culture relates to the question of power. Culture has been used to explain why some groups hold power, and how and why subordinate groups do, or do not, challenge those in power. For example, in Western countries education is linked with one's life chances, including the kind of job and income one is able to acquire. Pierre Bourdieu has focused on the educational system in Western industrialized countries to examine why children of middle-class parents tend to excel more than children of working-class parents (1973). Bordieu finds that although schools may seem neutral, in fact meeting the classroom expectations and doing well in assessments require certain cultural understandings. Bourdieu argues that in contrast to working-class parents, middle-class parents are able to endow their children with what he calls *cultural capital.* Just as money gives one the power to purchase consumer goods, cultural capital gives middle-class children the required language and cultural tools to succeed in education, to secure prestigious and well-paying jobs, and, ultimately, to perpetuate class inequalities generation after generation.

A third reason that culture is significant to the study of politics relates to the question of democratic justice. Is it enough to say that equality is achieved when all the laws in a country treat everyone the same? Or should there be distinct rights, treatment, or recognition for some groups on the basis of cultural difference? In Canada, for example, there were intense debates about whether the province of Quebec, which contains a majority of people whose first language is French, should actually be recognized as a "distinct society" in the Canadian constitution. Whether indigenous peoples and ethnic, racial, and religious minorities should have distinct recognition in the law has been the source of on-going debate.

In sum, culture is highly relevant to the study of politics because it pertains to differences between countries; relations of power and challenges to the status quo; and questions of democracy and justice. Each of these reasons in turn is associated with a particular approach to the study of culture. As outlined below, the question of explaining cultural differences between countries is tied to the approach to the study of culture known as *political culture.* The question of power relations is key to a *cultural studies* approach. And, last, the focus on questions of culture, democracy, and justice is central to examining *cultural identity.*

Major Themes and Debates

Political Culture

The term *political culture* was first employed by political scientist Gabriel Almond in the 1950s, when he attempted to distinguish political culture from culture generally. Almond drew on the influential political system framework established in the work of David Easton (1957), who suggested that the study of politics should be approached as a system of behaviour and institutions. For Easton, any country's political system consisted of institutions (such as political parties and legislatures). The political system, according to this model, was like a giant machine that would process inputs in the form of demands (what people want) and supports (how much support those making demands can obtain from other people) into specific outputs (decisions or policies). Easton's views are represented schematically in Figure 15.1.

But what is political culture? According to Almond, "every political system is embedded in a particular pattern of orientations to political action. . . . it [is] useful to refer to this as the political culture" (Chilcote, 1994, 179). For Almond, therefore, any given political system can be characterized by a population's pattern of feeling towards politics and political participation.

Political culture was subsequently elaborated in Gabriel Almond and Sidney Verba's well-known 1963 book entitled *The Civic Culture,* which examined the political cultures of Mexico, the United States, Britain, and Germany in order to explain their comparative political stability. For each country, the authors surveyed a *representative sample* of 1000

FIGURE 15.1

INPUTS ———>	POLITICAL ———> SYSTEM	OUTPUTS
Environment		Decisions
Demands		Policies
Supports		

SOURCE: Adapted from David Easton, "An Approach to the Analysis of Political Systems," *World Politics* 9, 3 (1957), p. 384. Center of International Studies, Princeton University.

people. Almond and Verba argued that their evidence indicated it is generally possible to speak of "attitudes that are characteristic of a nation" and, moreover, that political culture is key to explaining stability (51). They distinguish three distinct types of attitudes people have about their own role in the political process:

- *parochial*—people do not expect to participate and do not make any demands;
- *subject*—people have no expectation of being politically active, but they do expect that the system will provide them with the goods and services they want; and
- *participant*—people feel they can play an active role, and expect that the political system will deliver in return.

Almond and Verba's book argues that the best kind of political system has a "civic culture" which embodies a balance between democracy, as opposed to authoritarianism, and stability, as opposed to instability. The civic culture, demonstrating both democracy *and* stability is based on limited participation. The authors of *The Civic Culture* presumed that too much citizen activism creates instability. From their analysis, the countries that best characterize this ideal civic culture are Britain, and, especially, the United States. In contrast, Mexico was a far cry from being a civic culture. For the record, both Almond and Verba are American.

One major criticism is that *The Civic Culture* served as a justification for the status quo. The stress in this work was on stability, and the desirability of stability, as opposed to change. Indeed, for Almond and Verba, the limited participation of people was a positive thing precisely because it ensured stability. *The Civic Culture* has also been criticized for being *ethnocentric* and *ahistorical*. The book actually assessed the political culture of other countries in terms of how closely they resembled the American political culture. Moreover, the work did not address the historical differences between countries. Such historical differences are not captured by a "snapshot" glance at culture gleaned from administering a survey to a population at one particular point in time.

Finally, and not least, *The Civic Culture* has been criticized for its exclusive focus on national political cultures, to the exclusion of relevant subcultures within countries. This criticism emphasizes the idea of diversity because a **subculture** refers to a different, or distinctive shared way of life within the national cultural setting, characterizing a smaller grouping of people within a country. For example, in the case of the United States, African-Americans (who often hold specific attitudes towards politics) might be described as a subculture. Writing some twenty years later, Almond (1980, 23) admitted that they had not interviewed a sufficient number of African-Americans to study this important American subculture, and "hence we failed to deal with the political attitudes of American blacks."

These criticisms of *The Civic Culture* did not dissuade other political scientists from employing the concept of political culture to study the attitudes, beliefs, and rules that guide a political system, and in some cases to look at the question of subcultures within a given country, or even to debate the number of subcultures in a given country. In particular, political scientists turned their attention to the process of **political socialization** or the way individuals actually internalized political values. Many studies have focused on the **agents of political socialization**, which include the family, the media, educational institutions, and political parties.

Cultural Studies

In contrast to the political culture approach, the **cultural studies** approach is premised on the desirability of transforming power relations. Also emerging in the postwar period, the cultural studies approach is interdisciplinary. This means that analysts working in this

---

DEBATE BOX

Who is "Canadian"?

What is Canadian culture? Is there a distinct Canadian identity? What makes an individual "Canadian"? These questions have long provoked considerable debate because of the diversity of languages, regions, and ethnic groups in the country. While poets, writers, academics, and politicians have frequently been hard-pressed to conclusively define Canadian culture, it appears that advertisers are less reticent.

In 2000, the Molson beer company attempted to define Canadian culture and identity through a series of advertisements featuring a young man named Joe. Decked out in a plaid flannel shirt, in the first of these ads, Joe stands in front of a Canadian flag and challenges stereotypes many Canadians feel Americans hold of them. Joe argues "I am not a lumberjack, or a fur trader. I don't live in an igloo, eat blubber or own a dogsled. . . . I speak English and French, not American. . . . I believe in peacekeeping, not policing; diversity not assimilation; and that the beaver is a truly proud and noble animal" (Jacoby, 2000, A27). By the end of the ad Joe is shouting "Canada's the second largest country, the first nation of hockey, and the best part of North America. My name is Joe and I am Canadian" (Ibid.).

The first ad made an impact, and Joe Canadian quickly came to define the "quintessential Canadian guy" (Mallick, 2000, R1, R2). In fact, in her capacity as Minister of the Department of Canadian Heritage, Sheila Copps used the "I am Canadian" ad to explain Canadian culture abroad. As Copps put it to an international audience, "Yes the ad pokes fun at the U.S., and yes, there is a bit of chest thumping, but it also pokes fun at Canadians' efforts at self-validating by posing in contrast to Americans" (Craid, 2000, A9). Copps went on to assert that culture "is the expression of the soul and the identity of the country" (Ibid.).

The Joe advertisement also proved to be popular with the public, winning standing ovations in movie theatres, bars, and hockey rinks across Canada (Gatehouse, 2000, A1).

Some American commentators made fun of how Canadian culture was being defined by a beer commercial stressing that Canadians are not Americans (Jacoby, 2000, A27). However, Canadian marketing experts suggested that the ad was appealing because it tapped into a latent patriotism, especially amongst young Canadian males who were the target audience for the ad (Gatehouse, 2000, A2).

The popularity of this advertisement and its particular portrayal of Canadians and Canada raises a number of questions regarding national culture. Is there a single national culture in Canada? Do those who attempt to define Canadian identity and culture (e.g., writers, poets, politicians, advertisers) mainly or exclusively define it by what it is not (i.e., not American)? Can ethnic and linguistic diversity foster a national culture, and if so does it do so in Canada? Not least, what accounts for the success of this ad with the Canadian public?

SOURCE: Murray Campbell, "O Canada, our home and...?" The Globe and Mail (November 10, 1997), p. A1; A4.

tradition continually draw on a number of theories and methods from disciplines both in the social sciences and in the humanities. These disciplines include literary criticism, linguistics, philosophy, art history, sociology, and political science. There is no one single theory or methodology characterizing this approach. It moves from discipline to discipline, and theory to theory, and method to method depending on the analyst and his or her subject. In fact, for this reason, cultural studies has been described as anti-disciplinary (Nelson et al., 1992, 2).

Nonetheless, cultural studies is united by a core concern—to expose power relations and how these shape cultural practices, with a view towards challenging relations of subordination, especially in capitalist societies. In this sense, cultural studies analysts do not present their work as objective and value-free, in contrast to the stance taken by analysts seeking to develop a "science of politics" through the political culture approach. Cultural studies has been profoundly influenced by the work of Karl Marx (1818–1883), and his understanding of the importance of ideology. While the concept of ideology was used as far back as the French Revolution, in the post–World War II period the concept was largely associated with the writings and philosophy of Marx. Marx used the term to refer to those ideas which masked the uneven distribution of power between workers (the proletariat) and owners of the means of production (the bourgeoisie) in a capitalist system (McLellan, 1986, 5–15). Two important thinkers in the twentieth century, Louis Althusser and Antonio Gramsci, inspired by Marx, elaborated upon the factors that keep "bourgeois ideology" in place.

The French Marxist thinker Louis Althusser argued that under capitalism, people are conditioned through ideology that is passed on to people through what he termed "Ideological State Apparatuses" (ISAs) (1971). For Althusser, the ISAs include churches, schools, parties, unions, communications, literature, arts, and the family. All, in complementary ways, encourage people to believe in the value of capitalism. The ISAs identified by Althusser bear a striking resemblance to the agents of political socialization in political culture accounts. For Marxists, however, the specific problem with Althusser's account was that the ideological conditioning seemed so complete that it was impossible to imagine change, in particular how a working-class revolution would ever happen.

In much work in the Marxist tradition, culture is seen to be determined by economic relations. Antonio Gramsci (1891–1937) however argued that culture was relevant in its own right, and a key to understanding the possibility of change and revolution. Gramsci, one of the founders of the Italian Communist Party, was arrested by Mussolinis Fascists in 1926. While in prison he wrote on the role of culture (Gramsci, 1971). Gramsci believed that social stability could not be achieved through state coercion or force. Instead, social support for capitalism, he argued, was the result of cultural consensus or **hegemony**. For Gramsci, the persistence of the capitalist system was largely achieved by the bourgeoisie's ideological domination (hegemony) of the working class. Gramsci suggested that because hegemony was never total, or static, but ever-changing, there was always a potential for revolutionary consciousness in the working classes.

The influence of Marx and Marxist accounts of ideology/culture through such figures as Althusser and Gramsci are evident in cultural studies work. Most thinkers agree that cultural studies began with the publication of Richard Hoggart's 1957 book *The Uses of Literacy* (During, 1993, 1). This book describes changes in working-class life in postwar Britain, compared to the beginning of the century. It details how just one practice—reading mass publications—has profound consequences on morals and attitudes. Hoggart was dismayed by the cultural changes brought to everyday working-class life by the ever-widening number and reach of popular newspapers and magazines. He argued that "they make their audience less likely to arrive at a wisdom derived from an inner, felt discrimination in their sense of people and their attitude toward experience" (Hoggart, 1957, 339).

In 1964, Hoggart, along with other British Marxist-inspired thinkers established the Centre for Contemporary Cultural Studies (CCCS) at the University of Birmingham. Here, culture was defined broadly as "the entire range of a society's arts, beliefs, institutions, and communicative practices," and therefore explicitly considered both "high culture" and "popular culture" (Nelson et.al., 1992, 4). Analyses done at the CCCS tended to see culture as contested, and as a modern site of class struggle. In this context, the stress was on "how groups with least power practically develop their own readings of, and uses for, cultural products—in fun, resistance, or to articulate their own identity" (During, 1993, 7).

While cultural studies developed first in Britain, it has had considerable influence in countries as diverse as Canada, the United States, and France. In the process, it has become institutionalized within many universities, and taken on issues and concerns sometimes different from the original goals of the CCCS at the University of Birmingham. Given that cultural studies was originally identified as a movement committed to bringing about change, especially socialism, its institutionalization has in itself brought about one of the major criticisms of cultural studies. It has been argued that the increasing institutionalization of cultural studies has led to the "[Walt] Disneyfication of the left," that its linkage with the working class has been muted and abandoned (Davies, 1995, 159–60).

A second major criticism of cultural studies is that it pays little attention to Third World countries that experienced colonialism, and to diverse groups other than the working class who might experience disadvantage in advanced capitalist countries (such as women and ethnic and racial minorities). The importance of thinking about culture in broader terms than class and Western industrialized countries is clear when considering acts of cultural resistance, such as that of celebrated Kenyan writer Ngugi wa Thiong'o. In 1986 Thiong'o wrote *Decolonizing the Mind: The Politics of Language in African Literature.* As an act of resistance against a historical past marked by British colonialism, this book was expressly the last book he wrote in English. Since then, Thiong'o has written his novels and plays in his first language, Kikuyu. For Thiong'o, the imposition of the colonial language of English was aimed at undervaluing indigenous culture. It was also central to the maintenance of colonial power. As Thiong'o puts it, "Economic and political control can never be complete or effective without mental control. To control a people's culture is to control their tools of self-definition in relationship to others" (1995, 443).

Cultural Identity

The third approach to the study of culture, the **cultural identity** approach, stems from the branch of political science known as political philosophy. Political philosophers are interested in the normative question of "what ought to be," as opposed to the empirical question of "what is." A central normative question in political philosophy concerns identifying the best forms of government, and establishing the standards by which such a judgment can be made. Political philosophy is characteristically **deductive** in its method. That is, political philosophers start from an axiom (or principle) and then deduce from this principle.

When it comes to culture, today there is large-scale agreement among political philosophers that discrimination against individuals on the basis of membership in a cultural group is wrong because such discrimination contravenes the principle of equality (May et al., 1998, 396). However, there remains considerable debate over how equality is actually best achieved, particularly in Western industrialized countries where distinct cultural groups may experience discrimination, disadvantage, and inequality despite formal laws that provide for equal treatment.

Consider the case of Canada as an example. Canada is a settler-colony founded on French and British immigration, and the expropriation of land from Aboriginal peoples. Prior to European settler-colonization in the early seventeenth century, Aboriginal societies themselves where characterized by a rich range of cultural, linguistic, social, and political practices (Dickason, 1992, 63–83). As such, ethnic, linguistic, religious, and cultural diversity is a hallmark feature of this country's experience. According to the 1996 Census, immigrants constitute 17.4 percent of the Canadian national population (Canada, 1997, 2–13). Since the 1970s, there has been a steady decline of immigrants arriving from the countries of Europe, and an increase of immigrants arriving from countries in the Caribbean, Central and South America, Africa, the Middle East, and Asia. For much of Canada's history, state laws and policies explicitly limited the ability of racial minorities to access education, housing, and employment (Henry et al., 2000, 112). Today, overtly discriminatory laws and policies have been eradicated. Yet there is considerable evidence that racial minorities and Aboriginal peoples encounter subtle forms of discrimination and are therefore still disadvantaged in areas such as education, relations with the police, social services, and the justice system (Henry et al., 2000, 383–389).

The question of cultural groups and equality has become pertinent in Canada and other Western industrialized countries not simply because of diversity, or the existence of inequality, but because of the emergence and demands of what are termed "new social movements." During the 1960s, a variety of new social movements emerged, coalescing around the idea of identity; for example feminism, linguistic rights for minorities, Aboriginal rights, disability rights, and gay rights. This emphasis on identity often takes a cultural form. While we might expect certain ethnic groups who share a common language, history, and culture to make claims on the basis of cultural identity (for example, French-Canadians in Canada, Aboriginal peoples in the United States, or the Welsh in Great Britain) non-ethnic groups sometimes make claims on the grounds of a unique cultural identity that have striking parallels. The deaf have argued they share a cultural identity based on a shared language (sign language), past, and sense of community (Kymlicka, 1998, 95). The increasing relevance of cultural identity in Western liberal democratic countries, as Charles Taylor notes, raises the obvious question of whether equality is best guaranteed by principles of **universalism** and difference blindness or whether true equality requires special recognition and valuing of difference (1992, 37–44).

Difference blindness holds that through the policies and laws of the state, everyone should be treated equally and exactly the same no matter what differences may exist among them—whether in terms of gender, religion, ethnicity, or past history of oppression. The value attached to "difference blindness" is seen in many constitutions of liberal democratic countries. For example, the French Declaration of the Rights of Man and Citizens, the American Bill of Rights, and the Canadian Charter of Rights and Freedoms all include individual rights, based on the principle that the constitution should not draw any distinction among citizens because of their cultural, social, religious, or linguistic background. The rule of law holds that the basic laws of the land should be "difference blind."

An alternative perspective holds that real equality can not be achieved without recognition and valuing of difference, and even according differential rights on the basis of group membership. Within a liberal democratic state, group-differentiated rights in the form of language rights in education, a veto power in constitutional amendments, or territorial autonomy are rights that may enable minority cultural groups to overcome potential vulnerability and disadvantage from majorities (Kymlicka, 1995). For proponents of this perspective, if everyone is treated exactly the same, without regard to their special or unique context, inequality may actually be the result. Along with Charles Taylor, two other contemporary political philosophers, Iris Marion Young and Will Kymlicka (1995), are associated with passionate criticisms of "difference blindness" as the sole approach to equality. For example, Iris Marion Young has argued that "strict adherence to a principle of equal treatment tends to perpetuate oppression or disadvantage" (1989, 251). Young argues that special rights need to be given to groups defined as different in order to actually overcome oppression and disadvantage.

The critique of difference blindness, and advocacy of special rights and recognition, has generated its own criticism. Some argue that the official recognition of group rights on the basis of cultural identity might allow grounds to violate the rights of the individual (Fierlbeck, 1996, 21). Many continue to say that the best protection of the individual is difference-blind laws and rights only. Critics of differentiated rights on the basis of cultural identity also raise concerns about national stability, arguing that any recognition or emphasis on diversity is destabilizing. If minority cultures are accorded separate rights and recognition, can there still be a uniting national culture, or will there be unending fragmentation and disorder? These questions have particular pertinence in a country such as Canada, where the issue of national unity has been recurring, and is still salient in the twenty-first century.

The Challenge of Globalization

THE TERM GLOBALIZATION IS USED TO REFER TO THE INTENSIFICATION OF A world-scale re-orientation of economic, technological, and cultural processes and activities that transcend state boundaries. Today, capital rapidly crosses state borders, and markets have been enlarged and extended. Modern forms of transportation mean people too can rapidly cross state boundaries. Contemporary communication systems, such as satellite television, cellular phones, fax machines, and the World Wide Web allow information to quickly pass around the globe.

The processes associated with globalization may affect specific countries differently. Nonetheless, as a package, these processes suggest that culture must also be considered in a context larger than the national state. Yet, many analysts feel that in the absence of a world state, it is inappropriate to talk about "a global culture" as something akin to the national culture of a country. It is quite possible, however, to refer to the globalization of culture (Featherstone, 1990, 1).

Currently many kinds of cultural flows quickly transcend state boundaries, illustrating how there has been a globalization of culture. Cultural flows that criss-cross state borders include the movement of ideas (e.g., democracy or human rights), the movement of images (e.g., the world-wide television viewers of the 1990 Gulf War, and of the 1997 funeral of Princess Diana) and, not least, the movement of people (e.g., tourists, immigrants, refugees, guest workers, and exiles) (Appadurai, 1990, 295–310). Indeed, global migration has become a central form of globalization, and one which serves to contribute to the internal diversity of nation-states (Abu-Laban, 2000). Given this, it would seem that the study of culture would be best approached by combining a sensitivity to diversity within states, with a sensitivity to forms of political participation, power relations, and forms of resistance, and identity that transcend national borders.

Evidence of political participation at levels larger than the national state challenges the traditional study of political culture which has emphasized peoples' attitudes towards national participation. One of the things that has coincided with globalization is the deepening of regional integration, as seen in the 1993 North American Free Trade Agreement between Canada, the United States, and Mexico and especially developments in the fifteen European countries now making up the European Union. Along with a European Parliament, whose members have been elected Europe-wide since 1979, there is now a European passport, a European flag, and a European anthem. These were expressly designed with an aim to create a European (as opposed to simply national) cultural identity (Martiniello, 1995, 43–44). The case of Europe illustrates how political symbols, forms of identity, and even opportunities for electoral participation have transcended the national state.

Globalization also raises a number of important issues from the cultural studies perspective. It has been suggested that in many ways national governments are unable to exert control over global economic and technological processes. The Internet, for instance, has made it virtually impossible for governments to regulate or control the flow of information, particularly in the context of ever-changing technological developments (Brehl, 1998, A1). Given the economic and technological processes which challenge the national state, there are new ways less powerful groups (e.g., women, workers, minorities) may try to resist the spread of capital globally. Adequately addressing how resistance is demonstrated increasingly requires looking at how groups may join together across state boundaries. This was evident during the meeting of the World Trade Organization (WTO) in Seattle in December 1999. The WTO consists of the governments of over 130 countries (including Canada) committed to reducing trade barriers between countries. Seattle proved to be a lightning rod and meeting point for mass protest from an array of students, labour groups, and other non-governmental organizations in the United States, and also abroad, critical of trade liberalization for its impact on the environment, labour standards, and poverty (Coffield, 1999, A1, A7).

Finally, globalization spells changes for culture and cultural identity—the key concerns in much contemporary political philosophy. As one example at the level of the arts, consider world music, which has been described as a music without borders. World music is characterized as coming from parts of the developing world (Cuba, Brazil, Algeria, Senegal, South Africa, India, and Pakistan), drawing from sounds the world over, and making its way to Western markets. Mickey Hart, former drummer of The Grateful Dead, and 1991 winner of the Best World Music Album Grammy Award with his band, Planet Drum, describes it as such:

> It's not really "world music." It's the *world's* music. There is a difference. When artists come out of their culturally bound musical traditions and start using modern instruments, they mutate the sound, they make a new stew, a new blend. This is what is called world music. There is no pure music in the world. Everything is a fusion because that's the way it is intended ("Music," 1998, 76).

Just as world music reflects a fusion of a variety of sounds from across the globe, globalization creates a host of other opportunities for cultural inter-mixing, as people, images and ideas traverse state boundaries. What results from such fusions? The case of France suggests some distinct possibilities as to how the globalization of culture creates new cultural identities and political claims. During the 1950s and 1960s, migrants from Algeria, Tunisia, and Morocco came to France to work—typically in areas such as manufacturing and construction. The second-generation children of these migrant workers, born and raised in France, are popularly referred to as *les beurs*. This name is Parisian slang for "Arab," and signifies the sense of a distinct cultural identity among the second generation that is simultaneously neither and both North African and French. Notably, the second generation has also made unique claims on the French state for recognition and equality (Wihtol de Wenden, 1994).

These are just some examples of the implications of globalization for the study of culture. The wide-ranging processes relating to the globalization of culture raise political issues regarding participation, as well as power and identity. This suggests that in the coming years, as in the past, culture and politics will continue to command the interest of political scientists, and there will be a lot to discover.

Summary

This chapter has addressed three ways that the study of culture and politics has been approached in the period following the Second World War. The political culture approach places an emphasis on peoples' attitudes towards political institutions and participation. In contrast, the cultural studies approach draws from Marxism to highlight power relations, and how these shape cultural practices. Cultural studies, as an approach, has traditionally been concerned with transforming relations of power. Finally, many contemporary political philosophers examine the implications of cultural identity claims made by groups in liberal democracies, for equality, democracy, and justice. While each of these approaches is distinct, they share in common a tendency to look at culture and politics within the confines of a state. In an era of globalization, there are new themes and concerns related to culture that transcend state boundaries, suggesting the need to balance a state focus on politics and culture that is sensitive to diversity with a more global focus on culture and politics.

Discussion Questions

1. Outline the major similarities and differences between the political culture, cultural studies, and cultural identity approaches. Is there an approach you favour, and if so why?

2. Is there a distinct political culture to the place you live now? If so, how would you describe it?

3. Discuss whether popular culture forms (e.g., television programs, music, the popular press) serve to help maintain or challenge the status quo.

4. Is equality best served by treating all cultural identity groups the same, or by granting differentiated rights? Does special recognition of cultural identity groups lead to national fragmentation, or does lack of recognition lead to fragmentation?

5. Does globalization foster cultural uniformity or cultural diversity?

References

Abu-Laban, Yasmeen (2000). "Reconstructing an Inclusive Citizenship for a New Millennium: Globalization, Migration and Difference," *International Politics* 37, 4 (Forthcoming December).

Almond, Gabriel A. (1980). "The Intellectual History of the Civic Culture Concept." In Gabriel Almond and Sidney Verba (ed.), *The Civic Culture Revisited* Boston: Little, Brown, pp. 1–16.

Almond, Gabriel and Sidney Verba (1963). *The Civic Culture*. Princeton: Princeton University Press.

Althusser, Louis (1971). *Lenin and Philosophy and Other Essays*. New York: Monthly Review Press.

Appadurai, Arjun (1990). "Disjuncture and Difference in the Global Cultural Economy." In Mike Featherstone (ed.), *Global Culture: Nationalism, Globalization and Modernity.* London: Sage, 295-310.

Bourdieu, Pierre. (1973). "Cultural Reproduction and Social Reproduction." In R. Brown (ed.), *Knowledge, Education and Cultural Change.* London: Tavistock, 71-112.

Brehl, Robert (1998). "CRTC Asks If It Should Regulate Internet." *The Globe and Mail* (August 1), A1.

Canada, Statistics Canada (1997). "1996 Census: Immigration and Citizenship." *The Daily,* November 4. Available: [http://www.statcan.ca/english/census96/nove4/naliss.htm].

Chilcote, Ronald (1994). *Theories of Comparative Politics: The Search for a Paradigm Reconsidered* Second Edition. Boulder: Westview Press.

Coffield, Heather (1999). "Demonstrators mass for WTO Trade Talks." *The Globe and Mail* (November 29), A1, A7.

Craid, Susan (2000). "My Name is Sheila and I am a Canadian." *The Globe and Mail* (May 2): A9.

Davies, Ioan (1995). *Cultural Studies and Beyond* London: Routledge.

Dickason, Olive Patricia (1992). *Canada's First Nations: A History of Founding Peoples from Earliest Times.* Toronto: McClelland and Stewart.

During, Simon (1993). "Introduction." In Simon During (ed.), *The Cultural Studies Reader.* London and New York: Routledge, 1-25.

Easton, David (1957). "An Approach to the Analysis of Political Systems." *World Politics* 9, 3, 383-400.

Featherstone, Mike (1990). "Global Culture: An Introduction," in Mike Featherstone (ed.) *Global Culture: Nationalism, Globalization and Modernity.* London: Sage, 1-14.

Fierlbeck, Katherine (1996). "The Ambivalent Potential of Cultural Identity." *The Canadian Journal of Political Science.* XXIX, 1 (March), 3-22.

Gatehouse, Jonathon (2000). "With Glowing Hearts We See Thee Advertise." *The National Post* (April 12), A1, A2.

Gramsci, Antonio (1971). *Selections from the Prison Notebooks.* London: New Left Books.

Henry, Frances and Carol Tator, Winston Mattis and Tim Rees (2000). *The Colour of Democracy: Racism in Canadian Society.* Toronto: Harcourt Brace.

Hoggart, Richard (1957). *The Uses of Literacy.* Middlesex: Penguin.

Jacoby, Jeff (2000). "What if Means to be Canadian." *The Boston Globe* (April 20), A27.

Jary, David and Julia Jary (1991). *The Harper Collins Dictionary of Sociology* . New York: Harper Collins.

Kymlicka, Will (1995). *Multicultural Citizenship: A Liberal Theory of Minority Rights.* New York: Oxford University Press.

Kymlicka, Will (1998). *Finding Our Way: Rethinking Ethnocultural Relations in Canada.* Toronto: Oxford University Press.

Lipset, Seymour Martin (1990). *Continental Divide* New York: Routledge.

Mallick, Heather (2000). "Joe: The Man Behind the Myth." *The Globe and Mail* (May 2), R1, R2.

Martiniello, Marco (1995). "European Citizenship, European Identity and Migrants: Toward the Post-national State?" In Robert Miles and Dietrich Thränhardt (eds.), *Migration and European Integration: The Dynamics of Inclusion and Exclusion.* London: Printerm 37-52.

May, Larry, Shari Collins-Chobanian and Kai Wong (1998). *Applied Ethics: A Multicultural Approach*, Second Edition. Upper Saddle River, NJ: Prentice Hall, 1998.

McLellan, David (1986). *Ideology.* Milton Keynes: Open University Press.

"Music without Borders: Mickey Hart Charts World Beat's Sonic Boom."(1998). *Shift Magazine* (August), 76.

Nelson, Cary, Paula A. Treichler, and Lawrence Grossberg (1992). "Cultural Studies: An Introduction." In Lawrence Grossberg, Carly Nelson and Paula Treichler (eds.), *Cultural Studies.* New York: Routledge, 1-14.

Taylor, Charles (1992). "The Politics of Recognition." In Amy Gutmann (ed.), *Multiculturalism and The Politics of Recognition.* Princeton: Princeton University Press.

Thiong'o, Ngugi wa (1995). "Decolonising the Mind." In Stuart Hirschberg (ed.)., *One World, Many Cultures.* Boston: Allyn and Bacon, 428-437.

Wihtol de Wenden, Catherine (1994). "Immigrants as Political Actors in France." *West European Politics* 17, 2 (April), 91-109.

Young, Iris Marion (1989). "Polity and Group Difference: A Critique of the Ideal of Universal Citizenship." *Ethics* 99, 250-274.

Further Readings

Political Culture

Almond, Gabriel and Sidney Verba. *The Civic Culture: Political Attitudes and Democracy in Five Nations.* Princeton: Princeton University Press, 1963.

Nevitte, Neil. *The Decline of Deference: Canadian Value Change in Cross-National Perspective.* Peterborough: Broadview Press, 1996.

Cultural Studies

Sardar, Ziauddin and Borin Van Loon. *Cultural Studies for Beginners.* London: Icon Books, 1997.

Eagleton, Terry. *The Idea of Culture.* Oxford and Malden: Blackwell, 2000.

Cultural Identity

Guttman, Amy (ed.) *Multiculturalism and the Politics of Recognition: An Essay by Charles Taylor.* Princeton: Princeton University Press, 1992.

Kymlicka, Will. *Multicultural Citizenship: A Liberal Theory of Minority Rights.* New York: Oxford University Press, 1995.

Weblinks

Political Participation
http:www.umich.edu/~nes/resources/nesguide/gd-index.htm

Cultural Studies and Sociology Home Page
www.bham.ac.uk/cultural studies

Cultural Studies Central
home.earthlink.net/~rmarkowitz

CHAPTER 16

COMMUNITY

Objectives

This chapter focuses on various notions of political community that appear in popular discussion and political science. Although we all have the sense that we live in some sort of geographic community, community can mean much more than the local place where we reside. To draw a complete picture of what community means politically, this chapter distinguishes between three types of community, discusses the sentiment of community, and outlines the communitarian–liberal political theory debate about community. To appreciate the powerful but controversial contribution of communitarianism to current politics, three types of modern communitarians will be presented. Feminist and other critiques of communities are also reviewed. Finally, the chapter suggests how community is used as a political strategy, and why community should be seen as a flexible political concept.

JUDITH A. GARBER

Introduction

During one week in October 2000, "community" appeared in more than 70 articles in *The Globe and Mail* newspaper. A week's reading turned up: the anxiety caused by a contaminated community water supply, a community's demands that police identify pedophiles living in its midst, efforts throughout Canada to keep the peace between two communities supporting their warring brothers and sisters halfway around the world, a joint community-government-business drive to raise funds for playground equipment, a mayoral candidate campaigning as a member of various of the city's communities, and a woman seeking community in a neighbourhood of imposing homes and empty streets. For a word that is used so often, and so offhandedly, community's meaning turns out to be surprisingly elusive. Clearly, how we conceive of community depends on context, and although the variations in our understanding of community might be subtle, they are significant. Even if we restrict ourselves to using community to stand for dimensions of political life, its meaning remains open to interpretation.

Community always refers in some loose sense to a group of individuals who recognize themselves, or are viewed by others, as sharing something significant in common. This general description does not lead directly to a working definition of community that applies in all instances, as is obvious from the illustrations above. To begin with, it does not say what that "something significant" is, or why it is significant. The most helpful way to approach community, then, is to recognize it not as one single thing, but as a collection of related political concepts revolving around unity, connectedness, and sharing within groups of human beings.

The Importance of Community in Political Science

COMMUNITY HOLDS A SPECIAL FASCINATION FOR POLITICAL THEORISTS, WHO have sparred about it for centuries. Initially, this was a two-sided debate, between **communitarians**, who believed that democracy rests on strong, vital community, and liberals, who believed that democracy requires individual freedom from the demands of community. More recently, the debate has expanded to include feminists and other political theorists who are skeptical about the impact of community on the equality and rights of groups in society. Other political scientists talk more explicitly about states and nations than about community, but their studies of international trade agreements, peacekeeping, religion in politics, or constitutional negotiations are often implicitly tied up with an interest in such questions as who determines community boundaries, what happens when communities clash, and which political values are promoted by community.

Political scientists study community because it is at its core a political concept. Community is sometimes used in ways (*entering a New Age spiritual community* or *the physics community's prestigious award*) that are not particularly political, but the concept of community is inherently political because it contains the built-in assumption that people have a natural capacity to act publicly, together, for common purposes. Community does not assume that people's political interests and participation are always oriented towards the outlets provided by formal governments, such as elections and lawmaking. However, community definitely conjures up the deeply political notion of collective self-governance, as well as related issues concerning setting goals, distributing privileges and powers, enforcing rules, handling conflict, and reaching agreement within groups of individuals who hold something significant in common.

Political scientists are also interested in community because it is a live political issue. In Canada, for example, there are at least three visions of community vying for superiority. One stresses a national community made up of distinct communities that include, among others, Quebecers, Aboriginal Canadians, and immigrant groups. Another proposes self-governing communities that exist totally (Quebec) or partly (First Nations) apart from "the Canadian community." The third seeks a dominant community that is guided by "traditional" anglophone–British–Christian culture and values. Worldwide, it is an ongoing project of both ultra-nationalist political leaders and fundamentalist religious leaders to cultivate communities that are homogeneous, assertive, and closed to outside influences. Our conduct in the home, at work and school, over channels of communication, and on the streets is governed by rules that supposedly reflect "community standards" and "community values" of one or more authoritative communities.

Three Types of Community

COMMUNITY FUNDAMENTALLY CONCERNS GROUPS OF PEOPLE WHO HAVE something in common. To make this concept of community more specific and tangible, we can identify three major commonalities that underlie community: place, identity, and interest. While these categories sometimes overlap, they capture distinct types of community that come up in popular discussions and political science.

Place-Based Community

Place-based community is "a general term for a real territorial settlement" (Gusfield, 1975, 32). Here, community refers to geographical, usually local, places with identifiable boundaries such as city limits. When local places coincide with official political jurisdictions, community becomes little more than a synonym for municipality. Traditionally, community is associated with villages and towns, but the concept "has been generalized to the wider scope of urban communities" (Gusfield, 1975, 33). Thus, we see inner-city neighbourhoods, mobile home parks, and gated housing complexes, as well as Native reserves and suburbs, called communities.

What people hold in common in these communities is shared space. This may create shared interests and feelings of closeness that did not previously exist, and it frequently results from identifiable groups—gay men, retirees, upper middle-class professionals, Ukrainians—concentrating themselves in a particular location. Community does not necessarily go any deeper than geographic proximity, however, and it may not even exist in the eyes of all community "members." Laws or group rules set out conditions for belonging to place-based communities, such as property ownership (for membership in condominium associations), citizenship (for voting), an address (for attending schools), or payment of dues (for using the facilities of community leagues).

Place-based community is especially useful for contrasting localities with larger, more anonymous political jurisdictions. For many people localities are communities precisely because they are not provinces, countries, or continent-wide trading blocs. In a very important sense, this form of community emphasizes the perceived "grassroots" or democratic character of local places, as opposed to the more distant or elitist "higher" levels of government. Local places are seen as communities because it is believed that they support a closeness among people. Locality facilitates people's awareness of and participation in the decisions that affect their immediate, everyday lives in common. Mexico City, Toronto, and New York, with many millions of residents each, are hardly intimate places, but they are often seen as more politically accessible and thus more like communities than Mexico, Canada, or the United States, which are also geographical places.

Identity-Based Community

Groups whose members share at least one identifiable characteristic make up another significant form of community. Characteristics including national origin, language, religion, sex, sexual orientation, skin colour, or degree of physical ability may underlie people's personal and, thus, collective identity. This is how we come to hear so much about "the francophone (or Somali or deaf or Jewish) community." While these identities frequently produce political interests and claims, the basis of the community is the shared identity, which precedes and goes beyond political concerns.

Identity-based community can facilitate a group's self-awareness, appreciation of its culture and history, and organization for political action. Communities whose core is their identity may succeed in gaining official recognition, citizenship rights, inclusion in (or autonomy from) mainstream politics, or even the creation of a nation-state. In recent decades in various countries, indigenous peoples' communities have sought each of these things. On the one hand, in peaceful democracies, the ordinary disagreements and negotiations between identity-based communities whose practices or political claims are at odds may become pressing issues. On the other hand, powerful identity-based communities (or governments) can spawn civil wars and the suppression of vulnerable, disfavoured identity-based communities. In the 1980s and 1990s, the most systematic cases of violence against identity-based communities in Europe, Africa, and Asia produced the term *ethnic cleansing*.

It is interesting to ponder why some politically potent group characteristics are rarely identified as motivating identity-based communities and their actions. Compare how infrequently we hear about the "white community" with how regularly the "black (or Sikh) community" is mentioned, as if racial or ethnic visibility constitutes a noteworthy political fact only for certain groups. Moreover, identity-based communities may get labelled from the outside, especially by politicians and the media. The result may be an inaccurate portrait of the group and its members' interests. The "Hispanic community," for example, homogenizes Spanish-speakers with roots in several countries, and whose politics are shaped by differences in ethnicity, skin colour, class, gender, and citizenship status.

Interest-based community

Interest-based communities exist to provide their members with benefits, whether recreational, economic, or political. To take as examples the business and environmental communities, organizations within these communities provide their members with an array of benefits such as bumper stickers, seminars, and inexpensive insurance, but they can still reasonably be called political communities because they are bound by a set of concerns that bear directly on the members' political interests. The political quality of interest-based communities does not evaporate if the members' political concerns are articulated as protecting the "public interest." Members tend to carry these concerns into the political process, and the communities try to benefit their members politically by forming interest groups to influence policy making and elections. Indeed, the popular identification of many interest-based communities *as* communities (e.g., the gun-owning community or the medical community) is tied to their inserting their common interests (freedom to use firearms and maintenance of public health care) into the political sphere.

The label *community* makes political sense only when applied to groups whose common interests include political goals—politically, goldfish owners are not a community. Non-political interests may become politicized, though, as has happened with two well-publicized interest-based communities—divorced fathers and women with breast cancer. These communities began by providing emotional support and information to their members, but are now demanding favourable child custody rules and funding for breast cancer research, respectively.

Naturally, joining Greenpeace, the Chamber of Commerce, or Students Against Drunk Drivers may not create meaningful community. It is important to know whether members of interest-based communities are merely paying dues to a far-off headquarters, or whether many members are active in the life of the organization (Putnam, 2000).

Community and Social Capital

IT IS EASY TO NAME DOZENS OF EXAMPLES OF COMMUNITIES BASED ON CONCRETE commonalities among people; more abstractly, community is also a shared sentiment or feeling. Community as a sentiment "points to the quality or character of human relationships" (Gusfield, 1975, xvi). Just as one could argue that political relationships should be grounded in honesty or courage, some people insist that these relationships should rest upon community. Here, community is a concept that endorses shared values, common goals, participation in public life, and ongoing relationships. People bound by sentiment trust and help one another. Communal sentiment is mostly attributed to people who end up feeling like a community because they start out sharing territory, whether local (Downtown Eastside Vancouver) or national (Japan). For this reason, community feelings are often discussed in conjunction with localism or nationalism. In either case, community may go beyond describing some characteristic people have in common to defining a way of life.

Political scientists and sociologists increasingly refer to these communal sentiments—and our willingness to act on them—as **social capital**. Like other forms of capital, social capital adds value wherever it is expended. In this case, society and the political system are believed to be enriched if large numbers of people are community-minded, and impoverished if they are not. That individuals may use their social capital because it is in their self-interest to live among the community-minded does not diminish the notion of social capital and the perceived value of community sentiments (Putnam 2000).

On a day-to-day basis, volunteer work by community groups and philanthropy by local community foundations convey communal feelings, as does the formation of neighbourhood watches or cordial police–citizen relations as elements of community policing. Community justice programs are becoming popular. They try to instill feelings of attachment and responsibility in people who have committed crimes by sentencing them to make amends to their victims or to the community as a whole, instead of imposing jail sentences that isolate offenders from the community (Karp, 1998). Voting, aiding someone in distress, and even purely social activities may be deemed significantly communal acts. Other commentators are skeptical that participation in bowling leagues, for instance (Putnam 2000), contributes very much to healthy politics.

We also hear about "the **international community**." This expression is often associated with organizations such as the United Nations and the Commonwealth, which are expected to react to events on the global stage. In this sense the international community is more a group of governments than a sentiment-based community. However, the international community can also symbolize shared sentiments of people in different countries, as when it "expresses outrage" at countries that test nuclear weapons, the hunting of endangered species, or governments that execute political opponents. We can imagine a global public that shares moral values and common purposes—justice, health, safety, and peace—and extends empathy towards people around the world.

Classical Political Theories of Community

COMMUNITIES AND COMMUNITY APPEAR TODAY AS AN ALTERNATIVE TO PERVASIVE individualism; a cure for the fragmenting forces of the modern world, and a supplement to impoverished civic and moral lives. Community is presented as struggling against the momentum towards capitalism, urbanization, secularization, and privatization. In contrast to these powerful trends, the idea of community may appear to have lost its political relevance.

This account is partly accurate. Western history since the eighteenth century has largely been one of key communal structures (village, monarchy, tribe, family, religion) giving way to a new, powerful tradition of liberalism that emphasizes the individual and individual freedom. These changes occurred with lightning speed in the second half of the twentieth century, aided both by technological developments facilitating travel and access to information and by political movements that have weakened older structures of authority based on inherited status, religion, race, ethnicity, language, age, and gender.

Liberalism is actually the new kid on the block in the long history of Western political theories. Fully two thousand years before the English liberal philosopher John Locke emphasized the individual's rights to "life, liberty, and property," Aristotle praised community

DEBATE BOX

Communities and Conflicting Identities

Usually, in Canada, multiple identity-based communities within a single place-based community merely enhance local cultural diversity. When divergent practices and beliefs conflict, the question of which community (or communities) should prevail arises. In Markham, Ontario, a dispute concerned plans to construct a substantial mosque also containing a "cold-storage facility for keeping dead bodies awaiting burial, in accordance with Muslim law."

One issue was resolved easily—the mosque's minaret (tower), which would have loomed over the area, was scaled down after the neighbourhood, the Markham town council, and mosque officials compromised. However, some Chinese homeowners signed a petition protesting the mosque. They "feared that . . . proximity to corpses would lead to bad *feng shui*," a prescription for building design and building placement to increase harmony and reduce bad fortune. The Islamic Society of Markham submitted their own petition complaining of discrimination.

A Muslim town councillor and a Chinese-Canadian regional councillor helped calm the situation. The mosque was approved, and "a groundbreaking ceremony before hundreds of dignitaries and well-wishers" from different cultures took place. Tension remains, and some Chinese families threatened to leave Markham, but according to the mayor (who is neither Chinese nor Muslim), "'at some point, [municipal] planning will dominate'. He stresses the hard work that went into bringing the communities together, advising the town to 'never stop working to improve relations and build bridges'."

What are all the types of community involved in this story? Why was the issue of the minaret more easily addressed than the issue of the storage of bodies? What is the general community interest that the mayor and councillors were promoting? Does it seem that this dispute was genuinely resolved? Can this story about communities be applied to other situations you have heard of or encountered?

SOURCE: Ron Csillag. 2000. "When feng shui meets Muslim law," *The Globe and Mail*, January 10, R10. © Ron Csillag. Reprinted with permission.

as the foundation of a healthy polis, or political society. The precise understanding of community differed for ancient Greek, classical Roman, early Christian, and Renaissance European thinkers (Friedrich, 1959). Nevertheless, community's importance was not seriously challenged from the fourth century B.C.E. until the seventeenth century, when liberal Enlightenment thinkers began to argue that political communities only come into being to secure individual rights. Even in the late eighteenth century, after liberalism became dominant in England, France, and America, influential political philosophers such as Jean-Jacques Rousseau were "rediscovering community" (Sabine and Thorson, 1973, 529) and insisting, as Aristotle did so many centuries earlier, that people are naturally political animals. Thus, the recent interest in retrieving community as an alternative to the perceived weaknesses of liberal individualism should not be surprising, given the persistent belief in the value and virtue of community.

Contemporary Communitarianism

COMMUNITY IS A FAVOURITE TOPIC OF CONVERSATION AMONG POLITICIANS, religious leaders, journalists, and citizens today. Today's communitarianism always reflects an appreciation for classical communitarianism, as well as fervent hopes that it can be adapted for contemporary use. All communitarians take the sentiment of community very seriously.

Nevertheless, the communitarian label has been adopted by a highly diverse array of political thinkers. Whereas some communitarians propose novel models of community, such as a global eco-community for the twenty-first century, others reminisce about examples from living memory, such as the tranquil small towns of the pre–World War II era or hippie communes of the 1960s. Ideologically, communitarians may be religious conservatives, socialist feminists, or anything in-between. Communitarians can also be grouped into those who want to see a strong relationship between community and the public sphere of collective self-governance, and those who focus on the role of the community in the private sphere of family and friendship.

Participatory Communitarians

One main branch of communitarianism focuses on citizens' direct participation in democratic decision making and public affairs. **Participatory communitarians** envision community as a base for active, committed citizens. This type of community is heavily place-based (Boyte, 1984); workplaces and cooperatives are included as potential sites for participatory politics (Wilkinson and Quarter, 1996). As a way of governing entire countries, the participatory community framework would still need small-scale decision-making units so that everyone would have an opportunity to make their voice heard and to interact directly with other members of the community. Electronic forums such as "virtual dialogue" on the Internet might help support national-level participatory democracy (Etzioni, 1996).

Participatory community encourages open and equal participation and discussion, substitutes equality-producing structures such as worker or housing cooperatives for hierarchical (corporate or bureaucratic) ones, and teaches the habit of equal treatment and equal responsibility. Feminists (Gilligan, 1982) have sometimes been attracted to participatory communitarianism because it draws on so-called "feminine" qualities of caring, cooperation, and equality, rather than competition for power and prestige. Many feminists do not subscribe to the idea of essential "feminine" and "masculine" traits, but it is no coincidence that feminists have historically attempted (with varying success) to structure their organizations around the ideal of participatory community.

Civic Republicans

Most political theorists who value community for its public component are **civic republicans** (or republicans). Civic republicans are attracted to language like "the public good" and "the good society," and they often develop specific plans for realizing "the good." Civic republicans do not dismiss individual autonomy, but their predominant concern is with "we-identities as against . . . I-identities" (Taylor, quoted in Etzioni, 1996, 26). For these communitarians, an individual's moral and political development is rooted in rich communal frameworks, rather than in alienated economic pursuits or quests for personal "growth." Individual acts and achievements have meaning when they honour and enhance the goals of the group. Just as athletes generally earn greater respect when they perform as "team players," and superior teams are those that function well as a group, the health of society is judged by how well it inspires political and moral commitment on the part of its citizens; in other words, its amount of social capital. Generally, "the public good is that which benefits society as a whole and leads to . . . public happiness" (Bellah et al., 1985, 335).

This brand of communitarianism is largely American in origin. Civic republicans, who are intensely concerned with identifying and being faithful to a community's "tradition," draw tremendous inspiration from the American founding tradition. Liberal ideas ultimately won the day in the United States, but communal ideas and political practices were prominent in the late eighteenth and early nineteenth centuries. Civic republicans are often criticized for their American bias, but even within that national context there are problems. Notably, republicans do not often explore the possibilities of competing traditions within American history and downplay certain elements of the founding traditions in North America, such as colonizing Natives, enslaving Africans, and subordinating women.

Many other countries claim vital, intact communal traditions, though—how often is Canada ("peace, order, and good government") associated with community and the United States ("life, liberty, and the pursuit of happiness") with individualism? Whether or not this is an accurate picture of either country, there are plenty of Canadians who worry about Canada moving away from its communitarian roots and towards an "Americanized" tradition of individual rights and freedoms (Bogart, 1994).

Civic republicans recognize that the specific content of the public good depends on the traditions of different places. Whether Italy (Putnam, 1993), Egypt (Rutherford, 1993), the United States, or Canada, each society has its own, unique "pattern" of values and practices. If these are respected and nurtured, community life will be healthier and more stable. Because basic patterns differ, acceptable levels of political and economic equality may be higher or lower. "[C]ommunitarian societies do not all exhibit the same combination of order and [individual] autonomy." Certain communities, therefore, expect subgroups to commit only to selected "core values" (Etzioni, 1996, 92–93). Canadian political philosopher Charles Taylor (1993), a leading proponent of strong community, has argued that a type of community-of-communities model is appropriate to Canadian traditions. Within distinct communities, whether these are based on language, culture, territory, or some other commonality, communal ties are very important. Such a diversity of strong communities is key to the public good of the larger Canadian national community.

Private Communitarians

There are, finally, communitarians who are deeply skeptical of the public sphere of collective self-governance and politics. **Private communitarians** wish to tame individualism, social disorder, and value change by shoring up private-sector social structures and intimate relations. Marriage, family, religion, and neighbourhood are the backbone of private communitarianism. Consequently, private communitarians may seek to privatize institutions that are now predominantly public, such as schools; and home schooling and religious schools are popular among private communitarians (Stackhouse, 2000). They may also join groups like Promise Keepers, an evangelical Christian men's group.

In this communitarianism, public life is important if it reflects, upholds, and builds on these private communal structures, as they are defined by the community. Public life should not intrude on or contradict them. Religious and "pro-family" organizations, and their members, may therefore participate in electoral and legislative politics to gain political support for policies such as government funding for parent-controlled charter schools and tax deductions for parent-provided childcare. For the most part, though, private communitarians gravitate to and seek collective involvement in forums that are close to home, including the immediate local community, and in voluntary and religious organizations alongside people who share their values (Berger and Neuhaus, 1977).

This is a conservative communitarianism by any North American standard. It is doubly conservative in terms of its attitude toward government. First, it discourages government intervention into the private sector to redistribute wealth, guarantee group equality, or engage in large-scale social spending. Second, it demands that government use its powers to enforce law, order, and what it sees as traditional moral values. Private communitarianism is also conservative in its conception of community itself, because it rarely tries to promote equality or individual choice within the structures of intimate relationships. Civic republicans generally believe that families, neighbourhoods, and other close relationships should be strengthened, but should also be open and evolving. Private communitarianism, in contrast, extols the virtues of rebuilding community on the foundation of stable values, including distinct gender roles for men and women, the authority of parents and teachers over children, and adherence to one religion or another (Talbot, 2000).

Difference, Conformity, and Community

IN A WORLD WHERE COMMUNITY AND INDIVIDUAL LIBERTY ARE BOTH HIGHLY prized elements of democracy, they will always be in tension. However, and despite the real differences between liberalism and communitarianism, there is increasing agreement on some fundamentals. Present-day liberals typically acknowledge that individual autonomy can coexist with certain restrictions imposed by the community. If the will of the community is expressed through democratic procedures, and if there are protections for fundamental liberties, community priorities may actually be interpreted as enhancing individual autonomy. For instance, censoring "hard-core pornography that intends no political message" and is "harmful to the interests of members of the community" (Gutmann, 1993, 135–136) is acceptable to many liberals. Similarly, civic republicans and participatory democrats may work at "finding an equilibrium between universal individual rights and the common good . . . between self and community" (Etzioni, 1996, xviii). In practice, this might mean that the community refrains from heavily regulating or severely punishing individual lifestyle choices, unless they clash with core community values or endanger other people.

Liberalism and communitarianism, while still dominant voices, do not define the entire debate about community. Some political theorists point out that the demands of commonality that exist within communities may clash with the need to respect the great diversity among groups in society. These penetrating criticisms of the impact of community on women, on lesbians and gay men, on ethnic or racial minorities—on any group that is perceived as "different" from the community norm—present a major challenge to contemporary communitarians. If communities discourage internal diversity, and if they expect members to conform to a set standard of public activity, then community is not a particularly democratic model of political relationships.

In nostalgic pictures of small-town life, harmony and goodwill are guiding forces. People like and trust each other, identify with each other, can come to a consensus about matters of public concern, and, if they must leave to pursue opportunities in other places, aspire to return home some day. This comforting scenario is drawn more from myth than from the real world, however, and ignores that communities invariably contain factions, sub-cultures, outliers, and outright dissidents with values, opinions, characteristics, and interests that defy "the good of the community."

It is no secret that communities may ignore, discourage, or punish internal diversity and disagreement, since conflicting interests, desires, and needs go against the idea of the "sameness" of a community. There may not be adequate mechanisms within communities for resolving serious conflict, if it is neither expected nor welcomed; conflict may not even be openly acknowledged. The norm of closeness and caring that operates in communities may also dictate that people will simply not risk starting a conflict, since it might offend or embarrass others.

Silencing difference may harm individuals, but it is also a serious matter for groups of people who hold distinctive perspectives on what constitutes the public good or what is appropriate behaviour. Christine Sypnowich comments that "it is women in particular who found that if they challenged communal traditions, be they in the Greek polis, Old Quebec, or the New England village, they risked being cast out of the community as traitors, whores, or even witches" (Sypnowich, 1993, 493). The presence of poor people, disabled people, people of colour, immigrants, gays and lesbians, untraditional families, or strangers can so threaten a community's perceived identity that they may be shunned, threatened, or expelled, especially if they actually voice dissenting opinions (Rayside, 1989).

Exclusion can happen in any community. The "feminist community" appeared in the 1960s and 1970s to speak with one voice and share a unified set of goals. These included liberating women from the nuclear family and moving them into positions of economic and political equality with men. Unfortunately, this notion of a single community allowed the majority of feminists to passively ignore or actively silence many fundamental differences among feminists and among women generally. Working-class women were already in the labour force. Women of colour faced discrimination from white women as well as from men. Lesbians wanted access to the legal and economic benefits of heterosexual women. These differences were seen as disruptive or irrelevant to a feminist community that was predominantly middle-class, white, and publicly heterosexual, and which wanted to preserve the notion of common goals, benefiting "all women."

Communities may also have expectations for action in the public sphere that permanently disadvantage some groups. When it comes to political participation, one size does not fit all. A good analogy is students who are shyer, noticeably younger or older, less confident, or who have less background preparation than their classmates. Maybe they have transferred from another university, are not native speakers of the language of instruction, or hold opinions that are different from the professor or the majority of the students. These students may not participate effectively in class discussions and group exercises. They may seem uninterested. They may not, in short, meet the preexisting expectations about activity in the classroom community.

The larger public sphere presents a similar situation. Recall the assumption, built into sentiment-based community, that people are political, public creatures by instinct. Before actual communities ever form, then, community imposes basic expectations about political habits. For adults, political expectations involve extensive, often face-to-face, interactions within the public sphere, which is the core of the ideal of collective self-governance. Members of different groups in the community approach politics from unequal positions, though. Political practices that are heavily oriented toward debate or other public interactions favour the most assertive, verbal, and credible members of the group. Class, race, sex, and other characteristics affect the outcome of group interactions. Even in situations where everyone has equal political rights, some people participate but are not taken seriously or given equal time. This has been documented frequently when women speak in mixed-sex groups (Mansbridge, 1993). Even in communities that highly value democracy and participation, some people will lose the desire or energy to try to fit themselves into biased models of interaction (Mansbridge, 1983).

Some feminists believe that when community is tied to public speech and action it will always reinforce separate roles for women and men. The historical tradition, at least for white, middle-class citizens, of men acting in the public sphere—as "city fathers" (Bellah et al., 1985, 170)—and women staying in the private sphere—as wives, mothers, and volunteers—places these two groups in very different relationships to politics in the community. None of the three kinds of contemporary communitarianism escape this trap. For private communitarians, women's work is valued, but it is confined largely to the private sphere. For civic republicans and participatory democrats, women's work may not "count" as genuinely political. Moreover, women may not be able to conform to the rules of interaction in the public sphere.

Summary

Community is a collection of related political concepts pointing to groups of people who share something significant in common. For political scientists, community is important and interesting because it concerns collective self-governance and has relevance to political relationships in the real world. Community may be based on a geographic place, an identity, or an interest; it may appear as the sentiment of connectedness. Advocates of community are reacting to the dominance of individualism in modern life, but communitarianism is a far older political tradition than liberalism. Contemporary communitarians can be divided into those who see community as a search for the public good, and those who view community as a way of upholding private relationships. Some liberals and communitarians are moving toward agreement on how to balance individual freedom and community authority, but feminists and other political theorists worry that community is hostile to differences among groups in society.

Where do we go from here? Must we choose between those who think that community is basically a good thing and those who think that community is basically a bad thing? Isn't community more complex than that? What do we do if we agree that community often discourages diversity and conflict, but we also feel that our social and political relationships would be enriched if individuals were more connected to some sort of community?

One way of stepping out of the community-as-good/community-as-bad debate is to begin thinking of community as an idea and a strategy rather than a thing. Whereas things are rigid and static, ideas and strategies suggest the possibility of flexibility and change. Perhaps what we are looking for are approaches to community that are adaptable to the political challenges and possibilities posed by twenty-first century society.

As an idea, community supplies a framework for discussing, naming, and evaluating human relationships, including political ones. The term says as much about how we choose to characterize people's commonalities as about the commonalities themselves. It also indicates a lot about how we imagine that various kinds of people interact. On the one hand, ugly or pathological examples of community, such as white supremacist colonies or street gangs, rarely get called community. On the other hand, we persist in calling community places where neighbours detest neighbours because of who they are or what opinions they hold.

As a strategy, people use community to build support for their preferred solutions to political and social problems. The success of community as a political strategy depends on placing it in a flattering light. This can be done by contrasting it with things that are clearly bad, such as social chaos, or using it so vaguely as to discourage scrutiny. In the typical North American city, for example, far more people would rally to support a new stadium for "the community's football team" than for "the billionaire media mogul's team," even if it is the same team.

Still, we should not conclude that community is a "glittering and nearly empty term" (Fowler, 1991, 150). A better assessment is that the term *community* provides a relatively familiar and easy route into politics for a wide range of citizens, including people who are not politically experienced or powerful. Community helps attract people to a variety of activities falling under the heading of politics.

What community politics means in people's minds may begin with a public debate among candidates running for mayor, but it does not end there. Community also applies to residents of a Native reserve protesting against a hazardous waste facility that pollutes their air, a coalition of mothers from both sides of a divided nation searching for peaceful solutions to civil war, parents from various backgrounds organizing to take control of their troubled neighbourhood school, immigrant women starting a self-help program to combat domestic violence, or a virtual dialogue about free trade among university students on different continents. Community persuades people to act for their shared interests and values in all these ways precisely because it is not a rigid and static thing.

Discussion Questions

1. What are some differences between communities that people are born into and communities that people choose to enter into?

2. Do you believe that Canadian politics and society are suffering from low levels of communal sentiment and actions?

3. When should a community's priorities give way to the rights of its individual members or subgroups?

4. How is community used as a political strategy by politicians, the media, and interest groups?

References

Bellah, Robert N., Richard Madsen, William M. Sullivan, Ann Swidler, and Steven M. Tipton. 1985. *Habits of the Heart: Individualism and Commitment in American Life*. Berkeley: University of California Press.

Berger, Peter L. and Richard J. Neuhaus. 1977. *Community is Possible: The Role of Mediating Structures in Public Policy*. Washington, DC: American Enterprise Institute.

Bogart, William. 1994. *Courts and Country*. Toronto: Oxford University Press.

Boyte, Harry C. 1984. *Community is Possible: Repairing America's Roots*. New York: Harper and Row.

Etzioni, Amitai, 1996. *The New Golden Rule: Community and Morality in a Democratic Society*. New York: Basic Books.

Fowler, Robert B. 1991. *The Dance With Community: The Contemporary Debate in American Political Thought*. Lawrence: University Press of Kansas.

Friedrich, Carl J. 1959. "The concept of community in the history of political and legal theory." In Carl J. Friedrich, ed., *Community, Nomos II*. New York: The Liberal Arts Press, 3–24.

Gilligan, Carol. 1982. *In a Different Voice: Psychological Theory and Women's Development*. Cambridge, MA: Harvard University Press.

Gusfield, Joseph R. 1975. *Community: A Critical Response*. New York: Harper Colophon Books.

Gutmann, Amy. 1993. "The Disharmony of Democracy." In John W. Chapman and Ian Shapiro, eds., *Democratic Community, Nomos XXXV*. New York: New York University Press, 126–160.

Karp, David R., ed. 1998. *Community Justice*. Lanham, MD: Rowman and Littlefield.

Mansbridge, Jane J. 1983. *Beyond Adversary Democracy*. Chicago: University of Chicago Press.

Mansbridge, Jane J. 1993. "Feminism and democratic community." In John W. Chapman and Ian Shapiro, eds., *Democratic Community, Nomos XXXV*. New York: New York University Press, 339–395.

Putnam, Robert D. 1993. *Making Democracy Work: Civic Traditions in Modern Italy*. Princeton, NJ: Princeton University Press.

Putnam, Robert. 2000. *Bowling Alone: The Collapse and Revival of American Community*. New York: Simon and Schuster.

Rayside, David. 1989. "Small town fragmentation and the politics of community," *Journal of Canadian Studies 24*, 103–120.

Rutherford, Bruce K. 1993. "Can an Islamic Group Aid Democratization? In John W.

Chapman and Ian Shapiro, eds., *Democratic Community, Nomos XXXV*. New York: New York University Press, 313–335.

Sabine, George H. and Thomas L. Thorson. 1973. *A History of Political Theory, 4th ed.* Hinsdale, IL: Dryden Press.

Stackhouse, John. 2000. "The new suburbia," *The Globe and Mail* (October 28), A11+.

Sypnowich, Christine. 1993. "Justice, community, and the antinomies of feminist theory," *Political Theory 21*, 484–506.

Talbot, Margaret. 2000. "A mighty fortress," *The New York Times Magazine* (February 27), 34-41.

Taylor, Charles. 1993. *Reconciling the Solitudes: Essays on Canadian Federalism and Nationalism.* Montreal and Kingston: McGill-Queen's University Press.

Wilkinson, Paul and Jack Quarter. 1996. *Building a Community-Controlled Economy: The Evangeline Co-operative Experience.* Toronto: University of Toronto Press.

Further Readings

Anderson, Benedict. 1991. *Imagined Communities: Reflections on the Origin and Spread of Nationalism.* London: Verso.

Clairmont, Donald H. and Dennis William Magill. 1999. *Africville: The Life and Death of a Canadian Black Community, 3rd. ed.* Toronto: Canadian Scholars' Press.

Freie, John P. 1998. *Counterfeit Community: The Exploitation of Our Longingness for Connectedness.* Lanham, Maryland: Rowman and Littlefield.

Weiss, Penny and Marilyn Friedman, eds. 1995. *Feminism and Community.* Philadelphia: Temple University Press.

Weblinks

The Communitarian Network
www.gwu.edu/~ccps

Communities On-Line
www.communities.org.uk

Community Foundations of Canada
www.community-fdn.ca

Globe and Mail Family Matters Series
www.globeandmail.com/series/familymatters

The Greek Community of Metropolitan Toronto/The Greek Village Online
www.greekcommunity.org

Intentional Communities
www.ic.org

CHAPTER 17

CITIZENS AND CITIZENSHIP

Objectives

The political concept of citizenship can mean something as simple as legal membership in a country or a full menu of rights and obligations that define an individual's relationship with fellow citizens and with the state. In this chapter, we trace the origins of citizenship as a critical political concept. We explore the question of access to citizenship. Who historically has been included and excluded from citizenship status? Finally, we consider some of the tensions that underwrite recent uses of the term *citizenship* in contemporary politics. In particular, we focus on three primary tensions between rights and responsibilities, universality and difference, and the national and the global.

CHRISTINA GABRIEL

Introduction

In 1946, Secretary of State Paul Martin Sr. introduced Canada's first Citizenship Bill to the House of Commons. He declared that "citizenship is the right to full partnership in the fortunes and future of the nation" (Martin, Sr., 1993, 72). Despite this declaration, more than fifty years later many of us find it difficult to describe what it means to be a "Canadian citizen" beyond a narrow legal definition or, indeed, to specify the content of "full partnership." Key political questions in Canada and elsewhere revolve around immigration as a source of potential citizens as well as the meaning of citizenship itself. These questions are particularly germane because the way we choose to answer them has implications for the kind of society and political community to which we aspire (Mouffe, 1992, 225).

Consequently, it is not surprising that citizenship, both in theory and in application, has been the source of on-going debate. Some social theorists have characterized citizenship as a "slippery" concept (Riley, 1992). Others have highlighted its essentially "contested nature" (Hall and Held, 1989). At the most general level, however, differing conceptions of citizenship are characterized by some common concerns including the inclusions and exclusions that are constitutive of membership of a particular community; reciprocal rights in, and duties towards, the community; and full participation in practice (Hall and Held, 1989, 175).

Citizenship as a political concept has a long history. The classical ideal of citizenship can be traced to the ancient civilizations of Greece and Rome. In the Greek city-state of Athens, for example, citizenship granted the privileges and obligations of self-government to a fortunate few. A citizen, according to the Aristotelian ideal, "is one who both rules and is ruled" (Pocock, 1995, 30). Political participation was regarded as a civic duty.

The privileges of citizenship, however, were usually only bestowed upon a select small group: "The citizen must be a male of known genealogy, a patriarch, a warrior, and the master of the labour of others (normally slaves)" (Pocock, 1995, 31). Citizenship was predicated on a strict division of the private from the public. The earliest citizen had slaves and women to satisfy his needs, leaving him free to engage in politics. This citizen as well as his equals "left his household . . . behind" (Pocock, 1995, 32) when entering the realm of citizen politics. Such criteria excluded most of the Greek population, including women, slaves, foreigners, and resident aliens from citizenship. In this respect, Athens' solution to potentially disruptive social inequality was to confine access and influence within the political process to a select few and "to limit the definition of citizenship" (Jenson, 1991, 198). The issue of whether citizenship as status can transcend differences based on social relations of class, gender, race, and ability so citizens participate as equals remains with us today. The Roman Republic further defined the status of citizenship. It pronounced clear reciprocal links for Roman citizens between rights, for example voting in assemblies, and responsibilities, primarily military service. However, the Republic came to draw distinctions between civil rights and political rights: "A 'citizen' came to mean someone free to act by law, free to ask and expect the law's protection" (Pocock, 1995, 36).

Although the origins of citizenship are ancient, many current conceptualizations of citizenship-as-rights are informed by the liberal political tradition dating back to the seventeenth century. The French Revolution's principles of liberty, equality, and fraternity were the grounds upon which French citizens claimed "universal recognition on the basis of common equality" (Hall and Held, 1989, 176). The French and American revolutions in the late 1700s helped to "revive" the concept of citizenship. These events were deeply influenced by the English philosopher John Locke. His work emphasized that the relationship between government and the people was "consensual" and "contractual" (Kaplan, 1993, 248). According to Locke's ideas, formal equality between citizens is assured by civil and political rights guaranteed and protected by a limited state. Under the terms of Locke's "social contract," consent was the basis of authority. Locke was convinced that the business of government rested with the people. They and they alone were responsible for their own good. They would "elect representatives, delegate powers, and agree to abide by majority decisions, but ultimately the representatives and officials hold their powers on trust and are responsible to the people" (Goodwin, 1992, 221).

The "sovereign people," however, with the "natural right to liberty" were an exclusive association of property owners. "[W]omen, not usually possessing property in their own right, and embedded in the 'private' realm of the family, were not considered adequate contenders for political subjecthood" (Riley, 1992, 186). Nevertheless, Locke forwarded a critical political concept—equality among citizens. Citizens were recognized as independent, equal members of the sovereign people. As such they had equal natural rights that the government was obligated to protect (Goodwin, 1992, 222).

This ideal of equality gives the concept of citizenship its radical emancipatory potential. Previously, citizenship had been underwritten by a range of exclusions. Take for example the basic political right of voting in Canada. In the years immediately following Confederation, income and property requirements, as well as the exclusion of all women, meant only a small proportion of the population could vote. Most women won suffrage by the 1920s but people of Chinese, East Indian, and Japanese origin were denied the vote until the late 1940s. Each of these groups contested their marginal status using the language of citizenship, by making a claim for equality. In this respect, citizenship is a very powerful concept. The very idea of citizenship implies that there should be no exclusion from the political community on the basis of, for example, sex or race.

Citizenship as Belonging

THE ISSUE OF MEMBERSHIP IN A POLITICAL COMMUNITY IS A KEY ASPECT OF citizenship. Hall and Held contend that "issues around membership—who does and who does not belong—is where the politics of citizenship begins" (Hall and Held, 1989, 175). These processes of inclusion and exclusion operate both through formal and through less direct understandings of citizenship. Formal citizenship refers to a legal status—"the rules of access to citizenship." Less direct questions about citizenship revolve around "rights and obligations connected with being a member of a state." Often these two understandings do not correspond (Castles, 1994, 4). It is important to point out, however, that rights and obligations can also apply to those who are not formal members of the community. Similarly, possession of formal citizenship does not necessarily guarantee the benefits of substantive citizenship (Lister, 1997, 43). The latter is associated with the term "second-class" citizen.

This section considers the question of citizenship as a legal status—who is born a citizen and who can access the right to be a citizen. Some argue that, for citizenship to have any meaning, it should be restricted, granting rights to citizens not available to others. For example, recent American legislation has limited the right to welfare benefits and services for legal immigrants who have not yet become legal citizens (Lister, 1997, 46). Others, in contrast, argue that citizenship should be freely available to all settled members of a community and all individuals should be treated in the same way (Kaplan, 1993, 257). This debate has become particularly heated in the wake of the large-scale postwar migration to Western Europe and North America. These issues are a major challenge to conceptions of citizenship in modern liberal democracies.

Access to citizenship, in some ways, occurs along a spectrum. At one end are those born into citizenship. At the other end are groups of people resident in countries where their formal citizenship is in doubt or in question. The situation of Western European migrant workers (guest workers) is a good example. They were recruited under employment and residence permits in the postwar period. Today they participate in the economic realm. They pay taxes and many have children who were born in the host country. But many are excluded from political participation at both the local and national level. This situation has led to questions about the representativeness of government when large segments of the population are disenfranchised. Layton Henry argues that "[t]here is clearly a contradiction between the economic exploitation of immigrants . . . and the length of time that residence and membership in a state can be sustained without representation" (Henry, 1990, 22). How long does a person have to live in a country before he or she can expect political representation? The dilemma of the guest worker is not limited to Western Europe. In Canada, the number of work permits for people working in Canada on a temporary basis matches or exceeds the number of people applying for immigration to Canada (Stasiulis, 1997, 154). Foreign domestics, for example, enter Canada under the provisions of the Live-in-Caregiver program. These provisions include the granting of temporary "visitor" status and the condition that domestics live with their employers. These conditions effectively render these workers "non-citizens" (Bakan and Stasiulis, 1997).

Despite the growing number of migrants whose status is precarious in Canada, there is a popular perception that Canadian citizenship is relatively easy to obtain. Citizens are either born in Canada, or in the case of permanent residents, can apply for Canadian citizenship once certain conditions are met. These conditions currently include a three-year residency and a knowledge of Canada's geography and political system.[1] Permanent residents share many of the same rights as Canadian citizens, but they are unable to vote or run for public office. They may also be barred from certain jobs in the public service.

Increasingly, there are those who charge that Canadian citizenship amounts to little more than a passport and that as a country, we don't value citizenship. In an opinion editorial, University of Toronto Professor John Crispo argued that Canadian citizenship "is so precious, indeed priceless, that we should grant it only to the most deserving individuals" (Crispo, 1996, A6). The implication here is that citizenship should be earned. Neil Bissoondath has gone further by claiming many people treat Canadian citizenship in a cavalier manner, knowing that it allows them to return to former homelands secure in the knowledge that they are protected from unforeseen consequences. Canadian citizenship, he suggests, does not force immigrants to make a strong commitment to their new country (Bissoondath, 1993, 382).

The status and meaning of citizenship is currently on the political agenda in Canada. In 1994, the federal government initiated a process to rewrite the Canadian Citizenship Act. And in November 1999 they introduced a new Citizenship Act, Bill C-16. However, the 2000 federal election ended the Parliamentary session in which it was being considered. The Bill—had it been passed—would have been the first major reform of Canadian citizenship legislation since 1977. Among the changes suggested were a new oath; more precise residence requirements to attain citizenship; new provisions applying to children adopted abroad; promotion of citizenship values; and additional proposals to revoke citizenship (Young, 2000, 3—11).Whether such measures engender a greater feeling of "belonging" or "loyalty" to the national community or ensures the extension of status to only "deserving individuals" is open to public debate.

Tensions Underlying Citizenship

THE POLITICAL APPLICATION OF THE CONCEPT OF CITIZENSHIP IS NOT LIMITED to legal definitions of access. It also addresses more substantive aspects of citizenship. Three are particularly noteworthy. First, the postwar conception of citizenship-as-rights is increasingly being challenged by "active" models of citizenship that stress responsibility. Second, the liberal conception of citizenship is being criticized for exclusions based on categories of difference. And last, conditions of globalization are giving rise to new forms of citizenship.

Rights versus Responsibilities

The work of British sociologist T. H. Marshall is often taken as the starting point for thinking about the evolution of citizenship. Marshall's analysis of citizenship was concerned with addressing the fundamental contradiction between democracy and capitalism. He was concerned with the meaning of citizenship within the context of class-based inequities. Do rights have any relevance, asked Marshall, if people do not have the means or capacity to make citizenship meaningful in practice?

In *Citizenship and Social Class*, Marshall defined citizenship as, "a status bestowed on those who are full members of a community." Moreover, Marshall maintained that "[a]ll who possess the status are equal with respect to the rights and duties with which the status is endowed" (1950, 14).

Drawing specifically on the English example, Marshall mapped three elements of citizenship that had evolved in the modern liberal democratic state. The first element, civil rights, emerged in the eighteenth century and referred to rights necessary for individual freedom including "liberty of person, freedom of speech, thought and faith, the right to own property . . . the right to justice" (1950, 10). The second element encompasses political rights such as the right to vote and run for political office. These rights date to the nineteenth century. According to Marshall the twentieth century was associated with the social rights of citizenship. He defined this element as "the right to a modicum of economic welfare and security . . . according to the standards prevailing in society" (1950, 10). The law and Parliament were the institutions most closely associated with the first two elements of citizenship. However, the welfare state was the institutional mechanism for social rights. Welfare state arrangements, such as public education, universal health care, public housing, and income security programs, were designed to counteract the insecurities generated by the market economy in which liberal democratic citizenship was embedded. In this respect the welfare state added a social dimension to citizenship.

It is argued that social rights make possible a fuller expression of citizenship for those groups who are disadvantaged in terms of resources and power. As Lister states "without social rights, gross inequalities would undermine the equality of political and civil status inherent in the idea of citizenship" (1997, 17). Drawing on Marshall's framework, sociologist Esping-Andersen (1990) has argued that social citizenship rights "de-commodify labour" because welfare state provisions, such as unemployment insurance, allow individuals and families some protection in the capitalist workplace. Relatedly, Lister argues these social rights release people from absolute dependence on the labour market by "decoupling the living standards of individual citizens from their market value"(Lister, 1997, 17). Within this formulation the risks, economic insecurity, and inequalities associated with a competitive market economy are alleviated, but not eliminated, by new social entitlements that permit individuals as citizens to meet their basic needs.

The specific configuration of national welfare states and the nature of social entitlements have varied from country to country in the postwar period. A host of factors including the level of national resources, differing capacities of groups to advance claims, institutional practices, and ideas about the state play a role in the degree to which countries have protected and advanced social rights (Tuohy, 1993). In Canada social rights have also played an important role in fashioning postwar ideas about Canadian identity and citizenship. In a sense, social programs provided an important benchmark to assess our progress as a people. Some programs were "the standard by which Canadians could judge themselves vis-à-vis Americans. Canadians were more compassionate, more caring and had a greater sense of social justice" (Taras, 1997, 2). Our health care system offers a case in point. *Macleans* magazine recently reported that "medicare is a matter of enormous pride for Canadians, up there with the Maple Leaf flag as a symbol of what we are as a people" (Marshall, 2000/2001, 48).

However, compared to Western Europe, social citizenship in Canada has been relatively limited. Indeed the Canadian welfare state has been characterized as minimalist, "providing a basic level of benefits and services, designed to encourage labour-force participation regardless of working conditions" (Bakker and Scott, 1997, 289). Moreover, unlike some Western countries, social rights are not protected in the Canadian Constitution.[3]

T.H. Marshall's key point was that citizens in need were entitled to welfare provisions not in the form of charity but as an entitlement of citizenship itself. In contrast to liberal definitions of citizens, which construct citizens as individual members of a state, Marshall's conception emphasizes collective membership in a community (Yuval-Davis, 1997). As Ed Broadbent underlines, "it is the community that provides the social right and it as a member of the community that redress is to be sought . . . . The objective of social policy as a right of citizenship in the modern age is to ensure a high level of community standards equally accessible to all" (Broadbent, 1997, 8).

In recent times, this postwar idea about citizenship is sometimes labelled "passive." This is because it emphasizes passive social entitlements "and the absence of any obligation to participate in public life" (Kymlicka and Norman, 1995, 286). New Right critics such as the American social policy theorist Lawrence Mead have argued that social and economic rights to collective public goods cannot be separated from moral obligations to society as a whole. In particular, he emphasizes the obligation to work (Plant, 1991, 60). On the Left, there has been defence of the position that full citizenship requires social rights coupled with a recognition of the problematic nature of the welfare state and its practices, as it has developed in the past forty years. These critics advocate that the provision of social rights should be decentralized and democratized (Kymlicka and Norman, 1995, 290).

In the United Kingdom, Margaret Thatcher's Conservative government attacked the social dimensions of citizenship by praising the "active citizen." This individual discharges the duties of citizenship privately through neighbourliness, voluntary work, and charitable gifts. This notion detaches citizenship "from its modern roots in institutional reform, in the welfare state and community struggles" and rearticulates social welfare in the "Victorian concepts of charity, philanthropy and self-help" (Hall and Held, 1989, 175). This particular New Right construction of the "active citizen" marks an important shift in the way we experience citizenship. The social rights of the disadvantaged are transferred, in part, from publicly financed entitlements into the private sphere of charity and voluntary services (Yuval-Davis, 1997, 84).

There are other ideas apart from the New Right's about "active citizenship." One emphasizes "local people working together to improve their own quality of life and to provide conditions for others to enjoy the fruits of a more affluent society" (Lister 1997 citing Pahl, 1990, 23). This approach to active citizenship would embrace the community-based struggles of the disadvantaged groups, such as women and minorities, against particular forms of social exclusion. In Canada, the former president of the National Action Committee on the Status of Women (NAC), Judy Rebick, has called for greater and more meaningful citizen participation in public life as a necessary counter to the adverse effects of globalization (Rebick, 2000, 8). There are 17 points in her model of active citizenship including such measures as:

- combining direct and representative democracy;
- including citizens at every level of decision making;
- inviting people to participate directly in the decisions that affect their lives;
- reducing the power and influence of the corporate elite;
- redesigning democracy to be bottom up more than top down;
- including all demographic groups, especially those most marginalized in our current system (Rebick, 2000, 231).

The differing ideas of active citizenship show how the concept of citizenship can be deployed by different political actors. But it also begs a central question: what are the duties of citizenship?

One of the key duties, or obligations, embraced by the New Right is the requirement that citizens support themselves. These critics of the postwar welfare state have attacked social rights because they believe these rights create "quite the wrong incentives for the worst off groups in society who are encouraged to believe that others owe them a living and a status not earned by their own efforts" (Plant, 1991, 61). The welfare state far from ensuring a more meaningful expression of citizenship has, in the view of New Right critics, promoted passivity and encouraged a culture of dependence among disadvantaged groups (Kymlicka and Norman, 1995, 287). These ideas, which stress the obligation and duties of citizenship, are progressively displacing the postwar social rights paradigm (Lister, 1997, 19). The new notions of "active" and "responsible" citizenship call on people to take seriously their duties to the broader community instead of their right to make rights-based claims on it.

It is important to emphasize that this struggle to redefine the concept of citizenship is not taking place in an ivory tower. It finds expression in recent policy developments in Canada and elsewhere. The Organization for Economic Cooperation and Development (OECD) has adopted the "active society" as a policy rationale. Walters argues that the "active society" argument is premised on familiar assumptions including the belief that welfare or social security is not the solution to society's problems, but, instead, part of the problem. Moreover, social problems are argued to be best addressed through the promotion of "activity" such as paid employment (Walters, 1996, 224). These assumptions inform the policy directions of many OECD countries.

In Canada, the Unemployment Insurance Program was replaced by Employment Insurance in 1997. The Liberal Government policy papers suggested that the very provisions of the former program produced "disincentives" to work and these resulted in a rise in the national unemployment rate (Jackson, n.d., 1). Program changes to earning calculations and eligibility have significantly reduced the numbers of workers who are now able to claim benefits. The Canadian Labour Congress reports that "UI reform in the '90s had a disproportionate and very negative impact on women . . . The fall in coverage for women in many of the regions has been twice—even three and four times—as great as it has been for men" (CLC, n.d.,1). Individuals are compelled to search for and accept what may well be low-paid, unpleasant work.

At the provincial level both Ontario and New Brunswick are experimenting with *workfare* programs. Under Ontario's 1996 welfare reform it was suggested that all able-bodied welfare recipients be required to undertake work-for-welfare activities, job searching, training, and community service. These requirements became a condition for what was previously a social entitlement of all citizens.

Under the postwar social rights paradigm, basic entitlements were supported by tax dollars and available to all members of society. Current New Right thinking equates social citizenship rights and "entitlement" with the idea of dependency, privileges, the better-off in society, and tends to reinforce existing social inequalities. "The work obligation is presented as one that unites all citizens," but, as Lister points out, the target of the active citizenship model is overwhelmingly the poor (Lister, 1997, 20). In the debate over rights vs. responsibilities the New Right's attempt to promote "responsible" citizenship has significantly eroded the social dimension of citizenship.

Does citizenship require demonstrated physical presence in the country?

A number of discussion documents and reports have identified residency as a key requirement for Canadian citizenship. For example, in 1994 the Standing Committee on Citizenship and Immigration stated "residency is not a mathematical exercise. Residency is an experience, a Canadian experience, for which there can be no substitute" (Standing Committee, CIC, 1994, 12). A subsequent Immigration Advisory Review Group built upon this and added "We wish to encourage immigrants to work and raise their families here, to become part of the Canadian fabric. We want to encourage them to become citizens. One aspect of their commitment must be physical residence here" ... [which] "would be verified by three guarantors . . . and confirmed by T4 slips, telephone bills, credit card bills or other documentation" (Immigration Legislative Review, 1997, 39–40). The federal Liberal government addressed the issue of residency in its recent proposals for legislative reform.

Proposed criteria included a measure that people seeking to acquire Canadian citizenship must be physically present in Canada for a specific time in order to qualify. Current requirements demand than an applicant be in residence three out of four years. Problems have arisen because the residency requirement has not been clearly defined. An analysis of these provisions has suggested that differing judicial interpretations of the requirement have complicated the issue. The assessment highlighted a 1977 federal court decision that indicated actual physical presence was not necessary so long as the applicant could demonstrate "significant attachment to Canada throughout the period, even if absent." Evidence of attachment could be "Canadian bank accounts, investments,

club memberships etc." In other cases federal court judges have not been willing to overlook long absences from the country (Young, 2000, 5–6).

The Liberal government attempted to address this issue by proposing that a person must be in Canada for 1095 days (60%) of a five-year period before applying for citizenship. Under pressure, this was subsequently modified to 1095 days of a six-year period.

Many groups and organizations criticized such proposals on the grounds that they would adversely affect "international business travelers, academics and others who are often out of the country but want to make Canada their home" (Laghi, 1999, A5). Immigration lawyers suggested that these types of measures "would scare away investors whose global interests force them to travel extensively" (Murray, 1998, A1). Within the House of Commons similar concerns were raised. Additionally, while the new proposals set out clearer residency requirements, critics, such as Canadian Alliance MP Rob Anders, pointed out that there were no proposed mechanisms—presumably of the type suggested by the Immigration Advisory Group— to actually determine whether a person was physically resident in the country or not.

In your view, should physical presence within Canada be a necessary requirement for granting Canadian citizenship? If so, why?

In what ways does physical presence in Canada indicate the type of citizen a person may be?

Is it feasible to maintain this type of requirement in a global economy where many people move around for business purposes? Should business people or certain kinds of workers be exempt from such provisions?

Universality versus Difference

The politics of citizenship, both in theory and practice, is also centred around the issues of "universality" and "difference." Within the concept of citizenship is an ideal premised on the basis of equality or universal status. This ideal of universality is found in such phrases as "everyone is equal before the law." Critiques by feminists, people of colour, and other disadvantaged groups, however, have raised concerns about the exclusive nature of supposed "universalistic" concepts. These groups draw attention to the fact that formal citizenship rights have been no guarantee of full participation or full membership of everyone. We may be equal as citizens, yet may be "distinguished from other citizens by physical appearance, ethnicity, origin, culture or socio-economic position. Where such a separation gives rise to inequality, discrimination and racism, citizenship must be seen as incomplete" (Castles, 1994, 4). To some extent Marshall's conception of citizenship tried to address this issue. Marshall's key preoccupation was how the working class was cut off from a common culture and prevented from accessing a common civilization (Kymlicka, 1992). Yet, exclusion can take many different forms. People of colour, women, people with disabilities, and gay men and lesbians have been excluded from full participation "not because of socio-economic status but because of their socio-cultural identity—their difference." (Kymlicka and Norma, 1995, 302). Women, for example, may claim formal citizenship rights but this seeming parity is countered by the material aspects of their disadvantage as a group. What does citizenship mean in the context of the continuing sexual division of labour or increasing feminization of poverty?

Feminist accounts of citizenship have been instrumental in highlighting how this concept is deeply gendered. Noted political philosopher Carole Pateman, for example, has examined the ways in which women have been excluded and included in the category "citizen." Political theory, Pateman argues, despite its claim to universality presupposes sexual difference and this, in turn, structures women's status as citizens. She argues conceptions of citizenship are premised on a "patriarchal separation" between the public realm of politics and work and the private realm of sexual relations and domestic life. Anything that happens in the private realm, the space traditionally associated with women, is treated as insignificant to citizenship (Pateman, 1989, 189). Moreover, the qualities citizens are expected to display, such as impartiality, rationality, independence, and political activism are attached to men and the public realm (Lister, 1997, 70).

This public–private dichotomy, Pateman suggests, also informs the construction of the postwar welfare state. In "The Patriarchal Welfare State," Pateman takes exception to Marshall's theory of social citizenship. She argues that the very structure of the welfare state, Marshall's mechanism for the realization of social rights, far from ensuring full membership for women casts them as "social exiles." The welfare state was constructed around the notion of a male "breadwinner/worker." It presumed that men are full-time wage earners who provide for dependent wives and children. Women, in contrast, were assumed to provide unpaid domestic care at home. They were the "dependent wife." The development of the welfare state was premised on the notion that certain aspects of care should be provided in the home by women's unpaid labour instead of through public provision (Pateman, 1989, 192). Pateman argues that these assumptions created a gendered two-tier structure in the welfare state. Men could claim "benefits available to individuals as 'public' persons" because they were paid employees. Women, however, were seen as "'dependents' of individuals in the first category" (Pateman, 1989, 188). Women's access to the rights of social citizenship was only partial. Through their unpaid labour they could contribute to the welfare of men and society but women's welfare and social citizenship rights were contingent upon their relationship to breadwinner-males.

Explorations of citizenship, such as Pateman's, have demonstrated how women's relationship to political, civil, and social elements of citizenship is very different from that of their male counterparts. These works show how the emancipatory promise of citizenship's universal ideals, of full participation and membership, remain far from being realized by many. In exposing the "male" citizen that lurked behind the concept of modern citizenship, feminist analyses have provided insights into the differential positioning of other groups within discourses of citizenship.

Indeed, feminist theorist Iris Marion Young has argued that modern conceptions of citizenship can often serve to marginalize and oppress various groups of people. She begins from the starting point that a unitary conception of citizenship is unjust because, as she puts it, in societies "where some groups are privileged while others are oppressed, insisting that citizens should leave behind their particular affiliations and experience to adopt a general point of view, serves only to reinforce that privilege. . . . the perspectives and interests of the privileged will tend to dominate this unified public, marginalizing or silencing those of other groups" (Young, 1990a, 120). Young supports a democratic project that would incorporate people into the political community not only as individuals but as members of groups. Group representation becomes a method to "promote just outcomes within the democratic decision making process" (Young, 1990a, 126). Within this call is Young's conception of "differentiated citizenship" which requires the introduction of group-specific rights in order to confront oppression and disadvantage. She suggests specific measures are necessary for effective recognition and representation of disadvantaged groups. Such measures would include, among other things, public support of group organizations, group representation in the generation and evaluation of relevant key policies, and veto power over specific policies that affect any one group directly (Young, 1990a, 124).

In the case of everyday politics there have been a number of examples where policies have been directed at specific groups rather than at individuals. Many of these have proved very controversial. Multiculturalism policy in Canada, for example, has been the source of considerable debate. The policy has been criticized as "divisive" on the grounds that it emphasizes differences between citizens and produces "hyphenated Canadians." It has also been attacked on the basis that it grants "special status" and funding to ethno-cultural groups. The notion of differentiated citizenship has been identified as a "radical development in citizenship theory" and one that constitutes a serious challenge to an understanding of citizenship premised on "treating people as individuals with equal rights under law" (Kymlicka and Norman, 1995, 302–3). Regardless of one's personal perspective, this growing debate about universality and difference is central to the politics of citizenship in the twenty-first century.

The National versus the Global

Various forms of globalization have challenged traditional understandings of citizenship. First and foremost, it is generally taken for granted that the nation-state provides the infrastructure for citizenship status and citizenship rights. Increasing global interconnectedness challenges this understanding. David Held sees a number of "disjunctures" in the areas of law, polity, security, identity, and economy between the sovereign power of the nation-state and the current process of globalization. Globalization effectively narrows the actions and decisions of governments. It blurs the boundaries of domestic politics, changes the administrative and legal environment in which decisions are taken and effectively obscures "the lines of responsibility and accountability of national states themselves" (Held, 1995, 135).

How do these developments affect conceptualizations of citizenship that have been built upon the foundation of a sovereign nation-state? To what extent has citizenship been detached from particular states? Held, for one, draws attention to the "disjuncture" between citizenship, as a status with rights and duties stemming from an individual's membership in a national political community, and the growth of international law. The latter, he suggests "subjects government and non-government organizations to new systems of regulations" (Held, 1989, 198). These emerging systems produce mixed consequences.

For example, membership in the European Union has created opportunities for individual citizens of member states to challenge their own governments in forums such as the European Court of Justice. This supraterritorial means for citizens to challenge their governments has already had some effect on national legislation (Held, 1989,199). The development of international legal regimes may contribute to the erosion of the nation-state to the extent that they constrain national sovereignty. Importantly, however, these regimes also provide opportunities for citizens who seek to protect their rights from national laws that may violate them.

Held has also focused on the development of new forms of transnational activities, highlighting the disjuncture between new forms of governance and the sovereign states (Held, 1995, 108). Nation-states have developed a host of international links in areas as diverse as trade, banking, and environmental regulation leading to profound changes in decision making and decision-making capacity. Canada is a member of numerous international organizations, such as the UN. It participates in less formal but influential coordinating meetings, such as economic summits, by virtue of its membership in the G7. And, Canada is signatory to a number of trading agreements of which the North American Free Trade Agreement (NAFTA) is the most encompassing. This matrix of international links affects the ability of nation-states to pursue policies that are truly national. This has potential consequences on the state's very ability to guarantee rights of citizenship. Regional trade agreements and rapid economic changes have led many companies to adopt drastic fiscal restraint measures and public sector retrenchment. Within this environment the fate of social citizenship rights is in question (Stewart-Toth, 1996, 271).

Within the matrix of international linkages, however, Lister also draws attention to the "unaccountable power" of institutions of global capital, transnational corporations, the

World Bank, and the existing institutions of global citizenship. She argues that if the social and economic rights embodied in UN covenants are to be realized by countries that are less privileged, the imbalance of power would need to be confronted. Citizenship, she argues, "is tied to democracy and global citizenship should in some way be tied to global democracy" (Lister, 1997, 61). The implication here is that international institutions such as the International Monetary Fund should be reformed and made more democratically responsive to the people it regulates. There is a growing awareness among people that many political issues transcend national borders and thus cannot be addressed by national governments alone. This realization has led to transnational linkages among social movements and non-governmental organizations operating at an international level. The activities of organizations such as Amnesty International, women's groups, and environmental organizations are notable examples of transnational politics. These developments, it has been suggested, signal the "birth of an international global civil society" (Lister, 1997, 62).

The politics of environmentalism, in particular, challenges us to think about citizenship in new ways. This issue connects individual lifestyle and responsibility with the fate of the planet. It reinforces an international or global dimension to politics insofar as environmental issues, such as global warming, oil spills, and acid rain, very clearly transcend the borders of nation-states and the decision-making capabilities of individual governments. For these reasons, Fred Steward argues that a citizenship of the planet earth, the concept of "green citizen," offers a marked departure from current conceptions of citizenship. Green citizenship draws on our shared dependence on nature as the basis of equality. It expresses "the right to a common human inheritance regardless of nation—the rainforests and coral reefs, as well as the earth's planetary resources" (Steward, 1991, 740). It focuses on the need for supranational action to confront environmental issues and thus challenges elements of national and local sovereignty commonly associated with current notions of citizenship.

One attempt at a reconceptualization of citizenship suggests that the trends highlighted above will require individual citizens to have "multiple citizenships." That is, people will be members not only of the nation-states they were born in or brought up in, but of wider regions and of the wider global order. This view of "cosmopolitan citizenship" is elaborated by Held in what he terms a "cosmopolitan project." He calls for a rethinking of democracy in terms of double democratization—"the deepening of democracy within a national community, involving the democratization of states and civil societies over time, combined with the extension of democratic forms and processes across territorial borders" (Held, 2000, 426).

Summary

The starting point of this chapter was an exploration of the concept of citizenship. Conceptualizations of citizenship are generally characterized by issues of inclusion and exclusion, rights and duties, and full participation. The nature of each of these issues, however, as this chapter tried to demonstrate, is historically specific, shifting, and the object of considerable political debate. Not surprisingly, citizenship as a concept has been rightly described as slippery.

While the roots of this concept are ancient, our current conceptualizations are largely informed by liberal understandings. Postwar conceptions of citizenship have been greatly influenced by T.H. Marshall's model of citizenship rights. His formulation has been the focus of considerable criticism by those who suggest that his account pays insufficient attention to the duties or obligations of citizenship. More recently, a number of diverse social groups have challenged the dominant assumptions of citizenship to argue that formal citizenship rights have not been a safeguard against socio-economic exclusion. Such groups have advocated for forms of "differentiated citizenship" to ensure full participation in the polity. As we approach the millennium, citizenship as a concept remains highly relevant and politically charged. New developments signal the emergence of the nascent concept of "global citizenship" that will further challenge many of our current ideas about citizenship. For these reasons it is highly likely that citizenship will remain on the political agenda for some time to come.

As members of a political community we are all engaged in the larger ongoing project of defining who belongs to a community of citizens and what belonging means in practice. This chapter has attempted to demonstrate both the necessity and difficulty of engaging in this task by tracing some of the major lines of tension within the politics of citizenship.

Endnotes

[1] In highlighting these conditions, I am not dismissing or minimizing the difficulties experienced by those who seek to be "potential citizens" —that is become permanent residents/landed immigrants in Canada. As many have argued, Canadian immigration policy is inscribed by a host of systemic biases that makes it much more difficult for some groups of people to enter than others. For a discussion of racism and immigration policy see for example Simmons (1998).

[2] Among the proposals from a recent report "Not Just Numbers" are physical residence, fiscal responsibility, knowledge of an official language, minimum age, no serious criminality, and active participation in two of the following four areas: employment, education, voluntary/community service, homecare.

[3] In his discussion of social rights and the Canadian Federation, Morrison (1997) has pointed out that the Constitution has proved largely empty of content in respect to social citizenship and that the Charter of Rights and Freedoms has not offered any real protection against the erosion of the social safety net. (72)

Discussion Questions

1. To be a "Canadian citizen" is to enjoy the rights and privileges which flow from full membership of Canada as a nation-state. Discuss the ways in which some groups of people may feel excluded from the promise of full or effective citizenship in Canadian society. Are some groups in Canada "second-class" citizens?

2. How do processes of globalization challenge our understandings of citizenship? In the next century will more and more Canadians come to see themselves as global citizens?

3. Many citizenship debates focus on rights and duties. What types of duties should be required of Canadian citizens? Is it possible to strike a balance between rights and duties?

References

Bakan, A., and D. Stasiulis, 1997. "Foreign Domestic Worker Policy in Canada and the Social Boundaries of Modern Citizenship." In *Not One of the Family.* Toronto: University of Toronto Press, 29–51.

Bakker, I., and K. Scott, 1997. "From the Postwar to the Post-Liberal Keynesian Welfare State." In W. Clement, ed., *Understanding Canada: Building on the New Canadian Political Economy.* Kingston: McGill-Queens, 286–310.

Bissoondath, N. 1993. "A Question of Belonging: Multiculturalism and Citizenship." In W. Kaplan, ed., *Belonging: The Meaning and Future of Canadian Citizenship.* Kingston: McGill-Queens, 368–387.

Broadbent, E. 1997. "The Rise and Fall of Economic and Social Rights—Thoughts on Justice and Stability in the North Atlantic Democracies." In *Canada House Lecture Series No. 61.* London: Canadian High Commission.

Canadian Labour Congress (CLC). N.d. "Taken Away: Unemployment Insurance Losses in Communities Across Canada" http://www.clc-ctc.ca/policy/ui/takenaway.html

Castles, S. 1994. "Democracy and Multicultural Citizenship. Australian Debates and their Relevance for Western Europe." In R. Baubock, ed., *From Aliens to Citizens.* Aldershot, England: Avebury.

Crispo, J. 1996, June 24. "Canada Places too Little Value on Citizenship." *Toronto Star.*

Esping-Andersen, G. 1990. *Politics Against Markets.* Cambridge: Polity Press.

Goodwin, B. 1992. *Using Political Ideas. 3rd ed.* West Sussex, England: John Wiley & Sons.

Hall, S., & Held, D. 1989. "Citizens and Citizenship." In S. Hall & M. Jacques (eds.), *New Times* (pp. 173–188). London: Verso.

Held, D. 1989. "Decline of the Nation-State." In S. Hall and M. Jacques, eds., *New Times.* London: Verso, 173–188.

Held, D. 1995. *Democracy and the Global Order.* London: Polity Press.

Held, D. 2000. "Regulating Globalization." In David Held and Anthony McGrew (eds.), *The Global Transformations Reader* (pp.420-430). Cambridge: Polity Press.

Jenson, J. 1991. "Citizenship and Equity. Variations Across Time and Space." In J. Hiebert, ed., *Political Ethics, a Canadian Perspective. Vol. 12,* Royal Commission on Electoral Reform and Party Financing. Toronto: Dundern Press, 195–228.

Kaplan, W. 1993. "Who Belongs? Changing Conceptions of Citizenship and Nationality." In W. Kaplan, ed., *Belonging: The Meaning and Future of Canadian Citizenship.* Kingston: McGill-Queens, 245–264.

Kymlicka, W., & Norman, W. 1995. "Return of the Citizen: A Survey of Recent Work on Citizenship Theory." In R. Beiner, ed., *Theorizing Citizenship.* Albany: State University Press New York, 283–322.

Layton-Henry, Z., ed. 1990. *The Political Rights of Migrant Workers in Western Europe.* London: Sage.

Lister, R. 1997. *Citizenship: Feminist Perspectives.* London: MacMillan Press.

Marshall, R. 2000-2001. "Paying the Price." In *Macleans* December 25/January 1, Vol. 113 No. 52, 48-50.

Marshall, T.H. 1950. *Citizenship and Social Class.* Cambridge: Cambridge University Press.

Martin Sr., P. 1993. "Citizenship in a People's World." In W. Kaplan, ed., Belonging. *The Meaning and Future of Canadian Citizenship.* Kingston: McGill-Queens, 64–78.

Mouffe, C. 1992. "Democratic Citizenship and the Political Community." In C. Mouffe, ed., *Dimensions of Radical Democracy.* London, England: Verso, 225–239.

Pateman, C. 1989. "The Patriarchal Welfare State." In C. Pateman, ed., *The Disorder of Women.* Stanford, California: Stanford University Press, 179–209.

Plant, R. 1991. Social rights and the reconstruction of welfare. In G. Andrews (ed.), *Citizenship* (pp. 50–64). London, England: Lawrence & Wishart.

Pocock, J. 1995. "The Ideal of Citizenship Since Classical Times." In R. Beiner, ed., *Theorizing Citizenship.* Albany: State University Press New York, 29–52.

Rebick, J. 2000. *Imagine Democracy.* Toronto, Stoddart.

Riley, D. 1992. "Citizenship and the Welfare State." In J. Allen, P. Braham & P. Lewis, eds., *Political and Economic Forms of Modernity.* Cambridge, England: Polity Press, 180–211.

Stewart, F. 1991. "Citizens of Planet Earth." In G. Andrews, ed., *Citizenship.* London, England: Lawrence & Wishart Ltd, 65–75.

Stewart-Toth, J. 1996. "Ideologies, Identity and Citizenship." In R. Gibbons & L. Youngman, eds. *Mindscapes. Political Ideologies Towards the 21st Century.* Toronto: McGraw-Hill Ryerson, 266–288.

Taras, D. 1997. "Introduction." In D. Taras & B. Rasporich, eds. *A Passion for Identity. An Introduction to Canadian Studies (3rd ed.)* Toronto: Nelson Canada.

Tuohy, C. 1993. "Social Policy: Two Worlds." In M. Atkinson, ed. *Governing Canada. Institutions and Public Policy.* Toronto: Harcourt Brace, 275–305.

Walters, W. 1996. "The 'Active Society': New Designs for Social Policy." *Policy and Politics, 25* (3), 221–234.

Young, I. 1990a. "Polity and Group Difference." In *Throwing Like a Girl and Other Essays in Feminist Philosophy and Social Theory.* Bloomington: Indiana University Press.

Young, M. 2000. "Bill C-16: The Citizenship of Canada Act: Legislative History of Bill C-16 (:S-352E) Parliamentary Research Branch. (http://www.parl.gc.ca/36/2/parl-bus/chambus/house/bills/summaries/c16-e)

Yuval-Davis, N. 1997. *Gender and Nation.* London: Sage.

Further Readings

Kaplan, W., ed. 1993. *Belonging: The Meaning and Future of Canadian Citizenship.* Kingston: McGill-Queens.

Kymlicka, W., and Norman, W. 1995. "Return of the Citizen: A Survey of Recent Work on Citizenship Theory. In R. Beiner, ed., *Theorizing Citizenship*. Albany: State University Press New York, 283–322.

Lister, R. 1997. *Citizenship: Feminist Perspectives*. London: MacMillan Press.

Pateman, C. 1989. "The Patriarchal Welfare State." In C. Pateman, ed., *The Disorder of Women*. Stanford, California: Stanford University Press, 179–209.

Rebick, J. 2000. *Imagine Democracy*. Toronto: Stoddart.

Weblinks

Canadian government site for citizenship and immigration.
www.cic.gc.ca

Environment Canada's Primer on Environmental Citizenship
www.ms.ec.gc.ca/udo/primer1.html

A network of individuals and institutions working in the area of citizenship, political education and democracy in Europe.
www.politeia.net

CHAPTER 18

GENDER AND THE POLITICS OF FEMINISM

Objectives

Biology determines whether a person is male or female, but social, cultural, political, and economic forces shape what being male or female means in everyday life. **Gender**, then, is socially constructed, and includes the assumptions, roles, and expectations associated with one's sex. Although feminism has challenged rigid gender roles, such as the expectation that women marry, bear children, and care for them while relying on their husbands for social status and economic security, gender continues to shape both who we are and what we can aspire to achieve. Gender is about power, and is a crucial element of many political struggles. This chapter explains why gender is political, and shows how the politics of gender and feminism help shape contemporary Canadian political realities.

LINDA
TRIMBLE

Introduction

Comic moments in an American sitcom called "Daddio" reflect the determination of Chris, a stay-at-home Dad, to defend his new role against the skepticism voiced by his best friend, his surly neighbour, and even the members of his "Mommies group." "Daddio," like the label "Mr. Mom" captures societal unease with shifting gender roles. So does *The Contender*, a fall 2000 film about Laine Hanson, a fictitious female U.S. Vice Presidential nominee whose adversaries wage a deeply personal campaign against her during the confirmation hearings. She is attacked, not on policy grounds or issues of competence, but on the basis of her private life and sexuality. The production notes for the movie refer to various characters' reluctance to allow a woman in to the "boys' club" of American politics. Clearly North Americans continue to hold ambivalent attitudes towards women, and men, who step across unwritten, but socially enforced, gender role boundaries. That women who enter the male preserve of politics are still viewed with trepidation, and even suspicion, is illustrated by the following example.

On September 16, 2000, anticipating an early election call by the governing Liberals, the *Globe and Mail* newspaper ran a story that featured a tongue-in-cheek profile of Canada's five federal party leaders (McCarthy, 2000, A1, A4). Called "Ready to Rumble," the piece casts the leaders as pugilists, eagerly awaiting their turn in the electoral ring. A photograph of each leader is accompanied by a summary of his or her relative capacity to duke it out in the next election. Like a scorecard, the profiles list the leader's alias, age, "experience in the ring," "brag line," "most effective punch," and even provide a pithy assessment ("the skinny") of the leader's capacity to land a "knockout punch." The lone female party leader, the NDP's Alexa McDonough, is ostensibly treated like one of the guys in the article. McDonough, (aka "Lefty") is recognized for her punch, "the left jab," and for her "plodding but dogged style." But "the skinny" on McDonough is that she's a lightweight and a weakling; "Float like a butterfly, sting like a, er, mosquito," the article says.

The message underlying this leadership-as-boxing-match news frame is that women don't have the right stuff for the nasty business of politics. The "journalistic use of metaphorical language describing election campaigns as battles or sporting events subtly reinforces traditional conceptions of politics as a male preserve" (Everitt and Gidengil, 1998, 1). Canadian women party leaders are so far off the media map that Pat Duncan, who led her party to a surprise win in Yukon on April 17, was bemused by news reports of "Mr. Duncan's" victory. When Jean Charest left the federal Conservatives to take over the Quebec Liberals, neither the party nor the news media conjured up the names of any women who could lead the party. Similarly, no women were cited as possible contenders for the leadership of the Canadian Alliance. Party leadership remains masculine territory.

Why is politics, in this day and age, still assumed to be a bastion of male power and privilege? The obvious answer is that men do continue to dominate many aspects of political life. In Canada, women are as politically active as men in community politics, interest group and social movement activism, electoral activities, and everyday acts of political rebellion—activities which are sometimes called *mass politics*. They remain significantly underrepresented in formal arenas of political power such as legislatures, city councils, the leadership ranks of bureaucracy, and the courts (Vickers, 1997, 66–69). The more difficult question is why men's control of political institutions, ideas, and decisions is still considered the natural order of things. The next section explains how male dominance of politics (patriarchy) emerged as normal, or commonplace. But why is this understanding important? Why should we care that more men than women hold positions of political power?

Political decisions profoundly affect our private and public lives. Those who hold political power decide whether or not birth control, abortion, and new reproductive technologies are legal and available to women. Politicians can allow men who sexually assault women to claim an "honest though mistaken belief" that the victim consented to sexual activity, or they can make laws that ensure that "no means no." Political actors can provide economic support, child care, and job training for mothers on social assistance, or they can force single moms into workfare programs. Employment opportunities for female immigrants can be enhanced or constricted on the basis of access to government-funded language training programs. Women (and men) with disabilities can enjoy more, or less, mobility and autonomy, depending on policy makers' decisions about funding accessible public spaces and government services. Politicians, and judges, decide whether lesbians can legally marry or adopt children. The list is endless. Political decision makers can challenge or uphold patriarchal structures, with very real consequences for the everyday lives of men and women.

Gender, Patriarchy, and the Public–Private Divide

PATRIARCHY MEANS "RULE BY MEN." IN PATRIARCHAL SOCIETIES, MEN HAVE MORE power than do women and enjoy greater access to what is valued by the social group (Code, 1993, 19). Patriarchy conveys the core notion of systemic gender inequality, whether in the household or in the broader domains of economic and public life (Walby, 1996, 24).

Patriarchal thought prescribes power and authority to men, both as fathers in the household and as members of the legal profession, the business community, organized religion, and of course, the political arena. Patriarchy has been constructed and maintained through political practices and public policy. Governments, from archaic state forms to complex modern regimes, have passed laws designed to uphold the patriarchal family and keep women in their assigned place within the household, performing domestic duties appropriate to chaste daughters or monogamous wives and mothers. For instance, Mesopotamian city-states in the second and third millennium B.C.E. decreed that women, slaves, and children were legally the property of men, and they passed laws which allowed men to commit infanticide, pledge their children in marriage, and sell their wives, concubines, and children into slavery (Lerner, 1986, 88–91). In some feudal societies, political authorities upheld the so-called "rule of thumb" which decreed that a man could beat his wife, as long as he used a stick no thicker than his thumb. Control of women is a key feature of patriarchal power relations, so laws have regulated and restricted women's sexual and public behaviour. Legal strictures and cultural practices such as veiling, silencing, menstruation taboos, enforced marriage, genital mutilation, and penalties of death for errant wives, ensured male domination of the female body (Miles, 1989, 103–123).

Patriarchal power relations construct sexual difference as political difference by giving legal form to the belief that women, because of their sex, are fit only to serve as wives and mothers in the domestic sphere where they can be ruled by men. These presumptions are usually based on biological determinism and the public–private dichotomy. Biological determinism is "the belief that a woman's nature and all of her possibilities are determined by her biology" (Code, 1993, 22–23). This perspective sees women as bodies governed by hormones and reproductive destiny, not as bearers of minds with the capacity for intelligence, rationality, and free will. Biological determinism holds that biology is destiny, that since women are "naturally" subservient and inferior to men, it is also natural for women to be ruled by men.

Social, economic, and political forces have structured these assumptions into a foundation for mutually exclusive gender roles, called the *public/private dichotomy*. Characteristics, roles, and standards are separated into two distinct spheres—the private sphere of family and domestic life, and the public world of business, government, culture, sports, and organized religion. Women are regarded as emotional, family-focused, irrational, dependent, other-regarding, and nurturing; therefore "naturally" suited for private sphere roles. Men, on the other hand, are believed to be rational, independent, competitive, self-regarding, civic-minded individuals with the right stuff for engagement with public sphere activities and duties. The division between public and private remains the foundation for gender codes—different roles, characteristics, resources, norms, and expectations based on the meanings ascribed to sex differences.

Patriarchal assumptions form the foundation for laws and policies that oppress women. Oppression is "a system of interrelated barriers and forces which reduce, immobilize and mould people who belong to a certain group, and effect their subordination to another group" (Frye, 1983, 33). Post-confederation Canadian law provides a good example of political efforts both to render women subordinate to men and to cast non-white women as subordinate to white women. Canada's earliest electoral legislation, for example, explicitly excluded women, children, and so-called "mental incompetents" from voting. The very notion of equality for women (and other marginalized groups, including poor, Aboriginal, black, Indo- and Asian-Canadians) was ridiculed as a dangerous and outlandish idea in Canada's early years. The vote was almost exclusively limited to white male property owners.

Patriarchal assumptions guided the law, denying women economic liberty until at least the 1920s in most respects. Men were the legal heads of households, which gave them the exclusive right to control family finances (including their wives' wages), to own and sell property, to sign contracts, and to exercise guardianship rights over children (Burt, 1993, 213–214). Entry into prestigious professions, particularly medicine and law, was the exclusive privilege of men. Women who left, or were abandoned by, their husbands were not legally entitled to make any financial demands on their estranged spouses and were often left destitute as a result.

Canadian women did not have reproductive autonomy either. From 1892 until 1967, the Criminal Code banned the sale, advertisement, or distribution of birth control information, procedures, and devices. Laws reflected the patriarchal presumption that while men owned property in their own persons, they also owned their wives and daughters.

Rape laws provide a good example. As late as 1983, men could not be charged with raping their wives regardless of whether or not consent was given. Instead of protecting and promoting women's autonomy, Canadian laws and policies upheld women's economic dependence on the male head of the household and their physical confinement to the domestic sphere.

Biological determinism, coupled with racism, structured a hierarchy of womanhood in early Canadian society. Anglo-Saxon women who did not stray from the domestic fold could achieve the pinnacle of womanly superiority. In contrast, Eastern European women were stigmatized as prolific child bearers with loose morals, and women of colour were considered highly suspect, both morally and sexually. For example, the entrance into Canada of black women from the Caribbean was restricted in the 1950s because they were "construed as promiscuous and therefore a threat to the standards of Canadian morality" (Agnew, 1997, 19). Non-white women who sought to immigrate to Canada faced racist and patriarchal immigration laws designed to keep the country "white" and morally pure. During the post–World War II immigration surge, male European labourers and farmers, along with their immediate family members, were encouraged to come to Canada. White, single, European domestics, particularly women from England and Scotland, were favoured from the 1900s to the 1960s (Abu-Laban, 1998, 7). The wives and children of Chinese labourers were not allowed to enter the country until 1947, and although Japanese and South Asian women were not explicitly denied entry, immigration practices kept their numbers very low (Das Gupta, 1995, 153).

Laws governing citizenship—legal belonging to the Canadian state—clearly illustrated patriarchal thinking, as a woman's status was governed by that of her father or husband. Canadian women did not have the independent right to claim legal belonging to Canada until 1947, when the first Citizenship Act was passed. Prior to 1947, a woman married to a non-Canadian man lost her citizenship. In contrast, a man married to a non-Canadian woman both kept his citizenship and conferred it to his wife (Canada, 1970, 362). Similarly, until 1985, Aboriginal women with Indian status under the Indian Act who married non-status men lost their status and the rights attendant to it. These included the right to live on the reserve, to be active band members, and the right to confer Indian status upon their children. Yet Indian men who married non-status women kept their status and shared it with their women and children (Weaver, 1993, 95).

Canadian women were not passive victims of patriarchal ideas and structures; indeed, they took full advantage of the aspects of liberty they were not denied, especially freedom of expression, to claim their fundamental rights as citizens. Women were in the thick of political activity long before they won the right to vote, joining political parties, protest groups, church organizations, unions, and social movement groups, and lobbying for political rights, social supports, and legal reforms designed to improve the daily lives of men, women, and children. Even though women's political participation was met with protest, because it violated the norm of separate spheres for men and women, women's activism was remarkable in its tenacity and diversity. The women's movement's goals and strategies were based, in large part, on feminism.

Feminism

FEMINIST POLITICAL ACTION IS ABOUT THE PURSUIT OF WOMEN'S LIBERTY, justice, equality, and solidarity. Feminism seeks to change the gender order so women can enjoy autonomy and gain acceptance as socially valued members of the community. Yet feminism truly defies a compact definition. The feminist literature is diverse, complex, full of internal debates, and constantly evolving through self-criticism and introspection. There is no feminist orthodoxy. Feminism, however, must mean something, otherwise how can we identify a feminist approach to understanding political life?

Feminism is woman-centred. This does not mean that only women can be feminists, or that feminists are only concerned with women. It means that feminism presents ways of understanding women's experiences and offers strategies for demanding changes that will improve the everyday lives of women. Feminists ask why patriarchy exists, how gender codes have been socially and politically constructed so that women are seen as subordinate to men, and what types of institutions and ideas maintain women's oppression. Feminist theories offer diverse interpretations of the nature and origins of gender-based oppression. Feminist theories also offer different ideas about how to challenge and change the discrimination and dependence women confront because of their sex, and often also because of their ethnicity, sexual orientation, class, and physical or mental ability.

Feminism is shaped by culture; thus it differs from place to place. In North America, certain variants of feminism have been very prominent and have shaped women's social, cultural, and political movements. Radical, liberal, and socialist feminism are arguably the dominant threads, though postmodern feminism has made many important contributions to contemporary feminist thought and political practice. To briefly summarize these theoretical approaches is to grossly oversimplify complex and varied bodies of thought. Students seeking a more thorough account of feminist theories are encouraged to read further (see Tong, 1998).

Liberal feminism is the most familiar variant of feminist thought to North Americans, who are accustomed to claims for equal rights. Liberal feminists argue that inequality for women is the result of differential treatment. Patriarchal assumptions, rooted in biological determinism and manifested in the public/private dichotomy, created a set of political, legal, and economic structures that denied women a place beyond the household. As discussed above, women lacked basic citizenship rights such as equal access to education, politics, property, and employment. Liberal feminists argue that when women are denied the right to become free, self-actualizing individuals, they, not surprisingly, act like second-class citizens and form dependency relationships with men. Socialized and educated to be man's helpmate, women are unable to claim autonomy. The solution, for liberal feminists, is equal rights for women, accompanied by social and educational messages of liberty and equality. Women's subordination will end when discriminatory practices, such as denying women business loans, refusing to hire women on the grounds that they will take time off for child care, and barring women from certain professions, are eradicated. Women, then, should have the same opportunities, rights, and liberties as men.

Radical feminists would point out that even though women have won equal rights, and have entered the workforce, they continue to grapple with oppression. Radical feminism exposes the roots of the "sex/gender system"—the set of rules, assumptions, institutions, and understandings that uphold women's subordination to men. Biological determinism, or the "biology is destiny" perspective, leads to narrowly constructed gender roles for women (as wife, caregiver, mother). At the same time, women's traditional roles are undervalued and even ridiculed. Consider the oft-used phrase "I'm just a housewife." Radical feminists show how patriarchal thinking is manifested in everyday practices such as the traditional heterosexual family and expectations about gender roles. For instance, a radical feminist would notice the virulently negative reaction to American film star Julia Roberts' unshaven armpits, exposed to the media glare at a film premiere. As an icon of contemporary femininity, Roberts is expected to shave daily. More importantly, radical feminists focus on the ways in which legal, social, and political control of women's bodies leads to sexual exploitation, promotes economic dependency on men, and denies women a political voice. Women's lack of reproductive autonomy and fear of sexual assault on the job, in the home, and in the streets, maintains their subordination.

Early Canadian policies, outlined in the previous section, illustrate what radical feminists are talking about. Women did not have the right to control their bodies, and laws ensured their physical, emotional, and economic dependence on their fathers or husbands. For instance, until 1983, the law guaranteed a woman's consent to sexual activity with her husband. If she denied sex to her husband, legally he was entitled to force himself upon her, however violently, without recourse. In sum, the root of women's oppression according to radical feminists is male control of women's bodies.

Liberal feminists reveal legal, social, and political practices that prevent women from making free choices and from competing on a level playing field with men, and radical feminists show how sexual domination oppresses women in public and private spaces. *Socialist feminists* emphasize economic sources of oppression, arguing that capitalism and state patriarchy intersect to reinforce women's social marginalization and economic dependency. Women have been consigned to unpaid household duties because capitalism benefits from a sexual division of labour wherein women serve a nurturing and reproductive function. Increasingly women are entering the workforce to take up underpaid casual or part-time jobs, acting as a cheap, exploitable, and disposable "reserve army of labour" for the private economic sector. Governments uphold patriarchy and capitalist gender exploitation by reinforcing women's dependence on men and on low-income work. For example, workfare programs coerce single mothers into insecure, minimum-wage jobs, and "spouse in the house" rules cut women off social assistance when they form relationships with men.

Liberal, radical, and socialist feminists alike point to the role of the state in maintaining women's dependency. All point out that governments have done little to promote women's autonomy. Socialist feminists contribute another layer to the analysis by revealing how the state often acts in the interests of capital, which relies on the unpaid or underpaid work of women.

Postmodern variants of feminism are not well known or understood, since they are based on theoretical premises that challenge the foundations of modern epistemology (ways of knowing). Postmodernism challenges the very existence of universal truths or common understandings about things like justice, equality, citizenship, and democracy.

Postmodern thinkers believe that such "meta-narratives" are part of a symbolic order that is socially constructed by discourse (ideas, words, text, and images). As a result, reality is not set, but is continually being formed, challenged, deconstructed, and reformulated. In other words, there cannot be a single unassailable version of any event or communication. Postmodern feminists apply this thinking to social constructs such as "gender" and "woman," arguing that there can be no universal, comprehensive understandings of these concepts. For instance, women's diversity challenges the very concept of "woman," as different women have different contexts, realities and conceptions of their own identities. This idea—that there is no single, unifying woman's reality—has become very important within the contemporary women's movement, as early feminist thought and practice tended to ignore women's multiple, overlapping realities and oppressions, and to speak from the standpoint of the white, middle-class, able-bodied, heterosexual woman. A quest for the unifying policy goals of the "universal woman" did not encompass the experiences, social positions or political claims of many women who faced oppression on the basis of their sex and their ethnicity, sexual orientation, mental or physical ability, or class position. The willingness of postmodern feminism to fracture the category "woman" was paralleled by a difficult, but necessary, struggle within women's groups to recognize women's diversity and confront women's oppression by other women.

Another contribution of postmodern feminism is attention to language and discourse. Postmodern feminists argue that language, not laws, represents the main instrument of patriarchy, because discourse constructs a masculinist symbolic order. In other words, dominant discourses underpin political decisions about laws and policies. Feminists are paying increased attention to the symbolic gender order evidenced in popular culture. My own research has found that business advertising evokes images of the "corporate cowboy," associating economic power, digital mastery, and individual liberty with the white male businessman (Trimble, 2000).

Feminist Politics

The politics of feminism are evident throughout Canadian history and have fundamentally changed our social and political order. The women's movement "has touched the lives of many Canadian women, radically transforming the nature of their everyday experiences" (Burt et. al., 1993, 9). Liberal, radical, socialist, and postmodern variants of feminism have intersected to create a vibrant, constantly evolving, and multi-faceted women's movement.

The liberal feminist goal of basic citizenship rights for women represents an important part of this transformation, as many of the widely cited gains of the women's movement are legal equality guarantees. Early women's groups worked for decades to claim civil and political rights for women, including ownership and control of wages and property, custody of children, access to education and employment in various professions, and the right to stay in the workplace after marriage. The right to vote and run for political office was a central focus of the early Canadian women's movement, and women's groups struggled for decades to claim their role in democratic politics. Women's groups felt the franchise was essential to their ability to achieve other political goals. Obstacles to the attainment of basic political rights were set higher for women of colour, immigrant women, and Aboriginal women.

The federal franchise was not extended to Asian and Indo-Canadians until 1947 and 1948, respectively; and Aboriginal peoples classified as status Indians under the Indian Act could not vote in federal elections until 1960. Persons with mental disabilities were not granted the right to vote until 1991, and those with physical disabilities only gained full access to polling stations in 1992 (Valentine and Vickers, 1996, 155, 173).

TABLE 18.1 *Women and Political Power in Canada*

PERCENTAGE OF WOMEN REPRESENTATIVES IN FEDERAL, TERRITORIAL, AND PROVINCIAL LEGISLATURES, DECEMBER 2000	
Yukon	29.4%
British Columbia	29.3%
Alberta	26.5%
Manitoba	24.6%
Quebec	23.2%
Saskatchewan	22.4%
Prince Edward Island	22.2%
Canada	**20.6%**
New Brunswick	18.2%
Ontario	17.4%
Newfoundland	16.7%
Northwest Territories	10.5%
Nova Scotia	9.6%
Nunavut	5.3%

SOURCE: Jane Arscott and Linda Trimble, *Still Counting: Women in Politics Across Canada* (Peterborough: Broadview Press, forthcoming 2002). Reprinted with permission of the publisher and authors.

Even after white women were granted the federal franchise and the right to run for political office, women were excluded from appointments to the Bar and the Senate because they were not considered qualified "persons" as defined by the British North America Act. Five women from Alberta challenged this interpretation of the Canadian constitution in a reference case popularly known as the *Person's case*. In 1929, the British Judicial Committee of the Privy Council, which was Canada's highest court at the time, decided that women could be considered "persons" under the law (Baines, 1993, 246–258). In 2000, a monument to the "Famous Five" was unveiled on Parliament Hill.

It became clear to feminist activists that legal rights alone could not secure full participation in all aspects of society for all women. In the 1960s and '70s, women's groups turned to radical and socialist feminist ideas to explain their continued second-class status. Women still performed most of the domestic duties; could not find adequate, affordable child care; were woefully under-represented in politics; earned a fraction of the pay men earned; faced spousal abuse, sexual assault, and sexual harassment; and had no legal access to birth control. The slogan "the personal is political" captured social and radical feminist goals, and women's groups used it to draw attention to a range of issues previously considered private matters, unimportant to political decision makers. The women's movement politicized issues such as child care, job ghettos for women, unequal pay, reproductive autonomy, sex-role stereotyping in schools and by mass media, sexual violence, restrictive employment legislation, and the feminization of poverty. Some women's groups made demands on the state; others provided services to women; others organized women into collectives and labour unions; and many women's groups offered solidarity based on ethnicity, class, ideology, sexual orientation, and disability (Burt, 2000).

Years of activism by women's groups resulted in several concrete policy gains and improvements in the status of some women. Table 18.2 highlights various policy initiatives of the Canadian federal government since the 1950s. The list indicates that Canadian governments are more likely to respond to liberal feminist claims for formal, legal equality. Very few programs address the sexual division of labour and the feminization of poverty. For example, various governing parties since the early 1980s have promised a national day care program, and none have delivered. When governments do tackle an issue foregrounded by socialist or radical feminist activists, such as violence against women, their solutions focus on the justice system rather than on providing counselling for abusers or emotional and economic support for victims.

TABLE 18.2 *Canadian Government Policies for Women*

1955: Rules prohibiting married women from holding federal public service jobs revoked

1956: Legislation guaranteeing equal pay for equal work in industries under federal jurisdiction implemented

1967: Establishment of Royal Commission on the Status of Women (reported in 1970)

1969: Criminal Code amended to allow the promotion and use of birth control devices

1976: Criminal Code changed to re-define rape as sexual assault, and to limit scrutiny of victims' sexual histories

1977: Canadian Human Rights Act passed; forbids discrimination based on sex

1983: Canadian Human Rights Act amended to make workplace discrimination (including sexual harassment) illegal

1983: Additional changes made to sexual assault law; inclusion of "rape shield" provisions

1984: Federal government establishes the national Equal Pay Program for employees under federal jurisdiction (based on equal pay for work of equal value)

1985: Equality provisions of Canadian Charter of Rights and Freedoms (Section 15) come into effect

1985: Indian Act amended to restore status to many of the women who had lost status due to marriage.

1986: Employment Equity Act—employment equity requirements for all federal government departments, agencies, federally regulated companies with more than 100 employees, and corporations receiving government contracts

1986: Family Violence Prevention Division established in federal department of Health and Welfare

1988: Supreme Court strikes down abortion legislation in the Morgentaler case

1989: Canadian Human Rights Tribunal rules that most military occupations must be open to women by 1999

1993: More revisions to sexual assault law provide a definition of consent

1992: Child care tax deductions increased to $5000 per year per child

1996: Sexual orientation added as a prohibited ground for discrimination in the Canadian Human Rights Act

Are We Equal Yet?

HAVE ALL OF THESE LAWS AND POLICIES ACHIEVED EQUALITY FOR WOMEN? WHILE evidence suggests that progress has been made in many areas, economic independence, physical autonomy, and social self-determination remain elusive goals for many Canadian women. As Table 18.1 indicated, women are underrepresented in the legislative arena, holding fewer than 20 percent of federal and provincial elected offices in Canada. Judicial decision makers are increasingly important in Canada because of Charter reviews of legislation, but there are still few women on the bench. In 1998, only 14 percent of provincially appointed judges and 20 percent of justices appointed by the federal government were women.

In the labour force, women continue to experience glass ceilings (barriers to promotion), sticky floors (concentration in service jobs and low-ranking positions), unequal pay, and workplace harassment and discrimination. In 2000, Statistics Canada released its report, *Women in Canada*. It documents how Canadian women remain concentrated in traditionally "female" occupations—in 1999, 70 percent of all employed women worked in teaching, nursing, and health occupations; clerical or administrative positions; and sales and service occupations. Women's incomes are still significantly lower than men's. In 1997, the average annual pre-tax income of women aged 15 or older (from all sources) was just $19 800—62 percent of the comparable figure for men. Some of this wage gap is due to the fact that a large proportion of women—41 percent—work in part-time, casual, or temporary jobs. But even women employed on a full-time, full-year basis only earn 73 percent of what full-time male employees make. Women occupy only 22 percent of the country's highest-paying jobs, but hold 68 percent of the lowest-paying jobs.

That women's economic independence has yet to be realized is shown by Statistics Canada data on the feminization of poverty. Women make up a disproportionate share of the population with low incomes—54 percent in 1997. Elderly women and lone-parent mothers are particularly vulnerable to poverty. In 1997, 56 percent of single mother-led families lived below the poverty line. The unemployment rate for immigrant women, visible minority women, Aboriginal women, and women with disabilities is significantly higher than the national average, putting these groups of women at risk of poverty (Laghi, 1998, A4). The social and economic vulnerability of non-white women is not being addressed. Even though immigrant women have higher levels of education than Canadian-born females, they are less likely to have paid work and earn less at their jobs than other women in Canada. Visible minority women are less likely than other Canadian women to be employed, and more likely to be underemployed given their educational qualifications. They also earn less than white women. Aboriginal women endure serious economic deprivation, with the lowest employment and pay rates, and the highest rates of poverty compared to other groups of women.

Legal rights offer women an entrée into the public sphere but do not fundamentally challenge the sexual division of labour in society. Women continue to be held responsible for child rearing and domestic duties and are often compelled to layer public roles such as paid work, volunteering, and political activism on top of household obligations. The *Women in Canada* report shows that more women participate in volunteer activities than do men. Women with children under the age of 19 and full-time jobs continue to perform more of the domestic tasks, spending almost five hours per day on unpaid domestic work—an hour and a half more than their male counterparts. Despite their increased participation in the labour market since the early 1960s, women's share of domestic labour has remained about the same, about two-thirds of the total. Not surprisingly, married women with children and paid jobs are twice as likely to report levels of severe time stress than employed married men with children.

Bodily autonomy and security of the person are not yet guaranteed to Canadian women. For instance, women's physical security and mobility are curtailed by fear of male violence, both inside and outside the home. A survey conducted by Statistics Canada found that 25 percent of women had been physically or sexually abused by their marital partners, and more than half of the women surveyed had experienced at least one incident of physical or sexual violence since the age of 16 (Canada, 1995). Women report much higher levels of fear than do men about walking alone after dark or being home alone in the evening (Canada, 2000, 169).

Politics is about "who gets what," and the evidence continues to suggest that women get less. Women have less political power, fewer economic resources, less security, and lower social status than do men despite decades of feminist claims-making and despite the implementation of various policies designed to raise the status of women. Particular groups of women, including the poor, women with disabilities, immigrant and visible minority women, and Aboriginal women, get even less than other women. So the answer to the question "Are we equal yet?" is an unequivocal "No"; and some women are even less equal than others. The politics of gender remains a central concern of political analysts.

DEBATE BOX

Is Politics a "Man's Game?"

To win a seat in the U.S. Senate, Hillary Rodham Clinton found herself shifting gears with the skill of a Formula One racer. Making the switch from politician's wife to political office-holder was no easy task. A prototypical *political wife* is little more than an appendage, as she puts her own ambitions on hold so she can be the perfect helpmate to her husband. In contrast, the successful *politician* is an independent, fiercely competitive, sometimes unscrupulous individual who yearns for power. The phrase "lust for power" betrays the gendered nature of political yearning; after all, traditionally it is men who lust and women who submit. It is no accident that the language of elite political competition is borrowed from the boxing match, until very recently the exclusive territory of men. Imagine a woman stepping into the ring with the likes of Mike Tyson. Politics is still judged by masculine gender codes, women by feminine gender codes. Accordingly, assertive political women are often characterized as shrill and unfeminine; consider the "Iron Lady" label applied to former British Prime Minister Margaret Thatcher.

Do you agree or disagree with the portrayal given above? Does the public/private dichotomy continue to undermine women's quest for political representation and power? Is politics still regarded as a "man's game"? Or do women now compete on a level playing field, fully accepted as candidates and office holders? Can you think of examples where women politicians are treated in the same fashion as their male counterparts? What about examples of sex-stereotyping of female politicians?

Summary

Even though gender remains a key determinant of status, power, and social class, women's political claims are increasingly characterized as the self-interested demands of "special interest" groups (Brodie, 1995, 69–70). Women's groups are ignored altogether or castigated for making claims on debt-ridden, fiscally strapped governments. Neoliberals (often called "the new right") want to decrease the roles and expenditures of governments to make space for the free market. This increasingly popular approach has led to the erosion of social programs of particular importance to women (Dacks, Green, and Trimble, 1995; Burt, 2000). Moreover, many of women's claims are denounced by neoconservatives (sometimes called social conservatives) who say feminists have abused political power in an effort to discriminate against men, destroy the traditional family, and disrupt the "natural" moral order (see Gairdner, 1992).

The future of feminist politics is uncertain, but this does not mean we are in a post-feminist age. Feminism has evolved over the course of centuries, surviving many challenges and challengers. In an era of globalization the politics of gender may be played out on ever-shifting political terrain, but feminism will continue to inform women's political struggles and liberal democratic politics.

Discussion Questions

1. Describe some contemporary gender codes evident in daily life or popular culture.

2. Why were women once denied basic citizenship rights, such as the right to vote?

3. Different approaches to feminism inspire different political analyses. Apply liberal, socialist, radical, and postmodern feminism to a contemporary political issue such as pornography, pay equality, or child care.

4. Some observers argue that women have equality in Canada. Is there any evidence to the contrary?

5. Why is an analysis of gender key to understanding political life?

References

Abu-Laban, Yasmeen. 1998. "Keeping 'em Out: Gender, Race and Class Biases in Canadian Immigration Policy." In Joan Anderson, et al., eds., *Painting the Maple: Essays on Race, Gender and the Construction of Canada.* Vancouver; UBC Press, forthcoming.

Agnew, Vijay. 1997. *Resisting Discrimination: Women from Asia, Africa and the Caribbean and the Women's Movement in Canada.* Toronto: University of Toronto Press.

Brodie, Janine. 1995. *Politics on the Margins: Restructuring and the Canadian Women's Movement.* Halifax: Fernwood.

Burt, Sandra. 2000. "Canadian Women's Movements: Revisiting Historical Patterns and Considering Present Developments," in James Bickerton and Alain-G. Gagnon, eds., *Canadian Politics, 3rd edition.* Peterborough: Broadview Press, 393-412.

Burt, Sandra, et. al., 1993. "Introduction," in Sandra Burt, Lorraine Code, and Lindsay Dorney, eds., *Changing Patterns: Women in Canada.* Toronto: McClelland & Stewart, 9-18.

Burt, Sandra. 1993. "The Changing Patterns of Public Policy," in Sandra Burt, Lorraine Code, and Lindsay Dorney, eds., *Changing patterns: women in Canada.* Toronto: McClelland & Stewart, 212–242,

Canada, Statistics Canada. 2000. *Women in Canada, 2000.* Ottawa: Statistics Canada. (http://www.statcan.ca)

Canada, 1970. *Report of the Royal Commission on the Status of Women in Canada.* Ottawa: Government of Canada.

Code, Lorraine. 1993. "Feminist Theory," in Sandra Burt, Lorraine Code and Lindsay Dorney, eds., *Changing Patterns: Women in Canada.* Toronto: McClelland & Stewart, 19–58.

Dacks, Gurston, Green, Joyce and Trimble, Linda. 1995. "Road Kill: Women in Alberta's Drive Toward Deficit Elimination", in Trevor Harrison and Gordon Laxer, eds., *The Trojan Horse: Alberta and the Future of Canada.* Montreal: Black Rose, 271-80.

Das Gupta, Tania. 1995. "Families of Native Peoples, Immigrants and People of Colour," in Nancy Mandell and Ann Duffy, eds., *Canadian Families: Diversity, Conflict and Change.* Toronto: Harcourt Brace.

Everitt, Joanna and Elisabeth Gidengil. 1998. "Language and Gendered Mediation: Reporting the Speech of Party Leaders in the 1993 Canadian Federal Election," paper presented at the Annual Meeting of the Canadian Political Science Association, Ottawa Ontario, June 1998.

Frye, Marilyn. 1983. *The Politics of Reality: Essays in Feminist Theory.* Freedom, Calif: The Crossing Press.

Gairdner, William. 1992. *The War Against the Family.* Toronto: Stoddart.

Lerner, Gerda. 1986. *The Creation of Patriarchy.* New York and Oxford: Oxford University Press.

McCarthy, Shawn. 2000. "PM Pushes for Early Election," *Globe and Mail,* 16 September 2000, A1, A4.

Miles, Rosalind. 1989. *The Women's History of the World.* London: Paladin.

Tong, Rosemarie Putnam. 1998. Feminist Thought: A More Comprehensive Introduction, 2nd edition. Westview Press.

Trimble, Linda. 2000. "The Gender of Neoliberal Citizenship: An Analysis of *Report on Business* Magazine," paper presented at the International Political Science Association World Congress, Quebec City.

Valentine, Fraser and Jill Vickers. 1996. "'Released from the Yoke of Paternalism and 'Charity,': Citizenship and the Rights of Canadians with Disabilities," *International Journal of Canadian Studies 14,* 155–177.

Vickers, Jill McCalla. 1997. *Reinventing Political Science: A Feminist Approach.* Halifax: Fernwood.

Walby, Sylvia. 1996. "The 'Declining Significance' of the 'Changing Forms of Patriarchy,'" in Valentine Moghadam, ed., *Patriarchy and Economic Development.* Oxford: Clarendon Press.

Weaver, Sally. 1993. "First Nations Women and Government Policy, 1970–92: Discrimination and Conflict," in Sandra Burt, Lorraine Code and Lindsay Dorney, eds., *Changing Patterns: Women in Canada, 2nd editio*n. Toronto: McClelland & Stewart, 92–150.

Further Readings

Arscott, Jane and Trimble, Linda. 1997. *In the Presence of Women: Representation in Canadian Governments.* Toronto: Harcourt Brace.

Brodie, Janine. 1995. *Politics on the Margins: Restructuring and the Canadian Women's Movement.* Halifax: Fernwood.

Bashevkin, Sylvia. 1998. *Women on the Defensive: Living Through Conservative Times.* Toronto: University of Toronto Press.

Karam, Azza. 1998. *Women in Parliament: Beyond Numbers.* Stockholm: International Institute for Democracy and Electoral Assistance.

Vickers, Jill. 1997. *Reinventing Political Science: A Feminist Approach.* Halifax: Fernwood.

Weblinks

Canadian Women's Internet Association
www.women.ca/

Feminist.com
feminist.com/

National Library of Canada: Women in Canadian Legislatures
www.nlc-bnc.ca/digiproj/women97/ewomen97.htm

National Action Committee on the Status of Women (NAC) Home Page
www.nac-cca.ca

National Organization for Women (NOW) Home Page
www.now.org/

Status of Women Canada—Welcome
www.swc-cfc.gc.ca/direct.html

CHAPTER 19

ORGANIZING POLITICAL INFLUENCE

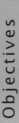

DANIEL COHN

The vast array of competing interests that characterize modern societies—citizens, groups, and corporate entities—all attempt to influence government decisions and the policy process. As we have already seen, citizens attempt to shape the conduct of government through individual action, the electoral process, and allegiance to political parties. In this chapter, we examine the numerous and diverse organizations known as interest groups that attempt to influence public policy, but, unlike political parties, do not seek to win political office. Interest groups differ widely with respect to their issue orientation, degree of formal organization, focus of activity, and political tactics. We explore these differences and assess the factors that help explain why some groups have more influence in politics than others. Finally, we discuss the Charter and the courts as a relatively recent avenue for interest groups to influence the conduct of government in Canada.

Introduction

Influence is a common term in our everyday conversations. *Webster's Dictionary* defines *influence* as "an effect on the condition or development of [something or someone] (1991, 621)." For example, Rap music may reflect an African-American influence, violence on television may be a bad influence on children, and it is a criminal offence to drive while under the influence of alcohol. In politics, influence is in play when an individual or group affects how decision makers think and act. To have influence is to have one's ideas or interests taken into account in the conduct of government and in the formation and implementation of public policy. Some people end up being influential in ways and in areas of life that they never planned. For example, a sport star's behaviour or comments can lead fans to take political actions in ways never consciously planned by the athlete. Maurice "Rocket" Richard, one of the greatest hockey players of all time, became a powerful symbol of the Quebecois nationalist movement, even though he avoided all involvement in politics (Ha, 2000). Other individuals quite deliberately try to affect political outcomes by exercising their personal influence. Richard Gere, for example, has used his fame as an actor to try to influence the foreign policy of countries towards Tibet (Greenberg, 2000). Such individual initiatives, however, are infrequent and rarely as influential as those carried out by large numbers of people joining together in a common cause. Consequently, when most people feel the need to exercise political influence they often become active in, or create, an organization.

Among the most common types of organization that people create in order to wield political influence are bodies that political scientists call "interest" or "pressure groups." *The Handbook of Political Science* defines an interest group as an "organized association which engages in activity relative to governmental decisions (Salisbury, 1975, 175)." This definition is a good place to start, but it makes it difficult to distinguish interest groups from other organizations such as political parties. It is also worth noting that many organizations engage in "activity relative to government" very infrequently. In this chapter, we will focus on organizations that have among their expressed purposes the goal of influencing public officials and the policy process. Finally the above definition does not allow us to distinguish interest groups from other types of organizations, such as think tanks, that expressly seek to influence public officials and the policy process but that do so by limited and often indirect methods. Therefore, we prefer to define interest groups as organizations created at least in part with the express purpose of directly influencing public officials and the policy process by engaging in any non-violent political activity short of trying to gain control of public office.

There is no way to calculate the exact number of interest groups in Canada. One political scientist estimated that, in the early 1990s, there were well over one thousand (Pross, 1992, 65). In Canada, there are few legal barriers to the creation of interest groups and few constraints on their activities. Indeed, the Charter of Rights and Freedoms guarantees Canadians the right to create interest groups by protecting free expression and free association (Section 2). However, as with almost all rights, these are not absolute, and interest groups have to respect certain limits on their behaviour. One such limit is contained in The Canada Elections Act (which governs conduct during federal elections and referenda). This statute limits how much money interest groups can spend during a federal election campaign to promote their viewpoints or the candidates they endorse.[1] Although all Canadians have the right to organize to influence government, this does not mean that they all have the same resources and capacity to do so. There is a great diversity among interest groups both in their nature and in what they are capable of accomplishing. In the next section we will take up this topic, exploring these differences and presenting a typology that can be used to differentiate interest groups.

A Typology of Interest Groups

POLITICAL SCIENTISTS HAVE SUGGESTED A NUMBER OF WAYS OF DISTINGUISHING among interest groups in order to study them. Pross (1992), dealing with the problem of how to differentiate the many interest groups active in Canadian politics, chooses to look at their degree of institutionalization. We will define institutionalization as the process whereby activities that were once random or done with little conscious planning become deliberate, formalized, and expected. In the case of interest groups this means attempting to give permanence to social relations that have been established to create political influence, both within an organization (through the creation of formal offices, duties, and procedures) and between the organization and the wider political environment (by establishing routine mechanisms and channels for communication and interaction). Institutionalization is an organizational task but it also requires cooperation from others outside the group who must decide to acknowledge the organization and agree both to the establishment of a means for working with the organization and to the range of issues open for discussion. In this chapter we will follow Pross's example and express institutionalization as a continuum (1992, 94–99). At one pole will be slightly institutionalized organizations and at the other will be fully institutionalized organizations.

   Another way to look at interest groups is to ask whether they are concerned with exercising influence on one specific issue or policy area, or across the whole range of governmental activities. This approach has the potential to explain something about how groups act. For example, a recent American study shows that in trying to exercise influence across the whole range of governmental activities, the United States Chamber of Commerce (the largest business interest group in the United States) tends to focus on a few pieces of legislation each year with implications for the entire relationship between business, state, and society. These "big" issues also tend to provoke public debates. Therefore, groups trying to exercise influence across the whole range of policy issues have to be more overt political players than those with narrower goals (Smith, 2000). Again we can create a continuum with an ideal type at each pole. At one pole we will place interest groups that seek to exercise influence over one specific issue or area of policy and at the other pole we will place groups that seek to exercise influence over the entire spectrum of issues and policy areas. We can refer to these two different ideal types respectively as issue-specific and omnibus interest groups.

   If we combine the two continuums as done in Figure 19.1, it is possible to produce a graph that shows the possible spaces that different interest groups can inhabit. In the lower

FIGURE 19.1   *Purpose and Institutionalization Continuums and Standards of Success for Different Organizations*

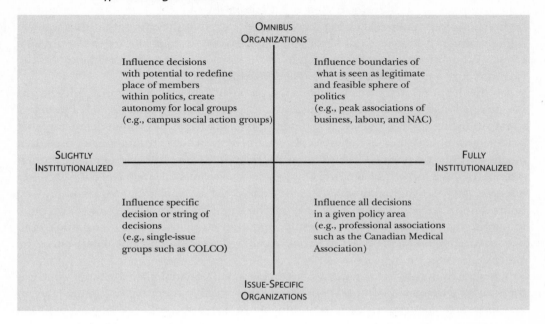

left quadrant are groups that are only slightly institutionalized and have a single-issue focus. These organizations either lack or have no interest in permanence. If they can influence a single decision or a few decisions they will have been successful. Sometimes this is all people want to do. A good example of this sort of group is the Coalition of Leaky Condo Owners (COLCO). The aim of this group is to secure compensation for British Columbians whose homes were improperly built and to change consumer protection laws so as to make this less likely to occur in the future (COLCO, 2000).

In the lower right quadrant are interest groups that are more fully institutionalized. These organizations have a degree of permanence that allows them to deal with both present and future issues. To the degree that others accept and wish to work with them they will become part of what is called a policy community, interacting with other groups, politicians, and bureaucrats in the community through a policy network of relationships and agreed-upon forms of behaviour. Coleman and Skogstad define a policy community as "all actors or potential actors with a direct or indirect interest in a policy area or function who share a common 'policy focus,' and who, with varying degrees of influence shape policy outcomes over the long run (1990, 25–26)." Examples of interest groups that fit into this category include the groups that represent professionals (such as lawyers and physicians), the associations that represent large social organizations (such as hospitals, universities, and colleges) as well as those that represent specific business sectors (such as pharmaceutical makers or the banks). These sorts of organizations command considerable political influence in their areas of expertise (we will discuss why this is the case in the next section of the chapter) and often have little inclination to move beyond these areas to engage in wider political and policy debates. Sometimes the members of a slightly institutionalized single-issue group choose to transform their organization into a more highly institutionalized body. They often make this choice because they find that the things that they want to achieve cannot be addressed quickly or with a single policy decision, but require a continual effort. A Canadian group that has made this transition in light of these factors is the Coalition for Gun Control (see Rathjen and Montpetit, 1999).

In the upper left quadrant are groups with a broad focus but only slight institutionalization. These arrangements have merits in certain circumstances. For example, some groups are deeply concerned about insuring a participatory form of democracy that makes institutionalization as described above difficult to achieve. Institutionalization often means the creation of a hierarchy that separates leaders from ordinary members. A good example of this is today's Greenpeace. Once a small environmental group based in Vancouver it is now a global organization with a structure and problems similar in many respects to the multi-national corporations that are so often the target of its campaigns (see for example Mintzberg and Westley, 2000). As a result, organizations that wish to foster participatory behaviour often find it necessary to remain small both in terms of membership and in the geographic range of their operations.

When many of these small groups focus on ideas that lead to similar large-scale concerns they can have tremendous impact even though they are only associated one to the other by very loose arrangements, or even by nothing more than a shared set of values. This is the logic behind the environmentalist slogan, "Think globally, act locally." Among the interest groups present in this quadrant are the many local organizations across Canada that came together with larger national groups (such as the Council of Canadians) to hold meetings, share information and ask questions about a plan to create an international treaty of investor rights (the Multilateral Agreement on Investment). Their efforts helped to defeat the plan (Kossick, 1999). These sorts of groups are as interested in reshaping our understandings of the relationships between the individual, society, the market and state, as they are with day-to-day policy successes. The growing number of interest groups that have omnibus concerns but are only slightly institutionalized is creating a problem for the state. Even when politicians and civil servants wish to engage such groups, difficulties often emerge, as the hierarchical and bureaucratic structure of the state is so out of line with the structures of these participatory organizations as to make working relationships difficult. This can lead to frustration on all sides (Phillips, 1992, 257–258; Stefanick, 1998).

In the top right corner are groups that seek to achieve omnibus influence that are more highly institutionalized. Such organizations not only have the potential to influence individual decisions, and participate in policy communities, but on a broader level they aim to change the perceived legitimate and feasible limits of politics and public policy—not just their own place within the political world but the places available to everyone. Such groups might participate in so many policy communities as to make themselves nearly as essential public policy participants as public officials. Possible examples of this in Canada are some so-called "peak associations" that claim to represent countrywide interests of business and labour (rather than "sectoral" associations that represent businesses or workers in a given industry, or "regional" associations that represent them in a given part of the country). Some of the better known peak associations include the Canadian Chamber of Commerce, The Alliance of Manufacturers and Exporters of Canada, and the Canadian Labour Congress. Another example of a peak association is the National Action Committee on the Status of Women (or NAC). NAC seeks to address issues of gender inequality throughout both public and private life in Canada. Although these four organizations have a similar strategy and all command relatively large resources, they do not wield equal power, as later portions of this chapter will explain.

Another possibility is that an omnibus and highly institutionalized interest group might concentrate on developing its relationships with the handful of central agencies and their surrounding policy communities that have a hand in almost all public policy due to their roles as coordinators within the state. Such agencies include the Prime Minister's Office, the Department of Finance, and the Department of Foreign Affairs and International Trade. An example of an omnibus and highly institutionalized interest group that has followed this strategy is the Business Council on National Issues (BCNI). The members of the BCNI include the chief executives of Canada's largest corporations. There is always debate about the level of influence wielded by a given group. However, it seems clear that the BCNI has played an important role in the two most important federal public policy choices of the last 15 years—the Mulroney government's negotiation of trade and investment liberalization with the United States, and the Chrétien government's decision to make deficit reduction its top priority during its first term of office from 1993 to 1997 (Clarke, 1997; Doern and Tomlin, 1991).

As formidable as the potential power of omnibus, highly institutionalized organizations might appear, one must not overestimate it. These organizations do not inevitably get everything that they want and sometimes suffer substantial defeats. They cannot take a government where it does not want to go. The BCNI's successes had as much to do with the dissatisfaction expressed by Canada's political leaders and bureaucrats with the country's previous situation, as with the skill that the BCNI displayed in mapping out an alternative policy agenda (Bradford, 1999, 37–41). However, by seeking to reset the boundaries of politics, omnibus and highly institutionalized pressure groups aim to create conditions that make getting what they want continuously more likely. For example, after having successfully convinced the federal government to sign trade and investment liberalization agreements, the BCNI then used the conditions created by these agreements to make further demands. The group began a campaign to convince the government and other Canadians that, given the mobility now available to business, Canada needed to cut taxes for businesses and executives or risk becoming an economic backwater (O'Brien et al., 2000). Speaking just before the November 2000 federal election, the BCNI's Chairman not only claimed credit for the Liberal decision to offer sweeping tax cuts as their main campaign pledge, but for changing the political climate in Canada so that it would be difficult for any party not to endorse the BCNI's policy agenda (O'Brien, 2000). Having examined the potential capability and objectives of interest groups it is now worth considering how they actually operate in the real world and what choices groups must make when they attempt to exercise influence.

The Political Context

THE FIRST QUESTION THAT AN INTEREST GROUP MUST CONFRONT IS HOW TO configure its structure so as to fit the political process it will have to work within. In Canada this especially means considering two factors:

1. whether the organization wishes to make its primary effort at gaining influence at the federal or provincial level, or both; and

2. how the organization intends to relate to the state given the closed nature of the Canadian political process at both federal and provincial levels.

A fundamental issue for those creating an interest group is whether they should create a single national body, separate provincial organizations, or both (Coleman, 1987). Many interests in Canadian society find it necessary to create separate groups to work at the federal and provincial levels given the sharing of jurisdictions in the policy areas of concern to these people or organizations. For example, although the provinces administer and regulate post-secondary education, much of the money spent in this field comes from Ottawa in the form of subsidies to the provinces, student loans and scholarships, as well as grants for specific infrastructure projects and research at individual institutions. Not surprisingly, therefore, universities and colleges find it necessary to have both a national association (The Association of Universities and Colleges of Canada) and separate organizations in each province as well.

The second obstacle that the Canadian political system poses for interest groups is that it is a relatively closed system. This is a result of several factors including our "Westminster" style of legislative–executive relations and the electoral and party systems which tend to combine so as to regularly produce majority governments. The net result of these factors is to produce a situation in which most major public policy decisions are made outside public sight by a small group including the prime minister, his or her cabinet, their top political aides, as well as the senior civil servants who advise both the individual ministers and the cabinet as a whole. These decision makers usually rely on recommendations prepared for them further down in the bureaucracy. It should also be noted that some prominent political scientists argue that the decision-making system found in Ottawa today is even more tightly closed than has been portrayed here (see for example Savoie, 1999). Once the prime minister (or a provincial premier) and their cabinet publicly adopt a position, it is very difficult to get them to change their minds and allow anything more than minor changes. This is because under our political system the government *is* the government because it can pass its agenda into law and rule in a way that maintains the confidence of the legislature. When a government fails to carry out its publicly stated plans or is criticized by its own backbenchers for its handling of public business it appears weak and incompetent. To avoid this, the government imposes strict party discipline on its parliamentary supporters in the backbenches, requiring them to vote with the party on almost all major issues (Franks, 1997). Therefore, groups that want to influence policy in Canada have a much better chance of success if they can make their contribution to the debate before the cabinet takes a public position, and an even greater opportunity if they can influence the thinking of the bureaucrats who craft the initial policy recommendations that the political decision makers rely on. In other political systems the policy-making process can be more diffuse. For example, in the United States—where the executive and two chambers of the legislature are elected with separate mandates—bargaining occurs between the President and Congress over almost every policy proposal (Peterson, 1990). The result is that American interest groups have access to the decision-making process at a much greater number of points than do Canadian groups.

Sometimes a Canadian government will make a wide-ranging public call for advice, appointing a body such as a royal commission to study affairs. However, more often than not, the bureaucracy quietly organizes consultations with groups outside the state over the shape and implementation of public policy. The groups contacted by the bureaucrats are those whom they believe have a stake in the matter and whom they have previously identified as being able to contribute to their deliberations (i.e., the policy community). Most Canadians will not know that a major decision is being made until it is announced. Needless to say, the organizations that are in constant contact with the government and its bureaucrats have a much better chance of influencing policy as they are far more likely to know that issues of concern to them are open for debate. Therefore, interest groups with the resources to support and sustain a highly institutionalized structure (including the professional staff necessary to maintain constant touch with the state) and the funds to commission and/or disseminate substantial amounts of research (that will assist bureaucrats in their work) will have a significant advantage over other organizations in this process.

 Interest groups that wish to wield influence are usually cautioned to behave in as constructive a manner as is possible when dealing with politicians and bureaucrats. In part this is because it is very easy for bureaucrats or politicians to exclude groups whom they feel have become too troublesome to offer constructive advice. However, there are other reasons as well and to understand them we have to briefly stop and consider why it is that the state might benefit from the presence of interest groups.

Government is a very complex business. As noted above, civil servants often rely on interest groups for advice. They consult interest groups on how to deal with issues and they also seek information from interest groups regarding the consequences attached to different choices. Beyond this, interest groups help create legitimacy and also provide a connection between the state and non-state actors who often are responsible for carrying out state policies (Pross, 1992, 114–139). In a democracy public policies are supposed to be beneficial for the people over which a government rules. If the perception grows that policies are not beneficial, the legitimacy of the governing party could be called into question, jeopardizing its re-election. In the extreme, if people come to believe that the entire system of government fails to work for their good, they may begin to question the legitimacy of the entire state. Interest groups can help in creating the impression that a government's policies are beneficial by speaking out in favour of them. In exchange for this support interest groups might indeed ask for input into decisions and the modification of details that they disagree with. Interest groups can also help as communications conduits for the state. Most public policy is not carried out directly by the state but is delegated to others. A good example is amateur sports. Governments spend money every year to support the participation of children and youth in amateur sports. However, the coaching, refereeing, and organizing of these activities is not carried out by civil servants but by countless volunteers from coast to coast. Interest groups can help in fields such as this, by bringing the ideas and concerns of those who ultimately carry out public policy to the ears of the state as well as by communicating the ideas and policies of the state to their members.

As a result, groups that are willing to work with the state often have an important say over policy. The proviso is that they must have something that the state wants, such as expertise, the ability to reach those who carry out public policy or the ability to confer legitimacy on decisions. Inherently those groups that represent the powerful people and organizations in society, and especially big business, have an advantage in doing this. They likely have the resources to develop fully institutionalized organizations, and they also benefit because their members or supporters are few in numbers. In larger groups people will attempt to "free-ride." A free-rider is a person, or an organization, who tries to take the rewards gained by collective actions without putting in the effort required to gain them. Consider a workplace with a union. All workers benefit from the improved conditions that the union negotiates, whether they choose to pay dues or not. Those who do not pay dues are free-riding. If others see some people getting something for nothing, they might also start to free-ride. If enough people adopt this attitude the union will fail and everyone will suffer. In smaller groups, such as the association representing the three major tobacco manufacturers in Canada, free-riding is next to impossible. The consequences would be catastrophic for this interest group if even one of its members were to leave. In this example there are only two alternatives open to the tobacco makers—bear the costs of cooperation or lose all the rewards that flow from it. Interest groups representing a small number of members, such as big businesses, can also often win greater rewards for each of their members—relative to the effort each member must expend to earn these rewards—than can interest groups with numerous members. As a result, big businesses often have greater incentive to form interest groups and to fight much harder for what they want. Imagine a proposal to regulate the service fees that the banks charge their customers. This might save each family a few dollars every year. However, the plan would cost each bank several million dollars every year. Therefore, the banks have a greater incentive to organize an interest group to fight against the proposal, than their customers have to organize and fight for it. Finally, smaller groups often find it easier to speak with one voice as they have more common interests and fewer divergent ones. A lack of dissenters makes its easier for them to lend legitimacy to policies that they support and to deny it to policies that they oppose. These factors help to explain why it is often easier for big business and their executives to organize, and why they often find it easier to achieve public policy decisions that they favour. This also explains why it is so difficult to organize wider publics such as workers, consumers, and students, or to shape public policy to reflect their concerns, even when they are well organized (Olson, 1965).

Lobbying

WHEN INTEREST GROUPS OR OTHER ORGANIZATIONS SUCH AS CORPORATIONS contact politicians or civil servants to influence policy they are said to be *lobbying*. A lobbyist is someone who contacts public officials on behalf of a client, or an organization that they belong to, or are employed by, so as to influence public policy in a manner beneficial to their client or organization. Interest groups must list themselves in the federal Lobbyist Registry if they make direct contact with ministers, civil servants, senators, or Members of Parliament (outside public venues such as giving testimony to Parliamentary Committees, Royal Commissions, or well-advertised events). Less institutionalized groups, or groups with less need to deal with Ottawa often choose to hire a "consulting lobbyist" who represents them in Ottawa for a fee. Consulting lobbyists are also sometimes hired by more institutionalized groups to augment their own staffs. Consulting lobbyists are required to list their clients in the Registry. Many lobbyists have previously been cabinet ministers or high-ranking civil servants, for example:

- Thomas Hockin was a minister in both the Mulroney and Campbell Conservative Governments and now leads the Investment Funds Institute of Canada.
- Marc Lalonde was a minister in the Liberal governments of Pierre Trudeau and one of Trudeau's closest advisors. After retiring from politics he undertook work as a consulting lobbyist as part of his legal practice.
- Catherine Swift was once a bureaucrat and later a bank economist. She now leads the Canadian Federation of Independent Business.

The knowledge that people such as these possess of how governments reach decisions, and what sorts of information public decision makers need, makes them useful advisors to the groups with the resources to employ them. In September 2000 the Lobbyist Registry (Office of the Ethics Counsellor, 2000) showed that approximately 360 lobbyists were institutionalized to such an extent at the federal level as to be required to maintain an active listing. More than 700 consulting lobbyists were also listed in the Registry as currently active.

The costs involved in mounting a successful lobbying effort tend to re-enforce the systems of power and privilege that already exist in Canada. Interested in opening up policy making to a wider range of groups and ideas, Canadian governments began a process of funding interest groups representing the concerns of women, minority official language groups, ethnic groups, and others. These groups were given public support with the clear assumption that they would engage in lobbying to champion the interests of people whose voices had been less clearly heard within the policy process, thus improving policy and also enhancing the legitimacy of both the resultant policies and of the Canadian state in general (Pal, 1993, 244 and 265–271; Pross, 1992, 68 and 71).

However, during the 1980s through to the mid-1990s such support was curtailed (Phillips, 1991; Bashevkin, 1998, 92–129). This was due in part to the financial problems the federal government encountered. It was also due to the adoption of a general policy aimed at reducing the role of the federal state in public life, by de-regulating international trade, privatizing assets, ceding policy responsibilities to the provinces, or by cutting spending and lowering taxes. The bottom line is that market forces are now being allowed a greater role in determining the life chances of each citizen. This new outlook on public policy is sometimes called "neoliberalism" (Broad and Antony, 1999, 10). As a result of it, many of the interest groups receiving federal funding ran afoul of the Canadian state's new direction.

Politicians and bureaucrats were now less interested in hearing from interest groups representing those lacking the resources to intervene in the policy process or to thrive in the market economy than they had been just a few years before. Equality-seeking groups once invited to consult with government in order to enhance both the legitimacy of policies and the system of government itself, were now branded as "special interests" (or worse) so as to justify their re-exclusion from the policy-making process.

This is the key problem with a strategy that involves behaving cooperatively so that one's interest group can gain a voice in decision making in a closed political process such as Canada's. It only works if the group can live with the general direction of public policy. Those groups most likely to fall into this category are those that already enjoy power and privileges and this is especially the case in today's Canada. The cooperative strategy is also unavailable to groups whose specific policy concerns are so opposed to those of the government that working quietly behind the scenes is not feasible.

The Changing Politics of Interest Groups

INTEREST GROUPS THAT ARE EITHER NOT INVITED INTO THE CORRIDORS OF power or disagree fundamentally with the decisions being contemplated, or even the entire structure of public policy making, still have a wide variety of options. Such options include strengthening ties to opposition parties in the hopes that bringing them to power will create a fundamental shift in public policy, denouncing the government in the media, holding demonstrations, and even civil disobedience. Such groups might also choose to approach a sometimes forgotten source of power in Canadian politics—senators. However, the same factors making it easy for some groups to work cooperatively with the government and its bureaucrats also influence the ease with which other groups can implement most of these alternative strategies. For example, if an interest group lacks the resources to participate in decision making with the government, it is likely to encounter similar difficulties when trying to develop a working relationship with the opposition parties and the media. The Senate has been described in one classic Canadian political science text as a lobbying group for big business within the governmental process (Campbell, 1978). On the other hand, public demonstrations and acts of civil disobedience are decidedly double-edged swords. They can just as easily lead to the destruction of a group's credibility as to an increased willingness on the part of decision makers to address its concerns (see debate box). One of the most important developments in terms of offering groups options was the constitutional entrenchment of the Canadian Charter of Rights and Freedoms in 1982.

The Charter significantly expanded the potential range of actions available to political-influence organizations when working with politicians and bureaucrats in a constructive manner seems impractical. Launching court challenges to the constitutionality of laws, intervening in court cases, and offering support and advice to litigants have become major activities for many interest groups in Canada. Interest groups representing large multinational corporations have used the Charter to advance their goals, as have groups representing minorities suffering social disadvantage and discrimination. An example of the former is the Association of Canadian Distillers. This interest group challenged the rules that once allowed beer and wine makers to advertise on television but prohibited liquor makers from doing so. They claimed that the rules were an unfair limitation on the right to free expression contained in Section 2 of the Charter and won (Federal Court of Canada, 1995). An example of the latter is Equality for Gays and Lesbians Everywhere (EGALE). This group has been involved in a number of Charter challenges to laws and regulations that EGALE's members see as discriminatory (Smith, 1999, 85–93). One of the more recent cases was that of *M v. H.* In this case the courts decided that provincial laws that protect people's financial interests in the event of family break-up apply equally to heterosexual and homosexual couples, and more generally, that the word "spouse" also applies equally to partners in heterosexual and homosexual families (Supreme Court of Canada, 1999).

DEBATE BOX

What do Public Protests Accomplish?

Demonstrations and public protests appear to be on the rise throughout North America. Do they help advance the goals of the interest groups that organize them? Critics say that demonstrations and protests only convince politicians and bureaucrats that a group is incapable of working constructively on the issues in question, further reducing the likelihood that the group will achieve its goals. For example, in September 1994 thousands of gun owners and their supporters showed up on Parliament Hill to demonstrate against any further gun control legislation. One of the founders of the Canadian Coalition for Gun Control considered the demonstration to be a great triumph for the gun control movement! The size of the pro-gun rally convinced gun control advocates to re-double their own efforts. It also allowed the Coalition to contrast their own well-reasoned arguments, and the suffering of gun victims, with the extreme rhetoric of the "scary" gun-owners for the benefit of the media and politicians (Rathjen and Montpetit, 1999, 158–167).

On the other hand, it is hard to think of a social group excluded from democratic participation that has ever managed to win full civil rights without holding some form of public protest. Many important changes in public policy have also been preceded by mass demonstrations and acts of civil disobedience. In November 1999 people from countless groups converged on Seattle. They were there to protest the beginning of a new round of global trade and investment liberation negotiations organized by the World Trade Organization (WTO). Numbering in the hundreds of thousands, they overwhelmed the entire city and temporarily shut down the meetings. Speaking to the WTO delegates, President Clinton warned them that although the WTO had an enviable record of promoting human welfare, it could not ignore the demonstrators. The organization would have to become more open and pay attention to the concerns of the demonstrators or lose its credibility (Clinton, 1999).

Do demonstrations and public protests help advance the goals of the interest groups that organize them? Why or why not?

The threat of litigation is now a serious problem for the federal and provincial states. It is compelling governments to take actions that they might not otherwise have chosen, either in response to court judgments or to avoid litigation in the first place. However, as with the more traditional ways in which Canadian interest groups operate, challenging the constitutionality of government actions is very expensive. Therefore, it is hardly an ideal strategy for those who wish to address historic inequality. This burden has been mitigated by the federal government to some degree, through a program that funds interest group involvement in selected court cases, with important implications for the interpretation of the Charter (Morton and Knopff, 2000, 54). It is also worth mentioning that litigation is something of a risk as no one can ever say with certainty how the courts will decide an issue. Furthermore, once they do decide an issue, a relatively permanent rule is often established in the matter that is extremely hard to change. Groups that lose a debate within a policy community or after an intensive lobbying effort often have a difficult choice to make. If they continue to work in a constructive manner within the political and bureaucratic decision-making systems there is always the possibility of achieving their goal at some future date. If they go to court they might achieve their goal more quickly, or relinquish it forever.

Summary

This chapter has explored the forms that interest groups take and how they attempt to influence the state. An argument has been presented that there should be no single standard for judging the success of an interest group. Rather such judgments should be based on what it is that the group wishes to accomplish and the limitations and possibilities of the organizational form that the group has adopted. In the long term however, highly institutionalized groups will find it easier to exercise influence, both because they have the capacity to engage in continuous dialogue with the state and because they tend to have a structure and forms of operation that facilitate cooperation with the public bureaucracy. Some forces in society find it easier to create highly institutionalized interest groups and to succeed in reaching their objectives. These are people and organizations that already enjoy power and privilege in society, especially big business. Big business has the resources to create powerful highly institutionalized interest groups, and given the logic of collective action, also usually finds it easier to create cohesive organizations than groups that seek to advance mass interests. Therefore, interest groups in Canadian society do little more than reflect the already-existing balance of social power. Given the closed nature of Canada's policy-making system, groups have traditionally been advised that working cooperatively with politicians and bureaucrats is the surest way to achieve their objectives. However, this cooperative strategy is only open to groups that can accept the overall policy direction of government in the policy fields that are of interest to them. These groups are most likely to be those that represent people and organizations already benefiting from the status quo, rather than groups seeking social change. Alternative strategies to cooperation and constructive involvement with the state also pose problems for groups representing the concerns of those lacking socio-economic and political power. For example, although the Charter has relieved the burden of discrimination and unfair treatment from some, litigation is very expensive. Litigation also represents a high-risk strategy because a loss in court can be relatively permanent.

Endnote

[1] In Libman v. Quebec, the Supreme Court of Canada (1997) ruled that it was acceptable for Parliament and the provincial legislatures to impose such limits as are reasonable in this area. However, at the time of writing the spending limits contained in the Canada Election Act are the subject of a court challenge and no one can say with absolute certainty whether or not the courts will find these limits to be within the range of "reasonable" measures that the Supreme Court authorized in its previous judgment. It must also be remembered that if a provincial legislature or the Parliament of Canada chooses, the rights to free expression and association can also be curtailed by use of the so-called "notwithstanding clause" (Section 33 of the Charter).

Discussion Questions

1. This chapter argues that the purpose for which interest groups are founded and their degree of institutionalization are important factors to consider when evaluating such groups. What are the four types of interest groups identified in this chapter by using these factors and how is their behaviour likely to differ?

2. What are some of the aspects of the political environment that people must consider when creating an interest group?

3. What are the costs and benefits that interest groups realize when they follow a strategy of constructive or cooperative behaviour with the state?

4. What are some of the advantages possessed by interest groups representing big business over other interest groups?

References

Bashevkin, Sylvia. 1998. *Women on the Defensive: Living through Conservative Times.* Toronto: University of Toronto Press.

Bradford, Neil. 1999. "The Policy Influence of Economic Ideas: Interests, Institutions and Innovation in Canada." *Studies in Political Economy* 59, 17-60.

Broad, Dave and Wayne Antony. 1999. "Citizenship and Social Policy: Neo-Liberalism and Beyond." In Dave Broad and Wayne Antony (eds.). *Citizens or Consumers? Social Policy in a Market Society.* Halifax: Fernwood Publishing.

Campbell, Colin. 1978. *The Canadian Senate: A Lobby from Within.* Toronto: Macmillan.

Clarke, Tony. 1997. *Silent Coup: Confronting the Big Business Takeover of Canada.* Toronto: James Lorimer and Company.

Clinton, William J. 1999. *President Clinton Delivers Remarks at the WTO Ministerial Meeting in Seattle* Washington, DC: Federal Document Clearing House. Accessed through Dow Jones Interactive on 15 September, 2000.

COLCO. 2000. *The Coalition of Leaky Condominium Owners.* Accessed on-line 21 September at: .

Coleman, William D. 1987. "Federalism and Interest Group Organization." In Herman Bakvis and William M. Chandler, eds. *Federalism and the Role of the State.* Toronto: University of Toronto Press.

Coleman, William D. and Grace D. Skogstad. 1990. "Policy Communities and Policy Networks: A Structural Approach." In William D. Coleman and Grace D. Skogstad (eds.), *Policy Communities and Public Policy in Canada* Mississauga, ON: C.C. Pitman.

Doern, G. Bruce and Brian W. Tomlin. 1991. *The Free Trade Story: Faith and Fear.* Toronto: Stoddart.

Federal Court of Canada. 1995. "Association of Canadian Distillers v. The Canadian Radio-Television and Telecommunications Commission." *Federal Court of Canada Reports* 1995 (2).

Franks, C.E.S. 1997. "Free Votes in the House of Commons: A Problematic Reform." *Policy Options* November, 33-36.

Greenberg, Susan H. 2000. "So Many Causes So Little Time Save the Rain Forests! Free Tibet! For Today's Stars, There is no Business like Fund-Raising Business." *Newsweek International* 21 February, 48.

Ha, Thu Thanh. 2000. "Maurice Richard: 1921-2000 Obituary." *Globe and Mail* 29 May, S2.

Kossick, Don. 1999. "The MAI Inquiry: Mobilizing Communities to Talk about the Impact of and Alternatives to the MAI." *Briarpatch* February, p.19.

Mintzberg, Harvey and Frances Westley. 2000. "Sustaining the Institutional Environment." *Organization Studies* 21, 71-94.

Morton, F.L. and Rainer Knopff. 2000. *The Charter Revolution and the Court Party.* Peterborough, ON: Broadview Press.

O'Brien David P. 2000. "Making Canada a Winner – Progress and Challenges: Remarks to the Autumn General Meeting, Business Council on National Issues, November 1." Accessed on-line 5 December at:

O'Brien David P. et al. 2000. "This is Your Captains Speaking: Tomorrow, the Business Council on National Issues Presents its 21st-Century Flight Plan for Canada." *Globe & Mail* 4 April, A13.

Olson, Mancur. 1965. *The Logic of Collective Action: Public Goods and the Theory of Groups.* Cambridge, MA: Harvard University Press.

Office of the Ethics Council. 2000. *Lobbyist Register.* Accessed on-line 15 September at:

Pal, Leslie A.1993. *Interests of State: The Politics of Language, Multiculturalism, and Feminism in Canada.* Montreal: McGill-Queen's University Press.

Peterson, Mark A. 1990. *Legislating Together: The White House and Capitol Hill from Eisenhower to Reagan.* Cambridge MA: Harvard University Press.

Phillips, Susan D. 1992. "New Social Movements and Unequal Representation." In Alain G. Gangon and Brian Tanguay, eds. *Democracy with Justice: Essays in Honour of Khyyam Zev Paltiel.* Ottawa: Carleton University Press.

Phillips, Susan D. 1991. "How Ottawa Blends: Shifting Government Relationships with Interest Groups." In Frances Abele, ed. *How Ottawa Spends, 1991-1992: The Politics of Fragmentation.* Ottawa: Carleton University Press.

Pross, A. Paul. 1992. *Group Politics and Public Policy: Second Edition.* Toronto: Oxford University Press.

Rathjen, Heidi and Charles Montpetit. 1999. *December 6: From the Montreal Massacre to Gun Control, The Inside Story.* Toronto: McClelland and Stewart.

Salisbury, Robert H. 1975. "Interest Groups." In Fred I. Greenstein and Nelson W. Polsby, eds. *Handbook of Political Science, Volume 4.* Reading, MA: Addison-Wesley.

Savoie, Donald J. 1999. *Governing from the Centre: The Concentration of Power in Canadian Politics.* Toronto: University of Toronto Press.

Smith, Mark A. 2000. *American Business and Political Power: Public Opinion, Elections and Democracy.* Chicago: University of Chicago Press.

Smith, Miriam C. 1999. *Lesbian and Gay Rights in Canada: Social Movements and Equality-Seeking, 1971-1995.* Toronto: University of Toronto Press.

Stefanick, Lorna. 1998. "Organization, Administration and the Environment: Will a Facelift Suffice, or Does the Patient Need Radical Surgery?" *Canadian Public Administration* 41, 99-119.

Supreme Court of Canada. 1999. "M v. H." *Supreme Court Reports* 1999 (2).

Supreme Court of Canada.1997. "Libman v. Quebec." *Supreme Court Reports* 1997 (3).

Vickers, Jill, Pauline Rankin and Christine Appelle. 1993. *Politics as if Women Mattered: A Political Analysis of the National Action Committee on the Status of Women.* Toronto: University of Toronto Press.

Webster's. 1991. *Webster's Ninth Collegiate Dictionary.* Springfield, MA: Merriam-Webster, Inc.

Further Readings

Coleman, William D. and Grace D. Skogstad (eds.) 1990. *Policy Communities and Public Policy in Canada* Mississauga, ON: C.C. Pitman.

Doern, G. Bruce and Brian W. Tomlin. 1991. *The Free Trade Story: Faith and Fear.* Toronto: Stoddart.

Morton, F.L. and Rainer Knopff. 2000. *The Charter Revolution and the Court Party.* Peterborough, ON: Broadview Press.

Olson, Mancur. 1965. *The Logic of Collective Action: Public Goods and the Theory of Groups.* Cambridge, MA: Harvard University Press.

Pross, A. Paul. 1992. *Group Politics and Public Policy: Second Edition.* Toronto: Oxford University Press.

Rathjen, Heidi and Charles Montpetit. 1999. December 6: From the Montreal Massacre to Gun Control, The Inside Story. Toronto: McClelland and Stewart.

Smith, Miriam C. 1999. Lesbian and Gay Rights in Canada: Social Movements and Equality-Seeking, 1971-1995. Toronto: University of Toronto Press.

Vickers, Jill, Pauline Rankin and Christine Appelle. 1993. Politics as if Women Mattered: A Political Analysis of the National Action Committee on the Status of Women. Toronto: University of Toronto Press.

Weblinks

The Association of Universities and Colleges of Canada
www.aucc.ca

The Business Council on National Issues
www.bcni.com

The Canadian Labour Congress
www.clc-ctc.ca

The Coalition of Leaky Condo Owners
www.myleakycondo.com

The Federal Ethics Commissioner (Lobbyist Registry)
www.strategis.gc.ca/SSG/oe00001e.html

The National Action Committee on the Status of Women
www.nac-cca.ca

TAO (A Pan-Canadian Telecommunications Resource for Activist Groups)
www.tao.ca

CHAPTER 20

NEW SOCIAL MOVEMENTS

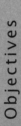

Objectives

The late 1960s and 1970s saw the widespread emergence of a new kind of citizen involvement in politics. Many people bypassed political parties and the electoral system and "took to the streets" to press for changes in their societies. These new social movements rejected many of the values dominant in earlier periods, such as those regarding the family, morality, authority, and economic "progress." They gave importance to issues that had been marginalized politically, among them, women's, Aboriginal, and gay rights, the environment, peace, and anti-racism. In this chapter we explore the origins, concerns, and defining characteristics of new social movements. We will ask whether they are really "new," and how their importance has been affected by developments in the late twentieth century. Finally, we will discuss how the study of new social movements reveals the changing nature of social and political conflict.

LAURIE E. ADKIN

Introduction

In the 1960s youth movements around the world began to challenge the cultural norms and the economic and political institutions of their societies. In Western Europe and North America, the baby boomers rejected the values and lifestyles which their middle-class parents had worked so hard to realize in the post–World War II era. Youth rejected, among other things, moral constraints on sexuality and personal freedom; the "materialism" which had replaced the search for a meaningful, creative life with the accumulation of objects; the so-called "rationality" of an economic and social system that reduced individuals to the roles of "workers" or "consumers" and degraded the environment; and a social system that enriched a privileged social class and empowered technocrats. The youth movements that emerged in the 1960s were anti-authoritarian, advancing a wide range of demands for the democratization of their societies. The cultural expression of these movements took the form of rock music and anti-conformist fads in dress and appearance—from the James Dean or Marlon Brando look to the "hippie" look of the 1970s. "Anti-Establishment" rock, originating in Great Britain with the Beatles and the Rolling Stones, rapidly created fans and imitators around the world. In North America, socially critical folk music came to express the utopian visions of a generation. The suburban life of the white middle-class family depicted in the 1950s "Leave it to Beaver" television series, in which father went out to work, exercised benevolent paternal authority at home, and mother played the homemaker with pearls, was challenged by the free-spirited rebellion depicted by events such as Woodstock and the classic 1960s' film *Easy Rider*.

Important political–ideological elements accompanied this cultural contestation. The "new left" in the Western industrialized countries had developed a Marxist critique of the postwar order, which was dominated militarily and economically by the United States. The new left argued that the American state was neo-imperialist because of its repeated political and military interventions in support of authoritarian, pro-capitalist regimes throughout the developing world, and in support of the interests of U.S.-based multinational corporations. The authoritarian nature of the regime in the Union of Soviet Socialist Republics (USSR) received less attention from the new left in the United States. In Europe, however, there was growing criticism of Stalinism, and the beginnings of a serious decline, among intellectuals, in support for the Moscow-aligned communist parties. The rupture between the new (socialist) left and the old (communist) left was deepened by the USSR's repression of movements for democratization in Hungary (1956) and Czechoslovakia (1968), and by the suppression of student-led protests in Poland (1968). Thus, the students' movement of May 1968 in France was anti-Stalinist, but not anti-Marxist. Indeed, many of its leaders came from the Marxist–Leninist and anarchist left.

The influence of the new left was particularly strong within the student movements, which linked their criticisms of oppressive authority to the struggle against U.S. imperialism. The American government's war in Vietnam—the first war ever televised—provoked massive reaction against its brutality, and solidarity with the struggle of the North Vietnamese, led by Ho Chi Minh. The war was viewed by many as a Third World people's struggle for liberation against a hegemonic world power seeking to keep Vietnam within its capitalist Cold

War sphere of influence. Moreover, the repressive nature of the South Vietnamese regime contradicted the American government's claims that this was a war being waged "for democracy." Thus there were large protests against American involvement in Vietnam, led mainly by university students, beginning in 1965. Opposition to American imperialism also united students' movements in North and Latin America, Africa, Asia, and Europe. In the wake of U.S. interventions in Nicaragua in the 1920s, in Guatemala (1954), in the Dominican Republic (1963), and in Cuba (the Bay of Pigs, 1961), as well as later in Chile (the U.S.-backed coup against the Unidad Popular government in 1973), Castro's Cuba was viewed by many as an embattled outpost against American hegemony. Che Guevara—the Argentinian-born revolutionary killed in Bolivia in 1967—symbolized armed struggle for the liberation of Third World peoples. Africa, too, had its heroes of Third-World resistance to American imperialism and European colonialism, such as Kwame Nkrumah of Ghana, and Eduardo Mondlane and Samora Machel of Mozambique.

New Social Movements

THE 1970s WAS A PERIOD OF LEFT-WING FERMENT; MANY DIFFERENT LEFT tendencies jostled for leadership. A feminist movement critical of the male-dominated left emerged, along with anti-nuclear, environmental, and anti-racism movements. In the United States, in the absence of the kind of historical socialist traditions and workers' organizations that characterized European societies, the student rebels went in a variety of directions. Some were marginalized or literally burned out in experimentation with mind-altering drugs. Some allowed themselves to be "recuperated" by the mainstream Democratic Party, often in the hopes of radicalizing it from within. Others joined the plethora of new radical or "progressive" struggles outlined in Table 20.1. In Western Europe and North America, the 1970s was the decade of the flowering of what came to be called *new social movements (NSMs)*.

In North America by the early 1980s, multiple women's movements had differentiated themselves from the predominantly white, middle-class women's movement, to take up questions which also divide women, including class exploitation, racism, and heterosexism. The gay and lesbian rights movement took its most political form in the United States, shaped by landmark events such as the Stonewall Riots of 1969, and the existence of evangelical Christian sects which have sustained a long "fundamentalist" campaign against challenges to their conceptions of the family, of sexuality, and of gender roles. Also in the United States, the black "civil rights" movement of the 1960s gave rise to the Black Power movement. By the 1980s, there was also a growing recognition in North America of racism against other minorities (Latino, Asian). In Europe, anti-racist movements were formed to protect immigrants and ethnic and racial minorities from harassment, violence, and discrimination (e.g., SOS Racisme in France). Aboriginal peoples' movements struggled in North America, Australia, New Zealand, and elsewhere against what were seen to be conditions of economic and institutional apartheid, or under-development. In the language of some of these movements, Aboriginal peoples constitute a "fourth world" of poverty within the affluent nations.

TABLE 20.1   *New Social Movements*

NAME	PERIOD	ISSUES AND EXAMPLES
Equal rights for women	1960s-	patriarchal sexism; reproductive freedoms (legalization of contraceptives, legal abortion on demand); economic discrimination against working women (e.g., the "equal pay for equal work" campaign)
	1970s-	racism, class exploitation, heterosexism
Equal rights for gays and lesbians	1960s-	decriminalization of homosexuality; freedom to be "visibly" (i.e., non-covertly) homosexual or bisexual without fear of harassment and discrimination; religious conceptions of the family, of sexuality, and of gender roles
Racial equality/anti-racism	1960s-	equal civil rights for racial minorities (especially the U.S. civil rights movement); "Black Power" movement seeking to establish a proud African-American cultural identity
	1980s-	protection of racial or ethnic minorities from discrimination, harassment, and violence (including in the police and justice systems); resistance to new far-right parties, skin-heads, and neo-Nazi groups; affirmative action policies to address economic and social inequalities
Self-determination for Aboriginal peoples	1960s-	defence of territorial sovereignty and self-government (e.g., the American Indian Movement, struggles in the Americas and South Pacific); economic and institutional forms of "apartheid" and "under-development" for Aboriginal peoples within the developed world; cultural forms of racial discrimination; re-creation or re-validation of cultural heritage, spirituality, and identities
International solidarity with Third World liberation movements	1960s-	opposition to the neo-imperialist policies of the advanced capitalist states; support for popular liberation struggles in the Third World against oppressive domestic regimes and foreign military intervention (e.g., the anti-apartheid movement, support for the Palestinian struggle for an autonomous homeland, support for revolutionary movements in Central America)
Peace and disarmament	1950s-	opposition to the arms race and cold-war thinking ("make love, not war"); demands for the dismantling of nuclear weapons ("ban the bomb") and the reallocation of massive military spending to socially useful purposes ("guns into ploughshares")
Anti-nuclear movement	1970s-	dangerous and undemocratic nature of nuclear power technology and its military uses; advocacy of alternative forms of energy production (more decentralized, less threatening to environment and health); critique of the ideas of "progress" which give rise to ever-increasing consumption of energy

TABLE 20.1   *New Social Movements (continued)*

NAME	PERIOD	ISSUES AND EXAMPLES
Environmentalism/ecology	1970s-	protection of the environment and of wilderness areas from resource exploitation and industrial pollution; health effects of toxic chemicals and emissions; urban living conditions (transportation, noise, green space); energy conservation; consumerism; sustainable development
Alternative or "counter-cultural" movements	1960s-	need for community, non-hierarchical relationships; human connectedness to nature and to other species; reduction of consumerism and simplification of life; exchange of goods and services outside the money economy (barter networks, co-operatives, communes)

Environmentalism grew out of concerns from the mid-1960s onward about industrial pollution and resource depletion (highlighted by the Club of Rome Report called *The Limits to Growth*) (Meadows, 1972). Citizens' associations concerned with the environment also emerged in the industrialized Soviet bloc (Allen, 1989; Jancar-Webster, 1993). The environmental movement had greater cultural influence in North America in the 1970s than in Europe, where the traditional left–right poles of political discourse made it difficult for politically "unlabelled" issues such as environmental protection to gain prominence. An exception was West Germany (the Federal Republic of Germany, or FRG), where conditions specific to that country encouraged the growth of important ecological, peace, and anti-nuclear movements in the 1970s (Müller-Rommel, 1989; Keller, 1993). The urban environment was also the focus of many struggles, in which citizens' groups sought to prevent various development projects, such as autoroutes or building projects entailing the destruction of historical quarters or green spaces.

The peace or disarmament movements were particularly strong in the FRG and the United Kingdom. West Germany was the site of NATO military bases, and positioned in the middle of the predicted war zone in the event of a nuclear exchange between the United States and the USSR. In 1979, the decision taken by NATO (at the initiative of the West German social democratic chancellor, Helmut Schmidt) to install Pershing and Cruise missiles in the FRG (to counter the SS 20 missiles of the USSR), triggered the formation of a massive peace movement (Hegedus, 1987; Johnstone, 1984). Between 1980 and 1983 an unprecedented extra-parliamentary resistance developed. In Britain, peace activists organized the Campaign for Nuclear Disarmament (CND), which had broad-based support, and led to the formation of the Europeans for Nuclear Disarmament network (END) (Thompson and Smith, 1981; Kaldor, 1991). Both of these movements formed outside the political party system, in contexts where the Social Democratic (FRG) and Labour (UK) parties had failed to adequately represent the concerns of the pacifists, or had allied with the positions of the United States in the NATO alliance.

The peace and anti-nuclear movements of the 1970s and early 1980s were closely related, particularly in the sense that the opponents of the civilian uses of nuclear power were also strongly opposed to the existence of nuclear weapons. (Not all peace movement activists were against the construction of nuclear reactors for the production of electricity.) In France, where both military and civilian uses of uranium were controlled by state agencies, the two movements were virtually fused in their opposition to atomic power. The anti-nuclear movement viewed the enemy as an anti-democratic, technocratic state, seeking to impose policy decisions with long-term, possibly irreversible, and destructive consequences (Touraine et al., 1983).

NSMs also took the form of "alternative" cultural movements or sub-cultures. These are essentially networks of interaction, communication, spaces, and services, aimed at creating and sustaining communities of persons sharing similar (alternative) values. Some examples are organic food co-operatives, community gardens and markets, systems of barter-exchange, communes, alternative (e.g., feminist; gay and lesbian) bookstores and publishing houses, discussion groups, co-operative child-care centres, coffee houses, and theatre groups. The feminist movements played an important part in promoting non-hierarchical ways of relating, tolerance of differences, and mutual support, as well as "consciousness-raising" activities. The slogan "the personal is political" drew attention to the various forms of domination and oppression in inter-personal relationships, and to the impossibility of transforming the social without transforming the personal. Ecological thought made similar connections between individual lifestyle choices and social responsibility for the future of the planet. Many young people chose to live in communal housing arrangements, in informal couple relationships rather than marriages, or to experiment with rural communes. The alternative or "counter-cultural" movements, as they are sometimes called, also include such things as household or neighbourhood measures to reduce energy consumption, locally organized recycling, boycotts of goods from countries with repressive regimes—as a means of exerting economic and political pressure for their downfall (as in the boycott of goods from South Africa during the apartheid era), patronage of shops selling products from cooperatives and small producers in the developing world (e.g., the OXFAM and Mennonite Central Committee shops), use of homeopathic medicine, and vegetarianism. One of the most radical of these currents—in the sense of being "counter" to the dominant culture—is what came to be known in Britain and North America as the animal rights or animal liberation movement, which has developed an ethical critique of anthropocentrism and "speciesism" (Garner, 1996).

From the 1970s to the mid-1980s, all of these movements influenced political agendas and won many concrete victories. For example, they succeeded in bringing about new reproductive rights for women, accelerated the decline in conservative religious authority, initiated reforms of the universities and other institutions, pressured governments to implement environmental legislation, advanced formal equality rights for racial minorities and women, and obstructed American military intervention in the Third World. Most importantly, NSMs transformed cultural values and called into question the paradigm of social conflict and the political party systems which had dominated since the nineteenth century. In the remaining sections of this chapter, we will look at explanations for the emergence of these movements, and ask what became of them in the 1980s and 1990s.

Explanations of New Social Movements

NEW SOCIAL MOVEMENT THEORY (NSMT) IS REALLY A SET OF CONTENDING interpretations of the nature of social conflict and change, predominantly in the advanced industrial societies, and in the latter half of the twentieth century. The schools of thought may be categorized in different ways. For example, some observers distinguish between a "European" approach, which seeks to explain the historical meaning of these movements in the context of sociological theories of conflict and change, and an "American" approach, which focuses rather on explanations of how these movements organize and exert influence on political institutions (Canel, 1992). The latter approach is also referred to as *Resource Mobilization Theory (RMT)*. While NSMT is concerned with explaining why NSMs emerged when and where they did, in terms of historical and structural contradictions, RMT is interested in the conditions that explain the relative success or failure of social movement organizations. These conditions include the ways in which movement actors manage the resources available to them, how they organize themselves internally, and how their objectives may be facilitated or obstructed by existing political institutions (Klandermans, 1995; Johnston and Klandermans, 1995). Resources may be material as well as non-material. Material resources include money, access to means of communication, labour, and meeting spaces. Non-material resources include moral authority, the creation of identities, group solidarity, organizational experience and networks, and appeals to traditions.

But why are these social movements called "new," when many of their elements have historical precedents in the Enlightenment, the Romantic rebellion against industrial society, the anti-slavery movements of the 1800s, the nature conservation movements of the nineteenth century, or women's demands for equal citizenship rights dating from the French Revolution to the struggles of the suffragettes?

First, the term *new social movement* serves to distinguish the movements that emerged in the late 1960s from the dominant "traditional" social movement, the labour movement, which had roots in the industrial revolution. A number of theorists of the new movements emphasized the decline in importance of the unions and working-class parties in Europe by the 1970s. The expansion of the public service, the relocation of industrial production from the old industrialized countries to areas of the Third World, and the shift to new information technologies and services-based growth, were among the trends that diminished the political importance of industrial workers and the parties that represented them. In a sense, the NSMs were viewed as the successors to the workers' movement of the nineteenth and first half of the twentieth centuries. They signified a period of transition in which political party systems had not yet integrated the new issues and conflicts, or adapted to the changing social composition of their societies (in particular, a growing new middle class).

Second, the NSMs are distinguished from the earlier social movements because their concerns are expressed in response to the postwar model of development in the Western industrialized societies (Hirsch, 1988; Lipietz, 1992). For example, industrial pollution and new technologies such as nuclear power and weapons of mass destruction created threats to human and planetary survival on an unprecedented scale. The postwar sexual division of labour in which women were once again relegated to the sphere of domestic labour and made the objects of intensive ideological campaigns constructing femininity, motherhood, and the ideal middle-class lifestyle, generated resistance that took the form of "second wave feminism." Also, the social-democratic state took on many areas of economic management previously left to the private market (through nationalizations and the creation of public corporations, particularly in the areas of resource exploitation, transportation, utilities, and production of weapons). As a result, a growing number of citizens' struggles— for example, against nuclear power development or the arms race—were in response to developments initiated by postwar states.

Third, the NSMs are seen by some authors to be "new" insofar as they reject some of the shared assumptions of liberalism, Marxism, and social democracy about what constitutes progress, development, or modernization. For all of these ideological traditions, industrialization and productivism have been viewed quite uncritically as beneficial to human progress. Moreover, the patriarchal relationships embedded in both capitalist and state–socialist economic systems have been granted only secondary, or marginal importance. Such NSM criticisms were reinforced by the crises in Eastern and Central Europe that led to the collapse of the state-socialist regimes. It became apparent that NSM concerns (such as environmental destruction and patriarchal relationships) were not unique to the Western industrialized countries, but had played an important part in mobilizing grassroots opposition to the model of development in the East, as well (Bahro, 1978; Einhorn, 1991; Kamenitsa, 1998).

Since the qualifier "new" tends to obscure important continuities and similarities, some theorists have preferred to use the term *alternative social movements*. "Alternative" signals transformative and critical social functions. It thereby distinguishes such movements as those for women's equality, peace, and ecology, from contemporary movements which are reactive. The latter represent social groups whose interests and identities are threatened by such changes as the entry of women into the workforce, or the growing presence of other racial or ethnic groups. Such movements may take the form of religious fundamentalism (e.g., the U.S. "Moral Majority"), ethnic nationalism, or violence perpetrated by skinheads and neo-Nazi groups. Politically, they are represented (and mobilized) by xenophobic–nationalist parties like the Front National in France, or the Republikaaner in Germany. However, many of the themes of far right parties (e.g., blaming immigration for unemployment levels), have also been incorporated in the platforms of more mainstream political parties.

The term *new social movement* remains a widely used label for the post-World War II women's, eco-pacifist, anti-racist, and other oppositional, change-oriented movements. The literature on new social movements, however, differs greatly in its explanations of why these movements emerged when they did, and what kinds of social change they signify, as well as in its predictions regarding the forms they may take in the future.

Differing Interpretations of the NSMs

LIBERAL THEORISTS VIEW NSMs AS INTEREST GROUPS PURSUING QUALITY-OF-LIFE goals. Such groups have arisen outside the traditional political party systems because these parties have ceased to reflect new social actors and their concerns. In this view, economic development in the West has succeeded in creating sufficient material affluence to render material concerns about economic security secondary to quality-of-life goals, such as a clean environment, recreational and cultural activities, self-development, and consumer choice. The emergence of these so-called "post-materialist values" is said to amount to a cultural revolution (Inglehart, 1977, 1990) that has changed the nature of our political systems.

In contrast to this evolutionary view, in which economic and technological progress eventually liberates humans from their material concerns, Marxists see NSM concerns as expressions of new forms of class structure and conflict. The class composition of capitalist societies has changed with the growth of the public sector, services, and in general white-collar employment, and the simultaneous relative decline of the traditional working class. However, this does not imply the disappearance either of classes or of social conflict. Instead, the problem has shifted to one of constructing alliances between the new middle class and the traditional working class in order to create alternatives to economic exploitation, inequality, and other oppressive social relationships. In this regard, arguments have arisen between traditional Marxists and post-Marxists. The former continue to assert that the industrial working class must take the leading role in any radical project for social change, because of workers' central place in the productive sector of the economy (Meiksins-Wood, 1986). Post-Marxists, on the other hand, view the primary economic concerns of most organized workers as being too narrow to encompass the diversity of contemporary social problems (such as racism, sexism, ecological destruction, undemocratic political institutions). Some unifying theme other than class struggle is needed to bring together all of the oppressed or exploited groups in society. At the same time, the traditional forms of action of the working class (strikes, economic bargaining) and its forms of organization (the union, the workers' party) no longer seem adequate to counter the diffuse nature of power (which is not simply economic, or invested in states, but also stems from the means and the authority to produce knowledge and information, among other sources).

Some have argued that the new middle class is in fact better positioned than the traditional working class to engage in the struggle of ideas, in the production of identities, and in the development of alternative policies and political agendas. The German sociologist, Klaus Eder (1993), draws attention to what he calls the "social opportunity structure" of middle-class radicalism. That is, members of the new middle class are generally highly educated, technologically skilled, and work in areas (such as the public sector) that provide them with knowledge of complex social issues. They therefore have the resources to develop criticisms of government policies and administration, as well as to envision alternatives. In addition, they produce the cultural resources (e.g., in the education sector and information and cultural industries), rather than the industrial goods, of modern societies. The cultural production of knowledge and identities is crucially important to the exercise of political influence, and to the success or failure of various political agendas. Eder argues, moreover, that the middle class has long been the carrier of radical critiques of modernization—the ways in which its processes are destructive of "the good life." The good life encompasses "consensual social relations" in which individuals interact as "equal and free persons"; hence its central feature is communication. The good life is also associated with a holistic vision of the human relationship to nature. Thus the vision of the new middle class extends beyond (but does not exclude) traditional class issues about the distribution of wealth, to questions about what we produce, why, and for whom. Does the predominant economic system reduce inequalities, meet basic needs, or provide a good and meaningful life? Is it environmentally sustainable? Is it the outcome of participatory citizenship and informed, democratic decision making? Do existing liberal-democratic institutions permit such participation or the consideration of alternatives? How are cultural values (such as consumerism or misogyny) transformed or reproduced? Note that Eder's analysis suggests that the future of the new social movements is closely related to the fate of the social opportunity structure for middle-class radicalism.

The work of the French sociologist Alain Touraine also falls into the category of a post-Marxist approach to NSMs. Touraine's analyses of the workers', students', and anti-nuclear movements, led him to conclude that the late 1960s signalled a transition to a *post-industrial society*. In it, the central conflict is no longer between industrial workers and capitalists, but between citizens and technocrats. This struggle brings citizens of industrialized societies into conflict with the elites and institutions that dominate decision making and the direction of social development. For Touraine, the French anti-nuclear movement of the 1970s was an example of this new kind of political conflict, its terrain, and its stakes. Anti-nuclear activists identified the enemy as the technocratic state and its instrumental logic of production. They tried to recast technocratic rationales for nuclear expansion into mere choices among many alternatives for future social development.

Another post-Marxist interpretation of the NSMs was presented in the work of Chantal Mouffe and Ernesto Laclau (1985) and developed in Mouffe's later work (1988, 1992, 1993). They argue that—in place of class struggle—the political stakes uniting the majority of the population against elites, currently, could be defined as democratic struggle. This includes struggles for equality, understood as freedom from unwarranted discrimination (as in blacks' struggles against white racism, which excludes them from equal enjoyment of citizenship and economic well-being); for autonomy, understood as respect for difference (e.g., the demand that different choices regarding sexuality be accepted, or that the ways in which women's needs or concerns differ from men's be taken into account in various kinds of policy formation), or freedom from unwarranted assumptions of sameness in relation to some pseudo-universal norm (as in the subsumption of the reality of gender differences in concepts such as "mankind"); and for deepened and broadened participation in decision making at all levels of society.

Mouffe views such demands as elements of a "discourse of radical and pluralist democracy" that permits the creation of bonds among, for example, anti-racist, anti-sexist, and anti-capitalist struggles. Forming a "rainbow coalition" or a common front for the organization of an event may bring different social subjects together, but it may not result in their examining both their conflicts and their commonalities. Without such a discussion, one subordinated group might tolerate discrimination against, or participate in the marginalization of another subordinated group. Thus, it is important for predominantly male trade unions to address issues of gender discrimination; for white feminists to recognize their privileged position, vis-à-vis women of colour, in the racial hierarchy of white supremacist societies; and for environmentalists to understand the importance of sustainable livelihoods for communities affected by the closure of polluting factories. Support for one another's democratic struggles for equality and autonomy may require the relinquishing of certain privileges, ending exclusionary practices, and questioning established identities.

The Future of New Social Movements

BY THE END OF THE 1980S, THE INFLUENCE OF WESTERN NEW SOCIAL MOVEMENTS appeared to be waning. Mass mobilizations had declined and organizations were paralyzed by seemingly irresolvable conflicts over strategies of change, particularly the question of whether movement goals were best served by grassroots organizations or more formal organizational and institutional structures. In Europe, new political parties formed to represent the issues of the NSMs, among them, the Ecology Party in Britain (1975; Green Party, 1985), Die Grünen in Germany (1980), and Les Verts in France (1984). Some observed the "reabsorption" of movement activists back into the traditional political parties, which were beginning to integrate NSM issues. These developments were taken, by some, as evidence that NSMs had become effectively integrated into mainstream politics. Others, however, argue that neoliberal restructuring has eroded the social opportunity structures of NSM actors. In this view, important aspects of political decision making have been transferred to the market, while broadly based movements for social change have given way to more localized and fragmentary forms of identity politics. Such characterizations of the contemporary period have given rise to speculation about the end of social movements.

The announcement of the decline of NSMs, however, may be premature. Some argue that the deepening inequalities and forms of marginalization created by neoliberalism or new nationalist ideologies have in fact made the need for coalition-building more urgent and more apparent to a wide range of social groups. There have indeed been renewed efforts in this regard, including the ongoing work of social justice and environmental coalitions in Ontario (the organizational base of the 1995 "days of action" protests against the Harris Government), the "movement unionism" of the Canadian Autoworkers (Adkin, 1998), the massive strikes in France in the fall of 1995 against the economic policies of the Chirac-Juppé government, and the international women's march against poverty and violence (culminating at the United Nations, October 17, 2000).

Local mobilizations against "neoliberal globalization" have become very widespread, and, thanks to Internet communication, are increasingly coordinated (see Table 20.2.) Such actions are directed against the institutions (Organization for Economic Co-operation and Development, International Monetary Fund, World Bank, World Trade Organization, etc.) and actors (multinational corporations, government leaders) seen to be most responsible for the extension and enforcement of an international "free trade" regime that serves the interests of elites (particularly in the North), while perpetuating global poverty and worsening environmental destruction. Agreements such as the North American Free Trade Agreement (NAFTA), the proposed Free Trade Agreement of the Americas (FTAA), and the stalled Multilateral Agreement on Investment (MAI) have been the targets of concerted opposition by networks of citizens' coalitions and non-governmental organizations (NGOs) around the world, such as those which organized the massive protest against the WTO in Seattle in 1999.

TABLE 20.2 *Some recent mobilizations against neoliberal globalization*

May 1998	anti-MAI protest in Montreal, Quebec
July 1999	protests against IMF in Ankara, Turkey
August 1999	protests against IMF policies in Ecuador
September 1999	protests against IMF policies in Columbia
	"Alternatives to the APEC Agenda" Forum in Auckland, New Zealand
December 1999	the "battle of Seattle" during WTO ministerial meeting
February 2000	protest against the World Economic Forum in Davos, Switzerland
	Anti-globalization protest in Bangkok, Thailand, during UNCTAD conference
May 2000	protests during Asian Development Bank meeting, Thailand
June 2000	protest in Calgary, Alberta, during World Petroleum Congress
	Anti-globalization festival in Millau, France
July 2000	protest in Windsor, Ontario, during Organization of American States (OAS) meetings
September 2000	People's Summit in New York City, paralleling the "Millenium Summit" of world leaders
	Prague protests against the IMF and World Bank during these organizations' 55th annual summit
October 2000	anti-globalization events planned for the meeting of World Bank and IMF officials, and central bankers from 19 countries (the G20), in Montreal, Quebec
	World March of Women 2000 to demand improved programs to eradicate poverty and violence against women, culminating at the UN, October 17 and co-ordinated by the Fédération des femmes du Québec
April 2001	protest against the negotiation of the Free Trade Area of the Americas (FTAA) in Quebec City

An estimated 50 000 protestors gathered in Seattle, representing diverse groups from many different countries: Philippine indigenous peoples, Canadian public health care defenders, French farmers, environmentalists, large trade unions (including representatives from more than 100 countries), human rights organizations, citizens' organizations for "fair trade," Indian opponents of "bio-piracy," women's activists, and many others. Over 1500 organizations from nearly 100 countries signed a declaration (set up on-line by Public Citizen, a consumer-rights group) demanding no further trade liberalization until the social and environmental impacts of existing agreements have been fully assessed (Weissman, 1999; *New Internationalist*, 2000). More recently, an estimated 60 000 protestors gathered in Quebec City to demonstrate against globalization and the negotiation of the FTAA.

Summary

The current study of new social movements poses a number of critical questions about what politics will look like in the twenty-first century. For example, what are the consequences of the emergence of new political parties and the poles of social conflict that they seem to represent? Green parties embrace many of the critical perspectives and the alternative agendas of the new social movements. But will their positions be deradicalized through institutionalization and the imperatives of electoral politics? What kinds of social coalitions will be constructed by the left-ecological political parties, on one hand, and the far-right parties, on the other hand? What influence will be wielded by new social movements that remain outside the formal sphere of politics? For example, will women's, Aboriginal, and gay and lesbian NGOs continue to play important roles in policy and constitutional debates? What new collective actors will arise? Will the future see the re-emergence of radical trade unionism in response to neoliberalism? Will there be a "globalization" of new social movements, uniting actors in the North and the South who are facing similar issues and adversaries? International NGOs or networks of NGOs are already important actors in negotiations on human rights and environmental conventions, and the terms of international trade. Or will politics increasingly revolve around identities based on race, ethnicity, and nationalism? These are just some of the questions on the agenda of social movements research.

The study of social movements that began with the attempts to explain the explosion of student-led protests in the 1960s has given rise to a number of schools of thought with regard to the broad outlines of social conflict and change in contemporary societies and their implications for political institutions. New social movement theory identifies such trends as changing social class composition, the "new paradigm" of politics suggested by the issues of the new social movements, and the emerging poles of conflict represented by left-ecology and far-right parties. Concepts such as "post-materialism," "post-industrial society," "the new middle class," or "radical democratic discourse" reflect some of the new ways in which we have come to understand these changes.

While there have been some shifts in focus, reflecting new developments (such as the re-emergence in the 1980s of far-right parties in Europe, movements of the unemployed, and resistance to neoliberal globalization), social movement theorists continue to study the important roles of non-institutional actors in shaping public opinion, revolutionizing cultural values, transforming political identities and representation, and redefining the meaning of citizenship at both local and global levels.

Discussion Questions

1. Have you participated in an organization that could be considered part of a new social movement? If so, what was the organization?

2. Do you think social movements have a significant impact on Canadian politics? Why or why not?

3. Which social movement do you think will have the greatest effect on political decisions? Why?

4. Which interpretation of NSMs—liberal, Marxist, or post-Marxist—do you find most convincing? Why?

References

Adkin, Laurie E. 1998. *The Politics of Sustainable Development: Citizens, Unions, and the Corporations.* Montreal, London and New York: Black Rose Books.

Canel, Eduardo. 1992. "New Social Movement Theory and Resource Mobilization: The need for integration," in William K. Carroll, ed. *Organizing Dissent: Contemporary Social Movements in Theory and Practice.* Toronto: Garamond Press.

Eder, Klaus. 1993. *The New Politics of Class: Social Movements and Cultural Dynamics in Advanced Societies.* London; Newbury Park; New Delhi: Sage Publications.

Einhorn, Barbara. 1991. "Where Have all the Women Gone? Women and the Women=s Movement in East Central Europe," *Feminist Review no. 39* (Fall).

Garner, Robert, ed. 1996. *Animal rights: the changing debate.* New York: New York University Press.

Hegedus, Zsuzsa. 1987. "The Challenge of the Peace Movement: Civilian Security and Civilian Emancipation." *Alternatives vol. XII.*

Hirsch, Joachim. 1988. "The Crisis of Fordism, Transformations of the `Keynesian' Security State, and New Social Movements," *Research in Social Movements, Conflicts and Change vol. 10.*

Inglehart, Ronald. 1977. *The Silent Revolution.* Princeton University Press.

——————. 1990. *Culture Shift.* Princeton University Press.

Jancar-Webster, Barbara. 1993. "Eastern Europe and the Former Soviet Union," in Sheldon Kamieniecki, ed. *Environmental Politics in the International Arena.* Albany: State University of New York Press.

Johnston, Hank and Bert Klandermans, eds. 1995. *Social Movements and Culture.* Minneapolis: University of Minnesota Press.

Johnstone, Diana. 1984. *The Politics of Euromissiles.* London: Verso.

Kaldor, Mary, ed. 1991. *Europe from Below: An East-West Dialogue.* London and New York: Verso.

Kamenitsa, Lynn. 1998. "The Process of Political Marginalization: East German Social Movements after the Wall," *Comparative Politics 30,* no. 3 (April).

Keller, Thomas. 1993. *Les Verts Allemands: Un Conservatisme Alternatif.* Paris: L'Harmattan.

Klandermans, Bert. 1995. *The Politics of Social Protest: Comparative Perspectives on States and Social Movements.* Minneapolis: University of Minnesota Press.

Lipietz, Alain. 1992. *Towards a New Economic Order: Postfordism, Ecology and Democracy,* trans. by Malcolm Slater. New York: Oxford University Press.

Meadows, Donella H. et al. 1972. *The Limits to Growth: A Report for the Club of Rome's Project on the Predicament of Mankind.* New York: Universe Books.

Meiksins-Wood, Ellen. 1986. *Retreat from Class.* London: Verso Books.

Mouffe, Chantal. 1993. *The Return of the Political.* London: Verso.

—————, ed. 1992. *Dimensions of Radical Democracy: Pluralism, Citizenship and Community.* London: Verso.

—————. 1988. "Hegemony and New Political Subjects: Towards a New Concept of Democracy," in Nelson, C., and L. Grossberg, eds., *Marxism and the Interpretation of Culture.* University of Illinois Press.

Mouffe, C. and Ernesto Laclau. 1985. *Hegemony and Socialist Strategy: Towards a Radical Democratic Politics.* London: Verso Books.

Müller-Rommel, Ferdinand, ed. 1989. *New Politics in Western Europe: The Rise and Success of Green Parties and Alternative Lists.* Boulder, Co.: Westview Press.

New Internationalist, The. 2000. "WTO shambles in Seattle," Issue 320 (Jan/Feb).

Thompson, Edward P. and Dan Smith, eds. 1981. *Protest and Survive.* New York and London: Monthly Review Press.

Touraine, Alain, Z. Hegedus, F. Dubet, and M. Wieviorka. 1983. *Anti-Nuclear Protest: The Opposition to Nuclear Energy in France.* Cambridge University Press.

Weissman, Robert. 1999. "Democracy is in the streets," *Multinational Monitor vol. 20,* Issue 12 (December).

Further Readings

D'Arnieri, Paul, C. Ernst, and E. Kier. 1990. "New Social Movements in Historical Perspective." *Comparative Politics 22,* no. 4 (July).

Carroll, William K., ed. 1997. *Organizing Dissent: Contemporary Social Movements in Theory and Practice. 2nd ed.* Toronto: Garamond Press.

Dalton, R. and M. Kuechler, eds. 1990. *Challenging the Political Order.* Cambridge: Polity Press.

Richardson, Dick and Chris Rootes, eds. 1995. *The Green Challenge: The development of Green parties in Europe.* London and New York: Routledge.

Weblinks

Canadian Autoworkers Union
www.caw.ca/

Canadian Federation of Students
www.cfs-fcee.ca/
Canadian Labour Congress
www.clc-ctc.ca/

Canadian Women's Internet Association
www.herplace.org

Citizens on the Web (Toronto) - News
www.interlog.com/~cjazz/action7b.htm

Co-operatives and non-profits on the Internet
csf.Colorado.EDU/co-op

French Greens
www.verts.imaginet.fr

Green Party of Canada
www.green.ca/

Green parties of the United States
www.greenparties.org/

Greenpeace International Homepage
www.greenpeace.org/

MAI links
http://userpage.fu-berlin.de/~timor/mai/mailinx.htm
    www.seattle99.org/links/links—mai.html

Peoples' Global Action
www.agp.org/agp/

The Magnus Hirschfeld Centre for Human Rights
www.angelfire.com/nj/hirschfeldcentre/index.html

World March of Women
http://www.worldmarch.org/

Global Perspectives

The politics of the early twenty-first century is marked by a movement from the level of the national state to the level of the global and transnational. For centuries, the national state was the most significant unit in the study of politics. The state contained key political institutions and largely determined what happened within its boundaries. Relations between states in the international system were and are influenced by power inequalities among states, which, as the early chapters in this part describe, structure foreign policy and the internal workings of international organizations. Foreign policy, whether pertaining to war, trade, human rights, or development assistance, as well as international organizations, are integral parts of the ongoing international matrix. However, the end of the Cold War and the globalization of the international political economy have ushered in a new era of uncertainties and challenges. The globalization of technological innovations has collapsed geographic distance and discredited the idea that national populations can be protected from outside forces. The fates of North and South have been drawn closer together, exposing in stark relief the growing and indefensible disparities in well-being and life-chances between the minority and the vast majority of the world's population. The current era has witnessed new roles for established international organizations and new agendas for multilateral action on a global scale. New transnational entities and international financial organizations hold increasing sway over politics within and between states. Driven by the promises of neoliberalism, these organizations largely elude the democratic procedures that were incorporated into the practices of national political institutions.

The final part of this text demonstrates that the sites of politics are rapidly shifting beyond the boundaries of the national state to the level of the transnational where the possibilities of politics are opened to the ideas of shared fates, universal human rights, and a global commons. In many ways, the substance of the new politics of the twenty-first century—issues of equality, democracy, and ethics—remain largely unchanged from the concerns of the ancient Greeks.

CHAPTER 21

POST–COLD WAR POLITICS

For nearly fifty years, the Cold War struggle between the superpowers—the United States of America and the Soviet Union—had a profound impact on political life among and within states and societies around the globe. The end of this rivalry in 1991 marked the onset of remarkable sea-changes in political affairs. Many analysts predict even more dramatic future changes that will challenge the conventional political expectations and categories that dominated the Cold War era. As James Richardson notes, "in groping for new landmarks, commentators have put forward a bewildering variety of diagnoses and prescriptions" (1992, 1). Like "globalization," the phrase "post-Cold War era" has become a cliché for all sorts of conflicting assumptions about politics in our times. This chapter aims to make explicit and place in context these assumptions. First, we review three distinct explanations for why the Cold War began and ended. These explanations focus on the importance of ideological struggle, domestic politics and leadership, and the international structure. Next we explore competing visions of politics in the post-Cold War era. We outline four popular and competing visions about the future—the end of history, McWorld versus Jihad, the Coming Anarchy, and the Clash of Civilizations. The chapter concludes with a critique of the assumptions underlying each of these four visions.

ANTONIO FRANCESCHET

Introduction

The **Cold War** was the antagonistic political relationship between the United States of America and the Soviet Union between approximately 1946 and 1991. Although these two superpower states (and their allies) frequently clashed, open fighting never occurred between them. Most political scientists agree that change has occurred with the end of the Cold War but disagree on *what* has changed, *why*, and *how* things will look in the future as a result. Additionally, scholars are divided over whether the Cold War was a period of stability and relative peacefulness or, by contrast, a dangerously unstable time that nearly brought us to nuclear suicide (as some argue the 1962 Cuban missile crisis nearly did). Whether the post-Cold War era is something to celebrate, as citizens of Eastern Europe did when the Berlin Wall fell and the Soviet Empire crumbled, or something to lament and fear is a central theme of this chapter.

Either/or options, polar opposite visions, and binary distinctions are the common features of political science scholarship on the Cold War and its aftermath. These stark dualities may obscure more than they illuminate about political reality today and about future alternatives (Brown, 1999, 56). Nevertheless, this approach also provides political science students with clearly defined images and concepts with which to contemplate the grand scope of global political change since the collapse of the Soviet Union. As Brown concludes, "The end of the Cold War was an event of great significance in human history, the consequences of which demand to be glossed in broad terms rather than reduced to a meaningless series of events" (1999, 41).

Why the Cold War Began and Ended

THE COLD WAR WAS NOT SIMPLY AN EVENT NOR EVEN A SERIES OF INTERRELATED occurrences. The Cold War was marked by important episodes, circumstances, and statements that either incited and perpetuated or moderated and dampened the tensions, suspicions, and antagonisms between the superpowers. Some important historical markers of the Cold War include Winston Churchill's famous "Iron Curtain" speech in Fulton, Missouri (5 March 1946); the Korean War (1950–3); the nuclear arms race; the Cuban Missile Crisis (October 1962); various "proxy" wars in the developing world sponsored by either the United States or the Soviet Union; a period of relaxed tension and mutual accommodation (*détente* in the 1970s); and a revived "Second Cold War" (in the early 1980s), during which American President Ronald Reagan referred to the Soviet adversary as an "evil empire" and the Soviets shot down a Korean airline jet full of innocent civilians (September 1983).[1] But while these events are part of the Cold War, they do not explain its outbreak nor why it ended. Facts like these need to be placed in context and interpreted as the result of larger political patterns. A number of explanations do this. They tend to focus on three elements:

- ideology
- domestic politics
- the international structure of military power

Ideological Struggle

A popular and compelling explanation of the Cold War is that it erupted because of—and was then sustained by—ideological differences. The 1917 Bolshevik Revolution that formed the Soviet Union was based on communist ideology; and the United States was fashioned on the basis of liberal democratic ideology. Although the two countries cooperated to defeat Nazi Germany in World War II, without a common enemy the deep incompatibilities between each state's fundamental political ideas and beliefs became apparent. The Cold War was therefore a contest over opposed visions of polity, society, and economy. Both superpowers engaged in a missionary attempt to convert other states around the globe to either liberal capitalism or communism, and to prevent them from being influenced by the rival's ideology.

The United States meddled in the domestic politics of Western European states to prevent the left—especially the strong Communist parties of France and Italy—from gaining power. It also intervened in and subverted states throughout the Third World to guard against a perceived Soviet agenda of "taking over the world." American foreign policy makers frequently referred to a **domino effect**, through which a single communist state such as Cuba would infect neighbours until the entire "free" world fell to this ideology. The Soviets relentlessly maintained control over an "empire" in Eastern and Central Europe through the so-called Warsaw Pact alliance. When Central European countries, especially Hungary (1956), Czechoslovakia (1968), and Poland (1981), attempted to gain greater autonomy and civil liberties, the Soviets cracked down with military and other means. Although the liberal capitalist and communist ideologies changed somewhat throughout the Cold War, the essential differences remained to drive the conflict until the Soviet Union abandoned the central features of its ideology. When Soviet leader Mikhail Gorbachev (1984–1991) introduced liberalizing political reforms and market economics, there was eventually little left on which the two sides could disagree.

Domestic Politics and Leadership

Another explanation of the Cold War is that domestic politics in each superpower state started and then exacerbated it. This explanation stresses the unique role and interests of political elites and leaders in both the United States and Soviet Union. In both societies an external threat or enemy helped to legitimate rule, consolidate power, and silence domestic dissent or opposition. Throughout the Cold War, leaders in both states depicted the enemy in mirror-like terms as evil, aggressive, expansionist, and unpredictable. Rather than ideological difference, then, leaders like U.S. President Harry Truman and Soviet Chairman Joseph Stalin fostered conflict in order to promote internal cohesion.

Certainly the United States is a democracy and the Soviet Union was a totalitarian system. There is little doubt that the Soviet leadership faced little serious internal opposition and could eliminate dissent almost at will. However, the Cold War gave an added, external rationale for Soviet executions, forced exile, and Siberian gulags—the usual fate of individuals deemed a threat to the state. During the early 1950s, an illiberal force known as McCarthyism affected the American political system. This was a series of political smear campaigns led initially by

Senator Joseph McCarthy against suspected Communist sympathizers. The so-called "witch hunt" that ensued in the U.S. targeted political enemies and dissuaded any criticism of an aggressive foreign policy. Famous Hollywood actors and directors were "blacklisted," unable to get employment for many years. The McCarthy episode sent a clear message to opinion leaders that any criticism of the Cold War would not be tolerated. The Cold War also favoured the interests of certain domestic coalitions both in and out of the state. For example, both superpowers had unique versions of what American President Dwight D. Eisenhower called the **military-industrial complex**. This referred to sectors within the defence industry and military establishment that had a vested interest in perpetuating Cold War conflict.

According to this explanation, "The Cold War ended when Gorbachev shifted the basis of authority" within his state. Gorbachev "needed to reward a different set of constituencies whose interests required a shifting of resources away from defence" (Lebow, 1999, 23). The Soviet leadership became interested in domestic economic and political reform and international accommodation as ways to overcome the crippling limits of a planned economy locked in a costly arms race.

International Structure

A school of International Relations known as **Realism** claims the Cold War was simply the result of a "bipolar" international structure.[2] Realists see conflict and antagonism among states as an essential and enduring reality, one that determines international events such as those of the Cold War period. Unlike politics within states, there is no international political authority to settle conflicts—there is instead only **anarchy** defined as the absence of overarching authority. Realists argue that the unequal distribution of military power among states in anarchy will have an effect on the international structure. For example, if there are— as in the Cold War—only two states of roughly equal military power, there is a bipolar structure; with several, a multipolar structure; and, when there is only one great power, as is currently the case, a unipolar structure emerges.

For Realists, the Cold War was a product of the bipolar international structure, inevitable after World War II had weakened Europe, dismembered the German state, and disempowered Japan. The pre-war multipolar structure of several great powers was displaced by a global political rivalry between the United States and Soviet Union. This rivalry produced two blocks of allied states that either chose or were compelled to "choose" affiliation with the superpowers.

Realists closely monitored the varying degrees of military capability possessed by the superpower protagonists, especially the nuclear balance. When things change in this dynamic—that is, when a state no longer possesses the military might to balance against the strength of the enemy—Realism predicts a change to the international structure. "The root cause of the Cold War and its demise," for Realists, was the "rise and fall of the Soviet Union as a global power" (Lebow, 1999, 22). We return to this thesis below because its chief exponents have predicted a post–Cold War era of instability and dangerous conflict.

The ideological, domestic–political, and international structure accounts of the Cold War and its ending provide partial perspectives on a complex phenomenon. To some extent, the first two can be synthesized to create a richer explanation of the conflict between the organizations (NGOs) around the world, such as those which organized the massive protest against the WTO in Seattle in 1999.

TABLE 20.2 *Some recent mobilizations against neoliberal globalization*

May 1998	anti-MAI protest in Montreal, Quebec
July 1999	protests against IMF in Ankara, Turkey
August 1999	protests against IMF policies in Ecuador
September 1999	protests against IMF policies in Columbia
	"Alternatives to the APEC Agenda" Forum in Auckland, New Zealand
December 1999	the "battle of Seattle" during WTO ministerial meeting
February 2000	protest against the World Economic Forum in Davos, Switzerland
	Anti-globalization protest in Bangkok, Thailand, during UNCTAD conference
May 2000	protests during Asian Development Bank meeting, Thailand
June 2000	protest in Calgary, Alberta, during World Petroleum Congress
	Anti-globalization festival in Millau, France
July 2000	protest in Windsor, Ontario, during Organization of American States (OAS) meetings
September 2000	People's Summit in New York City, paralleling the "Millenium Summit" of world leaders
	Prague protests against the IMF and World Bank during these organizations' 55th annual summit
October 2000	anti-globalization events planned for the meeting of World Bank and IMF officials, and central bankers from 19 countries (the G20), in Montreal, Quebec
	World March of Women 2000 to demand improved programs to eradicate poverty and violence against women, culminating at the UN, October 17 and co-ordinated by the Fédération des femmes du Québec
April 2001	protest against the negotiation of the Free Trade Area of the Americas (FTAA) in Quebec City

---

An estimated 50 000 protestors gathered in Seattle, representing diverse groups from many different countries: Philippine indigenous peoples, Canadian public health care defenders, French farmers, environmentalists, large trade unions (including representatives from more than 100 countries), human rights organizations, citizens' organizations for "fair trade," Indian opponents of "bio-piracy," women's activists, and many others. Over 1500 organizations from nearly 100 countries signed a declaration (set up on-line by Public Citizen, a consumer-rights group) demanding no further trade liberalization until the social and environmental impacts of existing agreements have been fully assessed (Weissman, 1999; *New Internationalist*, 2000). More recently, an estimated 60 000 protestors gathered in Quebec City to demonstrate against globalization and the negotiation of the FTAA.

Britain, Russia and China would compete—has yet to fully materialize, if indeed it ever will (Krauthammer, 1991, 23-4).

Liberal internationalism is Realism's main disciplinary rival. Liberals in international relations argue that conflict is not an inevitable nor permanent reality. Conflict can be reduced if not eliminated progressively through the dissemination of the ideals of democracy and the free market, as well as by international organizations such as the United Nations. Liberal internationalists claim that the collapse of the Soviet Union and end of the Cold War will cause progress and peace in international relations.

Michael Doyle (1995) has shown that in the past two hundred years, democratic states have never waged war against one another. As a result, the spread of democratic government that has resulted from end of the Cold War increases the prospects for international peace. Another liberal internationalist, Bruce Russett (1993), claims there are two intrinsic characteristics of liberal democracy that explain its pacifying nature. First, in democracies the political leaders are accountable to the public. Since the public has to sacrifice their lives and property in a war, they will be much more hesitant to authorize a war. Second, democratic states learn to apply the non-violent means of dispute resolution within society to their relations with other democratic states. The principles of law, moderation, and civility are used to mitigate international anarchy.

Liberal internationalism's hope of international peace through the spread of democracy is not without problems. First, democratic states have in fact been very aggressive and war-like against undemocratic states, as the Cold War foreign policy of the United States demonstrates. Second, as long as democracy remains only weakly entrenched in many parts of the world, the limited international peace achieved since the Cold War (at least among democracies) could conceivably be reversed.

Both realism and liberal internationalism focus on the implications of the end of the Cold War for relations among states. But is this too narrow a scope to consider the emerging political order? The Cold War affected not only sovereign states, "it encompassed deep-seated divisions about the organization and content of political life, economic and social life at all levels" (Brown, 1999, 41).

Global Politics

In the 1990s three political scientists and at least one popular journalist offered broad but starkly different images of the politics of the post–Cold War era. By and large, these images are all concerned with the implications or effects of the Cold War's termination. Like the Realists and Liberal internationalists, the main focus of their views is on whether we can expect conflict or peace in the future. However, there is also disagreement about what kind of political actors and forces will likely enjoy peace, suffer conflict, or simply engage in new and emerging dynamics.

The End of History?

In 1989, Francis Fukuyama proclaimed that the end of the Cold War meant the **"end of history"** (1989; 1992). He did *not*, as skeptical critics charged, mean that history, as events or occurrences in time, would stop. That would be absurd. Rather, Fukuyama was making a more profound philosophical point. Fukuyama adapted the "end of history" notion from philosopher G.W.F. Hegel (1770–1831), for whom political progress was considered to end once the liberal state became fully established. Fukuyama claims that progress is now impossible since the Soviet Union has collapsed and communism has been repudiated. The Soviet Union was the last great impediment to the universal recognition that liberal democracy and capitalist economics were the best of all possible regimes and systems, "free from…fundamental contradictions" (Fukuyama, 1992, xi). Consequently, Fukuyama predicts the democratization of all states; the flourishing of human potential, rights, and liberties; greater peace and stability among states and peoples, as the liberal internationalists predict; and growing prosperity for all in the very long term.

Along with greater peace and prosperity, Fukuyama claims that cultural diversity and ideological disagreement have simply come to an end in the post–Cold War, post-historical era. "Rather than a thousand shoots blossoming into as many different flowering plants, mankind will come to seem like a long wagon train strung out along the road" (1992, 338). This incredible homogeneity may seem boring, he concedes, but it is better than living with the terrible conflicts of history. The only disagreements now are simply over the means of political life, not the ends; that is, politics now is simply about implementing liberal capitalism. "[A]ll the really big questions [have been]…settled" (1992, xii).

CHURCHILL NAMES THE IRON CURTAIN

Excerpt from a speech by then former British Prime Minister Winston Churchill. The speech was delivered in Fulton, Missouri, USA, March 5, 1946 on the occasion of his honorary degree from Westminster College. The speech, which he called "The Sinews of Peace," has since become known as the "Iron Curtain" speech, a signal event in the Cold War's history.

A shadow has fallen upon the scenes so lately lighted by the Allied victory. Nobody knows what Soviet Russia and its Communist international organisation intends to do in the immediate future, or what are the limits, if any, to their expansive and proselytising tendencies. I have a strong admiration and regard for the valiant Russian people and for my wartime comrade, Marshal Stalin. . . . We understand the Russian need to be secure on her western frontiers by the removal of all possibility of German aggression. We welcome Russia to her rightful place among the leading nations of the world. . . . It is my duty however, for I am sure you would wish me to state the facts as I see them to you, to place before you certain facts about the present position in Europe.

From Stettin in the Baltic to Trieste in the Adriatic, an iron curtain has descended across the Continent. Behind that line lie all the capitals of the ancient states of Central and Eastern Europe. Warsaw, Berlin, Prague, Vienna, Budapest, Belgrade, Bucharest and Sofia, all these famous cities and the populations around them lie in what I must call the Soviet sphere, and all are subject in one form or another, not only to Soviet influence but to a very high and, in many cases, increasing measure of control from Moscow. . . . Whatever conclusions may be drawn from these facts—and facts they are—this is certainly not the Liberated Europe we fought to build up. Nor is it one which contains the essentials of permanent peace. . . .

I do not believe that Soviet Russia desires war. What they desire is the fruits of war and the indefinite expansion of their power and doctrines. But what we have to consider here to-day while time remains, is the permanent prevention of war and the establishment of conditions of freedom and democracy as rapidly as possible in all countries. Our difficulties and dangers will not be removed by closing our eyes to them. They will not be removed by mere waiting to see what happens; nor will they be removed by a policy of appeasement. What is needed is a settlement, and the longer this is delayed, the more difficult it will be and the greater our dangers will become.

The text of Sir Winston Churchill's "The Sinews of Peace" speech is quoted in its entirety from Robert Rhodes James (ed.), *Winston S. Churchill: His Complete Speeches 1897–1963 Volume VII: 1943–1949* (New York: Chelsea House Publishers, 1974) 7285–7293. Reprinted with permission of Chelsea House Publishers.

How does Fukuyama account for the civil strife, bloodshed, and nationalist fervour that also emerged after the Cold War? There has been ethnic cleansing in the Balkans and genocide in Africa. Fukuyama is clear to distinguish between two worlds: the liberal capitalist "post-historical" world in which advanced, industrialized states such as Canada and the United States reside, and the illiberal peripheral world that simply contains what he considers "irrational" peoples stuck in history, like Yugoslavs and Rwandan tribes (1992, 276). There may be short-term conflicts in the historical world and between the historical and post-historical worlds. Eventually, however, he argues that all humanity will be integrated into the post-historical world. In other words, although Fukuyama thinks the end of the Cold War is something to celebrate, residual and peripheral conflicts and discord will exist for the foreseeable future.

This last point is a major concession that weakens the power of Fukuyama's overall argument—the benefits and stability of the post–Cold War era are not evenly distributed. And the violence and poverty in the daily lives of the majority of the world's population have not been noticeably ameliorated since the triumph of liberal capitalism over communism. Other political scientists are thus rightly less confident or sanguine than Fukuyama about the prospects for peace, prosperity, and democracy in the post–Cold War era.

McWorld versus Jihad?

Benjamin Barber (1995) argues that the great ideological contradiction between communism and liberal capitalism has simply been replaced by an even more dangerous collision of forces—*McWorld* and *Jihad*. Barber uses these terms to signify a global battle between two dangerous threats to democracy and human liberty worldwide.

McWorld refers to the forces of global capitalism, consumer greed, and the cultural homogeneity they breed when unchecked by democratic politics. **Jihad** refers to the forces of intolerance that lead a people or state to reject universal political values, rights, and freedoms. McWorld is thus a symbol of the planet being artificially unified and transformed by corporate power and American consumer desire, such as the global dominance of McDonald's fast food restaurants. For Barber, Jihad represents (with remarkable cultural insensitivity) the world being torn apart by self-righteous, inward-looking, fanatical advocates of traditional religious, ethnic, national, cultural, historical, and political identities. These zealots spur on others to slaughter the threatening infidels from the outside world.

Barber does not draw a direct connection between the end of the Cold War and the eruption of the two conflicting McWorld and Jihad forces. However, he does suggest that Western states and publics have, in light of their victory over Soviet communism, become too complacent and accepting of free-market madness, that is, the unfettered and uncontrolled interests of global capitalism. McWorld has emerged as soulless corporations have emancipated themselves from the control of sovereign states. Barber claims we are paying the price for this in two related ways. First, we in the West are now enduring a destruction of public or civic culture by the mindless consumer advertising and "branding" of McWorld. Second, we must also now be on guard against the reactionary, mainly anti-Western Jihad forces that are provoked by the conformity, homogeneity, and cultural insensitivity of McWorld.

McWorld and Jihad may appear like contradictory forces. Yet Barber claims they actually reinforce and sustain each other: "Jihad not only revolts against but abets McWorld, while McWorld not only imperils but re-creates and reinforces Jihad" (1995, 5). McWorld and Jihad are two sides of the same anti-democratic coin, creating chaos and anarchy rather than reinforcing the popular control that a tolerant and respectful civil society ideally enjoys over the levers of government. "Antithetical in every detail," he adds, "Jihad and McWorld nonetheless conspire to undermine our hard-won (if only half-won) civil liberties and the possibility of a global democratic future" (1995, 19).

Unlike Realists, Barber sees conflict among sovereign states as less important and troublesome than the impact of McWorld and Jihad's struggle on all domestic political societies, namely, the erosion of a progressive, participatory, and culturally sensitive democracy. Unlike Fukuyama, Barber does not see convergence and harmony in the future but instead divergence and struggle between the worst excesses of our time. But Barber perhaps romanticizes the democratic credentials of Western and certainly developing nations prior to the McWorld and Jihad struggle he claims erupted so recently. And he offers little in the way of convincing solutions to the dilemmas he identifies.

The Coming Anarchy?

Realists assume that anarchy is an ever-present feature among sovereign states in the international system. But they largely assume the opposite about politics within states—that governments authoritatively settle disputes and uphold common laws among citizens. According to the journalist Robert Kaplan (1994; 2000), we can no longer take these assumptions for granted within states—anarchy is now emerging *within* them, and will in the future undermine domestic political orders and the individual security that states are supposed to provide.

Kaplan's influential reportage from the Balkans and Africa during the 1990s made the broad claim that the lawlessness, ethnic enmity, and criminally irresponsible government he found there would in future be reproduced in many more states and societies. He claims the causes of these terrible problems are "natural" disasters, rather than political and social breakdown. What Kaplan means by "natural" is that resource scarcity (especially water), environmental degradation, overpopulation, migration, and squalid urbanization are creating a powder keg in the developing world—domestic violence and struggle over the basic resources needed to sustain life. Unable to cope, governments are collapsing and states, particularly former European colonies in Africa, are incapable of upholding the law, providing welfare, and preventing the gross abuse of human rights. The anarchy in places like Sierra Leone and the Ivory Coast are, Kaplan claims, a part of our future simply because *all* humans depend upon scarce natural resources and are vulnerable to the limits of the physical environment. Moreover, the global population, particularly in the developing world, is exploding. But soon Western governments will face the same problems, not least because refugee migrants from the Third World will arrive on the shores of the wealthy states, thus spreading the anarchy.

How did the end of the Cold War unleash the coming anarchy? Kaplan explains that the end of European imperial control over the Third World left it populated with weak, ill-constituted states that could not independently cope with the challenges of governing. The Cold War provided a temporary stop-gap to the coming anarchy because the superpowers invested aid, trade, and support to these states to fight the battle against communism and/or capitalism. The end of the Cold War thus opened the flood gates to "a cruel process of natural selection among existing states," claims Kaplan, "No longer will these states be so firmly propped up by the West or Soviet Union" (2000, 40).

With the end of the Cold War, there is little interest or incentive in the West to help fight the tide of anarchy in the developing world. Military planners are concerned only with understanding new environmental security threats that are posed—particularly by migration—and how best to control and contain their impact on Western societies. Thus the Cold War strategies once adopted to protect American citizens from nuclear attack are no longer appropriate—the new front lines are the disorderly "hordes" and violence in the periphery.

As the political geographer Simon Dalby has noted, Kaplan constructs a new and alarming threat, one that is even more unpredictable and ominous for the Western way of life than was communism (1996). Quite simply, the privilege, prosperity, and rule of law (that we simply assume is part and parcel of the West) will start to erode when too many people compete for decreasing natural resources. In this lifeboat depiction of the future, Kaplan fails to consider that Western colonialism, privilege, and economic interests have created many of the problems the developing world must now confront. Thus the anarchy that undoubtedly arises from scarcity, overpopulation, and forced migration is not simply a product of natural limits, but also of political realities, many created by earlier Western imperial powers.

The Clash of Civilizations?

The political scientist Samuel Huntington claims that, "In the post–Cold War world, the most important distinctions among peoples are not ideological, political, or economic. They are cultural" (1996, 21). The bipolar international structure of the superpower rivalry has been eclipsed by a multipolar, multicivilizational order in which six to nine different civilizations have become distrustful rivals. These civilizations—Western, Islamic, Sinic (based principally in China), Hindu, Orthodox (principally Christians in East Europe and Russia), Japanese, Latin American, African—are based on different and, moreover, *incompatible* religious precepts and world views.

Huntington modifies or rejects the previous depictions of the post–Cold War era that we have reviewed. Realism is correct to focus on conflict emerging from a multipolar balance of power in anarchy, but wrong to think that sovereign states are the most important political units. States will in future perceive their interests on the basis of wider, cultural traits shared with other states of the same civilization. Huntington's argument contrasts with the others discussed above because he rejects the idea that the non-Western world will embrace liberal democratic values. Global harmony, Huntington argues, is an illusion because "enemies are essential" in creating political identities (1996, 19).

Huntington assumes that the basic dynamics of global politics will shift with the rediscovery of cultural identities by differing peoples after the Cold War. It is time, he warns, for Westerners to recognize they are not superior and that values such as individual freedom, the rule of law, and human rights will be rejected by other civilizations (1996, 51). It is also time to recognize that multiculturalism is a disastrous policy to adopt within Western domestic societies. Multiculturalism only weakens the sense of coherent identity required to meet the challenge of a multipolar world in which the interests of the American-led West must defend against the "Rest" (1996, 306). Finally, Huntington alarms his readers about the relative decline of Western global power and influence when compared to other civilizations. Other civilizations are experiencing population and economic growth that will soon render the existing power of the West less impressive than ever—and these other civilizations will not necessarily show mercy when they perceive Western weakness. A dangerous clash of civilizations can be averted only by carefully strengthening Western power while not provoking the wrath of the non-Western world, particularly its core states— China, Iran, and India.

Huntington almost certainly exaggerates the incompatibility among civilizations and ignores the shared characteristics among them. For example, although human rights may be a Western concept, all cultures share in common a belief in the value of human life and a prohibition against cruelty. Also, the distinctions he draws between civilizations are arbitrary and difficult to sustain. For example, why is Latin America separate from the West given that Catholicism is a common element in both cultures? If religion is not always the most important difference, why does Huntington separate Orthodox Christian civilization from Western Christendom? And so on. Finally, like Realism, Huntington's clash of civilizations thesis may contain the seeds of a self-fulfilling prophecy, feeding distrust and enmity between the West and the Rest rather than solving disputes that may arise in the future.

Summary

This chapter has described and evaluated the most influential explanations of the Cold War and the emerging post–Cold War order. Although there is substantial agreement in political science that the Cold War has ended, there is little agreement about what this means for current and future generations. This suggests that the so-called facts of international and global politics are highly conditioned by contradicting assumptions about the continuity or discontinuity of key elements of the Cold War era. In particular, scholars are divided over whether the post–Cold War era is likely to see greater peace or conflict and whether these basic trends will pertain equally to all states, societies, and other political identities or to only a particular subset of them.

The purpose of uncovering the main assumptions that different political scientists hold about the post–Cold War era is to develop a critical understanding of different trends in the discipline and in the larger realm of global politics. As the above analysis shows, clearly not all of these assumptions can be true: Realists, Liberal internationalists, Fukuyama, Barber, Kaplan, and Huntington disagree and there is little chance of synthesizing their contrasting visions of the present and future. They cannot all be correct, can they? Students will likely be attracted to some or only one of these competing visions of the future; or they may find grounds for rejecting all.

The alternative visions of the post–Cold War era presented in this chapter are also conditioned by another factor: all are formulated by Americans. Almost without exception, a subtext of the most influential post–Cold War scenarios evaluated above has been the future of the United States' foreign policy. There is good reason not to simply follow slavishly a limited number of political alternatives that reflect the concerns, values, and interests of the American polity after the demise of the Soviet threat. Certainly the material presented in this chapter does not exhaust all available options for the post–Cold War era—they may obscure more than they illuminate. One of the great difficulties of the Cold War period was the lack of choice and viable alternatives to the stark dichotomies of capitalism versus communism and the U.S. versus the Soviet Union. If we really have moved beyond the Cold War, our range of options concerning the future of politics ought to be much wider than is conventionally assumed.

Endnotes

[1] An excellent history of the Cold War is by LaFeber (1985).

[2] Realism is a diverse school of International Relations theory. In this chapter, the Realism described is often referred to as "neorealism" or "structural realism" because it emphasizes the effects of international structures on interstate behaviour. This contrasts with earlier, classical realists who focused on individual states or human nature as the causes of peace and conflict (see Keohane, 1986).

Discussion Questions

1. In light of the continuing ideological differences between the United States and communist states such as Cuba, China, and North Korea, why do you think political scientists generally agree that the Cold War is over?

2. In your opinion, which vision of the post–Cold War era presented in this chapter is most compelling and why? Rank from most to least persuasive the ideas of Fukuyama, Barber, Kaplan, and Huntington.

3. Are cultural differences more important than ideological differences in explaining conflict within and among states today? Why or why not?

4. Is the so-called Western world really declining in influence in global politics as Huntington claims? If this is so, what are the implications?

References

Barber, Benjamin R. 1995. *Jihad Versus McWorld.* Toronto: Random House Ltd.

Brown, Chris. 1999. "History Ends, Worlds Collide," *Review of International Studies*, 25 (Special Issue): 41-57.

Dalby, Simon. 1996. "Reading Robert Kaplan's 'Coming Anarchy.'" *Ecumene*, 3, 4.

Doyle, Michael W. 1995. "Liberalism and the End of the Cold War," in Richard New Lebow and Thomas Risse-Kappen, eds., *International Relations Theory and the End of the Cold War,* New York: Columbia University Press: 85-108.

Fukuyama, Francis. 1989. "The End of History?" *The National Interest*, 16: 3-18.

Fukuyama, Francis. 1992. *The End of History and the Last Man.* New York: Avon Books.

Huntington, Samuel P. 1996. *The Clash of Civilizations and the Remaking of World Order.* New York: Simon and Schuster.

Kaplan, Robert D. 1994. "The Coming Anarchy." *The Atlantic Monthly*, 273, 2: 44-76.

Kaplan, Robert. D. 2000. *The Coming Anarchy: Shattering the Dreams of the Post Cold War World.* New York: Random House.

Keohane, Robert O. 1986. "Realism, Neorealism and the Study of World Politics," in Robert. O Keohane, ed., *Neorealism and its Critics.* New York: Columbia University Press: 1-26.

Krauthammer, Charles. 1991. "The Unipolar Moment." *Foreign Affairs*, 70, 1: 22-33.

Lafeber, Walter. 1985. *America, Russia and the Cold War.* Fourth Edition. New York: Alfred A. Knopf.

Mearsheimer, John J. 1990a. "Back to the Future: Instability in Europe After the Cold War," *International Security*, 15, 1: 5-56.

Mearsheimer, John J. 1990b. "Why We Will Soon Miss the Cold War," *The Atlantic Monthly*, 266, 2: 35-50.

Lebow, Richard Ned. 1999. "The Rise and Fall of the Cold War in Comparative Perspective," *Review of International Studies*, 25 (Special Issue): 21-39.

Richardson, James L. 1992. *Questions About a Post-Cold War International Order.* Working Paper 1992/3, Department of International Relations, Australian National University, Canberra.Russett, Bruce. 1993. *Grasping the Democratic Peace: Principles of a Post-Cold War World.* Princeton: Princeton University Press.

Waltz, Kenneth N. 1993. "The Emerging Structure of International Politics," *International Security*, 18: 44-79.

Further Readings

Charlton, Mark. ed. 1999. *International Relations in the Post-Cold War Era.* Second Edition. Toronto: ITP Nelson.

Ned Lebow, Richard and Thomas Risse-Kappen. eds. 1995. *International Relations Theory and The End of the Cold War.* New York: Columbia University Press.

New Lebow, Richard and Janice Gross Stein. 1994. *We All Lost the Cold War.* Princeton: Princeton University Press.

Hogan, Michael J. ed. 1993. *The End of the Cold War: Its Meaning and Implications.* Cambridge: Cambridge University Press.

Weblinks

John Mearsheimer's "Why We Will Soon Miss The Cold War" is posted online:
www.theatlantic.com/politics/foreign/mearsh.htm

A version of Robert Kaplan's "The Coming Anarchy" is posted online: .htm
www.theatlantic.com/politics/foreign/anarcf.htm

A version of Benjamin Barber's "McWorld versus Jihad" is posted online:
www.theatlantic.com/politics/foreign/barberf.htm

Cable News Network (CNN) Documentary Report on the Cold War:
www.cnn.com/SPECIALS/cold.war/

Woodrow Wilson International Center for Scholars, Cold War International History Project:
www. cwihp.si.edu/default.htm

The Cold War Museum:
www.coldwar.org/eng/index.htm

artizans.com

CHAPTER **22**

FOREIGN POLICY

Objectives

'You know what I have to say to people when I hear they're writing anti-war books?

'No. What do you say, Harrison Starr?'

'I say, 'Why don't you write an anti-glacier book instead?'

— Kurt Vonnegut, Jr.

This chapter on foreign policy analysis focuses our attention on intergovernmental relationships between states. The foreign policy approach to global politics engages the student in the study of the nature of states, nations, and nation-states; their interests and goals; and their capacity or power. It also introduces a discussion of powerful ideas such as nationalism and national interest. But the core of the study of foreign policy is defined by asking and answering the question of why states behave the way they do when interacting with their international environment. It can be argued that all states behave in essentially the same way depending on their power position within the international system. Here we see state behaviour as the result of the impact of the international system with little or no room for domestically driven foreign policy. Another way of explaining state behaviour, the one chosen here, is to emphasize the importance and individuality of the state and look within the state for explanation. Here the focus is on the political processes within the state that lead to defining the national interest and specifying the content of foreign

JURIS
LEJNIEKS

policy—the process of foreign policy decision making with its emphasis on human behaviour. At this level of explanation there are a number of competing models that deserve our attention: a model that emphasizes national character or political culture; one that focuses on the nature of governments; the dominant class approach that highlights the important influence of the corporate elite; and finally, a model that emphasizes the nature of state leadership, whether defined by personality traits or belief systems.

Introduction

What do the following international events have in common?

1. Almost 24 years after it detonated its only nuclear explosion, India conducts a series of underground nuclear tests to signal to its neighbours and the rest of the world that it is a declared nuclear power and potentially a great power. India's Prime Minister Atal Bihari Vajpayee, leader of a Hindu nationalist party, implies that the next step is to arm Indian missiles with nuclear warheads.

2. A very young Thai girl helps her government by donating U.S. dollars in response to the currency collapse in her country.

3. Kim Bong So, who sells crunchy silkworm larvae in Seoul, is concerned with the International Monetary Fund's $57 billion (U.S.) bailout of South Korea. He says that it is a "national humiliation" and compares the rescue to Japan's seizure and occupation of Korea in the early 1900s. "I feel so ashamed" (*New York Times,* Dec. 11, 1997, A1).

4. At the same time as Palestinian negotiators are attempting to reopen Middle East peace talks with the Israelis, thousands of Palestinian mourners demonstrate, chanting "Death to Israel" while they bury their dead from the latest bloody clashes (*New York Times,* Dec. 16, 2000, A1).

5. For three years, the Caterpillar Company has been lobbying the United States government in an attempt to receive government-sponsored loans for the sale of earth movers to the People's Republic of China.

All of the examples above suggest that the existence of the state and the idea of the nation-state are alive and well in the system of global politics. Despite the claims of the globalists that the state has been crippled in its ability to determine its own economic destiny and despite the *liberal internationalist* and *functionalist* arguments as to the increasing significance of international institutions, the nation-state remains the focus for people's identification at the global level. The examples above point to the pervasive role that states play in our daily lives.

1. The Indian prime minister claims that the capacity for a big bomb has given India a new measure of international power. He further states that the tests were motivated by a concern for national security and that "millions of Indians have viewed this occasion as the beginning of the rise of a strong and self-confident India" (*New York Times,* May 17, 1998, A10).

2/3. The currency collapse in Thailand, Indonesia, Malaysia, and South Korea was mainly about unsound banking practices (cronyism and lack of regard for risk) and their consequences. Since state revenues will be the eventual solution to the problem, the citizens will face tax increases to support failing banks. While there is personal fear about unemployment and lost savings in all four countries, in South Korea there is an added concern about national honour and independence related to their long domination by China and Japan. In Indonesia, ethnic Chinese have been the targets of civilian discontent and have had their shops looted or burned. There is also evidence that the government of Indonesia has instigated some of the riots.

4. Palestinian negotiators say that they would attend a peace summit only on the condition that Israel withdraw from occupied territories including East Jerusalem. The talks would focus on Arab East Jerusalem which Israel occupied in 1967 and later annexed, an action not recognized by the international community.

5. Dani Rodrik, an economist at Harvard, states that "we have to keep separate that the mobility of corporations has increased from the notion that we are living in a completely seamless integrated world market that gives national governments no bargaining power to set standards" (*New York Times*, April 30, 1998, C3).

All of these examples also show how the state, or the desire for a state, interacts with the international arena as defined by other states with similar interests.

States, Nations, and Nation-States

WHAT DO WE MEAN WHEN WE SPEAK OF STATES, NATIONS, AND NATION-STATES? The **state** is an internationally recognized legal entity. Only states can be members of the United Nations, for example. States are characterized by the existence of a definable territory, a population, and a government. The most important characteristic of states, however, is their continuing claim to sovereignty. This means that there is no higher authority than the state and that there is a legal equality between all states. While independence is thus a significant attribute of sovereignty we should not assume that sovereignty is absolute. A reality of the state system is that some states are so influenced by their powerful neighbours that absolute independence is a chimera. Think how often we refer to the influence of the United States on Canada and yet we consider Canada to be a sovereign state.

A *nation* is less easily defined. James Kellas defines **nation** as a "group of people who feel themselves to be a community bound together by ties of history, culture, and common ancestry" (Kellas, 1991, 2). The core of the idea of **nationalism** lies in the feeling of community. That feeling focuses on such common characteristics as race, religion, and language that are expressed in a common historical experience, a common set of fears and expectations, and the idea that there is a common future for the members of the group. Nationalism is the result of a deep-seated need for humans to be part of a continuous cultural and historical community set in its own territory. We express our identity through such a community. Michael Ignatieff writes that it is possible to think of nationalism as a kind of narcissism. He argues that a nationalist uses otherwise neutral facts about a people (language, culture, religion, and tradition) to generate a national self-consciousness that leads to the belief in the right of self-determination. "A nationalist, in other words, takes 'minor differences'—indifferent in themselves—and transforms them into major differences. For this purpose, traditions are invented, a glorious past is gilded and refurbished for public consumption, and a people who might not have thought of themselves as a people at all suddenly begin to dream of themselves as a nation" (Ignatieff, 1998, 51). Whether or not the differences are minor is, of course, debated. While students of global politics might consider the differences to be insignificant compared to the needs of mankind, ethnic and religious nationalists such as Israelis and Palestinians, carrying out a struggle for the future of East Jerusalem, see the differences as too great to overcome except through violence.

When former president of Russia, Boris Yeltsin, announced that "the main goal of our foreign policy is consistent promotion of Russia's national interests," he expressed an oft-stated theme in foreign policy—*national interest* (*New York Times,* Sept 19, 1994, A10). The idea of national interest, has been a key feature of foreign policy analysis despite the difficulty of defining its nature. **National interest** refers to the idea that individual states possess a core set of interests that are readily identifiable. Since we live in an anarchical world, national interest often stands in conflict with international interests or the competing interests of other states. If we do not pursue our own interests, no one will pursue them for us. There are, of course, difficulties with identifying the national interest of a state. One main criticism is that there is no objective national interest; there are merely multiple subjective interests claimed to be "the" national interest by politicians or analysts. In other words, there is no common interest that unifies a people. A second criticism of national interest rests on the argument that today there are global interests that transcend national interests, making the notion outmoded and short sighted. If we are only concerned with our short-term domestic needs and wants, we will pay the long-term penalty of global violence for having neglected the international environment or the poorer states of the world. Yet, despite these problems, *national interest* is a commonly used term in reference to foreign policy.

Our third concept is the idea of the *nation-state*. It follows from the discussion above, that the **nation-state** is the desired objective of a communal group to have their own state and to govern themselves independently. Of course, a fit between the idea of the nation and the state is an ideal that is hardly ever achieved in practice. The first problem is that most states contain two or more nations within their boundaries. Canada's problems with achieving stable political unity is a prime example of the lack of fit. Japan, on the other hand, is an example where the fit is close to being perfect, with the exception of a small group of people (Ainu) in the province of Hokkaido who are fast disappearing as a unique culture. The second problem of fit is that of a nation that overlaps more than one state. Members of the Kurdish nation, for example, are citizens of many different states, namely Turkey, Iran, Iraq, Syria, and Armenia, all of which refuse to recognize Kurdish independence. The Kurds are powerless to change their state-less condition without outside assistance. The states in which they reside have the power to maintain their existing boundaries and deny the creation of a Kurdish state. Two competing ideas of nationalism are competing with each other; the distinction being based on the unequal access to power.

Power and Foreign Policy

The plight of the Kurds suggests another important dimension of the study of global politics and foreign policy—that of power. Power has been the staple of the study of international relations and foreign policy in the twentieth century. Joseph Nye conveys an apt image when he suggests that power "is like the weather. Everyone talks about it, but few understand it" (Nye, 1990, 12). Political scientists either embrace the term as a core concept in the study of global politics, see it as increasingly peripheral in a globalized world, or reject the term altogether as useless in explaining state behaviour or any political behaviour. For those who embrace the concept, the range of definitions is broad indeed. It is defined as a means or an end, and sometimes both. It has been defined as the ability to influence or as the ability not to be influenced. Power is seen as objective (the sum total of power components that can be measured and compared) or subjective, whereby we can do none of those things. It has been argued that it is situational—that the ability to influence depends on the context of the political problem. As an alternative, power has been defined as absolute—as something that some states have more of than others. It is for good reason that we refer to the United States as a superpower and Canada as a middle-power. Those labels have policy implications.

Probably the most influential definition of power was articulated by Hans J. Morgenthau. "When we speak of power, we mean man's control over the minds and actions of other men" (Morgenthau, 1967, 26). Holsti's definition is simpler but is based on the same idea of control: power is "the general capacity of a state to control the behaviour of others" (Holsti, 1995, 118). Note that Holsti introduces the idea of capability. There is good reason for this. States cannot achieve their objectives, say the well-being of their citizens in an increasingly integrated world, without having some capacity for action. The U.S. decision to pursue the Vietnam War and later to withdraw from South Vietnam is an example of a state with enormous military and economic capabilities being unable to bring sufficient force to bear on the North Vietnamese. The U.S. possessed overwhelming military force (including atomic weapons) but the use of those ultimate weapons presented strategic problems abroad and domestic opposition that finally resulted in U.S. President Johnson's decision not to run again and the loss of the war. The will to pursue the war at all costs was not there. This suggests an important aspect of the concept of power. Not only must a state have the physical capability to pursue particular foreign policy goals, but its government and citizens must also have the will to pursue those objectives. Power, therefore, is not just a question of having a physical capability, but more broadly of having the ability to pursue one's objectives and to act in global politics. The execution of foreign policy goals depends on the extent of a state's capabilities and the will to use those capabilities.

Foreign policy is policy formulated and executed by states in order to influence other international actors in order to achieve the state's goals. In a very broad sense all states attempt to achieve the same objectives: security (including the continuation of the existence of the state), well-being for its citizens (especially economic well-being), and identity (the fit between state and nation). But how do the governments that act on behalf of the state go about attaining these objectives? Foreign policy involves a decision-making process that takes place within a complex environment that includes the world inside and outside national boundaries.

The decision-making process itself is a political process that can involve a few key political leaders, or more often, numerous officials each representing and seeking their own competing interests. Thus decision making can be a lengthy and cumbersome process. Generally, it is possible to identify and focus on the key participants in the process. The making of U.S. foreign policy normally involves the president and White House staff, officials from relevant departments such as State and Defence, and agencies like the Central Intelligence Agency or the Drug Enforcement Agency. The Canadian situation is not as complex, as the prime minister and cabinet generally act as the key foreign-policy decision makers.

So the study of foreign policy turns our attention to the state and its domestic setting—the individual, societal, and governmental influences on policy formulation. This approach rests on two premises. First, the state is a multifaceted and complex polity that varies in its structure and function. Second, these differences lead to variation in the responses to external demands. States with different domestic political processes respond to the challenges of the global system with different foreign policy strategies. These differences are explained by differing institutional arrangements (democratic or authoritarian), differing institutional processes (presidential or prime ministerial), and the relationship of the government to societal actors (such as public opinion, media, or interest groups). The state is not a simple reactive mechanism like a thermostat. Also, the decision-making process is not the rational process sometimes assumed by analysts. It is not a process characterized by perfect information, where problems are defined accurately, goals are clearly articulated and prioritized, and all policy alternatives are considered resulting in optimum results. Instead, policy is driven by routines established by bureaucracies (standard operating procedures), bargaining and negotiating between competing interests, or by group dynamics that can impede creativity and emphasize conformity. The three foreign policy approaches discussed below will illustrate some of the promises and problems of foreign policy analysis.

Approaches to Foreign Policy

The Middle Power Approach

In order to understand the middle-power approach to foreign policy analysis generally, and as it is applied to Canada specifically, we first need to look at the foreign policy models currently applied to the study of Canadian political behaviour. Canadian foreign policy (CFP) approaches can be categorized in a number of different ways but here we will put them into two broad classes.

First, there is the systemic approach, which essentially places CFP within a broad international context without necessarily claiming that CFP is determined by the nature of the international system. A number of different assumptions are possible here. One possibility is that Canada is a principal power; a state that stands at the pinnacle of the international hierarchy with other influential states. After all, Canada is a member of a number of elite state groupings such as the G7. On the other hand, a satellite or dependency framework sees Canada as subordinate to the United States in both economic and military security areas. Canada is simply a junior partner to a large and powerful U.S. which dominates and limits

Canadian policy options. A third alternative sees Canada as a state which, because of its mid-level capabilities, has evolved a distinctive middle-power world view. Because it cannot act effectively by itself, it co-operates with other like-minded states in multilateral institutional settings that promote broader international interests as opposed to narrow national interests. This CFP is characterized by such themes as peacekeeping, mediation, and internationalism, and is often labelled "middle-powermanship."

A second broad category emphasizes the domestic sources of foreign policy. Examples of this approach are Pratt's dominant class approach in which CFP is the handmaiden of the Canadian capitalist economy and the business class that dominates it (Black and Smith, 1993, 750). Putnam, on the other hand, suggests that with the increasing importance of economic issues resulting from the end of the Cold War, domestic influences are at least as important as international interests in international bargaining situations; what he calls a "two-level" game (Putnam, 1998, 428). In fisheries negotiations, for example, the Canadian federal government negotiates on two levels—with other states and with domestic constituencies such as the provinces. Putnam's is a "modified statist" model that recognizes the dominance of the state in foreign policy, with some impact from domestic interests.

But here we will focus on a middle-power approach, one that blends these two viewpoints, for a number of important analytical reasons. First, Canadian middle-power analysis has a longer history, and probably more adherents, than any of the other approaches to CFP. Second, the origin of middle-power CFP lies in the overt practice of foreign policy rather than in academic analysis. The middle-power approach begins with Canadian dissatisfaction with its lack of influence and status on World War II boards and in postwar institutional planning. Canadian policy makers understood that Canada is not a world power on the one hand, nor a minor power on the other. Third, the concept of middle-power behaviour does not have to be static. In fact, most analysts today recognize that changes in system dynamics modify middle-power behaviour. Fourth, the middle-power concept fits well with the realist idea of national interest that assumes that there is a collective state vision of the good although not everyone will agree as to how to achieve that good. And finally, the concept is amenable to bridging the gap between the domestic and the international approaches.

So what is a middle power? There are two basic approaches to the definition of a middle power. The first is to define a middle power in terms of its material and non-material capabilities. A middle-power is, as its name implies, a state with middle-level power usually defined by such criteria as Gross National Product (GNP) or GNP per capita. Here Canada is usually grouped with states such as Australia, New Zealand, Sweden, and Norway. This approach to middle-power behaviour begins with an empirical definition of middle powers and then proceeds to look at and define middle-power behaviour.

Second, as the Canadian middle-power model became more sophisticated, the definition of middle power became associated with particular foreign policy activities—peacekeeping, mediation, and participation in and support of international institutions (multilateralism). The problem with defining middle power this way is the inherent danger of circular reasoning: Canada is a peacekeeper because it is a middle power and conversely, Canada is a middle power because it is a peacekeeper. But having first established a particular level of capability, it is possible to move on to describe specific examples of middle-power behaviour as mentioned above.

In Canada there is an oft-cited pride in the normative behaviour associated with being a middle power. Canada behaves as a good international citizen with a sense of moral superiority in contrast to other states which are defined as either smaller "free riders" or egotistic superpowers (Cooper, 1997, 21). This moral superiority, more often than not, begins to fade under closer scrutiny as will be discussed later. But whether Canada is or is not a good international citizen, this argument has a significance that is little appreciated by CFP analysts. Middle-power identity is an important aspect of being a middle-power. Canadian foreign policy makers have made a good deal of Canada's support of multilateralism, promotion of the land mines treaty, and commitment to the preservation of the international environment. Canadians in turn, take great pride in Canada's international accomplishments, especially as a peacekeeper. The issue is not whether or not Canada's foreign policy is moral but that decision makers see themselves as supplying international norms and Canadians feel good about themselves. In fact, a study published in 1979 concluded that Canadians "like to be liked," and that Canada is a "sensible, responsible country, but not exceptionally influential in global affairs" (Lyon and Tomlin, 1979, 77). Acting like a Canadian was described as being generous, peace-promoting, internationalist, and responsible.

Despite the normative underpinnings of middle-power behaviour, the key point to remember is that middle-power origins rest on a "realpolitik" calculation of Canada's capabilities. During the discussions at Dumbarton Oaks and the San Francisco Conference, it became clear that Canada saw a role for itself that ran counter to the views of the larger powers. Canada, during the Second World War, was a major contributor to the Allied war effort against the Axis powers, and in any postwar institution realignment, Canada was not willing to be relegated to a secondary status along with all "smaller" states. Canadian policy makers of the day made the forceful argument that influence, status, and membership should be commensurate with levels of ability. Canada's war-time role was not as great as that of the world powers—the United States, Great Britain, and the Soviet Union—but neither was it as minor as the contributions of states such as Mexico. Canada, as a power of medium rank, felt it should have an influence that reflected that middle rank. One of the results of this strong stance by Canada (and Australia) was the acceptance, by the large powers, of the idea of non-permanent seats at the UN Security Council table. Canadian middle-power policy is rooted in the pragmatic view of influence reflecting levels of capability. The normative aspects of middle-power behaviour are a much later addition to these humble beginnings.

Two specific middle-power approaches deserve our attention because they have something to add to our understanding of middle powers and their policies. One study by Cranford Pratt focuses on the question of why the foreign policies of some middle powers are more responsive to humanitarian issues (humane internationalism) than those of most larger states. The answer to this question is found in the domestic political cultures of Western industrialized states whose citizens understand that they have an ethical obligation to others beyond their own borders. This sense of obligation is transferred to their governments and pursued as foreign policy (Black and Smith, 1993, 763).

A different approach is one applied by Robert Cox in a unique study entitled "Middlepowermanship, Japan, and the Future World Order" (Black and Smith, 1993, 764). The significant point made by Cox is that middle-power behaviour is more than an "idiosyncratic invention," in this case by Canadian policy makers (Black and Smith, 1993, 764). It is a generalized foreign-policy behaviour that has manifested itself in the past (historically), the present, and probably future world systems. Today, middle-power solutions to international disputes are characterized by the pursuit of multilateral activity and compromise. Cox emphasizes that possession of middle-power capabilities is a necessary, but not sufficient, condition to a disposition to play this role. In addition, the ability to stand a certain distance from involvement in major conflicts also involves some autonomy from major powers and "a commitment to . . . the facilitation of orderly change in the world system" (Black and Smith, 1993, 765). Middle-power policy, in some future world order, may look nothing like middle-power behaviour today.

Middle-power states and their foreign policies are defined by a number of characteristics. Middle-power states must have:

1. the ability to distance themselves from major conflicts;
2. a degree of autonomy from major powers that allows for meaningful foreign policy choices; and
3. the characteristics of a "democratic" power that is committed to orderly change in the global system.

Middle-power behaviour is characterized by a commitment to multilateralism to solve contentious international issues and by the pursuit of a higher good defined by the needs of international society, such as preservation of the environment or limiting ethnic violence within states. Finally, middle-power behaviour provides the state and its citizens with an identity as a significant international actor. As opposed to the negative identity of not being American, a middle-power identity is positive—one that is structured on international norms characterized by the promotion of civil society through multilateralism and peacekeeping. Canadians have a psychological investment in that identity. But ultimately it must be remembered that middle-power policies are not a guide to foreign-policy behaviour; instead, middle-power policies are pragmatic in the sense that they must be seen as a constraint and an opportunity for foreign policy action that may change with the times.

In fact, recent writing on CFP suggests that the era of "Pearsonian internationalism"—the formula for altruism, multinationalism, and liberal engagement in global affairs—may be coming to an end. Rioux and Hay, for example, argue that due to significant cut-backs in defence budgets, Canada has "limited means to project an international profile." Thus, Canada must practise a "selective internationalism," one more consistent with the post–Cold War era. Rioux and Hay endorse the view of several influential commentators that "prosperity and security can be ensured without devoting inordinate resources to foreign affairs" (Rioux and Hay, 1998–9, 57–8).

More interesting is the question of why CFP suffered in the 1990s. It is obvious that the end of the Cold War prompted a reevaluation of Canada's foreign policy. The end of the Cold War pointed to a new set of threats, needing new solutions, including ethnic conflict; disease;

environmental degradation; small arms proliferation; and transnational crime, including drug trafficking; all of which require new and different responses. Along with the international changes came two domestic concerns of successive Conservative and Liberal governments—the problem of budget deficits and the political question of the place of Quebec in Canadian confederation. Budget difficulties were felt especially strongly by the departments of Foreign Affairs and National Defence because they were easier fiscal and political targets than departments that were responsible for more immediate domestic programs. These attitudes were nicely expressed by the Canada 21 Council which published a controversial report in 1994 that stressed that the Cold War was indeed over. The Council recommended that Canada could now "make choices about its foreign policy based on comparative advantage and within constraints posed by domestic economic priorities" (Rioux and Hay, 1998–9, 66). It remains to be seen whether future Canadian governments will pursue an equally limited foreign policy or return to the earlier years of liberal international engagement.

The Two-Level Perspective

An alternative model of foreign policy decision making is the "two-level" model which rests on the idea that decision makers cope simultaneously with both domestic and international pressures (Putnam, 1998, 427). Foreign policy is not simply a response to outside pressures but is the result of a complex domestic foreign-policy process. First, foreign policy makers face multiple pressures from domestic political interests often in direct opposition to each other. Second, the impact of these domestic interests varies with the decision makers' choice of alternative political strategies. Third, the domestic side of the two-level model has a direct effect on the foreign policy of a state in that it influences both the strategy and the content of that policy (Hagan, 1995, 121).

An example of this type of analysis is Andrew Cooper's discussion of Canada's strategy leading to the Canada–Spain fish war of 1995 (Cooper, 1997). In March of that year, Canadian Fisheries and RCMP officers chased the Estai (a Spanish trawler) beyond Canada's 200 mile EEZ (Exclusive Economic Zone), forced it to stop by firing warning shots, and arrested and charged its captain with illegal fishing. What makes this a fascinating example is that the action flew in the face of Canada's traditional diplomatic reputation as a helpful fixer and ardent internationalist. "The whole episode . . . might be described as 'rock 'em, sock 'em' tactics (more commonly associated with Don Cherry's robust brand of hockey videos than with the tradition of quiet and skilful diplomacy)" (Cooper, 1997, 146).

What is important here, however, is not the gun-boat diplomacy exhibited by Canada, nor whether it was pursuing its national interest or promoting global governance (although these are important issues), but the nature of the bureaucratic struggle exhibited by two departments—the Department of Fisheries and Oceans, and the Department of Foreign Affairs and International Trade (DFAIT). Cooper calls it a textbook example of intergovernmental tension. Brian Tobin, upon assuming the Fisheries and Oceans portfolio after the federal election in 1993, was faced with the problem of depleting fish stocks and a very visible foreign fishery on the East Coast. For Fisheries and Oceans and Tobin, this was both a challenge and an opportunity. The challenge was that his department did not possess the fiscal resources to be able to cushion the decline of the East Coast fishery with the income replacement package of his predecessor, John Crosbie. The opportunity was provided by his powerful political position within the Chrétien government, his charismatic personality, and his political power base in Newfoundland.

The Department of Fisheries and Oceans also presented an opportunity; the Department had the reputation of a "loose cannon." Tobin played up the reputation with a more aggressive approach to over-fishing not only to pressure foreign fisheries, but also to differentiate his department from the traditional quiet diplomacy of DFAIT. Success against over-fishing would enhance the position of Fisheries and Oceans and detract from DFAIT's ability to carry out its diplomatic role in this context (Cooper, 1997, 157–159). Tobin's decision to challenge DFAIT on the over-fishing issue resulted from experiences by the Mulroney government. EAITC (External Affairs and International Trade Canada, the department's name from 1989 to 1993), under Barbara McDougall, had put a brake on Crosbie's efforts to make over-fishing a visibly successful issue at the 1992 Rio Conference. EAITC opposed any unilateral action against foreign fishing vessels. EAITC's concern was that any forceful action would be counter-productive to an international settlement of the issue. EAITC rejected unilateralism and coercion in favour of traditional Canadian diplomacy of negotiation and coalition building. Barbara McDougall said in March 1992 that "I don't believe in gunboat diplomacy . . . we believe in multilateralism" (Cooper, 1997, 160). While Canada was successful in getting the over-fishing issue on the agenda at the Rio Conference, and in the convening of a high seas conference in 1994, the effort had little direct impact on over-fishing and decreasing East Coast fish stocks.

Tobin was determined to pursue a different path. He decided to keep up the pressure with a plan that raised the level of confrontation both domestically and internationally. In May 1994, parliament passed amendments to the Coastal Fisheries Protection Act that gave greater domestic legitimacy to Canadian enforcement outside the 200-mile exclusive economic zone. The targets of this legislation were fishing vessels flying flags of convenience or no flags of any kind. A March 1995 amendment extended the legislation to other fishing vessels including Spanish ones. He called reflagged vessels "modern-day pirates" and said that Canada had the determination to halt over-fishing as an act of conservation. According to Tobin, DFAIT was emphasizing procedure instead of attempting to get results. Instead of low-key procedure, Oceans and Fisheries would get results by a policy that would be clear, forceful, and unilateral. DFAIT considered Tobin's "get tough" policy to be disruptive and potentially harmful to Canada.

The "get tough" approach did have a number of dangers. Canada invited international condemnation by deviating from its former international principles; a tactic which could have resulted in Canada's reputation suffering. It was also possible, of course, that Canada's actions would lead to an escalation of the conflict at an economic or political level, or by Spain sending vessels to the Grand Banks that could effectively support and defend Spanish fishing vessels. But rather than these possibilities, the fish war led to a compromise settlement negotiated by DFAIT who took over the negotiations with the European Union. In effect, this stage of the issue bypassed Tobin and his department. In good Canadian tradition, DFAIT worked out a compromise by giving up a portion of Canada's fish quota and allowed the

EU a transition period to adjust to a reduced catch for their vessels. Canada in turn, received a "set of firm and effective enforcement mechanisms" (Cooper, 1997, 166). Had Tobin succeeded? It was probably a draw between Tobin and DFAIT. Tobin's approach had certainly forced the issue into serious negotiations with the EU. DFAIT had its revenge by negotiating the final agreement and compromising on an important issue to East Coast fisheries interests—the number of fish that Canadians could catch. The fish war with Spain was over.

The Cognitive Approach

The third example of foreign-policy models does not focus on the decision-making process but rather on the leaders of states. The cognitive approach has the advantage of identifying the key decision makers of states, and of seeing them as creatively responding to their environment and shaping that environment rather than merely responding to external stimuli. Cognitive approaches assume that individuals rely on "existing beliefs and schema—that is, mental constructs that represent different clumps of knowledge about various facets of the environment—for interpreting information." (Rosati, 1995, 53). The beliefs and images of foreign policy decision makers may be partial or general, unconscious or conscious, carefully thought out or instinctive. Whatever the sources, all decision makers possess a set of images that control their foreign-policy behaviour (Brecher, Steinberg, and Stein, 1969, 86–87). Schema, or what can be called world views, make the external environment accessible by structuring and simplifying that environment. It is the basis by which decision makers interpret new information.

In this genre is a study by Janice Gross Stein, a Canadian academic at Toronto, who analyzed the role of Gorbachev in the ending of the Cold War (Stein, 1994). Essentially she argues that the shifts in Soviet foreign policy in the 1980s cannot be explained without reference to Gorbachev and his "new thinking" on the Soviet security issue. She argues that "through trial-and-error learning stimulated by failure, Gorbachev developed a new representation of the 'ill-structured security problem'" (Stein, 1994, 156). How did this new thinking deviate from long-standing Soviet strategic principles? Gorbachev repudiated the Marxist class-based interpretation of global politics in the nuclear era. Gorbachev came to believe that "all human values" must take precedence over the class struggle. He pointed to the interdependence of capitalism and socialism and argued that "security was mutual." The solution to the struggle of the past forty years would be political negotiation instead of the escalating arms race of the 1980s (Stein, 1994, 157). The most obvious reason that Gorbachev saw a need to reevaluate Soviet strategy was the absolute and relative decline of the Soviet economy in the context of the international system. Stein rejects the realist argument that it was a relative economic and military decline that prompted the reevaluation. Her reasoning is that other states, including the United States, also showed a decline in economic fortunes during the 1980s. It is true that there was not the kind of relative decline that is an important aspect of structural realist explanation. The answer to this is not to reject a relative decline argument, but to recognize that a decline in Soviet economic fortunes is more destabilizing in the long-term than the same decline in the United States. The Soviet economic infrastructure is significantly weaker than that of the U.S., so cannot sustain the same level of economic slowdown as can the United States. This is especially true when looking at military expenditures. While Soviet military expenditures did expand at the beginning of the 1980s, the real question is whether or not the Soviets could sustain that level of military expansion.

While we can dismiss a simple structuralist explanation of the shift in Soviet policy, we cannot dismiss Gorbachev's understanding of the structural shifts by saying that the systemic changes were open to differing interpretations. It could be that Gorbachev interpreted the potential for relative long-term decline quite accurately. While the same data about Soviet economic performance were available to Andropov and Chernenko, it was Gorbachev who was able to project the implications of that decline into the future.

There are several reasons to come to this conclusion. As Stein herself argues, Gorbachev was a more complex thinker than his predecessors. She argues this by analyzing Gorbachev's and Brezhnev's thinking about peaceful coexistence by comparing a Brezhnev speech from 1971 with a Gorbachev speech from 1986. She concludes that Gorbachev demonstrated "significantly greater complexity in the number of distinct arguments that he considered" (Stein, 1994, 167). Brezhnev, for example, "focused almost exclusively on the nuclear threat to survival. Gorbachev spoke of global threat to survival that emanated not only from nuclear weapons and the arms race but also from the fragility of the ecosystem, the widening gap between the rich and the poor, and the tight linkages across those dimensions" (168). In addition, Brezhnev argued that the Soviets could support revolutionary movements in the Third World while still pursuing peaceful coexistence. Gorbachev recognized the necessity for compromise, for trade-offs, where even superpowers accommodated each other's interests. Another argument in favour of a more perceptive leadership in the 1980s is that Gorbachev's background before he became General Secretary was in domestic economics, at the local level rather than international. It was because his experience was not in security affairs that Gorbachev was more perceptive regarding the downward drift of the Soviet economy.

But Stein's main emphasis is on Gorbachev's learning process. According to Eduard Shevernadze, Gorbachev, in the early 1980s, had very few ideas about the kind of foreign policy he wanted. He knew that he wanted to stop the Cold War, but not how to proceed to that end. In Stein's words, he "was a largely uncommitted thinker" on security issues (174). Much of his motivation resulted from the Soviet version of the Vietnam War. "The 'failure' in Afghanistan was a powerful incentive to learn. With no personal responsibility for the war, Gorbachev concluded . . . that it was a costly error" (175). Not only was he motivated, but he had an interest in acquiring the necessary knowledge. According to Dobrynin, the then-Soviet ambassador to the U.S., of all of the leaders of the Politburo, Gorbachev was the one who asked the most questions and showed a surprising interest in U.S. affairs. He also asked new questions, was open to a broader range of answers than his peers and was motivated to search for new ideas. Gorbachev rigorously approached sources that helped to crystallize his new thinking. He looked for ideas from specialists both inside and outside the government. After he became General Secretary, Gorbachev ordered critical studies on security issues from various government ministries, the Soviet versions of "think tanks," and journalists who had been critical of Soviet defence policy. Not only was a community of critical intellectuals available, they provided new ideas about security and made explicit some of the difficult trade-offs mentioned earlier (Stein,1994, 178).

Finally, Gorbachev learned by experimentation, by relating policy to action and then responding to the feedback. In 1985 he suspended Soviet countermeasures to INF deployment by NATO, established a moratorium on deployment of SS-20s, and proclaimed a unilateral moratorium on nuclear testing. Despite the initially slow response by the U.S., he persevered. It led to a personal relationship with U.S. President Ronald Reagan who talked of a chemistry that was close to friendship. The Cold War was soon over.

But no single explanation of leadership motivation and world view change can explain foreign policy change. In any analysis we must put decision makers into their institutional and policy-process setting. If individual learning is translated into policy change, "learning must be institutionalized in the central political agencies, a dominant political coalition must be committed to the new representations. . . . Institutions with a stake in the old order must be restaffed, reorganized, given new missions, or otherwise marginalized" (Stein, 1994, 180).

Summary

What do these examples and concepts tell us about the study of foreign policy? First, explaining a state's foreign policy is more than describing what states do. It is more than saying that Canada is a middle power that chooses to pursue foreign policy objectives through multilateral channels, or that Canada fought (although that term is probably too strong) and seemed to win a fish war with Spain, or that policy shifts by the Soviets led to the end of the Cold War. Students of foreign policy pursue the questions of why Canada is or is not multilateralist, or why Canada fought the fish war, or why the Cold War ended.

Second, as much as we speak about Canada doing this or the United States pursuing those goals, foreign policy is made and carried out by individuals (decision makers) who act on behalf of the state in an institutional context. We have to ask and answer questions such as: How do decision makers view the world? What is the impact of leaders' beliefs on foreign-policy processes and content? What influences help to define the leader's beliefs and their images of the world? What is the nature of the routine and non-routine decision-making process?

Third, we have to recognize that the beliefs, motivations, and world views of foreign policy decision makers are the same beliefs, motivations, and world views that allow us to define our environment and respond to it in a constructive manner. Viewing decision makers and group dynamics in this way helps students of foreign policy to better explain and appreciate foreign policy behaviour. World leaders are neither omniscient nor perfect in their understanding, nor even necessarily moral.

Fourth, much of our political tradition assumes the rationality of the individual. The study of foreign policy forces us to reevaluate that assumption and focus on why individuals do not apply optimum decision-making strategies or why individuals pursue individual political objectives that may or may not coincide with state interests.

Fifth, the study of foreign policy does not make predictions, as attractive as that idea is in our scientific environment. It is not even clear whether or not we can make forecasts (like we do with the weather) that are based upon probabilities as opposed to definable pre-conditions that force a particular outcome. Thus it is futile to talk of theory in the same sense as physicists or chemists use the term. In the study of foreign policy, we talk of models that help us to structure the events that we study in the same way that we built model airplanes when we were young, and gained a rudimentary understanding of flight as a result. The foreign policy process is the result of multiple influences or variables that call for multi-causal explanations. At the same time as we attempt to be rigorous about the study of foreign policy by generalizing about behaviour and its causes, that same research raises ever more questions and puzzles for us to explain and speculate about. The suggestion that in order to understand the events here we must take a realist perspective or liberal, or neo-Marxist, or feminist is doomed to failure.

Sixth, the decision-making approach is heavily data dependent. Unless we have access to data about the decision process or the world views of individuals, we can not plug data into our models. One reason why American foreign policy is so extensively studied is because we have the necessary data though access to documents and the revelations of participants.

Seventh, all three examples either explicitly or implicitly address the ultimate question of peace and conflict. While the three studies are interesting in their own right, they become more significant when seen in the context of why individuals, governments, and states pursue conflict instead of accommodation. The study of foreign policy takes on a vitality only insofar as it addresses that larger issue. We can argue that once we understand, we have the potential not to repeat the mistakes of history.

On the other hand, maybe Vonnegut is correct. Maybe attempting to stop conflict is like attempting to stop a glacier. Maybe conflict is inherent in our nature and our need for political association. When it comes to our attachment to nation-states we are forced to balance two mutually exclusive sets of ethical rules. On the one side is the rule—my country right or wrong. On the other side are the interests of the broader community, which often demand that we ignore or overthrow the nationalism rule, as Gorbachev appears to have done. This struggle is also expressed in the conflict between expediency and morality. Pragmatism argues that the ends justify the means, tempered by the normative nature of society underlying the acting state. Foreign policy more often than not takes the form of pragmatism or pursuit of the national interest.

Discussion Questions

1. Some argue that nationalism is an unchangeable, fundamental attitude based on emotional identifications (such as religion, language, race, and culture), while others suggest that globalization is slowly eroding national identification as it erodes state borders. How important is nationalism in an era of globalization?

2. Was the end of the Cold War inevitable? Why or why not?

3. Is it possible to identify a Canadian national interest?

4. Does the recent Canadian shift away from Pearsonian internationalism reflect changes in the international system (the end of the Cold War) or is it a reflection of changed domestic circumstances?

References

Black, David R. and Heather A. Smith. December, 1993. "Notable Exceptions? *New and Arrested Directions in Canadian Foreign Policy Literature, 26*:4, 745-774.

Brecher, Michael, Blema Steinberg, and Janice Stein. March, 1969. "A Framework for Research on Foreign Policy Behavior," *Journal of Conflict Resolution*, 13:1, 75–101.

Cooper, Andrew F. 1997. *Canadian Foreign Policy: Old Habits and New Directions*, Scarborough: Prentice-Hall.

Hagan, Joe D. 1995. "Domestic Political Explanations in the Analysis of Foreign Policy." In Laura Neak, Jeanne A.K. Hey and Patrick J. Haney, *Foreign Policy Analysis: Continuity and Change in its Second Generation*, Englewood Cliffs: Prentice-Hall.

Haney, Patrick J. 1995. "Structure and Process in the Analysis of Foreign Policy Crises." In Laura Neak, Jeanne A.K. Hey and Patrick J. Haney, *Foreign Policy Analysis: Continuity and Change in Second Generation*, Englewood Cliffs: Prentice-Hall.

Ignatieff, Michael. 1998. *The Warriors Honour: Ethnic War and the Modern Conscience*, Toronto: Viking.

Kellas, James G. 1991. *The Politics of Nationalism and Ethnicity*, New York: St. Martins'.

Morgenthau, Hans J. 1967. *Politics Among Nations: The Struggle for Power and Peace, 4th ed.* New York: Alfred A. Knopf.

Nye, Joseph S., Jr., "The Changing Nature of World Power*," Political Science Quarterly*, *105*, 177–192.

Putnam Robert D. Summer 1988. "Diplomacy and Domestic Politics: The Logic of Two-level Games," 42 *International Organization*, No. 3, 427–460.

Rioux, Jean-Francois and Robin Hay. Winter,1998-9. "Canadian Foreign Policy," *International Journal*, 57-75.

Smith, Steve, and Michael Clarke. 1985. *Foreign Policy Implementation*, London: George Allen & Unwin,

Stein, Janice Gross. Spring 1994. "Political Learning by Doing: Gorbachev as Uncommitted Thinker and Motivated Learner," 48 *International Organization*, No. 2, 155–183.

Further Readings

Brehony, Kevin J. 1999. *Nationalisms Old and New*, New York: St. Martin's Press, Inc.

Gray, Colin S. Spring, 1996. "The Continued Primacy of Geography," *Orbis*, 40:2, 247–259.

Guibernau, Montserrat. 1996. Nationalisms: The Nation-State and Nationalism in the Twentieth Century, Cambridge, UK: Polity Press.

James, Paul. 1996. *Nation Formation: Towards a Theory of Abstract Community*, London: SAGE Publications.

Rourke, John T., Ralph G. Carter & Mark A. Boyer. 1994. *Making American Foreign Policy*, Guilford, Conn.: Dushkin.

Rourke, John T. 1997. *International Politics: On the World Stage*, 6th ed. Dushkin/McGraw-Hill.

Weblinks

ASEAN Web
www.asean.or.id

Asia Gateway
www.asiagateway.com/index.html

Foreign Policy Association
www.fpa.org/links.html

International Network Information Center
www.inic.utexas.edu

Japan Ministry of Foreign Affairs
www.mofa.go.jp

Political Science RESOURCES
www.psr.keele.ac.uk/psr.htm

US Department of State
www.state.gov/index.html

World Wide Web Virtual Library
www.etown.edu/vl/

THE SOUTH IN GLOBAL PERSPECTIVES

Objectives

Political science, along with the larger family of social sciences, is currently paying close attention to the processes of globalization. Optimists express the hope that globalization will end underdevelopment and world poverty, closing the great socio-economic divides so apparent in the twentieth century. For nearly fifty years, the term *Third World* was synonymous with those divides and with the other inequalities of power in both international political and economic relations.

FRED JUDSON

As with all such inclusive terms in the social sciences, "Third World" suffered many inadequacies and attracted many justified criticisms. Nonetheless, it captured certain global realities of hierarchy and domination, and of socio-economic polarization and marginalization associated with modernity and especially with the post–World War II period of global history. In using the term *the South*, we can examine those same realities in the context of globalization and post–Cold War international relations. While the term embraces the dynamics of global and national transformations in economic, social, and political dimensions of human societies, it also underlines the enduring, even deepening divides in the global system. It also points to growing divides *within* virtually all the world's societies. The South, it is frequently said, doesn't end at national borders. In examining the South as a central element of today's world, this chapter maintains a historical-structural and critical approach, exploring global perspectives useful for understanding the world's political, economic, and social composition in the twenty-first century.

Introduction

A fundamental aspect of modernity has been development. The expansion of European colonial empires in the period between 1500 and 1800 was followed by the industrialization, urbanization, and administrative bureaucratization of nation-states; all of which are associated with modernity. The historical and social sciences, in general, have termed these processes **modernization**. They have sought to explain these processes, along with their stresses, contradictions, and consequences. It could be argued that the modern social sciences (particularly economics, sociology, and political science) began with that theorization and modelling of development. Classical liberal economic theory was concerned with the unprecedented economic growth and wealth-creation which accompanied capitalist industrialization. Political theory focused on the formation of the modern nation-state and the exercise of power within its varied institutional contexts, especially as that state had to manage the social transformations brought about by industrializing development.

Sociology evolved as a more specific examination of those social transformations and of the social structures of modernity, as manifested in Max Weber's concern about the destabilizing and potentially revolutionary effects of modernization. A powerful critical approach within more traditional political economy emerged in the latter half of the nineteenth century in the form of Marxism. It too concentrated on capitalist modernization, social transformation, and questions of power, theorizing the contradictions of modernity in a particular and militant way, both predicting and advocating *socialism* as the historic successor of capitalism. Marxism had repercussions in all of the social sciences and their agendas in relation to modernization and modernity.

The desire to understand, manage, and redirect the historical transformations of modernization thus predates the twentieth-century specifications of "Third World" and "underdevelopment." As many critics of development studies insisted in the closing decades of the twentieth century, the social sciences' approaches to modernization have been more Eurocentric and Western than global. Fundamental and complex ontological and political issues arise at this point, their treatment and resolution lying far beyond the scope and capacity of this chapter[1]. Ethical choices, value judgments, and considerations of justice also enter the arena when development, underdevelopment, modernization, and globalization are the subjects. Postmodern and postcolonial discourses, as well as feminist and environmentalist perspectives, have mounted articulate and concerted critiques of social science treatments of modernization and development/underdevelopment. The result is a richer and more diverse, but also more diffuse, chorus of voices on the subject.

Without directly representing the diverse voices, but remaining alert to them, we can consider the central features of a contemporary global social reality; *the South.* Patterns and experiences of modernization, development/underdevelopment, colonialism, capitalism, imperialism, international relations, and globalization have all had roles in shaping this South. The analysis offered here starts from the premise that the term *the South* captures the fundamental asymmetry or polarization that characterizes the contemporary human socio-economic condition at the planetary level. Acknowledging that theories of "the global development gap" are sharply divergent, we seek neither to synthesize nor resolve the various debates. The approach here is to construct a narrative of the South as a global historical structure of modernity. The narrative will develop a series of critical "global perspectives" as it proceeds.

The Emergence of a World System

THERE IS GENERAL AGREEMENT AMONG HISTORIANS THAT THE BROAD CONTOURS of a truly global system of political, economic, and social interactions among world populations were established around 1500 AD. Although there is incontrovertible evidence that earlier civilizations, such as China, had developed trade routes that reached westward, Wallerstein (1974) argues that there are two key factors that signal the emergence of a world system in the early sixteenth century. The first was the institutionalization of a global economy—permanent globe-circling trade and commercial networks—that regularly moved commodities between defined geographic spaces. This movement of goods (luxury items, primary commodities, and mass consumer goods) and the accumulation of wealth and power that attended it became "global" instead of "regional" or "inter-regional." The second feature of the emerging world system was the "state system." At this historical juncture centralized nation-states were in the process of becoming the dominant, if not the most numerous, form of organized political authority. States related to each other in an international political system as sovereign units responsible for their own interests and territorial integrity. Each of these two features of the world system had a complicated historical evolution. But both the world market and the international state system of the current era have their origins in the early sixteenth century.

Three other features of the modern world system are important to note. First, both the world market and the international state system are hierarchically structured: power is unevenly distributed. Clearly, some states are dominant and thus have the capacity to influence the world system and benefit disproportionately from it. A number of other states are dependent, weak, or barely functioning. Economic capacity and performance is just as concentrated and differentiated among societies. Both dimensions—states and the global market—can be understood as a pyramidal structure which houses a few states at the apex as global powers and the vast majority at the base as lesser states. A concentric-circle model with "core," "semi-periphery," and "periphery" labels also captures the essential hierarchy of both dimensions of the world system.

Second, economic and political power in the world system are concentrated in spatial or geographic centres. Europe (Spain, Holland, France, Britain) functioned as the earliest centres or "core" in the world system, followed in the twentieth century by the United States. During the Cold War, we came to use the spatial term *West* to denote the economic and political centres of the system. *East* was a term applied to the socialist parts of the world—the Soviet Union and its associated Eastern European states, China, and a loose, often isolated grouping of socialist-oriented states in Africa and Latin America. Today, given

FIGURE 23.1 *World-Systems Models*

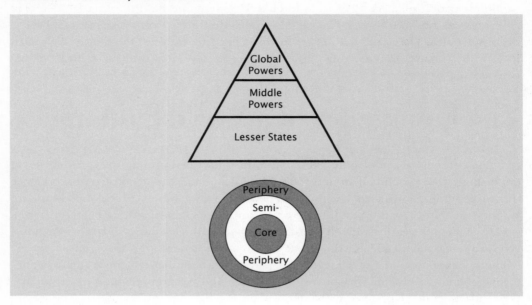

historical changes to the world system, we are more inclined to name the capitalist core *the North* rather than *the West*. This reflects the changes in the former Soviet Union, the end of the Cold War, and the rise of East Asian countries, especially Japan, in the world economy.

Third, the world system's dominant economic activity has been capitalist. Northern capitalism has been dominant in its commercial, financial, and production relations with the economies of the South since the sixteenth century. As a result, the North has been the economic centre of the world system and presents itself as the model of development that should be followed by the South. Of course, as critics of capitalism and the world system's asymmetry have long pointed out, the dominance of the capitalist North has included exploitation, violent coercion, and the concerted political shaping of global economic relations in its favour. Capitalism's dominance was challenged by a variety of socialist experiments in the twentieth century, but they were never close to establishing a strong alternative force within the world system, despite shaping the lives of some 40 percent of humanity.

Creating the South Historically

The Colonial Period (1500–1900)

Classic European colonialism (1500 to 1900) established many of the features of the world system. These features have come to be associated with the social science concepts of *underdevelopment*, *Third World*, and *South*. In this period, colonial powers such as France,

Great Britain, Portugal, and Spain claimed territories in the Americas, Africa, and Asia. Colonial representatives established local control over indigenous populations—often by violent means. Indigenous political and cultural authority was destroyed and resistance was crushed or co-opted. Whole populations were enslaved and economies restructured to serve the demands of metropolitan (European) economies and the social forces controlling them (merchant capital, financiers, monarchic state apparatuses). As a result of the colonial invasions, a new world system was created that subjected the colonized territories and peoples to a sovereign (European) power. Commerce was controlled by the colonial power and colonies emptied of their natural resources (and labour) to the benefit of the centre. The "centralization" of colonialism effectively created a world system in which the newly colonized territories were seen as "peripheral" to the core. The Americas represented perhaps the most complete "insertion" of non-European territories into the world system through colonialism. Indigenous populations faced catastrophic death tolls due to disease, wars of resistance, social disintegration, and population displacements during the first century of colonialism. The Americas, in turn, were transformed by the reorientation of agriculture and mining for export to European markets. Subjugated indigenous populations and imported slaves provided the labour force.

Such early "economic restructuring" created an **international division of labour** that characterized the world system for centuries. Core countries were able to colonize the periphery and thereby extract raw resources and use cheap or slave labour. For the Americas in particular, long-term export commodity cycles became the norm. A succession of profitable agricultural commodities controlled by merchant capitalism, produced by non-capitalist labour relations (usually slavery), and administered by colonial regimes were transported out of the country of origin. Some of the same patterns occurred, especially in later colonial territorial expansion and economic restructuring, in Asia and Africa. Metropolitan (European) state managers and merchant elites considered the colonies as sources of wealth for the core economies rather than as sites for autonomous economic development.

The world system's international division of labour established by classic colonialism was driven by the combination of two powerful social forces—merchant capital and absolutist monarchy. Together they promoted **mercantilism**, an economic philosophy that, among other things, granted certain European merchants the exclusive right to conduct commerce and trade in different parts of the world. Mercantilism also stressed the importance of the accumulation of gold and silver in state treasuries. The Americas, especially Mexico, Peru, and Bolivia, were the primary sources for gold and silver. Development strategy thus focused on mining and the collection of revenues from commerce and transportation to Europe. To a considerable degree, such wealth financed the dynastic and territorial wars among rival absolutist monarchies as well as the bureaucratization of monarchic states. It also has long been argued that wealth from the Americas was the primary source of capital for financing the industrial revolution and the transformation of European economies from merchant to industrial capitalism.

Classic colonialism thus established three of the central features of the South within the world system. First, it circled the globe with long-distance commercial networks drawing wealth to Europe. Second, colonialism forcefully and unevenly absorbed the South into an international division of labour designed to benefit the core economies. Finally, and significantly, colonialism extended European sovereignty across most of the geographic spaces we have known as the "Third World." These features have a historical—structural relationship with the set of conditions and processes termed *underdevelopment* and *development*. Colonialism's "inclusion" and "insertion" of the South in the world system delayed, prevented, obstructed, or distorted local development, while advancing economic development at the core. Moreover, colonialism promoted a definition of development that was self-referencing; that is, to be considered "developed" colonized peoples and spaces had to emulate the development values and path entrenched at the core. However, in reality, the result of colonialism, as we have already discussed, was to structure economies and societies of the South in such a way that they would always be subject to the control of the North.

Colonialism was both a North/South and centre/periphery dynamic as well as an arena of Great Power rivalry, conflict, and struggle for power and position within the newly forming state system. For the core states, geopolitics, military strategy, and economic competition merged and had no boundaries during the mercantilist period, as is demonstrated by the wars waged among European colonial powers on the territories, with the economies, and among the populations of the periphery. These expansionist urges, if anything, increased with the accelerated economic growth brought on by the expansion of industrial capitalism in the nineteenth century. By the close of the nineteenth century, there was a rush by Great Powers to accumulate more territories and exert increased economic, social, and political control over peripheral areas in Africa, South East Asia, and Latin America—a phenomenon generally referred to as **imperialism**.

The South in the Twentieth Century

In the first half of the twentieth century, three major economic and political events in the world system marked the beginning of the end of familiar patterns of colonialism and imperialism and the emergence of new patterns of interaction between the North and the South—the core and the periphery.

The first, World War I, significantly restructured Great Power relations by both destroying the Austro-Hungarian and Ottoman Empires and by placing the United States close to being first-among-equals. By the early 1920s Japan had assumed a place among the few Great Powers at the apex of the system and brought a new challenge to European colonial and imperialist interests in Asia and the Pacific. The war's destruction and debt burden (with the United States as the major creditor) weakened the major European colonial powers. Ironically, the war's outcome also presented new opportunities for the expansion of colonial and imperialist engagements with the South, namely in the Middle East. Britain and France "inherited" much of the region that had formerly constituted the Ottoman Empire. In effect, the North consolidated its grip on the Middle East's oil and delayed or diverted the various nationalist projects of the region which had been percolating in the dying days of the Ottoman Empire.

It is not easy to assess the impact of World War I on the South. Nonetheless, we can point to the emergence of articulate independence thinkers and organizations in a number of colonized South regions after the war: Southeast Asia (especially Vietnam), East and West Africa, North Africa and the Middle East, India, Indonesia, and the Phillipines. All were anti-colonial and called for "national self-determination." Somewhat paradoxically, both U.S. President Woodrow Wilson and Leninists in the USSR also engaged in anti-imperialist rhetoric. To some degree, the spectacle of European powers engaged in a brutal, industrialized and murderous "civil war," in which colonial troops took a significant if involuntary part, must have eroded some of the colonial mystique of invincibility and civilization. As well, even the distorted and extractive economic development of the colonies impelled by imperialism during the twenty-five years before the war generated local social forces (educated middle classes and professionals, organizations of workers) that expressed and organized struggles for independence. The efforts of colonial powers to modernize administration and economic activity, both before and after the war, often included conscious efforts to create "native" bureaucracies, managers, and intermediaries. Some of the latter became independence leaders.

The Great Depression of the 1930s was the second world system event centred in the North that had repercussions for the South. The colonial economies of South and Southeast Asia, the Middle East, and Africa foundered as the core economies rapidly contracted. The same mass unemployment, sharp curtailment of investment, devaluation of assets, financial system chaos, and collapse of purchase power that prevailed for nearly a decade in the North were repeated in the South and, indeed, were often much more severe. The Depression shook the colonial systems as nothing had before, helping to set in motion mass participation in independence movements, most notably with Mahatma Gandhi in India.

There had been prior global depressions but the "Great Depression" of the 1930s was the deepest the South had ever experienced. This was due to the closer integration of the South (via investments and financial, commercial, and productive activity) in the international division. In Latin America, national bourgeoisies, which had acquired more momentum in the 1900–1930 period, developed broad policy alternatives when their economies' position in the international division of labour was essentially trumped by the Depression. Global, meaning European and American, markets for Latin American agricultural and mineral commodities rapidly shrank. The means to purchase imported capital goods and manufactured mass consumer goods, not to speak of luxury items for the wealthy elites, also evaporated.

In response, a variety of nationalist, populist, corporatist, and semi-authoritarian regimes in Chile, Argentina, Uruguay, Brazil, and Mexico undertook what came to be called **import substitution industrialization** (ISI). This development strategy called for government subsidies and tariff protection of domestic industries producing mass consumer and capital goods, which would then be able to provide what formerly had been imported. In these countries, as well as in Cuba, Colombia, and the Dominican Republic, the state assumed an extended public sector role to provide infrastructure, energy, transportation, even heavy industry and consumer goods. The state also promoted cooperation among business and organized labour and expanded public employment, thus reinforcing a professional and urban middle class. Although currently ISI development policies are shunned by international financial institutions, in the 1950s to 1970s they fostered significant economic growth as measured by sustained GNP increases and by degrees of industrialization in Latin America. This period also saw advances in levels of literacy, life expectancy, and education, while infant mortality rates and malnutrition declined. Latin America's place in the global economy cannot be understood without acknowledging the historical importance of ISI.

World War II was the third world system event with great significance for the global construction of the South before 1950. This great bloodletting and destruction was essentially two wars—one among capitalist Great Powers (the liberal democracies of Britain, France, the United States, and "lesser" Allies) versus the fascist and authoritarian states of Germany, Japan, Italy, and "lesser" Axis states—and another between certain capitalist Great Powers (the Axis) and the Soviet Union. It was, thus, both an inter-imperialist conflict and a systemic conflict between capitalism and socialism that continued the confrontation of the West with Bolshevism at the end of World War I and prefigured the systemic conflict known as the Cold War. In the grand Asian theatre of the war, more than anywhere else, the inter-imperialist conflict was specifically about control of the South. At the same time, there was a systemic conflict waged for the independence and future development path of the colonized areas and China.

In a struggle for their very survival as states, European colonial powers involved, in varying degrees, their respective colonies. They drew upon the resources and wealth-extraction structures in these colonies. They used colonial troops more extensively than in World War I. And, in some cases, they granted some concessions and loosening of colonial rule. For the most part, however, the colonial powers, as evidenced by the behaviour of Britain, France, Belgium, and the Netherlands in their respective possessions, hardly considered the prospect of decolonization and independence. But the forces within colonial countries advocating independence, including those convinced of the necessity of socialist revolution, gathered strength during the war.

As in the postwar settlements and treaties between 1918 and 1922, the United States officially took an anti-colonial and anti-imperialist position at the end of the war. Even more than in World War I, the war-time propaganda and ideology of the victorious Allies was laden with the rhetoric of democracy and freedom. Hence, it was more than a little hypocritical for states that had fought to "liberate Europe from the Nazi/fascist yoke" and to "defeat Japanese militarism and its nefarious 'Greater East Asian Co-Prosperity Sphere'" to so determinedly return to their colonial possessions. The United States also deployed an anti-colonial rhetoric because it wished to end the colonial/imperial protectionisms, especially in the British and French empires, that denied it those markets. Just as Britain had come to advocate "free trade" at the height of its own commercial, industrial, and financial hegemony in the nineteenth century, a consolidated American globalism at the end of World War II championed its own version of "free trade."

In the end, World War II shaped the South/periphery as we came to know it in the second half of the twentieth century in four important ways. First, the war weakened the grip Europe's colonial powers had on their respective empires. Second, it strengthened the pro-independence forces within the colonies, with the portent of the South assuming greater agency in the world system. Third, as in World War I, a Marxist revolution took place in a "backward" capitalist social formation (China), sharply shifting both the balance of power and the panorama of economic development. Communist China, moreover, established a "Third World" Marxism as an alternative development path for the South.

Lastly, World War II created the global political structure of superpower bipolarity between the United States and the Soviet Union. In so doing, it signalled the end of the South as an arena of colonial empires and rivalry among a group of Great Powers. Instead, the South became an arena of contention in the Great Contest between the U.S. and the USSR. The remaining colonies, soon to gain independence in the 1960s, as well as already-independent states in the South would become the critical arena in the battle for global supremacy waged by the forces of capitalism and communism in the post–World War II era.

Discourses and Imagery of the "Third World"

LOGICALLY, PRIOR TO A "THIRD WORLD," THERE MUST BE FIRST AND SECOND Worlds. "Third World" very generally captured, at least in the North's cultural understandings of modernity and global realities, the "development gap"—the marginalization and structural weakness of the South in the world system's political and economic dimensions. Implicit was the consideration of First and Second Worlds as more advanced and more empowered. But the discursive origins of the term are in the Cold War as a bipolar and contentious global structure. The Third World was the "rest of the world"—those areas not explicitly included in that structure and its alliance systems. These areas were, from this perspective, objects of superpower agency, areas to be won or lost, in which to exercise influence or hegemony, and in which to be prevented from so doing.

For certain political and intellectual elites within a South configured in Cold War discourses as the Third World, such a position between East and West (or between First and Second Worlds) was a positive and active location. It lent peoples and states of the South a certain leverage as subjects and agents within the world system. As the Cold War hardened into its classic structures (economic militarization of superpowers, balance of nuclear terror, alliance systems, "proxy wars" and "client states" in the Third World), this perspective developed as *non-alignment*. **Non-alignment** is generally associated with neutrality, promotion of Third World cooperation in the United Nations, and disarmament. In 1955 at Bandung, Indonesia, outstanding Third World figures (Nehru of India, Sukarno of Indonesia, Nasser of Egypt, and Tito of Yugoslavia) met to found the Non-Aligned Movement. Very broadly, the non-alignment perspective contested the very idea of a bipolar world and especially the notion that the South was "available" to be aligned behind one superpower or the other.

Non-alignment was closely associated with anti-colonialism and the movements for independence that surged in the South after World War II. It was a sentiment shared in an extremely diverse South, a kind of common front that rejected the Cold War content of the term "Third World." The message there was that in lumping together such a diversity of peoples, who were then and remain today by far the majority of the world's population, under the same category the First and Second Worlds were indicating that they saw them as inferior and secondary in importance. In order to contrast the "othering" and the racism embedded in the term, "Third World" was proactively grasped by many in the South. In the post-World War II period of decolonization and wars of national liberation, there was a considerable optimism and pride in the South's agency within the world system. To be "Third World" meant liberation from colonialism and a brighter and independent future of equality and sovereignty. In this sense, "Third World" was empowering.

In the South's appropriation of the term "Third World," there were also some very strong feelings of resentment, rebellion, rage, and even hatred. These were expressed, for example, in the classic *The Wretched of the Earth* (1965) by the Martinique (French colonial possession in the Caribbean) psychiatrist Frantz Fanon. Writing about the ferocious Algerian struggle for independence (1956–1962) from France, but in reference to many national liberation struggles in the South, Fanon sought to understand and channel the visceral anti-colonial passion and hatred of the colonial oppressor not only into militant and implacable struggle for liberation, but also into a positive Third World redirection of humanity and the world system: "Europe undertook the leadership of the world with ardour, cynicism and violence. Let us decide not to imitate Europe, let us combine our muscles and our brains in a new direction."

It has been a reality of our hierarchical world system that cultural discourses have been dominated by the powerful. Hence, whatever the North may know or appreciate about the empowerment and positive appropriation of the designation "Third World" in the South, what has prevailed in both the North and the South are the more negative connotations. In the imagery of the South as Third World it is often identified, especially in popular culture and the media, as subject to constant upheavals and revolutions, instability, and brutality. It is also the realm of horrors. As Eleanor O'Donnell writes: "The accepted image is that in the Third World there is only misery; the land is parched and good for nothing, there is no food to eat, diseased children grow up in filth, poverty and illiteracy—the places we imagine are grossly overpopulated, and the brutality of daily life is so commonplace that only the most unbelievable of atrocities become significant" (1991, 277–78).

In the West's popular acknowledgement of uneven development and its global divides of North/South, the South is also depicted as that part of the world that has to "catch up"; and it has to do so by following the paths of the North. It has been the North that has trodden and proven the necessary paths of modernization and development. In the worst expressions of such Third World imagery and in a backlash against post-colonial thought emerging from the South, the Third World is deemed ungrateful and not properly appreciative of the civilization brought to it by colonialism or of the maps of modernization and development the West/North have provided it.

Whose Development and Modernization?

THE MODERNITY OF THE WORLD SYSTEM AFTER WORLD WAR II STRUCTURED the South as Third World, as we have seen, by inserting it into superpower bipolarity and making it an arena of geopolitical and ideological contention. It also did so with the extension, over several decades, of the "modernized" sovereign state system to almost all of the colonized areas of the world. This occurred either via decolonization—the formal agency of the North in relinquishing direct control—or through prolonged wars of national liberation. The economic structuring of the South in postwar modernity is perhaps what has most fundamentally filled out its contemporary identity within the world system. The expression "combined and uneven development" can be updated to express that structuring.

It is an old cliché that "the world doesn't stand still for anybody." The predicament for much of the South over the past fifty years has been that they were supposed to "catch up" with national economic development projects in an era in which, arguably, such projects were concluding in the North. The very viability of such projects became more and more questionable as capitalist accumulation cycles, particularly those with high technological content, accelerated and became more global. At the same time, the stakes and penalties in the economic development sweepstakes became higher and more severe. Failures and reversals could immediately widen the "development gap," since competition for niches in the global circuits of finance, investment, production, and market access sharpened the difference between winners and losers. The market, seemingly, has been a harsh taskmaster as well as a generous rewarder over the last half-century.

There is no doubt that capitalism staged a tremendous come-back in the decades after World War II, with spectacular growth in global production, international trade, and wealth-creation. And the South had a variety of roles within that historic long wave of expansion, ranging from "dependent development" and ISI to peripheral socialist accumulation and the **export-oriented industrialization** (**EOI**) of Asian newly-industrialized countries (NICs). Sites of production for the global market have historically been part of the South since its insertion into the world system, but they proliferated at a much greater rate during the postwar expansion of global capitalism. And while we should be cautious about generalizing across well over one hundred social formations that constitute the modern South, we can still acknowledge the hierarchical structuring of the wealth created by processes of production.

In the 1950s and 1960s, numerous voices noted the transfer of wealth from South to North through a variety of mechanisms—unequal trade arrangements, multinational corporations' pricing practices, differential interest rates in global finance, debt burdens, appropriation of pre-capitalist labour, local elites' corruption and looting of national resources, and capital flight, among others.[2] They also noted that international financial institutions (IFIs), stock markets, commodity cartels, and monopoly structures of global capitalism tilted the dynamics of the market towards the powerful actors of the North, especially banks and corporations. Together, these economic agents of the North institutionalized what Pierre Jalée (1968), using United Nations trade and investment statistics for the 1950s and early 1960s, dramatically termed "the pillage of the Third World"—consistent and very large flows of wealth from the South to the North. Dependency and "unequal exchange" theorists developed their arguments in the 1960s and 1970s, and they became the basis for campaigns by the Non-Aligned Movement and the Group of 77, a "Third World Coalition" in the United Nations General Assembly, for a New International Economic Order (NIEO).[3] Similar arguments and campaigns for a debt moratorium arose in the 1980s at the height of the debt crisis. In the face of these wealth flows and widening development gaps, both radical and moderate voices in the South and North called for "delinking"of the South's economies from global capitalism.

What was going on? We might well ask. Does the widening development gap of the past fifty years mean that in global capitalism's competitive environment there are bound to be more losers than winners? Are there really so many peoples and countries that are just incompetent, so backward and incapable of seizing opportunities presented by insertion in the world market? Was it colonialism's fault for not more adequately preparing the South for economic modernity? Is the problem climatological, geographic, locational, or cultural? Such questions indicate what a minefield of issues, debates, perspectives, and conflicting explanations the field of development theory is.

To simplify very crudely, there are two counterposed notions of development within modernity. First, there is what is usually called *the modernization model.* It assumes a progressive upward path of all human societies from the simple and traditional, largely agrarian beginnings (underdevelopment) towards the complex, secular, industrialized, high-consumption societies. In the Western/Northern social science traditions of later modernity, it is assumed that such a goal is natural, inevitable, desirable and, of course, possible. To be Third World/South, then, is not to have arrived at that state yet, but to be at various "stages of growth," to echo the famous title of United States modernization theorist Walt Rostow's (1962) book, en route to that goal. To be in the South is to have the historical task of confronting and overcoming the various obstacles on the "pathways from the periphery."[4] The goal is to leave behind the designation "Third World" or "South," to move, in the United Nations economic agencies' language, from "underdeveloped" to "developing" to "developed."

The second and opposing notion, embodied in world systems and dependency theories and in Marxism very generally, holds that underdevelopment is not a primary condition of all human societies, but that it is a condition created by domination. More specifically, underdevelopment is the product of the historical development of capitalism as a world order, with colonialism and imperialism being logical elements within such an order. From this perspective, "development" is a two-edged historical sword of transformation, an uneven and dialectical set of global experiences. Hence it is understandable that many post-colonial and critical voices would decry "development" as the hegemonic discourse and skewed accumulation dynamic of the powerful in the world order[5]. Development, as John Isbister suggests (1998), has been "promises unkept" for hundreds of millions, even billions of human beings in the twentieth-century South.

The South Today

The Making and Unmaking of the Third World

It would be misleading to suggest that the "debate" about the reasons and solutions for underdevelopment is over. In fact, as the processes of **globalization** intensify, it is likely that the debate will become increasingly important for social scientists, governments, and activists alike. However, as tentative as current processes are, it is important to sketch out the recent history of the South as it has emerged from experiences of decolonization and intensified insertion in the global economy. For our purposes, four events and processes have been key in forming the South as we see it today. These are: decolonization and independence; revolution; the expansion and acceleration of global accumulation; and, differentiation among the countries of the South.

Decolonization and Independence

The wave of decolonizations in the 1950s and 1960s added scores of sovereign states to the world system, and they quickly made their presence felt, especially in the United Nations. During these years there was an epochal sense that the South was "coming of age." Humanity's *majority* was finally enfranchised and the South's societies were emerging to take their place alongside the established and developed nation-states of the North. The nation-state form of governance was little questioned, and the political leaderships of the newly independent countries expected to shape citizenship, economic development, and political institutions by mobilizing nationalist sentiments. Where there had been little "national consciousness" under colonialism the new states expected that nationalist independence would create a shared national identity and social cohesion.

These new and "late" nationalisms were as contradictory and artificial as many of the borders inherited from arbitrary colonial boundaries. Many new countries have had what must be recognized as spectacular successes in creating a national citizenship from multi-lingual, multi-cultural, and multi-ethnic populations. Others have been either tragic failures or have suffered from very low levels of government legitimacy and effectiveness. Such fraught nationalisms have often been accompanied by problematic authority. Many formal democracies in newly independent African, Asian, and Middle Eastern states were soon transformed into authoritarian regimes (personal, single-party, or military dictatorships).

Whether authoritarian or democratic, institutions and practices of governance often have had to tolerate or encourage "pre-colonial" forms of local and national authority (religion, caste, clan, tribe, monarchy). Establishing and administering what would seem routine practices in much of the North (generally effective tax collection, norms of regulation, expectations of the citizenry for common standards and governance throughout the national territory, low levels of corruption, equality before the law, among others) have been difficult to realize. That many countries in the South are ethnically, culturally, and linguistically much more complex and diverse than those in the North is part of the explanation. That newly independent states in the South were faced with "more to do, with much less" infrastructure and resources is another part. That sovereignty, economy, society, and political institutions were fragile created a preoccupation that Caroline Thomas (1987) termed "the search for security." Such, it might be said, are the conditions and realities of underdevelopment.

Revolution

Modernization theory and development studies were essentially "invented" to consider the multi-faceted problems faced by the independent countries, new and old, in the so-called Third World. Development paradigms imported from the West advocated calculated, incremental, and non-violent change. But it was often revolution that presented itself in much of the South in the second half of the twentieth century. Broadly, Third World revolutions of the period had three elements, which combined differently in the many manifestations in Asia, Africa, and Latin America. First, anti-colonial struggles for independence and sovereignty were identifiably nationalist and anti-imperialist. Second, these struggles, and those elsewhere against dictatorial and authoritarian regimes, were democratic in the sense that they sought popular empowerment, much as had the bourgeois democratic revolutions of core social formations in the eighteenth and nineteenth centuries. Third, many revolutionary experiences had a strongly socialist character, emphasizing anti-capitalist perspectives and the pursuit of mass-oriented development strategies as alternatives to prevalent elite and externally oriented patterns.

The Cold War structures of the world system and the institutionalized confrontation of capitalism and socialism constituted a crucial environment for the dozens of revolutionary experiences in the South. To attribute revolutionary surges to the machinations of the Soviet Union or a more abstract "international communist conspiracy" appears unfounded in the aftermath of the Cold War and belittles the struggles and aspirations of the peoples of the South. It also diminishes the tremendous diversity of social forces where revolutionary experiences occurred and their specific responses to uneven development and underdevelopment. From the world system and historical-structural perspectives, then, it was dependent, uneven, extractive and "underdeveloping" patterns of economic activity in the South that were the underlying causes of revolutions.

Global Economic Expansion

As in all previous periods of capitalist economic expansion within national economies and global regimes of accumulation, the great post–World War II growth cycle was uneven across and within the North and South and across time. As Satoshi Ikeda (1996, 38) expresses it, "the overall productive capacity of the world economy expanded, allowing an unprecedented increase in world production . . . [but this was] not linear over time, nor was its spatial distribution uniform." Within the prevailing international division of labour, the South's inclusion in this expansion had three expressions: the intensification and modernization of raw materials production, either agricultural or mineral; significant industrialization, in both traditional heavy industrial products and in consumer goods; and increased marginalization (much of Africa) or socialist de-linking (China, Vietnam, North Korea, Ethiopia, etc.) from the capitalist global market.

Of the many dynamics and episodes of the South's experience during global economic expansion in the second half of the twentieth century, we can highlight the emergence of Asian newly developing countries (NICs); an intensified financial integration of the South via direct and portfolio investment as well as loans from the North; significant industrialization in Latin America, both for import substitution and for export. In world systems terms, global economic expansion structured much of the South as "semi-periphery" (crudely defined as "developing" rather than "underdeveloped") while maintaining the rest as "periphery." Global economic expansion in the South was both disintegrative and integrative. As Samir Amin writes, "this period was simultaneously . . . one of the progressive dismantling of autocentric national production systems and their recomposition as constitutive elements of an integrated world production system" (1997, 2).

Differentiation

The discourses of Cold War bipolarity, which cast the Third World as the arena of superpower contention, discouraged neutrality and thus divided the South into broad "spheres of influence." Revolutionary and counter-revolutionary episodes, with imperialist interventions and authoritarian regimes, also produced differentiations. But it was global economic expansion and its varied experiences in the South that produced the most marked differentiations, which are now integral characteristics of the current era. The dual processes of integration and marginalization produced, on the one hand, high-income global production sites such as Singapore and the EOI "Asian tigers" so celebrated until the 1997 financial crises and recessions. Within both Asia and Latin America, a minority of industrialized and industrializing economies have distanced themselves from their regional neighbours, as was symbolically recognized by Mexico and Korea becoming OECD (Organization of Economic Cooperation and Development, a grouping of "developed countries") members. On the other hand, many more countries in the South have "regressed," as measured by economic and social indicators. With such differences, let alone all the other problems with the term, it is no wonder that Susan George could write, more than a decade ago: "I am fully aware that 'Third World' is no longer a valid concept, if indeed it ever was" (George, 1988, xiii).

The South in the Twenty-First Century

CHANGE IS THE CONSTANT IN THIS CHAPTER'S HISTORICAL-STRUCTURAL NARRATIVES of the South within the world system. Given the hierarchy and inequality of the system, it is not surprising that the stress has been on change from "outside," though clearly internal dynamics have also structured change. The South's contemporary realities continue to be driven by the latest organization of the world system through the multiple processes of globalization. Thus, it is important to briefly examine the economic, political, and social conditions that define and will continue to challenge the South.

The Economic: Debt, Market, and Accumulation

Canadian economist Michel Chossudovsky uses World Bank data to draw a stark portrait of the South's position in the global and globalizing economy of the 1990s: "By [2000], the world population will be over six billion of which five billion will be living in poor countries." Over half the world's population in 1995 received only 5 percent of world income, at under $400 U.S. per capita, while 15 percent of the world's population disposed of nearly 80 percent of world income, at just over $23 000 U.S. Some 20 percent of the world's population living in "middle-income Third World" countries, such as Mexico, drew about 12 percent of world income, at $2400 U.S. (1997, 38–39). Such comparative statistics are impressive, but don't begin to capture realities of poverty or the continuing impoverishment inherent to economic globalization, in both the South and the North.

The development gap has clearly increased and global socio-economic polarization is accelerating, notwithstanding "islands of success" within the South. But even in cases where macro-economic indicators seem to show success, it is often accompanied by a more unequal income distribution structure and marked declines in wages, per capita income, and purchase power for the particular country's majority.

For "free market" enthusiasts, some of these problems of expanding poverty during the current era of intensifying globalization are attributed to poor management by governments or incomplete implementation of the reforms required by programs of structural adjustment. The result is a failure to achieve full competitiveness in an exacting global market. Other analysts argue that the legacies of ISI, economic nationalism, protectionism, and Keynesian policies between the 1930s and 1980s all over the South are deeply entrenched and that it will take a generation or more for the benefits of deregulation, privatization, and liberalization to be apparent.

The broad point of agreement shared by supporters and critics of free-market globalization as it concerns the South is that the dominant dynamic of capitalist accumulation is indeed global. For critics, the debt-cycle and restructuring are coercive instruments for global capitalism's targeting of the South as its "solution" to a prolonged crisis of accumulation. Hence, globalization's division of labour casts the South in a triple role: the cheap-labour manufacturer and source of raw materials; a place to invest when conditions are not ripe in the North; and the market for the North's goods, from technology to consumer products. But a number of critics point out the limits of this logic. Continuing to produce goods for sale at "First World prices" and "Third World wages" sooner or later leaves fewer consumers. It becomes, structurally, an over-supply and under-demand situation that increases competition between firms as well as jurisdictions (countries, regions, cities) in the search for markets and investors. At its worst, it becomes "the race to the bottom" in the South, as capital leaps from one country to another in search of the lowest wages and the fewest regulations on their activities.

The Political: The State of the South

Globalization has transformed public policy environments for states in both the North and the South by narrowing their latitude for action and diminishing sovereignty. At the same time, the stresses of modernization and underdevelopment have increased social demands on states of the South. Structural adjustment and its externally required conditionalities have placed states in a world system dependency structure somewhat distinct from earlier eras. In a number of cases, states of the South have in fact collapsed, in effect leaving territories and populations without effective governance. In others, states are occupied by World Bank, International Monetary Fund and core state functionaries, becoming "hybrid and transnationalized regimes of accumulation and governance."[6] Another potential "management solution" for states of the South is regionalization. So far, such solutions primarily imply economic association for the ease of market dynamics and the logic of competitiveness, rather than for political governance.

Such conditions of the state and governance in the South are not absolute, but rather matters of degree. The same can be said for the global trend of democratization. Few would lament the disappearance of the authoritarian regimes and dictatorships prevalent in much of the South in the latter half of the twentieth century, but formal democracy accompanied by the globalization of poverty may make little material difference to billions. As Borón (1999) argues, as states "decay" and democracy becomes "decadent," as capital effectively rules and democratic institutions fall under the principle of "all the democracy that money can buy," globalization brings a new crisis of political authority to the South. In response, social disintegration and citizen apathy are as likely an outcome as "the strengthening of civil society" or the proliferation of viable local and regional "democratic governance alternatives." While a new wave of dictatorships and authoritarian regimes is not necessarily on the agenda for the South, they remain possibilities embedded in the contradictions and deprivations of the current era of globalization.

The Social: Violence and its Governance

With the end of the Cold War, some argue that a truly global governance is taking shape as an epochal replacement of bipolarity and unchallenged state sovereignty. However, while violence between major powers seems unlikely today, violence between states is considered to be a problem of the South (the Balkans notwithstanding). The North has responded in several ways. When a significant shift in a regional balance of power might result, as in Iraq's invasion of Kuwait in 1991 or in the prior Iran–Iraq War, either direct military intervention (the U.S.-led Gulf War against Iraq) or massive arming/finance of one side (Iraq was backed against the threat of Iran) is a likely response. Direct intervention is most likely when a strategic resource, such as oil, is at stake. But with cases of "low-intensity conflict" within "collapsed states" (for example, Somalia and Sierra Leone) or in areas of little material interest for the North (Rwanda, Sudan, Afghanistan), there may be no intervention. Thirdly, there may be approval if a regional hegemon (Nigeria, for example, in West Africa) or surrounding states (Uganda, Angola, Zimbabwe, Rwanda, Namibia, in the case of Congo) sends troops to regional conflict zones.

Violence in our global era, as Mary Kaldor (1999) perceptively writes, has actually proliferated, increasingly within states rather than between them. Some of it arises from the privatization and enfranchisement of security forces, some from the breakdown of state authority and from conflicts between powerful economic interests rather than states. As well, there is a tremendous commerce in arms that enables small groups within states and beyond states (mercenaries, criminal organizations, terrorists, outlawed political organizations) to engage in violence. Other actual and potential sources of violence that are being explored by serious scholarship are cultural and civilizational differences. The stresses of a North-dominated globalization, on the one hand, contribute to identity-based backlash (ethnic, religious, cultural) and rejection within the South, producing confrontations neatly encapsulated in popular language as "Jihad versus McWorld" (Barber, 1995). On the other hand, as states decay or are diminished by the cultural and economic forces of globalization, underlying "civilizations" (defined in a variety of ways) become the entities comprising global political encounters. Hence, present and future conflict and violence may reflect "the clash of civilizations" (Huntington, 1997).

The South and Social Globality

FROM THE HISTORICAL-STRUCTURAL AND CRITICAL PERSPECTIVES DEPLOYED IN this chapter, the South's globalization within the world system is primarily the extension of capitalism's accumulation dynamics and contradictions to its social formations. Hence, the social impacts are predictable and linked to the same patterns in the North, producing a social globality. Since the social and economic forces of globalization are trans-national, their effects are as well. Very broadly, those effects are an advancing differentiation within and between the South's social formations. Integration of some social strata with their counterparts in the North (high consumption, entrepreneurial, and technical elites) proceeds alongside the socio-economic marginalization of others—the enlarged "informal" and economically disenfranchised strata, the impoverishment of large swathes of the middle class, the army of under- and unemployed, the landless rural populations, and the urban poor majority. The result is the polarization and fragmentation of national social formations.

The optimistic view of such social globalization in the South is that it may well constitute a restructured civil society which becomes a protagonist for democratization and resistance, which engages in transnational linkages, and which eventually can make a bid for political power on the basis of its eclectic social pluralism. As such, the South, as the majority, is a crucial player in the formation of a "global civil society."[7] In a more militant interpretation of such social globality, Samir Amin (1997, 148–152) advocates the intellectual and political "reconstruction of the social power of the popular classes" of the South, since otherwise "the cycle of spontaneous and inadequate reactions from peoples crushed by the new worldwide polarization is bound to continue, and the energies generated will just as surely be harnessed by the dominant regimes in their determination to manage the crisis." Amin is concerned that "various centrifugal ethnic and communal forces, the nostalgic cultural revivalists, and especially the religious antiquarians active these days" will gain the upper hand. In the absence of cross-class and regional coalitions capable of reconstructing popular development projects, "the ordinary classes try to cope as best they can, sometimes coming up with creative feats in their daily struggles for survival [but] the crisis will not be resolved until popular, democratic forces capable of dominating the society get together again."

The Human Global Condition

IN EVERY ECONOMIC TRANSFORMATION OF MODERNITY, OBSERVED KARL POLANYI (1944), the gains and strains of accumulation ("the first movement") were followed by society's assertion of control and regulation ("the second movement") over the unfettered market forces that made such accumulation possible. Contemporary theorists of globality such as Cox (1987) and Amin (1997) echo Polanyi's lead in locating the social forces capable of leading that "second movement." With the contradictions and crises of accumulation on a world-scale deepest and most evident in the South, it is reasonable to look there for the "second movement" within social globality. Writers like Shiva (1993, 1997) and Esteva (1998) similarly focus on the South, preoccupied with its economic, cultural, and social plunder by the North but convinced that its historical depth and diversity hold the keys to what would be a "global double movement."

Canadian social philosopher John McMurtry (1999), identifying the "civil commons" as that realm of collective social activity and spaces available and necessary for society's sustainability, looks to a global ethical maturity arising in both North and South social formations in the face of the "development gap," ecological deterioration, and the "cancer stage of capitalism." The resulting social forces, cognizant of their civilizational diversity but as well of their existential equality, would be the forces seeking a "second movement" within globality. That "second movement" would have to pursue balance and sustainability in ethical, ecological, economic, and political terms; and necessarily as a global project. En route, perhaps, we will cease seeing the South in global perspectives and start to perceive the globe from the South, the home of most of humanity.

Summary

This chapter demonstrates how the geographic and political entity called "the South" is very much a creation of and reaction to historical changes in the organization of the world system. During the past five hundred years, the South has taken on many identities, among these: the colony, the underdeveloped, the "other," the non-aligned, and the Third World. These terms are less descriptions of autonomous entities than relational concepts— results of the ongoing power imbalances between the North and the South. During the current era of globalization, the fate of the South seems shaped by extreme poverty, a growing income gap with the North, failed states, and states with an inability to exercise effective governance due to both external and internal constraints.

Others, however, view the future of the South within the context of globalization more optimistically. They argue that, with globalization, the fates of the North and the South have become intertwined. This relationship facilitates the formation of transnational linkages among the marginalized as well as the proponents of democratization. The South constitutes the vast majority of the world's population and, thus, is and must be a crucial player in the emergence of a global civil society. The emergence of such social globality, it is argued, is necessary in order to realize balance and sustainability in ethical, ecological, economic, and political terms in the new global order. En route, maybe, we will cease seeing the South in North/South terms and, instead, perceive the globe as the home of and for all.

Endnotes

[1] For provocative recent treatments of the origins of global developmental differences, see Diamond (1999) and Landes (1998).

[2] See Baran (1957) for a characterization of the global economy taking shape on the basis of transnational monopoly capitalist firms' extraction of wealth from the South to the North. For him, it constituted "neo-imperialism," that is, without the need for actual empire, and it was centred in the United States-based multinational corporations.

[3] See Mortimer (1984) for an extended discussion of the "Coalition" and its campaign for the NIEO.

[4] Taken from Steven Haggard's book (1990).

[5] There are some compelling examples of such critiques in Rahnema (1997)

[6] Though my term, the work of Robert Cox (1987, 2000) is crucial for a theoretical understanding of such "transnationalized governance." Chossudovsky (1997) and Dasgupta (1998) provide concrete examples.

[7] See Cox (2000) for an expression of this conception of social globality. Another compelling interpretation is found in McMurtry (1998).

Discussion Questions

1. What are the possible explanations for the "development gap" that divides the world into North/South, First World/Third World, or The West and The Rest?

2. In what ways did imperialism shape modernization experiences in the South?

3. What are some possible meanings of the expression "uneven development" as applied to the South?

4. How has "modernity" structured the South in the latter half of the twentieth century?

5. What does globalization portend for a differentiated South?

6. If we don't use "South" or "Third World," how should we speak of humanity's 80-percent majority in the twenty-first century?

References

Amin, Samir. 1997. *Capitalism in the Age of Globalization. The Management of Contemporary Society*. London: Zed Books.

Baran, Paul. 1957. *The Political Economy of Growth*. New York:Monthly Review Press.

Barber, Benjamin. 1995. *Jihad Versus McWorld*. New York:Times Books.

Borón, Atilio. 1999. "State Decay and Democratic Decadence in Latin America", in L.Panitch and C.Leys, eds. *Global Capitalism Versus Democracy. Socialist Register 1999*. London:Merlin Press, pp.209-226.

Chossudovsky, Michel. 1997. *The Globalisation of Poverty: Impacts of IMF and World Bank Reforms*. Penang, Malaysia:Third World Network.

Cox, Robert. 1987. *Production, Power and World Order: Social Forces in the Making of History*. New York:Columbia University Press.

——————. 2000. "Political Economy and World Order: Problems of Power and Knowledge at the Turn of the Milennium", in R.Stubbs and G.Underhill, eds. *Political Economy and the Changing Global Order*. 2nd Ed. Don Mills, Ontario:Oxford University Press, pp.25-37.

Dasgupta, Biplab. 1998. *Structural Adjustment, Global Trade and the New Political Economy of Development*. London:Zed Books.

Esteva, Gustavo and Madhu Suri Prakash. 1998. *Grassroots Post-Modernism: Remaking the Soil of Cultures*. London: Zed Books.

Fanon, Frantz. 1965. *The Wretched of the Earth*. Trans. Constance Farrington. New York: Grove Press.

George, Susan. 1988. *A Fate Worse Than Debt*. New York: Penguin Books.

Harvey, David. 1989. *The Condition of Post-Modernity: An Enquiry into the Origins of Social Change*. Oxford: Blackwell.

Huntington, Samuel. 1997. *The Clash of Civilizations and the Remaking of World Order*. New York: Touchstone.

Ikeda, Satoshi. 1996. "World Production", in Terence Hopkins, Immanuel Wallerstein, et al. *The Age of Transition. Trajectory of the World system 1945-2025*. London: Zed Books.

Jalée, Pierre. 1968. *The Pillage of the Third World*. New York: Monthly Review Press.

Kaldor, Mary. 1999. *New and Old Wars: Organized Violence in a Global Era*. Stanford: Stanford University Press.

McMurtry, John. 1999. *The Cancer Stage of Capitalism*. London: Pluto Press.

Mortimer, Robert. 1984. *The Third World Coalition in International Politics*. 2nd ed. Boulder: Westview.

O'Donnell, Eleanor. 1991. "Mass Media Worldviews: Canadian Images of the Third World", in Jaimie Swift and Brian Tomlinson, eds. *Conflicts of Interest: Canada and the Third World*. Toronto: Between the Lines, pp.275-294.

Polanyi, Karl. 1944. *The Great Transformation*. Boston: Beacon Press.

Rostow, Walter W. 1962. *The Stages of Economic Growth: A Non-Communist Manifesto*. Cambridge: Cambridge University Press.

Shiva, Vandana. 1997. *Biopiracy: The Plunder of Nature and Knowledge*. Toronto: Between The Lines.

Thomas, Caroline. 1987. *In Search of Security: The Third World in International Relations*. Boulder: Lynne Rienner.

Wallerstein, Immanuel. 1974. *The Modern World system*. New York: Academic Press.

Further Readings

Amin, Samir. 1997. *Capitalism in the Age of Globalization: The Management of Contemporary Society*. London: Zed Books.

Diamond, Jared. 1999. *Guns, Germs and Steel: The Fates of Human Societies*. New York: Norton.

Frank, Andre Gunder. 1967. *Capitalism and Underdevelopment in Latin America*. New York: Monthly Review Press.

Hoogvelt, Ankie. 1997. *Globalization and the Postcolonial World: The New Political Economy of Development*. Baltimore: Johns Hopkins University Press.

Isbister, John. 1998. Promises Unkept: *The Betrayal of Social Change in the Third World*. 3rd ed. West Hartford, Connecticut: Kumarian.

Landes, David. 1998. *The Wealth and Poverty of Nations: Why Some Are So Rich and Some So Poor.* New York: W.W. Norton.

Mason, Mike. 1997. *Development and Disorder: A History of the Third World Since 1945.* Toronto: Between The Lines.

Weblinks

Third World Network
www.twnside.org.sg/

Post-Colonial Studies
www.emory.edu/ENGLISH/Bahri/

Jubilee 2000 Campaign
www.jubilee2000.org/

North South Institute
www.nsi-ins.ca/

CHAPTER 24

GLOBALIZATION, POSTMODERNITY, AND INTERNATIONAL RELATIONS THEORY

MALINDA S. SMITH

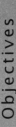

Objectives

Today it is impossible to pick up a newspaper, turn on the television, or surf the Internet without encountering the word *globalization*. Although globalization is now part of our everyday political discourse, its widespread use is very recent. A survey of social science books or journal articles prior to the mid-1970s reveals few references to *globalization* or *globalism*. The explosion of this concept's use since the late-1980s has led skeptics to characterize it as buzzword or as "globaloney." Even those sympathetic to the idea have suggested that "'globe-babble' has penetrated all social science disciplines" (Hoogvelt, 1997, 116). Given the concept's pervasiveness, one would think its meaning and significance would be clearly understood. However, this is not always the case, although at the end of the twentieth century and since, a number of essays and readers have offered useful critical readings of the concept (Lecher and Boli, 2000).

The main objective of this chapter is to explain the concept of globalization, its use within the field of international relations, and the challenges it poses to the field. First, we look at key elements that are constitutive of our ideas of globalization as a complex political, economic, and cultural phenomenon. Second, we locate globalization within international relations and political theory. In order to do this the chapter examines realism as the dominant paradigm within international relations, and globalization within the broader theoretical debates about modernity and postmodernity. Third, we explore the shift from traditional concepts such as international and transnational, to the now prevalent concepts of global and globalization. Finally, this chapter concludes by examining five contradictions of globalization that promise to be with us well into this third millennium.

Introduction

Modern disciplinary boundaries within the social sciences and humanities have become somewhat exclusive in terms of what they study and the terminology each discipline invents to clarify increasingly specialized subject areas. Globalization challenges this disciplinary exclusivity, whether the separation is between political science and economics or philosophy and literature. It also poses new challenges to field borders within disciplines, such as the artificial separation between local, national, and international politics. However, of all the fields within political science, the concept has been particularly vexing for international relations theory and, to a lesser extent, international political economy (IPE). With few exceptions, scholars within these two fields have only recently embraced the concept with analytic rigour.

This reluctance to seriously engage globalization as a concept was surprising given the three main goals of international relations theory—description, prediction, and prescription. The first goal, *description*, entails the complex task of sifting through disparate data in order to determine if there are any discernible patterns that might make sense of historical developments. For example, is globalization a new phenomenon or merely the intensification of older established processes? The second goal, *prediction*, requires theorists to use the data "to provide a reasoned argument for what they expect to happen" (A. George, 172). Given the role of random events, accidents, luck, and other unforeseen phenomena in international relations, scholars have learned that the search for "infinite predictability" is foolhardy. Instead, prediction calls for reasoned and contingent judgments based on the discernible patterns that have unfolded in international affairs. Finally, the normative (or *prescriptive*) component of international theory entails the two-fold process of making a judgment about the subject matter (e.g., the case for or against globalization) and the prescription of policy (e.g., to promote or resist globalization). Competing international theories produce different descriptions, predictions, and prescriptions, based on various assumptions about the central actors, important interests, and relevant units of analysis.

Explaining Globalization

THE FIRST OBJECTIVE OF THIS CHAPTER IS TO ANALYZE GLOBALIZATION AS A political, economic, and cultural phenomenon. To do this, we begin with a genealogy of globalization and its constitutive components particularly as they relate to international relations theory and IPE. Explaining "when" one historical moment ends and another begins is an imprecise if not a highly contestable exercise. This is certainly true of the shift from the international era to the era of globalization. Some scholars, such as Gamble (1994), suggest we have been engaged in processes of globalization since the dawn of human civilization. Others, such as Modelski (1988), claim globalization began sometime at the outset of modernity. Sweezy (1992) traces globalization's genesis to about four or five centuries ago, during the heyday of exploration, imperialism, and colonialism. Many other scholars locate globalization's genesis sometime between the middle of the nineteenth century (Robertson, 1992) and the mid-1970s (Harvey, 1989).

Perhaps a more useful way to think of globalization is as a process in which earlier manifestations were shaped by the particularities of time and place. According to this view, the "new" globalization "is simply a convenient description for a collection of processes under way today" and, particularly, for the reorganization of capitalism (Davis, 1998). This capitalism in the electronic age, which enables "a high degree of integration of world production, markets, finances, culture, politics, at the expense of the local or national—only exists because of what new technologies like electronics, bioengineering, 'smart materials,' etc., make possible" (Davis, 1998). By contrast, the "old" globalization was theorized by Lenin's notion of imperialism or what Hobsbawn (1987) later characterized as "the age of empire," followed by the end of the Cold War and what Fukuyama subsequently dubbed "the end of history."

A genealogy of the words *global* and *globalization* reveals shifting definitions over time and space, with contemporary meanings very much marked by developments in the information and communications technology (ICT) revolution. The word *global* has a long history; it is a much older word than *international*. It first emerged in public discourse in 1676, some twenty years after the Peace of Westphalia gave rise to the modern state-system, the legal notion of state sovereignty and, subsequently, modern notions of national self-determination. *Global* was used primarily to designate the entire world as a globe or sphere. Later it was used to characterize phenomena that were worldwide in scope, application, and significance. In contrast, *globalization* was not used until 1944. Its geopolitical significance did not warrant either a dictionary or encyclopedia entry until some fifteen years later (see Webster unabridged, 1961).

Recently, a number of definitions of globalization have emerged in the academic literature and in everyday conversations, but it is possible to distinguish two broad groupings. The most frequent use of globalization is in relation to transformations in the international political economy and, particularly, within the organization of capitalism. The most popular terms for characterizing these changes is "economic globalization" or "globalized capitalism."[1] What these terms try to do is make sense of transformations in the creation of wealth since Adam Smith's *An Inquiry into the Nature and Causes of the Wealth of Nations* and Karl Marx's *Communist Manifesto*. The main thesis of economic globalization is that the ability of sovereign nation-states to protect their domestic economies and citizens is diminished by the global economy. Instead of wealth being created by national governments—through finance, investment, production, distribution, and marketing—it is now created at the global level, outside the control of national governments and domestic public policies.

Globalization—What is Really New?

According to the United Nations Development Report (1999) these are some of the things that are truly distinctive about the current era of intensifying globalization.

- growing global markets in services—banking, insurance, and transport
- new financial markets which are deregulated, globally linked, and working around the clock
- global consumer markets with global brands
- multinational corporations dominating world production
- regional blocs proliferating—e.g., European Union, Nafta, APEC, Mercosur
- a booming international network of NGOs
- an international criminal court in the making
- Internet and electronic communications linking people simultaneously
- market economic policies spreading around the world
- new multilateral agreements which are more binding on national governments
- conventions and agreements on the environment
- widespread adoption of democracy as the choice of political system
- growing awareness of human rights conventions and instruments
- globalization of crime
- consensus on goals and agendas for development

Adapted from United Nations Development Program, *Human Development Report –1999* (New York: Oxford University Press, 1999) 30. Reprinted with permission of Oxford University Press.

The globalization debate raises important questions about whether we are shifting from an international political economy to a global political economy. IPE is seen both as a subfield of the disciplines of political science and economics and as a distinct field. When the term "political economy" was first coined in 1615 by the French writer, Montchrétien de Watteville, it meant "the science of wealth acquisition common to the State as well as the Family" (Hoogvelt, 3). International political economy can be defined as a perspective on international relations that emphasizes the inseparability of economic factors such as the creation of wealth and political factors such as the allocation of resources and the distribution of power. Both at the national and international levels, political economy approaches examine the interaction of states, markets, modes of production, social forces, and culture.

Since the 1970s, changes in production, labour, and finance have been dramatic. Production is now significantly de-localized. In the past, goods and services were produced by workers within a national territory for local consumption and later for international markets. Today, workers produce components to be assembled worldwide for a global market. Instead of workers being part of a national economy, they are increasingly integrated into a global economy. For example, workers in the maquiladoras of Mexico and the free trade zones of Southeast Asia produce brand names such as Nike and Alfred Sung for worldwide distribution. Indeed, local workers often cannot afford to buy these "global products" advertised by multimillionaire global icons such as Venus Williams and Tiger Woods. The "world car,"produced by Ford and Mitsubishi is another example. The British Ford Cortina produced in Britain for local consumption after World War II is now produced for worldwide distribution as the Ford Escort. This car is assembled in some fourteen different countries including Spain, Switzerland, and Germany.

Globalizing National Economies

Globalization, that is, the "new" globalization, has brought profound changes in labour practices. While many workers today are tied to a national economy, most others are inextricably integrated into a "global factory" and a new international division of labour. Some scholars, concerned with the deepening divisions between North and South represented by the global factory argue that we are witnessing the reproduction of old colonial relations. Manufacturing and financial services are now more heavily concentrated in the industrialized countries and production takes place primarily in low-income and industrializing countries. Mexico's **maquiladoras**, which were set in place as early as 1965, now employ some 500 000 low-income workers who produce goods overwhelmingly for export. These burgeoning export processing zones (EPZs) located across the South were developed to exploit cheap labour, to evade labour and environmental regulations, and to avoid domestic taxes and import restrictions in the North.

International finance, that is, the system by which credit is created to finance production and trade has likewise witnessed fundamental changes. In the postwar period, financial structures were very much territorially based. Both the Bretton Woods institutions and the development of the welfare state in the North assumed significant national control over the movement of capital. The Bretton Woods system had been designed to shape international monetary and financial relations in the postwar period. In 1973 the agreements also created the World Bank and the International Monetary Fund (IMF). In this new post–Bretton Woods era, technological developments have enabled financial transactions to move across multiple national borders in nanoseconds, thereby inhibiting effective state control. Moreover, there has been a change from primarily nationally based currencies to a handful of globally recognized (or supraterritorial) currencies such as the U.S. dollar, the Japanese yen, the British pound, and the German deutschmark. Most significant has been the change from "hard currency" to digiCash and electronic money due to technological developments such as automatic banking/ATMs, e-banking on the Internet, and the rise in globally accepted credit cards such as Visa and American Express. Banking has also moved beyond the national state with the growth of transnational loans, deposits, and money transfer.

These changes in the international political economy do suggest an intensified shift to something new. Over a decade ago, political economists began writing about the breakdown of distinctions such as *national* and *international*. According to Charles-Albert Michalet (1982), "ideas of national and international, of domestic and foreign, of exterior and interior, and of frontier limits that used to define the existence of an international economy, are losing their validity. The outline of nation-states is becoming blurred and the power of the state over economic activity is lessened." The international political economy involved distinct national economies shaped by national governments and their institutions, and in their national interest. The globalizing economy is increasingly non-territorial, involves integrated production and services, and is shaped by global actors whose views of global competitiveness and interests cannot be reduced to the interests of specific national actors.

Globalizing National Cultures

Globalization is also invoked to characterize cultural transformations. In this case, the study of global processes is an attempt to understand changing notions of culture, nationality, and identity. By *culture* we mean the complex matrix that includes customs, conventional practices, national myths, ethnic heritage, and artistic and creative genres by which a people imagine themselves. The nation-state form as a cultural unit is only about two hundred years old. Thus, the embeddedness of national cultural societies and identities is fragile and, in fact, has been subject to contestations by "deep identities" based on ethnicity and religion (Cerny, 1996, 628).

In the past, different cultures were seen as incompatible within the international system. Those who were not members of one's own cultural group were characterized as infidels, barbarians, uncivilized, or "aliens." In fact, U.S. immigration policies and forms still refer to foreigners as "aliens" or "enemy aliens." Today, there are at least two competing and contradictory views about the significance of globalization for the heterogeneity of national cultures: the first view focuses on clashes and tensions, the other on the emergence of a global multicultural and cosmopolitan civilization. On the one hand, Samuel Huntington (1993) suggests the post–Cold War period is characterized by a "clash of civilizations." Civilizations are the broadest form of culture and identity. For Huntington, the ideological antagonisms of the Cold War—between East and West, communism and democracy—have given way to a clash of cultural values between "the West and the Rest." Thus, Western liberal values are juxtaposed against so-called orthodox civilizations that include Islam, Confucianism, Hinduism, and Buddhism. Ultimately, Huntington sees Islam as the West's main nemesis, leading him to oversimplify difference and, ultimately, to stereotype Islam and Muslims, who differ from Indonesia and Malaysia to Bosnia or to the Nation of Islam. A related argument is offered by Fukuyama (1992) who associates the post–Cold War with the worldwide hegemony of Western liberalism and forms of governance, as well as the "end of socialism" because socialism fails to satisfy deeply felt human yearnings.

Similarly, Benjamin Barber maps a clash between two competing tendencies—what he calls *McWorld vs. Jihad*. The first term is meant to capture the homogenizing values and internationalization of American consumer culture that sees everyone wearing Tommy Hilfiger, eating at McDonalds, using Microsoft, watching Hollywood movies, listening to the unhip hip-hop of Puff Daddy and Eminem, and espousing the vacuous values of "Survivor" or "Sex and the City." Apparently in stark contrast, *Jihad* connotes the fragmenting tendencies of ethnic and cultural nationalism that led to the disintegration of the former

Yugoslavia and the kind of genocide and "ethnic cleansing" that occurred in Bosnia and Rwanda.[2] Stereotypes notwithstanding, what Huntington and Barber attempt to do is to think through the fact that globalization does involve paradoxical forces—of homogenization and integration as well as of fragmentation and disintegration.

The other dominant view about culture is that all of the complex interconnections, relations, and social ties are leading to a new global infrastructure that links individuals, households, associations, and communities across nation-state boundaries into "the reality of world society" (Modelski, 1972, 227). Other scholars go further and suggest we are witnessing for the first time in human history a global civilization or a new world order with shared values, processes, and structures whereby nations and cultures become more open to influence by each other; whereby there is recognition of the identities and diversities of peoples in various groups, and ethnic and religious pluralism; where people of different ideologies and values both cooperate and compete but no ideology prevails over all the others; and where the global civilization becomes unique in a holistic sense while still being pluralist and heterogeneous in its character (Perlmutter, 1991, 898, 902).

Perlmutter goes on to say that despite the plurality of values and the interpretations of these, there is increasingly a perception that these values are shared worldwide. Consequently, "for the first time in human history and with all the help of major political and technological changes, we have the possibility of real time . . . global civilization." This idea of shared values is elsewhere referred to as globalism or cosmopolitanism. Globalism is not the same as globalization. Rather, "globalism . . . points to aspirations for a state of affairs where values are shared by or pertinent to all the world's more than 5 billion people, their environment, and their role as citizens, consumers, or producers with an interest in collective action to solve common problems" (Rosenau, 1997, 361). Globalism can thus be distinguished from globalization by its emphasis on values. *Cosmopolitanism* derives from the Greek words *cosmos* and *polis* which, combined, literally mean "world city." It also connotes a conception of political identity and ideology that is worldwide.

Thus the cultural focus of globalization tends to be on a worldwide phenomenon that includes "interconnections, interchanges and movements of people, images, and commodities" across national territorial frontiers (Friedman, 195). This cultural focus pays close attention to the growing number of relations that transcend the nation-state, and the movement of cultures, people, commodities, images, icons, fashion, and lifestyles that cannot be understood within paradigms that subordinate cultural and social relations to the national states. With these movements and interconnections has come a change in consciousness. Susan Strange (1997) argues there has been a transformation from national consciousness to what might be called "global consciousness," which involves changes in "perceptions, beliefs, ideas, and tastes." What this means is that "while cultural differences persist, the sensitivities and susceptibilities of individual human beings are increasingly being modified by the processes of global homogenization" (Strange, 365). These processes are enhanced by developments in media and information technologies and by the declining costs of transportation and increased travel that reinforce the perception that the globe is "shrinking" and is finally becoming the "global village" first imagined by Marshall McLuhan (1964). McLuhan's global village conceived of the world as one community, as well as a world in which geographical space was transcended by electronic media (the television).

Although global consciousness is facilitated by technology, its emergence is attributable to other factors as well. For Anthony Giddens (1990), "globalisation can thus be defined as the intensification of world wide social relations which link distant localities in such a way that local happenings are shaped by events occurring many miles away and vice versa" (64). These intensified relations may be:

- *ecological*—involving the worldwide recognition of planetary climatic change, deforestation, and desertification;

- *economic*—involving awareness of the low wages associated with the global factory or the economic uncertainty resulting from round-the-clock stock market transactions and crashes (e.g., the impact of the 1994 Mexican peso crisis and the Asian currency meltdown of the late 1990s);

- *strategic*—involving the implications of global weaponry such as nuclear and chemical weapons, intercontinental ballistic missiles (IBMs) and spy-satellites, which have made the world into one strategic sphere; and

- *ethical*—involving the supraterritorial discourse about democracy, human rights, cultural values, poverty, and unemployment.

To summarize, in its broadest sense the concept of globalization encompasses both economic transformations and wide-ranging social and cultural transformations. It is what Edward Soja (1989) calls a new political–cultural governing order. This new governing order entails "the notion of a 'brake,' if not break, in secular trends, and a shift toward a significantly different order and configuration of social, economic and political life" (Soja, 159). This new order embraces an emergent global economy characterized by changes in production, labour, and finance. As well, it includes notions of global governance, global civil society, and the idea of an emergent global civilization.[3]

In a philosophic reflection on globalization, Frederic Jameson identified four common responses to globalization and what it represents (Jameson, 1998b, 54–77). The first response is that there is no such thing as globalization. It is dismissed as nothing more than "'globaloney,' a great myth, an illusion, and therefore not to be taken seriously" (Strange, 1997, 365). The second response claims globalization is nothing new. It suggests the processes we see as signs of globalization have been with us since as early as the neolithic age when cultural artifacts were exchanged across trade routes well before the emergence of the nation-state system. In other words, what we now call globalization has been a fact since the earliest times; current technologies only enable an intensification of these relations and exchanges. A third response relates globalization to the changes in the world market and capitalist networks. It maintains that capitalism has always been globalizing. The difference today is more a matter of degree than kind. Finally, globalization is seen as a new stage of capitalism. Some call it a third stage of capitalism or multinational capitalism. This fourth response maintains that our understanding of globalization is inseparable from transformations in capitalism. For Jameson, multinational or finance capitalism is also inseparable from what is elsewhere called postmodernity.

Modern and Postmodern International Relations Theory

THE SECOND OBJECTIVE OF THIS CHAPTER IS TO LOCATE GLOBALIZATION WITHIN international relations and political theory. In order to do this, it is helpful to consider both the modern orthodox approach to the subject matter and how this has been challenged by transformations associated with postmodernity and globalization. Despite the debate about when globalization began, an important marker for international relations and international political economy was the fall of the Berlin Wall and the relatively peaceful collapse of the Soviet Union at the end of the 1980s. Some scholars like Fukuyama (1992) triumphantly claimed that the end of the Cold War was "the end of history," implicitly referring to the worldwide spread of neoliberalism and democratization. Regardless of what one thinks of these claims, it is true that some dramatic changes have occurred. These changes have made obsolete the Cold War institutional framework that dominated international relations since 1945. Thus, the East–West axis and logic, along with the centrality of the Warsaw Pact and North Atlantic Treaty Organization (NATO) alliances have given way to the rhetoric of multilateralism, regional trade blocs, and reforms to international organizations such as the United Nations, and those of the international financial architecture.

The end of the Cold War changed what we thought both about international relations as well as about the main characteristics of the international arena. Jim George associates the post–Cold War period with significant transformations in "patterns of thought and behavior identified as corresponding with an enduring, universal 'essence' of global existence" (J. George, 1994, 1). In particular, it transformed old ideologies, and led to the restructuring of alliances like NATO, the redrawing of territorial borders to accommodate newly independent states in the Baltic and Eastern Europe, the reunification of Germany, and changes in symbols of identity. These events suggest that globalization marks a rupture from earlier historical moments and, as such, could pose dramatic challenges to international studies. As the following section explains, however, there are both continuities and discontinuities between earlier historical moments and what we now call globalization.

Modern International Relations Theory

Modern international relations have been shaped by key elements of modernity: rationalism, science, progress, industrialization, capitalism, and the nation-state system. Modern international relations perspectives have been derived primarily from explanatory theories. These theories assume the world is "outside" or external to the theory about it. The aim of explanatory theories is to uncover the enduring patterns, regularities, and continuities of human life, in this case, regularities of international relations and political economy. Explanatory theories, at least until the 1980s, found their justification in positivism. What positivism assumed is quite important to understanding the limits of orthodox international relations theory and its principal method of inquiry. Modern positivism evolved from the data-gathering approaches of Comte and Durkheim, the skepticism of Hume, and the British empiricism of Bacon. Positivists made several assumptions: first, they assumed the "truth" of international relations could be determined by observing the "facts"; second, they thought facts were distinct from values; and third, they believed that there were underlying patterns (or foundations) to the social and cultural world that could be uncovered and understood. The assumption was that as social scientists discovered the "laws" of international politics, they would be better placed to understand and forecast the evolution of the international system.

Orthodox international relations theory assumed there were various "truths" about the international sphere. In the postwar years, political realism was the dominant theory of international relations in Anglo-American academies. First, it assumed the state was the most fundamental unit of analysis in the international system and that state sovereignty was the governing principle of that system. In addition to sovereignty, a state was characterized by territory, population, government, diplomatic recognition of other states, and national loyalty to the state (patriotism). Second, realism maintained that states act in accordance with the idea of "national interest" and this overrides all other interests. Relatedly, they believed that human beings were, by nature, selfish and, thus, acted in their own self-interest. Third, they assumed the international system was anarchical, meaning there was no world government or authority higher than the state. Conflict and war were inevitable because of the power struggle for control over limited resources. All of these assumptions have been called into question by globalization. Thus, globalization represents a powerful challenge to realist assumptions.

The ways in which globalization challenges realism are both theoretical and methodological. The first challenge is to realism's narrow view of the international sphere. As Fred Halliday points out, "the subject-matter of the academic discipline of international relations is often thought of as being very much a question of facts: tracing the foreign policy of one country here, the relations between states in a particular region there" (Halliday, 1988, 187). According to Mervyn Frost, realism "seeks to verify conclusions by reference to the 'facts' which are in some sense 'hard' and there for all to see . . . [it draws] a radical distinction between the status accorded to factual judgments, to which the discipline of international relations should aspire and that accorded to value judgments" (Frost, 1986, 10). This limited focus on factual analysis of current affairs, and the failure to address issues of ethics and morality, led Frost to characterize international relations as the "backward discipline."

In contrast to this narrow focus, Halliday suggests the core of the discipline is also concerned with two other areas. First, the discipline is concerned with fundamental concepts used "to analyze relations between states and across frontiers." This includes concepts such as international, transnational, and global, to which we will return later. Moreover, the core of the discipline is also concerned with "a question of values, of the normative." Normative considerations require us to think about what obligations, if any, we have to the particular state we are born in or migrate to, as well as to "foreign" nationalities and states. These perennial questions—first engaged by Socrates in the *Apologia* and, subsequently, by political thinkers as diverse as Hobbes, Bukharin, Goldman, Gandhi, and King—have been dismissed by realism. Nonetheless, the processes of globalization and notions of cosmopolitanism and global consciousness are forcing a rethinking of this normative silence. Finally, Halliday suggests it is important to consider what forms of international political institutions, economic transactions, and social relations are preferable as a matter of justice (Halliday, 187). In other words, international relations theory is best when it weaves together empirical, ethical, and philosophical considerations.

The Limits of Realism

In light of the observations by theorists such as Halliday, the first difficulty we encounter with realist orthodoxy and why it has been slow to understand global phenomena is partly a story about modernity and how modernists have understood the world. Political realism represented "reality" from within a modern scientific consensus: the "real world" is believed to be entirely knowable through empirical observations, whether of institutional dynamics, current events, or human behaviour. Following Weber, realists dealt with "only the facts," which they believed could be separated out from normative questions about values or justice (Hekman, 1983, 98–115). Consequently, international reality has been framed within a modernist thought that constructed the world in terms of simplistic dichotomies: realism/idealism, anarchy/order, fact/value, is/ought, and theory/practice. For the modern realist, the world is simple: it is anarchical, factual, knowable from observing what "is," and based on an unchanging human nature and predictable state practice. Realism, however, is only one perspective on international reality. Its "primitive" representations (Berki, 6–8) are increasingly subject to critique by a number of new perspectives.

International relations methodology has also suffered because of the influence of nineteenth-century conceptions of science and the epistemological assumption that we could know the world through detached empirical observations of things "out there." Epistemology is a theory of knowledge; put simply, it is the study of what we know and how we know it. Realist epistemology is empirical. Realism assumes we can take our disparate observations and determine what is factual or true, versus what is probable, false, or an illusion by following a positivist method. Thus, the second difficulty with realist orthodoxy is the influence of positivism, and the attempts to bring scientific certainty to the "chaos" of international phenomena. This positivism is reflected in the writings of major postwar realists.

Empiricism and positivism have been central to constructing the modern international relations story that there is one reality that is fixed, stable, unchanging, and inalterable. And, in Carr's words, "the function of thinking is to study a sequence of events which it is powerless to influence or to alter" (Carr, 1964). This has been called *path dependency*. This approach assumes that events are dependent on the sequence or path of prior events, as in the evolution of the species. One criticism of this approach is that it is reductionist and does not easily distinguish what is important in the sequence from what is trivial. Moreover, at times, it can attribute major importance to minor or incidental events.

Postmodern Interventions

Realism's simplistic representations of reality are being challenged by a host of radical new perspectives. In recent times, realism has been challenged by critical theorists, including postmodernists, feminists, and ecologists. There is no single critical theory, rather it is made up of a number of related perspectives. They do, however, share some assumptions. Among these are that the structures of the international system are not natural or inevitable but socially constructed (the product of politics). Critical theorists also believe that the orthodox ways of thinking about the international system, including the assumptions about human nature and power politics, can lead to self-fulfilling prophecies. Postmodern theorists in particular extend these views to give primacy to ideas, texts, and discourse in the construction of international relations. They also argue that a shared global discourse can help create "epistemic communities." What this means is that media and information technologies are helping to create knowledge-based communities beyond the territorial limits of the modern nation-state.

A shared criticism of realism is that it constructed "a simplistic . . . image of the 'real' world, which is fundamentally detached from the everyday experiences of so much of that world" (J. George, 1994, 11). Critical theorists, particularly those influenced by Foucault and neo-Gramscian arguments, suggest our understanding of reality, and in this case global reality, can never be complete or entirely intelligible (Maghoori and Ramberg, 1982). Moreover, global reality is not made up of a simple aggregate of facts or produced by inexhaustible data-gathering as suggested by early positivism. For critical theorists, "reality is always characterized by ambiguity, disunity, discrepancy, contradiction, and difference" (J. George, 1994, 11).

Globalization discourse is partly related to the broader social science debates about modernity and postmodernity. Globalization has, in fact, been characterized as "the culture of postmodernity" (Jameson, 1991). When the prefix "post" was first invoked in the mid-1960s by Leslie Fielder, it represented a kind of anarchical counter-culture. It was against all establishment elitism and orthodoxies, and celebrated radical concepts such as "post-humanist, post-male, post-white, post-heroic . . . post-Jewish," long before they became fashionable (Fielder quoted in Jencks, 1991, 23). In contrast to the modernist assumptions embedded in political realism, postmodernism is highly skeptical that any human truth is a mirror image of an objective reality "out there" (Kvale, 1995, 18). Borrowing on the work of Thomas Kuhn, postmodernists argue that notions of science and objectivity are best understood when they are placed in a human context. What becomes clear is that "truths," even scientific truths, are socially constructed within the context of the dominant scientific communities of the time (Kuhn, 1970). Postmodern thought is thus quite compatible with the complex ideas associated with the emergence of global civilization.

As noted above, postmodernism pays close attention to words and discourses, particularly the ways in which human beings and societies use language and myths to construct personal and collective realities, that is, "who" we are and "how" we imagine our own communities (Anderson, 1991). Relatedly, postmodernism recognizes that there can be quite different descriptions of reality and that, ultimately, the choice between one or the other is not objective. Put differently, instead of an attempt to find the final frontier of some true reality, postmodernism focuses on "social and linguistic construction of a perspectival reality" and the ways in which global electronic media increase our exposure to "a multiplicity of perspectives, undermining any belief in one objective reality" (Kvale, 19).

What this enquiry suggests thus far is that globalization is not the exclusive domain of any particular discipline or field of study within political science. It reinforces the notion of an epochal shift from modernity to postmodernity, as well as the view that critical theory is better able to understand globalization than is realism. As well, the complex and multidisciplinary character of globalization constantly requires the quest for conceptual clarity. Instead of resulting in clarification, globalization has become "the modern or postmodern version of the proverbial elephant, described by its blind observers in so many diverse ways" (Jameson, 1998a: xi). Below, we examine the conceptual shift from traditional notions such as international and transnational to globalization.

From International to Global

THE THIRD OBJECTIVE OF THIS CHAPTER IS ONE OF CONCEPTUAL CLARIFICATION. What we do next is critically analyze the shift from international to global. Critical theorists argue that words and discourse are important in the construction of politics and our ideas about the international or the global sphere. Unlike realists, they do not see words as simply a mirror reflection of an external reality. Nor is discourse simply a linguistic copy of reality. Rather, discourse produces, and is produced by, a web of social relations and practices that give meaning and significance to the way people understand their identities, actions, and communities. Thus, words and discourse are constitutive—meaning they help produce—what we come to think of as international or global political reality. What is prescribed as meaningful within discourse in large part becomes what is understood as "real." Thus, critical theorists pay close attention to "the linguistic and social construction of reality," and to the "interpretation and negotiation of the meaning of the lived word" (Kvale, 21).

Given the centrality of words and discourse to politics generally, the poverty of realist theorizing is somewhat surprising. It brings to mind Shakespeare's lament in *Love's Labour's Lost*: "They have been at a great feast of language, and stolen the scraps." Sometimes globalization discourse itself seems made up of "scraps" from various disciplinary tables. Nonetheless, as with all scraps, some are more worthy of consumption and digestion than others. Below, we turn our attention to some of the major conceptual precursors to globalization.

International, Internationalize, Internationalism

In the 1980s, the concept of globalization seemed to suggest a fundamental rupture with the earlier notion of *inter*-national. It suggested a shift to *trans*-national or *supra*-national relations. Appropriately, this change in prefix and the corresponding replacement of the older concept with newer ones raised questions about the constitutive elements of both the international and the global. Moreover, given the excess of related terms already in circulation, there was a need to explain the relationship of globalization to the older notions of international relations and world politics, as well as to terms such as *internationalism* and *transnationalism*.

By definition, in both international relations and the narrower postwar realist conception of international politics, the subject matter is conceptually limited to transactions between nation-states. To minimize this limitation, some scholars opt for the terms *world politics* or *global politics* which more readily lend themselves to the study of political, economic, and cultural transactions both between state and non-state (or transnational) actors, as well as within and across different levels of analysis (e.g., city, nation-state, or transnational). This breakdown in levels of analysis—tantamount to a breakdown in disciplinary borders within political science—has enabled the articulation of hybrid terms such as *intermestic* and *glocalization. Intermestic* addresses the increasing analytic inseparability between international and domestic spheres due to interdependence. The idea of local globalization or *glocalization*, signals the increasing synergy between local and global relations and political economy.

When English philosopher Jeremy Bentham first coined the notion of "inter-national" in the 1780s, it was seen as marking a transition from an earlier era of relations within empires or between city-states, to one characterized by increasing diplomatic, political, and economic relations between nation-states. In 1864 the verb *internationalize* was used to capture the process of making something international or of placing something, such as a company or city, under international control (Encyclopedia Britannica, 1998). Today, *internationalize* is used to indicate a process in which relations between national territories are intensified. Importantly, the frontiers of these territories, as distinct national domains, remain separate.

Bentham, followed by Immanuel Kant, became the intellectual architect of liberal internationalism[5]—the outgrowth of the Enlightenment's belief that from reason a law-governed community of states could be constructed. In effect, they extended the modern social contract prescribing rights and duties between individuals in civil society—as articulated by Hobbes, Locke, Rousseau, and others—to an international society of states. These early contract theorists associated interdependence with peace and, minimally, the regulation of conflict and war without any correlate notion of world government. Interdependence—through commerce, transportation, communication, and human interaction—narrowed the physical and psychic spaces between sovereign states. These liberal internationalist ideas about an international society of states were thus early precursors to the contemporary idea of a global civil society and global civilization.

There is an important distinction to be made between internationalization and globalization and between interdependence and globalization. In contrast to the nationally distinct spheres of internationalization, globalization implies *supraterritoriality* (above nations) and a web of transborder connections and relations. Although today interdependence and globalization are used interchangeably, it is better to think of interdependence as compressing the geographical space between sovereign states whereas globalization entails expanding or intensifying cross-national interactions (Reinicke, 1997, 127–8).

Transnational, Transnationalism

Like internationalism, transnationalism is an important precursor to the phenomena we call globalization. *Transnationalism* was first used in 1921 to designate phenomena that transcended the territorial borders of the nation-state. Today, the concept is used in one of two ways. First, within international theory, transnationalism is used to describe the proliferation of non-state or non-government actors—social, cultural, humanitarian—on the world stage. Transnational actors are non-governmental actors from one state who have relations with actors from another state or international organization. The concept's use reinforces the view that, contrary to the assumptions of realism, meaningful international relations are engaged in by actors other than the nation-state or governments. Transnational actors include transnational corporations (TNCs) such as Microsoft and Shell; single-state non-governmental organizations (NGOs) such as the Sierra Club (U.S.) and Médecins sans Frontières (France); international non-governmental organizations (INGOs) such as Amnesty International, the International Red Cross, and the World Council of Indigenous Peoples; and intergovernmental organizations (IGOs) such as the Organization of African Unity and the European Union. Given the heterogeneity of actors collected under the umbrella of *transnational*, some scholars differentiate between NGOs and regional IGOs such as the Organization of American States and international organizations such as the UN.

The second main use of *transnationalism* is within political economy literature and diplomatic circles, where it tends to be more narrowly defined in terms of firms or corporations. The focus is on corporations engaged in transactions due to more open borders (liberalization) and intensified cross-(state) border transactions (e.g., multinational or transnational corporations). Multinational and transnational are frequently used interchangeably to refer to any corporation that is registered and simultaneously operates in more than one country. Over the past fifty years, this generally meant a corporation having the parent company or headquarters in one state and subsidiaries in multiple other states. Today, there are some 40 000 TNCs with over 250 000 affiliates worldwide.

Ankie Hoogvelt argues that the difference between transnationalism and globalization is, at worst, a matter of what is linguistically fashionable and, more probably, an indicator of the degree of change rather than the kind of change. Thus, globalization seeks to "replace terms like 'internationalisation' and 'transnationalisation' as a more suitable concept for describing the ever-intensifying networks of cross-border human interaction" (Hoogvelt, 114). Put differently, transnationalism anticipates globalization and, specifically, the ways in which the realist focus on the duality of state versus non-state actors—with the latter seen as secondary—unduly limits our understanding of worldwide relations.

The Contradictions of Globalization

THUS FAR WE HAVE ARGUED THAT GLOBALIZATION CAN BE DEFINED AS A PROCESS of worldwide integration of heterogeneous individuals, nationalities, cultures, and economies. In addition to the empirical reality of deepening integration, there is a worldwide perception or consciousness of this integration in everyday life. This is due, in part, to the media. However, this chapter's fourth objective shows that we should approach all claims about globalization with prudence.

Global processes are fundamentally contradictory, but this is often not reflected in the most prevalent metaphors of globalization. On the one hand, globalization is seen as a universalizing tendency that is producing a world that is one, borderless, seamless, integrative, and convergent. Thus, we hear talk about a global society alongside a global political economy. On the other hand, it is argued that globalization is a particularizing tendency that is creating a world characterized by fragmentation, disintegration, divergence, balkanization, and tribalism. Postmodern perspectives suggest a third view, one that tries to capture the internal paradoxes of the concept and the diverse processes it covers. New words have been invented to capture these intermixings: some scholars talk about mongrelization of identities and cultures; others talk about hybridity, polyglotism and multiculturalism, *mestizaje*, and creolization.

Globalization in the third millennium will continue to be shaped by complexity and contradiction. Nine of the most significant contradictions associated with globalization have been laid out by Stephen Castles (1998, 179–87).[6] Below I discuss five of these contradictions as a launching pad for discussions about the future of globalization:

1. Inclusion and exclusion;
2. Wealth and impoverishment;
3. Economy and environment;
4. Modernity and postmodernity; and
5. National citizen and global citizen.

Inclusion and Exclusion

Globalization is a profoundly ideological process that differentiates between classes, genders, nationalities, and regions. It has created new "winners" and "losers." Put differently, "rather than reaching out and including everybody, globalization is more like deciding who to pick to be part of the central economy and who to exclude" (Collier, 1998). Several broad exclusionary trends are evident. The first trend is in the political sphere, as observed in the European Union (EU). While the EU is improving rights for the citizens of its fifteen member states, these same states deny similar rights to the millions of residents of the EU, mainly migrant workers, who are not citizens. The EU is thus reinforcing unequal relations and privileges between citizens of member states and "other" residents.

A second exclusionary aspect of globalization is in the economic sphere—economic trade, finance, and investment are concentrated in fewer states than in the past. This is happening in one of two ways: the deepening of economic relations within a triad (EU, Japan/Southeast Asia, and NAFTA), and a reduction in the number of states in the South that are included in global economic relations. Between 1989 and 1992, 70 percent of all foreign direct investment (FDI) to developing states went to 10 countries (China, South Korea, Malaysia, Thailand, Indonesia, Brazil, Argentina, Venezuela, Mexico, Nigeria). By 1993, the percentage of FDI to the top ten countries had increased to 90 percent (Mexico, Brazil, Argentina, Venezuela, South Korea, China, Thailand, Hungary, Turkey, Greece). Thus, none of Africa's 53 states were included. Globalization is also structuring relations in which some peoples and states are "irrelevant." Within the North and the South, we are witnessing "the structurally irrelevant fourth-world in our midst in the inner cities of advanced countries" (Hoogvelt, 1998). The poor, the homeless, often refugees and migrants, experience economic and social exclusion and thus do not enter global civilization on an equal footing. Many of the world's refugees, primarily women, the elderly and children, are without home or native land (Castles, 2).

Growing Wealth and Impoverishment

In the 1970s and 1980s, liberal modernization theory promised that developing countries would "take off" if they opened their economies to free trade, that wealth would "trickle down" from the rich to the poor. It is clear this linear progression to wealth has not materialized. Today, the rich are getting richer and the poor are getting poorer both within the North and the South, and between the North and South. In 1960, the poorest 20 percent of the world's population accounted for 2.3 percent of the world's income; by 1997 this number had declined to 1.1 percent.

Other indicators of global inequality, particularly between the North and the South, have been mapped by Bradshaw and Wallace (1997, 15–39). Daily, more than thirty-five thousand children die worldwide from preventable or treatable diseases, including pneumonia, diarrhea, malaria, measles, tetanus, and whooping cough. Bradshaw and Wallace associate this with the difference in "life chances" between rich and poor countries. Inequality between rich and poor countries is also reflected in the average annual income. In rich countries such as Canada, Australia, Japan, Germany, and the United States, the average income is $21 174 (U.S.). By contrast, in the poorest 42 states including Nicaragua, Haiti, and most of sub-Saharan Africa, the average income is $307.56 (U.S.). A third indicator is a state's ability to "cope" with emergencies such as new diseases like Ebola or HIV/AIDS and natural disasters such as the 1998 hurricane and flooding in Central America that led to over ten thousand deaths and millions of dollars of damage. The main point here is that the economic effects of globalization are uneven. This unevenness is exacerbated by a host of political, economic, and social problems associated with development in post-colonial states.

The Economy and the Environment

Rapid economic growth in the context of an unregulated global market places a tremendous strain on the earth's ecological system. This strain is exacerbated by international migration and urbanization. Deforestation, desertification, pollution, the depletion of the ozone layer, and resource depletion are not confined within the territorial borders of the national state. However, where there has been the political will to develop trans-territorial regulations for trade, finance, and investment, there has been no comparable commitment for the environment. Stresses on environments are exacerbated by migration. International migration is the result of many factors—the move for family reunification and employment, or from civil conflict and, increasingly, environmental disasters. All of these factors put pressure on the ecosystem. Migration due to environmental disasters has given rise to a new category of refugee: in addition to political refugees fleeing persecution, we now have "environmental refugees." Finally, urbanization also causes strains on the global ecosystem. It is estimated that by 2025, 61 percent of the world's population will live in cities. With hyper-urbanization and "megacities" come a host of political, economic, and social strains. Among these are overpopulation, the wretched condition of slums from Latin America to Asia, and the spread of disease especially in the absence of clean water and sanitation. Postmodern notions of hybridity due to migration and cultural intermingling, in other words, are mostly experienced by the wealthy.

Modernity and Postmodernity

The globalization debate reveals why it is best to think of postmodernity as both a continuation of and a break from modernity. Fundamental to the project of modernity was the idea of progress—human societies were on a continuous path toward the good society. This optimistic view contrasts sharply with postmodern perspectives that reject the idea of progress. Postmodernism also displays a healthy skepticism toward the idea of "the good society," and questions whether there is such a thing at all. A second paradox concerns the postmodern rejection of "grand narratives"—basically theories that purport to explain all human relations. In some respects, globalization discourse is a current example of a grand narrative. It is seen as all-embracing, with dictates of the market overriding all other logics, whether that of the state, democracy, civil society, or principles of equality and justice. However, while globalization seems to fulfill the economic vision of modernity, the political and cultural projects remain underdeveloped. In Castles' words, "globalization means a modern integrated economy, but a postmodern fragmented political sphere" (7).

National Citizen and Global Citizen

The idea of a democratic citizen is an invention of the modern nation-state. According to this idea, each individual is a bearer of rights and duties, and an active participant—through voting, party politics, local associations and the like—in the governing of the nation-state. This idea is applicable to only a handful of the world's states. Moreover, the idea of democratic citizenship is, itself, paradoxical. On the one hand, it assumes membership in a nation-state, equal civic belonging in a political community, and cultural belonging in a national community. However, the belief in equal belonging in a political community is contradicted by a history of discrimination on the basis of race, ethnicity, gender, sexuality, and religion. On the other hand, throughout history, processes of nation-formation have entailed brutal conquest, incorporation, and colonialism. Nation-building aimed either to annihilate or assimilate ethnic and cultural difference. Additionally, as the French historian Ernest Renan (1992) put it, nation-formation also involved long processes of "forgetting difference." A good example of this is the way in which settler-societies such as Canada, Australia, and the United States imagined themselves by "forgetting" the differences of indigenous peoples.

The modern nation-state and its conception of citizenship are being challenged by various forces. International migration is giving rise to ethno-cultural communities in old societies that previously had imagined themselves as homogeneous. In societies as diverse as Germany, France, Canada, South Africa, and India, the persistence of ethnic and cultural minorities is leading to two contradictory dynamics: one sees individuals celebrating their multiple and conflicting (or transcultural) identities, while the other witnesses ethnic tensions, conflict, and violence. In either case, the modern notion of individuals belonging to a single political and cultural community is obsolete. Most states today are multi-ethnic and multi-national and will be increasingly so in the next millennium.

This situation has raised the idea of a global citizenship, but this conception is underdeveloped, as are notions of a global governance. The call for a global citizenship is more a matter of necessity than choice and is due, in particular, to two developments. The first development relates to the transformation of the nation-state, including the erosion of state sovereignty and the state's growing inability to protect its citizens from the vagaries of globalization. The second development focuses on the complex and contradictory forces of globalization which cannot be subjected to control by a single national state or government.

For Castles, these two developments suggest the need to, among other things, strengthen the role of supra-national institutions to curb the excesses of the global economy; minimize social marginalization and exclusion; ameliorate growing inequality and impoverishment; and confront global environmental problems (8). If this sounds like "peddling utopias," Castles also recognizes that in order for a global citizenship to emerge, supra-national institutions have to be open, accessible, democratically accountable, and reflective of the needs and aspirations of the world's citizens. Thus far, institutions of global governance— whether the Organization for Economic Corporation and Development, the World Trade Organization, or the Asia Pacific Economic Community—have suffered from a "democratic deficit," with much of their deliberations being conducted in secret and with few or no mechanisms for input by individuals, groups, or movements within civil society. The paradox at this moment, then, is between a diminished national citizenship and an underdeveloped global citizenship.

Summary

Globalization promises to become a central concept in the discipline of political science and especially in the vocabularies of international relations and international political economy. This chapter examines the concept of globalization and its significance for international relations theory. It suggests that the dominant paradigm—realism—as a product of modernity, is conceptually limited by its own assumptions. These assumptions about the reality of the international sphere have been analyzed and rejected by a number of new perspectives associated with critical theory. In particular, postmodernism rejects realism's empiricism, positivism, and exclusive focus on the national state. It argues that global reality is ambiguous and contradictory. Moreover, while realists are correct in pointing to the persistence of the state, they are shortsighted in not seeing the change in state form and philosophy of governance. The changes to the state have been wrought from above by international institutions and agreements, horizontally by regional agreements, and from below by the activism of new civil society movements.

There is considerable debate as to globalization's novelty. This debate can be seen in the competing views of when globalization began as well as the four main responses to globalization mapped by Jameson. This chapter suggests globalization can be engaged as a cultural phenomenon as well as an economic one. It also argues that in both instances there have been historical precursors to globalization, including internationalism, transnationalism, and globalism. Both have also been reconfigured by new information and communications technologies. However, conversations about globalization have been dominated by economic globalization, particularly changes in international production, labour, and finance. Globalization as a cultural phenomenon engages the emergence of a world *polis*, global civilization, and transculturation. Complex mechanisms of global governance have emerged in the economic sphere, such as the OECD and WTO; however, no comparable institutional arrangements exist in the political, cultural, and environmental spheres. Thus, globalization can be seen as realizing the economic project of modernity, while leaving the political and cultural project of modernity underdeveloped.

Globalization is an elusive concept. This chapter argues that globalization is best understood as a historical process of transcending (the nation-state), rather than as the opening up of borders or the crossing of borders. However, ideas of transcending the state are not without problems, as the contradictions of globalization reveal. While five major contradictions are discussed, there are many others which promise to engage international relations theorists in the future. The debate about globalization in the new millennium will be profoundly political, not least because it will involve contestations of power in relation to how globalization unfolds, who benefits, and substantive issues of equality and justice related to an emergent global polity and global citizenship. The fundamental challenge of the new millennium will be finding new ways to re-insert the political into both the global and local spheres.

Discussion Questions

1. What do you understand by the concept of globalization?

2. Is globalization a better concept than internationalization or transnationalization for explaining some or all of the present political, economic, and cultural transformations? Why?

3. What are some of the forces driving globalization?

4. In your judgment, which theoretical perspective best explains globalization?

5. What do you think will be the implication of globalization for national politics and culture?

6. What role have the technological revolution and the new media played in shaping ideas of global community?

7. What are some of the problems and prospects of the new global economy?

References

Anderson, Benedict. 1991. *Imagined Communities: Reflections on the Origin and Spread of Nationalism.* London: Verso.

Barber, Benjamin. 1998. "Democracy at Risk: American Culture in a Global Culture," *World Policy Journal, 15,* 2 (Summer).

———— 1995. *Jihad vs. McWorld.* New York: Times Books.

Berki, R.N. 1981. *On Political Realism.* London: J.M. Dent.

Bradshaw, York, and Michael Wallace. 1997. *Global Inequalities.* Pine Forge Press/Sage.

——————— 1995. *Politics on the Margins: Restructuring and the Canadian Women's Movement.* Halifax: Fernwood.

Castles, Stephen. 1998. "Globalization and Migration: Some Pressing Contradictions," *International Social Science Journal, 50*, 2, 179–87.

Carr, Edward Hallett. 1964. *The Twenty Years Crisis, 1919-1939: An Introduction to the Study of International Relations*, 3rd ed. New York: Harper and Row.

Cerny, Philip G. 1996. "Globalization and Other Stories: The Search for a New Paradigm for International Relations," *International Journal, L1*, 4 (Autumn).

Collier, Ken. 1998. Interview with Ankie Hoogvelt, Aurora Online (March), http://stud1.acad.athabascau.ca/html/ejour/aurora/talks/hoogvelt.htm.

Davis, Jim. 1998. "Rethinking globalization," *Race and Class*, (October).

Fielder, Leslie. 1970. "The New Mutants" (1965). *In The Collected Essays of Leslie Fielder, vol. II.* New York: Stein and Day.

Flax, Jane. 1981. "Why Epistemology Matters: A Reply to Kress," *Journal of Politics, 43*: 1006–24.

Frost, Mervyn. 1986. *Towards a Normative Theory of International Relations.* Cambridge: Cambridge University Press.

——————. 1996. *Ethics in International Relations: A Constitutive Theory.* Cambridge: Cambridge University Press.

Gamble, C. 1994. *Timewalkers: The Prehistory of Global Colonization.* London: Sutton.

George, Alexander L. 1994. "Some Guides to Bridging the Gap*," Mershon International Studies Review, 39.*

George, Jim. 1994. *Discourses of Global Politics: A Critical (Re)Introduction to International Relations.* Boulder, Colorado: Lynne Rienner Publishers.

——————. 1989. "International Relations and the Search for Thinking Space: Another View of the Third Debate," *International Studies Quarterly, 33*, 3: 269–79.

——————. 1988. "International Relations and the Positivist/Empiricist Theory of Knowledge: Implications for the Discipline." In *New Directions in International Relations? Australian Perspectives, 23*, ed., R. Higgott. Canberra: Canberra Studies in World Affairs.

Giddens, Anthony. 1990. *The Consequences of Modernity: Self and Society in the Late Modern Age,* Cambridge: Polity Press, and Stanford: Stanford University Press.

Grinspun, Ricardo, and Robert Kreklewich. 1994. "Consolidating Neoliberal Reforms: 'Free Trade' as a Conditioning Framework", *Studies in Political Economy, 43* (Spring).

Harding, Sandra and Merrill Hintikka, eds. 1983. *Discovering Reality: Feminist Perspectives on Epistemology, Metaphysics, Methodology and the Philosophy of Science* (Dordrecht: D. Reidel).

Heckman, Susan. 1983. "Beyond Humanism: Gadamer, Althusser and the Methodology of the Social Sciences", *Western Political Quarterly, 36*, 98–115.

Hirst, Paul and Thompson, Grahame. 1996. *Globalization in Question: The International Economy and the Possibilities of Governance.* Cambridge: Polity Press.

Hoogvelt, Ankie. 1997. *Globalization and the Postcolonial World: The New Political Economy of Development.* Baltimore, Maryland: The John Hopkins University Press.

Huntington, Samuel. 1996. *The Clash of Civilization and the Remaking of the World Order.* New York: Simon and Schuster.

Jameson, Frederic. 1998a. "Preface" in *The Cultures of Globalization,* (eds.) F. Jameson and M. Miyoshi. Durham, N.C.: Duke University Press.

————1998b. "Notes on Globalization as a Philosophical Issue" in *The Cultures of Globalization,* (eds.) F. Jameson and M. Miyoshi. Durham, N.C.: Duke University Press.

————1991. *Postmodernism or, the Cultural Logic of Late Capitalism.* London: Verso.

Jameson, Frederic and Miyoshi, Masao. 1998. *The Cultures of Globalization.* Durham, N.C.: Duke.

Jencks, Charles. 1991. *The Language of Post-Modern Architecture.* London: Academy Editions.

Kanter, Rosabeth Moss. 1995. *World Class: Thriving Locally in the Global Economy.* New York: Simon and Schuster.

Kleinknecht, Alfred and Wengel, Jan ter. 1998. "The myth of economic globalization," *Cambridge Journal of Economics, 22,* 5. September.

Kuhn, Thomas. 1970. *The Structure of Scientific Revolutions.* Chicago: University of Chicago Press [1962].

Kvale, Steinvar. 1990. "Postmodern Psychology: A Contradiction in Terms?" *The Humanist Psychologist, 18,* 1.

Lechner, Frank J. and John Boli (eds). 2000. *The Globalization Reader.* (Malden, Massachusetts: Blackwell Publishers).

Maghoori, Ray and Bennet Ramberg. 1982. *Globalism versus Realism: International Relations' Third Debate.* Boulder: Westview Press.

Marshall, Don. 1996. "Understanding Late-Twentieth Century Capitalism: Reassessing the Globalization Theme," *Government and Opposition, 31,* 2 (Spring), 193–215.

Michalet, C-A. 1982. "From International Trade to World Economy: A New Paradigm." In: K. Makler et al., *The New International Economy.* Thousand Oaks, California: Sage, 37–58.

Modelski, G. 1988. *Sea Power in Global Politics* 1494–1943. Seattle: University of Washington Press.

Offe, Claus. 1985. *Disorganized Capitalism.* Cambridge: Polity.

O'Meara, Patrick, Howard D. Mehlinger and Matthew Krain, (eds.). 2000. *Globalization and the Challenges of a New Century.* Bloomington: Indiana University Press.

Perlmutter, H. V. 1991. "On the Rocky Road to the First Global Civilization," *Human Relations, 44,* 9, 897–1010.

Rajaee, Farhang. 2000. *Globalization on Trial: The Human Condition and the Information Civilization.* Ottawa, Canada: International Development Research Council.

Reinicke, Wolfgang. 1997. "Global Public Policy," *Foreign Affairs, 76,* 6 (November).

Reiser, O.L. and Davies, B. 1944. *Planetary Democracy: An Introduction to Scientific Humanism and Applied Semantics.* New York: Creative Age Press.

Robertson, Roland. 1992. *Globalization: Social Theory and Global Culture* (London: Sage).

Rosenau, J.N. 1990. *Turbulence in World Politics.* Princeton: Princeton University Press.

Sachs, Jeffrey. 1998. "Interlocking Economics: Unlocking the Mysteries of Globalization." *Foreign Policy, 110,* 15 (Spring).

Scholte, Jan Aart. 1997. *Globalization: A Critical Introduction.* London: MacMillan.

Schumann, Harald and Martin, Hans-Peter. 1997. *The Global Trap.* London: Zed Books.

Singh, Kavaljit. 1999. *The Globalization of Finance: A Citizen's Guide.* London and New York: Zed Books.

Soja, Edward. 1989. *Postmodern Geographies.* London: Verso Books.

Strange, Susan. 1997. "The Erosion of the State," *Current History* (November), 365B69.

————1996. Retreat of the State: *The Diffusion of Power in the World Economy.* Cambridge: Cambridge University Press.

Sweezy, Paul M. 1997. "More (Or Less) Globalization," *Monthly Review, 49,* 4 (September): 1–4.

———— 1992. "Globalization—To What End?: Part II," *Monthly Review, 43,* 10 (March), 1–19.

Webster. 1961. *Webster's Third New International Dictionary of the English Language Unabridged.* Springfield, Mass.: Merriam.

Further Readings

Brecher, Jeremy, Tim Costello and Brendan Smith. 2000. *Globalization from Below: The Power of Solidarity.* Cambridge, Massachusetts: South End Press.

Chossudovsky, Michel. 1998. *The Globalisation of Poverty: Impacts of IMF and World Bank Reforms.* New York: Zed and Halifax, Nova Scotia: Fernwood Publishing Ltd.

Held, David, and Anthony McGrew (eds.). 2000. *The Global Transformations Reader.* Malden, Massachusetts: Blackwell Publishers Ltd.

Hirst, Paul, and Grahame Thompson. 1999. *Globalization in Question. 2nd edn.,* revised. Cambridge: Polity Press.

Khor, Martin. 2000. *Globalisation and the South: Some Critical Issues.* Third World Network.

Weblinks

Guides: Globalization
http://www.oneworld.org/guides/globalisation/front.shtml

Global Exchange—Economic Alternatives
http://www.globalexchange.org/economy/

After Seattle—InTheseTimes
http://inthesetimes.com/index2403.html

Worldlink Online—Pro-globalization
http://www.worldlink.co.uk/

Corporate Watch—Globalization and Corporate Rule
http://www.corpwatch.org/trac/globalization/

UNDP Poverty Initiatives
http://www.undp.org/poverty/initiatives/pgm.htm

Globalization: Myth vs. Reality
www.indolink.com/Analysis/globaliz.htm1

Global Policy Forum
www.globalpolicy.org

Global Environmental Facility, World Bank:
www.worldbank.org/htm1/gef/geftext.html

CHAPTER 25

INTERNATIONAL ORGANIZATIONS

Objectives

In this chapter we shift our focus to the arena of world politics. International organizations are a central part of politics at the global level. To gain a fuller understanding of international organizations in all of their variety and complexity, this chapter will provide an introduction to international organizations and an overview of their place in the wider arena of world politics. Every country in the world belongs to international organizations. These organizations, in turn, are shaped by the major organizing principles of world politics, among them, state sovereignty, anarchy, and global governance. This chapter discusses these principles as well as the origins and evolution of international organizations. It describes the critical distinction between intergovernmental and nongovernmental organizations. Finally, it identifies some of the central preoccupations influencing the future role of these organizations in world politics.

TOM KEATING

Introduction

International organizations are a prominent feature of world politics. As we enter the twenty-first century, there are thousands of these organizations active on the world stage. Every country in the world is a member of at least one international organization, and most countries participate in many. Canada has been one of the more active participants in these organizations, having joined dozens of them through the years, ranging from the United Nations to the Arctic Council formed in the 1990s. These organizations have also been a very important forum for conducting Canadian foreign policy. In addition, many individuals belong to organizations whose membership and activities cross national borders. International organizations have a long history, but have proliferated most dramatically in the second half of the twentieth century. They have become a permanent and, often influential, feature in the daily lives of billions of people throughout the planet. It is possible to learn a great deal about international organizations by studying particular organizations such as the United Nations or the European Union and nongovernmental organizations such as the International Committee of the Red Cross or Amnesty International. The immense variety of organizations, however, suggests a slightly different approach, one that examines features common to many different organizations.

As an integral part of world politics, international organizations have been influenced by many of the principles and practices of world politics, particularly as they differ from those in domestic politics. It is particularly beneficial to understand the meaning and significance of *state sovereignty, anarchy, global governance,* and *multilateralism.* An understanding of these concepts provides a good starting point from which to examine the origins, evolution, current practices, and possible futures of international organizations.

The International Context

INTERNATIONAL ORGANIZATIONS HAVE BEEN TRACED BACK TO 1397. SINCE THE time of Dante, in the early 14th century, international organizations, including those proposing world government, have been advocated as an alternative or complement to the system of independent sovereign states. Since that time they have been invented and reinvented repeatedly in attempts to find effective means for facilitating and regulating political, economic, and social interactions that cross national borders. Proposals for institutions that closely resemble the United Nations and the European Union date back to the seventeenth century (Hinsley, 1963). Many of these proposals were concerned primarily with eliminating or reducing international conflict. They were also primarily concerned with European states. While the authors of these proposals, writers such as Sir Thomas More, William Penn, and Immanuel Kant, might be impressed with the extensive network of international organizations that exists today, they would likely be disappointed that these organizations have not prevented warfare within and between states. By the latter half of the nineteenth century international organizations were more likely to be devoted to matters of international commerce than to conflict. This trend has continued and international organizations involved in matters of international trade and finance are among the more numerous and influential in the contemporary period.

As with most political institutions, international organizations do not operate in a vacuum. Instead they exist amid a vast array of political, economic, social, and cultural activity. This activity has had a significant influence on the origins and evolution of international organizations. Particularly noteworthy are two prominent features of the global political arena in which international organizations operate—*state sovereignty* and *anarchy* (Schmidt, 1998). The first distinguishes the participants in world politics, separating national governments or states as they are most commonly labelled from the private individuals, groups, and corporations who also participate in world politics. *State sovereignty* refers to the legal (*de jure* sovereignty) and empirical (*de facto* sovereignty) condition whereby states recognize no higher authority either domestically or externally and are thus free to act as they wish. Sovereignty emerged as an influential governing principle of world politics after the Thirty Years War ended with the Peace of Westphalia in 1648. The war and the resulting peace settlement legitimated the autonomous power of states over and against that of the Church and the Emperor as well as potential domestic challengers. Sovereignty is an absolute term suggesting both autonomy and capability, but few states possess absolute sovereignty. Most states are constrained in their actions by their limited capabilities and by the restrictions imposed on them through international agreements including those established by international organizations. The widespread acceptance of the principle of state sovereignty, however, has meant that states must give their consent to be bound by international law and other commitments that might arise from being members of international organizations.

The principle of state sovereignty reflected and reinforced a second feature of world politics—the absence of a single central authority or government to regulate world politics and enforce international law. *Anarchy* refers to the absence of government at any level. The significance of anarchy at the international level has meant in effect that sovereign states operate in a political context in which there is no permanent authority that makes and enforces laws to regulate state behaviour or the behaviour of other actors in world politics. As a result, states (increasingly with private individuals, groups, and corporations) make their own rules, and determine how and by whom they are to be administered and enforced. The process by which rules are made and enforced in world politics is both complex and fascinating because of the absence of clearly defined authoritative procedures and institutions. When private citizens and groups are added to the mix the process becomes even more complicated. This process is often referred to as *global governance*. It has been defined as "governing, without sovereign authority, relationships that transcend national frontiers" (Finkelstein, 1995, 369). Attempts to establish more authoritative institutions of government at the global or regional level necessarily imply restrictions on the sovereignty or freedom of states to do as they please, something that many states have resisted. Thus, the establishment of international organizations and the process of global governance generally involve a delicate and complicated balance between the preservation of state sovereignty and the development of authority structures at the international level. Such a process has been the foundation of many intergovernmental organizations that exist today. It has also been a process in which these organizations, once established, play a major role.

Multilateralism is a term that has been used to describe both the process and the end result of co-operative efforts by states to establish rules and organizations to resolve common problems and support co-operation among states and other actors in world politics. At its simplest, multilateralism refers to a diplomatic process involving more than two states. Multilateralism has also been used to describe a particular form of international politics, one where co-operation among states has been marked by three distinct characteristics (Ruggie, 1993). First, that the costs and benefits of co-operation are shared by all participating states. Second, that co-operation is based on certain substantive principles of state conduct that influence the relations among states. And finally, that states are committed to this co-operative behaviour for the long term and do not necessarily expect immediate results. Multilateralism thus entails a specific form of inter-state co-operation, one that has a significant role for international organizations. Critical scholars have also called attention to the increasing influence of nongovernmental or civil society organizations in the process of global governance. These scholars have referred to the involvement of these actors alongside states as exemplifying a "new multilateralism," a process of co-operation that is initiated and sustained by groups emerging out of civil society (Schechter, 1999).

Classifying Intergovernmental Organizations

AN INTERNATIONAL ORGANIZATION MAY BE DEFINED AS A FORMAL INSTITUTION that facilitates regular interaction between members of two or more countries across national boundaries. Such a definition would yield thousands of entities (see, for example, http://www.uia.org). There are, however, several criteria by which one can sort out the vast array of international organizations that populate this planet. One important initial distinction is to identify two separate categories of international organizations. The first, intergovernmental organizations or IGOs, are composed of national governments or states. There are between three and four hundred IGOs actively involved in world politics. These organizations are among the most prominent. Most people have heard of the United Nations (UN), the preeminent example of an IGO. The European Union (EU), the Commonwealth, the North Atlantic Treaty Organization (NATO) and the World Trade Organization (WTO) are other well-known examples. A second category of international organization is nongovernmental organizations or NGOs. These organizations have as their members private citizens or national affiliates of groups composed of private citizens. In the mid-1990s there were over 10 000 NGOs. Most NGOs are of little interest for students of world politics, while others occasionally emerge as important political actors for selected issues. Some, however, such as the Red Cross (formally known as the International Committee of the Red Cross), Greenpeace, and Amnesty International have an active and ongoing involvement in world politics. Later in this chapter we will return to take a closer look at these NGOs and their involvement in contemporary global politics. For now, however, we will examine the origins and evolution of intergovernmental organizations and the competing perspectives of their role in world politics.

Intergovernmental Organizations

Intergovernmental organizations (IGOs) have become a permanent feature of world politics in the twentieth century. As suggested above, one of primary motivating factors in establishing these organizations has been warfare, or more specifically a desire to limit or prevent warfare between states. The words of French novelist Victor Hugo in the mid-nineteenth century captured a common sentiment. "A day will come when bullets and bombshells will be replaced by votes, by the universal suffrage of nations, by the venerable arbitration of a great sovereign senate, which will be to Europe what the Parliament is to England." (Cited in Goodspeed, 1959, 3). For many people concerned about the recurrence of warfare, some form of world government through international organizations offered the best solution to continued bloodshed. Consequently, scholars and practitioners devised elaborate plans for international organizations as the core of a world government[1] (Hinsley, 1963). Perhaps for this reason, one finds that the most elaborate efforts to establish intergovernmental organizations have taken place during or immediately following major wars (Holsti, 1995). For example, the two major institutional experiments of the twentieth century were set up after the world wars. The League of Nations was established as part of the Treaty of Versailles ending the First World War in 1919. The UN was established in 1945. In the latter case, the commitment of states to establishing an international organization was so strong that discussions on the UN began as early as 1942, long before the outcome of the war was known. The preamble of the UN Charter identifies the organization's primary objective of preserving the peace: "We the peoples of the United Nations are determined to save succeeding generations from the scourge of war, which twice in our lifetime has brought untold sorrow to mankind."

While peace may have been the primary motive in most proposals for international organizations, at a more practical level, the vast majority of international organizations have been created to serve economic and social needs. In an analysis of international organizations, Murphy identified their two principal tasks as fostering industry and managing social conflicts. He also noted two secondary tasks for these organizations, that of strengthening states and the state system and of strengthening society (Murphy, 1994, 32-37). Murphy also argued that, in addition to warfare, an equally important influence on the creation of international organizations has been the different phases of expansion and reform of the international political economy commencing with the second industrial revolution in the late eighteenth-century. "They have helped create international markets in industrial goods by linking communications and transportation infrastructure, protecting intellectual property, and reducing legal and economic barriers to trade" (Murphy, 1994, 2).

The vast and at times contradictory range of activities that have engaged international organizations is illustrated in the UN and its network of Specialized Agencies. While the primary objective is to maintain peace and security, as a multi-purpose organization the UN has also been involved in a number of other areas such as economic development (UN Development Program), health (World Health Organization), communications (International Telecommunication Union), human rights (Office of the UN High Commissioner for Human Rights), and other social concerns such as refugees (Office of the UN High

Commissioner for Refugees), women (UN Development Fund for Women), and children (UN Children's Fund). The UN has also been the principal forum in which newly independent states seek confirmation of their independence and sovereignty. At the same time, it has been pursued by human rights advocates as the organization through which the rights of individuals against the state are to be advanced and ultimately protected and by civil society organizations to gain recognition and participation in the process of global governance. Other intergovernmental organizations were established to serve a more limited and specialized mandate. The World Trade Organization (WTO), for example, which was established in 1995 focuses primarily on matters related to international trade. It developed out of the General Agreement on Tariffs and Trade (GATT) first signed in 1947. The GATT's original objective was to reduce and eventually eliminate tariff barriers to international trade. It has since become involved in a wider, yet still fairly limited, range of trade-related issues. The restricted purpose of the WTO, however, has been challenged by critics who argue that it is not possible to separate trade from other issues such as the environment and labour practices. To date, attempts to have the organization deal with some of these effects of trade have been strongly resisted by many members of the organization.

The UN, and other intergovernmental organizations, can also be distinguished on the basis of their membership. Organizations like the UN, which are open to all states are described as universal. There are very few of these. Other intergovernmental organizations restrict membership to particular regions or to states with similar historical roots or strategic concerns. The Organization of African Unity (OAU), for example, is primarily restricted to countries on the continent of Africa and originated in 1963, in part, to unify African states. The Commonwealth is composed of countries who were former colonies of Great Britain. The North Atlantic Treaty Organization (NATO) unites countries of Europe and North America that share common strategic and security interests, whereas the Association of Southeast Asian Nations (ASEAN) was created to serve the regional security interests of its members. Regional organizations have, in certain instances, emerged as important alternatives to the more universal institutions, particularly in matters of trade and finance. The European Union (EU), the North American Free Trade Agreement (NAFTA), and Asia Pacific Economic Co-operation (APEC) stand as the most important regional organizations in the international political economy. These and other regional organizations raise additional concerns and debates about the relationship between and among international organizations as they compete for recognition and influence (Fawcett and Hurrell, 1995).

Intergovernmental organizations vary extensively in their structures, procedures, capabilities, and budgets, but there are some common elements worth mentioning. Most organizations have a permanent secretariat that oversees the day-to-day operations of the organization. Members of the secretariat are drawn from member countries, and become the employees of the organization. Frequently they view their position as an international civil servant and represent the interests of the organization as a whole rather than their previous home country. Most of these organizations are led by a secretary general, president, or director who is selected by the member governments of the organization. The budgets of IGOs are based on the contributions of member governments. IGOs do not have any independent sources of revenue and thus remain dependent on member government contributions.

The representation of states in intergovernmental organizations is generally based on the principle of political equality. At the same time the decision-making structures and procedures actually employed in these organizations commonly accept a certain inequality in status and power, allowing more powerful states a greater opportunity to control the decisions of the organization. In some organizations this inequality in status is formally acknowledged. For example, the UN Charter recognizes the political equality of all of its members, yet only the UN Security Council can make decisions that are binding on all member states. The United States, Great Britain, France, China, and Russia as permanent members of the Council, have been given a veto that allows any one of them to prevent the Council and hence the UN from undertaking an action with which they disagree. In the International Monetary Fund (IMF) and the World Bank, inequality of status is recognized by granting member states voting shares based on their monetary contributions, much like private corporations and their stockholders. Other organizations, such as NATO, that lack such formal mechanisms, often take decisions only if and when, the mst powerful member governments support the decision. While the support of major powers is most often required if an international organization is to undertake effective action this does not necessarily mean that major powers always dominate the process of global governance. On occasion, the agreement and support of more powerful states can be obtained through the efforts of smaller states or members of the organization's secretariat. For some observers, IGOs provide the best opportunity for less powerful states in the global system to influence the course of global politics. The Canadian government, for example, has relied extensively on international organizations to advance its interest and objectives in the international political realm, as has Australia and other states of comparable power (Keating, 2001). The influence of such states, especially when they act as members of coalitions of states, is apparent in such areas as international trade negotiations and the extensive negotiations at the UN on the law of the sea in the 1970s (on trade see Winham, 1990; on the law of the sea see Sanger, 1987).

The decision-making process in most IGOs is based on some combination of negotiation, consensus-building, and formal votes. The sources of influence within this decentralized and diffused policy-making environment are extremely varied. Obviously, one's power in the world at large has some effect on one's ability to wield influence. Beyond this, and the more formal power structures found in places such as the UN's Security Council, states can employ a variety of techniques, such as diplomatic skills or technical expertise, to shape the outcome of the decision-making process within international organizations, as Young's work in the area of environmental policy making, among others, has suggested (Young, 1994). Unlike a national legislature, there are no organized political parties, but there are often coalitions of states that share common views and that co-operate to achieve specific objectives. These coalitions have become an active part of the process of global governance in international organizations. As early as the 1960s, in the UN, seventy-seven poorer countries formed a coalition known as the Group of 77 to pressure other UN members to devote more attention and resources to global economic inequalities. The Group of 77 later expanded to more than 100 members, and continued to serve as an effective coalition for articulating the demands of these governments. Similar coalitions can be found in institutions such as the WTO and the IMF.

One of the ongoing dilemmas that confronts international organizations is the balance between the sovereignty of member states and the power of the organization to take and enforce binding decisions that infringe on this sovereignty. Part of the difficulty arises from the fact that most intergovernmental organizations are explicitly designed to protect and reinforce the sovereignty of their member governments. The view was made explicit in the fourteenth point of U.S. President Woodrow Wilson's war aims in 1918 which partly inspired the League of Nations. Wilson called for "a general association of nations . . . formed under specific covenants for the purpose of affording *mutual guarantees of political independence and territorial integrity* to great and small states alike" (Baker and Dodd, 1925, 161). Most intergovernmental organizations recognize the independence, sovereignty, territorial integrity, and formal equality of member governments. This, in turn, makes it difficult for these organizations to take action against a member government unless that member government consents to such action. At the present time, however, there has been widespread acceptance of the position that the domestic practices of sovereign states are a matter of international concern. "The old notion that what goes on within the state is a matter of sovereign privacy . . . has been swept away. In its stead, we have installed the doctrine that world order entails political stability, democratic governments, respect for human rights, general economic well-being, ethnic harmony, and peaceful resolution of conflicts within states, no less than co-operative and peaceful relationships among them" (Claude, 2000). This has raised a whole series of new issues and responsibilities for international organizations without any concomitant attempt to expand their capacity or authority to address such issues.

Nongovernmental Organizations

Nongovernmental organizations have been defined in various ways. One of the more encompassing definitions can be found in two UN resolutions which refer to "any international organization which is not established by intergovernmental agreement . . . including organizations which accept members designated by government authorities, provided that such memberships does not interfere with the free expression of views of the organizations" [UN General Assembly Resolutions 288 (X) and 1296 (XLIV)]. The term NGOs is also generally restricted to non-profit organizations and thus excludes multinational corporations and other more nefarious commercial activities such as drug cartels that operate across national boundaries. Many groups have taken to calling themselves civil society organizations (CSOs) so as to distinguish themselves more explicitly from the government and to reinforce their connections with civil society. First it should be noted that most of these nongovernmental organizations have absolutely nothing to do with world politics as it is most commonly understood. As an individual you might take some interest in the World Ninepins Bowling Association or the World Rock 'n' Roll Confederation, but these groups are likely to contribute little to ending the conflict in the Middle East or alleviating poverty in Haiti. On the other hand, the World Jewish Congress or Oxfam might have a significant role in the Middle East peace process or reducing poverty in Haiti. NGOs have been around for a very long time and have been actively involved in the politics of global governance for centuries. In contrast to IGOs where there is a considerable amount of similarity in organizational structure and decision-making processes, there is an amazing degree of variety among the more than 10 000 nongovernmental organizations in terms of such things as organizational structure, decision-making procedures, and budgets.

In contrast to intergovernmental organizations, most nongovernmental organizations have developed out of concerns for specific issues on the part of individuals and groups. Amnesty International, for example, emerged as a result of the work of British lawyer, Peter Beneson, who in the early 1960s began to advocate for the humane treatment of prisoners in foreign countries. It has since developed into the world's most active and effective defender of individual rights. In 1977 Amnesty International was awarded the Nobel Peace Prize. The International Committee of the Red Cross, which originated in the mid-nineteenth century, also as a result of an individual's (Jean Henri Dunant) concern for the welfare of injured combatants, was awarded the first Nobel Prize for peace in recognition of its work in providing humane treatment for victims of conflict. The Red Cross remains one of the world's most active humanitarian assistance organizations. Médecins sans Frontières illustrates the disregard that NGOs have often displayed for principles such as state sovereignty and non-intervention, as they have responded to emergencies regardless of the state or situation. They too have been recognized for their work by receiving the Nobel Peace Prize in 1999. In 1997, another NGO, the International Campaign to Ban Land Mines (ICBL), was awarded the Nobel Peace Prize in recognition of its work to pressure governments to sign the Ottawa Treaty which calls for a comprehensive ban on anti-personnel land mines. This group developed as a result of a number of individual efforts, in many countries, to press governments to eliminate their reliance on anti-personnel land mines. It subsequently developed a close working relationship with the Canadian government to push for the adoption of an international treaty. The landmines treaty-making process (often referred to as the Ottawa Process) illustrates the dynamics of NGO involvement in global governance. It is, for example, interesting to note that the ICBL was led by an American, Jody Williams, but found that it was able to work more effectively with Canadian government officials in Ottawa than it was with its own government in Washington. The American government did not even consent to sign the Ottawa Treaty that had been so strongly promoted by this American-based NGO. It is also worth noting the extensive and direct involvement of NGOs alongside state representatives in the diplomatic process leading to the Ottawa Treaty (Cameron, Lawson, and Tomlin, 1998).

Not all NGOs win peace prizes. Nor are they as effective as these three have been in influencing the course of world politics. Most NGOs are rather modest operations established by groups of concerned individuals in different countries in the hope of pressuring governments to adopt policies that support their particular cause. Their political activity is generally focused in three directions (Lipschutz, 1996). First, they seek to influence national governments to adopt foreign policies that support their cause. Second, they lobby intergovernmental institutions to promote their policy concerns. Finally, they publicize their concerns with the intent of generating popular support and funds to enable them to continue to pursue the first two. Nongovernmental organizations, however, are becoming an increasingly important political actor in world politics (Matthews, 1997). The evolving nature of the relationship between intergovernmental organizations and nongovernmental organizations has thus become an important issue for both entities and for national governments. Groups such as Amnesty International, the Red Cross, CARE, Oxfam, Save the Children, Greenpeace, World Wildlife Fund, to mention just a few, have taken an increased interest in the activities of international organizations and have sought to articulate their concerns and demands to an international audience. Additionally, some NGOs are in the centre of international politics in such areas as conflict prevention and resolution, economic development, and human rights. In recognition of this increased involvement, certain NGOs have pressed for and been granted more direct participation in the policy-making process of global governance. The Canadian government has been among those that have pressed for improved access for NGOs at the UN and other international organizations. As mentioned, the Canadian government worked closely with NGOs in the negotiations on the landmine treaty and facilitated their involvement on negotiations leading to the Rome Treaty of 1998 establishing the International Criminal Court. Canadian officials have also advocated for greater access for NGOs at the UN and other institutions such as the World Bank and the WTO.

In response to these and other pressures, IGOs such as the UN and the World Bank have begun to develop more extensive contacts with NGOs. Many states, as well as IGOs however, have been reluctant and slow to respond to the substantive demands of these groups and as a result, NGOs have been less than successful in influencing policy. Their efforts, however, point to a potentially significant development in the area of global governance. More extensive, direct, and effective involvement on the part of NGOs would see traditional nationally based political activity leading to inter-state negotiations replaced by policy making at the international level involving representatives of national governments acting through intergovernmental organizations and representatives of nongovernmental organizations representing the interests of the "public" before these same IGOs. To date nongovernmental organizations have acquired consultation status with some intergovernmental organizations, most notably in the UN. NGOs have also become particularly active around various UN conferences that were held during the 1990s on such issues as population, women, human rights, and social development. NGOs have used these venues as an opportunity to voice their concerns about policies at both the national and international level and have achieved some success in shaping the agenda of these conferences. The UN Security Council has also consulted with representatives of selected NGOs in areas such as human rights and peacekeeping. All of this activity reflects an increasingly significant role for NGOs in the process of global governance.

Competing Perspectives

THERE ARE A VARIETY OF THEORETICAL DEBATES SURROUNDING THE CURRENT status and future direction of international organizations, multilateralism, and global governance. These reflect the major theoretical debates in the literature on international relations (Cox, 1992). We will briefly review three of the most prominent arguments about the sources and potential role of IGOs in world politics. The first, or realist view, holds that international organizations play at best marginal roles in world politics and are little more than a reflection of the interests of the governments that created them (Mearsheimer,

1994–5). Viewed from this perspective, international organizations have no independent influence of their own. States are the most significant actor in world politics and states are primarily concerned with maximizing their own power. States are therefore primarily interested in relative gains or improving their position relative to other states in the system, and thus use IGOs to protect or enhance their relative power position in the system. Among realists, hegemonic stability theorists argue that a dominant power (hegemon) uses IGOs to organize support and compliance from other states. In their view a hegemon is essential for the creation and maintenance of IGOs (Gilpin, 1981; Keohane, 1984). Realists maintain that IGOs act only in response to the pressures of their member governments and therefore are very much at the mercy of the most powerful states in the international system. For most realists, nongovernmental organizations are relatively insignificant players in world politics and can only be effective to the extent that they gain the support of powerful national governments. Viewed from a realist perspective international organizations have no independent influence and cannot control or shape what states do. They last only so long as states wish them to last.

An alternative view usually labelled *liberal institutionalist* holds that international organizations are both important and influential on the world stage (Young, 1994). This view holds that states co-operate out of a sense of common purpose that emphasizes absolute gains and mutual interests rather than narrowly defined self-interest. As a result states are not only concerned with maximizing their own gains relative to other states in the system, but are more generally concerned with the effects of co-operation on the system as a whole. While accepting the importance and influence of states, liberal institutionalists also argue that organizations, once created, acquire a degree of independence from their member governments and are effective in shaping the behaviour of these governments. Further, they argue that states tend to comply with many of the rulings of international organizations and abide by the principles embedded in them. International organizations are, in this view, considerably more than a mere reflection of states' interests and power. Some liberal institutionalists go further in arguing that there has been a transfer of authority from the states to international organizations such that these organizations have taken on responsibility for areas previously under the jurisdiction of national states.

A final collection of views takes a more critical perspective on international organizations. Proponents of these critical approaches argue that international organizations hold the potential for bringing about a radical transformation in the practice of world politics (Cox, 1992). For example, while they may accept the view that IGOs reflect the interests of their more powerful member states, they argue that these institutions provide an opportunity for less powerful states to pursue their own interests and perhaps design policies in opposition to those being pursued by more powerful states. This view has also emphasized the potential influence of NGOs to alter the course of world politics and argues that international organizations are a critical area for global political and economic reform. More than the other two approaches, these critical approaches emphasize the historical and political context in which international organizations operate and argue that changes in areas such as technology and in the increased globalization of economic activity create a different environment in which these organizations must exist and respond (Murphy, 1994). Some of these analysts take an explicitly normative view of international organizations and identify them as a source of global governance which is more democratic, just, and humane than the existing international system (Falk, 1995).

Current Issues and Debates

THERE ARE A NUMBER OF IMPORTANT AND INTERESTING ISSUES INVOLVING international organizations at the beginning of the twenty-first century. One such issue has been institutional reform. While much of the interest in reform has been sparked by the 50th anniversary of the UN in 1995, it has also been inspired by the end of the Cold War in 1989 and the increased activism of IGOs and NGOs in the global political economy. Institutional reforms touch on many issues, from the more practical concerns with budgets and administration to the more complicated and politically charged issues of NGO representation and democratization. Numerous studies, commissions, and reports undertaken in the 1990s examined organizational reform in IGOs such as the UN, the WTO, and the EU. The attention to reform reflects a perceived growth in the influence or relevance of these institutions and, as a result matters of accountability, transparency, and legitimacy of decision-making structures and processes; and concerns about representation and democracy take on greater significance.

The concern for representation and democracy has become an especially interesting area of debate. It pertains to the need for and mechanism by which national communities and ultimately individual citizens are to be represented in these organizations. As international organizations assume greater responsibility for public policy, questions are raised about the extent to which and means by which the public is to be represented in these organizations. There is increased attention given to the need to democratize these organizations, to open up their decision-making procedures to allow for representation by NGOs, or other representatives of private citizens in addition to the national governments currently represented. In the European Union a Parliament was established in 1977. Members of the European Parliament are elected directly by constituents in all of the member states of the Union. Proposals for popular assemblies and for elected parliaments along the lines of the European Parliament have been suggested for other organizations, but have yet to be adopted. Alternatives which have been tried or proposed include such mechanisms as regular consultations between representatives of IGOs and NGOs; periodic meetings of NGOs and other groups such as has occurred around various UN conferences. Each of these proposals seeks to provide a more direct link between individuals and IGOs (Held, 1995).

A final significant and related area of concern is the scope of responsibilities to be accorded to these institutions in the arena of global governance. Many people have looked to international organizations as a preferable alternative form of government to that of the nation state. For them international organizations should expand their responsibilities to govern an ever-widening set of policy areas. To some extent this has been occurring. A number of areas of international and domestic politics are now regulated by international organizations. This is especially evident in Europe where the EU has assumed responsibility for vast areas of domestic politics. For the most part, however, responsibility for those

State Sovereignty versus Human Rights

Events in Kosovo, Bosnia, and Rwanda have raised concerns about the morality and practicality of international organizations intervening in the domestic affairs of member governments to stop civil conflict and human rights abuses. In a discussion paper prepared for the Millennium Summit held at the UN in September 2000, United Nations Secretary General Kofi Annan wrote that " . . . if humanitarian intervention is, indeed, an unacceptable assault on sovereignty, how should we respond to a Rwanda, to a Srebrenica—to gross and systematic violations of human rights that offend every precept of our common humanity? . . . surely no legal principle—not even sovereignty—can ever shield crimes against humanity. . . . Armed intervention must always remain the option of last resort, but in the face of mass murder, it is an option that cannot be relinquished."

Others have maintained that intervention in the domestic affairs of sovereign states is unacceptable for a number of reasons.

On September 15, 2000, the Canadian government established the International Commission on Intervention and State Sovereignty to examine this issue. The mandate of the Commission is to promote a comprehensive debate on the issues surrounding the problem of intervention and state sovereignty. The purpose of the Commission is to contribute to building a broader understanding of those issues, and to fostering a global political consensus. The Commission will focus on determining the appropriate international reaction to massive violations of human rights and crimes against humanity. As part of its mandate the Commission will solicit the views of a variety of interested parties.

You have been requested to prepare a submission for the Commission that addresses the following question: Should international organizations intervene in the domestic/internal affairs of sovereign states in response to gross violations of human rights?

areas that most affect our daily lives—such as education, health, and social welfare—remains with the nation state. Moreover, if and when international organizations have intervened in domestic affairs it has generally been at the behest of their member states. Nevertheless, increasingly international organizations whose mandate was not initially concerned with selected issues have moved into these areas. For example, international trade and financial institutions increasingly intervene into domestic social affairs by imposing monetary and fiscal constraints on national governments. The result has been to transfer responsibilities and power for some policy areas to international organizations. Former Canadian Prime Minister Joe Clark once suggested that "The rules of the GATT are as important to Canadians as the rules of the Canadian constitution." The net effect has been to increase the salience of international organizations and international agreements in national policy debates. This is particularly true of poorer countries, but is to varying degrees significant for all countries that are extensively involved in international trade and other activities. The increased involvement of international organizations in areas previously within the domestic jurisdiction of national governments suggests that there has occurred a diminution of state sovereignty.

This also raises important and challenging questions about the acceptable degree of institutional interference in the domestic affairs of states. For example, many advocates would like to see international organizations interfere to protect the human rights of oppressed peoples in countries such as Burma, Rwanda, or China. At the same time, others worry about the possibility that international organizations might interfere to protect the interests of foreign investors or interfere with domestic environmental and labour standards. Additionally there are profound differences among member states over the nature and scope of intervention by international organizations. Many governments in the developed capitalist countries support international organizations which act in support of free market principles, while governments of weaker countries are concerned that more powerful states will use international organizations to control their policy options. The balance between effective international institutional intervention and respect for state sovereignty will be one of the major considerations shaping the future role of international organizations.

These are but a sample of the many issues surrounding international organizations. Global governance has always been an important issue, but the increased number and variety of organizations on the world stage have made it one of the more important and complicated issues for the twenty-first century.

Summary

International organizations have become a permanent and prominent feature of world politics. There has been a tremendous growth in the number and variety of international organizations especially in the last half of the twentieth century. International organizations refer to nonprofit organizations of which there are two general categories—governmental and nongovernmental. Intergovernmental organizations refer to organizations of two or more states. Nongovernmental organizations refer to organizations of individuals and/or groups from two or more countries. There are more than 300 intergovernmental organizations and more than 10 000 nongovernmental organizations active in the world today. Intergovernmental organizations can be further classified according to membership (universal or regional) and objectives (multi-purpose or single-purpose).

Intergovernmental organizations have originated out of a concern for the elimination of war and a shared concern for managing trans-border problems. Many advocates of a more peaceful international system have argued for the need for international organizations to provide for global peace, order and justice. Others argue that international organizations merely reinforce the position of powerful states and interests in the international system. Three competing perspectives—realist, liberal institutionalist, and new multilateralist—posit different views on the salience and influence of international organizations and their relationship with national governments. While interpretations on the role and influence of international organizations varies, it is evident that as a result of the salience of cross-border issues such as environmental pollution, the AIDS epidemic, refugees and economic globalization, international organizations will continue to be a central part of world politics in the years ahead.

Discussion Questions

1. Should more responsibility be given to international organizations to manage political, and economic, and social affairs at the international level?
2. Would a world government be a good thing?
3. Have international organizations such as the World Trade Organization acquired too much power?
4. How could intergovernmental organizations be made more democratic, allowing for more direct representation and participation by nongovernmental organizations and/or private citizens?
5. How effective has the United Nations been in facilitating peaceful co-operation among states?

References

Baker Ray S. and William E. Dodd, eds. 1925. *The Public Papers of Woodrow Wilson, War and Peace Volume I.* New York: Harper.

Cameron, Maxwell A., Robert Lawson and Brian Tomlin. Eds. 1998. *To Walk Without Fear.* Don Mills, Ontario: Oxford University Press.

Cox, Robert. 1992. "Multilateralism and World Order." *Review of International Studies.* *18*:61-80.

Falk, Richard. 1996. *Humane Governance.* University Park, Pennsylvania: Pennsylvania State University Press.

Fawcett, Louise and Andrew Hurrell. Eds. 1995. *Regionalism in World Politics: Regional Organization and International Order.* Oxford: Oxford University Press.

Finkelstein, Lawrence. 1995. "What Is Global Governance?" *Global Governance,* 1:376-372.

Gilpin, Robert. 1981. *War and Change in World Politics.* Cambridge: Cambridge University Press.

Goodspeed, Stephen S. 1959. *The Nature and Function of International Organization.* New York: Oxford University Press.

Held, David. 1995. *Democracy and the Global Order.* Stanford: Stanford University Press.

Hinsley, F.H. 1963. *Power and the Pursuit of Peace.* Cambridge: Cambridge University Press.

Keohane, Robert. 1984. *After Hegemony.* Princeton: Princeton University Press.

Lipschutz, Ronnie. 1996. "Reconstructing World Politics: The Emergence of Global Civil Society," in Rick Fawn and Jeremy Larkins, eds., *International Society after the Cold War.* New York: St. Martin's Press.

Mathews, Jessica. 1997."Power Shift" *Foreign Affairs.* January/February

Mearsheimer, John. 1994-5. "The False Promise of International Institutions." *International Security.* 20:82-104

Mitrany, David. 1966. *A Working Peace System* Chicago: Quadrangle.

Murphy, Craig. 1994. *International Organization and Industrial Change*. Cambridge: Polity Press.

Ruggie, John. Ed. 1993. *Multilateralism Matters*. New York: Columbia University Press.

Sanger, Clyde. 1987. *Ordering the Oceans*, Toronto: University of Toronto Press.

Schechter, Michael. 1999. *Future Multilateralism*. New York: Palgrave.

Schmidt, Brian C. 1998."Lessons from the Past: Reassessing the Interwar Disciplinary History of International Relations" *International Studies Quarterly* 42:433-460.

Winham, Gilbert. 1990. "GATT and the International Trade Regime." *International Journal. 45*:796-822

Young, Oran. 1994. *International Governance*. Ithaca: Cornell University Press.

Further Readings

Bennett, A. LeRoy. 1995. *International Organizations: Principles and Issues*. 6th ed. Englewood Cliffs, N.J. : Prentice Hall.

Commission on Global Governance. 1995. *Our Global Neighborhood*. Oxford: Oxford University Press. Also see the Commissions website at: http://www.cgg.ch

Claude, Inis L. 1971. *Swords into Plowshares: The Problems and Progress of International Organization. 4th ed*. New York: Random House.

Keck, Margaret and Kathryn Sikkink. 1997. *Activists Beyond Borders: Advocacy Networks in International Politics*. Ithaca, NY: Cornell University Press.

Weiss, Thomas David P. Forsythe, and Roger Coate, 1997. *The United Nations and Changing World Politics, 2nd edition*, Boulder: Westview.

International Organization, Global Governance, and *International Peacekeeping* are quarterly journals devoted to issues and debates involving international organizations.

Weblinks

Most international organizations have their own web sites, including:

United Nations
www.un.org

The Organization of American States
www.oas.org

World Trade Organization
www.wto.org

Most nongovernmental organizations also have their own sites, including:

International Commission of the Red Cross
www.icrc.org;

Amnesty International
www.amnesty.org

Medecins sans Frontieres
www.msf.org

For other nongovernmental organizations check
www.oneworld.org.

There are also some comprehensive listings of international organizations and
issues involving these organizations on the Internet, including:
www.uia.org
www.globalpolicy.org

The International Commission on Intervention and State Sovereignty
www.iciss.gc.ca

CHAPTER 26

INTERNATIONAL FINANCIAL INSTITUTIONS

SUSANNE SOEDERBERG

Objectives

Among the growing number of international governmental and non-governmental organizations, international financial institutions (IFIs) have gained unprecedented prominence and power in the current era. This current importance of IFIs is directly related to the changing nature of the international economic environment in which they operate. In the late twentieth and early twenty-first centuries international financial markets have become a dominant aspect of the international economy. These financial markets engage in the trade of currency, securities, and equity and have emerged as dominant players in the international political economy. For instance, every day trillions of dollars move around the globe with lightening speed and profoundly influence the decision-making and policy priorities of national governments in both the North and South. Nevertheless, while financial markets now dominate the global economy, there are few (and often inadequate) regulatory mechanisms to govern them. The key task of this chapter is to examine the role that IFIs, such as the IMF and the World Bank, play within the new economic environment. Do these organizations function to effectively regulate the international economy in the interests of all states? Or do they merely facilitate the continuance of the current status quo that works for the benefit of particular states and actors within the global economy? Because IFIs are intimately involved in the functioning of the current international political economy, it is essential to look at their historical emergence in the postwar period in order to understand their current role. This chapter traces the regulation of international trade back to the Second World War when world leaders established a rule structure called the Bretton Woods system. Next, the chapter describes the key roles of the IFIs within this larger regulatory structure. It then explores the three main factors leading to the collapse of the Bretton Woods system: the oil crises during the 1970s; the underlying financial crisis within the world economy; and the emergence of the London Eurocurrency market. We then survey the volatile landscape of the post–Bretton Woods world economy. Following this discussion, we turn our attention to the roles of IFIs within the current era of globalization. Finally, we consider the critical issue of who benefits from the deregulated and often chaotic post–Bretton Woods era.

Introduction

Archaeologists tell us that humans for most of recorded history have been traders. The earliest market economies depended on **barter**, or the trading of goods directly for other goods. Yet barter proved to be complicated and expensive as individuals searched for satisfactory exchanges. The invention of money helped individuals bypass the inconvenience of barter. Money also greatly assisted trade between nation states. Economists argue that money also allowed nation states to adhere to the **principle of comparative advantage**. This principle holds that the best way for countries to achieve prosperity is to trade those things they can produce most competitively and buy those things that other countries produce most competitively. The principle of competitive advantage, however, does not fully capture the nature of economic relations between nation states. Because some states are more economically powerful than others, they enter into exploitative relations, such as imperialist relations. A historical example of imperialism is the exploitation of natural resources and labour power in the "new world," such as between Spain and its former colonies which we now know as Latin America, and between the United Kingdom and Canada. Trade between states has also become complicated by periods of protectionism when some states create national barriers to block the import of goods from competitor states. For example, England and the Netherlands used heavy protectionist measures in the 1660–1715 period. Equally, France attempted to protect its industries from British exports between 1715 and 1815, as did Germany throughout the nineteenth century. Tariffs, which are duties or taxes levied on certain imports, are the most common way that states have implemented protectionism through public policy.

As nations continued to trade goods with one another, they became more economically and politically interdependent. Modern-day examples of this interdependence include the European Union or the North American Free Trade Zone. As we saw with protectionist tendencies, trade relations between states are not always harmonious, especially if one state feels that it is losing its competitive edge to another state. Economists speak of this unequal trading relation between states in terms of balance-of-payments problems. A **balance of payments** is essentially a summary record of a country's transactions that involve payments or receipts of foreign exchange, including the current account (goods and services) and the capital account (short-term and long-term money). If a country is experiencing a capital accounts deficit, this means that more money is leaving the country than entering. When a nation state experiences a balance of payments deficit, it usually becomes protectionist in its relations with other states. This in turn can have detrimental economic effects for a nation state that depends on foreign markets for its exports. For example, approximately 80 percent of Canada's export trade is with the United States. If the U.S. became protectionist overnight, Canada's economy would be seriously hurt.

Protectionism and other forms of economic conflict between trading nations present problems in global relations because of the inherently unequal and increasingly interdependent nature of the world economy. How have nation states sought to mitigate the occurrence of conflict and to regulate the international economy? An early attempt was undertaken by Great Britain in the nineteenth century. Under the hegemonic rule of Great Britain, the world economy was temporarily stabilized through the application of the Gold Standard from 1870 to 1914. Nevertheless, the formalization and institutionalization of trade regulation is relatively recent, occurring only at the end of World War II with the establishment of the Bretton Woods Agreement.

Bretton Woods

AFTER WORLD WAR I, THE USE OF THE GOLD STANDARD AS A MEANS OF ORGANIZING and managing the world economy came to a close with the erosion of the economic might and hegemonic position of Great Britain in the international political sphere. During the late 1920s, national economies entered into a period of stagnation, which was marked by the shrinking of foreign investment, large increases in unemployment rates, bankruptcies, and tumbling levels of international trade. The culmination of this turmoil was the New York stock market crash in October 1929 which propelled the era of the Great Depression. During this period, many states turned their attention to the mounting internal social problems brought about by massive unemployment and growing poverty. In doing so, governments embraced highly protectionist policies to deal with their worsening domestic economic conditions. This form of state intervention represented a unilateral action undertaken by a country in pursuit of its own self-interest in international trade, regardless of how the action might adversely affect the economy of other countries. Examples of such **beggar-thy-neighbour** policies included imposing tariffs; dumping, which involves the use of government subsidies to domestic companies so that they may sell their goods in other countries far below the cost required to manufacture them (i.e., unfair pricing); and competitive currency devaluation, which occurs when a government decreases the external value of a currency to make a country's exports cheaper to prospective buyers in other countries. Because states exist in an interdependent world, other states reacted to beggar-thy-neighbour policies usually by adopting similar policies. A good example of this was the Smoot-Hawley tariff in the United States, which became law in June 1930. The Smoot-Hawley tariff essentially sanctioned gigantic escalations in tariff prices by the United States on imported goods. Of course, the Smoot-Hawley tariff prompted other countries, which traded with the U.S., to impose retaliatory measures. The increasing economic problems within states and escalating economic trading tensions between states was interrupted by World War II (1939–1945).

Although World War II effectively derailed any international efforts to reform the rules of trade, by the war's end world leaders, anxious not to repeat the disasters of the 1930s, turned their attention to the regulation of world trade. In July 1944, representatives of 44 countries met at Bretton Woods, New Hampshire, to design a multilateral postwar system through which the trade and monetary relations of the non-communist world could be regulated in a stable manner. An overriding concern for the policymakers who were present at Bretton Woods was to avoid another Great Depression. The policymakers at Bretton Woods believed that the length and severity of the Great Depression was exacerbated by the lack of commitment by individual states to the maintenance of a stable world economic regime and the absence of formal international rules to guide state action.

To avert the economic ills brought about by the beggar-thy-neighbour trade policies of the Great Depression, the key policymakers present at the Bretton Woods conference attempted to construct an international agreement that would promote international political and economic co-operation. The architects of the Bretton Woods system were implementing a basic liberal premise that expanding international trade held the key to stable economic reconstruction and development and that it would make states more accountable to other states for the international effects of their domestic policymaking. How was this achieved? The Bretton Woods System (BWS), which was the formal agreement that emerged from the meeting in July 1944, comprised a set of rules that would govern the economic relations between member countries through a fixed-but-adjustable exchange rate system arrangement that was based on the par (equal) value system. Under this system the United States defined the value of its dollar in terms of gold: one-ounce of gold was to be equal to (or at par with) $35 U.S. The Bretton Woods System established that world trade would be conducted in American dollars. The U.S., however, was required to maintain gold reserves to back up its dollar. Traders thus could, at any time, exchange their American dollars for gold at the set price of $35 U.S. per ounce. Other countries fixed the value of their currency in relation to the US dollar. The Canadian dollar, for example, was fixed at a rate of $.925 U.S. between 1962 and 1970 (Crow, 1993). Under the *fixed exchange rate system*, member countries agreed to keep the value of their money within one percent of this par value. If they thought that change in the value of their currency would help their economy, they discussed this issue with other members in the forum of the International Monetary Fund (IMF) and obtained their consent before doing so. The underlying motivation behind this mechanism was to keep currencies stable and predictable. Thus, in contrast to today's economy, there was little motivation for currency speculation—buying and selling currencies for profit. This par value system lasted from 1944 to 1971.

The policymakers of the BWS regarded unfettered financial markets with much suspicion both because of the harmful effects of financial speculation on national economies and their strong association with the Great Depression. Advanced economies in the postwar period were driven by manufacturing and mass consumption of the new technologies of the period, especially cars, home appliances, and televisions. National governments kept a watchful eye on the flow of money within the national economy in order to ease inflation or to prevent recession. The architects of the BWS championed the use of capital controls to regulate the amount and type of capital (i.e., direct investment or loans) entering a national economy. Regulating the flow of capital both into and inside the national economy was one of the many policy instruments that national governments regularly employed to maintain a healthy economy. As such, in the postwar era government priorities outweighed those of the market. The invisible hand of the market was steered by the decidedly visible hand of the state.

One basic dilemma in the international political economy is the contradiction between domestic economic autonomy and international economic stability. The BWS overcame this paradox through an inter-state agreement that all forms of domestic intervention into the economy should be compatible with the requirements of international stability (Ruggie, 1982). John Ruggie refers to this form of multilateralism as an *embedded liberal compromise*. It should be stressed that not all countries benefited equally from the new international regime. The economies of Europe, the United Kingdom, and Japan had been demolished by World War II and, thus, the United States stood unchallenged both economically and militarily in the international economy. It would be American products, aided by the new international financial regime (and by the Marshall Plan) that would rebuild these economies as well as those of newly decolonized countries in the 1960s. The United States benefited greatly from this embedded liberal compromise, not least because it progressively opened the world markets for American products. This reinforcing relationship between an ordered international trade and monetary system, on the one hand, and the political and economic power of the United States, on the other, has led to the description of this period as Pax Americana. This term refers to the unchallenged political, economic, and military rule of the United States within the Western capitalist world.

Later in this chapter we will explore some of the reasons why the economic stability created by the BWS began to erode in the 1970s. First, however, we will take a closer look at the "twin institutions" of the BWS, namely the World Bank and the International Monetary Fund (IMF), as well as at the General Agreement on Tariffs and Trade (GATT).

The IFIs of Bretton Woods

The World Bank

The initial role of the World Bank was that of a financial intermediary providing finance for postwar reconstruction in such sectors as agriculture, transportation, and energy. The World Bank provides creditworthy countries access to international capital markets on more favourable terms than they could obtain otherwise because it acts as a guarantor. For some developing countries now, and in the past, borrowing from the Bank has been the only way to obtain long-term finance. When the many colonies of European imperialism gained independence in Africa and elsewhere in the 1960s, the World Bank began to play a larger role as lender for large-scale development projects such as dams, bridges, and power plants. In most instances, the contracts to build these large infrastructural projects in developing countries were obtained by enterprises from the developed world, especially the United States.

By late 1950s, it became clear that a growing number of developing countries were having problems meeting the requirements to borrow on the World Bank's terms. To address this problem, in 1957, the World Bank created the International Finance Corporation (IFC) to assist these states in obtaining finance from private lenders, that is, commercial banks. In 1960, the International Development Association (IDA) was established to finance projects in poorer countries on more favourable terms than the World Bank's. By the 1970s, developing countries increasingly turned to the private banks for development capital while the World Bank began to focus on the elimination of poverty. Aid given by the World Bank to fight against poverty was tightly linked to the recipient country's economic and social reforms.

Up to the time of the Third World Debt Crisis, which occurred in the early 1980s, World Bank lending, IFC loans, and IDA credits were increasing in importance as a source of development finance. The perceived success of the Bank in its early years led to regional multilateral development banks that were modelled closely on the World Bank, and included the Asian Development Bank, the Inter-American Development Bank, and the African Development Bank.

The International Monetary Fund

The fundamental role of the IMF was to oversee exchange rate relationships in a fixed, but adjustable exchange rate system. As mentioned earlier, the fixed exchange rate system was established to encourage worldwide economic growth and stability by enabling member countries to pursue domestic growth polices that would be reflected in positive balance of payments statements. Drawing on the experience of the 1930s, the IMF sought to alleviate trade deficits because of the fear that they might eventually threaten the entire world economic system. To avoid the possibility of disrupting economic stability, the IMF lent money to countries facing a balance-of-payments problem. Where did this money come from?

The IMF does not make loans in the conventional sense. Rather, it swaps one type of monetary asset for another. For example, "a member with a weak balance-of-payments position and in need of hard currencies will exchange some of its own currency for the currencies of members with strong balance of payments" (IMF, 1999c). To illustrate, after the 1994 peso crisis, Mexico could hypothetically purchase one million U.S. dollars with an equivalent amount of Mexican pesos (one million pesos), even though a peso was only a fraction of the value of a U.S. dollar. Within a certain period of time, however, Mexico would have to buy back its pesos with U.S. dollars. This purchase–re-purchase strategy explains why the Fund's resources do not change—"only the composition of its currency holdings" (IMF, 1999c).

IFIs are structured in a similar manner to corporations. A member government owns a number of shares which is determined by how much money it has paid into the IMF. Clearly, some shareholders are far more powerful than others. The U.S. and other affluent countries have had a much higher proportion of shares and thus higher representation in the IMF and World Bank. For example, the Group of Seven industrialized countries plus the rest of the European Union, representing a mere 14 percent of the world's population, account for 56 percent of the quotas and thus voting rights in the IMF executive board (Krueger,

1997). The size of a country's shares or quotas clearly establishes an internal pecking order among Fund members, since these quotas determine the voting power in the Fund. It should be noted that the original rationale behind the shareholder regulatory structure of the IMF was to avoid the gridlock that is common to many international organizations, such as the United Nations. Nevertheless, to get particularly significant changes or decisions through the IMF, such as a change in the Fund's articles, an 85 percent majority is required. Thus, any member or group of members capable of collecting 15 percent of IMF shares possesses the ability to block decisions. In order for the required majority to be obtained, the United States must agree to the changes being proposed because it holds 18 percent of the Fund's quotas (Krueger, 1997). This highly unequal shareholder-based power structure means that the IMF has a serious democratic deficit.

While the IMF was created to prevent financial instability and the World Bank was devised to finance economic recovery, the General Agreement on Tariffs and Trade (GATT) was created to prevent discriminatory trade practices, such as those that flourished in the 1930s. The basic goal of the GATT was not to regulate trade, as its successor the World Trade Organization currently is empowered to do. Rather the GATT was aimed to facilitate freer trade on a multilateral basis. Freer trade has been facilitated through a series of international negotiations (known as "rounds") over the past 50 years, each lasting several years. The number of states involved in these rounds has grown over this period as well. In 1947, for example, 23 states participated whereas the last seven-year (Uruguay) round, which concluded in 1993, included 107 states.

The GATT attempted to centralize trade negotiations as well as to make certain that trade liberalization would be in turn applied to all states. The core principle of the GATT is non-discrimination, aimed at preventing the emergence of privileged trading blocs that act in a protectionist or discriminatory manner against third states. To deter this type of discriminatory practice, the GATT relied on the *most-favoured-nation* clause (MFN). The MFN is invoked when a concession established with one state would automatically be applied to other states. In effect, the MFN turned out to be a powerful policy tool in seeking greater trade liberalization in the world economy. For example, if Canada agreed to lower tariffs on American beer, it would be required to apply that same tariff to all other countries selling beer to Canada.

The Collapse of the Bretton Woods System

THREE INTERRELATED WORLD EVENTS LED TO THE BREAKDOWN OF THE BRETTON Woods System in the early 1970s:

1. The rise in the Euromarkets;
2. Two significant hikes in the price of oil by the Organization of Petroleum Exporting Countries (OPEC); and
3. The increasing problems in the world economy, particularly the U.S.

First, the Euromarkets or Eurodollar markets began to emerge as a major force within the world economy. Simply stated, the Euromarkets are an organized market for foreign currency deposits. A Eurodollar deposit, for example, is nothing more than American dollars deposited in a bank outside the U.S. Banks were attracted to these foreign currency deposits due to the perceived profit opportunities arising from the comparative regulatory freedom accorded such activity. American banks in particular found the offshore market irresistible in that it allowed them to bypass domestic reserve requirements and interest-rate limitations as well as the widening array of capital controls imposed by Washington in the 1960s to cope with the U.S. balance-of-payments problem (Cohen, 1986, 24).

Second, the growth and power of the Euromarkets was closely tied to further acceleration in the internationalization of banking activity, especially with the skyrocketing oil prices in 1973–74 and again in 1978–79. Two immediate consequences of the oil shocks were the rise in imbalances in the pattern of global payments, and the phenomenon referred to as *petrodollars*. Because most countries were experiencing a downturn in their economies during this period, many, particularly in the developing world, found it difficult to make payments on the rising cost of petroleum. Simultaneously, the cartel known as OPEC purchased U.S. dollars with their huge profits and reinvested these dollars in the unregulated Euromarkets, where their investments would receive the highest return. Banks operating in the Euromarkets, and especially American banks, lent this money to cash-strapped governments. During the late 1970s, these banks were providing huge loans to the developing world.

The third, and decisive, factor that led to the demise of the BWS was the recessionary climate of most countries, particularly the United States. The effects of economic "stagflation" (high unemployment mixed with high inflation rates) translated into growing balance-of-payments problems for the country. In response to mounting domestic pressures, the Nixon administration in the U.S. turned inwards, taking a protectionist stance. In doing so, the U.S. government found itself engaging in beggar-thy-neighbour tactics. In 1971, for example, President Nixon introduced tax legislation that discouraged U.S. investment abroad by providing a tax credit for domestic investment and encouraged exports as opposed to foreign direct investment. A surcharge was also imposed on imports to the United States. In the same year, the U.S. government suspended the dollar's gold convertibility. This move was motivated by the fact that there were simply not enough U.S. gold reserves to adequately meet international demand for gold, which in those inflationary times was regarded, at $35 an ounce, as an irresistible bargain. In 1973, the U.S. government abandoned the fixed exchange rate system and effectively did away with the fundamental logic of the BWS. From this point onwards, national currencies would be determined by the forces of supply and demand in the world market. This is what is meant by floating exchange rates. Governments became responsible for maintaining the value of their currencies at market value.

With the abandonment of the BWS and the subsequent loss of its political and economic scaffolding (the *Pax Americana*), embedded liberalism, which had constituted the principle guiding inter-state relations for almost three decades, would also come to an end. International trade and monetary relations had thus become a free-for-all as each country attempted to deal with the effects of crisis.

The Post–Bretton Woods Era

THERE ARE TWO DEFINING FEATURES OF TODAY'S WORLD ECONOMY—FIRST, THE meteoric rise of financial markets, which undermine the regulatory capacity of any single state and, second, swathes of private, unregulated capital flows that dominate the "real economy" (i.e., the production and trade of goods and services). What does this mean in practical terms? Although the trade in goods and services is more beneficial to society as a whole because it helps create and maintain jobs, global financial markets have become more influential in terms of shaping domestic policymaking, which in turn affects both our daily lives and the relations between states. The fate of our domestic economies is largely determined by the activities in the complex and powerful international financial markets. Yet the private sector is not the only segment of a country which is dependent on financial markets for investment flows. Governments have become equally reliant on global financial markets to sustain their countries' balance of payments. As such, governments compete with one another to attract these capital flows into their national boundaries. To this end, governments attempt to implement "investment friendly" policies, such as low taxation, high interest rates, stable currencies, and so forth. In this sense, the international financial markets can and do influence state policy. The following quote provides an idea of the type of power these international markets wield vis-à-vis domestic markets: "The daily turnover in the foreign exchange market, which was about $15 billion in 1973 and about $60 billion in 1983 is now approximately $1.3 trillion, an amount perhaps sixty times the volume needed to finance trade, one that dwarfs the less than one trillion dollars available to the governments of advanced countries for exchange rate stabilisation purposes" (Crotty and Epstein, 1996, 132).

How did this situation come about? In times of crisis, money flows throughout the world in search of secure and profitable outlets. Not only falling levels of profit mark the ongoing crisis, but also relatively low economic growth rates. As William Greider observes "[s]ince the early 1970s, long-term growth in the major industrial countries has been cut in half, from about 5 percent a year to about 2.5 percent a year" (Greider, 1997). Instead of investing in the real economy (i.e., in workers, machinery, and factories), money flows in search of speculative, often very short-term means of profit (Holloway, 1995). Seen in this light, the initial expansion of the private financial markets was directly related to the breakdown of the BWS. The U.S. paved the way in granting freedom to market players through liberalizing initiatives and opting not to implement more effective controls on financial movements. Both the UK and U.S. governments explicitly supported the largest *offshore market* at the time, namely the London Eurocurrency markets. As mentioned above, American banks in particular found the offshore market irresistible in terms of bypassing American monetary policy. It was precisely the unregulated nature of offshore markets that made them attractive, since large profits could escape national financial regulation. To get an idea of how quickly the Euromarket was growing, in 1964 its net size was $9 billion, but by 1982 it had skyrocketed to $702 billion. This is an increase of more than 7500 percent (Cohen, 1986).

Where was all of this money destined? A large part went to finance the public (government) and private (corporations) sectors of the advanced industrialized countries.

However, a good chunk of these capital flows also went to developing countries, which were in desperate need of funding. In fact, U.S. banks engaged in overbanking to certain countries, particularly Brazil and Mexico. Overbanking refers to an unwise (or, "imprudent") extension of large amounts of credit by commercial banks to borrowers who are already highly indebted. For example, in 1976, Mexico's debt service ratio, which is an indicator of the ability of a country to pay back its debt, climbed steeply from 49 percent to 69 percent (Kapstein, 1994). This precarious financial situation was not to last long, however. In August 1982, Mexico announced that it could no longer meet the interest payments on its loan, never mind the principal amount. After Mexico's proclamation, several countries in Latin America, East Asia, and Eastern Europe followed suit and threatened to default on their loans. This event was known as the Debt Crisis and, as we will learn below, it had important ramifications for the role of the IMF.

Governments have encouraged the incredible power and regulatory freedom that finance enjoys today both by responding to corporate demands and by themselves having become dependent on capital flows from the financial markets. As William Greider notes, the "fastest and largest component in the growth of global financial assets is debt, especially government debt. Capital is lending to enterprise and national government of nearly every major economy to finance their deepening indebtedness" (Greider, 1997). The immediate implication for the inter-state system is that nation states compete with each other for capital flows. In fact, signalling creditworthiness and demonstrating the investment potential and benefits of a country have become overriding preoccupations of governments in order to lure and maintain capital investments. This competition for capital from international lenders, in turn, has led to the reordering of policy agendas. Beginning in the 1980s, governments have turned their backs on their postwar political commitments to promote social equity. Instead, government support for education, pensions, and social welfare has been reduced (and sometimes eliminated), all in the name of remaining competitive and creditworthy in the global economy.

How should we make sense of this post–Bretton Woods system marked by competing nation states? The embedded liberal compromise seems to have shifted to what could be called *neoliberal orthodoxy*; that is, the diehard and naïve belief that the constant liberalization of financial markets and trade will lead to some sort of magical self-healing and self-adjustment of the economy in which all societies will benefit equally. This new set of principles mirrors a new model of economic development, that has been called the *Washington Consensus*. This model is based on the premise of neoliberalism which suggests that market liberalization, privatization, economic stabilization, and deregulation will lead to greater prosperity and sustainable economic development. As we will see later, this neoliberal orthodoxy is the underlying principle of the policies implemented by the IMF and World Bank.

While neoliberal orthodoxy is affecting all states, it has had especially important ramifications for emerging market economies. The several devastating economic crises over the past decade in Mexico, Thailand, Indonesia, South Korea, Russia, and Brazil should be seen as a result of abusive and rampant speculation caused by financial deregulation and the greed of banks (Baily et al., 2000). This view is opposed to the post facto finger pointing of American economists and officials at the IMF and World Bank, who blame the crises on corruption as well as inadequate banking and finance regulations in the crisis-hit countries.

IFIs in a Globalizing Era

The World Bank

With the increasing intensity of the world economic crisis in the late 1970s, the World Bank gradually began to become more cognizant of the importance of a sound macro-economic policy framework for economic development. Macro-economic policies are governmental techniques designed to influence broad aspects of the domestic economy such as economic growth, unemployment, inflation, and money supply. These policies include balanced budgets, low interest rates, decreased levels of government spending, and the transference of responsibilities from the public to private sector. From the perspective of the World Bank, loans to improve a country's infrastructure were ineffective without a healthy economy to sustain developmental progress. Of course, the other important motivation behind the Bank's desire that the countries implement sound economic management was to ensure that they could also pay back their loans to the international financial institutions. Hence, in the 1980s, the World Bank shifted its focus from development or aid to *structural adjustment policies* (SAPs), a type of conditional loan which we will discuss below. This modification in the World Bank's policy orientation represented a significant departure from its earlier focus on infrastructure development. Taking a lead in the establishment of the new neoliberal model of economic development, the World Bank now swiftly disbursed money to support policy reforms, such as market liberalization, privatization, economic stabilization, and deregulation. It was assumed that these fundamental neoliberal policies would lead to prosperity and sustainable economic development. Thus, the SAPs, which are issued by the World Bank, may be seen as an attempt to lock in nations to the principles of the Washington Consensus.

While SAPs and neoliberal policy practices have assisted in transferring wealth to the Northern hemisphere by ensuring that loans issued by large transnational banks (mostly American-based) were repaid, they have, however, done little to alleviate poverty levels in the Southern hemisphere. Indeed, the 1999 United Nations Development Program's *Human Development Report* indicates that the income ratio between the fifth of the world's people living in the richest countries and the fifth in the poorest countries was 74 to 1 in 1997, up from 60 to 1 in 1990, and 30 to 1 in 1960 (United Nations, 1999). All in all, SAPs and neoliberal policies have gone hand-in-hand to erode already low levels of social spending, and to encourage the privatization of health and education, as well as the forced export of food products. Clearly such policies have led to increases in malnutrition and illiteracy, and to deteriorating levels of basic health standards for the general population. In the early 1990s, the World Bank admitted that SAPs have had a deleterious impact on the developing world and has once again turned its focus to poverty elimination albeit within a neoliberal framework.

The IMF

Because of its ability to wield larger amounts of money and to interfere more deeply with a country's macro-economic policymaking processes, the IMF has been far more controversial than the World Bank in recent years. The chief concern of the IMF's critics are the SAPs that it has consistently forced on developing countries since the early 1980s. Individuals across the ideological spectrum have heavily criticized SAPs for appropriating a large chunk of a developing country's economic sovereignty, and for contributing to increasing poverty, economic dependence, and financial instability. These criticisms have particularly been levied at the IMF's response to the Asian crisis of 1997. SAPs had been a key policy instrument of the IMF as it arranged new loans for the crisis-hit debtor nations and tried to ensure that these loans would eventually be paid back. For the debtor countries, new money was available only to pay off old debts. These new loans were negotiated through new stand-by arrangements with the Fund. In this way, the IMF was able to assure that the debtor governments would co-operate with its so-called *conditionalities*. Basically this term refers to a commitment that debtor nations must make to the IMF before receiving any funds. In effect, the debtor country is pressured to adhere as closely as possible to the Fund's SAPs, or risk being cut off from external markets and experiencing a lengthy loss of access to external sources of funding such as development aid.

SAPs involve two basic phases; first stabilization and then neoliberal restructuring. The first phase, economic stabilization, aims to engender what the IMF considers sound economic fundamentals. To this end, the Fund encourages the debtor nation to undergo budget cuts, currency devaluation, interest rate increases, and outward-oriented trade and investment policies and credit squeezes. The second phase involves "necessary" neoliberal structural reform, such as trade liberalization, privatization of state enterprises, deregulation of the country's banking system, liberalizing capital movements, and tax reform (Chossudovsky, 1997).

Since the collapse of the Bretton Woods System, the IMF has increasingly changed its role from an institution that managed a stable international exchange rate system to one that manages economic crises (primarily in countries of the South), especially after the debt crises of the early 1980s. In the process the IMF has helped ensure that developing countries implement and adhere to neoliberal policy practices and, more generally, to the narrow contours of the Washington Consensus. To this end, the Fund has become the main organizer of international debt agreements by lending to countries facing debt crises, and serving as the axis around which negotiations occur. Private international lenders insist on linking their rescheduling agreements to the Fund's seal of approval for a debtor's economic policies.

It is important to stress that the SAPs are tied to two interlocking objectives, which are in turn linked to the interests of powerful global financial players and the governments of industrialized states. First SAPs discipline the governments of developing countries to adopt the same neoliberal macro-economic policies as found within the G7, now expanded to the G10. Through this enforced policy adoption, the second concern of the powerful political and economic elite can be addressed, namely the avoidance of another global economic crisis that could have obvious detrimental effects on the wealthier nation states.

Although SAPs ensure that international lenders are reimbursed, they have been less than successful in promoting sustained economic development in the developing world. SAPs have created harrowing social and economic experiences for the majority of residents of the debtor nations. Almost two decades of IMF-inspired economic restructuring has been marked by increased poverty rates in the developing world. In response, the Fund's former Managing Director, Michel Camdessus, has stated that poverty in the developing world is a key threat to the growth and stability of the world economy (IMF, 1999a). In fact, as in the case of the World Bank, the IMF has responded by making reducing poverty one of its two key policy pillars, the other being, of course, macro-economic reform. However, experience suggests that the two goals may be contradictory.

It should be stressed that the SAPs were quite successful as "debt collection devices" in that they produced a large and sustained net resource transfer from many developing countries to the developed world. Although the IMF's apparent role as crisis manager was to facilitate aid in crisis-hit countries, as the crises grew the IMF became a net recipient of capital from developing countries (Bienefeld, 1993). As mentioned above, the SAPs were designed to ensure that debtor countries earned hard currency (i.e., money that is in demand such as the U.S. dollar) to pay back their loans. The SAPs, for example, forced debtor countries to export more than they import so that they could pay off their debt to the banks. To keep their own banks afloat, and thus stabilize the wider global economy, the U.S. government used public money to provide a bail-out for their banks. In effect, the taxpayers in the United States and the debtor countries bear a significant portion of the debt. It becomes clear why this process of debt conversion, whereby the government takes over large amounts of debt incurred by large corporations and commercial banks, as it did in the early 1980s, is referred to as the **socialization of debt.**

By 1987, primarily due to the SAPs, the banks had largely recovered from the debt crisis, and were reluctant to re-enter the game of debt financing in the developing world (Kapstein, 1994). This had two important implications regarding the changing role of the IMF. First, official lending (i.e., loans largely from the IMF and individual governments) supplanted commercial funds by the mid-1980s. Second, new, more mobile and less vulnerable players, such as **mutual funds** arrived on the scene as a source of financing in the debtor countries. A mutual fund is basically a collection of bonds or stocks that allows investors to avoid risking all their money on one single company. As we saw earlier, the amount of money wielded by these new financial actors dwarfs government economic resources in the more prosperous industrialized world, not to mention the Southern hemisphere.

Against the backdrop of embedded financial orthodoxy, these two factors led to increased instability for debtor nations. In this light, the new role of the IMF may be seen as either a financial intermediary or a crisis manager. Both these roles are geared towards stabilizing the world economy. After the Mexican Peso crash in December 1994, for instance, the Fund's role as crisis manager took on new dimensions in avoiding collapses of the international payment system. In April 1995, financial ministers and central bank governors of the leading members of the Fund committee called for "stronger and more effective IMF surveillance of its members," especially with respect to "unsustainable flows of private capital," overextended credit, and speculative activity in member countries (Pauly, 1997, 127).

This move was designed to further strengthen the Fund's primary mandate of surveillance over the economic policymaking in the developing countries. To promote this new role, the G7 countries agreed in June 1995 to establish an emergency financing facility, which would provide quicker access to IMF arrangements with strong conditionality, as well as larger up-front disbursements in crisis situations. In addition, the IMF was to use its new leverage to encourage countries to become more transparent. This meant that debtor countries should regularly publish economic data about their levels of short-term indebtedness, the amount of international reserves (i.e., U.S. dollars) held by the countries' central banks, and so forth (Pauly 1997, 128; IMF, 1999b).

World Trade Organization (WTO)

In 1995 the GATT was transformed into the WTO. The WTO, which is a multilateral institution designed to promote, monitor, and adjudicate international trade, builds on the GATT framework and covers all areas of trade such as manufactured goods, services and intellectual property. Almost all of the world's key trading countries were members of the WTO. As of 2000, the WTO had 136 member states. The WTO, like the World Bank and the IMF, possesses a democratic deficit in that its decision-making processes (an international bureaucracy of 500 people) take place largely out of the parameters of public scrutiny. An equally disturbing aspect of the WTO is its ability to override or change democratically passed laws concerning trade at the national level. Thus the issue of state sovereignty seems to be in contradiction with the fundamental aim of the WTO, namely to widen trade liberalization.

These transparency requirements were based on the assumption that the root causes of the recent economic crises in the developing world were largely due to policy error if not outright corruption on the part of the governments involved. This assumption was clearly articulated during the Cologne Summit of the G7 industrialized countries in June 1999. The primary directive of this summit was a call for greater openness and accountability among debtor countries while meeting the basic objective of integrating emerging market economies more fully and flexibly into the global financial system. Interestingly enough, the highly deregulated international financial markets, whose players are motivated by insatiable voracity and risk-seeking thrills, have not been admonished.

Summary

This chapter has examined the changing roles of the international financial institutions (IFIs) within the international economy. As we saw, both the World Bank and the IMF were created at the Bretton Woods conference in 1944. They were formed in an attempt to avoid the economic ills of the Great Depression as well as to overcome the basic paradox in the inter-state system—national policy autonomy versus international economic stability. These institutions functioned fairly well up to the early 1970s when the United States abandoned the gold standard. The general crisis of the world economy created new tensions between national policy autonomy and international economic stability. The emerging landscape of the global political economy is marked most notably by powerful international financial markets. This phenomenon has had great implications for national governments and domestic economies, since both are highly dependent on private, unregulated capital flows. States have become increasingly competitive in attracting capital investment. Given the uneven nature of inter-state relations, the wealthier nation states are able to secure a larger amount of capital flows than those in the Southern hemisphere. Against this backdrop of the globalized world economy, IFIs have become preoccupied with stabilizing the volatile world economy, and in doing so, have perpetuated economic inequality between rich and poor countries.

In light of such criticisms, the IMF and World Bank have attempted to present a new and more caring face. Nevertheless, as the critics rightly point out, both these institutions, as well as the WTO, operate behind closed doors and are largely accountable to no-one. This distinct lack of democratic accountability has furthered the charge that today, as well as during the time of the BWS, the IFIs reflect the interests of the most powerful national economies in the world, and particularly those of the United States.

Discussion Questions

1. Compare the past and present roles of the IFIs. How have they changed and why? Do you think that these changes are for the better?

2. Lately there has been much talk about erecting a post–Bretton Woods system. Do you think it would be beneficial, both politically and economically, if a new international system were established to regulate monetary and trade relations between states?

3. Do you think that the decision-making process of the IMF and World Bank should become more democratic? Should debtor countries be able to determine the nature of financial assistance from the IFIs?

4. Many countries of the South are caught in the vicious cycle of so-called "debt trap." Do you think that the recent campaign for debt forgiveness might mitigate the swelling levels of abject poverty associated with this "debt trap"?

References

Bienefeld, Manfred. 1993. "Structural Adjustment: Debt Collection Device or Development Policy?" Paper prepared for Sophia University Lectures on "Structural

Adjustment: Past, Present and Future" given at Sophia University Tokyo on 24-25 November 1993. mimeo.

Chossudovsky, Michel. 1997. *The Globalisation of Poverty: Impacts of the IMF And World Bank Reforms.*

Cohen, Benjamin. 1986. *In Whose Interest? International Banking and American Foreign Policy.* New Haven: Yale University Press.

Crotty James and Gerald Epstein. 1996. "In Defence of Capital Controls." InLeo Panitch (ed.) *The Socialist Register 1996: Are there Alternatives?* London: Merlin Press.

Crow, John W. 1993. "Monetary Policy Under a Floating Exchange Rate Regime" Lecture by John W. Crow Governor of the Bank of Canada given at the Stockholm School of Economics. April 22, 1993. Ottawa: Bank of Canada

Greider, William. 1997. *One World, Ready or Not: The Manic Logic of Global Capitalism.* New York: Penguin Press.

Held, David, Anthony McGrew, David Goldblatt, and Johnathon Perraton. 1999. *Global Transformations: Politics, Economics and Culture.* Stanford: Stanford University Press.

IMF (1999a) "International Financial Policy in the Context of Globalisation." Remarks by Michel Camdessus Managing Director of the International Monetary Fund at the Konrad Adenauer Foundation Frankfurt, Germany, October 11, 1999. http://www.imf.org/external/np/speeches/1999/101199.HTM.

IMF (1999b) "IMF Surveillance." September 5, 1999. http://www.imf.org/external/np/exr/facts/surv/htm.

Krueger, Anne O. 1997. *Whither the World Bank and the IMF?* Stanford: Washingon: National Bureau of Economic Research (NBER) Working Paper No. 6327.

Pauly, Louis W. 1997. *Who Elected the Bankers? Surveillance and Control in the World Economy.* Ithaca: Cornell University Press.

Ruggie, John Gerard. 1982. "International regimes, transactions and change: Embedded liberalism in the post-war economic order" in *International Organization.* No. 36, 2 (Spring).

United Nations. 1999. *Human Development Report 1999.* New York: Human Development Report Office, United Nations Development Programme.

World Bank. 2000. *World Development Report 2000/2001: Attacking Poverty.* Washington, DC: World Bank.

Further Readings

Cerny, Philip G. (ed.) 1993. *Finance and World Politics: Markets, Regimes and States in the Post-Hegemonic Era.* Aldershot, England: Edward Elgar.

Cohen, Benjamin J. 1998. *The Geography of Money.* Ithaca: Cornell University Press.

Germain, Randall D. 1997. *The International Organization of Credit: States and Global Finance in the World-Economy.* Cambridge: Cambridge University Press.

Gowan, Peter. 1999. *The Global Gamble: Washington's Faustian Bid for World Dominance.* London: Verso Books.

Hewson, Martin and Timothy J. Sinclair (eds.) 1999. *Approaches to Global Governance Theory*. Albany, New York: SUNY Press.

MacEwan, Arthur. 1990. *Debt and Disorder: International Economic Instability and U.S. Imperial Decline*. New York: Monthly Review Press.

Weblinks

International Monetary Fund
www.imf.org

The World Bank
www.worldbank.org

World Trade Organization
www.wto.org

I'M GONNA MISS HAVING YOU AROUND, LLOYD.

CHAPTER 27

THE NEW MULTILATERALISM IN A GLOBAL ERA

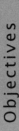

Objectives

The last decades of the twentieth century witnessed profound shifts in the nature of international relations. A growing number of global and domestic forces were unleashed that constrained the ability of all governments to formulate a coherent foreign policy. While there is still much evidence of continuity in the global political and security environment, it is also clear that this environment is filled with uncertainty, turbulence, and change. In this chapter we explore some of the new directions in global politics that are emerging in the twenty-first century. First, the chapter reviews some of the changes that characterize today's international context and discusses the transition from traditional *multilateralism* to *new multilateralism*. Second, we examine what is now referred to as the "new human security agenda." Advanced by both the United Nations and Canada in the 1990s, this agenda stresses the new, more aggressive multilateralism, which is less concerned with the mutual defence of states than with the human rights and needs of people throughout the world. In the final section of the chapter we examine Canada's growing role in the new international context, particularly in the areas of *peacekeeping* and *peacebuilding*.

W. ANDY KNIGHT

Introduction

A number of factors, some more positive than others, underlie the uncertain global politics of the early twenty-first century. The thawing of the Cold War, the fall of the Berlin Wall, the disintegration of the Soviet empire, and the accompanying dissolution of the Warsaw Pact were, without question, the most dramatic and potentially positive, changes disrupting the organization of global politics. The end of long-standing political, economic, and ideological rivalries in the early 1990s promised a genuine rapprochement between the two superpowers. There were, nonetheless, other less dramatic but also foundational shifts during these years, among them, the acceleration of Western Europe's economic and political integration and the creation of the European Union. Several former members of the Warsaw Pact entertained the notion of merging their economies with the "Western" world and of joining the North Atlantic Treaty Organization (NATO). Major shifts and political configurations were also being experienced in the Middle East, Central and South America, and Asia. Decade-long conflicts between Iran and Iraq had come to an end. Conflicts in Cambodia were sufficiently settled that the country was able to, with the assistance of the UN, put in place a new governmental administration. Hostilities in Central and South America were being extinguished through a series of peace initiatives. Many of the political changes seemed so positive that then-U.S. President George H. Bush claimed that the international community was on the threshold of a "new global order."

Others, however, saw the period in a less optimistic light, more indicative of a "new world disorder." Violence and bloody civil wars were prevalent in Angola, Burundi, the Congo, Eritrea, Ethiopia, Liberia, Mozambique, Namibia, Nigeria, Rwanda, and Sierra Leone. The Rwandan genocide represented the apogee of this new disorder. A civil conflict in the former Yugoslavia ripped that country apart and threatened to disrupt the peaceful conditions in surrounding European states. The atrocities in Kosovo exacerbated the problem so much that NATO was forced to intervene directly with military action in order to prevent further atrocities. Just as appalling was the violence in East Timor, which resulted, belatedly, in United Nations (UN) intervention. All of these were examples of *intra*-state rather than *inter*-state violence—threats to human security coming from inside rather than outside national territorial boundaries.

These intra-state examples of a new world (dis)order are compounded by the ongoing threat of interstate conflict around the globe. One only need look at the Indian sub-continent where Pakistan and India are engaged in a Cold War-like nuclear arms race. China still acts as though it is living in a Cold War environment in continuing its disputes with Taiwan. The Oslo Peace Process has been eroded beyond recognition and stands on the brink of rejection at the beginning of 2001. Ongoing violence in the Middle East is a constant reminder of the potential danger which countries in the region face if the Palestinian/Israeli conflict spills over borders as it has in the past. Moreover, the renewed commitment of the United States, with the election of George W. Bush, to build a new missile defence system to shield the continent against aggression from so-called "rogue states," may ignite a new arms race among global superpowers.

All of these factors, both positive and negative, mean that states now navigate in uncharted waters. Their power to establish the parameters and substance of international politics, moreover, is increasingly challenged by new actors in political systems. While the state is still very much the primary actor in the international system, authority appears to be dispersing, as well as elevating the importance of non-state actors such as nongovernmental organizations (NGOs), multinational corporations (MNCs), grassroots movements (GROs), and even transnational criminal organizations (TCOs) in global politics. The growth in number and influence of civil society organizations, in fact, is rapidly becoming a distinguishing mark of the politics of the twenty-first century. The Centre for Civil Society at John Hopkins University, for example, reports that the current growth in NGOs is "unprecedented in modern history," perhaps as significant an historical development as the elaboration of the nation state in the twentieth century (Barlow and Clarke, 2001, 3). The current era has also witnessed a shift in power in some parts of the globe as peoples' movements took down dictatorships (in the Philippines, Romania, Haiti, and Yugoslavia, to name a few places). As a corollary of this trend, democracy has begun to take root in these countries and a greater interest in human rights protection is slowly becoming the norm.

At the same time, issues of poverty, inequality, injustice, and abuses of human rights still plague the international community. The immense wealth created by liberal economic reforms at the global level (part of the globalization phenomenon) has not trickled down to the vast majority of the world's people. Some regions of the globe appear to have benefited from these reforms, notably South Asia, but, as the Asian economic meltdown of 1997 clearly demonstrated, these benefits can be precarious and short-lived. Other regions, especially sub-Saharan Africa, have stagnating economies and their people live in increasingly abject poverty. This economic disparity, if left unchecked, promises to generate major tensions and outright conflicts both within and between countries. Related to this is the emergence of clan, ethnic, and religious violence in places like Somalia, Rwanda, the Congo, Sierra Leone, the former Yugoslavia, and Algeria, to name a few. These tensions have fed local, regional, and international terrorism and have led, in some cases, to major civil wars and the collapse of some states.

In this changing international context, non-traditional threats to national and personal security have outpaced traditional ones. These non-traditional (i.e., non-military) threats include international crime, global pandemics such as AIDS, global warming, environmental degradation, overpopulation, mass involuntary migration, and ethnic cleansing. These new threats to national and global security have forced us to reconsider the nature and meaning of security and to develop new strategies for dealing with its expansion in the global environment.

This context of turbulence, transition, and disorder on a global scale has renewed debate about the need for multilateral solutions to global problems, a re-conceptualization of security, and a development of the governance structure at the global level that can handle problems that states, acting individually, cannot. Canada is at the forefront of this debate and can be considered, both in terms of rhetoric and action, a leader, norm entrepreneur, and promoter of human security and global governance. However, since Canada is not a major power, it has had to advance the new global security agenda by acting in concert with other states through a new multilateralism. We will briefly discuss multilateralism before exploring in greater detail the new human security agenda.

From the Traditional to the "New" Multilateralism

MULTILATERALISM HAS TRADITIONALLY BEEN DEFINED IN REFERENCE TO THE state system and a state-centred understanding of world order and global governance. **Multilateralism** is the institutionalization of coordinated behaviour and reciprocal practices among three or more states around a given issue area. According to John Ruggie, the factors that distinguish multilateralism from more limited arrangements, such as **unilateralism** and **bilateralism**, are generalized principles of conduct, principles of "indivisibility" (non-discrimination between the members of the arrangement), and the practice of "diffuse reciprocity" (a rough equivalence of give-and-take between members of the arrangement) (Ruggie, 1993, 571).

Advocates of traditional multilateralism assume that international institutions are able to maintain equilibrium in an otherwise anarchic inter-state system through instruments and processes of coordination, formal and ad hoc arrangements, reciprocity, and predictability. Multilateralism, in this view, provides an escape valve for states which allows the inter-state system to function with the minimum amount of disruption and violence.

Robert Keohane, for example, argues that multilateralism is "the practice of coordinating national policies in groups of three or more states, through *ad hoc* arrangements or by means of institutions" (1990). John Ruggie also holds a similar position, but is more analytical in his definition of multilateralism. He suggests that the essence of multilateralism is that it embraces certain principles and norms that order the relationship of states with each other. Thus multilateralism is conceived by Ruggie as "an architectural form" or "deep organizing principle" of global society (1993, 567).

These definitions of multilateralism share similar assumptions about the desirability of maintaining order and minimizing violent conflict through co-operative efforts and about the central role of the national state in international affairs. Multilateralism is viewed as an activity to be engaged in by states. From the signing of the Westphalia Treaty in 1648 until the end of the nineteenth century, multilateral activity was concerned with maintaining peace among European states. This was manifested through such institutional vehicles as the Concert of Europe (1815), congresses of Vienna, Paris, and Berlin (1815, 1856, and 1878 respectively), the London conferences (1871 and 1912–1913), the Berlin congresses (1878 and 1884–85), the Algeciras conference (1906), and the Hague conferences (1899 and 1907). By the end of the nineteenth century, multilateralism had evolved to include the activities of a broader range of states through formal, more permanent intergovernmental organizations (IGOs) brought into existence by the self-same states to facilitate their interactions. The Permanent Court of International Justice (PCIJ), the League of Nations, and the United Nations (UN) are obvious examples.

Traditional multilateralism is more than simply a state-centred principle of the inter-state system. It also perpetuates the dominance of states that are at the apex of the international hierarchical state system (Nye, 1990). The constitutive principles or underlying ideas of world politics are generally those that are promoted by these leading states and are more often than not embodied in multilateral bodies. However, some states that are not at the top of the international hierarchy have, from time to time, challenged and modified the traditional notion of multilateralism, often in collaboration with non-state entities. These states are thus playing a key role in defining what multilateralism will mean for the future.

The new multilateralism refers to a set of long-term policies and actions designed to solve problems and issues raised by a complex interdependent, globalized, and multilateral world and formulated with the specific goal of facilitating the building of a new global order for this century in a potentially post-hegemonic, post-international environment. The problems and issues that emerge in such a context cannot be adequately resolved by individual states acting on their own (i.e., through unilateralist strategies). Neither can they be satisfactorily resolved by a couple of states acting together through bilateral strategies nor even by a group of well-meaning states acting in concert through international strategies. This is the position taken by a growing school of thought within the international community and, especially by Canada. This new approach emphasizes building new institutions of global co-operation from the bottom up, involving both states and civil societies in a new vision of the global order.

Elevating Human Security

THE NEW MULTILATERALISM IS AT THE HEART OF PERHAPS THE MOST SIGNIFICANT change in global politics during the current era—the decided shift away from issues of national security (the security of states) to those of human security (the security of people). Security is central to humanity's individual and collective existence. It is a fundamental public good. All people want to feel secure. Governments have traditionally been considered guarantors of the security of the people over whom they rule. From that perspective traditional views of security were naturally state-centric; dependent upon the military defence of a nation state's territory. According to this view, national security thus rests with the ability of a state government to defend its territory, institutions, and population against possible attacks from outside its national boundaries.

Similarly, international security relied on the extent to which all states within the international system felt secure. However, as traditional international relations theorists remind us, the quest for security by states often led to a "security dilemma." As one state beefs up its military to protect itself and its population, other states may view this action as threatening and may decide to strengthen their own military defence to counter the perceived initial threat. The outcome of this dilemma has been the proliferation of weapons (particularly those of mass destruction) as well as increased insecurity for states and their populations.

To the majority of the world's population, national and international security have very little meaning for their individual personal security. The major threats to people's security now come from diseases, crime, malnutrition, environmental degradation, and domestic violence (usually targeting women and children). Indeed, threats to human security often come from domestic governments themselves. Amnesty International's files are filled with examples of citizens who have been tortured, incarcerated, and killed by the very state that is supposed to provide them with security.

The notion of "human security" has long historical roots. The ideas that underpin this concept can be traced back to the 1860s when the International Committee of the Red Cross introduced a doctrine that was based on the safety and protection of individuals during times of war and violent conflicts. During the Second World War, the genocide of European Jews forced a serious examination of the place of international moral standards and codes in the conduct of world affairs as well as a re-examination of the principles of national sovereignty. The Nuremberg trials indicated that people's rights mattered as much as states' rights. Similarly, the United Nations Charter, the Universal Declaration of Human Rights, and the Genocide and Geneva Conventions all recognize the inherent right of people to personal security. They challenged conventional notions of sovereignty where serious violations of rights occur.

Currently, the term *human security* conveys the idea that meaningful security entails freedom from all types of threats from the political, economic, social as well as military spheres. Military security is only one element of security and military threats only one type of threat to human beings. Ken Booth has argued further that true international security can only be had if humankind is emancipated from war or the threat of war, from poverty, poor education, political oppression, scarcity, overpopulation, ethnic rivalry, environmental destruction, and disease (1991). These military and non-military threats to humanity must be taken seriously into consideration because they emerge from "issues on which the future conditions of life on the planet may well depend." Thus, terms like "human security," "common security," and "comprehensive security" have been commonly used recently to embrace the range of issues being placed on the revised security agenda of our emerging global polity. Increasingly, people, regardless of country of citizenship, share the same, often global, security concerns.

Thinking that broadened and deepened the concept of security began to gain in prominence during the 1990s. Boutros Boutros-Ghali, then-UN Secretary-General, for instance, used his *An Agenda for Peace* document published in 1992 to redefine threats to global security. He claimed that such threats could come from a porous ozone layer, from drought, or from disease just as easily as they could from weapons of war (1992). These are threats not just to nation states but to the people who occupy them. By placing human beings as the referent object of security and by linking security to human rights protection, freedom from state violence, and freedom from non-military as well as military threats; the conception of security underwent substantial change.

The human security agenda became commonplace after 1994 with the publication of a report by the United Nations Development Programme (UNDP). This *Human Development Report* linked security and development issues in a way that privileged people over states. The Report argued that "For most people today, a feeling of insecurity arises more from worries about daily life than from the dread of a cataclysmic world event." The UNDP definition of security in that report was broadened to include security from crime, job and income security, economic security, food security, health security, environmental security, personal security, communal security, and political security. At the heart of this definition of human security was the notion of "freedom from want" and "freedom from fear" for each individual on the face of the planet. To accomplish these goals, the UNDP report contended, there must be a decisive reorientation of the concept of security away from the state-centric preoccupation to a people-centred one. Thus, it should not come as a surprise that the UNDP Report called for a global safety net and what amounts to a "human welfare" strategy (UNDP, 1994, 3).

Around the same time as the publication of this report, there was an increase in the level of human rights abuses, civil conflicts, and internecine violence. Most conflicts in the 1990s have been civil conflicts, internal to states, that have dramatically increased the global population of refugees as well as the number of civilians killed in war. For example, around the time of the First World War, the ratio of military to civilian casualties in war was eight-to-one. Today, the ratio is exactly reversed. Every military combatant killed is matched by eight civilian deaths (Kaldor, 1999, 8). The main victims have been women, children, the poor, and the weak. This situation has prompted a movement that seeks to solidify human rights norms and to introduce new norms such as humanitarian intervention. Such norms place the individual more firmly at the centre of security strategy and thinking. They also invite practitioners at both state and international levels to reconsider the questions of what constitute the main threats to people and how security is to be achieved.

Reconceptualizing security in the above manner implies the need for a careful rethinking of how states and their multilateral institutions confront this subject. Clearly, such rethinking of security will have implications for the traditional way in which state-centric institutions deal with security threats. It may also imply a global interest in peace and security that transcends (and even contradicts) the more exclusive interests of individual sovereign nation states. The Canadian government has undergone such a rethinking in its approach to security and has placed human security as the central element of its foreign policy.

The Canadian Approach to Human Security

BY THE EARLY 1990S, CANADIAN FOREIGN AFFAIRS OFFICIALS BEGAN TO incorporate this new thinking about security into the government's foreign policy. References were made to new threats to international security coming from unsustainable practices in the environment and from economic and political sources, for example. The conception of the threat to Canada's security was also broadened to include threats from the drug trade, illegal immigration, AIDS, terrorism, small arms, cyberwars, environmental disasters, and trafficking in women and children. The mid-1990s white papers on defence and foreign policy adopted this conception of security and noted that the international security context had changed, bringing with it transnational threats that affected not just single countries but broad regions of the globe and perhaps the globe itself. Individual governments could not address these threats on their own. Thus multilateral devices would have to be introduced to counter such threats as international crime, global diseases, mass voluntary or forced migration, social inequity, environmental degradation, overpopulation, and lack of economic opportunity. Canada used mulitlateral instruments to address some of these security threats through such strategies as the promotion of democracy and good governance, of human rights and the rule of law, and of prosperity through free trade and sustainable development (DFAIT, 1991–2).

There is little doubt that the driving force behind the new human security agenda in Canada was DFAIT minister Lloyd Axworthy—so much so that the policy has been termed "the Axworthy Doctrine." In the mid-1990s, Axworthy announced that the Cold War approach to security was antiquated and that a new approach was necessary, one that put people's security needs first. He argued that the concept of human security "recognizes the complexity of the human environment and accepts that the forces influencing human security are interrelated and mutually reinforcing." He went on to say that the minimum requirement for human security would be that the needs of individuals are met. According to Axworthy, "sustained economic development, human rights and fundamental freedoms, the rule of law, good governance, sustainable development, and social equity are as important to global peace as arms control and disarmament" (1997, 184).

The human security agenda adopted by Canada can be summed up under the following categories:

1. Supporting multilateral peacekeeping and peacebuilding activities;
2. Lending assistance to civilians, particularly children, affected by war; and
3. Helping to build multilateral institutions of humanitarian governance.

Multilateral Peacekeeping and Peacebuilding

Canada has played a leadership role in UN peacekeeping since the 1950s when Lester B. Pearson invented the concept. Indeed Canada has been involved in almost every single peacekeeping operation under the UN auspices. Keeping the peace requires putting Canadian military and civilian personnel at risk in faraway places. But the Canadian government views this risk as necessary to its goal of bringing about human security. Today, Canadian Forces personnel, civilian police, and civilians participate in UN peacekeeping missions in Bosnia and Herzegovina, Croatia, Korea, Cambodia, Iraq, Iraq-Kuwait, Egypt, Israel, Guatemala, Haiti, the Western Sahara, and Cyprus.

The new emphasis on human security has meant a rethinking of the function of UN peacekeeping. Canada recognized that in the post–Cold War security environment, the UN's approach to peacekeeping would have to be modified to address the predominance of intra-state conflicts. These conflicts differ from interstate ones in that they pose a heightened threat to civilians and require multifaceted action ranging from the promotion of the rule of law to overcome a state of lawlessness, to the provision of humanitarian assistance, to the protection of human rights, to the reconstruction of civil administration and economies. All of these activities fall under the rubric of peacebuilding. It is considered a conflict resolution and management process that involves economic and institutional rehabilitation, development and technical assistance programs, and the establishment of democratic and judicial processes, usually in war-torn societies or in countries whose state apparatus has collapsed.

The spread of democratic practices has also been at the centre of Canada's human security policy. Democracy is a fundamental Canadian value. Thus, it is not surprising that Canada has focused a great deal of attention on helping to design, organize, and monitor elections all across the world. It has done so primarily through the multilateral institutions of which it is a member, among them, the UN, the Organization of American States (OAS), the G7/8, the Commonwealth, and La Francophonie. Because Elections Canada's expertise in electoral processes is well known, the Canadian government has been called upon to organize and monitor elections in places such as South Africa, Cambodia, Haiti, Mozambique, El Salvador, Namibia, and East Timor.

However, it is important to realize that importing election processes is not sufficient for democracy to take root in a society. Democratic cultures have to be carefully nurtured. They have to be part of an overall environment that allows for political participation across all sectors of society, not simply among the elite. This environment must also be one in which the rule of law is respected, in which independent judiciary is the norm and not the exception, and in which military force is subjugated to civilian authority. All of this requires the commitment of substantial financial, human, political, and occasionally military, resources.

Canada has been criticized for being stingy when it comes to actual commitment of such resources. For instance, a peacebuilding fund set up by the Canadian government to be managed by the Canadian International Development Agency (CIDA) was allocated a mere $10 million for fiscal years 1997–98 and 1998–99. An additional $1 million was also assigned for this purpose to the Department of Foreign Affairs. However, as Rioux and Hay note, in 1996 the budget of $2.1 billion for international assistance was cut by $150 million. Effectively this has meant that since 1991–2 Canada's Official Development Assistance (ODA) has been cut by over 40 percent. By the end of 1999, the ODA/GDP ratio which was expected to be at least 0.7 percent was in fact about 0.2 percent—less than half the percentage expended by countries such as Denmark and Norway (1999, 69–70). One may reasonably ask if Canada has been willing to "put its money where its mouth is."

Lending Assistance to Civilians Affected by War

In February 1999, Canada chaired an open Council debate dealing with the impact of armed conflict on civilians. The result of this discussion was the path-breaking report entitled "Protection of Civilians in Armed Conflict: Towards a Climate of Compliance" which was tabled by UN Secretary-General Kofi Annan. This report pointed out the disturbing fact that about 90 percent of the casualties in post–Cold War conflicts are civilians. Indeed, over the past decade, wars have killed over two million children and disabled another four million. It is estimated that at the beginning of the twenty-first century over 300 000 children were serving in military armies or within irregular forces— some as combatants, some as sexual slaves, and others as messengers.

In response to the Secretary General's report, Canada drafted a resolution in the Council which called on the UN to address this problem. In Canada's second turn as President of the Council, it sponsored another resolution that condemned in the strongest terms the practice of deliberately targeting civilians who are normally on the sidelines of conflicts. That resolution which was endorsed by the Council in April 2000 went further than the previous one in spelling out a number of provisions that would enhance the physical protection of civilians caught in the crossfire of internecine struggles.

Some of these provisions include strengthening the UN's ability to respond rapidly to freshly brewing conflicts; ensuring that civilians in a theatre of conflict have unimpeded access to humanitarian assistance; providing for the protection of civilians (particularly women, children, and vulnerable groups) explicitly in UN peacekeeping mandates; authorizing UN peacekeeping forces and other peace operations to close down hate media outlets in the countries experiencing conflict; paying special attention to the issues of disarmament, demobilization, and reintegration of former combatants (including child soldiers) into post-conflict societies; and ensuring that the UN and the international community become

---

"The Protection of Civilians in Armed Conflict"

NEW YORK, FEBRUARY 12, 1999

Notes for an address by The Honourable Lloyd Axworthy,
Minister of Foreign Affairs to the United Nations Security Council.

The victimization of civilians in war is as old as time, but never more so than in our century. This has never been acceptable. What is more recent and disturbing, what provides the global community with a compelling reason for engagement today, is the increasing "civilianization" of conflict. More than ever, non-combatants—especially the most vulnerable—are the principal targets, the instruments and overwhelmingly, the victims of modern armed conflict. The number of casualties from armed conflict has almost doubled since the 1980s to about one million a year; and of those, 80 percent are civilians.

. . . It is a fact of our time that the threats to human security—the risks that individuals, communities, people face in their daily lives—outweigh the risks to security occasioned by conflicts across borders, which have been the more traditional concern of the Council. The promotion of human security is the bedrock upon which all other objectives of the UN Charter must rest—from economic and social development, to human rights and freedom, to the free flow of commerce. . . .

The Security Council has a vital role to play in confronting these threats. There should be no mistake. Promoting the protection of civilians in armed conflict is no sideshow to the Council's mandate for ensuring international peace and security. On the contrary, it is central to it. The ultimate aim of the Council's work is to safeguard the security of the world's people, not just the states in which they live. Clearly, faced with the disproportionate toll that modern conflict takes on civilians, the protection of individuals should be a primary consideration in the Council's activities.

The Council does not have to do it all; other parts of the UN and the wider international community also have their responsibilities. However, in the absence of resolute and effective Council leadership, civilians in situations of armed conflict are left in a security void. . . .

The Council's responsibility to protect civilians in armed conflict is therefore compelling, from a human security perspective, in terms of fulfilling the Council's own mandate and in the interest of enhancing state sovereignty. . . .

In Canada's view, the challenges facing the Council are fourfold:

First is preventing conflict. Averting the outbreak of armed hostilities is the optimal means to avoid needless destruction and suffering—in particular, the victimization of civilians. There is nothing new in this observation. Yet the United Nations record is not all it might be, in taking pre-emptive steps, or building strong human rights institutions, or ensuring early warning of impending crisis, or offering concerted support for peace processes, or having the capacity to act quickly—for example, in the absence of the Rapidly Deployable Mission Headquarters. The Council needs to reassert its leadership in this area. The second challenge is insuring respect for international humanitarian and human rights law. We have developed a considerable body of international law and standards regulating the conduct of belligerents and the protection of civilians—both local residents and international personnel—in conflict situations. In this regard, the situation of children and refugees merits special attention. And we are developing new standards for adapting to the changing nature of conflict, for example, with regard to the treatment of internally displaced persons. Too frequently, however, these standards are flagrantly violated or ignored by the belligerents—and are too often left unanswered.

The third challenge facing the Council is supporting the pursuit of those who violate humanitarian norms and standards. The impunity of individuals who commit gross violations of humanitarian law during armed conflict is a widely acknowledged problem. The tribunals established for the former Yugoslavia and Rwanda were a significant step forward. Backing is needed for more systematic prosecution of alleged war criminals—for example, through support to make the International Criminal Court operational sooner rather than later.

The fourth challenge is taking aim at the purveyors and instruments of war. Those who are accessories to these crimes and violations—the merchants of conflict—who illicitly traffic in the means of war, must likewise not be left unaccountable. Conflict areas are often awash with arms, especially military small arms and light weapons. When these fall into the wrong hands, their misuse compounds the misery of civilians, who are overwhelmingly their victims. Urgent attention must be given to the flow and misuse of weapons that terrorize, maim and kill.

These are complicated challenges with no easy solutions. Nevertheless, we believe that the Council has the capacity to respond—provided its members have the political will to act.

. . . . The plight of civilians in armed conflict is urgent, growing and global in the threat it poses to human security. It goes to the core of the Council's mandate, and deserves continued attention. The Council has a responsibility to act vigorously and resolutely. To do otherwise risks diminishing the Council's standing, and opens the way to a more disorderly and far less secure world. We look forward to the Secretary-General's report, and to working with other Council members to address this issue, starting now.

SOURCE: http://www.un.int.Canada/html/s-12feb99axworthy.htm. Reproduced with permission of the Minister of Public Works and Government Services Canada, 2001.

more responsive to threats of genocide, crimes against humanity, and war crimes (Canada World View, 2001, 2).

Canada's rhetoric was, in this case, matched by its actions. During its time on the Council (1999–2000), three new peacekeeping missions, launched in Sierra Leone, East Timor, and the Democratic Republic of the Congo, were given explicit mandates aimed at the protection of civilians. This was in direct response to Canada's advocacy of a human security discourse within the Council. In fact, Canada also pushed for the inclusion of Child Protection Advisors to all UN peace operations. Canada also supported the negotiation of an Optional Protocol to the Convention on the Rights of the Child which aims at raising the legal age of recruitment and participation of children in armed forces from 15 to 18. It was the first country to sign that Optional Protocol, thus becoming a public advocate and a moral voice for this cause. In April 2000, the Canadian government joined with Ghana in hosting a regional conference in West Africa on war-affected children. This was followed by the first-ever International Conference on War-Affected Children, which was held in Winnipeg in September 2000.

Multilateral Institutions of Humanitarian Governance

Given the ethical concerns that Canada has exhibited, one can understand this country's obsession with building multilateral institutions of humanitarian governance. The Canadian government has publicly expressed concerns about anti-personnel land mines and the proliferation of small arms. Not only do these two issues demonstrate the extent to which Canada's post–Cold War perception of the international security context has changed; they also point out the need for the development of an ethical and moral basis in policy making by all governments. Anti-personnel land mines are weapons that, even after they have fulfilled their military purposes, pose great harm to ordinary citizens. Small arms have reached an epidemic level in developing countries, in particular, and have tended to destabilize societies, increasing their level of insecurity. The situation becomes even more morally repugnant when those small arms get into the hands of children. The child soldier has become a major problem for the international community. For even after wars are over, children who were recruited to fight may take these weapons with them and become a threat to their own societies as criminals.

While Axworthy was the foreign minister for Canada, he called for the solidification of international humanitarian and criminal law. He clearly and consistently backed the notion of establishing a draft code of crimes and a permanent International Criminal Court (ICC) to try such international criminals. Consistent with the model of diplomacy employed during the Ottawa Process—the campaign to ban anti-personnel land mines—Canada joined with a bloc of like-minded small and medium-sized states and became a leading force for the establishment of the ICC. Canada became the chair of this group of states and was influential in guiding the multilateral process and negotiations involved in the creation of this court. Canada signed the statute that established the framework for the first permanent ICC on 18 July 1998.

A large part of the Canadian strategy in the above effort was to play a major role in all of the preliminary discussions and bodies which established the ICC. This has meant supporting the work of the International Law Commission (ILC) for decades. Canada's most recent contribution on the ILC was framed in the context of the need for a new international security agenda. Realizing that most of the conflicts since the end of the Cold War were civil ones and that most of the victims of those conflicts were civilians, Canada pressed for the creation of humanitarian law that would more effectively address this problem. The most exigent quandary of international relations seemed to be the insecurity that individuals feel, rather than the insecurity of states per se. Thus human security was pushed higher up on the agenda of Canadian foreign policy decision makers. Canada also realized that existing international institutions were not equipped to deal adequately with this problem.

Since the new security and justice demands were seen by Canada as requiring either new or reformed institutions, emphasis was placed on developing a novel international legal institution that would deter some of the most serious violators of international humanitarian law and that would have sufficient "teeth" to protect the vulnerable and innocent and punish those who commit war crimes, genocide, and crimes against humanity. Canada thus became one of the leaders in the attempt to create a body that would have the power to bring those accused of committing genocide, war crimes, aggression, and crimes against humanity to justice. It pushed for a Court that would have inherent jurisdiction over these core crimes and that would not be paralyzed either by norms of sovereignty or by *realpolitik*. Canadian representatives stressed the need for an independent, highly professional Prosecutor for the Court who would be in a position to initiate proceedings against state or individual actors involved in the above international crimes. Canada also argued that the Court should be sensitive to the issue of gender and required that both the statute and the day-to-day operations of the Court must integrate a gender perspective. Thus, rape, sexual slavery, and other forms of sexual violence were recognized as war crimes in the draft statute to create a permanent ICC.

Summary

The context of international politics is in a period of great flux, putting pressure on states to adapt their foreign policies to meet new and emerging demands. States are not always able to meet such demands on their own, hence the need for multilateral approaches and strategies. Canada has been one of the strongest supporters of multilateralism over the past 55 years. It has adopted a distinct multilateral strategy for its foreign policy which to some extent takes into consideration the input of civil society and draws on collaboration with like-minded states.

The central feature of recent Canadian foreign policy has been human security—known as the Axworthy doctrine. Canada has supported this concept both rhetorically and with action. However, while it seems to reflect the changes that are occurring in the international security environment, not everyone has reacted positively to this new shift in Canadian foreign policy. The very concept of human security is not without its own difficulties. Often these human security strategies are band-aid solutions which fail to address underlying problems of the state. Ken Bush has called this "bungee cord humanitarianism" (1996, 75). If the Canadian government is to take the goal of human security seriously, according to its critics, it will need to put greater resources into state-rebuilding processes and into strengthening civil societies within war-torn states. This requires a sustained and coherent long-term strategy which may mean that Canada will have to disburse substantial development funds.

While we may not yet be in a new world order, at the beginning of the twenty-first century the Canadian government finds itself at a transitional juncture between the old post–World War II world order and an embryonic post–Cold War global order which is not yet well defined. Canada has embraced assertive multilateralism as its main tool of foreign policy. In particular, over the past decade, the Canadian government has done much, both rhetorically and substantively, to shore up its image as a multilateralist state by embracing a human security agenda and by contributing to the building of a global governance architecture.

Discussion Questions

1. What are the most significant factors that characterize the current era in international politics? Why?

2. Discuss the ways in which governments might pursue a human security agenda in international politics. Would these strategies conflict with older concerns about state security? How?

3. Canada has been a world leader in peacekeeping and peacebuilding in global conflict zones during the past half century. Should Canada maintain this role in the twenty-first century? What factors might help or hinder Canada's future role as a mediator in inter- and intra-national conflicts?

4. What do you think are the most significant elements of human security? What are the most important elements in your daily life?

References

Barlow, Maude and Tony Clarke. 2001. *Global Showdown: How the New Activists are Fighting Global Corporate Rule.* Toronto: Stoddart Publishing.

Booth, Kenneth. 1991. "Security and Emancipation." *Review of International Studies, Vol. 17:4.*

Boutros-Ghali, Boutros. 1992. *An Agenda For Peace.* New York: United Nations Department of Public Information.

Bush, Kenneth. 1996. "Beyond bungee cord humanitarianism: towards a development agenda for peacebuilding." *Canadian Journal of Development Studies*, Special Issue. 75-81.

Franceschet, Antonio and W. Andy Knight. 2001. "International(ist) Citizenship: Canada and the International Criminal Court." *Canadian Foreign Policy Journal.* February.

Hay, Robin, and Jean-Francois Rioux. 1999. *Human Security and National Defense.* Ottawa: Department of National Defense.

Keohane, Robert. "Multilateralism: An Agenda for Research." *International Journal. Vol. XIV*:4 (Autumn)

Ruggie, John. "Multilateralism: the anatomy of an institution." *International Organization. Vol. 46*:3 (Summer).

United Nations. *United Nations Development Report.* 1994. New York: United Nations.

Further Readings

Axworthy, Lloyd. 1999. "NATO's New Security Vocation." *NATO Review* (Winter) -

Franceschet, Antonio and W. Andy Knight. 2001. "International(ist) Citizenship: Canada and the International Criminal Court." *Canadian Foreign Policy Journal.* February.

Keating, Tom. 1993. *Canada and the World Order: the Multilateralist Tradition in Canadian Foreign Policy.* Toronto: McClelland and Stewart.

Knight, Andy W. ed. 2001. *Adapting the United Nations to a Postmodern Era: Lessons Learned.* Palgrave/Macmillan Press.

Weblinks

Department of Foreign Affairs and International Trade
www.dfait-maeci.gc.ca

Canadian International Development Agency
www.acdi-cida.gc.ca

CANADEM: Resource Bank
www.web.net/~canadem

Canadian Centre for Foreign Policy Development
www.cfp-pec.gc.ca

United Nations
www.un.org

Cause Canada
www.cause.ca

War Affected Children
www.waraffectedchildren.gc.ca

Save the Children
www.savethechildren.net

Child Soldiers
www.child-soldiers.org

UNICEF
www.unicef.org

United Nations High Commission for Refugees
www.unhchr.ch

International Committee of the Red Cross/Crescent
www.icrc.org

Amnesty International
www.amnesty.org

Glossary

absolute monarchy A state form resting on the claim that absolute power is vested in the monarch by God.

Access to Information Act A law that establishes the right of citizen access to certain documents and information held by the Government of Canada. Similar laws are often called Freedom of Information Acts.

accountability The answerability of government representatives for their actions and inactions. It is a multifaceted concept that usually implies such questions as accountability to whom, for what, and by what means?

accumulation policies Governmental actions designed to ensure that businesses operate as profitably as possible. Examples would include low rates of taxation, minimal regulations, and investment in infrastructure such as roads and telecommunications.

act utilitarianism A moral theory that stresses the utility likely to result from one's action or choice. In its moral context, utility tends to be defined in terms of the increase of pleasure and the decrease of pain.

ad-hoc committee A legislative committee established to investigate particular issues or events that normally disbands at the conclusion of its review.

agency A force, an acting subject, capable of transforming society.

agents of political socialization Institutions that serve to socialize people about the political system and political action. Agents of socialization include the family, educational institutions, the media, and political parties.

ahistorical A theory or approach to politics that discounts the importance of history in explaining political outcomes.

anarcho-syndicalism A form of anarchism that calls for workers to be organized into "management" groups (syndicates) to collectively make decisions and organize production.

anarchy The absence of government at any level. The significance of anarchy at the international level is that it means in effect that sovereign states operate in a system in which there is no permanent authority that makes and enforces laws to regulate the behaviour of these states or the behaviour of other actors in world politics.

auditor general An officer of Parliament whose role it is to annually examine the government's financial management and report the findings to Parliament.

authoritarian A dictatorial regime based on force, or the threat of force, and obedience to authority among the ruled.

authority Socially approved power and legitimacy. Weber identified three types of authority—traditional, charismatic, and rational-bureaucratic.

autonomy Self-direction; the ability to think, choose, and act solely on one's own, without guidance from another person or group. Individuals are described as autonomous when they are able to give themselves their own moral and intellectual guidelines.

baby boomers The generation born in Western societies between 1944 and 1965.

backbenchers Assembly members in parliamentary systems who are not members of cabinet. These members sit in the back of the assembly since the front benches are reserved for cabinet members.

balance of payments A summary of a country's transactions with the rest of the world. It effectively reports receipts earned through export trade of a country's goods and services as well as payments made to other countries for the import of goods and services. The balance of payments also tracks financial flows entering (recorded as gains) and exiting (recorded as losses) the country.

barter A system of exchange that transpires without money.

beggar-thy-neighbour Any policy that aims to increase a country's competitive edge at the expense of another country's economic performance.

behaviouralism An approach in political analysis, dominant in the United States in the 1960s, that emphasizes the study of observable and quantifiable political attitudes and actions of individuals and the scientific search for enduring laws of politics.

bicameral system A political system in which the legislative assembly consists of two independent chambers.

bilateral An action or agreement taken by two parties, generally states.

bilateral opposition Non-cooperative behaviour among opposition parties, who cannot unite to oppose the government as their internal differences are at least as significant as their differences with the government.

biological determinism An assumption that a person's nature and possibilities are determined by biological factors alone.

bourgeois ideology A term associated with Marx that refers to those belief systems that serve to mask the inegalitarian nature of power relations under capitalism, and preserve the power of the bourgeoisie.

bourgeoisie A term most often used in Marxist analysis to refer to the social class that owns the means of production, often also referred to as the capitalist class.

brokerage party A party that takes a non-doctrinal approach to politics and focuses on maintaining unity by providing all groups it perceives as significant with a voice.

bureaucracy An organization defined by a hierarchy of offices, by written communications and rules, by a clear division of labour, and by employment based on technical qualifications. Bureaucratic organizations are the norm today.

bureaucratic-authoritarian The alliance of the military, state bureaucracy, domestic economic elites, and international actors in several Latin American dictatorships from the 1960s to the 1980s.

cadre political party A type of political party, small in membership and focused on winning elections. It is financed by a small number of large donors, usually corporations.

canvassing The act of going door-to-door asking voters for support. This enables a party to identify voters likely to vote for it and ensure that such voters get out to vote.

capitalism An economic system organized on the basis of private ownership of the means of production and the employment of wage-labour.

cartel party A new form of party organization funded by the state.

categorical ballot A form of ballot that requires the voter to make a simple choice among a set of candidates or political parties, indicating that those chosen are preferred to all other options without further distinction.

caucus A group of sitting legislators from each party or a meeting in which the group discusses party policy and strategy.

charismatic authority Power and legitimacy accorded to individuals on the basis of their extraordinary personality or other personal qualities.

checks and balances A set of institutional measures adopted in presidential systems allowing the legislative and executive branches to effectively check the power of the other branch.

citizenship Membership in a nation-state defined by territory and sovereignty. Membership is typically accompanied by various rights and obligations. There are three important aspects of citizenship in liberal democracies—liberty (freedom), equality, and solidarity (feelings of belonging).

city-regions Used as a synonym for census metropolitan areas. In Canada this refers to an urban core, and its working commutershed, with a population over 100 000. Although one city is usually the focus, the region may contain many other municipal governments containing the larger part of the population.

civic republicanism An approach to community that encourages commitment on the part of individual citizens to the public or community good.

civil rights Citizenship rights that are necessary for the protection of an individual's freedom. Examples include freedom of speech and the right to own property.

clash of civilizations A phrase coined by political scientist Samuel Huntington to describe emerging conflict between peoples and states of different civilizations. Civilizations are wide identities based on fundamentally different religious and cultural world views.

class analysis An approach to the study of politics and society that assumes that the most important explanatory factor is the division of populations by economic class and that politics is primarily about the necessary antagonisms between the owners of the means of production and non-owners or workers.

class politics A form of national politics, especially party politics, that is organized around citizen/voter identification on the basis of class position (working class, middle class, upper class) instead of on the basis of, for example, religion or ethnicity.

Cold War The antagonistic relationship between the United States of America and the Soviet Union between approximately 1946 and 1991. Although these two superpower states (and their allies) frequently clashed, open fighting never occurred directly between them.

collective ministerial responsibility A principle found in parliamentary systems that requires cabinet members to be collectively accountable to the legislature for executive actions.

colonialism A practice of appropriating, dominating, and in some cases settling other territories and peoples, usually associated with European expansionism of the 15th to 20th centuries.

common law Judge-made law that is sometimes synonymous with unwritten law.

communitarianism Set of political ideas that emphasizes the importance of community ties, or of social relationships, to human happiness and the good life, in opposition to liberal-individualist interpretations of human needs or human nature.

community A group of individuals who identify themselves, or are viewed by others, as having something significant in common.

comparative advantage An economic principle that holds that a country will benefit the most if it specializes in trading the goods and services it can produce with the greatest relative efficiency and at the lowest cost (i.e., relative to other countries).

conditional grant A transfer of funds from one government to support the more local administration of its priorities and programs by another level of government on the condition that the recipient agrees to meet the donor government's terms and conditions.

confidence chamber A legislative chamber in parliamentary systems where the loss of a legislative vote normally requires the resignation of the executive.

consequentialism A set of political or moral beliefs that emphasize the moral importance of the consequences of one's actions and decisions.

conservatism An ideology based on the belief that society is an organic (collective) whole. Moreover, conservatives believe that the best form of society is hierarchical—a society in which everyone knows their place, a society where some rule and the rest are ruled. Order and tradition, not freedom and reason, are key political values.

constituency A designated group of citizens who are entitled to elect a public official whose duties are to act for them as their representative. The term is also used in its plural form to refer to a set of electoral districts each containing its own set of constituents.

constitutional convention A non-legal constitutional rule that is not enforceable by the courts.

constitutional interpretation A method by which the judiciary undertake interpretation of written constitutions.

constitutionally entrenched rights Rights that are constitutionally guaranteed and thus may only be removed or added to by an amendment to the constitution rather than by ordinary legislation.

core A term used in dependency theory to describe the developed capitalist countries (North) which exploit the underdeveloped periphery (South).

corporatism State control and mediation of relations among business, labour, and organized civil society sectors.

crisis From the Greek *kreinen*, which means decision, this word usually refers to a turning point after which things will be different.

Crown corporation A corporation owned by the government that engages in commercial activity often in competition with private firms. In most countries, such firms are called public corporations or government corporations.

cultural capital A term that stems from the work of sociologist Pierre Bourdieu, who argues that success in the educational system is determined by the extent to which individual students have internalized and conform with the dominant culture.

cultural identity A form of group identification resting on shared cultural characteristics rather than, for example, shared class position. The term raises a central debate about whether equality in liberal democracies is best achieved by "difference blindness" or by recognizing and valuing "difference."

cultural studies An interdisciplinary (also called antidisciplinary) approach to understanding power and culture. It draws from Marx and other writers to examine how groups with the least power use culture as a means to express resistance or identity.

culture A shared way of life that is transmitted socially, not biologically.

decision makers Individuals in government who make authoritative policy decisions on behalf of their states; such as presidents, prime ministers, foreign secretaries, secretaries of state, members of parliament or legislatures, etc.

deductive method Analytic method that characterizes the normative field of political philosophy. Political philosophers start from an axiom (or principle) and then deduce from this principle.

de facto In reality, despite what may be prescribed in a constitutional document.

de jure That which is prescribed in law.

delegate A representative who votes the way those he or she represents indicate. In practice the term refers to anyone elected to a party convention regardless of how they approach their representative role.

democracy Rule by many, characterized by leadership selection through elections, constitutionalism, and the rule of law. From the Greek *demos* (people) and *kratos* (rule).

democratic deficit A phrase used to describe the lack of trust in politicians and political institutions. Such cynicism is understood to reduce direct public participation in the process of politics because of a perceived inability to influence public policy.

deontology A liberal, individualist approach to ethics and politics that emphasizes the principles upon which one acts or judges. It is strictly a formal, rule-based moral theory, because it ignores substantive questions concerning the consequences of one's actions, one's relationship to others, or one's commitment to particular traditions or communities.

department A government administrative body over which a cabinet minister has direct management and control.

dependency theory A theory of development that attempts to explain the gap between living standards in the rich core-industrial countries and the poor peripheral countries of the South. It argues that under development in the periphery is the result of the exploitation of the countries in that area by core industrial countries, which perpetuates a situation of dependent relations that keeps the countries in the periphery "poor."

deputy minister A non-elected member of the bureaucracy who reports to a cabinet minister who assumes administrative responsibility for a government department.

deregulation The process of placing matters that had been subject to overseeing by state agencies outside the state's jurisdiction. Deregulation is a governmental practice associated with the neoliberal state. It is justified on the basis that regulations needlessly impede the profitability of business.

devolution A transfer of political authority, usually by law or regulation, from one actor to another.

dialectical relationship A concept that proposes that history progresses through a process of thesis–antithesis that results in synthesis. A dialectical relationship argues that ideas and material circumstances interact to create historical change. Marx traces key outcomes of dialectical relations as the movement in history from slavery to feudalism to capitalism.

dictatorship An authoritarian or semi-authoritarian regime headed by one individual or a very small group.

dictatorship of the proletariat The stage immediately following socialist revolution, according to Marx. The dictatorship represents the empowerment of workers, the public ownership and management of production, and a transition phase to communism.

differentiated citizenship A conceptualization of citizenship that calls for an explicit recognition of group difference to ensure inclusion and full participation. This recognition would entail the public provision of resources and institutional mechanisms for the recognition and representation of disadvantaged groups.

direct democracy A system of government in which political decisions are made directly by citizens.

direct representation The idea or claim that a person can be represented only by someone whom they directly authorized to do so by voting for that candidate. Those who voted for a losing candidate in an election cannot be and are not represented by the winning candidate.

disciplinary power The ability to produce appropriate behaviours through social definitions of what is normal and expected. Conveys the idea of self-policing and the realization of social interests and goals without resort to force.

discourse An internally coherent story or worldview. Popularized in the work of Foucault, it advances the idea that the naming of things and their description through written or spoken language shapes both individuals and the material world around them. Different understandings of truth and reality are contained and find their meaning within discourses.

district magnitude The number of representatives (seats) assigned to represent a particular electoral district or constituency in an elective body who can be chosen by their constituents.

dividing practices Stigmatizing, controlling, and excluding different groups through the practice of naming as deviant, for example, homosexuals or welfare dependents.

division of labour An economic system's determination of the specific roles and functions performed, and by whom, within production processes.

doctrinal party An avowedly ideological party that seeks to fit policies into rational value-oriented schemes. Ideological fidelity is more important than winning elections.

doctrine of utility The proposition that the standard by which all human action, public and private, should be judged is the greatest happiness of the greatest number.

domino theory or domino effect The idea that if one state falls to communist domination, other neighbouring states will also fall, either through direct aggression or subversion.

egalitarianism A concept that encompasses a belief in the essential equal worth of all persons, and the view that social institutions should ensure equality of opportunity (economic, social, and political) for each individual to realize his or her needs and goals.

electoral system A set of laws and regulations specifying the rules to be followed and the procedures to be used in organizing and conducting an election, especially as these pertain to indicating who may participate, the number of choices to be made, how voting is to take place, and by what rule offices are to be awarded to candidates based on their vote totals.

elite theory An approach to politics that assumes that all societies are divided into only two groups—the few who rule, usually in their own self-interest, and the many who are ruled.

empirical theory An approach to political analysis resting on the belief that knowledge is derived from what is observable, experienced, and/or validated by experimentation.
It seeks to generate general explanations for seemingly distinct events through observation and comparison.

end of history A phrase used by political scientist Francis Fukuyama to describe the growing convergence of states and societies with a single, liberal democratic model of governance. The end of history refers to the end of the historic debate about superior systems.

epistemology A branch of philosophy concerned with issues of knowledge, its definition, what it is, how we acquire it, and the relationship between the knower and what is known.

equality A term conveying the idea of equal access to the political sphere, equal access to and benefit of the law, and equal access to social entitlements provided by the state.

essentialism The assumption that, by nature, all members of a group share the same core personal and social qualities. Essentialist thinking, for example, assumes that all women share the capacity to nurture.

ethics The philosophical study of standards of moral conduct and principles of moral judgment. Also called "moral philosophy." In general, a principle, belief, or value about what is morally good, or a system of such principles, beliefs, or values. From the Greek *ethos*, which means the general way of life of a culture or a people.

ethnic cleansing The systematic and forced removal or murder of members of an ethnic group from their geographic communities to change the ethnic composition of a region.

ethnocentric Prejudicial attitudes held by one group that feels its own values, customs, or behaviour are superior to any other. The term is also used in relation to political scientists who, often unconsciously, import assumptions or values from their own society into comparative research.

exclusive economic zone (EEZ) The zone of sea that extends 200 nautical miles from a state's shores over which the state has exclusive economic jurisdiction.

executive committee A part of council, chaired by the mayor and sometimes including the heads of standing committees, intended to coordinate municipal business and to give some limited political direction to council.

export-oriented industrialization (EOI) An economic development strategy based on maximizing the export of national unprocessed and processed goods.

faction A division in society based on narrow group loyalty. Factions are seen as being at odds with the idea of the public good.

false consciousness A term, common in Marxist analyses, that conveys the idea that working-class consciousness is influenced by the dominant ideology of the bourgeoisie in ways that are not in the real interest of workers.

fascism A form of repressive authoritarian governance that eliminates democracy and maintains capitalism.

fatalism A belief that our fate is pre-determined by external forces such as destiny or God.

federal constitution A constitution in which the sovereignty of the state is divided between national and subnational governments.

federalism A political system in which constitutionally assigned powers are divided between one or more levels of government.

feminism A diverse set of ideas, grounded in the belief that patriarchal societies have oppressed women and united by the goal of claiming full citizenship for all women. Beyond this, feminists disagree about the roots of women's oppression, the appropriate strategies for contesting patriarchy, and about visions for a post-patriarchal society.

feudalism An agrarian form of social and economic organization characterized by a strict hierarchy between the property-owning aristocracy and the landless peasants.

franchise The legal right to vote in the election of some governmental official. Although the term "suffrage" is also used with this meaning, "franchise" specifies a right or privilege that is constitutional or statutory in its origin, that is, a formal legal right to vote in elections held in some jurisdiction.

free vote A legislative vote that drops the requirement of party discipline normally adhered to in parliamentary assemblies.

fused ballot A term with two different meanings. It is applied where a candidate is endorsed or formally nominated by two or more parties and listed separately under those party names on the ballot but the vote totals for the candidate are combined in the final count. It is also used to describe a ballot form in which a given political party's nominees for a set of offices are listed together or where candidates run as a slate, as the presidential and vice-presidential candidates in the United States do, and the voter can choose all of them, that is, vote a "straight party ticket" just by marking one place on the ballot.

fusion of power The integration of the executive and legislative branches in the parliamentary system.

gender A socially, politically, and economically constructed sex-code that prescribes what it means to be male or female in daily life.

gerrymandering The alteration of electoral boundaries in order to advantage one party, usually the one in power.

global economy Characterized by interconnected production sites all over the world that produce different component parts of a final product.

global governance The mechanisms and processes by which transnational actors—individuals, governments, non-governmental organizations, corporations—make decisions for and about the global community.

global insertion The economic and political location of a country within the global system of states and markets.

globalization The intensification of a world-scale reorientation of economic, technological, and cultural processes and activities that transcend state boundaries.

governance The organized exercise of power; the manner in which we organize our common afffairs.

government bill A legislative bill introduced by cabinet in parliamentary systems.

head of government The position that assumes responsibility for the political and effective administration of government.

head of state The symbolic position that is assigned formal and ceremonial powers.

hegemony A term associated with the work of Antonio Gramsci to refer to the bourgeoisie's ideological domination of the working class, which results in the persistence of the capitalist system. Hegemony or hegemon is also used to describe the dominant country in the international system.

historical materialism A social-science approach based on the premise that a society's structure and political dynamics are driven by its mode of production.

humanism A philosophical belief system that puts an ideal person at the centre of philosophical reflection. This philosophy suggests that knowledge, happiness, and social and political fulfillment are entirely within human purview; religious or supernatural intervention in human affairs is not considered necessary. Rather than lament human imperfections, early humanists celebrated the human body, the ability to reason, and the capacity to produce beautiful art.

hybrid regimes Regimes that contain characteristics of two or more types.

ideal-type A mental model in the social sciences for categorizing and understanding social events.

identities The tendency of individuals and groups to develop a sense of who they are in relation to their shared cultural, sociological, and political attachments to each other.

identity-based community A group of people who share at least one identifiable characteristic, which members may carry into politics.

ideology A coherent set of ideas that explains and evaluates social conditions, helps people understand their place in society, and provides a program for social and political action. Ideology also consists of those beliefs and values that serve to legitimate a certain social order, the so-called dominant ideology, and those values and beliefs that may be said to oppose or challenge the dominant ideology.

imperialism An organization of the international political economy where the globe is divided among great powers into empires; associated with colonialism; for Marxists, the expansion of capital beyond single national markets.

import substitution industrialization (ISI) An economic development strategy wherein the state supports national industry through tariffs and subsidies to produce goods for the national market, goods which otherwise would be imported.

indirect election A procedure for choosing office-holders in which the members of some group, organization, or governmental body who are themselves directly elected by the citizens or by the members of their organization select the persons to hold an office from a set of candidates by voting among themselves.

individual ministerial responsibility Principle in parliamentary systems that requires ministers to assume responsibility before the legislature for the bureaucratic departments they direct.

inductive method An analytic method that aims to build empirically based theory or explanations from the observation of concrete events.

institutionalization A process whereby things that were once random or done with little conscious planning become deliberate, formalized, and expected.

institutionalized pressure group A group with a permanent and ongoing interest in, and influence on, the policy process that is also often supported by a permanent staff.

interest-based community A group formed around concerns that bear directly, but not exclusively, on the members' political interests and that are usually represented in the political arena by organizations or interest groups.

interest party A political party that seeks to represent a particular interest in the electoral process such as a region or a specific issue of concern. It does not make a full attempt to win power but raises consciousness about its concerns.

intergovernmental organizations International organizations that are composed of state governments, the United Nations being the preeminent example.

international community A group of governments, such as the United Nations, or the symbolic expression of the shared sentiments of people in different countries.

international division of labour A way of organizing the international economy wherein the factors of production (materials, labour, finance) are divided among countries.

international political economy (IPE) A perspective on international relations that emphasizes the close relationship between economic factors such as trade and investment, and political factors such as policy settings and issues of distributive justice. IPE approaches generally analyze the interaction of states, markets, modes of production, class, politics, and culture in the international sphere.

internationalization of production The ability of companies to consider the productive resources of the globe as a whole and to decide to locate elements of complex globalized production systems at points that will produce the greatest cost advantage. It is reliant on an environment in which capital, technology, raw materials, and component parts are allowed to cross national jurisdictional boundaries with minimal or no regulation.

internationalization of the state The erosion of state authority in favour of external international forces that are able to exert tremendous influence on domestic agencies and on national policies.

international relations A field of political science concerned with relations among nation-states that engages philosophical, ethical, epistemological, and ontological questions in order to understand relations within the international sphere.

Jihad An Arabic word for "holy war" that is used by political scientist Benjamin Barber to describe the fanaticism of different cultural and national groups. These fanatics are allegedly at war with the growing influence of global consumer capitalism in their particular societies (see also McWorld).

judicial review The process whereby the courts judge the legality of political/administrative actions. Judicial review of the constitution refers to when the courts are asked to determine whether political/administrative actions conform to constitutional requirements.

Keynesianism An approach to the management of national economies that was developed by the British economist John Maynard Keynes. This approach was implemented by Western industrialized countries between 1945 and the mid 1970s. The central concern of Keynesianism was to counteract the boom and bust tendencies of capitalist economies. In periods of economic downturn, Keynesianism advocated increased public spending and lower levels of taxation to ensure that people would continue to purchase goods in the market. In periods of economic growth, public spending was to decrease and tax rates would rise thereby curbing excessive growth and restoring balance to the public finances.

laissez-faire capitalism A principle espoused by classical economists such as Adam Smith that government should minimize intervention in the capitalist market.

law of capitalist accumulation The tendency of capital to become concentrated in fewer hands and to the benefit of fewer people.

legal institutionalism An approach to politics that emphasizes the centrality of formal procedures, constitutions, and institutions.

legal-rational authority Power and legitimacy accorded on the basis of laws, formal rules, and impersonal procedures.

legitimation Justification of the actions of the state to the population at large through policies that contribute to the authority of the state. Public health care, education, and transportation networks are examples of areas of public investment that are broadly supported by citizens, and thus provide a rationale for the role of the state in their lives.

less developed countries (LDCs) A term of relative economic development that is normally used with reference to the poor Third World of Africa, Asia, and Latin America. Least developed countries were defined in 1971 by the United Nations Conference on Trade and Development (UNCTAD) as those with very low per-capita incomes ($100 or less at 1968 prices), a share of manufacturing in GDP of under ten percent, and a literacy rate under twenty percent.

liberal democracy The form of government prevalent in contemporary Western countries. Governments are selected through regular elections in which all citizens of voting age are eligible to participate. Liberal democracies are particularly concerned with protecting the freedom of individual citizens against the arbitrary use of power by the state. Hence, some formal expression of the rights of citizens can be found in the constitutional documents of liberal democracies.

liberal democratic theory A political theory arising out of the Western European liberal revolution of the 16th, 17th, and 18th centuries that emphasizes the importance of freedom, equality, rights, reason, and individualism.

liberal feminism A perspective that sees women's oppression as resulting from unequal treatment of women and men by laws, opinions, and social practices; and that regards equal rights and empowerment through gender socialization as the solution.

liberal internationalism A belief that the natural global order has been subverted by non-democratic leaders and by policies such as the balance of power. Adherents believe that contact between people, who are essentially good, will lead to a more pacific world order.

liberalism A political theory and ideology that stresses the primacy of the individual and individual freedom.

Freedom, in this instance, refers to the freedom of individuals to do as they wish without interference from others, whether these be governments or private persons. Liberals believe in a limited state where the power of government is restrained by such devices as constitutions. This ideology arose alongside capitalism.

libertarianism A "softer" variant of individualist anarchism which rejects government intervention in the market and social life. Libertarian thought is evident in today's political rhetoric, which promises to "downsize" government.

liberty Freedom from bodily harm, freedom of expression, economic independence.

lobbyist A person who contacts public officials on behalf of a client or an organization that they belong to or are employed by so as to influence public policy in a manner beneficial to their client or organization.

logrolling An agreement between members of the U.S. Congress in which each promises to support the other's bill when it comes up for vote.

Magna Carta An important written element of Britain's constitution dating from 1215. It limited royal authority and strengthened the political position of the English aristocracy.

majoritarian electoral system An electoral system organized to reflect the principle of majority rule by requiring that candidates or parties obtain an absolute or a relative majority of the total valid vote cast to win control of an elective office.

majority government A situation in which the governing party controls more than half of the seats in the legislative assembly in a parliamentary system.

maquiladora Foreign-owned business enterprises that have been set up in Mexico in order to exploit cheap labour and low production costs, and where local labour is afforded little legal protection. Maquiladora often entail a system in which components are made in the United States, shipped to Mexico for assembling, and re-shipped across the U.S. border duty-free.

mass party An avowedly democratic political party organization possessing a large membership and active in recruitment. Joining the party involves agreement with principles, and members provide a good deal of financial support. Party conventions decide on policy.

mass politics Political activities citizens can engage in without having to invest large amounts of time, effort, or money. Examples include voting, signing petitions, protesting, writing elected officials, and joining political parties or interest groups. Mass politics must be distinguished from elite political participation, which requires special skills, intense levels of commitment, and particular resources. As well, entrance to elite political roles such as candidate or officeholder, union leader, or president of an interest group, is partly determined by factors such as public opinion, voting behaviour, and/or by the gatekeeping functions of activists within the organization.

McWorld Derived from the name of the fast food restaurant chain, McDonalds. This term was coined by political scientist Benjamin Barber to describe the negative cultural and political influences of global corporations. These influences include cultural homogenization, the erosion of democratic values, and the provocation of the "intolerant fanatics" around the world (see also Jihad).

means of production The physical and human factors of economic production processes (land, technology, infrastructure, capital, labour).

means-tested social programs Social programs available only to those citizens who can demonstrate that they do not have adequate resources to purchase a service in the marketplace. People in this position are required to reveal their level of income and are often required to provide information regarding the conduct of their personal lives.

mercantilism A governing philosophy, common in Europe prior to the Industrial Revolution, that measured a country's wealth by the amount of precious metals it held. It is also associated with colonialism and the division of the world by the Great Powers for exclusive commerce.

military-industrial complex A concept that refers to an interest in high defence spending shared by military professionals and military weapons producers.

minimum winning coalition The minimum number of votes needed to win. If electoral victory is the key, any votes above the minimum needed to win are in essence superfluous.

minority government A situation in which the governing party controls less than a majority of seats but more than any other party in the legislature in a parliamentary system.

mixed-member proportional system A type of electoral system that combines a primary tier of seats in a representative assembly assigned to single-member districts with a pool of seats in the assembly assigned to a secondary tier composed either of a single national district or a set of regional districts. A majoritarian electoral system is used to elect the members representing single-member districts, whereas a proportional representation procedure is used to allocate seats in the secondary pool in a compensatory fashion to achieve overall proportionality between the vote shares of parties and the share of seats they won.

mode of production The way that a society organizes its means of production.

modernity A concept historically associated with the Enlightenment and its ideas of reason, progress, emancipation, and universality; as well as with the rise of commercial and industrial capitalism.

modernization A process and endpoint which all societies were assumed, by development theory, to evolve into. Modernization brought rational authority, industrialization, and societies with a complex division of labour.

morality A principle, belief, or value; or the system of principles, beliefs, and values applied to conduct and judgment. Related to the Latin word *mores*, which means the general codes and guides for living that are accepted by a social group.

movement party A political party that arises out of a broad-based movement pursuing non-electoral goals such as national self-governance.

multilateralism A form of co-operation among states marked by three distinct characteristics. First, that the costs and benefits of co-operation are shared by all participating states. Second, that co-operation is based on certain principles of state conduct that influence the relations among states. Finally, that states are committed to this co-operative behaviour for the long term and do not necessarily expect immediate results.

mutual fund A collection of bonds or shares that allow investors to spread and diversify their money, which in turn reduces levels of risk. Mutual funds are especially useful in international investments where information about foreign companies and markets is not accessible to the average individual investor.

nation A group of individuals who identify with each other (sense of community) based on common history, language, culture, and religion.

national interest A concept referring to the basic irreducible interests of a state (material and ideal) and criteria for action from a realist perspective.

nationalism A belief system that prioritizes or gives special significance to the nation as a focus of loyalty. The nation, in turn, is a particular form of community, with a history, tradition, and identity that it desires to promote and preserve.

nation state An international legal entity defined by a specific territory, population, and government, possessing sovereignty. Because almost all states comprise diverse ethnic, national, and racial groups, some prefer the term *national state*.

negative rights An understanding of rights, entitlements, and liberty associated with classical liberalism. Negative rights entitle individuals to act without any interference from others. They are commonly associated with the freedoms of speech, assembly, religion, and press.

neoliberalism A modification of nineteenth-century economic and political theory which advocates deregulation of the market, a non-interventionist state, minimal controls on international economic interaction, and individual freedom and responsibility.

new multilateralism Cooperation among states to protect the security of people rather than the security of states.

new public management A combination of structures, practices, and processes of public management that were in vogue in liberal democracies in the 1990s. At the heart of new public management is a critical analysis of traditional Weberian bureaucracy and the view that government agencies must be driven by a desire to achieve clearly measurable results.

non-aligned states A group of states, the majority in the South, that were not aligned with either the Soviet Union or the United States during the Cold War.

nongovernmental organization (NGO) An organization that has as its members private citizens or national affiliates of groups composed of private citizens.

nonpartisanship The conduct of elections in the absence of political parties. In its pure form, individuals stand for election as independents.

normative Related to the establishing of moral norms or principles. Normative claims, statements or questions tend to contain such prescriptive words as *should, ought,* or *must.*

normative theory A theory that inquires into ethical questions, and considers what is moral, good, and true.

notwithstanding clause A clause in the Canadian constitution that shields an act of the legislature from a judicial declaration of constitutional invalidity.

ombudsman An officer of the legislature with independence from government whose role is to investigate citizen complaints about improper or unfair treatment by civil servants and/or government agencies.

oppression The systematic and systemic subordination of one group to another.

oral question period A time set aside in parliamentary assemblies during which opposition parties question the executive about its actions and policies.

ordinal ballot A ballot form in which the voter is asked to rank the candidates or parties to indicate his or her relative preferences among them. Also known as a preferential ballot.

packing A strategy used in candidate-nomination or leadership-selection processes. It involves bringing members (often new and uninformed members) to selection meetings in order to vote for a particular candidate (sometimes called *stacking*).

paradigm shift A shift in the intellectual framework that structures thinking about a set of phenomena.

parliamentary system A system of government in which the executive is chosen from and derives its authority from the legislature.

participation Direct action or involvement in processes of decision-making.

participatory communitarianism An approach to community that is focused on people's direct participation in democratic decision-making and that has the goal of political and economic equality.

party discipline An established principle in parliamentary systems that requires members of a party's legislative caucus to vote collectively on legislation.

party list ballot A ballot form in which each party's candidates for seats in a multi-member constituency are presented as separate lists, and voters must choose among the lists, rather than choosing among the individual candidates appearing on them.

patriarchical family A family form in which the father is the head and primary bread winner and the mother stays at home and takes care of the family.

patriarchy In the anthropological sense, the rule of the father over his wife and offspring (family, kingroup, or clan). In the modern sociological sense, the structuring of social relationships and institutions in such a way as to preserve the dominance and privileges of men in relation to women.

peacebuilding Intervention by foreign actors into conflict zones to build governmental institutions, democratic practices, and civil society.

peacekeeping Intervention by foreign actors into conflict zones to maintain peace among warring factions.

periphery A term used in dependency theory to describe the lesser developed regions of the world, which are dependent on and exploited by the developed core.

personal party A political party founded and organized around a single influential and/or charismatic leader.

place-based community A group of people who share geographical, usually local, space and who may also have common interests or feelings of closeness.

pluralist theory An approach to politics that assumes that society is composed of individuals who join groups to influence political outcomes. Politics is seen as the competition among groups for preferred policies. It assumes that all citizens can form groups and that no group has a permanent advantage in society.

plurality electoral system An electoral system in which the candidate who gains the most votes wins the office being contested even though that total may constitute less than a majority of the total valid votes cast. A plurality outcome is also known as a relative majority.

policy community All actors or potential actors who share expertise and interest in a policy area or function and who in varying degrees influence policy.

political culture A term popularized by Gabriel Almond that refers to a particular patterned orientation towards political action. The political culture approach attempts to empirically describe and explain these patterns by measuring the attitudes characteristic of a national population.

political rights Citizenship rights that encompass the exercise of a citizen's democratic rights within the political community. Examples include the right to vote and the right to stand for elected office.

political socialization The process by which people acquire their knowledge of the political system and attitudes towards political action.

political sociology A social-science approach that emphasizes the social and cultural composition of society and its relationship to the state.

politics-administration dichotomy A view of democratic politics whereby politicians make policy decisions which in turn are implemented by civil servants. Few observers see the dichotomy as a valid description of reality.

positive rights An understanding of rights, entitlements, and liberty associated with ideologies such as reform liberalism or democratic socialism. Positive rights entitle individuals to the conditions where they can maximize their chances for full development. They are commonly associated with an interventionist state and specific initiatives such as public education, social assistance, and affirmative action.

postmodern feminism A stream in feminist thought that challenges any universalizing or essentializing explanations for women's oppression, arguing that there is no single, unifying women's reality; focuses on exposing the patriarchal ideas inherent in language and discourse.

postmodernism A perspective in the social sciences and humanities that holds that reality is not given; rather it is constituted by ideas, texts, and discourses (writing, talking). It displays skepticism toward Enlightenment notions of truth, arguing instead that many "truths" can co-exist. Postmodernism holds that modern political ideologies, with their emphasis on reason and a single political identity, silence social differences and impose uniformity and homogeneity on society.

post-sovereign A depiction of the current era in which the state has lost its capacity to exercise sovereignty within its territorial boundaries.

power The capacity of individuals, groups, and political institutions to realize key decisions.

power of the purse A power of review over the expenditure of public moneys.

power over The idea that individuals, groups, or states are unable to realize their interests and goals due to external influences, constraints, and inequalities in resources.

power to The idea that individuals, groups, or states can realize their goals.

pragmatic party A non-doctrinaire party that competes strategically for public office. It is concerned with practicality and with winning elections and gears its campaigns to programs it believes will most likely lead to victory.

precedent Past judicial decisions declaring legal principles that have a bearing on present controversies.

presidential system A system of government in which the executive and legislative branches are independent and assigned distinct powers.

principle of commodification Marxist notion that, under capitalism, items are prized because of their exchange value rather than their use value. This makes all items (including labour) commodities of exchange.

principle of comparative advantage Economic theory that economic growth is best achieved when countries focus production on those things they do best, or that are associated with abundant natural resources.

private The realm of society that has been deemed "natural" and thus beyond the possibility of debate or change (often this has included the "market" and the family).

private communitarianism An approach to community that is primarily interested in strengthening private social structures such as marriage, family, and religion, often in their traditional forms.

private member bill Legislation introduced by non-cabinet members in parliamentary systems.

privatization A process of shifting public or governmental services and functions performed by the state into the realm of the market and the home.

Privy Council Office An agency of the Government of Canada that provides administrative support to and policy analysis for the cabinet.

productivism A characterization of industrial societies (both capitalist and state-socialist), referring to the priority given to the maximization of production of goods, even when this cannot be shown to enhance quality of life and may even result in its deterioration.

proletariat A term used by Marx for the social class that does not own the means of production, but is instead forced to sell its labour-power in exchange for wages.

proportional representation A system of vote-counting wherein the share of seats in a representative body that a party wins in an election is proportional, if not equal, to the share of the total valid votes cast for it in the election.

protectionism A government policy that protects a national industry or sector from foreign competition through subsidies or tariffs.

public The realm of society that has been deemed open to debate and thus change.

public/private dichotomy The gender-based division of personality characteristics, roles, and values. Women are associated with the private sphere of home and family and its accompanying traits, such as passivity, subjugation, and emotion. Men are linked to the public sphere of business and government and its virtues of individualism, rationality, intelligence, and freedom.

radical feminism A view of women's oppression as resulting from systematic subordination of women to men, especially male control of women's bodies; advocates the eradication of sexual violence and the promotion of bodily autonomy for women.

rational decision making A process whereby important policies are undertaken only after careful delineation of the problem at hand, a thorough analysis of policy options, and a detailed comparison of the costs and benefits of different options. Most public policy making is thought, for many reasons, to fall short of such standards.

rationality A claim to a systematic way of thinking.

realism The dominant international relations theory in Anglo-American academies. It purports to explain the world by holding that the international sphere is dominated by sovereign states, that states act in their own interests, and that international politics is a struggle for power between states.

regime A mode of governance over the organized activity of a social formation within and across four spheres—the state, society, market, and global insertion.

regulatory agency A government body, enjoying independence from the government of the day, that makes and enforces rules for sectors of the economy.

representation by population A principle applied in the apportionment of seats in a representative assembly among regions, provinces or states, or electoral districts. It holds that the number of seats assigned to a given region, province, or district should be directly proportional to the share of the population of the nation (or higher regional unit) that resides in that region, province, or district.

representative bureaucracy A view that argues that the civil service should reflect in its composition the major social groups of the society.

representative democracy or **indirect democracy** A democratic system in which citizens elect representatives who, in turn, make political decisions on behalf of all citizens.

representative sample A term used in survey research to refer to a sample that is a reflection of the larger population; that is, it has the same profile in terms of gender, age, income levels etc. of the larger population. It is crucial that a sample is representative if it is to give valid information about the larger population.

republicanism A political belief that holds that we are political animals. Republicans extol the virtues of positive freedom—the freedom of individuals to participate in the affairs of government.

responsible government A convention in parliamentary systems whereby the executive remains in power for so long as it maintains the confidence of the legislative branch.

revolution The overthrow of a given socio-economic and political order and implementation of a radical transformation.

rostovian model A model of development that posits a number of stages of growth that countries traverse in their transition toward development.

rule of law A fundamental principle in liberal democratic political systems. All citizens of a country are governed by a single set of legal rules. These rules are applied equally and impartially to all. No political official is above the law. The rule of law empowers and constrains political behaviour.

sentiment-based community A community based on a sentiment that endorses shared values, common interests and goals, participation in public affairs, and ongoing relationships that bind groups of people together.

separation of powers An institutional arrangement reflecting the idea that the liberty of citizens is best secured in those regimes where the executive, legislative, and judicial powers are separated and not fused into one single authority.

sexual division of labour The division of jobs and duties along gender lines.

simple candidate ballot A ballot on which only the names of the candidates, often with optional identifying information, appear, and voters are simply asked to indicate which one or more of these candidates they prefer, depending on the district magnitude that applies.

single transferable vote A voting procedure employing a preferential (ordinal) ballot in which a person's vote can be transferred from one candidate to another in successive rounds of the counting procedure.

social capital Communal sentiments and actions stemming from these sentiments that add value to society and the political system. Individuals have social capital when they have the education and skills to integrate successfully into society.

social contract The argument by Hobbes and Locke that individuals in a state of nature by mutual consent and agreement form societies and establish governments.

social democracy A democratic regime that uses the state to implement egalitarian redistribution of the wealth produced by a largely capitalist economy.

social formation A term applied to a "country" encompassing its given societal, economic, and political systems.

socialism An ideology founded on the recognition of a fundamental division and conflict in capitalist society between social classes. Class divisions are based upon those who own the means of production (the capitalist) and those who do not (the working class or proletariat). The solution to class conflict lies in the public or common ownership of the means of production, a solution to be achieved either through revolution or by working democratically within the existing capitalist system.

socialist feminism A stream of feminist thought that sees women's oppression as fostered and maintained by capitalism and the patriarchal state; the solution lies in challenging the sexual division of labour in the home and the workplace.

socialization of debt A governmental action wherein it takes over the debt incurred by the private sector. In doing so, the burden of responsibility to pay back this converted public debt shifts from private businesses to the average taxpayer. One important consequence of this is the channeling of taxpayers' money towards bringing down the public debt and away from spending in areas such as health, education, and welfare.

social rights Citizenship rights that are necessary for well-being and thus for full membership and participation in the political community as defined by the standards and norms prevailing in that community.

social stratification A heirarchically based division of society

social welfare liberalism A philosophy of governing resting on the idea that the basic necessities of life should be provided by government for those who are truly in need, for those who are unable to provide for themselves through no fault of their own.

socio-economic growth (development) An ability to produce an adequate and growing supply of goods and services productively and efficiently, to accumulate capital, and to distribute the fruits of production in a relatively equitable manner.

solidarity Membership in the political community, and feelings of belonging associated with acceptance by that community.

sovereignty A legal (*de jure*) and actual (*de facto*) condition whereby states recognize no higher authority either domestically or externally and are thus free to act as they wish. A state's right to manage its affairs internally, without external interference, based on the legal concept of the equality of states.

Speaker of the House A legislative official responsible for overseeing and controlling activity in the legislative assembly.

stakeholders A group of individuals who have identified a common interest in a portion of the more general public interest. They may consider themselves as having a common, sometimes a proprietary, interest in a specific policy area.

Stalinism Refers to the regime of Joseph Stalin, who ruled the Communist Party of the Union of Soviet Socialist Republics (CP-USSR) and the government of the USSR from 1924 to 1953. The regime oversaw the rapid industrialization and increasing military power of the USSR, but exercised extreme coercion over citizens, imprisoned, exiled, or "liquidated" suspected dissidents, and is widely viewed as having betrayed the democratic, proletarian principles of the international communist movement. Communist parties in the West which emulated the top-down bureaucratic structure of the CP-USSR, and which continued to defend the legacy of Stalinism, were also labelled "Stalinist" by their new left opponents.

standing committee A relatively permanent legislative committee with set responsibilities.

standing orders A set of rules governing activity in the Canadian House of Commons.

state See nation-state.

state of nature An imaginary existence without government where all people are equal and free to act as they please.

statute A written law enacted by the legislature.

subculture A different shared way of life within the national cultural setting, characterizing a smaller grouping of people within a country.

subjective Situation in which the observer is part of what is observed or is affected by values and preferences.

surplus value A key relationship of exploitation between capitalists and workers. Surplus value represents the profit that the capitalist gains as a result of selling a product for more than is paid to the worker in wages.

theory A coherent interpretation or story which orders and makes sense of the world.

Third World A term used to describe the majority of countries in the world or the vast majority of the world's population who live in conditions of poverty, underdevelopment and, often, political instability.

totalitarian An ultra-authoritarian regime which controls virtually all aspects of politics, society, and economy.

traditional authority Power and legitimacy accorded to individuals on the basis of custom or heredity.

traditional society A society characterized by inherited authority and low levels of industrialization, consumption, technology, and diversification.

transnationalized regime A form of governance carried out by international actors.

Treasury Board Secretariat A central agency of the Government of Canada with responsibility for overall administrative and management policy.

tyranny of the majority A potentially omnipotent power of the majority. Constitutional guarantees are required so as to curb the majority's potential excesses.

unicameral A regime in which the legislature consists of only one chamber.

unilateral Actions taken by one actor or government.

unitary constitution A constitution in which the sovereignty of the state rests in one government.

universalism A view that laws and policies should treat all citizens the same, irrespective of membership in distinct cultural or identity groups. Universalism collides with demands for recognition and valuing of difference whereby cultural groups are granted distinct rights or treatment in laws and policies.

universal social programs Programs available to all citizens regardless of their income level or their need.

unwritten constitution A constitution where most of a country's key governing principles are not contained in a single document. These principles exist in a combination of written laws and conventions.

vanguard A cadre of dedicated revolutionaries. The concept of the vanguard was put forward by Lenin as a means to lead the working class to revolution.

virtue ethics An approach to moral philosophy that emphasizes the human good. Virtue ethicists draw attention to both the consequences of one's decision or act (as in consequentialism), and also to the principles guiding the decision or act (as in deontology), but they do so more with a view to judging the individual's moral character than with a view to judging the actions themselves.

vote of no confidence A vote of parliament that determines whether the executive maintains the support of the legislature.

welfare state A form of governance wherein government programs and policies are designed to protect citizens from illness, unemployment, and long term disability. In modern political debate; a welfare state is said to have a "social safety net."

world city A modern-day city that has elaborate and independent economic, social, and political links with communities abroad that either subordinate, or bypass entirely, national and regional governments. Governing, social, and economic elites measure their community's success against other world cities outside their own national borders.

world system The idea that the international state system and capitalism have constituted an evolving single global system since the sixteenth century, with a core, periphery, and semi-periphery.

world view A collection of integrated images of the world that serve as a lens through which one interprets the world. It helps the individual to orient to the environment and to organize perceptions as a guide to behaviour, and it acts as a filter for selecting relevant information.

Index